Secure Computing

Other McGraw-Hill Books of Interest

COBB • *The NCSA Guide to PC and LAN Security*, 0-07-912168-3

KABAY • *The NCSA Guide to Enterprise Security*, 0-07-033147-2

MIORA • *The NCSA Guide to Disaster Recovery Planning*, 0-07-042904-9

RUTSTEIN • *The NCSA Guide to Windows NT Security*, 0-07-057833-8

SAMALIN • *Secure UNIX*, 0-07-054554-5

Secure Computing

Threats and Safeguards

Rita C. Summers

McGraw-Hill

New York San Francisco Washington, D.C. Auckland Bogotá
Caracas Lisbon London Madrid Mexico City Milan
Montreal New Delhi San Juan Singapore
Sydney Tokyo Toronto

Library of Congress Cataloging-in-Publication Data

Summers, Rita C.
Secure computing : threats and safeguards / Rita C. Summers.
p. cm.
Includes Index
ISBN 0-07-069419-2
1. Computer Security I. Title.
QA76.9.A25S85 1997
005.8—dc21 96-45108
CIP

1 2 3 4 5 6 7 8 9 0 DOC/DOC 9 0 1 0 9 8 7 6

ISBN 0-07-069419-2

The sponsoring editor for this book was John Wyzalek, the editing supervisor was David E. Fogarty, and the production supervisor was Suzanne W. B. Rapcavage. It was set in Century Schoolbook by Dina E. John of McGraw-Hill's Professional Book Group composition unit.

Printed and bound by R. R. Donnelley & Sons Company.

This book was printed on acid-free paper.

To Stan, First Reader

Contents

Part 3 Security in Computer Networks

Part 4 Management and Analysis

Preface

Computer security is a broad subject that includes many specialized topics. As a result, many books about computer security are specialized; they are about UNIX security, or viruses, or cryptographic protocols. I believe there is a need for books that pull it all together. This is so because making computing secure requires looking at the whole picture. This book covers the entire subject of computer security, placing each specialized topic within the whole.

The book is intended for computer professionals, managers, and students. It describes principles and methods in a real-world context, using case histories and discussing standards, legislation, technology trends, and market characteristics. The book covers topics in moderate depth; for the reader who wants to delve deeper, there are extensive bibliographic notes. The reader needs no specific expertise, but familiarity with operating systems is helpful.

System designers and developers will learn the basic security principles and methods as well as specialized material that is relevant to their projects. They will learn about security standards.

People who acquire hardware or software and *people who market products with security features* will learn about the main security threats and how to guard against them. They will learn how to evaluate security features. They also will begin to understand the issues motivating customers.

Security practitioners, such as security administrators and security auditors, will gain both general understanding and practical guidance. The book will help them prepare for certification examinations.

Managers with computer security responsibility will obtain an overall perspective on security and will learn about setting up and implementing security programs.

Senior or graduate students in computer science or information systems will get thorough coverage in a well-organized, readable form. Overviews, figures, summaries, examples, exercises, and bibliographic notes are provided.

I believe that all *computer professionals* and many *computer users* will find the book interesting, illuminating, and useful. For all readers, the book will serve as a comprehensive reference and a guide to other literature.

The book has four parts. Part 1 describes the societal and technological forces that affect computer security. It introduces important threats and lays a theoretical foundation. Part 2 describes technical methods: cryptography, secure design and development, protection mechanisms, operating system services, and database security. Part 3 is devoted to the security of networks and distributed systems. It deals with local area networks and Internet security. Part 4 gives practical information about management of security programs, administrative controls, physical security, risk analysis, and auditing.

Rita Summers

Acknowledgments

I appreciate having been able to work on secure computing at IBM and to follow security developments over many years.

I am grateful to Eduardo Fernandez for his help in the planning of this book and to Ruth Batterton for supplying important material. The Internet and the libraries of the University of California, Los Angeles and the California State University, Northridge were essential resources, and the Inglewood Public Library (especially Frank Francis) gave invaluable help.

I would like to thank my editors at McGraw-Hill—Neil Levine, Daniel Gonneau, Marjorie Spencer, John Wyzalek, and the manuscript team headed by David Fogarty.

Part

1

Foundations

Chapter

1

Introduction

Computers and computer networks are woven into the fabric of society. Bank or university, manufacturer or grocer, no organization can function long without its computing systems. For all organizations, crucial decisions depend on accurate, timely data and correct processing. Computer systems represent, hold, and transfer assets of enormous value. Personal and public safety depend on computers embedded into products—from antilock brakes to x-ray machines. Computing systems have major responsibility for transport safety. They make up much of the communications system. Personal data about individuals are collected and stored in great detail.

Are computing systems secure enough for their crucial roles? Often, they are not. Can they become more secure? Emphatically, yes. A great deal has been learned about the threats to secure computing and about guarding against them. The purpose of this book is to make that knowledge more accessible so that it can be applied.

Concepts

SafeCare is a fictional for-profit health maintenance organization that operates hospitals and clinics. It relies on information technology to keep it competitive. SafeCare needs to keep secure many kinds of information, including patient records, employee records, and business plans. SafeCare's computing systems must be there when they are needed.

A secure computing system provides three properties: *confidentiality, integrity,* and *availability.* All three are essential. *Confidentiality* (or *secrecy*) means that information is disclosed only according to policy. *Integrity* means that information is not destroyed or corrupted and that the system performs correctly. *Availability* means that system services are available when they are needed. *Computer security,* then, is the protection of computing systems against threats to confidentiality, integrity, or availability. By *computing systems,* I mean computers, computer networks, and the information they handle. The threats may be deliberate, such as fraud or hacker attacks, or accidental, such as human errors or power failures.

> SafeCare's policy is not to release a patient's records without the patient's consent except to persons who need the records for the patient's treatment. If an unauthorized employee, or an outsider, sees a patient record, confidentiality is violated. If someone maliciously alters a patient record to show the wrong medication, integrity is violated. If a nurse who administers medications cannot get prompt access to a patient's record, availability is violated. An accidental security breach occurs if an employee makes an error in entering a drug dosage into the pharmacy system.

Many people have a stake in SafeCare security—plan members, employer clients, employees, stockholders, and the public. SafeCare must abide by laws and standards about health care, privacy, and the protection of assets. The people who contribute to computer security follow various professions. They do research, develop systems and products, and strive to make systems secure for their organizations. As shown in Fig. 1.1, computer security at SafeCare depends, directly or indirectly, on

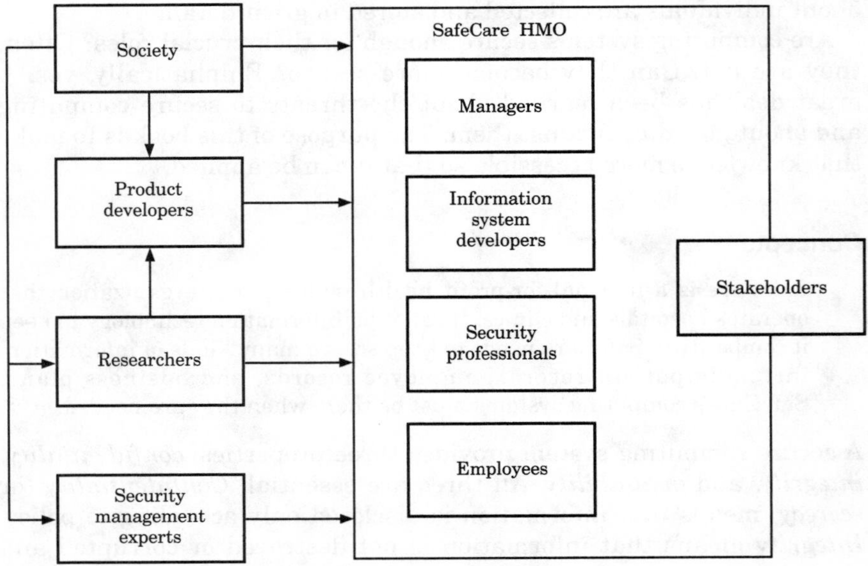

Figure 1.1 Influences on computer security at one organization.

- SafeCare managers and employees
- Security professionals
- Computing professionals
- The security of products
- Research results
- Actions of society in general

To summarize, computer security is a goal to be achieved—protecting computing systems against threats to confidentiality, integrity, and availability. Computer security is also a field of study and a set of activities aimed at achieving that goal.

Computer security policy

An organization's security policy specifies what security properties the system must provide. Real-world needs dictate security policy. If patients have the legal right to their medical records, then SafeCare's policy must be to release records to a patient who signs the right forms. In this example, the information is on paper. A *computer security policy* must interpret real-world policy for computer-based resources such as files and transactions. The policy also must consider threats, specifying which threats the organization chooses to guard against and how. For example, SafeCare's computer security policy specifies who may enter a prescription into the pharmacy system; the policy also states that the pharmacy system cannot be used over telephone lines. (Unlike SafeCare, many organizations do not have explicit security policies.)

Vulnerabilities, threats, and safeguards

The concepts of vulnerability, threat, and safeguard make up a framework for thinking about computer security. A *vulnerability* is some weakness of a system that could allow security to be violated. The weakness could be in system design or implementation or in the procedures for managing the system. A *threat* is a circumstance or event that could cause harm by violating security. A threat often exploits a vulnerability. A *safeguard* is any technique, procedure, or other measure that reduces vulnerability. Safeguards make threats weaker or less likely. Safeguards are also called *countermeasures,* and management safeguards are called *controls.* This framework—vulnerability, threat, and safeguard—is useful for analyzing and evaluating security and for deciding what safeguards to use.

The threats faced by SafeCare might include

- A power failure that takes down the computing system (availability)
- A deranged employee who corrupts pharmacy records (integrity)
- A hacker break-in that discloses personal data about plan members (confidentiality)

The corresponding vulnerabilities are

- Dependence on a single, interruptible source of power
- Poor employee selection and inadequate control of access to data
- Inadequate protection against network attacks

And possible safeguards are

- Backup power supply
- Better personnel practices, strong security software
- A "firewall" to limit system access over networks

Approaches to providing security

There are different basic approaches to providing security.

Cost-benefit approach. Most safeguards cost money. If SafeCare decides to install security software, it has the costs of the license fee, employee training, time spent using, administering, and maintaining the software, and additional computing resources. Since it cannot afford every possible safeguard, SafeCare must decide which threats to control and with which safeguards. The management of computer security can be viewed as *risk management*—identifying threats and vulnerabilities and selecting safeguards to control them. *Risk analysis* involves estimating the potential losses and how much the safeguards could reduce them in order to determine if the safeguards are worth their cost. Risks can be immediate and local (SafeCare loses money from insider fraud) or longer term and broader (the economy as a whole is slow to benefit from electronic commerce because security is weak).

Baseline approach. Sometimes a minimum level of security must be maintained, regardless of cost. This minimum level is called a *baseline.* For example, if security weaknesses of a new pharmacy system endanger patients' lives, SafeCare must either improve the system's security or go back to the old system. Often, minimum security requirements are expressed as standards that are promulgated by governments, international organizations, or industry groups. The standards apply both to specific products, such as operating systems, and to complete operational systems. Governments traditionally require high baseline security for military systems, especially when there are strong adversaries. In such circumstances, cost is secondary. The U.S. Department of Defense developed computer security standards called the *Trusted Computer System Evaluation Criteria* (TCSEC). Rather than a single baseline, the TCSEC define different classes of security, corresponding to different levels of need.

Combined approach. The cost-benefit and baseline approaches can complement one another. The baseline approach protects the people (such as hospital patients) who have a stake in a system's security. For example, an association of hospitals might require its members to provide the security defined for a specific TCSEC class. However, since cost always matters, risk management is essential.

Security, safety, and quality

Security is not the only problem that must be solved for systems to be trustworthy. The related problem of *safety* involves reducing the risk of harm due to system failures. Suppose that a patient at a SafeCare hospital dies from an overdose of intravenous medication because of an error in the software of the instrument that delivers the medication. This is a problem of software safety. If someone had changed the patient's prescription maliciously, that would be a security problem. The distinction between safety and security is not always so clear. A safety failure can make a system vulnerable to a security threat. Further, many traditional security threats do not involve human error or subversion. For example, a disk failure may damage the SafeCare pharmacy's database.

More general than security or safety is *quality.* A system must be suitable for its intended use, meet its technical specifications, and satisfy its users. Although a system can be technically secure without meeting quality requirements, such a system would not be much good to anyone.

Although it discusses safety and quality, this book concentrates on security.

Security Principles

Some general security principles have evolved gradually and have become widely accepted. These principles are mainly about people's responsibilities. Although the principles are not technical, they have implications for security technology.

OECD guidelines for the security of information systems

An excellent set of general principles or guidelines was adopted in 1992 by the Organization for Economic Cooperation and Development

(OECD). These guidelines are intended as a foundation for a total framework of laws, policies, technical and administrative measures, and education. Paraphrased, the OECD guidelines are

1. *Accountability.* All parties concerned with the security of information systems (owners, providers, users, and others) should have explicit responsibilities and accountability.
2. *Awareness.* All parties should be able to readily gain knowledge of security measures, practices, and procedures. A motivation for this principle is to foster confidence in information systems.
3. *Ethics.* Information systems and their security should be provided and used in ways that respect the rights and legitimate interests of others.
4. *Multidisciplinary principle.* Security measures should take into account all relevant viewpoints, including technical, administrative, organizational, operational, commercial, educational, and legal.
5. *Proportionality.* Security measures should be appropriate and proportionate to the value of and degree of reliance on the information systems and to the risk of harm.
6. *Integration.* Security measures should be coordinated and integrated with each other and with other measures, practices, and procedures of the organization so as to create a coherent system of security.
7. *Timeliness.* Parties should act in a timely and coordinated way to prevent and to respond to security breaches.
8. *Reassessment.* Security should be reassessed periodically as information systems and their security needs change. (Threats may change because the user population changes. For example, SafeCare may decide to allow its suppliers to access some systems directly.)
9. *Democracy.* The security of information systems should be compatible with the legitimate use and flow of information in a democratic society. (For example, SafeCare should protect the privacy of medical records and employee records.)

Principles underlying security policy

Some additional principles are so fundamental that most security policies support them.

1. *Authorization.* Explicit rules are needed about who can use what resources and in what ways. For example, SafeCare's pharmacy

needs rules about who can prescribe medication for a patient and who can look at prescriptions. Rules also are needed about who can authorize the use of resources.

2. *Least privilege.* People should be authorized only for the resources they need to do their jobs. When applied to confidentiality, this principle is also called *need-to-know.* Following the least-privilege principle reduces the risk that people will do harm (accidental or intentional) in the course of doing their work.
3. *Separation of duty.* Functions should be divided between people so that no one person can commit fraud undetected.
4. *Redundancy.* The principle of redundancy applies to procedures, information, and computing resources. For example, multiple copies of files should be kept, and there should be a backup power supply.

These principles, along with others, also apply to the design of secure systems.

Overview of Threats and Vulnerabilities

Security threats come from widely differing universes. Some come from natural forces (such as flood or earthquake), accidents (such as fire), and failures of services (such as power or telephone). Other threats come from people, both insiders and intruders. The greatest total losses are caused by insider errors and accidents. Insider errors also can provide the opening for deliberate misuse by outsiders or other insiders. Some insiders commit fraud, usually by abusing the authority they have been given. Often, fraud is possible because separation of duty and other control principles are not observed.

Intruders have many avenues of attack. Malicious software—such as viruses—makes its way into computing systems uninvited and carries out unwanted actions. Intruders exploit flawed operating system software, gullible privileged users, and vulnerable phone systems. Often, careless system administration worsens another vulnerability: products that are delivered with insecure configurations. Intruders often subvert safeguards. Network communications are vulnerable to eavesdropping and other communications security threats.

Overview of Safeguards

Safeguards are at least as varied as threats, ranging from personnel practices to hardware devices. Safeguards vary in their basic protection strategies.

Protection strategies

Security can be enhanced by four basic strategies: avoidance, prevention, detection, and recovery.

- *Avoidance* means just not exposing assets to threats. Instead, organize tasks so that threats can be avoided. For example, rather than printing a sensitive report on a shared network printer, SafeCare could print it in a secure room using equipment with no network connection.
- *Prevention* includes hardware and software security functions. It includes setting up and enforcing security policies. It includes many management controls. Prevention is by far the most heavily used strategy.
- *Detection* seeks to discover misuse while it is occurring or after the fact. For example, SafeCare employees analyze logs of system activity. Detection serves four purposes. It deters misuse (and thus doubles as prevention). It allows threat events to be detected in time to reduce the damage. It allows perpetrators to be identified and prosecuted. And it reveals vulnerabilities.
- *Recovery* follows a security breach. Recovery includes restoring the damaged resources and trying to remove the vulnerabilities that allowed the breach.

Safeguards in three realms

Safeguards belong to three interrelated realms: societal, management, and technical. The general safeguard environment is set by governments, international bodies, industry and professional groups, educational institutions, the media, and other influences. Laws about fraud, computer crime, and privacy deter misuse and provide recourse for victims. Standards promote baseline security and due care. Education promotes ethical and prudent behavior for computer users. The media spotlight security breaches. Computer security organizations promote security and help with achieving it. Societal safeguards have great influence on the other two realms.

Management safeguards are the steps taken by organizations for their own computer security. Organizations select, motivate, and educate employees so as to promote security. They physically protect computing resources against fire, flood, theft, and other hazards.

Technical safeguards are equally broad in scope. They include, for example, coding information to conceal its content, controlling (with software and hardware) who gets access to computers and information, and detecting when information has been modified improperly.

Safeguards from each realm apply to every problem area of computer security and are discussed throughout this book. However, Chapter 2 focuses on societal safeguards and Chapter 12 on management safeguards. Portions of Chapters 4, 6, and 13 also describe management safeguards. The remaining chapters focus on technical safeguards.

Framework for technical safeguards

A system is secure if it satisfies its security requirements. The requirements, in turn, must be specified correctly and precisely. There should be an explicit security policy, and if possible, the policy should be translated into a model that describes precisely how the system will enforce the policy. The system's design and implementation must enforce the policy correctly, and therefore, the engineering process is an important aspect of secure systems.

The functions that a system provides in support of security are known as *services*. For example, *authentication* of user identity is a service, and providing confidentiality of network messages is a service. A technique that is used to implement a service is called a *mechanism*. For example, the *password* mechanism is used to implement authentication, and the *encryption* mechanism is used to implement message confidentiality. The field of *cryptography* is the source of many security mechanisms. Cryptography is the art of hiding or transforming information to ensure its secrecy or authenticity or both.

Even with the best services and mechanisms, a system is not necessarily secure. The parts of the system must fit together in a good *security architecture*. The system must be secure as an integrated whole.

Some of the most important services are

- *Authentication*—verifying a user's claim of identity. Authentication supports the principle of accountability.
- *Access control*—ensuring that all access to resources is authorized access. Access control supports the principles of authorization, least privilege, and separation of duty. It protects both confidentiality and integrity. With *discretionary* access control, a user who owns or controls some objects (such as files) can freely authorize anyone to access them. With *mandatory* access control, an overall policy constrains what an authorizer can do. For networks, access control enforces policy about which computers connect to one another and what data can pass on the connections.
- *Integrity*—ensuring that information is not modified in unauthorized ways, that it is internally consistent and consistent with the real-world objects that it represents, and that the system performs

correctly. For networks, integrity means ensuring that a received message has exactly the same message contents that were sent.

- *Audit*—providing a chronological record of events, called an *audit trail*. Audit supports the principle of accountability by recording individuals' actions so that auditors can review them. Audit is a safety net: If access control fails to block misuse, audit can detect it. If authorized persons misuse their rights, audit can detect that.
- (*Network*) *confidentiality*—preventing access to the information that is transmitted or making it incomprehensible to an eavesdropper

Preview of the Chapters

Chapter 2, "The Context for Computer Security," describes the societal and technological forces that affect computer security. Topics include

- Relevant trends in computing and computer applications
- Privacy
- Computer fraud and abuse
- The legal environment
- Computer security standards
- Government policy on cryptography
- Ethics and computer security

Chapter 3, "Threats," focuses on misuse of computing systems by people, especially intentional misuse. Topics include

- Case histories of misuse
- Types of misuse and types of vulnerabilities
- Perpetrators—insiders, hackers, and spies
- Methods used in attacks
- Malicious code—Trojan horses, viruses, and worms

Chapter 4, "Policies and Models," describes real-world security policies and their counterparts in computer security. Topics include

- Principles underlying security policies
- The role of security models
- Policies and models for access control, information flow, and integrity
- The *multilevel* security policy and model

- How computer security policy is applied

Chapter 5, "Cryptography," deals with cryptographic theory and methods that are relevant to secure computing. Topics include

- Theoretical foundations and classical techniques
- The Data Encryption Standard
- Public key methods
- Threats to information integrity
- Digital signatures
- How cryptographic keys are handled
- Cryptographic protocols

Chapter 6, "Designing and Building for Security," treats the problem of developing systems that meet their security requirements. Topics include

- Software engineering in relation to security
- Security flaws in software
- Principles of secure design
- The main architectural approaches
- Criteria for evaluating security
- The process of developing secure systems

Chapter 7 is "Protection Mechanisms in Hardware Architecture and Operating Systems." Topics include

- Problems that protection must solve
- Domains and rings
- Memory protection
- Capabilities
- File protection
- Security kernels

Chapter 8, "Security Services in Operating Systems," describes what the services accomplish, how they are implemented, and how people use or abuse them. Topics include

- Authentication using passwords, token devices, and biometric techniques

- Availability, integrity, and audit services
- Security facilities for people who use, operate, administer, and audit operating systems
- Security in UNIX, MVS, OpenVMS, and Windows NT
- Add-on security products

Chapter 9 is "Database Security." Topics include

- Special security requirements of databases
- Access control and integrity for databases
- Multilevel secure database systems
- Security of statistical databases
- Security features of database management systems

Chapter 10, "Network Security," covers threats and safeguards that apply to computer networks. Topics include

- The role of network standards and the major standards frameworks
- Network architecture and network security architecture
- Network security threats
- The use of cryptography for network security
- Authentication for networks
- Access control, confidentiality, integrity, and nonrepudiation
- Internet vulnerabilities and safeguards
- Firewalls to protect networks
- World Wide Web security issues

Chapter 11, "Security in Distributed Systems," continues with network security, concentrating on modes of distributed processing. Topics include

- Local area networks—security threats and services
- Security for distributed file systems
- Security in the Novell NetWare network operating system
- Single sign-on to multiple systems
- Remote access over telephone lines

- Security problems of mobile computing
- Security for distributed computing

Chapter 12, "Managing Computer Security," covers what has to be done and how to get it done. Topics include

- Organizational structures for security management
- How security policy is formed and implemented
- People and security—employee selection and training, security roles, organizational and administrative controls
- How to operate computing systems securely
- Physical security—protecting against intrusion, electrical problems, fire, and flood
- Contingency planning—planning for harmful events such as natural disasters
- Response to computer security incidents

Chapter 13, "Analyzing Security," describes ways to analyze and evaluate security. Topics include

- Risk analysis
- Information systems auditing
- Testing systems for vulnerability
- Intrusion detection

Note on Terminology

The word *system* appears again and again in this book, referring to very different kinds of things. A *system* is a collection of components that work together to achieve some purpose. Often, the components themselves are systems. Depending on the context, a system may be something quite small (such as a wallet-sized smart card) or something very large (such as an airline reservation system). In between there are computers, operating systems, and database management systems. Many systems involve people, procedures, software, and hardware. For this reason, the term *information systems security* often is preferred to *computer security. Information Systems Security* would be an accurate title for this book. However, because of the weight given to technical aspects, a more fitting title is *Secure Computing.*

Chapter

2

The Context for Computer Security

This chapter is about the context for computer security—the conditions that pose threats and that shape the development and use of safeguards (Fig. 2.1).

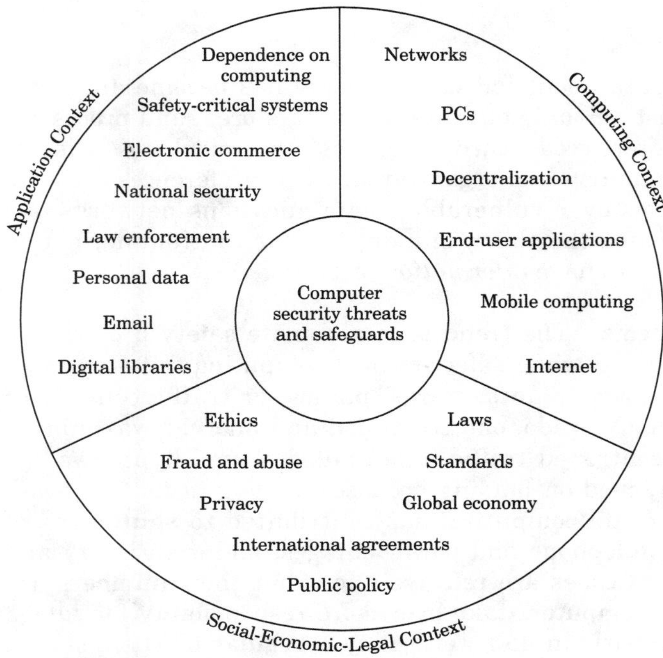

Figure 2.1 The context for computer security.

Overview of the Chapter

The technology and practice of computer security must respond to rapid changes in the context. This chapter begins by examining some of these changes. First, computer application trends that have strong security implications are considered. The chapter looks briefly at developments in technology, organizations, the economy, and government policy. Some of the topics surveyed are then taken up in more detail. The first of these is information privacy. The concept of privacy, threats to privacy, and privacy law and policy are discussed. The next section describes computer fraud and abuse—types of abuse, examples of loss from abuse, and the legal situation. Standards are the next topic—computer security standards and other relevant standards. Next comes a discussion of U.S. government policy on cryptography, giving historical background and treating issues about standards and export policy. The chapter concludes by examining ethics as applied to computer security.

The Changing Context

Security needs grow and change with new applications and new ways of doing computing.

Application trends

Personal data. Data about individual people has become abundant and valuable. Vast amounts of it are collected, stored, and processed. Our medical records, credit card purchases, and telephone calls are all studied by computers and organizations. Our preferences are sold. Personal data flow over vulnerable communications networks. All these trends threaten the ability of individuals to control information about themselves—to have *information privacy.*

Safety-critical systems. The trend is to automate safety protections. Lives are endangered when safety-critical computing fails—in medical equipment, power plants, trains, planes, or traffic control. In Colorado Springs, Colorado, one child died and another was injured when computer-controlled traffic lights failed. A prototype Swedish military plane crashed on landing because of a bug in its flight-control software. Unsafe computing has contributed to shutdowns of stock exchanges, telephone and power outages, and even injury and death. The serious cases are relatively few, but their numbers are likely to grow as computers take over more responsibility for safety. Industries vary greatly in how well safety is regulated. There should be (as there are for aviation) reporting requirements for safety or security incidents. The incidents should be investigated and the results published.

Electronic commerce. For many years, companies have done business with each other electronically. For example, U.K. retailers Marks & Spencer and W. H. Smith exchange purchase orders, invoices, and other data with their suppliers. This allows them to react quickly in an industry where products change quickly. These companies use *electronic data interchange* (EDI), exchanging common business documents electronically and processing the documents automatically. Organizations use EDI because they expect to communicate faster and better, reduce costs, and increase data accuracy. The U.S. government requires EDI for some of its procurement. EDI uses mainly private networks or *value-added networks,* which provide some security services.

Electronic commerce includes, along with EDI, any type of commerce over the Internet or private networks, on-line services such as Prodigy, or electronic bulletin boards. For example, merchants can offer items (digital or physical) for sale on the World Wide Web, and buyers can use credit cards or *digital cash* to buy them. People can do banking from their home PCs. The framework can accommodate large and small participants, including individual buyers and sellers. The main obstacle to the growth of electronic commerce is weak security. Traditional paper-based commerce has many protective measures, such as contracts and signed documents. Electronic commerce needs equivalent measures as well as safeguards for computer and network security threats. Participants in electronic transactions need certain assurances:

1. *Integrity.* The receiver of a message must be able to detect if the message was altered. Transactions must not be lost, duplicated, or reordered.
2. *Confidentiality.* There must be no unauthorized disclosure of the content of transactions.
3. *Authentication.* Each party (individual or organization) must be able to verify that the other parties are who they claim to be.
4. *Nonrepudiation.* A sender must not be able to deny sending a message or a receiver deny receiving it.
5. *Timely service.* Each party must meet the timeliness needs of its trading partners. This implies good availability of the computing systems that support the transactions.
6. *System security.* The systems must be protected against intrusion and insider abuse.

7. *Record keeping.* The records kept must satisfy legal requirements for business records. For example, a date and time stamp may be needed. Some record keeping requires the services of an impartial third party—a *trusted entity.* The legal standards for electronic commerce, which would include the responsibilities of trusted entities, are not yet well developed.

Another requirement for some commerce is *anonymity.* For example, we should be able to buy information or other products on the Internet without disclosing our identity, much as we buy at stores using cash.

Many projects are under way to expand electronic commerce on the Internet; for example:

> A group of major companies, including computer and aerospace companies and banks, set up CommerceNet to provide an infrastructure for electronic commerce. Expected uses include (in addition to EDI) on-line catalogs, collaboration on design and manufacturing, and payment services.
>
> American Express and America Online formed ExpressNet, to let cardholders pay bills, review their transactions, and download data into their home financial software.
>
> CyberCash planned to provide *digital cash.* A user presents a digital check to his or her bank and the bank sends the user digital cash that can be paid to on-line merchants. Digital cash can make very small purchases practical, and unlike credit cards, it provides anonymity.

All these projects emphasize security. The potential of electronic commerce motivates speedy adoption of computer and network security measures.

Computing environment trends

The computing environment is changing as rapidly as the applications.

Decentralization and networking. Computing in organizations has decentralized. Mainframes and professional information systems organizations have been joined by personal computers (PCs), departmental computing, and end-user application building. Technical and administrative security measures lagged behind this change so that security control loosened just as the transformed computing structures created new threats and vulnerabilities. These difficulties are compounded by frequent organizational changes. As Ross Anderson points out, "It can take many years for a security capability to mature and become effective. Continuity matters; and we do not really understand how to maintain effective control in an organization whose structure is constantly changing" (1994b: 37).

Accompanying and enabling decentralization is networking. Local-area networks (LANs) allow users to share files and specialized servers, update their software, schedule meetings, and work cooperatively. Many computer users are mobile, using wireless connections, which are less secure than wires. Network applications keep multiplying and crossing organizational boundaries. On-line services (such as America Online) provide electronic mail (*email*), discussion forums, news, shopping, product support, and database access. Internet use has grown exponentially.

Fraud and abuse. It is not surprising, given their importance, that computing systems are prominent targets of fraud and other abuse. Some perpetrators maliciously damage or disrupt computing systems or networks. Others steal computing or telephone services, violate individual privacy, steal property, and commit financial fraud. Much of this fraud and abuse could be controlled by improved computer security.

Networking gives anyone with a computer and modem the potential (given some skill and widely available knowledge) to access a great many computers without authorization. Hackers break into systems—mainly for the challenge but sometimes for profit. The proper legal response to nonprofit hacking is being debated, with the penalties tending to become more severe for disruptive episodes. Meanwhile break-ins continue.

The market for computer security. The market for computer products is international. Many U.S. computer and software companies, for example, get at least half their revenue outside the country. Potentially, the market for computer security products is also international. Standards and criteria (developed by governmental or other bodies) are a significant factor in computer security, and they are increasingly international. The European Union first harmonized criteria for its member nations and then worked with the United States and Canada toward common criteria.

Traditionally, security has been a hard sell. There would be few security products if not for government support of research and development and government procurement. Despite concern about abuse, many managers are unwilling to spend on technical safeguards. Vendors consider the security market risky because of high development costs and a market that is perceived as small. Also, a vendor who introduces a security feature can charge a premium for only a short time before the feature becomes standard. "Thus the pace of change and competition in the overall market for computer technology may be inimical to security, subordinating security-relevant quality to creativity, functionality, and timely releases or upgrades" (National Research Council 1991: 145). Another inhibition in the United States has been control of the export of some security products.

It is quite possible that the market will change dramatically. Some security products have become less expensive. For example, encryption hardware is affordable, and software encryption is practical. In some industries—especially communications—revenue losses to computer fraud have been great enough to motivate security measures. Perhaps most important, profitable commercial applications of networked computing have emerged, and their acceptance depends on security.

Government policy. Government policy strongly affects both security needs and security solutions. Government policy usually tries to clear the way for the development and rapid application of new technology. At the same time, governments have responsibilities for safety and for individual rights, both of which may be threatened by rapid adoption of new technology. In the United States, government support of research and development directly led to major technological developments such as the Internet. The government supported nearly all the technical work in computer security for many years, mainly through the Department of Defense (DoD). The government has a great deal of control over which cryptography products are produced and deployed, and it restricts export of many computer security products. Through standards for its own procurement, it strongly influences the entire market for computer security.

Computer networks are part of an emerging *national information infrastructure* (NII) that also includes telephone, cable, and broadcasting. According to a National Research Council committee, the NII "can provide a seamless web of...information networks, computers, databases, and consumer electronics that will eventually link homes, workplaces, and public institutions together. It can embrace virtually all modes of information generation, transport, and use" (1994: 1). Although the infrastructure is already international, national policy will affect how it develops.

Privacy

Privacy has been defined as "the claim of individuals, groups, or institutions to determine for themselves when, how, and to what extent information about them is communicated to others."

Background

Computers and privacy. From the earliest days of computers, their effect on privacy has been recognized. That effect grows almost unimpeded. One reason is that current technology makes it far easier to collect, store, manipulate, and share data. Another reason is that changes in our lives (many technology-driven) make personal data more abundant, available, and valuable. Our medical records are perused by people and computers at our insurance companies, employment, and doctors' offices. Our credit card purchases are studied by the computers of credit card issuers. Information about our telephone calls is recorded in databases. Our preferences, our addresses and telephone numbers, our incomes, even our Social Security numbers all are sold routinely. Personal data flow over vulnerable communications networks. The expected growth in network use and electronic commerce will only strengthen the impact on privacy. Public concern about computers and privacy in the 1970s led to legislation in some countries and to some self-regulation by government and industry. In general, however, the response has lagged far behind threats and public concern. In a 1994 U.S. survey, 84 percent of the respondents were "somewhat concerned" or "very concerned" about threats to their privacy. In 1995, 80 percent agreed that "consumers have lost all control over how personal information about them is circulated and used by companies."

Privacy law. Few national constitutions explicitly guarantee a right of privacy, but legal scholars find a basis for privacy in constitutions or in common law. The United Nations Declaration of Human Rights states that everyone has the right to protection against interference with his privacy. A milestone in the United States was an 1890 article by Samuel Warren and Louis Brandeis (later a Supreme Court justice) defining privacy as the right "to be let alone." Just as privacy advocates are now concerned about computers, Warren and Brandeis were concerned about the new technology of photography and invasions of privacy by newspapers. They argued that the common law already recognized the right of privacy and that this right extended to new means of publication.

The law about privacy in the United States includes constitutional protections, federal and state statutes, common law, and government regulations. Canada, Japan, the United States, and many European nations have privacy laws. In Europe, privacy is increasingly governed by international agreements, which can affect all countries that do business with Europe. Privacy legislation is broader and more general in Europe than in the United States, where it deals with specific problems and specific industries. For example, the United States has one law covering credit bureaus and another law covering cable television operators.

Information privacy is not an absolute good or an absolute right. There are legitimate exceptions: A person may consent to the access of information about himself or herself; governments must enforce laws and protect national security; monitoring is needed to maintain and protect computers and networks. It is important to strike a balance—allowing legitimate exceptions but not weakening privacy protection unnecessarily.

Privacy and computer security. Two main categories of privacy protection are relevant for computer security: protection from surveillance and personal data protection. Examples of surveillance include wiretapping by government or by intruders, monitoring of employees' keystrokes or whereabouts, and monitoring of credit card holders' purchases or cable television subscribers' selections. *Personal data protection* is the protection of the confidentiality and integrity of data about persons, as in medical, educational, or tax records. A *data subject* is the person that a data record is about. Surveillance and data protection are closely related, since surveillance generates personal data, and personal data are vulnerable to surveillance during transmission and use.

Privacy and computer security are closely related. Computer security is a prerequisite for privacy protection, since privacy is at risk if personal data lack integrity or are vulnerable to intruders and unauthorized insiders. Privacy law and privacy ethics impose computer security requirements. It is appropriate, then, that privacy is a traditional part of the field of computer security.

Threats to privacy

Computer and communications technology makes possible activities that threaten privacy.

Collection of personal data. It is technically possible to collect personal data in the minutest detail. Credit card purchases are stored and analyzed. Not only the payee and amount are recorded but also the time and the location. Every item we purchase at the grocery store is scanned, and (unless we pay cash) there is no technical barrier to associating this record with our identity. Not only is it possible to collect all these data, but the data have market value. The grocery chain or its partner could sell our food preferences to other companies. Citicorp started such a program in 1991, marketing lists of weight-conscious consumers or fancy food buyers. Businesses collect whatever information they can, to use or sell for targeted marketing. Computing technology supports the market in personal data by making feasible their collection, storage, and analysis.

As more commerce goes on-line, it becomes still easier and more profitable to collect computerized personal data. For example, interactive television and on-line shopping are expected to generate masses of data.

Another major source of personal information is telephone activity. Some information (such as name, address, and type of service) is collected directly from individual customers, and other information is generated by telephone transactions. Records of calls made, which are kept for billing purposes and disclosed to customers, include date and time, location, and number called. Less detail is disclosed in Europe, and Japanese subscribers have a choice of privacy options. U.S. rules do not restrict *automatic number identification,* which allows businesses that own 800 or 900 numbers to learn what numbers call them. Such data are valuable to them and to other organizations for targeted marketing. The Caller ID service also reveals the caller's number.

Another way to collect personal data is to eavesdrop on communications. It is quite feasible (if illegal) to tap local telephone lines. Wireless technologies, used for mobile phones, are more vulnerable than wire-based communications. Mobile computers expose location information not only to eavesdroppers but also to email correspondents and computer services that are used.

Personal data about employees are collected in the workplace. People who enter transactions (such as orders and insurance claims) are monitored routinely for speed and accuracy. The employee's work may appear directly on a supervisor's screen whenever the supervisor wishes. Many employers monitor email. Insurance companies make medical records available to employers in small batches, making it possible to deduce medical information about an individual. "Active badges" transmit continuously, revealing employees' locations. Computers and networks are monitored to detect problems—including security problems—and this means monitoring the users. Authenticating people who wish to use computers or enter buildings often involves collecting biometric data such as retinal patterns or hand shape.

Finally, governments collect great quantities of personal data about drivers, taxpayers, welfare recipients, students, possible criminals, and (in the census) everybody.

Maintenance and use of personal data. Every organization should have an explicit policy about the privacy and security of personal data that it maintains. Some organizations are also covered by privacy laws. Despite policy and law, however, personal data are often erroneous, and the confidentiality of such data is not protected.

> In 1991 it was learned that TRW (one of three major credit bureaus) had listed all the taxpayers of a Vermont town as tax delinquents. Similar errors occurred with other towns. Also in 1991, TRW settled a suit by 14 states over the inaccuracy of its database; TRW agreed to take steps to prevent errors. Still, in 1993 the major credit bureaus were receiving half a million disputes a month from people who believed their credit records had errors. Hackers have stolen credit card numbers and credit information from credit bureaus and telephone card information from telephone companies. A journalist tells of readily getting an account at a "super-bureau" (which buys data from the big three and resells it) and, using his home computer, obtaining then-Vice President Dan Quayle's credit report.

Serious problems were found by H. Jeff Smith (1993) in a survey of the privacy policies and practices of health and life insurers, banks, and credit card issuers. The study found that privacy policy often was lacking or in conflict with practice. Policy tended to drift until the organization reacted to an external threat—from publicity or legislative action. Competition sometimes led to a progressive weakening of controls. For example, as the customers of health insurers (employers) became more cost-conscious, the insurers responded by giving them more and more detailed information.

Like commercial organizations, government agencies sometimes fail to protect personal data.

> The National Crime Information Center (NCIC) contains over 24 million records and is used by thousands of law enforcement agencies. A study found (in the 1980s) that more than half the records had some significant quality problem, and 20 people were indicted in 1991 for selling information they had obtained from NCIC. Confidential data on more than 10,000 people, passed by a Social Security employee, were used to activate credit cards stolen from the mail. The Internal Revenue Service disclosed in 1994 that it had investigated 1300 employees since 1989 for unauthorized access to tax files. One IRS employee was indicted for illegally looking for information on a political candidate. The IRS mailed tax forms that exposed recipients' Social Security numbers. Employees of the California Department of Motor Vehicles teamed up with outsiders to sell DMV information. (Some DMVs sold data themselves before it was prohibited.)

Powerful parallel computers mine mountains of data for targeted-marketing nuggets. Seeking efficiency, organizations push more decision making into automated systems that base decisions on personal data. Authorized users of personal data download them to their personal computers for analysis, so organizations have difficulty knowing just where the personal data are. Personal data cross national borders (this is called *transborder data flow*). For example, multinational companies transfer personnel data, and transaction entry tasks are shipped abroad. Countries with strong legal protections for personal data may try to limit the flow of such data to countries with weaker protection.

Marketing of personal data. Perhaps the most striking trend affecting privacy is the marketing of personal data. In 1990 this was a $3 billion industry, with tens of thousands of lists for rent. Everybody from America Online to the Postal Service sells personal data. Businesses that collect data for one purpose keep those data for their potential value in another context. An industry of information brokers has come into place. One firm developed a list of 1.5 million wealthy people for use by nonprofit organizations to find donor prospects. From various sources, "prospect researchers" can develop detailed biographic and financial profiles. The Postal Service sells change-of-address information, saving itself work and making money—but exposing the mover to direct mail and possibly to danger. CompuServe rents subscriber lists that reflect subscribers' interests. Public reaction stopped two ventures in selling personal data. Equifax (another of the big three credit bureaus) and Lotus had planned to sell, on CD-ROM, data about U.S. households. New York Telephone had planned to rent directory information but received 800,000 requests from customers to omit their names.

Computer matching. Data about you collected by your bank are worth more when combined with data collected by market researchers. One personal record can be connected with another about the same person by matching identifiers such as name, Social Security number, and birth date. This is called *record linkage* or *computer matching*. Matching has a long history of use by government agencies, especially in connection with benefits. Welfare recipients, for example, have been checked against lists of government employees. Matching is seen as a cost-effective way to reduce fraud and abuse. Matching techniques are used by the private sector as well. Information bureaus and others build detailed records based on data from many sources. Data are also shared between the private and public sectors. For example, welfare recipients' records have been compared with credit bureau records.

Universal identifiers. Some countries (Sweden, for example) assign each citizen a number and use it for all records. In other countries, including the United States, public opinion traditionally has opposed *universal identifiers*. One reason for the opposition is a fear of the social control implied by linking all government records about a person into an inclusive dossier. (However, record linkage does not depend on a universal identifier; other identifying information can be used to link records.) Another reason for the opposition is that a universal identifier is seen as dehumanizing. A U.S. commission investigating privacy concerns was asked by a citizen to "prevent us from becoming our Social Security numbers." That was 20 years ago; now we are used to being numbers. The U.S. Social Security number (SSN) was not designed as a universal identifier but has evolved in that direction. Despite legislation designed to reverse the trend, the SSN is used by the federal government not only for Social Security but for tax records, medical benefit records, and many other purposes. State and local governments use the SSN for driver's licenses and welfare. Legislation introduced in 1995 would use it in federal databases aimed at deadbeat parents and employers of undocumented workers.

The private sector also depends on the SSN for identification. Nearly all health insurance uses it, as do banks and other financial institutions. Knowledge of the SSN is widely used as a proof of identity, allowing telephone access to bank accounts and other records.

> Using the SSN (available in public filings) of Robert Allen, chairman of AT&T, a reporter accessed Allen's AT&T stockholder records. In 1993, the U.S. Court of Appeals ruled in favor of a man who challenged Virginia's law requiring people to provide their SSNs when registering to vote (which made the SSNs publicly available). In 1994 the Ohio Supreme Court ruled that the city of Akron could refuse to publish the SSNs of its employees. The court heard testimony from an employee "Young 1" who had been denied credit because his SSN was revealed. Another person of the same name ("Young 2"), who had attended the same university, received by mistake Young 1's transcript, which showed his SSN. Young 2 opened several accounts using Young 1's SSN and was delinquent in payment. The court pointed out that the SSN allows an intruder to discover intimate details of a victim's personal life without the victim's knowledge. Indeed, the intruder here assumed the victim's identity.

Privacy law and policy

There are three main types of protection for personal data: (1) law and public policy, (2) policies and practices of organizations and individuals, and (3) technical measures. Laws, government policies, and codes of ethics establish rights of data subjects, place responsibilities on government and the private sector, and set up enforcement mechanisms. Law and public policy protections are increasingly international. Organizations—public and private, large and small—are the keepers of personal data; their policies and everyday practices are crucial. Technical protections for personal data range from encrypting electronic mail to ensuring that people who access databases are authorized to do so and accountable for their actions. Organizations can protect privacy by their policies, practices, and technical measures; individuals can take steps to protect their own privacy. Other chapters describe policies, practices, and technical measures; this section surveys privacy law and public policy.

Fair information practices. An important step toward data protection was the development in 1973 of a code of *fair information practices* (by the U.S. Department of Health, Education, and Welfare). This code has influenced legislation and practice in the United States and other countries. The code sets up five principles of fair information practices:

1. There must be no secret personal data record-keeping system.
2. There must be a way for individuals to discover what personal information is recorded about them and how it is used.
3. There must be a way for individuals to prevent personal information obtained for one purpose from being used or made available for other purposes without their consent.
4. There must be a way for individuals to correct or amend information about themselves.
5. An organization creating, maintaining, using, or disseminating records of identifiable personal data must ensure the reliability of the data for their intended use and must take reasonable precautions to prevent misuses of the data.

These principles are the basis for the Privacy Act of 1974, which covers federal databases.

International agreements. International guidelines for privacy come out of attempts to harmonize the legislation of different countries. One set of guidelines was adopted in 1980 by the Organization for Economic Cooperation and Development (OECD), whose members are industrialized nations. The OECD guidelines are based on the following principles:

- *Collection limitation.* Data should be obtained lawfully and fairly and, where appropriate, with the data subject's consent.

- *Data quality.* Data should be relevant to their purposes, accurate, complete, and up-to-date.
- *Purpose specification.* The purposes for which personal data are collected should be specified when they are collected. Data should be used only for those purposes or compatible ones.
- *Use limitation.* Data should not be used for purposes other than the specified ones, except with the data subject's consent or by authority of law.
- *Security safeguards.* There should be security safeguards against loss and misuse.
- *Openness.* There should be a general policy of openness about developments, practices, and policies. Means should be readily available for establishing the existence, nature, and use of personal data and the identity of the *data controller*—the responsible party.
- *Individual participation.* Individuals should have the right to find out what data are kept about them and to challenge data and have them erased or corrected.
- *Accountability.* A data controller should be accountable for complying with measures that implement the principles.

The OECD guidelines have been endorsed by all the member governments and by many private companies. In 1980, the Council of Europe adopted a similar set of fair information practices.

The OECD and Council of Europe guidelines are voluntary. Legally binding is the Council Directive on data protection for the European Union (EU), adopted in 1995. The directive calls for each EU nation to enact laws governing the processing of personal data. These laws must guarantee protections like those of the OECD guidelines, as well as others. Personal data must not be kept in an identifiable form any longer than is necessary for their original purpose. Restrictions are placed on the processing of data to reveal certain types of information, such as ethnic origin, political opinions, or health or sexual life. Individuals must have access to their records and the opportunity to correct them; the only exceptions are for national security, defense, law enforcement, public safety, or states' "paramount economic and financial interest...." Data subjects must be able to have their data erased before they are used for direct-mail marketing. The directive also establishes security requirements. Each state must set up an independent public authority to supervise data protection. There must be penalties for noncompliance and civil remedies for breach of rights. EU states may not restrict the flow of personal data among themselves for privacy reasons, but they must prohibit transfer of data to nonmember nations that do not ensure an adequate level of protection. This requirement raised concern in the United States, since U.S. law provides no comprehensive privacy protection, and since data transfers within multinational companies would be covered. Revisions eased these concerns by suggesting a flexible interpretation of "adequate level of protection."

National privacy laws. The first privacy legislation was enacted in the German state of Hesse in 1970. Since then, many European countries have enacted general data protection laws. In Japan, the constitution guarantees a right of privacy and secrecy of communications; there is also a general privacy protection law. The U.S. Privacy Act of 1974 covers federal records. The United States and Canada do not have broad privacy laws that apply to the private sector. Privacy laws in Europe typically set up a data protection commissioner, whose responsibility it is to oversee enforcement. However, privacy scholar David Flaherty (1988) warns against having created "only the illusion of data protection" as the "watchdog's teeth and claws become dull with age."

The Privacy Act of 1974. The U.S. Privacy Act of 1974 is based on the 1973 fair information principles. It applies only to federal agencies and does not cover private organizations. The Privacy Act is widely seen as ineffective, even within its limited scope. Some of the limitations are

- Although agencies must publish information about their record systems annually (in the *Federal Register*), this is not an effective way to notify individuals.
- The burden of enforcement is placed entirely on the individual, who must file a civil suit to get an injunction or damages.
- The act requires no specific measures to protect privacy.
- The penalties are inadequate.
- A loophole called "routine use" allows disclosure without the subject's consent for purposes compatible with (but different from) the original purpose. The loophole permits extensive computer matching.
- The act is outmoded. The extent of electronic access and information sharing that is demanded could not be foreseen in 1974. For example, the states have electronic access to Social Security data.

The Computer Matching and Privacy Protection Act of 1988 was intended to control matching. It requires agencies conducting a match to have written agreements specifying the purpose of the match, what records will be matched, and what the costs and benefits will be. Each agency involved in matching is also required to have a Data Integrity Board to oversee matching. The Computer Matching Act seems to have been ineffective, however. A General Accounting Office report (GAO 1993) concluded that cost-benefit analyses were done poorly or not at all and that proposed matches were not reviewed fully and earnestly. Some groups have recommended establishing a federal data protection board.

U.S. law and the private sector. A Privacy Protection Study Commission, reporting in 1977, rejected the idea of a comprehensive privacy law for the private sector. Some of the reasons stated were: (1) economic incentives for voluntary compliance are more effective; (2) a single standard is inappropriate for widely varying practices; and (3) a comprehensive law would involve too much government control over private flows of information. Instead, the commission recommended laws tailored to each industry but based on common principles. It recommended three basic objectives for privacy policy:

- Minimize intrusiveness
- Maximize fairness
- Establish obligations about using and disclosing personal data

The commission recommended legislation to establish a legally enforceable expectation of confidentiality for the records of certain private-sector organizations: credit bureaus, banks, insurance companies, doctors, and hospitals. Some of this legislation has been enacted at the federal level, some by individual states, and some not at all.

The Fair Credit Reporting Act (FCRA), passed in 1970, covers consumer reporting agencies such as Equifax, TRW, and Trans Union, as well as information brokers. These organizations provide both credit reports and more detailed investigative reports. A credit report contains a credit history, as provided by the person's creditors, landlords, utilities, banks, and others. It also contains the person's address, Social Security number, and employment and may include legal items such as marriage, divorce, and bankruptcy. An investigative report can include information about character, reputation, and lifestyle. If a report is used in a decision to deny credit, insurance, or employment, the act requires that the person be told the source of the report. Disclosure of credit reports without the person's consent is prohibited except for a "legitimate business purpose" or on court order. (Those who have a legitimate business purpose include potential creditors, landlords, insurance companies, and potential employers.) Agencies must disclose a credit report to its subject on request and must correct errors on the subject's request. The act requires some measures that help maintain data integrity and timeliness. Agencies must have procedures to verify the identity and purposes of recipients of reports. The preparation of an investigative report must be disclosed to the subject.

Many privacy advocates believe that the FCRA needs to be strengthened, and some states have stronger laws. There have been abuses of the law as well. Nearly anyone with modest determination can get credit reports, and errors are common. In 1994 the Federal Trade Commission ordered Trans Union to stop selling credit information for direct marketing purposes. Earlier, TRW had consented to stop such practices and Equifax had stopped voluntarily.

Many federal laws affect privacy in some way. The Right to Financial Privacy Act protects bank records against federal government access. Cable television companies cannot use the cable system to collect personal information without the subscriber's consent and cannot disclose such data. Purchasers and renters of videotapes have privacy protections. The Electronic Communications Privacy Act is discussed below.

U.S. law and the public sector. The Census Confidentiality Statute prohibits disclosure of census data that would allow an individual to be identified. National health research organizations are prohibited from disclosing data that would identify an individual. The Family Education Rights and Privacy Act gives students and parents the right to inspect educational records and challenge their accuracy and completeness. Individuals may see and correct information about themselves in criminal justice information systems. The crime bill of 1994 prohibits motor vehicle departments from selling most personal information.

Employee privacy. Except for the Privacy Act, information privacy of employees is largely unregulated. Many employers, however, have adopted codes of fair information practices, and an explicit employer policy is legally binding. (Such policies protect both employer and employee.) The main concerns are about personal data privacy, especially of medical records, and workplace monitoring. Some employers monitor the screens of employees' PCs and examine stored files. Keystrokes are often monitored to measure how much work an employee is doing. Email and voice mail are also monitored. Employers have the legal right to monitor business telephone calls. They often collect information about what numbers were called and how much time was spent on each call. Several attempts have been made to pass laws protecting workplace privacy, but none has succeeded.

Communications privacy

Most of us feel that our telephone calls should be private, and the law backs up our feelings. Calls and on-line personal data are exposed to communications security threats. Personal data gleaned from communications can be used for fraud or other purposes that harm the data subject. In addition, telephone calls generate personal data that are used for marketing or other commercial purposes.

Aspects of communications privacy. Privacy advocate Marc Rotenberg (1993) distinguishes three separate communications privacy interests: confidentiality, anonymity, and data protection. A confidential communication is one whose *content* and *existence* are known only to the parties to the communications (caller and callee or sender and receiver). *Anonymity* allows a person not to disclose his or her identity. For many communications, anonymity is no hindrance at all; for others, it may be essential (such as calls to health services that treat people with drug problems). Full communications privacy means not disclosing telephone numbers called from or called to. It means not disclosing the location of a person using a mobile telephone. The principles of personal data protection, originally devised for record-keeping systems, are being extended to communications networks. This is necessary because communications generate personal data and because personal data are used in on-line applications such as credit checks, electronic funds transfer, and benefit authorization.

Unfortunately, eavesdropping on telephone conversations is done, although it is illegal. Only law enforcement agencies can wiretap legally, and they must have court authorization based on probable cause.

EU Directive. The EU data protection directive (described earlier) contains several provisions about telephone transaction data. Traffic data are to be erased or made anonymous after the call terminates, unless they are needed for billing or other legitimate purposes. The directive recommends that itemized billing exclude the last four digits of called numbers. The directive also recommends strong protections against Caller ID service.

U.S. laws and policy. The Electronic Communications Privacy Act of 1986 (ECPA) prohibits eavesdropping or the interception of message contents. This law extends earlier wiretap protections to new technologies. It applies not only to telephone calls but also to national email, data transmission, and radio communication. It also applies to stored forms of the communications (such as those held by an email service provider). The ECPA does not, however, restrict private-sector use of transactional data, so it only protects a part of the confidentiality interest—content but not existence—and does not protect anonymity or personal data. A service provider can disclose transaction information without subscriber consent. Cable subscriber data are covered by a separate cable act, which does protect transaction data. A company's email system is not covered by the ECPA, and the courts have not established an employee's right to email privacy.

The Communications Assistance for Law Enforcement Act of 1994 (called the "digital telephony bill") was sought by the Federal Bureau of Investigation (FBI), which wanted to preserve its wiretap capabilities in the face of new technologies. The act requires all communications carriers to make it possible for the government to intercept communications and call-identifying information. The act authorizes $500 million to help the carriers provide this capability. The bill alarmed many privacy advocates, and some of them worked with Congress to get privacy protections included in the act. The act does not allow law enforcement agencies to initiate a tap directly; they must ask the carrier to do it. The call-identifying information to be provided does not include location information (except for telephone numbers). The act makes it harder for law enforcement agencies to get access to transactional data, and it requires carriers to protect the privacy and security of communications and call-identifying information that are not authorized to be intercepted.

In a related effort (discussed later in this chapter) the government has tried to curtail the total confidentiality of telephone calls that is technically possible.

Fraud and Abuse

The terms *computer fraud, computer abuse,* and *computer misuse* refer to a broad range of activities and effects. The categories of abuse include damaging or disrupting computing systems, corrupting information, stealing services (computing or telephone), violating privacy, stealing property (including information or intellectual property), and committing financial crimes.

Types of abuse

Abusers cause damage and disruption by maliciously erasing files or planting viruses (which copy themselves from one place to another) and in many other ways. Perpetrators steal telephone services by breaking into telephone system computers and then either subverting the system or stealing subscriber card numbers and other data. Authorized users of systems may violate the privacy of people whose records are in databases. For example, users of the National Crime Information Center checked whether friends had criminal records. An example of a computer property crime is using the computer system to have merchandise delivered to the criminal. Another example is the theft of trade secrets through computer espionage. Financial crimes range from fraudulent use of ATM cards, through bogus transactions that transfer funds out of bank accounts, to massive management frauds enabled by the computing system. The magnitude of loss from computer abuse is not known accurately, since organizations are not required to report it and they have incentives not to. Many individual cases involve losses of over a million dollars. A 1994 study conducted by the U.K. government found an average cost per fraud incident of £196,000 (roughly $300,000). The average bank robbery, in comparison, nets only $10,000. Clearly, computers are where the money is.

Examples of abuse

Probably the most common and most costly incidents involve insider fraud.

> Three technicians at AT&T's London headquarters were charged with unauthorized modification of computers and conspiracy to defraud. They had set up their own 900 telephone number and then programmed AT&T's computers to call that number repeatedly. (The caller of a 900 number is charged, and the owner is paid.) AT&T ran up and paid huge bills.
>
> An employee at Pinkerton Security & Investigation Services in California wire-transferred money from Pinkerton's bank account to the accounts of bogus companies that she controlled. The employee was given a code for accessing the Pinkerton bank account. She needed a superior's approval for the wire transfers, but—conveniently—she had been given the task of canceling a former superior's code. Instead, she began using the code to authorize her transfers. Over 2 years, she moved more than $1 million to her own accounts.
>
> In 1994 an MCI employee was charged in a fraud that compromised 100,000 telephone calling cards. He was alleged to have written software for MCI's switching systems that trapped calling card numbers from various telephone carriers. Through a fraud ring, the card numbers were sold to "phone phreaks" in the United States and Europe, who used them for hacking and network access. The Secret Service said that tens of

> thousands of customers were victimized, with the total fraud value estimated at $50 million.

Another type of abuse is corporate espionage.

> In 1993, Virgin Atlantic Airways and British Airways settled a case in which British Airways was accused of breaking into Virgin's reservation system to obtain passengers' travel plans and phone numbers and then calling the passengers and trying to get them to change to British Airways flights.

As the commercial use of networks grows, networked computers become increasingly attractive targets for hackers.

> Members of the hacker ring MOD (for Masters of Deception or Masters of Disaster) were indicted in 1992 and charged with computer tampering, computer fraud, wire fraud, illegal wiretapping, and breaking privacy laws. The ring members, who were 18 to 22 years old, all pleaded guilty, and some received substantial prison terms. The ring broke into telephone switching systems operated by telephone companies (including Southwestern Bell, Nynex, and Pacific Bell) and stole credit reports from systems owned by TRW and others. The case marked a government crackdown on hacking and was the first time that the government tapped hackers' computer transmissions.

One target of hackers is licensed software. The stolen software is sometimes distributed through electronic bulletin board systems, which pay a fee to the hackers and distribute the software free to their paying members.

> A bulletin board operator was indicted in 1994 for federal copyright infringement and wire fraud. Subscribers to the bulletin board, who paid $99 a year, could download software for free. The programs included Lotus 1-2-3 and Norton Utilities.

Sometimes the system of an unwitting third party is broken into and used to distribute stolen software.

> A system administrator at Florida State University noticed unusually high activity on one computer, with many users logging on from abroad. He discovered that his computer had been enriched with a wealth of proprietary software, including beta-test versions of Microsoft and IBM operating systems.

The legal environment

Computers and computer networks have changed commerce and the nature of fraud dramatically, and the law is only gradually reacting to the changes. For example, the Statute of Frauds requires contracts to be in writing and to be signed. Copyright law must cope with the explosion of digital information—music, video performances, software, and books are all stored and transmitted in the same form.

Computer crime law. The first U.S. federal computer crime law was passed in 1984 and amended in 1986 and 1994. Nearly all the states of the United States also have computer crime laws. Computer crimes are also prosecuted under other federal laws, such as wire fraud laws. The 1984 law was quite narrow, covering only (1) classified defense or foreign relations information, (2) records of financial institutions or credit reporting agencies, and (3) government computers. Unauthorized access or access in excess of authorization became a felony for the classified information and a misdemeanor for the financial information. The law made it a misdemeanor to knowingly access a U.S. government computer without or beyond authorization if the government's use of the computer would be affected. Few cases were prosecuted under the 1984 law. The Computer Fraud and Abuse Act of 1986 was much tougher. It clarified the 1984 law and added three new crimes:

1. Where use of a "federal interest" computer furthers an intended fraud
2. (Later amended) Altering, damaging, or destroying information in a federal interest computer or preventing the use of the computer or information when this causes a loss of $1000 or more or could impair medical treatment
3. Trafficking in computer passwords if it affects interstate or foreign commerce or permits unauthorized access to government computers

The Computer Abuse Amendments Act of 1994 changed "federal interest" to "a computer used in interstate commerce or communications" and amended the section to clarify authorization and to cover viruses and worms. Included are both intentional damage and damage done "with reckless disregard of a substantial and unjustifiable risk...." Imprisonment for the unintentional damage is limited to 1 year. The act also provides for civil action to obtain compensatory damages or other relief.

The Electronic Communications Privacy Act makes a crime of unauthorized access to stored electronic communications, such as electronic mail.

In the United Kingdom, the Computer Misuse Act of 1990 defines three offenses, all for intentional unauthorized access. The first offense is unauthorized access to computer material, punishable by a maximum prison term of 6 months. A second, more serious offense is unauthorized access with intent to commit or facilitate commission of further offenses, such as fraud; the maximum term is 5 years. The third offense is unauthorized modification of computer material, also with a maximum prison term of 5 years.

Computer security legislation. The laws just described target perpetrators of abuse. Other laws aim at preventing or detecting abuse through requiring better computer security. Laws that are not explicitly about computer security can impose requirements. An important one in the United States is the Foreign Corrupt Practices Act of 1977, which applies to companies registered with the Securities and Exchange Commission. The act requires these companies to keep accurate and fair records about transactions and disposition of assets. They must maintain controls that provide reasonable assurances that

1. Transactions are executed in accordance with management's authorization.
2. Transactions are recorded as necessary to permit preparation of financial statements and to maintain accountability for assets.
3. Access to assets is permitted only in accordance with management's authorization.
4. Records of assets are compared with existing assets at reasonable intervals, and action is taken about any differences.

The U.K. Companies Act requires companies to take precautions to guard against falsification of records and to facilitate discovering falsification.

The United States has no laws explicitly requiring private organizations to secure their computers. The Computer Security Act of 1987 places requirements on federal government agencies in order to improve the security of information in government computer systems. The act states that security and privacy of federal computer systems are in the public interest. It gives to the National Institute of Standards and Technology (then called the National Bureau of Standards) the computer security mission, including developing standards. The act requires each agency to provide its employees with training in computer security awareness and practice and to set up a security plan for each of its systems.

Privacy laws also impose requirements. The Privacy Act of 1974 requires federal agencies to set up administrative, technical, and physical security safeguards. The Fair Credit Reporting Act requires data brokers to maintain security procedures, including verifying the identity of the recipients of credit reports. The Data Protection Act of the United Kingdom requires organizations that keep personal data to take security measures.

Law on electronic signatures and evidence. In U.S. federal law, under the Statute of Frauds, a party who claims that a contract was made must provide some proof. The traditional method of proof is a signed written document. Cryptography can be used to put signatures on electronic messages, and these *digital signatures* probably will be accepted as legal. The Federal Rules of Evidence allow computer data to be admitted as business records if a foundation for their reliability is established. U.K. laws about evidence have similar provisions.

Standards and Criteria

The dictionary defines a *standard* as "something that is established by authority, custom, or general consent as a model or example to be followed." A *standard* is also "a definite level or degree of quality that is adequate for a specific purpose." Standards have enormous influence on computer security. For computing in general, standards serve two main purposes. First, every system is made of components that are designed and built by different organizations. The components must fit together, and standard interfaces are the way to accomplish this—for both hardware and software. When computers are networked, they must be able to understand one another; they must communicate according to standard *protocols*. Security components must fit with and communicate with one another and with other components. An *open* system has well-defined and public interfaces, services, and protocols.

The second role of standards is to assure users and other stakeholders that a product or system provides a "definite level" of some property. For security properties, a standards body publishes the criteria for meeting some level of security and then certifies that specific products do meet the standard. Standards apply not only to products and systems but also to people and procedures. For example, auditing standards specify how an audit should proceed when controls for fraud appear weak.

Standards come from a variety of sources: government and nongovernment standards institutes, professional societies, industry organizations, and ad hoc groups that organize around a specific need. Often a set of interfaces or protocols that was developed for a specific purpose or product becomes (through wide use) a de facto standard. Formal standardization often follows. Computer security is affected by many types of standards, as shown in Fig. 2.2.

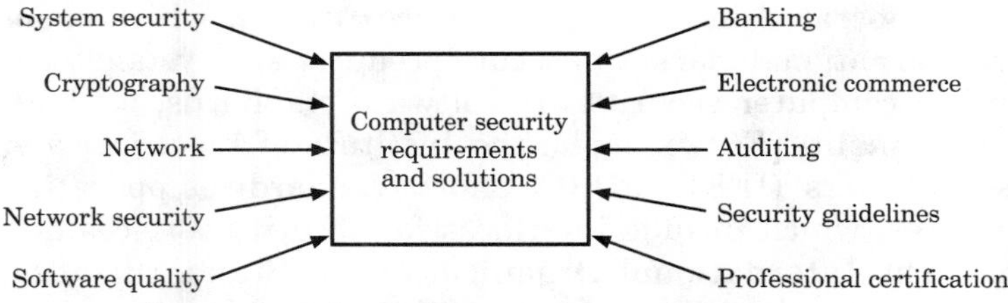

Figure 2.2 Types of standards affecting computer security.

Computer security standards

Criteria for products and systems. The early computer security standards arose in response to military needs and were developed by the DoD. First issued in 1983 and revised in 1985, the *Trusted Computer System Evaluation Criteria* (TCSEC) are important historically and continue to be very important. They have been adopted by other countries and have influenced other standards. The TCSEC include two kinds of requirements: required security features (*functionality*) and *assurance* requirements—in other words, what the computing system must do about security, and how we can know that it really does it. Systems developed according to the TCSEC are called *trusted systems.* The TCSEC emphasized confidentiality and did little about integrity and availability. They were developed by the National Computer Security Center (NCSC) of the National Security Agency (NSA), which is in the DoD. The main document, which has an orange cover, is called the "Orange Book"; related documents are red, blue, etc., leading to the name "Rainbow Series."

France, Germany, the Netherlands, and the United Kingdom cooperated in developing *Information Technology Security Evaluation Criteria* (ITSEC), which address both commercial and government requirements, considering attributes other than secrecy. The ITSEC serve as de facto standards for much of Europe. The *Canadian Criteria* cover integrity, availability, and accountability as well as confidentiality. The ITSEC and the Canadian Criteria separate functionality ratings from assurance ratings more completely than the TCSEC.

The world changed a great deal after the TCSEC were developed. Military secrecy was no longer the overriding computer security concern; of equal concern were integrity, availability, and confidentiality for commercial systems. Multiuser mainframes lost their dominance, and networking became the norm. As commerce became more international, an obstacle was that countries did not recognize each others' security certifications. The United States, the European Union, and

Canada have cooperated in drafting *Common Criteria,* which could facilitate an international market in secure products and systems.

Also affecting computer security are software standards, for both uniformity and quality. For example, the Institute of Electrical and Electronics Engineers' (IEEE) POSIX effort standardizes operating system interfaces, which include interfaces for security services and mechanisms. The International Organization for Standardization (ISO) has quality standards for manufacturing, with interpretations for software development. Quality certification is required by EU countries. The DoD has encouraged its contractors to demonstrate a level of software development maturity according to a Capability Maturity Model developed by the Software Engineering Institute.

Standards for finance and commerce. Banks are leading users of cryptography and other security technology, and electronic data interchange (EDI) transactions also must be secure. Voluntary security standards for wholesale banking transactions and automatic teller machines (ATMs) are developed by the American Bankers Association. The American National Standards Institute (ANSI) also develops standards for business and finance, as do ISO groups. Encryption of financial transactions is based mainly on the *Data Encryption Standard* (DES) of the U.S. government. EDI standards are still evolving. The two main ones are ANSI standard X12, which is used in the United States and Canada, and EDIFACT (EDI for Administration, Commerce, and Transport), which was developed by the United Nations Economic Commission for Europe. EDIFACT is expected to predominate for international EDI. Both standards groups recognize the need for security services for EDI transactions, and some ANSI encryption standards have been adopted. Both X12 and EDIFACT were adopted for U.S. government use.

Auditors' standards also affect computer security. These standards are promulgated in the United States by the American Institute of Certified Public Accountants and by the Institute for Internal Auditors, which is an international organization.

U.S. government standards. U.S. government standards affect security developments in all arenas—public and private, United States and international. The National Institute of Standards and Technology (NIST) has through the years issued a series of Federal Information Processing Standards. Although the standards apply only to federal procurement, their effect is far more widespread. The federal government is an enormous market with a corresponding influence on computer industry decisions about what products to build.

Standards requirements and responsibilities within the government changed with the passage of the Computer Security Act of 1987. This act was a response to two concerns: (1) the increased vulnerability of government operations to information system vulnerability and (2) the attempt by the Reagan administration (in National Security Decision Directive 145) to give the National Security Agency (NSA) responsibility for the security of "sensitive but unclassified" information. NSDD-145 shifted government information protection from civilian control to military control. With the act, Congress tried to change course; the act made NIST responsible for security and privacy standards and guidelines for sensitive unclassified information in government systems. NIST is to use technical advice and assistance of the NSA where appropriate. NIST and NSA developed a memorandum of understanding about their working relationship. Many observers feel that NSA continues to dominate work on security standards, especially cryptography standards. In 1994, Presidential Decision Directive 29 set up a Security Policy Board, which promptly recommended that it have authority over both classified and unclassified sensitive systems.

Generally Accepted System Security Principles. In its 1991 report *Computers at Risk,* a National Research Council committee recommended establishing a set of *Generally Accepted System Security Principles,* analogous in their breadth and wide acceptability to financial accounting standards or building codes. These would build on the TCSEC but enlist a much broader consensus by reflecting the "widest possible spectrum" of computer users. A few examples of such principles are

- The best known software engineering methods must be used, and a means of independent evaluation must be provided.
- Systems must be able to control which operations users can perform on specific data objects.
- Programs should be recognizable as, for example, "production" or "trusted" and protected against improper modification. It should be possible to restrict which classes of programs can access specific data.

In 1992 the OECD developed a set of Guidelines for the Security of Information Systems (Fig. 2.3). These guidelines are intended as a foundation for a total framework that includes laws, policies, technical and administrative measures, and education. Also in 1992 an effort began that follows up on the *Computers at Risk* recommendation. An international committee was formed to develop and promulgate Generally Accepted System Security Principles (GSSP). The committee decided on a hierarchy of principles, with *pervasive* principles

1. *Accountability.* All parties concerned with the security of information systems (owners, providers, users, and others) should have explicit responsibilities and accountability.
2. *Awareness.* All parties should readily be able to gain knowledge of security measures, practices, and procedures.
3. *Ethics.* Information systems and their security should be provided and used so as to respect the rights and legitimate interests of others.
4. *Multidisciplinary principle.* Security measures should take into account all relevant viewpoints, including technical, administrative, organizational, operational, commercial, educational, and legal.
5. *Proportionality.* Security should be appropriate and proportionate to the value of and degree of reliance on the information systems and to the risk of potential harm.
6. *Integration.* Security measures should be coordinated and integrated with each other and with other measures, practices, and procedures of the organization so as to create a coherent system of security.
7. *Timeliness.* Parties should act in a timely and coordinated way to prevent and to respond to security breaches.
8. *Reassessment.* Security should be reassessed periodically as information systems and their security needs change.
9. *Democracy.* The security of information systems should be compatible with the legitimate use and flow of information in a democratic society.

Figure 2.3 OECD Guidelines for the Security of Information Systems (paraphrased).

at the top of the hierarchy. In a 1994 draft the OECD security principles were adopted as pervasive principles, and others were proposed. NIST has drafted generally accepted system security principles and practices for the U.S. government.

Professional certification. The practice of information security is quite a new discipline, whose practitioners have varied educational and work experience backgrounds. Professions such as accounting, in contrast, have well-established prerequisites, common understandings and knowledge, and professional certification. The International Information Systems Security Certification Consortium [(ISC)^2], a consortium of professional organizations, is developing a certification program for information security professionals. A code of ethics has been defined and a testing program established.

Network standards

For computer networks, standards make it possible to master enormous complexity and heterogeneity. A network standard is tied to a *network architecture,* which describes the functions performed by the network and the protocols by which they are performed. (A *protocol* is a set of rules or an algorithm by which parties cooperate to accomplish some task.) Network architectures are *layered.* The lowest layers concern physical aspects, middle layers deal with messages and connections, and the highest layers deal with applications and how data are presented to users. Any or all layers may include security services. The two leading open architectures are (1) *ISO/OSI* (Open Systems Interconnection of the International Organization for Standardization) and (2) the layered protocols used for the Internet.

The *OSI Reference Model* provides a foundation for the many OSI standards, and the *OSI Security Architecture* is a foundation for OSI security standards. It identifies the security services and mechanisms that are needed and positions them within the layers. There are dozens of OSI standards pertaining to security. In contrast to the OSI Reference Model (which came out of a conscious top-down effort at architecture), the Internet architecture took shape gradually and less formally, tracking developments in the Internet itself. Its protocols (including the *TCP/IP protocol suite*) serve as standards. The Internet has well-developed procedures for formulating, reviewing, and approving its protocols. The Internet Society oversees the development of protocols by the Internet Engineering Task Force (IETF). The defining documents are all available on the Internet.

There are strong motivations to reach a single family of open network standards. There has been much cross-fertilization between TCP/IP and OSI, and there is hope for eventual convergence. In the U.S. market, TCP/IP is clearly dominant.

Cryptography Policy

Cryptography is the art of transforming information to keep it confidential or to protect its integrity. The process that transforms the information is called *encryption.* The historical uses of cryptography were military and diplomatic. The current uses are more comprehensive, driven by the needs for communications privacy and secure electronic banking and commerce. Advances in cryptography and computing power have broadened the range of applications for which cryptography is practical. The worldwide market is estimated at $1.8 billion. Cryptography is used to

- Authenticate retail transactions and transactions between organizations.
- Secure electronic funds transfers.

- Protect the secrecy of military and commercial communications.
- Protect email privacy.
- Protect the integrity of software and stored data.
- Authenticate the identity of network users.

Cryptographic methods and applications are covered in Chaps. 5 and 10. This section discusses U.S. cryptography policy.

Background

Two government agencies play major roles in cryptography. NIST promulgates standards for encryption of unclassified information. NSA develops cryptographic technology and influences policy. NSA also *uses* cryptography to conduct electronic surveillance for intelligence purposes. "This dual role seems suspect to some people: if codes influenced by NSA are crackable, the agency's intelligence mission becomes easier" (Adam 1992: 29). Some cryptographers in universities and the private sector have not trusted NSA, in part because its secrecy conflicts with their strong beliefs about open algorithms and public review. The most prominent cryptographic standard is the Data Encryption Standard. DES is implemented in hardware and software products throughout the world. Most encrypted financial transactions use it. Its algorithm is public. Although the DES has proved secure against attack (as far as is known publicly), its life is limited. Increases in computing power will soon make DES vulnerable to "brute force" attack. This means that new standards are needed.

With the DES, the sender and receiver of a message (and the encryption and decryption processes) both use the same *secret key*. One problem with secret key methods is the difficulty of distributing the keys securely. *Public key* methods use two keys: a public one and a private one; the sender only has to know the receiver's public key. Key distribution is much more feasible. Since public key encryption is very much slower than DES, it is used mainly for exchange of secret keys and not for bulk encryption of data.

Cryptography can be used for signing electronic messages, much as we sign paper documents. A *digital signature* identifies the sender of a message and prevents the sender from repudiating the message. A digital signature also confirms the integrity of the message—that it was not altered during transmission or later. Digital signatures are crucial for secure electronic commerce. The wide use of digital signatures (which use public key methods) requires a framework of law and procedures—a *public key infrastructure.*

Policy issues

Several overlapping cryptography policy issues have been controversial.

The Digital Signature Standard. The *Digital Signature Standard* (DSS) was adopted in 1994 after a long delay due to many criticisms. A major criticism is that the DSS provides only digital signatures and not encryption for confidentiality (to replace the DES) or support for key distribution. Both digital signatures and confidentiality can be provided by another method, *RSA*, which has become a de facto international standard. One reason given for NIST's decision not to use RSA is that it is patented. However, patent issues arose for DSS also.

The Escrowed Encryption Standard. Even more controversial is the *Escrowed Encryption Standard* (EES), originally known as the "Clipper Chip." The goals of the EES are to provide strong encryption for confidentiality and to assist law enforcement. If voice phone calls are digitized and encrypted, law enforcement officials cannot understand what passes on tapped wires. The EES solution is to design the encryption scheme so that law enforcement agents can (once they obtain a secret key) understand encrypted calls. A secure telephone contains a physically secure device that implements an encryption-decryption algorithm called *SKIPJACK*. The device also transmits a Law Enforcement Access Field (LEAF) that identifies the telephone. If the LEAF is intercepted and used with the secret key, a conversation can be decrypted. At the factory, each secret key is split into two pieces; then each piece is placed with a different escrow agent. The agents are to release keys only to law enforcement officials who present appropriate authorization. The SKIPJACK and LEAF algorithms are secret and can be implemented only in tamper-resistant hardware. These restrictions make it hard to study or imitate them—in contrast with DES.

The EES has been opposed by privacy advocates, professional organizations (including IEEE-USA and USACM), and computer and communications industry groups and companies. Privacy advocates are concerned about the escrow agents (initially NIST and the Treasury Department) holding keys so that individuals cannot communicate by phone with total privacy. They point to past improper government intrusions on privacy. Other criticisms are about the secrecy of the algorithms, availability only in hardware, and the lack of appeal to non-U.S. buyers. Opponents criticize the secrecy of the process leading to the EES, which sought no public input. The NSA and FBI point to the danger from criminals and terrorists, who could communicate without fear of interception. The EES was adopted in 1994 as a voluntary standard. At this writing, the plan is proceeding, and it is anticipated that the EES will be revised to cover computer network communication. Encryption software has been developed that defeats the EES scheme, allowing confidential communication over EES devices attached to computers.

The key escrow issue is closely related to another policy issue—export control.

Export control. For purposes of export control, cryptography for confidentiality has been considered inherently military. It appears on the Munitions List and is controlled by the State Department, which relies on NSA. Some cryptography exports, principally those used for banking and money transactions, are controlled by the Commerce Department. Both hardware and software confidentiality products are controlled, and export requires a license that can take months to obtain, if it is obtained at all. Only weak encryption can be exported routinely. These difficulties become more important with the use of cryptography in everyday software such as word processing and email systems. The developer of the public key software Pretty Good Privacy (PGP) was investigated because PGP was put on the Internet (which made it available overseas). In 1994 the State Department ruled against export of the electronic version of a book that contained source code for cryptographic algorithms. U.S. companies cannot use DES in communicating with their facilities abroad. However, EES technology apparently *can* be exported, since the hardened implementation prevents study of the algorithm.

The export policy is designed to reduce the availability of advanced cryptography to other countries, since its use can interfere with U.S. intelligence gathering. However, the policy also affects U.S. production of cryptographic products. Since many U.S. computer and software companies rely on the international market, they may not produce or adopt advanced cryptographic products that they cannot export. An explicit design goal for some products has been to avoid export-restricted technology. Export of somewhat stronger encryption has been allowed if portions of the keys were placed in escrow. There also is a softening of the presumption that all cryptography is weaponry. Legislation introduced in 1996 would greatly alter the export policy.

Constitutional issues. Cryptography policy raises important constitutional issues. Increasingly, communications that once were face-to-face or by paper are electronic; many of them will be encrypted. If encrypted communications are protected speech under the First Amendment, then the government's retaining the ability to decrypt them may violate free speech rights. It also may violate privacy rights. Key escrow might violate the Fifth Amendment protection against self-incrimination. Export restrictions may violate First Amendment rights. In 1995, an encryption researcher sued the government, claiming that not being allowed to post his source code on the Internet violated his right to free speech. In 1996, a judge allowed the case to proceed, ruling that source code *is* speech.

Ethics and Computer Security

Often, computer security involves deciding how things *should be*. Society in general must make some of these decisions. How important is privacy compared with law enforcement? How safe do systems have to be? Computer professionals face questions about the systems they build and manage. Should the system have additional features (and cost) to protect privacy? Has the system been tested enough? How much should we invest in physical security? Computer users have their own questions. Should I buy software or copy my friend's? Ethics helps us find answers to such questions. Principles of ethical behavior seem to be universal in social life; they derive from religion, views of human nature, philosophical analysis, or other sources.

In philosophy, ethics is a systematic method for deciding what is moral. Ethical analysis involves formulating an argument, critically evaluating it, reformulating it, and so forth in a continuing process. The process moves from principles to cases in which the principles are applied, and back to principles, and so on. Even if no final conclusion is reached, the analysis usually clarifies the arguments and reveals which arguments are inadequate. Michael McFarland (1991) distinguishes three basic modes of ethical analysis. *Normative ethics* seeks to arrive at ethical rules. The *ethics of virtue* asks what kind of person does the right thing. *Social ethics* asks what social structures are needed to support values such as justice and human dignity.

Who must apply ethical principles and ethical analysis to computer security issues? First, computer professionals. Second, leaders of businesses and other organizations who make decisions and set the ethical tone for their organizations. Third, computer users. Finally, all of us—as citizens in deciding which laws and government policies are right and as consumers, employees, and stockholders in "voting" for ethical companies.

Ethical principles

Three fundamental principles often are used in analyzing issues of computer ethics. These principles, developed by European philosophers, are (1) the promotion of happiness (utilitarianism), (2) justice, and (3) duty with respect for the humanity of others.

Utilitarianism. The thesis of *utilitarianism* (as articulated by John Stuart Mill in the mid-nineteenth century) is that "actions are right in proportion as they tend to promote happiness, wrong as they tend to produce the reverse of happiness. By happiness is intended pleasure, and the absence of pain; by unhappiness, pain and the privation of pleasure." What must be considered is the net happiness over unhappiness, and sometimes one must choose an action that produces a net unhappiness—if that action produces less unhappiness than alternative actions. That is, we may have to choose the lesser of two evils. It is not enough for a chosen action to produce net happiness; the action must produce more happiness than any possible alternative action.

Happiness is an *intrinsic good*. Moral rules such as "do not kill" or "do not break the law" are not intrinsically good, but in general they are useful—have utility—in promoting good. Although moral rules are generally useful, they may have exceptions. A utilitarian might say that killing is wrong because it always diminishes happiness. Or a utilitarian might say that under some circumstances killing is not wrong because it increases happiness—for example, assassinating Hitler in 1943.

This difference shows where disagreements arise in applying utilitarian theory. Consider the syllogism:

> *The action which promotes the maximum happiness is right.*
> *This action is the one which promotes the maximum happiness.*
> Therefore, *This action is right* (Hospers 1990: 32).

People who accept the first premise (the utilitarian ethic) still disagree about the conclusion because they disagree about the effects of a specific action. For example, people disagree about whether treating software as property promotes the maximum happiness.

Utilitarianism is criticized because it says nothing about how happiness is distributed. For example, we might imagine a situation where a few unhappy slaves created great happiness for many people. But slavery and other unequal distributions of good conflict with our notions of *justice* and with our feelings about the rights of all human beings.

Justice. Two important aspects of justice are *distributive justice* and *just deserts*. Most people, given a choice, would prefer a society having the largest total amount of good. And many would prefer a society where good is pretty equally distributed. The problem comes when these two choices conflict. Many people are dissatisfied with an equal distribution of good as an ideal because they feel that justice is getting what one *deserves*. Different criteria have been proposed for determining what reward is just. These criteria include an individual's achievement, effort, ability, and need, as well as societal criteria such as the market for work.

Duty and human dignity. According to the ethics of duty, what makes an action right or wrong is not its consequences (as in utilitarianism) but the internal nature of the action. Immanuel Kant believed that a moral action is one that is undertaken from a sense of duty and from understanding what that duty is. Kant believed that human beings, uniquely among all beings, are rational and moral agents who can set their own goals and decide about their own conduct. They are the embodiment of moral law. For this reason, the value of human beings is absolute, not comparable with the value of anything else. Kant's fundamental ethical principle is: Always treat another human being as an end and never merely as a means to some other end.

Privacy

The earlier discussion of privacy touched on the reasons for valuing privacy. Warren and Brandeis (1890) argue that the principle behind protection of personal writings and the like against publication is not the principle of private property, "but that of an inviolate personality." The philosopher Charles Fried analyzes why we value privacy so highly. He concludes that we do not value privacy as an end in itself but that it provides a "rational context" for our most significant ends, including love, friendship, trust, and respect. "Privacy is not merely a good technique for furthering these fundamental relations; rather, without privacy they are simply inconceivable" (Fried 1990: 53). In relations with others, privacy is control over knowledge about oneself and is therefore an aspect of personal liberty. In the privilege against self-incrimination, for example, society recognizes the great value of controlling information about oneself. This control cannot be absolute, since it must be limited by the rights of others. Fried proposes that legal protections for privacy will be just if (1) the process that produces them is just, representing all interests fairly, and (2) the outcome protects basic dignity and provides "absolute title to at least some information about oneself."

Some of our essential relations are with impersonal organizations, such as the Internal Revenue Service (IRS), the bank, an employer, or an insurance company. In these relations, personal information held by organizations gives them power, and individuals lose autonomy.

Professional ethics

For many of us, issues of computer ethics arise primarily in the context of our professions or our professional training.

Professionals. The term *professional* usually refers to people who have special skills and knowledge and substantial autonomy in their work. Most people recognize doctors and lawyers as good examples of professionals (although they have lost some autonomy). Doctors and lawyers are licensed to practice by professional boards and are subject to sanctions if they violate professional ethics. Some professionals involved with computer security, such as auditors who are CPAs, are also licensed. It is less clear if most computer people are indeed professionals. Although they need special skill and knowledge, many have little autonomy in their work. Software developers can become licensed, but few do. Computing organizations have established codes of ethics, but sanctions are generally lacking. Most computer people do think of themselves as professionals, and their responsibilities are often more comprehensive than those of more traditional professions.

Professionals have a special obligation to behave ethically because they have a special capacity to affect the world. They have the skills and knowledge, and their work can dramatically affect property, the quality of life, and life itself. Just as a doctor has life-and-death impact, so does a developer of software for an x-ray machine. A major difference, however, is that doctors know their patients and see the results of their decisions. The software developer may never see the technicians and patients who depend on the software or learn about the machine's safety record.

Obligations to others. A professional has obligations to employers, employees, clients, professional colleagues, and the public. The code of ethics of the Data Processing Management Association explicitly recognizes the professional's obligations to management, fellow members, society, employer, and country. In general, employee loyalty to an employer is a good, but loyalty to the employer may conflict with other ethical responsibilities. For example, the employer may insist on releasing a product that the employee knows to be inadequately tested. If all else fails, an employee may choose to "blow the whistle," probably at great personal cost. Some employee-employer obligations are matters of debate. For example, can an employee who changes jobs use the specialized knowledge gained with the former employer? The employer may feel that trade secrets are being taken away. Do restraints on working in that specialized area limit the former employee's autonomy? Is he or she being treated only as a means? Employers who want to treat employees as ends, not just means, should respect their employees' privacy and provide opportunities to learn, grow, and exercise autonomy. They should heed employee warnings about unsafe or insecure products. A professional's responsibilities to clients include honoring contracts, being honest about the status of work, and striving for the highest possible quality of work. Perhaps the most difficult to fulfill are obligations to society; these are easy to overlook in the daily press of getting work done on time and within budget. (A 1994 survey of U.S. workers found that 29 percent felt pressure to violate ethical standards to meet business needs such as tight deadlines and aggressive business goals.) A professional should behave in a way that contributes to the greater society and that does not harm it.

Codes of ethics. Most of the professional organizations that computer security professionals belong to (Fig. 2.4) have codes of ethics and professional standards. The codes serve multiple purposes. One purpose is to encourage the public to view the profession as ethically responsible. The code thus benefits both the public and the members of the profession. The code also may promote self-regulation, as opposed to government regulation, which most groups prefer to avoid. Most important, however, the code speaks to and for the organization's members. It embodies a set of values, and it sets standards for professional behavior. It sensitizes members and others to ethical issues, educates them, and helps them make decisions. Most probably, only a small percentage of members participate in crafting codes of ethics, and many join an organization without accepting (or even thinking about) its code of ethics. Still, if members strongly disagree with the code, their views are likely to be voiced and debated.

Figure 2.5 summarizes the ACM code of ethics, which was revised in 1992. The old 1972 code listed violations of ethics and specified sanctions. The 1992 code deemphasizes sanctions, aiming at an educational role. The code has four sections. The first section states basic

American Institute of Certified Public Accountants (AICPA)

ACM

British Computing Society

Data Processing Management Association (DPMA)

EDP Auditors Association (EDPAA)

Institute of Electrical and Electronics Engineers (IEEE)

Institute of Internal Auditors (IIA)

Figure 2.4 Some professional organizations of computer security professionals.

1. General Moral Imperatives
   1.1 Contribute to society and human well-being
   1.2 Avoid harm to others
   1.3 Be honest and trustworthy
   1.4 Be fair and take action not to discriminate
   1.5 Honor property rights including copyrights and patents
   1.6 Give proper credit for intellectual property
   1.7 Respect the privacy of others
   1.8 Honor confidentiality
2. More Specific Professional Responsibilities
   2.1 Strive to achieve the highest quality, effectiveness and dignity in both the process and products of professional work
   2.2 Acquire and maintain professional competence
   2.3 Know and respect existing laws pertaining to professional work
   2.4 Accept and provide appropriate professional review
   2.5 Give comprehensive and thorough evaluations of computer systems and their impacts, including analysis of possible risks
   2.6 Honor contracts, agreements, and assigned responsibilities
   2.7 Improve public understanding of computing and its consequences
   2.8 Access computing and communication resources only when authorized to do so
3. Organization Leadership Imperatives
   3.1 Articulate social responsibilities of members of an organization unit and encourage full acceptance of those responsibilities
   3.2 Manage personnel and resources to design and build information systems that enhance the quality of working life
   3.3 Acknowledge and support proper and authorized uses of an organization's computing and communications resources
   3.4 Ensure that users and those who will be affected by a system have their needs clearly articulated during the assessment and design of requirements. Later the system must be validated to meet requirements.
   3.5 Articulate and support policies that protect the dignity of users and others affected by a computing system
   3.6 Create opportunities for members of the organization to learn the principles and limitations of computer systems

Figure 2.5 Code of Ethics and Professional Standards of the ACM.

moral principles. The second section gets more specific about professional ethical concerns. The third section specifically addresses leaders in organizations. This is appropriate and necessary, since leaders have the most autonomy and since they strongly influence others. (Not shown in Fig. 2.5 are a section on sanctions and the guidelines for applying each imperative.) Computer security is prominent in the ACM code. Integrity and availability are essential to contributing to society and human well-being (1.1) and avoiding harm to others (1.2). The confidentiality attribute of computer security is essential to privacy (1.7) and confidentiality (1.8).

An important technique of ethics is to pose hypothetical cases and analyze them in terms of ethical principles. Ronald Anderson et al.

(1993) have analyzed several cases in terms of the ACM code. Here is a summary of one case:

> Diane, who owns a consulting business, is designing a database management system for the personnel office of a medium-sized company. She has described to the client several options about the kind and degree of security to build into the system. Because the system costs more than planned, the client has chosen a less secure system. Diane believes the information to be stored in the system, which includes medical records and salaries, is extremely sensitive. The data will be vulnerable to unauthorized access by employees and even hackers. Diane feels strongly that the system should be much more secure. She has tried to explain the risks, but the CEO, director of computing, and director of personnel all agree that less security will do. What should Diane do?
>
> The authors apply principle 1.7 on privacy as well as 3.4 and 3.5 on the obligations of organizational leaders. Diane's first obligation is to try to educate the company officials (imperative 2.7). If that fails, Diane needs to consider her contractual obligations (imperative 2.6). She may have to choose between her contract and her obligation to honor privacy.

As in many real-life situations, the professional in this case must reconcile or choose between conflicting obligations. If Diane had been an employee, she also might have faced a conflict between the standards of her employer and the standards of her profession.

Codes of ethics and professional standards are not limited to professional organizations. A statement of ethics about Internet use was adopted in 1989 (Fig. 2.6). Every organization should adopt standards and a code of ethics for its employees and officers. Organizations that develop systems should spell out the steps for employees to take if their supervisors do not respond to their complaints about system security.

Case study: The software process. The problem of ensuring that systems are secure is tackled through technical methods, through train-

> The IAB strongly endorses the view of the Division Advisory Panel of the National Science Foundation Division of Network, Communications Research and Infrastructure which, in paraphrase, characterized as unethical and unacceptable any activity which purposely:
>
> (*a*) seeks to gain unauthorized access to the resources of the Internet,
>
> (*b*) disrupts the intended use of the Internet,
>
> (*c*) wastes resources (people, capacity, computer) through such actions,
>
> (*d*) destroys the integrity of computer-based information, and/or
>
> (*e*) compromises the privacy of users.

Figure 2.6 Excerpt from Internet RFC 1087, Ethics and the Internet.

ing and certifying system developers, and through laws and standards. Rarely is the problem approached through ethics, although ethical factors may be as important as any. W. Robert Collins et al. (1994) apply ethical analysis to the software process and specifically to the issue of when a system is ready for use. They start with a hypothetical case, summarized here:

> At Mercy Hospital, a new software system for the pharmacy has been developed and put into use. The hospital is expanding rapidly, and the new system is intended to improve accuracy, speed treatment, and decrease costs. Rachel (vice president in charge of records and automation) and George (chief pharmacist) worked out the specifications, which were approved by the hospital administrators. The system was implemented by consultants, who took the user interface software from an existing system for warehouses. Helen was the consultant in charge of installing the system and training the users (pharmacists, doctors, and nurses). Two months after the installation, Rachel and George ask Helen to return because the staff is having trouble using the system. Helen finds that most of the doctors and several pharmacy employees have complained that the system is unworkable and could be dangerous. There have been two close calls—a drug dosage 10 times too concentrated and a switching of prescriptions between patients. In both cases, staff claim that someone else entered the wrong information. Since there is no transaction log, there is no way to tell. Software error seems unlikely, but possible. Helen recommends going back to the paper system until the new system is really ready.

The authors analyze this case in terms of an ethical framework for software as a social process. Their framework makes use of the theory of justice of John Rawls, which is based on the traditional theory of the social contract. The participants in the software process are a provider, a buyer, a user, and the "penumbra"—other people affected by the software, such as patients in the pharmacy case. If the participants could negotiate *fairly* the rules for the software process, they might come up with the following:

- Don't increase harm to the least advantaged. (The harm can be financial or personal.)
- Don't risk increasing harm in already risky environments.
- Use the *publicity test* for difficult cost-benefit tradeoffs. That is, tradeoffs between financial benefit to one party and personal harm to another "should be made on the basis of a cost-benefit ratio that, if made public, would not enrage most members of the public. That is, make only those decisions that you can defend with honor before an informed public" (Collins et al. 1994: 86).

The case analysis has three steps: (1) identify the players, (2) review the principles, and (3) check the responsibilities of each player to the others and identify the actions each could take to advance the principles.

1. Here Helen represents the provider, George and Rachel are buyers, the pharmacy staff, doctors, and nurses are the users, and patients make up the penumbra.

2. Reviewing here only the "risking harm" principle, the general question is whether the new system makes harm more likely. Errors occurred using the paper system, but users who were accustomed to that system compensated by more careful checking of each other. Another issue is whether the warehouse software should have been used. Its years of use argue for it, but that was in a different environment. Reliance on this past use may have led to inadequate testing in the new, high-risk environment.

3. We consider here only the software provider, who has the greatest responsibility in the issue of system readiness. The provider must help the buyer make an informed decision about acceptance. (Although there is a conflict of interest here, self-regulation is inherent in professional ethics.) The authors conclude that the providers have not given the buyers enough information about the new system. The providers also have responsibilities to the users. They must ensure that the system is used safely and that only trained people will be authorized to use the system. This education effort must be a long-term commitment. The responsibility to the penumbra is to establish the safety of the software well enough to pass the publicity test. The providers should give patients and the public enough information to allow them to evaluate the new system.

Software as property. Computer security professionals deal with proprietary software in their roles as researchers, system designers and developers, security administrators, and users. In the United States and some other countries, software is intellectual property that can be protected by copyright. In the United States, those who make copies in violation of copyright are subject to civil and possibly criminal prosecution. (A criminal case was brought against an MIT student who had distributed copyrighted software over the Internet. The case was dismissed by the U.S. District Court in 1994 for lack of applicable criminal law.) We have seen that the legal framework lags behind rapid developments in technology and in the market. Some believe the law is wrong. A group of distinguished computer scientists objected to the ACM code imperative, "Honor property rights including copyrights and patents." The objectors felt that "the spirit and practical effect of the code is to endorse the current intellectual property system and discourage independent judgment about it" (Steele et al. 1993). Some computer scientists feel strongly that computer programs should be free.

Ethics and the user

People often apply different ethical standards to computer use than to other situations. One reason is that the victims of computer misuse are anonymous or faceless. It is easy to forget they are human beings, and that makes it acceptable to use them as ends. They may be perceived as "the computer" or "the phone company." Perpetrators who plant viruses are protected by distance and anonymity from fully realizing the effects of their actions. A supervisor may see no moral problem with monitoring her employees' work by computer, although she would not do the same kind of monitoring in person.

An issue facing users is whether it is right to copy proprietary software. Many people do it and believe it is justified for private or educational use. The software industry calls it piracy. The ethics of this issue are complex, and the reader who wants to probe further will find leads in the "Bibliographic Notes."

Many people in industry and government believe that teaching computer ethics to children and students is essential to reducing computer misuse. The U.S. Departments of Justice and Education, for example, started a program of encouraging elementary and secondary schools to teach the responsible use of computers. A campaign backed by corporate and other sponsors encouraged teaching and discussion about ethics.

Hackers often claim that they are acting ethically. A person may believe that software should be freely available to all and that it is moral to break into systems to make it available. Another person may believe it is moral to attack the tools of what are perceived as impervious and unethical large organizations. Of course a perpetrator may *not* believe his or her action is moral but carry it out anyway. Although some hacker break-ins are for profit—to gain phone system access, to learn credit card numbers, to obtain software—many others are not. They are done for intellectual challenge or, perhaps, to teach society about the hazards of the technology it relies on. Deborah Johnson has summarized the arguments in defense of hacking: (1)"All information should be free, and if it were free there would be no need for intellectual property and security"; (2) break-ins illustrate security problems so that they will get fixed; (3) hackers are doing no harm and are learning; and (4) "hackers break into systems to watch for instances of data abuse and to help keep Big Brother at bay"

(Johnson 1994b: 48). In analyzing the first argument, Johnson points to three areas where information is constrained for the sake of other values: (1) allowing the ownership of information in order to foster a competitive economy (the argument for this is utilitarian), (2) national security, and (3) individual privacy. Johnson feels the hacker argument goes wrong in claiming that *all* information should be free, rather than that freedom of information is a good but that some information needs to be private.

Summary

Many factors make up the context for computer security, posing threats or shaping the development and use of safeguards. Security needs grow and change with new applications and new ways of doing computing. Computerized personal data are being used in new ways that threaten individual privacy. Safety protections are being automated in safety-critical systems. Companies do business with each other by electronic data interchange, and other electronic commerce is conducted over the Internet, private networks, on-line services, or electronic bulletin boards. Participants in electronic transactions need assurances of integrity, confidentiality, authentication, nonrepudiation, timely service, system security, record keeping, and sometimes anonymity. Encryption and cryptographic digital signatures can fill some of these needs. Computing in organizations has decentralized, with technical and administrative security measures lagging behind. Accompanying and enabling decentralization is growth in networking, bringing increased threat.

Government policy strongly affects security needs and safeguards. In the United States, the government supported nearly all the technical work in computer security for many years, and it has a great deal of control over cryptography. Through standards for its own procurement, it strongly influences the entire market for computer security.

From the earliest days of computers, their effect on privacy has been recognized. Technology makes it increasingly easy to collect, store, manipulate, and share personal data, which have become more abundant, available, and valuable. Sources of personal information include electronic commerce, dealings with governments, telephone activity, and workplace activity. Computer security is a prerequisite for privacy protection; privacy law and privacy ethics impose computer security requirements. Every organization should have a policy about privacy and security of personal data that it maintains, and some organizations are also covered by privacy laws. Nevertheless, personal data are often in error, and their confidentiality is not protected. The Social Security number was not designed as a universal identifier but has evolved in that direction. It is used by the federal government, state and local governments, health insurers, banks and other financial institutions. Knowledge of the SSN is widely used as proof of identity, allowing telephone access to bank accounts and other records.

The main types of protection for personal data are law and public policy, policies and practices of organizations and individuals, and technical measures. Many nations have privacy laws, and there are international agreements. Privacy legislation is broader and more general in Europe than in the United States. It is important for laws to strike a balance—allowing legitimate exceptions to privacy while maintaining strong privacy protection. The 1973 U.S. Code of Fair Information Practices has influenced legislation and practice in the United States and other countries. The code sets up five principles: (1) there must be no secret personal data record-keeping system; (2) there must be a way for individuals to discover what information is recorded about them and how it is used; (3) there must be a way for individuals to prevent personal information obtained for one purpose from being used for other purposes without their consent; (4) there must be a way for individuals to correct or amend information about themselves; and (5) an organization must ensure the reliability of the data for their intended use and must take reasonable precautions to prevent misuses. The 1980 guidelines of the OECD are based on the following principles: collection limitation, data quality, purpose specification, use limitation, security safeguards, openness, individual participation, and accountability of the data controller. The 1995 Council Directive on data protection for the European Union calls for each EU nation to enact protections like those of the OECD guidelines.

The United States and Canada do not have broad privacy laws that apply to the private sector. The U.S. Privacy Act of 1974 applies only to federal agencies and is widely seen as ineffective. The 1970 Fair Credit Reporting Act covers consumer reporting agencies. Many federal laws affect privacy in some way. For example, the Right to Financial Privacy Act protects bank records against federal government access.

Telephone calls and on-line personal data are exposed to communications security threats. Communications privacy should provide confidentiality, anonymity, and data protection. In the United States, the Electronic Communications Privacy Act of 1986 prohibits eavesdropping or the interception of message contents. The act does not, however, restrict private-sector use of transactional data. The Communications Assistance for Law Enforcement Act of 1994 requires all communications carriers to make government wiretaps possible.

Computer fraud and abuse include damaging or disrupting computing systems, corrupting information, stealing services, violating privacy, stealing property (including information or intellectual property), and committing financial crimes. A 1994 U.K. study found an average cost per fraud incident of £196,000. Insider fraud is probably the most common and most costly. There is corporate espionage. Computers are increasingly attractive and increasingly accessible targets for hackers.

The law reacts slowly to the changes caused by computing and computer networks. The first U.S. federal computer crime law was passed in 1984 and strengthened in 1986 and 1994. In the United Kingdom, the Computer Misuse Act of 1990 defines criminal offenses. Other laws aim at preventing or detecting abuse through better controls. However, no U.S. law explicitly mandates computer security for private organizations in general. The Computer Security Act of 1987 places requirements on federal government agencies, and privacy laws impose requirements on the organizations they cover.

Standards and criteria are significant for computer security. Developed by the DoD and first issued in 1983, the Trusted Computer System Evaluation Criteria include two kinds of requirements: required security features (functionality) and assurance requirements. Other criteria were developed in Europe and in Canada. The United States, the European Union, and Canada have drafted Common Criteria. Standards for finance and commerce also deal with security, as do network standards. The two leading sets of network standards are ISO/OSI and the Internet protocols. Under the Computer Security Act of 1987, NIST is responsible for the security of U.S. government "sensitive but unclassified" information. It sets standards for security products used by the government. However, NSA has much influence over security standards.

The 1991 report *Computers at Risk* recommended establishing Generally Accepted System Security Principles, analogous to financial accounting standards. In 1992 the OECD developed guidelines to serve as a foundation for a total security framework that includes laws, policies, technical and administrative measures, and education. A certification program for information security professionals has been developed.

U.S. cryptography policy has been controversial. NIST promulgates standards for encryption of unclassified information. NSA develops cryptographic technology and influences policy. The most prominent cryptography standard is the Data Encryption Standard. Since increases in computing power will soon make DES vulnerable, new standards are needed. The Digital Signature Standard, adopted in 1994, was criticized because it provides only digital signatures and not encryption for confidentiality. The Escrowed Encryption Standard is intended to provide strong encryption for confidentiality and to assist law enforcement in tapping encrypted voice phone calls. The EES has been opposed by privacy advocates, professional organizations (including IEEE-USA and USACM), and computer and communications industry groups and companies. For purposes of export control, cryptography for confidentiality has been considered military. Only weak encryption can be exported routinely. The export policy is designed to protect U.S. intelligence gathering, but it also affects U.S. cryptographic products.

Often, computer security involves deciding how things should be. The field of philosophy called *ethics* helps us with such decisions. Ethical analysis involves formulating an argument, critically evaluating it, reformulating it, and so forth. Philosophers have tried to find fundamental principles from which to derive all morality. The thesis of utilitarianism is that "actions are right in proportion as they tend to promote happiness, wrong as they tend to produce the reverse of happiness." According to Kant's ethics, what makes an action right or wrong is not its consequences (as in utilitarianism) but the internal nature of the action. Kant's fundamental principle is: Always treat another human being as an end and never merely as a means to some other end. Ethics is important for computer professionals, leaders of organizations, computer users, and all of us. Computer professionals have a special obligation to behave ethically because they have a special capacity to affect the world. A professional has obligations to employers, employees, clients, professional colleagues, and the public.

Bibliographic Notes

The changing context

Branscomb (1991) discusses legal issues that arise with networked computing. A report prepared for the U.S. Congress (OTA 1994) assesses security and privacy needs in a networked environment. Neumann (1995a) provides many examples of computer-related risks in safety-critical systems. Security requirements for EDI are covered in NIST (1993), Banarjee and Golhar (1994), and Commission of the European Communities (1993). Parfett (1992) provides a general treatment of EDI. Gebase and Trus (1994) describe electronic commerce and the services needed to support it. Chapters 5 and 10 describe digital cash and cryptographic support for electronic commerce. Morgan (1995) surveys payment systems for the Internet. Copyright law and proposed changes to it are discussed by Samuelson

(1993, 1994). The National Research Council (1994) discusses the NII. Computer Professionals for Social Responsibility published its vision of the NII (CPSR 1994).

Privacy

In 1967 Alan Westin published an influential book, *Privacy and Freedom,* that calls attention to the surveillance enabled by computing and communication technologies. The book considers the origins of claims to privacy, types of intrusions on privacy, and the history of U.S. privacy law. I quote Westin's definition of privacy. Tuerkheimer (1993) discusses the legal roots of privacy protection. An excellent survey of privacy issues was published by Turn (1990). Camp (1994) proposes guidelines for computer professionals about (1) the functions available to data subjects and (2) the responsibilities of data collectors. The story about Dan Quayle's credit report is told by Rothfeder (1992). Garfinkel (1995) describes proposed databases to be indexed by SSN. The health insurers electronic processing network is described by Winslow (1993). Laudon (1986) describes the study of NCIC data quality.

The description of the code of fair information practices is based on OTA (1994: 81). International agreements on privacy and privacy legislation are described by Rotenberg (1993) and in the OTA report. The discussion of the Council Directive for the EU is based on the OTA report and European Commission (1995). Oz (1994a) considers laws affecting transborder data flow. U.S. privacy legislation is reviewed by Plesser and Cividanes (1992), OTA (1994), and Rotenberg (1993). H. Jeff Smith (1993) describes how a federal data protection board might operate. Flaherty (1988) calls attention to the frailty of data protection laws and efforts in the face of massive surveillance. Californians who want to protect their privacy can get information from the California Privacy Rights Clearinghouse in San Diego. Dietz (1994) discusses law pertaining to email privacy. Schaefer (1992) discusses privacy implications of monitoring to detect computer system intrusions. Want and colleagues (1992) discuss privacy concerns for active badges. Agre (1995) discusses privacy as affected by automated tracking of vehicles.

Rotenberg (1993) discusses communications privacy. Telecommunications privacy policy documents are IITF (1995) and NTIA (1995). Hiramatsu (1993) reviews telecommunications privacy law for Japan. Spreitzer and Theimer (1993) discuss the privacy of location information. Technical safeguards for communications privacy are treated in Chaps. 10 and 11. Some of the debate on the Communications Assistance for Law Enforcement Act can be found in

Hanson (1994). In 1995, the FBI stated its need for greatly expanded wiretap capabilities.

Fraud and abuse

The 1994 U.K. survey results are summarized in *Computers & Security* **13**(2): 96–97. In all fairness to bank robbers, £196,000 represents the cost to the organization, not the gain of the defrauder. The U.K. Audit Commission defined *computer fraud* as "any fraudulent behaviour connected with computerization by which someone intends to gain dishonest advantage" (quoted in Dixon, Marston, and Collier 1992: 308). The fraud and abuse cases are taken from news stories by Bauman (1994), Carley (1992), Heichler (1993), Meyer and Underwood (1994), Moses (1992), and Woo (1994). Griffith (1990) surveys the history of the 1984 and 1986 computer crime laws and argues for laws requiring businesses to take security measures and report security incidents. Martin Smith (1993) summarizes U.K. legislation relevant to computer security. Anderson (1994a) argues that many computer security systems are designed more to shed liability than to reduce risk. He proposes the principle that "a trusted component or system is one which you can insure." Brown (1994) analyzes whether digital signatures will be accepted as legal signatures.

Standards and criteria

The TCSEC are published in NCSC (1985)—the "Orange Book." The other criteria are ITSEC (1991), Canadian System Security Centre (1993), and Common Criteria Editorial Board (1996). Security criteria are covered in Chap. 6 and network standards in Chap. 10. Chapin (1994) gives the status of network standards. Madsen (1992) discusses the importance of making standards international and summarizes weaknesses of existing standards. OTA (1994) discusses the history of the Computer Security Act of 1987. The GSSP effort is led by the Information Systems Security Association (ISSA); a draft has been circulated (GSSP Draft Subcommittee 1994). Power (1994) interviews Donn Parker about the GSSP and gives the draft principles. NIST (1995b) is a draft of the NIST version. Schou et al. (1993) discuss professional certification.

Overbeek (1992) concludes that standardization efforts for security in open systems ignore real-world needs and lack integration among standards for applications, operating systems, and networks. Ross Anderson recommends, based on a study of ATM fraud, that "future security standards take much more account of the environments in which the components are to be used, and especially the system and human factors" (Anderson 1994b: 39). A longer report on this work (Anderson 1993) is worth reading. EDI standards are described in Banarjee and Golhar (1994) and NIST (1991).

Cryptography policy

References on cryptography policy include NIST (1995a), Landau et al. (1994a, 1994b), Hoffman (1993, 1995), Hoffman et al. (1994), Banisar (1993), Adam (1992), Neumann (1995b), OTA (1994), and National Research Council (1996). The position of the ACM public policy committee on the EES is stated in USACM (1994).

Ethics and computer security

Sources on computer ethics include Johnson (1994a, 1994b), Ermann et al. (1990), and Parker (1990). The *Communications of the ACM* covers current ethical issues in computing. The December 1995 issue has an ethics section; especially relevant are the articles by Laudon and by Johnson and Mulvey. The discussion of ethical analysis is based on Johnson (1994a) and McFarland (1991). The discussion of ethical principles is based on Hospers (1990a, 1990b), Rachels (1990), and Johnson (1994a). The ethics of privacy is discussed by Fried (1990). The discussion of professional ethics draws from Johnson (1994a) and Anderson et al. (1993), who describe and reprint the ACM Code of Ethics. The Code of Ethics of the IEEE is reprinted by Johnson (1994a). Saltzer (1989) describes the ethical standards for the use of MIT's Project Athena. Vanasco (1994) presents the Code of Ethics of the Institute for Internal Auditors, considering its appropriateness as an international code. Whistle blowing is discussed by Bok (1990). Oz (1994b) describes a dramatic software development failure and how lax professional standards contributed. Stallman (1990) presents arguments for software being free, and Johnson (1994a) analyzes the philosophical basis for intellectual property. Logsdon et al. (1994) found little relation between business students' "level of moral judgment" and their attitudes toward unauthorized copying. There was high tolerance of unauthorized copying. Nissenbaum (1994) describes barriers to accountability in computing and suggests ways to promote accountability. Steps that managers can take to encourage ethical behavior are described in Chap. 12.

Exercises

2.1 Analyze the reasons for protecting personal data. Consider ethics, law, and practical effects.

2.2 A business wants to sell electronic documents over the Internet, charging for each copy. If technical measures enforced the charges, what security attributes would be assured? Would they be integrity and confidentiality, or is some new attribute needed?

2.3 Explain why the market for security products traditionally has been weak. Do you think it will improve?

2.4 Discuss the relationship between information privacy and security. Consider how each affects the other.

2.5 What privacy threats are posed by mobile computing?

2.6 What is computer matching? What legislation governs its use by government? What legislation governs its use by the private sector?

2.7 Explain the difference between confidentiality and anonymity of communications.

2.8 Name the laws discussed in this chapter that (directly or indirectly) impose computer security requirements.

2.9 What is an *open* system? Why is it important for systems to be open?

2.10 What is the purpose of the Generally Accepted System Security Principles? Give an example of a *pervasive* principle.

2.11 Explain escrowed encryption.

2.12 In what sense does the National Security Agency have a "dual role" in cryptography?

2.13 In utilitarianism, what is meant by *net happiness?*

2.14 In your profession or intended profession, what main groups of people do you have obligations to? If you had a conflict between these obligations, how would you go about resolving it?

2.15 What purposes are served by professional codes of ethics?

References

Adam, John A. 1992. Cryptography = privacy? *IEEE Spectrum* (August): 29–35.

Agre, Phil. 1995. Looking down the road: Transport informatics and the new landscape of privacy issues. *CPSR Newsletter* **13**(3): 15–20.

Anderson, Ronald E., Deborah G. Johnson, Donald Gotterbarn, and Judith Perrolle. 1993. Using the new ACM code of ethics in decision making. *Communications of the ACM* **36**(2): 98–107.

Anderson, Ross J. 1993. Why cryptosystems fail. *Proceedings of the 1st ACM Conference on Computer and Communications Security,* 215–227. New York: ACM Press.

———. 1994a. Liability and computer security: Nine principles. *Computer Security—ESORICS 94. Proceedings of the Third European Symposium on Research in Computer Security,* 231–245. Berlin: Springer-Verlag.

———. 1994b. Why cryptosystems fail. *Communications of the ACM* **37**(11): 32–40.

Banarjee, Snehamay, and Damodar Y. Golhar. 1994. Security issues in the EDI environment. *International Journal of Operations & Production Management* **14**(4): 97–108.

Banisar, David. 1993. Battle for control of encryption technology. *IEEE Software* (July): 95–97.

Bauman, Adam S. 1994a. Massive phone calling card fraud found. *Los Angeles Times,* October 3: D2.

———. 1994b. The pirates of the Internet. *Los Angeles Times,* November 3: A1.

Bok, Sissela. 1990. The morality of whistle-blowing. In Ermann, M. David, Mary B. Williams, and Claudio Gutierrez, eds. *Computers, Ethics, and Society,* 70–78. New York: Oxford University Press.

Branscomb, Anne W. 1991. Common law for the electronic frontier. *Scientific American* **265** (September): 154–158.

Brown, Patrick W. 1994. Digital signatures: Are they legal for electronic commerce? *IEEE Communications Magazine* **32**(9): 76–80.

Camp, L. J. 1994. Privacy: From abstraction to applications. *Computers & Society* (September): 8–15.

Canadian System Security Centre. 1993. *The Canadian Trusted Computer Product Evaluation Criteria,* Version 3.0e. Ottawa: Communications Security Establishment, Government of Canada.

Carley, William M. 1992. In-house hackers. *The Wall Street Journal,* August 27: A1, A5.

Chapin, A. Lyman. 1994. Status of standards. *Computer Communication Review* **24**(2): 109–136.

Collins, W. Robert, Keith W. Miller, Bethany J. Spielman, and Phillip Wherry. 1994. How good is good enough? An ethical analysis of software construction and use. *Communications of the ACM* **37**(1): 81–91.

Commission of the European Communities. 1993. *Green Book.* Draft 4.0, October 1993.

Common Criteria Editorial Board. 1996. *Common Criteria for Information Technology Security.* Version 1.0, January 1996.

CPSR. 1994. Serving the community: A public interest vision of the National Information Infrastructure. *CPSR Newsletter* **12**(1): 1–30.

Dietz, Lawrence D. 1994. Electronic mail and the law. *Computer Security Journal* **X**(2): 37–45.

Dixon, R., C. Marston, and P. Collier. 1992. A report on the joint CIMA and IIA computer fraud survey. *Computers & Security* **11**(4): 307–313.

Ermann, M. David, Mary B. Williams, and Claudio Gutierrez, eds. 1990. *Computers, Ethics, and Society.* New York: Oxford University Press.

European Commission. 1995. Council definitively adopts directive on protection of personal data. Press release, July 25, 1995.

Flaherty, David H. 1988. The emergence of surveillance societies in the western world: Toward the year 2000. *Government Information Quarterly* **5**(4): 377–387.

Fried, Charles. 1990. Privacy: A rational context. In Ermann, M. David, Mary B. Williams, and Claudio Gutierrez, eds. *Computers, Ethics, and Society,* 51–63. New York: Oxford University Press.

GAO. 1993. *Computer Matching: Quality of Decisions and Supporting Analyses Little Affected by 1988 Act.* Report to the House of Representatives, GAO/PEMD-94-2, October 1993. Washington: U.S. General Accounting Office.

Garfinkel, Simson L. 1995. Risks of Social Security numbers. *Communications of the ACM* **38**(10): 146.

Gebase, Len, and Steve Trus. 1994. *Analyzing Electronic Commerce.* NIST Special Publication 500-218, June 1994. Gaithersburg, Md.: National Institute of Standards and Technology.

Griffith, Dodd S. 1990. The Computer Fraud and Abuse Act of 1986: A measured response to a growing problem. *Vanderbilt Law Review* **43:** 453–490.

GSSP Draft Subcommittee. 1994. *Generally Accepted System Security Principles (GSSP)*. Exposure draft, August 1994. Glenview, Ill.: ISSA.

Hanson, Robin. 1994. Viewpoint: Can wiretaps remain cost effective? *Communications of the ACM* **37**(12): 13–15.

Heichler, Elizabeth. 1993. Airline hacking case reveals CRS' security shortcomings. *Computerworld,* January 18: 2.

Hiramatsu, Tsuyoshi. 1993. Protecting telecommunications privacy in Japan. *Communications of the ACM* **36**(8): 74–77.

Hoffman, Lance J. 1993. Who holds the cryptographic keys? The government key escrow initiative of 1993. *Computer* **26**(11): 76–78.

———, ed. 1995. *Building in Big Brother: The Cryptographic Policy Debate.* New York: Springer-Verlag.

Hoffman, Lance J., Faraz A. Ali, Steven L. Heckler, and Ann Huybrechts. 1994. Cryptography policy. *Communications of the ACM* **37**(9): 109–117.

Hospers, John. 1990a. Justice as part of an ethical theory. In Ermann, M. David, Mary B. Williams, and Claudio Gutierrez, eds. *Computers, Ethics, and Society,* 35–44. New York: Oxford University Press.

———. 1990b. Utilitarian theory. In Ermann, M. David, Mary B. Williams, and Claudio Gutierrez, eds. *Computers, Ethics, and Society,* 26–34. New York: Oxford University Press.

IITF. 1995. *Privacy and the National Information Infrastructure: Principles for Providing and Using Personal Information.* Task Force Report, June 1995. Information Infrastructure Task Force.

Internet Activities Board. 1989. *Ethics and the Internet.* RFC 1087, January 1989. Internet Request for Comments.

ITSEC. 1991. *ITSEC: Information Technology Security Evaluation Criteria.* Luxembourg: European Communities—Commission.

Johnson, Deborah G. 1994a. *Computer Ethics.* 2d ed. Englewood Cliffs, N.J.: Prentice-Hall.

———. 1994b. Crime, abuse, and hacker ethics. *Educom Review* **29**(5): 40–51.

Johnson, Deborah G., and John M. Mulvey. 1995. Accountability and computer decision systems. *Communications of the ACM* **38**(12): 58–64.

Landau, Susan, Stephen Kent, Clint Brooks, Scott Charney, Dorothy Denning, Whitfield Diffie, Anthony Lauck, Douglas Miller, Peter Neumann, and David Sobel. 1994a. Crypto policy perspectives. *Communications of the ACM* **37**(8): 115–121.

Landau, Susan, Stephen Kent, Clint Brooks, Scott Charney, Dorothy Denning, Whitfield Diffie, Anthony Lauck, Doug Miller, Peter Neumann, and David Sobel. 1994b. *Issues in U.S. Crypto Policy.* Report of a Special Panel of the ACM U.S. Public Policy Committee (USACM), June 1994. New York: Association for Computing Machinery, Inc.

Laudon, Kenneth C. 1986. Data quality and due process in large interorganizational record systems. *Communications of the ACM* **29**(1): 4–11.

———. 1995. Ethical concepts and information technology. *Communications of the ACM* **38**(12): 33–39.

Logsdon, Jeanne M., Judith Kenner Thompson, and Richard A. Reid. 1994. Software piracy: Is it related to level of moral judgment? *Journal of Business Ethics* **13**(11): 849–857.

Madsen, Wayne. 1992. International information technology (IT) security cooperation into the 21st century. *IT Security: The Need for International Cooperation. Proceedings of the IFIP TC11 Eighth International Conference on Information Security, IFIP/Sec '92,* 5–12. Amsterdam: North-Holland.

McFarland, Michael C. 1991. Ethics and the safety of computer systems. *Computer* **24**(2): 72–75.

Meyer, Michael, and Anne Underwood. 1994. Crimes of the "Net." *Newsweek,* November 14: 46–47.

Morgan, Lisa. 1995. Cashing in: The rush is on to make net commerce happen. *Internet World,* February: 48–51.

Moses, Jonathan M. 1992. Wiretap inquiry spurs computer hacker charges. *The Wall Street Journal,* July 9.

National Research Council. 1991. *Computers at Risk: Safe Computing in the Information Age.* Washington: National Academy Press.

———. 1994. *Realizing the Information Future: The Internet and Beyond.* Washington: National Academy Press.

———. 1996. *Cryptography's Role in Securing the Information Society: Overview and Recommendations.* World Wide Web document, May 30, 1996. Committee to Study National Cryptography Policy.

NCSC. 1985. *Department of Defense Trusted Computer System Evaluation Criteria.* Report DOD 5200.28-STD. Fort Meade, Md.: National Computer Security Center.

Neumann, Peter G. 1995a. *Computer-Related Risks.* Reading, Mass.: Addison-Wesley.

———. 1995b. Reassessing the crypto debate. *Communications of the ACM* **38**(3): 138.

Nissenbaum, Helen. 1994. Computing and accountability. *Communications of the ACM* **37**(1): 73–80.

NIST. 1991. *Security Issues in the Use of Electronic Data Interchange.* Computer Systems Laboratory Bulletin June 1991. Gaithersburg, Md.: National Institute of Standards and Technology.

———. 1993. *Good Security Practices for Electronic Commerce and Electronic Data Interchange.* Contract final report. Gaithersburg, Md.: National Institute of Standards and Technology.

———. 1995a. *The Data Encryption Standard: An Update.* Computer Systems Laboratory Bulletin, February 1995. Gaithersburg, Md.: National Institute of Standards and Technology.

———. 1995b. *Generally Accepted Principles and Practices for Securing Information Technology Systems.* Draft document, December 1995. Gaithersburg, Md.: National Institute of Standards and Technology.

NTIA. 1995. *Privacy and the NII: Safeguarding Telecommunications-Related Personal Information.* NTIA Report, October 1995. Washington: National Telecommunications and Information Administration.

OTA. 1994. *Information Security and Privacy in Network Environments.* Report OTA-TCT-606, September 1994. Washington: U.S. Congress, Office of Technology Assessment.

Overbeek, Paul L. 1992. Secure open systems: An investigation of current standardisation efforts for security in open systems. *IT Security: The Need for International Cooperation. Proceedings of the IFIP TC11 Eighth International Conference on Information Security, IFIP/Sec '92,* 87–100. Amsterdam: North-Holland.

Oz, Effy. 1994a. Barriers to international data transfer. *Journal of Global Information Management* **2**(2): 22–29.

———. 1994b. When professional standards are lax: The CONFIRM failure and its lessons. *Communications of the ACM* **37**(10): 29–36.

Parfett, Martin. 1992. *What Is EDI? A Guide to Electronic Data Interchange.* 2d ed. Manchester, U.K.: NCC Blackwell.

Parker, Donn B. 1990. *Ethical Conflicts in Information and Computer Science, Technology, Business.* Wellesley, Mass.: QED Information Sciences.

Plesser, Ronald L., and Emilio W. Cividanes. 1992. *Privacy Protection in the United States: A 1991 Survey of Laws and Regulations Affecting Privacy in the Public and Private Sector Including a List of All Relevant Officials.* NIST PB92-173228. Gaithersburg, Md.: National Institute of Standards and Technology.

Power, Richard. 1994. Computer security as folk art: Why we need the GSSP. *Computer Security Journal* **X**(2): 1–4.

Rachels, James. 1990. Kantian theory: The idea of human dignity. In Ermann, M. David, Mary B. Williams, and Claudio Gutierrez, eds. *Computers, Ethics, and Society,* 45–49. New York: Oxford University Press.

Rotenberg, Marc. 1993. Communications privacy: Implications for network design. *Communications of the ACM* **36**(8): 61–68.

Rothfeder, Jeffrey. 1992. *Privacy for Sale: How Computerization Has Made Everyone's Private Life an Open Secret.* New York: Simon & Schuster.

Saltzer, Jerome H. 1989. Teaching students about responsible use of computers. *Communications of the ACM* **32**(6): 704.

Samuelson, Pamela. 1993. Computer programs and copyright's fair use doctrine. *Communications of the ACM* **36**(9): 19–25.

———. 1994. The NII intellectual property report. *Communications of the ACM* **37**(12): 21–27.

Schaefer, Lorrayne. 1992. Employee privacy and intrusion detection systems: Monitoring activities on the job. *EDPACS* **XX**(6): 1–7.

Schou, Corey D., W. Vic Machonachy, F. Lynn McNulty, and Arthur Chantker. 1993. Information security professionalism for the 1990s. *Computer Security Journal* **IX**(1): 27–37.

Smith, H. Jeff. 1993. Privacy policies and practices: Inside the organizational maze. *Communications of the ACM* **36**(12): 105–122.

Smith, Martin. 1993. *Commonsense Computer Security: Your Practical Guide to Information Protection.* 2d ed. London: McGraw-Hill.

Spreitzer, Mike, and Marvin Theimer. 1993. Scalable, secure mobile computing with location information. *Communications of the ACM* **36**(7): 27.

Stallman, Richard M. 1990. The GNU manifesto. In Ermann, M. David, Mary B. Williams, and Claudio Gutierrez, eds. *Computers, Ethics, and Society,* 308–317. New York: Oxford University Press.

Steele, Jr., Guy L., Danny Hillis, Richard M. Stallman, Gerald J. Sussman, Marvin Minsky, John McCarthy, John Backus, and Fernando J. Corbato. 1993. Code of ethics reconsidered. *Communications of the ACM* **36**(7): 17–19.

Tuerkheimer, Frank M. 1993. The underpinnings of privacy protection. *Communications of the ACM* **36**(8): 69–73.

Turn, Rein. 1990. Information privacy issues for the 1990s. *Proceedings of the 1990 IEEE Computer Society Symposium on Research in Security and Privacy,* 394–400. Los Alamitos, Calif.: IEEE Computer Society.

USACM. 1994. USACM position on the Escrowed Encryption Standard. *Communications of the ACM* **37**(9): 16.

Vanasco, Rocco R. 1994. The IIA code of ethics: An international perspective. *Managerial Auditing Journal* **9**(1): 12–22.

Want, Roy, Andy Hopper, Veronica Falcao, and Jonathan Gibbons. 1992. The Active Badge location system. *ACM Transactions on Information Systems* **10**(1): 91–102.

Warren, Samuel D., and Louis D. Brandeis. 1890. The right to privacy. *Harvard Law Review* **IV**(5): 193–220.

Westin, Alan F. 1967. *Privacy and Freedom.* New York: Atheneum.

Winslow, Ron. 1993. Insurers activate nine-state network to process health data electronically. *The Wall Street Journal,* September 7: B5.

Woo, Junda. 1994. Copyright laws enter the fight against electronic bulletin board. *The Wall Street Journal,* September 27: B10.

Chapter

3

Threats

This chapter describes threats to computer security. A history of misuse attests to the gravity of these threats, but history may not warn us enough. A National Research Council report warned in 1991 that "emerging trends...point to growth in both the level and the sophistication of threats....There is reason to believe that we are at a discontinuity: with respect to computer security, the past is not a good predictor of the future" (NRC 1991: 10). Events since 1991 have validated this belief.

This chapter focuses on misuse of computing systems by people, especially intentional misuse. Other types of threats (such as natural disasters and theft of hardware) are considered in Chap. 12. This chapter first reviews the concepts of vulnerability, threat, and safeguard. Then several case histories of misuse illustrate threats and vulnerabilities. Types of misuse and types of vulnerabilities are outlined. The chapter discusses perpetrators of computer misuse: insiders, hackers, and spies. The chapter then describes the methods used in attacks: how they are planted and activated, their missions, and how safeguards are attacked. The threat of malicious code is introduced. The last three sections deal with three types of malicious code: Trojan horses, viruses, and worms.

Concepts, Cases, and Categories

This section reviews concepts, gives examples of misuse, and categorizes misuse and vulnerabilities.

Vulnerability, threat, and safeguard

The concepts of vulnerability, threat, and safeguard were introduced in Chap. 1. A *vulnerability* is some weakness that could be exploited to violate security. A *threat* is a circumstance or event that could cause damage by violating security. A threat is thus the potential for exploiting a vulnerability. A *safeguard* is any technique or procedure or other measure that reduces vulnerability. A safeguard makes threats weaker or less likely. (*Countermeasure* is also used. I like the term *safeguard* because it fits general security measures. If safeguards are only countermeasures to specific threats, they will always be a step behind.)

A threat can aim specifically at one vulnerability, or it can exploit more than one. Although some safeguards are specific to threats, others (such as backups) guard against a wide variety of threats. Some threats aim at safeguards such as passwords. Figure 3.1 shows how these concepts relate to one another. Inside the box are the computing system and its procedures and controls. Outside the box is the rest of the world, including the authorized users. Safeguard S_1 in the figure guards against threat T_1 exploiting vulnerability V_1, and S_2 guards against T_2 exploiting V_2. S_3, represented by the curved boundary, guards against any of the threats exploiting any of the vulnerabilities.

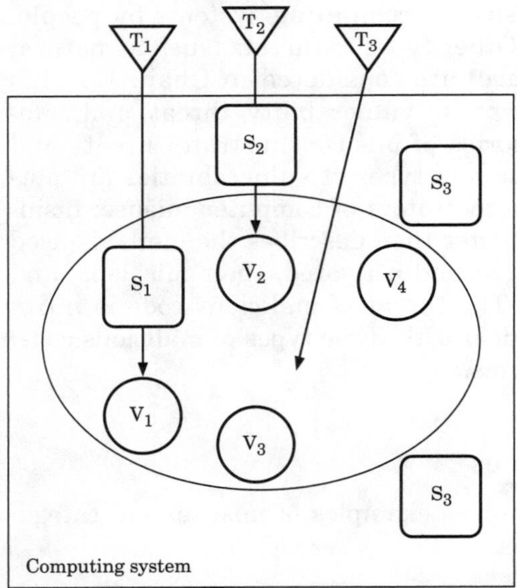

Figure 3.1 Vulnerability, threat, and safeguard.

A case of *misuse* is an event that violates security policy; it is a threat realized. Some cases are crimes, and others violate an organization's policies. The term *intrusion* is often used for outsider misuse, and *attack* is used for an attempt at misuse. We know too little about the losses due to computer misuse and the details of the incidents. Many organizations do not report or prosecute misuse, fearing embarrassment or lacking solid evidence. A 1996 survey found that fewer than 17 percent of organizations would report misuse to authorities.

Case histories

The California state lottery was closed 3 hours early on a Saturday in 1995 because of an error by an employee of the company that operates the lottery. The employee entered the command to close the lottery while carrying out another task. Purchasers discovered that their tickets were dated the following Wednesday—the next lottery day. The lottery honored tickets purchased during the "closed" period (totaling $1 million) for both Saturday and Wednesday—no doubt costing the lottery operators dearly.

In 1985, at a Texas insurance company, the program that computed commissions for agents failed miserably. Many records of the commission files had been destroyed. An unauthorized power-down of the computer occurred a few days later. Donald Burleson, a former employee, was later convicted of a felony—harmful access to a computer with loss and damages over $2500. The company was also awarded civil damages.

In England, a bank clerk stole £8600 from a customer's account. The clerk changed the customer's address to his own, then issued an extra card for the account (which he received), and then changed the address back again. He withdrew the money from ATMs. The customer did not notice the thefts for a long time because of the way the bank's system worked: When a customer got a statement from an ATM (as the clerk always did), that transaction did not appear on the full statement that was mailed.

In 1986 an intruder (dubbed the "Wily Hacker") gained system manager privileges for a computer of the Lawrence Berkeley Laboratory. From that computer the intruder broke into more than 30 others, many operated by the military or by defense contractors. After almost a year of detection effort, the intruder was identified as a West German spying for the East Bloc.

In 1988 a *worm* attack spread rapidly through the Internet. Within hours, several thousand Sun and VAX computers running UNIX went down. Robert Tappan Morris, a Cornell computer science graduate student, was later convicted under the Computer Fraud and Abuse Act of 1986.

This small sample of cases shows a variety of motivations, outcomes, vulnerabilities, and methods. The lottery system evidently had weak safeguards against error. The bank clearly was lax in its systems and procedures. The clerk should not have been able to change the address by himself, and the mailed statement should have shown all transactions. The Wily Hacker exploited known vulnerabilities in operating systems. The Internet worm was the most dramatic and the most technical of these examples; it arouses our worst fears about breakdowns of the systems we count on.

Types of misuse

Incidents of misuse vary in their outcomes. The outcome can be loss of confidentiality (the British Airways case of Chap. 2), loss of information integrity (the Burleson case), theft of computing services, theft of resources controlled by the computing system (the bank clerk case and the MCI fraud case of Chap. 2), or denial of service (the lottery, Burleson, and Internet worm cases). Incidents that violate confidentiality only are *passive misuse,* and cases that alter data are *active misuse.* A 1989 survey of over 1200 organizations found that the main outcome was misuse of computer service, followed by data integrity loss and program integrity loss.

Cases of misuse also vary widely in method or technique. The most common threats are accidents and human error. Not only do they cause damage in themselves, but they also provide opportunities for further damage by malicious perpetrators. Next most common is abuse of authority by authorized users, like the bank clerk. Misuse by outsiders is increasingly important because of increased connectivity. Outsider threats include viruses, worms, and other *malicious software.* Outsiders use technical knowledge to attack safeguards, such as passwords. Once the authentication safeguards have been breached, an outsider has insider privileges and can go on to breach other safeguards, thus acquiring special privileges. Many cases involve a combination of methods, only some technical. For example, a hacker may use "social engineering" to trick a systems administrator into revealing a password. The hacker may search trash bins for technical manuals or other helpful information. Then, gaining system access with the purloined password, the hacker can mount an informed technical attack.

An attack or case of misuse has a *perpetrator,* and that person has a *motivation* (such as financial gain or revenge). Sometimes the motive is complex and hard to understand, and the perpetrator gains no conventional benefit. The attack has a *method of operation*—a way of exploiting vulnerability. There is a *mission,* such as destruction of data, and a *target.* Some examples of targets are files, passwords, and messages. More than one target may be attacked, and intermediate targets (such as passwords) may be used in attacking the ultimate targets.

The *damage* is in effects such as loss of assets, delay in billing clients, or advantage gained by competitors. When critical systems are attacked, lives can be lost. These attributes (perpetrator, motivation, method of operation, mission, target, and damage) are shown in Fig. 3.2.

We learn from cases of misuse. A case may be significant because its method of operation is new or widely applicable or because it reveals some weakness in safeguards.

Types of vulnerabilities

Vulnerabilities are also extremely varied, ranging from poor physical security to obscure software errors. Poor management is often to blame. Poor system administration is a common problem that becomes grave when coupled with another vulnerability: products that are delivered with unsafe configurations. For example, an operating system may be delivered with built-in accounts that have high privileges and well-known user IDs and passwords. If the person who configures the system is unaware of the hazard, these account names and passwords never get changed. Other hazards may lurk in a system configuration. Also, software often has security flaws. An operating system may have a fundamentally insecure architecture or a design flaw. Its code may have a "bug" that affects security. These

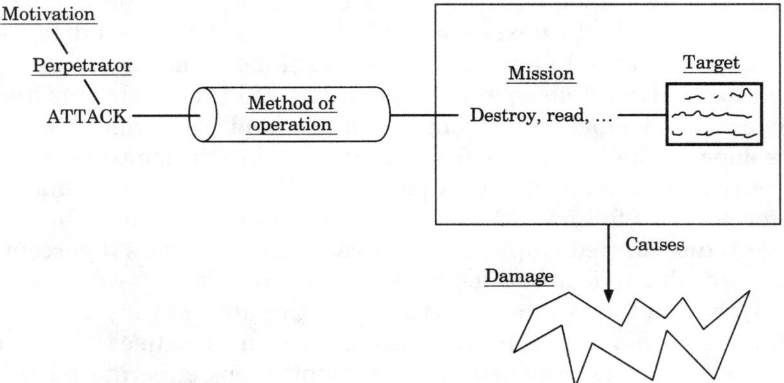

Figure 3.2 Attributes of cases of misuse.

flaws are probably better known to the hacker community than to the system administrator community. Hardware also may have flaws that can be exploited for security breaches.

Perpetrators

We need to understand how perpetrators' behavior interacts with technical vulnerabilities, attack methods, and safeguards.

Insiders

Insiders are the most serious threat as perpetrators. Insiders can include not just employees but also contractors, vendors, customers, and the families of employees. Their errors can be costly (the California lottery shutdown) or disastrous. Their deliberate abuse may be fraud or theft, or it may be sabotage. Unauthorized insider browsing (as with the IRS employees described in Chap. 2) destroys confidentiality and privacy. Legitimate authorizations can be exploited to modify information in unauthorized and harmful ways (the bank clerk). Insiders can steal services; for example, an employee uses her employer's computing system to support her own side business. Insiders can deny service by deliberately overloading the system or crashing it. They can encrypt data for secrecy and forget (or hold hostage) the key for decrypting it.

Some insider misuse involves disgruntled employees; trends such as downsizing and outsourcing are swelling their ranks. Disgruntled ex-employees also are a threat because they know the system. Finally, some employees cooperate with outsiders in criminal acts. The MCI fraud case, with losses estimated at $50 million, shows that the stakes are high. A 1989 survey of computer misuse found that the motivations were personal gain (30 percent), ignorance of proper conduct, misguided playfulness, and maliciousness. Other studies (of crime, not just misuse) found a different ranking of motivations: (1) the need to resolve intense personal problems, (2) peer pressures and challenges, (3) idealism or extreme advocacy, and (4) financial gain. Studies done in the late 1980s found that mistakes of honest employees were responsible for about 65 percent of the financial loss due to computer security failures. Dishonest employees were responsible for 13 percent, disgruntled employees 6 percent, and outsiders 3 percent. (The rest was due to factors such as power failure and water damage.) Errors by insiders also interact with other threats. A study of fraud involving ATM machines found a combination of causes in most frauds. Insider errors provided the opportunity for deliberate misuse by outsiders or other insiders.

The Burleson case shows the avenues for misuse open to an insider.

> The prosecutor has described the methods alleged in the state's argument. These methods were not technically sophisticated. Instead, the defendant used his status as a privileged insider; he was the company's computer operations manager and computer security officer. When he was fired and his privileges were revoked, he had already prepared for the misuse. He had set up an extra account and given it authorization to the security functions. No one thought to delete this account when he was fired. He also wrote programs to delete records from the commission files. A few days after his firing, Burleson entered the company's building in the middle of the night, used the clandestine account, and then could sign on as security officer and as another user. He ran the programs that he prepared earlier. The computer's history log provided the main evidence of these events.

In this case the perpetrator was a former employee, the motive apparently revenge. The methods included *masquerading* (described later in this chapter) and abuse of authority. No great expertise was needed. The culprit programs were straightforward. The mission was file corruption; the target was the commission files. The damage included $26,000 in lost employee time and $3800 for computer downtime. Relations with clients and agents surely were harmed as well.

Hackers

The term *hacker* originally referred to a programmer who loves to exercise great skill on operating systems and software tools. The term evolved to refer to someone who breaks into computers. The prototype hacker was young (as young as 14), a fan of cyberpunk literature, and motivated by the technical challenge and thrill of entering forbidden worlds. A hacker subculture evolved, with its own bulletin boards, newsletters, and conferences. Favorite targets were telephone companies and credit reporting companies.

Probably the best-known hacker of the older generation is Kevin Mitnick, whose career spans two decades.

> As a high-school student, Mitnick broke into school district computers. Still a juvenile, he hacked into the North American Air Defense Command computers and was convicted of stealing Pacific Bell manuals. In 1988 he was convicted (under the 1986 computer crime law) of stealing programs from Digital Equipment Corporation and using unauthorized MCI long-distance service codes. Mitnick had obtained the source code of Digital's VMS operating system and caused damage that Digital estimated at $4 million in downtime and repair time. Although Digital security people had been aware of the break-ins to their internal network for 18 months, they were unable to stop them or to identify the

hacker; he eventually was caught through an associate. Mitnick was sentenced to 1 year in prison and 3 years of probation—the stiffest sentence a hacker had ever received.

In 1992, Mitnick disappeared. He was suspected of stealing software and data from cellular telephone manufacturers. Reportedly, by subverting a phone system, he could wiretap the very agents who were searching for him. Wiretapping FBI calls to the California Department of Motor Vehicles, he learned access codes that enabled him to access drivers license information; this helped him set up false identities. In 1995, Mitnick was arrested and charged with computer fraud and illegal use of a telephone access device. He allegedly broke into systems used by Apple Computer and Motorola and copied credit card information for 20,000 users of an Internet access provider. Mitnick was convicted.

Mitnick used "IP spoofing" attacks (described in Chap. 10). He attacked one computer from another that he had already penetrated at the most privileged level, causing the penetrated computer to masquerade as a computer that is "trusted" by another computer. One penetration method was to take over an existing connection, sometimes by subverting phone-system computers. He might then call the computer operator, posing as the systems programmer, and ask for "super-user" privilege. Mitnick stole programs and data and stored them on other penetrated systems. After Mitnick broke into the computer of Tsutomu Shimomura and stole computer security tools, federal agents (with Shimomura's help) found Mitnick.

Mitnick's story illustrates some of the many weaknesses that a hacker can exploit: flawed operating systems software, careless system administration, gullible privileged users, and phone system computers. It also illustrates the application of the new computer crime laws.

As far as is known, the only profit Mitnick obtained from his exploits was free phone service. He was a hero for many hackers. But the hacker culture seems to be at a crossroads. Tougher laws and crackdowns may be a deterrent. System-cracking information and tools are readily available on the Internet, taking away the challenge. At the same time, criminals have that same ready access to tools and more incentive than ever to use them. Intrusion services are offered for sale. It appears that more intrusions are malicious. Whether or not the hacker culture persists, hackers' exposures of vulnerability will have a lasting effect.

Spies

In the history of computer security, foreign espionage is the prototypical threat. Little information is publicly available, but the threat was certainly great during the Cold War, and espionage continues. A government intelligence-gathering organization can pose a "high-grade threat" that is quite different from the threats posed by hackers or unorganized criminals. Such an organization is well-funded and staffed and has a long-term approach. It can even build replicas of systems that it would like to attack. It is good at circumventing physical and procedural safeguards. In contrast to other attackers, it can afford to look for obscure system vulnerabilities that could be exploited for a long time.

Industrial espionage threatens individual companies. For example, a New England manufacturer lost a competitive bid because its computer system was cracked. Government agencies also are targets, and the perpetrators are either individual companies or governments trying to help their domestic industry—*economic espionage.* Industrial computer spies have stolen information about manufacturing and product development, as well as sales and cost data, customer lists (as in the British Airways case), and planning information. According to the FBI and CIA, the main target of economic espionage is information on technology. Other targets are "policy deliberations concerning foreign affairs and information on commodities, interest rates, and other economic factors...corporate proprietary information such as negotiating positions and other contracting data..." (NIST 1994).

Attack Methods

An attack on a computing system has three main stages. In a preparatory stage, the method of the attack is put into place (*planted*) or other preparations are made. For example, an account with special privilege is set up or a system program is modified. Then (perhaps quite some time later) the attack is *activated,* or *triggered.* Finally, the *mission* is carried out—to bypass controls, violate secrecy or integrity, deny service, steal services, or just make the attack known. Along the way the attacker may try to destroy or confuse evidence about the attack.

Preparing and planting the attack

Information gathering. Information is the attacker's greatest weapon. Insiders may simply collect the system information that they are authorized to see. Outsiders must be more ingenious. They collect discarded manuals and computer output from trash bins—*dumpster diving.* In order to learn which telephone numbers provide computer access, they do *war dialing*—computer-controlled dialing of all the numbers in a range. To obtain passwords or other secrets, outsiders use *social engineering*—tricking the people who know the secrets into revealing them. For example, a hacker might call a system administrator and claim to be an employee who has forgotten his or her password. Posing as an executive is another trick. One break-in leads to information that can help in further attacks. For example, Kevin Mitnick took operating system source code and computer security tools.

Trojan horse. During the Trojan war, according to Homer, the Greeks left a magnificent wooden horse outside the walls of Troy. The Trojans brought it inside their defensive walls—only to discover that Greek soldiers were hidden within the hollow horse. Analogously, a computer user brings a rogue program into his or her realm of protection; when the program runs, it has the user's privileges. The victim becomes an unwitting accomplice. A system programmer, for example, finding a faster version of a file backup utility, does not know that it makes clandestine copies of certain files. A programmer obtains an editor with useful new features; what is not apparent is that it sends data from his or her files to the perpetrator.

Programmed propagation. By introducing itself into new target computers, malicious code can multiply its scope and damage. Viruses spread by propagating themselves, and so do worms, which spread across networks.

Trap doors. Software is sometimes delivered containing hidden mechanisms that allow the developers (or anyone who knows the secret) to bypass controls. This kind of mechanism is a *trap door* or *back door.* A trap door in a login program, for example, could allow a developer to log on without providing a valid password. Mainframe trap doors are sometimes put in by systems programmers—to make maintenance easier in emergency situations. This is a risky practice, however, because a trap door can be exploited by anyone who knows about it. A software or hardware implementation of an algorithm, or even the algorithm itself, can have a trap door. In the 1970s it was alleged—apparently incorrectly—that the Data Encryption Standard had a trap door. A trap door in the UNIX mail service was used in the Internet worm. In a variation on the trap door, the software vendor Logisticon, reacting to nonpayment by its customer Revlon, remotely disabled its software.

Masquerading and spoofing. Donald Burleson, when he was no longer system security officer, masqueraded in that role. *Masquerading* or *spoofing* means pretending to be someone else in order to obtain that person's access rights. Often, masquerading involves an attack on the authentication controls. A system also can masquerade as another system, tricking the user into disclosing information. For example, an application program can display what appears to be the operating system's logo on a shared terminal, tricking the next user of the terminal into entering a name and password. The masquerading program stores away these tidbits, simulates an error that terminates login (to avoid arousing suspicion), and terminates its own session. The logo reappears, and the user has no idea that the password has been compromised.

Spoofing has been used with ATM machines. The perpetrator either builds a phony ATM machine or outfits a real ATM with a phony input device. The masquerading unit then collects users' account numbers and PINs.

Other forms of masquerading serve to prevent identification of the perpetrator. Burleson gave his clandestine account a name intended to suggest an IBM service account, and he ran jobs with legitimate names. Network attacks typically come by way of sites that were penetrated precisely because they would not look suspicious.

Scanning. Before masquerading can be attempted, the attacker needs to learn telephone numbers of computers, account identifiers, and passwords. A method frequently used is *scanning*—presenting sequentially changing information to a computer in order to find values that get positive responses. Scanning works because it can be automated. War dialing is an application of scanning. Scanning is no longer useful for learning passwords, because good countermeasures are widely used.

Misuse of authority. Preparation is much easier if the attacker has legitimate access to the computing system and the targets. Burleson easily planted penetration tools while he was still security officer.

Activating the attack

If the preparation stage took over an operating system interrupt (a common method), the attack code is invoked whenever that interrupt is issued. We have seen that an unsuspecting user may be enticed to invoke a threatening program. A perpetrator can, of course, invoke a program directly that carries out the mission. Burleson apparently did that, since the computer log showed mysterious logins close in time to discovery of the attack.

A more sophisticated attack imposes a delay between preparation and activation. This makes identifying the attacker much more difficult. Delay also can make the attack more destructive, especially for viruses. A *time bomb* is set to go off at a specific date and time. It may *hook* itself to some regularly executing program (such as an operating system interrupt), check for the appointed time, and when the time arrives, carry out the mission. A time bomb does not even have to check the time itself; it can be planted in a cyclically run program, such as month-end processing. Burleson used a time bomb to power down the computer a few days after his other attack. A time bomb is one type of *logic bomb*; a logic bomb is triggered by any combination of conditions, such as a particular input transaction or change in a file. An extortionist can claim to have a transaction that will disable the logic bomb; unless that transaction is run, the logic bomb will explode according to its criteria.

Missions

Active misuse. Active misuse affects information integrity or availability of services. Files can be destroyed or subtly altered. Communications messages can be altered, deleted, or inserted; they can be misrouted; their apparent origin can be modified. An insider like Burleson can destroy valuable data, set up trap doors, alter authorization status, cause a system crash, and destroy evidence.

Passive misuse. When confidentiality is violated but the state of the system is not affected, the misuse is *passive.* One passive technique is *eavesdropping*—unauthorized snooping. Eavesdropping ranges from sophisticated electronic listening on communications to looking at displays and keystrokes over someone's shoulder (*shoulder surfing*). Local telephone connections can be tapped quite readily, and so can local-area networks. Long-distance lines are harder to tap, but eavesdropping can be done through subversion of telephone system computers.

Experiments in the mid-1980s showed that inexpensive equipment could eavesdrop on video display terminals from distances of thousands of feet. Some displays and PCs are now specially built to minimize emanations. (The term *TEMPEST* is used for the study and control of compromising emanation.)

Most security policies aim at protecting information, not the data objects (such as disk sectors and memory segments) representing that information. Some threats exploit the imperfect relationship between the two. An open file is partly represented by segments of memory, and the data may remain in those segments when they are reallocated for other purposes and other users. A magnetic tape may be allocated to a new user with its old data still readable. A client of a time-sharing service exploited this vulnerability to learn about its competitors who used the same service. The U.S. Air Force even sold surplus tapes without first erasing them. The vulnerability here is known as the *residue* or *object-reuse problem,* and the threat as *scavenging.* Scavenging also can occur outside the computing system, on discarded program listings or outputs of test runs.

Browsing means searching through storage (or more generally, through available information) without knowing in advance exactly what information is sought or if it exists. For example, an attacker might look for logged-on accounts whose names suggest special privilege. The Wily Hacker used the UNIX commands **who** and **finger** to learn account names. Alternatively to browsing, an intruder might search for specific patterns, such as character strings that seem relevant to the goals of the intrusion. Browsing and searching are effective in systems that are quite open or in systems that have been penetrated by other means.

The technique of *inference* puts together pieces of accessible information to arrive at information that is supposed to be secret. For example, information about an individual can be inferred from a database that releases only statistical summaries of medical data, especially if information from the database is combined with outside information. The inference vulnerability for society as a whole is increasing because there are more databases containing personal data and more details in each database.

A system whose policy is to control information flow is vulnerable to the use of *covert channels.* According to the *multilevel* security policy, for example, a Secret level user cannot transfer Secret information to a Confidential user. However, if the two users cooperate, they can transfer information in subtle ways, using channels not intended for such a purpose. They can modify stored information or control the timing of events; that is, they can use *storage channels* or *timing channels.*

Denial of service. Denial-of-service attacks are probably the easiest to mount. Networks can be overwhelmed with traffic. On mainframes, operating systems prevent looping programs from monopolizing computing service. Still, there are vulnerabilities. For example, user-added operating system calls and interrupt handlers may disable interrupts. Such code can loop to deny or badly degrade service. Dial-up ports can be monopolized to prevent users from even getting in. Local-area network (LAN) file servers can be deluged with work. Any traumatic crash, whether power-down of a mainframe or failure of a virus-infected PC, denies service.

Theft of service. Hackers steal computing and communication services from systems they penetrate. Authorized users can play games, send personal electronic mail, maintain personal businesses, and sell services to outsiders. Although many of these activities are harmless, even game playing can be fraud—for example, where computer time is charged to customer projects. Because it diverts computing resources, theft of service on a shared system involves some denial of service.

Attacks on safeguards

As computer security matures, attackers spend relatively more effort on disarming the safeguards.

Authentication. An intruder must get by the login controls in order to proceed further. Login to the vast majority of computing systems is protected *only* by passwords. The person logging on must supply a user or account identifier plus a password associated with that identifier. Some systems also use passwords to control access to applications and other resources. Unfortunately, passwords are often weak safeguards.

Users typically choose their own passwords. If this were not so (e.g., if the computer generated an arbitrary character sequence), users would have trouble remembering their passwords and would write them down in convenient places—where intruders could find them. Many users choose passwords that are easy to guess, such as their own names or account identifiers or common first names. When this tendency is combined with weak protection of password files, the result is weak authentication.

In some UNIX systems, passwords are stored in a pseudoencrypted form, having been put through a one-way transformation. The file of transformed passwords can be read by any user. Since it is essentially impossible to go from the stored encrypted password to the original password, this approach might seem quite secure. The problem is that passwords are chosen from a limited number of names and words. In a *dictionary attack,* a program on the attacker's own computer encrypts all the words in a list; the attacker hopes that some will match encrypted passwords in the password file. This worked for the Internet worm and for the Wily Hacker, who was observed moving the encrypted password files to his own computer and a few days later using passwords from those very files.

Other attacks can get at passwords in clear (not encrypted) form. In 1994, a series of *sniffer* attacks compromised hundreds of thousands of passwords. Attackers first penetrated a system (using well-known vulnerabilities), then obtained privileged status (using other well-known vulnerabilities), and then installed software that collected information from all new network sessions. This information included account IDs and passwords for other computers. The information was stored for later access. Usually, the attackers also installed Trojan horse versions of operating system programs; this was done to make it easy to get back in and also to hide the illicit access. The attacks snowballed, as the compromised passwords gave access to other systems and the opportunity to compromise more passwords. The attacks made obvious what was already known: The familiar "reusable" password is vulnerable, and in a networked world, one system's vulnerability is another system's vulnerability.

Another problem is that some installations neglect to change the identifiers and passwords for accounts shipped with a operating system. An attacker who knows these could sign on, for example, as system programmer or security administrator. Other account names and passwords are easy to guess. One attack used an account named GUEST with password GUEST.

Work that is started without direct user interaction—batch jobs, remote batch jobs, sign-on sequences for remote computers—involves files containing account names and often passwords. These are open to scavenging by those who have gotten by other safeguards. Often these files reside on computers with far weaker security than the remote computer being compromised.

Tunneling attacks. Another way to defeat safeguards is to attack below the level of the safeguard. If there is access control on files, attack the disk sectors where the file is stored. If an application transaction has strict controls, attack the transaction program object module. An attack that goes "under" the controls in this way is called a *tunneling attack* (Fig. 3.3).

Tunneling attacks have used system utilities designed for just that purpose—bypassing normal procedures to correct emergency problems. This has been called the *Superzap threat* after an IBM disk repair utility. A first step in a tunneling attack can be to create an emergency that damages system files; this provides the Superzap opportunity. A tun-

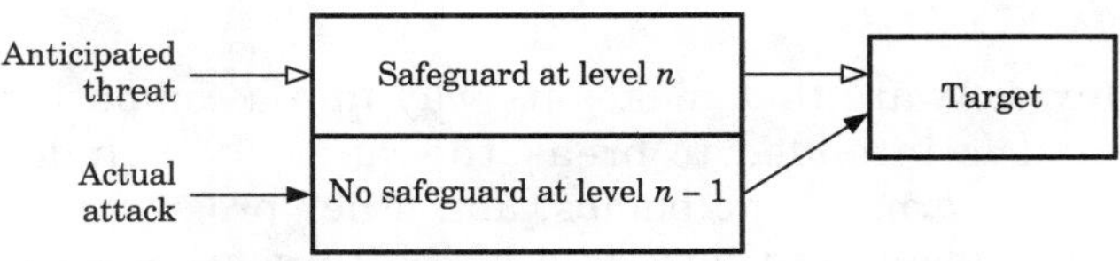

Figure 3.3 Tunneling attack.

neling attack also could modify hardware or microcode (in disk-storage controllers, for example) to allow bypass of controls.

Compromise of encryption. Some encryption methods are effective only if encryption keys are chosen carefully. A key could be learned by an intruder. The encryption system could be broken. An implementation of an encryption algorithm could contain errors. Increasingly, encryption is part of complex protocols used to solve specific security problems—such as authorization of transactions. These protocols can have errors. Finally, encryption is always used in a larger system context. The total system may be poorly designed or poorly managed.

Destruction of evidence. In Burleson's trial, the prosecution relied heavily on the computer history log. Logs or audit trails are valuable because they are general and often well protected. Hard-copy logs helped solve the Internet worm case. On-line logs could be bypassed, altered, or destroyed (if their controls are subverted), and off-line or hard-copy logs could be destroyed (if physical security is lax).

Subversion of application controls. Many of the most effective safeguards operate at the application level. They include accounting controls (such as control totals), integrity and reasonability checks on data input, and enforcement of separation of responsibility. It was an accounting control that first detected the Wily Hacker. Even without modifying programs, an insider who knows an application intimately may be able to exploit weaknesses in its controls. Persons with access to the application programs can alter them (during development or during maintenance) to generate fraudulent transactions, to bypass control checks on certain accounts, or to remove or alter records of transactions. One method is the *salami attack,* so called because thin slices at a time are taken, without noticeably reducing the whole. Each victim loses only a tiny amount, and controls are not violated. One variety of salami attack is the round down fraud. Suppose the monthly interest on a bank account is computed as $35.19387 but rounded down to $35.19. A subverted application can accumulate fractions such as $.00387 and add them to an accomplice's account.

Malicious Code

Malicious code is any software that makes its way into a computing system uninvited and is intended to break the rules. It includes Trojan horses, viruses, worms, logic bombs, and other programmed threat methods. (This widely used term is a bit off target, since the code is only the agent of a malicious person.) Viruses and worms thrive on sharing and interconnectedness. They spread from program to program, from computer to computer.

Malicious code often exploits flaws in operating systems and associated software. It also exploits insecure configuration. Most systems are delivered with insecure configurations, no doubt because such configurations are the easiest to install and use. At the same time, many systems are administered by people who do that job in addition to their main work. Security may not be a salient concern. Perhaps the increased awareness of the interdependence of systems will encourage vendors to deliver securely configured systems and administrators to become savvy about security. The Internet has increased interdependence but also has made security information and tools readily available.

Unless the exchange of information is severely limited, there is no simple protection from malicious code. There are safeguards, but none is complete and foolproof. Mandatory access controls can be used. Users can be wary of software obtained from uncertified sources. Systems can be dedicated to one or a few applications. Strict controls can be placed on changes to program libraries. Developers can follow the best practices to avoid distributing malicious code in their products. Organizations can set up procedures to certify updates received from vendors. However, with information exchange getting easier all the time, the malicious code threat will not soon go away.

Trojan Horses

The Trojan horse was the first type of malicious code to be recognized, and it stimulated many computer security efforts. A *Trojan horse* is an apparently useful program containing hidden functions that can exploit the privileges of the user, with a resulting security threat. A Trojan horse does things that the program user did not intend. A Trojan horse is most dangerous when the user is a system administrator or other privileged user.

> At a computer show, one manufacturer offered a prize to anyone who could compromise its secure operating system. The winner asked the system manager for help with a program he had written (which contained a Trojan horse). The system manager, while helping, inadvertently ran the program under his own account.

Games and graphics make good Trojan horses.

> A program (call it MERRYX) was sent over a company network a few days before Christmas. When invoked, MERRYX displayed a Christmas tree, then screens of "file deleted" messages—one for each of the user's

files. Although MERRYX only simulated deletion, it could well have deleted the files, since it ran with the privileges of the user who invoked it.

Recently, the term *Trojan horse* has been used more broadly to include threats that do not depend on a user's cooperation. For example, a penetration may substitute a Trojan horse for a standard system utility, or a Trojan horse received in the mail may exploit weaknesses in controls to cause its own execution. The Internet worm exploited a trap door in the mail program that caused immediate execution of received mail. This kind of threat is called a *letter bomb*.

A Trojan horse is extremely dangerous, because discretionary access controls are powerless against it. Many other techniques are built on the Trojan horse.

Perpetrator steps

Morrie Gasser has listed the steps that a perpetrator must take in order to succeed with a Trojan horse:

1. Write a program that carries out the mission in a way that will not be noticed by the victim or by the safeguards. The program also must be useful or enticing.
2. Provide a way for the victim to get the program. For example, place it in a shared library (if access controls permit) or on the Internet. Hand it to the victim, or send it as electronic mail.
3. Get the victim to run the program. The victim can invoke it directly, or it can run without the victim's knowledge (e.g., if it replaces a legitimate utility program).
4. Provide a way to reap the benefit. For example, send confidential information from the victim's files as mail to the perpetrator's account.

Networking multiplies the ways that victims can get programs. For example, many network applications include code that runs on the user's computer, some code even being sent "just in time" to execute.

Threats to integrity and confidentiality

As has been emphasized, discretionary access controls do not protect against a Trojan horse. Although a Trojan horse cannot subvert mandatory controls, it can violate policy in mandatory-control systems, since most policies also involve discretionary controls. One might think that careful scrutiny of source code would reveal a Trojan horse, but even if such certification were practical, it could not be relied on. Ken

Thompson has demonstrated, with a few lines of code and a few pages of words, that self-reproducing programs can be written, that a Trojan horse can be installed in a compiler without leaving any trace in the compiler source (his example compiles the login program to always accept a specific password), and that the compiler Trojan horse can maintain itself even if the compiler is rebuilt from source.

A Trojan horse can violate integrity much more easily than it can violate confidentiality. This seems strange at first, but it follows from the definitions. Since the Trojan horse has the user's rights, it can modify or destroy any objects that the user can modify or destroy. In fact, the perpetrator needs no access at all to the user's system, only some way to get the Trojan horse executed. To violate confidentiality, the Trojan horse must move information to some place the user can write and the perpetrator can read (Fig. 3.4), and such a place may be hard to find. In some systems the perpetrator can create a file writable by the user (or by anyone). The Trojan horse can send messages or mail to the perpetrator, but such activity might be prevented by mandatory controls, recorded by the system, or observed by the user.

An integrity violation can prepare the way for a future confidentiality violation. If the access-control software can be invoked by a program (and generally it can), the Trojan horse can modify access rights to the user's files, granting read access to the perpetrator.

Viruses

A *virus* is a program that attaches itself to a *host* program so that when the host is executed, the virus will execute. When the virus is executed, it tries to copy itself (or a modified version of itself) to some other host program. The new host is modified in memory or on a disk. Then the virus typically carries out a destructive mission, such as destroying the boot record or the file-allocation table on a disk. In fact, the mission can be almost anything; some viruses merely expose

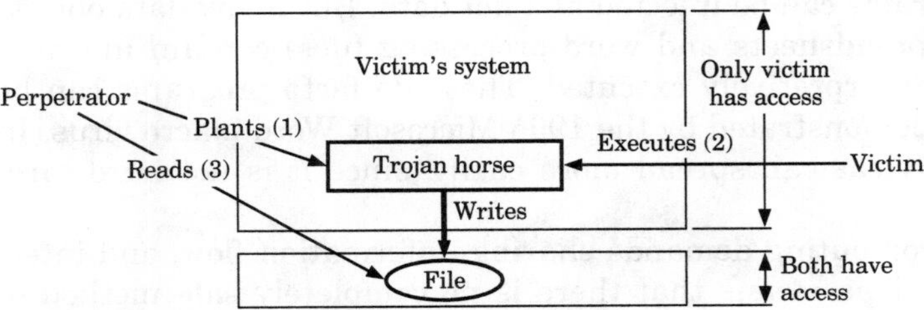

Figure 3.4 Confidentiality-violating Trojan horse.

themselves, and others are wantonly destructive. The victim experiences a terrifying betrayal; a trusted tool suddenly behaves in arbitrary and harmful ways.

Viruses are dangerous because they propagate themselves and infect other computers. There may be a long transmission path and long delay between the first infection and any noticeable effect. The infected programs usually perform their normal functions. The virus can reside on disks or backup tapes and then appear long after it was planted or reappear long after it was supposedly eradicated. This indirectness makes it nearly impossible to identify the perpetrator. (In fact, some authors "sign" their viruses to get proper credit.) Most viruses have not brought any concrete gain to their authors. The hacker motivations seem to prevail: meeting a technical challenge and projecting one's presence and influence. The number of different viruses seems to be growing exponentially. The prevalence of any one virus seems to increase linearly over quite a long time and then level off at a low level, perhaps because of safeguards.

Most "in the wild" viruses (as opposed to experimental ones) have infected personal computers, especially those running the DOS operating system. A 1992 survey of large organizations that used antiviral measures showed a rate per quarter of about 1 virus incident per 1000 PCs. PCs are vulnerable because protection hardware and software have been weak, and PCs provide what viruses thrive on—a large population of homogeneous systems and much exchange of software.

Theory

Fred Cohen was the first to study viruses systematically. He showed that infection can occur wherever there is sharing or uncontrolled information flow. If a program *E* belonging to user *A* is infected and user *B* executes *E,* then *B*'s files can become infected. Moreover, if there is a path from user *A* to user *B* and a path from user *B* to user *C,* then there is a path from *A* to *C,* even without *B*'s knowledge. This path could be as simple as a diskette being passed from *A* to *B* to *C,* or it could be a circuitous network path.

Only programs can be infected and not data. But many data objects (including spreadsheets and word-processing files) contain information that is interpretively executed. These de facto programs can be infected, as demonstrated by the 1995 Microsoft Word macro virus. In fact, such a virus can spread more easily, since it is not hardware-dependent.

Effective computing demands sharing, information flow, and interpreted data. This means that there is no completely safe method of preventing infection. Where information flow is controlled, infections can only pass according to the flow policy. This, however, turns out to be inadequate protection.

Cohen proved that we cannot *in general* decide whether a program is a virus. That is, we cannot write a program to decide whether another program is a virus. Although the general problem is undecidable, we can devise a detection method for any particular virus. However, the virus can always modify itself—*evolve*—to elude any specific detection method.

These theoretical conclusions should not dishearten us, however, because there are highly practical ways to detect viruses.

How a virus works

A virus has three stages: (1) it is activated, (2) it infects other programs, (3) it carries out its mission or *manipulation* task or *payload.* The activation and mission can use any of the methods already described. The virus may be triggered by a time bomb or logic bomb, or it may be hooked to frequently invoked software, such as operating system interrupts. A virus that delays its mission with a time bomb or logic bomb is especially dangerous, since backup copies of the host program will be infected before the virus is noticed. In a PC without memory protection, the virus has access to all the computer's resources. In a better-protected environment, the virus may wait until it is executed by a user with the authority to carry out its mission.

The virus may use various strategies for replication and infection. It can try to replicate itself every time it is executed or a certain percentage of times. It can choose only certain kinds of files or certain memory locations to infect. It can infect every file that is executed or every file that is opened. Typically, a virus leaves a *signature* in the infected program—a unique pattern that it tests to avoid reinfecting the same program.

A *boot-sector virus,* as opposed to a *file-infecting virus,* infects the boot sector of a disk (a fixed disk location containing the code to be executed when the operating system is booted up). Some file-infecting viruses (called *direct-action viruses*) spread only when an infected file is executed. Most become memory-resident and infect every file that is executed or even opened. Some virus variations do not literally infect host programs but have a similar effect. One type alters the directory entries for executable programs, causing the virus to be executed first; it is the disk that is infected. Another method takes advantage of the way DOS carries out commands: DOS searches for a file extension of COM first, then EXE. A *companion virus* creates a .COM file with the same name as an existing .EXE file.

Increasingly, viruses are designed to elude detection. A *stealth virus* may intercept the system calls that read files or disk blocks and forge the results of the calls. The forgery causes the software using the calls (including antiviral software) to see the original uninfected form of the file so that the virus is not detected. Viruses also elude detection by modifying themselves when they replicate. Viruses that do this are called *polymorphic*. For example, a virus may encrypt itself differently each time it replicates, using a different encryption key or even a different algorithm. Virus writers can link their viruses with *mutation engines*—components that make the viruses polymorphic.

Sources of viral infection

A computer or disk is exposed to infection any time software is created or acquired. Many epidemics have occurred in open environments (such as universities) that have lots of sharing of PCs and diskettes. Office computers catch viruses from infected home computers. Viruses spread through file sharing on LANs. Free software obtained from bulletin boards or from acquaintances is a possible source. No source is free of danger. Vendors have shipped software that was infected during development. In 1995, Microsoft distributed to hundreds of software developers a disk that contained a common virus. Even preformatted new diskettes have been infected.

Safeguards

Protecting against viruses takes both the right procedures and multiple layers of technical defenses. Virus safeguards include prevention, detection, containment, and recovery. This section describes the main approaches, and Chaps. 8 and 12 give more detail.

Prevention. The only sure ways to prevent virus spread are to limit sharing and information flow or to restrict function. Mandatory access controls cannot prevent viruses from spreading, but they can limit the damage the virus does. There have been attempts to "inoculate" files against viruses by making it appear to the virus that the file is already infected. However, the great number and variety of viruses make inoculation impractical.

Protection hardware and access-control software can inhibit the virus at each stage of its life cycle. Preventing unauthorized or unintended modification of programs prevents their infection (except by a Trojan horse). Organizations and individuals can use restraint and caution in accepting software.

Detection. The patterns of computer behavior caused by viruses can be recognized by people or programs. A common symptom is an unexplained change in the size or time stamp of a file (the result of the virus being added to the file). Programs may take longer to start or may run more slowly than usual. There may be unexpected failures, such as rebooting or attempts to write on write-protected media. Screen or printer output may be garbled. The system date or time of day may change inexplicably. The amount of available memory may decrease, and bad areas on disk may increase.

Antiviral software is a large industry. Most of the products include several programs that use different techniques. *Scanners* check for known viruses, looking for specific code sequences associated with each virus or for the virus signatures. Scanning can be done on demand, or memory-resident scanners can check each program just before it executes. Scanners are limited because new viruses come along very rapidly and because viruses evolve to thwart detection. Since virus detection cannot be perfect, a scanner will have false positives (it detects viruses where they are none) or false negatives (it fails to detect viruses) or both. Nevertheless, scanning is effective. *Generic scanners* look for properties that are common to all viruses or to classes of viruses. *Generic monitors* try to detect and prevent malicious program behavior. Other antiviral programs emulate the execution of programs in order to detect viruslike behavior. This approach seems to be successful for detecting polymorphic viruses. Many organizations use multiple antiviral products to increase the coverage and reduce the false negatives. The products may conflict, however. Changes made by one product, or strings that it leaves in memory, may be interpreted as viruses by another product.

Change detection is an important tool for more than just virus protection. Automated change detection computes a *baseline* at a time when files are considered to be intact. A baseline table contains file names and corresponding checksums for executable files and other files designated as unchanging. Of course, the table has to be protected. Some software computes a "checksum" from only the file's size, attributes, date, and time. However, a virus could manipulate date and time and could compress an expanded file to arrive at the same size. A *Cyclic Redundancy Check* (CRC) is based on the entire file contents. However, an intruder who knows the CRC algorithm can change a file and still leave the checksum unchanged. Most secure is a checksum based on cryptographic methods.

Change detection has the advantage that it guards against any kind of integrity threat, not just viruses. It has the disadvantage that it does not identify the virus. Change detection can be applied periodically or on demand, for entire disks or for specified files.

Alternatively, an *integrity shell* checks programs on each invocation, ensuring that they were not changed since the last check. The checking code also can be attached to each executable file so that it does a *self-test* just before execution. However, the virus could get control first, disinfect the file, and then reinfect it after the checking.

Containment and identification. Once a virus has been discovered, the first objective is to keep it from spreading. The infected computer should be isolated (from networks and from sharing of media) until it is clearly disinfected. The virus should be identified or analyzed so that its behavior is understood.

Recovery. Recovery consists of replacing every infected file with an uninfected version and restoring other files that may have been damaged. Most antiviral tools can try to disinfect and repair infected files. Although repair minimizes down time and may be the only option (if backups are not available), it is risky. Some viruses damage files irreparably. Software products should be restored from the original copies. Backups themselves may be infected or damaged (if they were made after the infection), so they must be checked before being used. Once recovery is completed, the system must be checked once more for infection.

Worms

Worms are programs that propagate themselves; a worm makes a copy of itself and causes the copy to execute. Worms often spread from computer to computer across network connections. A worm attack may involve several different programs that cooperate across the network. Unlike a virus, a worm does not infect a host program. In order to spawn an executing replica of itself, a worm needs a multitasking system.

The worm concept (introduced in the science fiction book, *The Shockwave Rider*, by John Brunner, 1975) was developed and implemented by John Shoch and Jon Hupp at Xerox Parc. The concept is of "a program or a computation that can move from machine to machine, harnessing resources as needed, and replicating itself when necessary" (Shoch and Hupp 1990: 265). These early worms were benign creatures that could take advantage of idle machines on a LAN. Later worms were far from benign.

Worm incidents

In 1988, the Father Christmas worm attacked VAX/VMS systems at several U.S. government laboratories, using a DECnet network. The worm exploited network features and insecure configurations and accounts. When the worm succeeded in penetrating a system, it reported its success to a specific network site. In 1989, the similar WANK worm attacked. If it succeeded in taking over a privileged account, WANK changed the system banner to "Worms Against Nuclear Killers." The CHRISTMA attack (dubbed a worm) brought down IBM's internal network in 1987. When CHRISTMA was invoked by an unsuspecting user, it read the file containing names and addresses of the user's network correspondents and sent a copy of itself to each name in that file, rapidly clogging the network. CHRISTMA was a Trojan horse that propagated itself, rather than a true worm, which propagates without user cooperation. The terms *bacterium* and *rabbit* have been used for a malicious program that, like CHRISTMA, just replicates itself, using up resources. These are denial-of-service threats.

Worms are far less common than viruses—probably because writing them demands broader knowledge and skill. When they do attack, the effect is swift and dramatic.

The Internet worm

Here we analyze the Internet worm to show the vulnerabilities it exploited and its methods of operation. Computer scientists starred in the media-heightened drama of this event—diagnosing the problem, immunizing their computers, and repairing the damage. Fortunately, some of them wrote detailed articles, examining the incident from both technical and social points of view.

It was no secret that the UNIX operating system attacked (BSD 4) had security vulnerabilities. Many of its users chose that operating system precisely because it was open and convenient. Some of the system administrators were researchers doing system management on the side or not at all. They were unconcerned about internal threats (because they supported trusted users) and unaware that they faced threats from their network connections.

The Internet worm involved several methods of operation. First, the worm got a "grappling hook" or bootstrap program into execution at some computer by trying each of three vulnerabilities. The first was a feature that makes remote execution easier to use—"trusted" remote logins. (This is described later.)

The second vulnerability was a design weakness in a basic routine of the C language I/O library—a failure to check for inputs that will overrun a buffer. The worm used this flaw by connecting to a UNIX system program running on another computer (**finger**) and passing it a carefully constructed string that overflowed the buffer and changed a return address on the stack. As a result, the worm's own code in the buffer was executed. That code attempted connection to a shell on another computer.

The third vulnerability was a trap door—a debug option in the **sendmail** program. This option (so useful that system administrators often left it in) allowed the worm to send its commands as mail and get them executed on a remote computer.

Once ensconced on a computer, the bootstrap program used normal network functions to communicate with its parent and receive the complete worm code. The worm tried to break each user password, exploiting vulnerabilities in password controls. Many of the tries succeeded. Once running in a user's account on a computer, the worm used information available in that account's files or on that computer generally to select other computers and accounts to attack. It would try to break into remote computers where the user had accounts. For this, it exploited two UNIX features for trusted remote login. The administrator can specify a list of trusted computers from which remote logins are accepted without passwords. A user can specify a similar list of additional trusted computers. When the worm hit a list where its current computer was trusted, it got its hook into still another computer.

The worm tried to avoid detection. Its main code was encrypted during transfer and was not left in the file system. It ran under an innocuous name. It kept forking a new process and terminating its old one (to avoid a long-running process being noticed). Still, its activities appeared in the on-line system logs, which turned out to be crucial in fighting the worm.

Lessons from the Internet worm

What was learned from the Internet worm about threats, vulnerabilities, and safeguards? All the technical and procedural vulnerabilities were well known to the UNIX community. This does not mean, however, that all system administrators and users knew about the dangers or took them seriously. The worm made the hypothetical threats intensely real and drove home the importance of safeguards such as safe operating system configuration, a least privilege policy, good passwords, logging, and good backups. It also showed the value of having diverse implementations of UNIX; many computers were unaffected, and their continued functioning benefited the whole network.

People learned how to organize to combat worm attacks. Centralized incident-response centers were set up. It was learned that crisis teams should be set up in advance, along with ways to communicate that do not use the very network being attacked. Network gateway computers (through which all traffic must flow) could be instrumented to detect unusual volume or patterns of traffic or to diagnose an ongoing attack.

The 1988 attack also led to programs of training in ethics and to revised computer crime law.

Summary

The concepts vulnerability, threat, and safeguard make up a framework for thinking about computer security. A threat is a circumstance or event that could cause damage by violating security. A case of misuse is a threat realized. The outcome of a case of misuse can be loss of confidentiality or integrity, theft of computing services, theft of resources controlled by the computing system, or denial of service. The most common threats are accident and error, followed by abuse of authorization. A case of misuse has a perpetrator, motivation, method of operation, mission, target, and damage.

Perpetrators include insiders, hackers, and spies. Insiders have been responsible for most losses, and mainly through error. Dishonest insiders have the opportunity for costly computer fraud. Many fraud cases involve insider error that is exploited by outsiders or other insiders. Hackers are an increasing threat. The story of Kevin Mitnick shows that a hacker can exploit flawed operating systems software, careless system administration, gullible privileged users, and vulnerable phone systems.

An attack has three stages: preparation, activation, and carrying out of the mission. One method of preparation is to give a victim a Trojan horse—an apparently useful program containing hidden functions that can exploit the privileges of the user, with a resulting security threat. Software can contain trap doors—hidden mechanisms for bypassing controls. Access to systems and targets is often obtained by masquerading—pretending to be someone else. Masquerading may follow scanning—for example, war dialing sequential telephone numbers until a computer is reached. A delay between preparation and activation makes detection less likely and also can make the attack more destructive. A time bomb delays the attack until a specific date and time; a logic bomb can be triggered by any conditions.

Active misuse affects information integrity or availability of services. For example, files can be destroyed or subtly altered. When the mission violates secrecy but the state of the system is not affected, the misuse is passive. One passive technique is eavesdropping. Scavenging exploits the residue or object-reuse vulnerability. Browsing is fishing for information that might be useful. Inference puts together pieces of accessible information to arrive at information that is intended to be secret. A covert channel transfers information in a way that violates security policy. Misuse can deny service to users. Computing services can be stolen.

Most misuse involves subverting safeguards. Passwords are vulnerable to scanning, guessing, dictionary attacks, and eavesdropping. A tunneling attack defeats a safeguard by working at a lower level. Audit trails can be destroyed. Application controls can be bypassed by an insider who knows their weaknesses, and application programs can be altered to bypass controls.

Malicious code is any software that makes its way into a computing system uninvited and is intended to break the rules. It includes Trojan horses, viruses, and worms. Viruses and worms propagate themselves. A Trojan horse is dangerous because discretionary access controls do not protect against it. A Trojan horse can violate integrity more easily than it can violate secrecy.

A virus is a program attached to some host program. When the virus is executed, it copies itself to some other host program. Viruses propagate themselves, infecting more programs and more computers. Infection can occur wherever there is sharing or uncontrolled information flow. According to virus theory, we cannot in general detect a virus by examining a program. Nevertheless, there are practical ways to detect viruses. A virus has three stages: (1) it is activated, (2) it infects other programs, and (3) it carries out its mission.

Virus safeguards include prevention, detection, containment, and recovery. The only sure ways to prevent virus spread are to limit sharing and information flow or to restrict function. Mandatory access control can limit damage, as can protection hardware and access-control software. Users can be cautious about accepting software and can learn to detect virus-induced computer behavior. Antiviral software products check for known viruses. Another method is to check for modified files. Once a virus has been detected, it must be kept from spreading by isolating the infected computer. Recovery consists of replacing every infected file with an uninfected version and restoring other files that may have been damaged.

Worms are programs that replicate themselves, often spreading from machine to machine across network connections. The Internet worm of 1988 made UNIX and network vulnerabilities vividly apparent, and it led people to organize for combatting future attacks.

Bibliographic Notes

Computers at Risk (National Research Council 1991) includes good discussions of threats and safeguards. It describes the high-grade threat. Surveys of misuse and its motivations are Hoffer and Straub (1989) and Neumann and Parker (1989). Neumann (1995) has many case histories. Frizzell et al. (1994) describe intrusion threats to national security and emergency preparedness telecommunications. The Burleson trial is described by McCown (1990). Industrial espionage is discussed in NIST (1994). Baker (1993) covers computer crime law and its applications to hackers. A letter by Dr. Morton Grosser, reprinted in Denning (1990), discusses the origins of the word *hacker.* The description of Kevin Mitnick's career is based on Baker (1993), Johnson (1995), Babcock (1995), and CF&SB (1994). The bank case and cases of ATM fraud are described by Anderson (1994). The case of the Wily Hacker is described by Stoll (1988, 1989).

The problem of object reuse is discussed in Chap. 7. Inference is discussed in Chaps. 4 and 9. Covert channels are discussed in Chap. 6. The eavesdropping threat from video display terminal emanations is discussed by van Eck (1985). The salami attack is discussed by Donn Parker (1989). Parker uses the term *crimoid* for "an elegant, intellectually interesting method of computer abuse that receives extensive coverage in the news media" (1990: 544). Colorful names such as *virus* or *salami* help turn a threat technique into a crimoid.

The collections of articles edited by Peter Denning (1990) and Lance Hoffman (1990) are excellent sources on malicious code and other threats. Many of the papers cited here are reprinted in one or both of these collections.

According to Landwehr et al. (1994), the term *Trojan horse* was first used for a computer security threat by Dan Edwards and first published in the Anderson report (1972). Gasser (1988) gives a lively and thorough discussion of Trojan horses. Our list of steps comes from there.

Applications tend to have predictable behavior. Karger (1987) proposed using that predictability to guard against discretionary Trojan horses that violate secrecy. An application's pattern of file access could be documented in an application profile. A trusted piece of software would then check all file accesses and would query the user about unexpected ones. Authentication safeguards and vulnerabilities are described in detail in Chap. 8. The computer-show Trojan horse incident is described by Smith (1988).

Virus theory is described by Cohen (1987, 1989, 1990). The proof of undecidability appears in the 1989 paper, which introduces the concept of *viral sets* to handle viruses that evolve. Overviews of viruses are provided by Spafford et al. (1990), White et al. (1990), Bowles and Peláez (1992), Bassham and Polk (1992), Ferbrache (1992), and VIRUS-L (1992). Polk and Bassham (1992) discuss antivirus tools. Kephart and White (1993) report the results of surveys of virus prevalence and describe epidemiologic models of virus spread. Cohen (1992) considers defenses against viruses.

The June 1989 *Communications of the ACM* was a special issue about the Internet worm of 1988, with three technical articles (Rochlis and Eichin, Seeley, and Spafford 1989) plus the report of the Cornell commission and several statements of ethics. The 1988 event is also described by Reynolds (1991). The 1986 break-ins using trusted accounts are described by Reid (1987). UNIX security features and flaws are described in Chap. 8. Other network attacks are discussed in Chap. 10. Chapter 12 deals with response to computer security incidents.

Exercises

3.1 Discuss the possible misuse outcomes, such as loss of confidentiality. Think of an organization that you are familiar with. Which type of outcome would be most dangerous to that organization?

3.2 Compare the vulnerabilities that an insider might exploit with the vulnerabilities that hackers exploit. Which do you think are easier to correct?

3.3 Discuss the ways that an attack can be planted.

3.4 Why is tunneling attack an appropriate choice of terminology?

3.5 Why is it to a perpetrator's advantage to use a time bomb or logic bomb?

3.6 Why is a Trojan horse so dangerous?

3.7 Is it easier for a Trojan horse to commit passive misuse or active misuse? Why?

3.8 Can a virus infect data as well as programs? Explain.

3.9 Describe the stages in the life of a virus.

3.10 What are the main safeguards against viruses?

3.11 What is the most significant difference between a virus and a worm?

3.12 How did the 1988 Internet worm use a trap door?

References

Anderson, James P. 1972. *Computer Security Technology Planning Study.* Report ESD-TR-73-51. Bedford, Mass.: Electronic Systems Division, AFSC.

Anderson, Ross J. 1994. Why cryptosystems fail. *Communications of the ACM* **37**(11): 32–40.

Babcock, Charles. 1995. A hacker's lines of attack. *Computerworld,* March 6: 8.

Baker, Glenn D. 1993. Trespassers will be prosecuted: Computer crime in the 1990s. *Computer/Law Journal* **XII:** 61–100.

Bassham, Lawrence E., and W. Timothy Polk. 1992. *Threat Assessment of Malicious Code and Human Threats.* NISTIR 4939. Gaithersburg, Md.: National Institute of Standards and Technology.

Bowles, John B., and Colón E. Peláez. 1992. Bad code. *IEEE Spectrum,* August: 36–40.

Brunner, John. 1975. *The Shockwave Rider.* New York: Harper & Row.

CF&SB. 1994. FBI frustrated by most wanted hacker. *Computer Fraud & Security Bulletin,* August: 4–5.

Cohen, Fred. 1987. Computer viruses: Theory and experiments. *Computers & Security* **6:** 22–35.

______. 1989. Computational aspects of computer viruses. *Computers & Security* **8:** 325–344.

______. 1990. Implications of computer viruses and current methods of defense. In Peter J. Denning, ed., *Computers Under Attack: Intruders, Worms, and Viruses,* 381–406. New York: ACM Press.

Cohen, Frederick B. 1992. Defense-in-depth against computer viruses. *Computers & Security* **11**(6): 563–579.

Denning, Peter J., ed. 1990. *Computers Under Attack: Intruders, Worms, and Viruses.* New York: ACM Press.

Ferbrache, David. 1992. *A Pathology of Computer Viruses.* London: Springer-Verlag.

Frizzell, Joseph, Ted Phillips, and Traigh Groover. 1994. The electronic intrusion threat to national security and emergency preparedness telecommunications: An awareness document. *Proceedings of the 17th National Computer Security Conference,* 378–388. NIST/NCSC.

Gasser, Morrie. 1988. *Building a Secure Computer System.* New York: Van Nostrand Reinhold.

Hoffer, Jeffrey A., and Detmar W. Straub, Jr. 1989. The 9 to 5 underground: Are you policing computer crimes? *Sloan Management Review,* Summer: 35–41.

Hoffman, Lance J., ed. 1990. *Rogue Programs: Viruses, Worms, and Trojan Horses.* New York: Van Nostrand Reinhold.

Johnson, John. 1995. A cyberspace dragnet snared fugitive hacker. *Los Angeles Times,* February 19: A1.

Karger, Paul A. 1987. Limiting the damage potential of discretionary Trojan horses. *Proceedings of the 1987 IEEE Symposium on Security and Privacy,* 32–37. Washington, D.C.: IEEE Computer Society.

Kephart, Jeffrey O., and Steve R. White. 1993. Measuring and modeling computer virus prevalence. *Proceedings 1993 IEEE Computer Society Symposium on Research in Security and Privacy,* 2–15. Los Alamitos, Calif.: IEEE Computer Society.

Landwehr, Carl E., Alan R. Bull, John P. McDermott, and William S. Choi. 1994. A taxonomy of computer program security flaws. *ACM Computing Surveys* **26**(3): 211–254.

McCown, Davis. 1990. The Burleson trial—A case history. *Computer Security Journal* **V**(2): 21–35.

National Research Council. 1991. *Computers at Risk: Safe Computing in the Information Age.* Washington, D.C.: National Academy Press.

Neumann, Peter G. 1995. *Computer-Related Risks.* Reading, Mass.: Addison-Wesley.

Neumann, Peter G., and Donn B. Parker. 1989. A summary of computer misuse techniques. *Proceedings of the 12th National Computer Security Conference,* 396–407. NIST/NCSC.

NIST. 1994. *Threats to Computer Systems: An Overview.* Computer Systems Laboratory Bulletin, March 1994. Gaithersburg, Md.: National Institute of Standards and Technology.

Parker, Donn B. 1989. *Computer Crime: Criminal Justice Resource Manual,* 2d ed. Washington, D.C.: U.S. Dept. of Justice.

______. 1990. The Trojan horse virus and other crimoids. In Peter J. Denning, ed., *Computers Under Attack: Intruders, Worms, and Viruses,* 544–554, New York: ACM Press.

Polk, W. Timothy, and Lawrence E. Bassham, III. 1992. *A Guide to the Selection of Anti-Virus Tools and Techniques.* NIST Special Publication 800-5. Gaithersburg, Md.: National Institute of Standards and Technology.

Reynolds, Joyce K. 1991. The helminthiasis of the Internet. *Computer Networks and ISDN Systems* **22:** 347–361.

Rochlis, Jon A., and Mark W. Eichin. 1989. With microscope and tweezers: The worm from MIT's perspective. *Communications of the ACM* **32**(6): 689–698.

Seeley, Donn. 1989. Password cracking: A game of wits. *Communications of the ACM* **32**(6): 700–703.

Shoch, John F., and Jon A. Hupp. 1990. The "worm" programs—Early experience with a distributed computation. In Peter J. Denning, ed., *Computers Under Attack: Intruders, Worms, and Viruses,* 264–281. New York: ACM Press. Reprinted from *Communications of the ACM* **25**(3): 172–180, 1982.

Smith, Kirk. 1988. Tales of the damned. *UNIX Review,* February: 45–50.

Spafford, Eugene H. 1989. Crisis and aftermath. *Communications of the ACM* **32**(6): 678–687.

Spafford, Eugene H., Kathleen A. Heaphy, and David J. Ferbrache. 1990. A computer virus primer. In Peter J. Denning, ed., *Computers Under Attack: Intruders, Worms, and Viruses,* 316–355. New York: ACM Press.

Stoll, Clifford. 1988. Stalking the Wily Hacker. *Communications of the ACM* **31**(5): 484–497.

______. 1989. *The Cuckoo's Egg: Tracking a Spy Through the Maze of Computer Espionage.* New York: Doubleday.

Thompson, Ken. 1984. Reflections on trusting trust. *Communications of the ACM* **27**(8): 761–763.

van Eck, Wim. 1985. Electromagnetic radiation from video display units: An eavesdropping risk? *Computers & Security* **4:** 269–286.

VIRUS-L. 1992. Frequently asked questions on VIRUS-L/comp.virus. *VIRUS-L Forum,* November 1992.

White, Steve R., David M. Chess, and Chengi Jimmy Kuo. 1990. An overview of computer viruses and how to cope with them. *Computer Security Journal* **V**(2): 37–55.

Chapter

4

Policies and Models

Policy defines security for a computing system; a system is secure if it lives up to its security policy. The policy specifies what security properties the system must provide. Similarly, policy defines computer security for an organization, specifying both system properties and the security responsibilities of people.

The needs of the real world dictate security policy. A *real-world security policy* is the set of laws, rules, and practices that regulate how an organization manages, protects, and distributes resources to achieve its security objectives. Those objectives come from the goals and environment of the organization. Consider, for example, a hospital whose policy is to release records to a patient who signs the right forms. In this example, the resource is information, on paper. The resource could also be a physical object or an action. For example, a radiation dose can be given only if two operators verify the radiation machine's settings. Even if an organization has no explicit security policy, policy assumptions guide its actions.

A *computer security policy* must faithfully represent real-world policy and must interpret that policy for resources that have a computing base, resources like databases and transactions. It must also consider threats to computers, specifying which threats the organization chooses to guard against, and how. Some threats (viruses, for example) bear little relation to real-world policy elements. So computer security policy has two parts: (1) an interpretation and partial automation of the real-world policy—sometimes called the *automated security policy*—and (2) policy about computer security in general (see Fig. 4.1). For example (1) security software enforces rules about who can initiate or approve a banking transaction, and (2) a bank requires

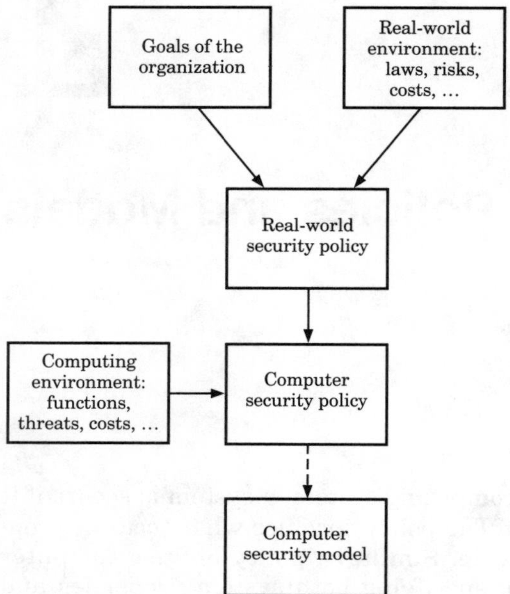

Figure 4.1 Sources of computer security policy.

employees to change their passwords every 30 days. An organization may have different policies for its different applications and systems.

A computer security policy is expressed in a language such as Spanish or English or Japanese. Natural language can be vague or ambiguous, especially if the policy is complex, or if different rules of the policy interact with each other. Most of the time we live with ambiguity, designating who is to interpret the policy when interpretation is needed. Sometimes, however, policy is expressed in a model. A *computer security model* restates the policy in more formal or mathematical terms, allowing its implications to be more fully understood. One purpose of a computer security policy is to guide the design of the security aspects of computing systems. The designers of a system need a clear statement of what policy the system is to carry out. A security model fills that need, defining what services will be provided and, often, what mechanisms will implement them. The model allows designers to get a handle on a complex enterprise.

Of the three computer security properties—confidentiality, integrity, and availability—confidentiality has received by far the most attention. The policies and models for integrity are less developed, and models for availability are in their infancy. This situation resulted in part from the Trusted Computer System Evaluation Criteria (TCSEC) emphasis on confidentiality. All along, however, integrity has been at least as important for both commercial and military needs. For many applications it is clearly more important—financial systems or medical equipment, for example. As more and more critical devices and activities incorporate computing (communications systems, air traffic control, missile launching, radiation treatment) we depend more and more on the integrity of that computing and its data.

This chapter begins by considering security policy apart from computing, then shows how real-world policy needs carry over into the computing world, where additional needs arise. The idea of security models is introduced. Three major categories of models are considered—access control, information flow, and integrity—along with work on denial of service. The chapter closes with a few words on how computer security policy is applied in building and managing systems.

Real-World Security Policy

Security needs have a long history, with computers entering the picture only late in that history. Everyone is familiar with the need to protect secrets—personal, business, or military. For military secrets, this need led to the encoding of messages so that the enemy could not read them. Almost everyone is familiar with policies designed to control fraud and error in the business world. For example, a large cashier's check must be signed by two bank employees, including a manager. This rule is designed to prevent one person alone from committing fraud and to ensure supervisory control.

Principles underlying real-world security policies

Real-world security policy has been defined as the set of laws, rules, and practices that regulate how an organization manages, protects, and distributes resources to achieve its security objectives. Although the laws, rules, and practices reflect that organization's goals and situation, they also reflect principles that apply broadly. These principles underlie the management controls that are applied in nearly all business practice to reduce the risk from fraud and error. (Many of these real-world security principles were introduced in Chap. 1.)

Individual accountability. Individual persons are held answerable for their actions. The principle implies that people are uniquely and accurately identified and that records of their actions are kept and reviewed.

Authorization. Explicit rules are needed about who can use what resources, and in what ways. For example, only authorized technicians can operate SafeCare's imaging equipment. Rules also are needed about who can authorize the use of resources and how the authorization can be delegated. At SafeCare, the head of the radiology laboratory authorizes access to the equipment and can delegate that authority temporarily.

Least privilege. People should be authorized only for the resources they need to do their jobs. Privileges should be "least" in time as well as scope; they should persist only as long as they are needed. This aspect of least privilege is sometimes called *timely revocation of trust.*

Separation of duty. Functions should be divided between people, so that no one person can commit fraud undetected. For example, two bank officials must sign large cashier's checks. Applying this principle may involve "split knowledge"—no one person knows everything. Separation of duty works best when the different people have different roles and viewpoints.

Auditing. Work and its results must be monitored both while the work is being done and after it is done. Information must be checked for internal consistency and for consistency with other criteria. For example, the linen store's inventory record must be consistent with its records of inventory received and sold, and also with the sheets and towels on the shelves. An *audit trail* must be kept—a record of all actions—that supports a later reconstruction of who did what. The audit trail supports the principle of individual accountability.

Redundancy. The principle of redundancy affects both work and information. Important steps are done twice or more (sometimes by different people—separation of duty), and the results are checked for consistency. Multiple copies are kept of important records, and the copies are often stored in different places. There are backups for critical resources like electrical power.

Risk reduction. It is rarely practical or even possible to enforce security policy absolutely. The strategy must be to reduce risk to an acceptable level, keeping the cost of enforcement proportional to the risks.

Roles in real-world security policy

Security policy involves roles that recur in many situations, and also application-specific roles. For paper documents the following generic roles apply:

- *Originator.* The person who issues a document, often the author or the manager of the responsible unit.
- *Authorizer.* The person with control over access to the document. The authorizer may or may not be the originator.
- *Custodian.* The person who physically keeps the document and carries out the authorizer's intentions about access to it.
- *User.* The person who reads or alters the document.

If the resource is not a document but a commercial transaction, other roles come into play, including:

- *Creator.* The person who designs the transaction and writes the rules about its steps.
- *Customer.* The person on whose behalf the transaction is carried out.
- *Executor.* The person who actually carries out the transaction—prepares a check or debits a bank account.
- *Supervisor.* The person who authorizes the transaction.
- *Auditor.* The person who checks the actions, results, and controls.

Some roles make sense only for a specific application or transaction. For example, the process of obtaining a prescription drug involves the roles of physician, pharmacist, and patient. Each has certain rights in the process. The physician has the right to prescribe. The pharmacist can dispense, but not prescribe. The patient has the right to receive a copy of the prescription. Security policies refer to both general roles and application-specific roles.

Real-world policies for confidentiality

Of the three computer security properties—confidentiality, integrity, and availability—the first two clearly reflect real-world security properties. We first describe traditional policies for confidentiality, especially of documents.

Some highly sensitive documents are kept secret from everyone, except as explicitly approved by the originator. More typically, documents are grouped or *classified,* according to the type of confidentiality that is needed. Similarly, people are given *clearances.* The policy then can be stated as a relation between the classification of the document and the clearance of the person. In the confidentiality policy of the U.S. military, for example, both documents and people have levels of classification or clearance: Top Secret, Secret,

Confidential, or Unclassified. Access is allowed only if the person's clearance level is at least as high as the document's classification level. A person cleared for Top Secret can see documents at any level. A person cleared for Secret can see Secret, Confidential, and Unclassified documents. Many commercial organizations also classify information according to its level of sensitivity, usually with three or more levels.

Some confidentiality policies cannot be handled with levels alone, however. According to the least-privilege principle, Lieutenant Ray, who works in Army missile procurement, has no need to know about enemy troop number estimates, no matter what her clearance. To meet the least-privilege objective, organizations describe people in terms of *categories* that are relevant to their work, and documents in terms of the categories they cover. The policy for access then states that the categories of the person have to include all the categories of the document. (The military policy is described more precisely later in this chapter.) The categories of a commercial organization may describe the functional areas of its business, such as Engineering and Manufacturing. Also used are categories such as Business Confidential (for sensitive business results), Personal and Confidential (for personnel information), and Proprietary (for trade secrets).

With all this emphasis on confidentiality, it is important to remember that some policy limits confidentiality. The Freedom of Information Act mandates the availability of information, with constraints for confidentiality. A policy of *maximized sharing* would be appropriate for a research database or for a library.

Regardless of its other policies, an organization usually explicitly gives people access to resources, or explicitly denies people such access. Lieutenant Ray has been authorized to see a report summarizing the year's procurement activities for ground-to-air missiles. Many of her colleagues cannot see that report. Another rule denies Lt. Ray access to a report showing vendors' production costs.

Organizations that are concerned about confidentiality devote much effort to classifying documents, labeling them with their classifications, and giving them proper custodial care. For example, BioWidget numbers the copies of its highly sensitive documents. It keeps records about who receives each copy, and it prohibits making new copies. A sensitive document must be kept in a reinforced, fireproof safe, and the location of the document must be audited every three months. Classification is especially important for trade secrets. Not only does it help keep the information confidential, but it is important for obtaining legal recourse if the information does get out. By enforcing its classification policies, BioWidget demonstrates that certain information is proprietary and that it tried to protect it.

Policies and controls for integrity

Management control policies are directed mainly at integrity rather than confidentiality. Many integrity policies are so familiar that they are scarcely noticed. A few of the most important and most common are described here, with a caution to the reader that the definitions and terminology for integrity are very much in flux.

The policy of *authorized actions* states simply that people can take only those actions they are authorized for. (Of course there are realms in any organization where people have implied authorization to act. The policy of authorized actions applies for important resources, such as money in a restaurant cash register. Anyone may retrieve a napkin from the floor.) Another common policy is *supervisory control*—certain actions must be approved by a supervisor. The manager in charge must approve the cashier's going off duty early.

The principle of separation of duty is reflected in many common policies. Dividing a task into parts that are performed by different people is a time-honored way of preventing fraud by one person acting alone. According to the related policy *rotation of duty,* a task should not always be carried out by the same person. If it were, the person would have a better shot at committing fraud without being discovered. Many organizations rotate tasks among employees and insist that employees take their vacations. The policy of *N-person control* requires people to cooperate to carry out an action. To launch a missile, for example, two physically separated controls must be operated simultaneously. This is an example of a *dual-custody* rule.

The policy of *operation sequencing* requires the steps of some task to be carried out in a specific order. Often this policy is combined with separation of duty and N-person control, so that a different person or group carries out each step in the sequence. For driver's license renewal, for example, the old license, new forms, and fee go to one clerk, who issues a written exam. A second person corrects the exam. If a driving test is needed, a third person gives it. A fourth person checks vision and takes a picture. Finally, the license is mailed from a different place to the address of record.

The policy of *constrained change* requires data to be changed only in prescribed and structured ways. Forms, such as purchase orders, are a common way of constraining change. In double-entry bookkeeping, every transaction involves at least two changes, and debits must equal credits for every transaction. If a business buys a computer, the asset account is credited and the cash account is debited by the same amount. A transaction that is constrained and structured has been called a *well-formed transaction.*

Closely related to constrained change is *consistency.* Data must be internally consistent (as in double-entry bookkeeping) and also consistent with external reality. An example of inconsistency is given by the U.S. employment estimates for September 1992. The national figure was 400,000 larger than the sum of the 50 state estimates.

Not all data is as highly structured as accounting data. A written document, for example, cannot be constrained in analogous ways; the best assurance of integrity may be knowing who wrote it. The policy of *attribution of change* aims at attesting to the authorship or "pedigree" of some data. Since various people may change a document, this policy might be enforced by keeping a log showing the description, author, and date of each change. For logs and other history-type documents, a *no-change* policy applies. Once an entry is made, it is never changed or erased.

Real-world policy examples

A few specific policies are worth keeping in mind as test cases for the models described later in this chapter. Since real requirements led to these policies, a good model should handle them.

Chinese Wall policy. Consider an analyst who works for an investment banking firm in the United Kingdom. To do her work for a client—a financial software company—she must obtain insider knowledge about the company. By law she may not advise other competitive software companies but she may advise, for example, a copier manufacturer. According to a model of this policy, information is grouped into "conflict of interest classes," and a person is allowed at most one set of information in each class. Once the analyst has insider information about financial software, a wall is built around all information of that class. Anything else inside the wall is forbidden to her; anything outside is allowed. This is called the *Chinese Wall* policy.

Originator controlled. Another test case is the *originator controlled* (ORCON) policy of the DoD, which is outside the DoD classification and category scheme. A document marked *ORCON* may be released only to organizations on a list specified by the originator of the document. Any other release must be explicitly granted by the originator.

Core policy elements

Although security policy often is tailored to applications, some elements are common to many application-specific policies. A key element of many policies is the concept of *role*. Real-world security policy is often role-based; along with a role come rights to use resources in designated ways. People have these rights because they have to do a job. Once they leave the job, they lose the rights.

One study of tactical military applications (Sterne et al. 1991) identified the same core elements of policy in different applications. These elements included: protection of information from unauthorized disclosure and modification, role-based access control, role exclusion rules (a person who plays one role cannot play another—as in separation of duty), delegation of authority, orders that may not be repudiated, two-person and *N*-person controls, operation sequencing, identification and authentication, and auditing.

Security Policy in the Computing World

The policy principles of the real world continue to hold for the computing world, but the scope of security policy becomes much broader. First, the real-world security policy must be automated faithfully. This means that it must be specified unambiguously. An ambiguous or vague policy may work when it is interpreted by human beings, but it does not work for automated policy. Second, policy choices must be made about the computing situation itself, such as physical security of the computing equipment, or how users identify themselves to the computing system. These choices concern what threats are guarded against and what safeguards are used. Security policy choices must be made when hardware, operating systems, and applications are designed and built, and when they are selected for use. In the computing world, as in the real world, many of the same policies apply to both confidentiality and integrity. More than in the real world, however, confidentiality and integrity may conflict.

Although a few policy needs have been studied intensively, security policy in general is not highly developed. The National Research Council report concluded that "the lack of a clear articulation of security policy for general computing is a major impediment to improved security in computer systems" (National Research Council 1991: 51). The report recommended developing a set of generally accepted system security principles, analogous to those developed over the years by the accounting profession. This means codifying and promulgating principles (about access control, user identification, and auditing, for example) that are applicable to nearly all systems.

A computer security policy is specified in a natural-language document, as clearly and unambiguously as possible. The document specifies what security properties are to be provided, and (to a lesser extent) how. Some policies are abstract and apply to many different computing environments—for example, the DoD policy of classification and categories. Others pertain to a specific organization or site. Still others pertain to a computing system or an application.

Jonathan Moffett and Morris Sloman (1988) have characterized security policy for an organization as general or specific. Examples of general policy include

- Access rules should refer to positions or roles, not people.
- An authorizer should be able to grant rights only to positions in his or her organizational domain.

Examples of specific policies would be

- Security administration for the marketing department is delegated to the administrative manager of that department.
- A wire transfer of funds may be executed by any teller assigned to the window authorized for wire transfers. It must be approved by the assistant manager or (if the amount is over $100,000) by the assistant manager and the branch manager.

Security Models

Models serve three purposes in computer security. The first purpose is to provide a framework that aids understanding of concepts. Models designed for this purpose often use diagrams, charts, or analogies. One example is the "threat-vulnerability-safeguard" model. Another example is the original access matrix model of Butler Lampson (1971), represented in Fig. 4.2.

The second purpose is to provide an unambiguous, often formal, representation of a general security policy. One example is the Bell-LaPadula model, which formalizes the military security policy of classification and clearance. Formal methods of reasoning can be used with that model to reveal the detailed implications of the policy. A model like Bell-LaPadula is an *abstract model,* in that it deals with abstract entities like subjects and objects. A *concrete model* translates these abstract entities into the entities of a real system, such as processes and files. The abstract and concrete models also can be seen as one model at different levels of abstraction; there can be intermediate levels between the most abstract and most concrete.

The third purpose for a model is to express the policy enforced by a specific computing system. A precise expression of policy is needed to guide the design of a system; a formal expression opens the way for proving mathematically that a design does enforce the policy. The

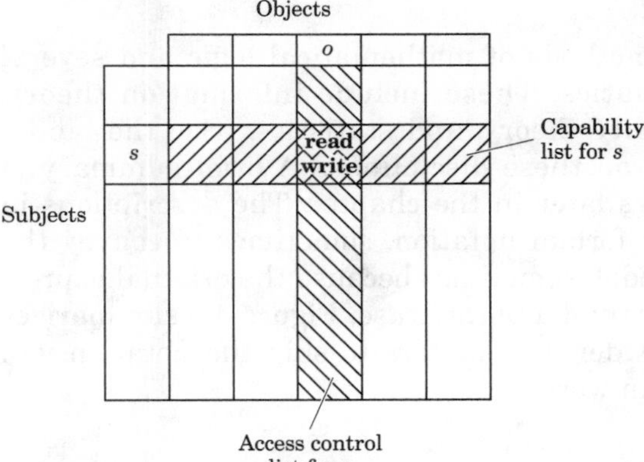

Figure 4.2 Access matrix.

National Computer Security Center (NCSC) definition of a "security policy model" is "a formal presentation of the security policy enforced by the system. It must identify the set of rules and practices that regulate how a system manages, protects, and distributes sensitive information" (NCSC 1988: 42).

The three purposes for models overlap. Conceptual frameworks may evolve with time into abstract formal models. This did happen for the access matrix model. Abstract formal models such as Bell-LaPadula provide a base for concrete models of systems.

History of computer security models

The earliest modeling work, beginning in the 1960s, was stimulated by the development of time-sharing systems, which had to face the problem of sharing information securely. The early systems were developed and used at universities, so the models reflected the university environment. The 1970s and 1980s saw a great expansion of research and a shift to work reflecting military needs. In the late 1980s another shift occurred—toward incorporating the needs of the commercial world and the expertise represented by security controls in business. The 1990s have seen a realization that many different security policies must be modeled (not just one), and that often a single system must be able to support multiple policies. There has been soul-searching about the role that models and formal methods have played—whether the right policies have been modeled, and whether the models have helped or hindered.

Disciplines used in models

Formal models draw on methods of mathematical logic and several fields of applied mathematics. These include information theory, automata theory, complexity theory, and statistics. (See the bibliographic notes for sources on these disciplines.) A brief summary of information theory appears later in the chapter. The descriptions in this chapter include some formal notation, sometimes to convey the essence or flavor of the model, sometimes because the original expression is simpler and clearer than a paraphrase. Figure 4.3 summarizes the notation used. The reader who prefers to skip the notation will always find a paraphrase in words.

Criteria for good models

Assuming that the security policy is appropriate, the first demand on a model is to faithfully represent that policy. There is no way to prove mathematically this faithfulness, since the policy statement is informal. Rather, the model builders must clearly explain in words just how the model corresponds to the policy and must justify the validity of the correspondences.

Another criterion is expressive power. Can the model express all the wrinkles and twists of the policy? For example, the policy may be that a person who has **write** access to a file may grant **write** or **read** access to another person. How can the model express that policy?

A good model helps understanding by clarifying concepts and expressing them forcefully and precisely, focusing attention on the

Notation	Meaning
$X = \{a, b, c, d\}$	X is the set whose elements are a, b, c, and d
$x \in X$	x belongs to the set X
$X \subset Y$	X is a subset of Y; all elements of X belong to Y
$X \cup Y$	All elements of X with all elements of Y
(x, y)	An ordered pair
$X \times Y$	The set of all possible ordered pairs whose first element is a member of set X and whose second element is a member of set Y
$F: X \rightarrow Y$	Function f with domain X and range Y
$y = f(x)$	Function f applied to $x \in X$
$A \Rightarrow B$	A implies B
A iff B	A is true if and only if B is true
$\sum_{i=1}^{n} x$	$x_1 + x_2 + \cdots + x_n$

Figure 4.3 Notation used in describing models.

essentials. A formal model can lead to better understanding of the general problem by way of new truths derived from the axioms of the model. For example, a formal description of the access matrix model led to new understanding of its limitations.

A security model should support decisions about *safety*. The question is whether there is some state of the modeled system in which a specific security property is not preserved. The model should support answering this question, and the decision must not be too complex computationally. Unfortunately, the models that are strong on expressive power tend to be weak in regard to safety. There is a tension between safety and precision. If the model is restricted in order to make safety decidable, it may not represent the security policy precisely enough.

A security model should provide a good foundation for building systems. A system based on the model must be reasonable to build and must perform adequately. A convincing argument must be made that the system is a true implementation of the model. If the model is a formal one, and if the system design is also expressed formally, some steps of the argument can be proved mathematically. This formal *verification* enhances confidence in the security of a system; the TCSEC criteria require formal verification for the highest level of certification. So it is an advantage for the model to be expressed in precise mathematical terms and in a form that can map clearly to design specifications and eventually to code. Since verification is exceedingly difficult, it is a further advantage to express the model in a form that allows proofs to be carried out by computer programs. (This process of going from formal model to implemented system is discussed more fully in Chap. 6.)

It should be possible to model complex systems in parts and then put the parts together. Each part is simpler and more understandable than the whole. It is more likely that the formal specifications and verification will be correct—since they are simpler. Also, parts of the model can be reused when the specification changes as a system evolves. For modeling in parts, formal models of security properties must be *composable*. If two systems are shown individually to have some composable property, and the systems are then hooked together, the resulting system also has that property.

In summary, then, a security model should:

- Validly and precisely represent security policy
- Aid understanding through focused and exact expression and through proofs of properties
- Support safety analysis

- Support system building and system verification
- Allow systems to be modeled in parts that are then put together.

Access Control Models

Access control is the process of ensuring that all access to resources is authorized access. Access control enforces the fundamental security principle of authorization. It supports both confidentiality and integrity.

The access matrix model

The *access matrix model* of access control is simple and intuitive, and it can express many protection policies. The access matrix relates subjects, objects, and rights. *Objects* in the model represent the resources to be controlled. Although objects are abstract entities, they can be thought of as representing files or areas of memory. (Access matrix models were developed in the early 1970s for operating systems, motivated by the protection problems that arose in multiuser systems.) *Subjects* are the active entities of the model. A subject can be thought of as a user or as a process executing on behalf of a user.

The *access matrix* has a row for each subject and a column for each object. In the access matrix *AM,* cell *AM[s,o]* specifies the *rights* that subject *s* has to object *o*. A right represents a type of access to the object, such as **read** or **execute.** In Fig. 4.2, for example, subject *s* has **read** and **write** rights for object *o*. Types of rights are sometimes called *access modes* or *access types*. Subjects may also appear as objects, as when a program subject has **call** rights and also is the object for other programs' **call** rights. A row of the access matrix corresponds to a *capability list*—the list of all the rights of a subject. A column corresponds to an *access control list*—the list of all the rights held by subjects to some object.

The access matrix model can represent many access control policies that support both confidentiality (through controlling reading of objects) and integrity (through controlling modifications to objects and invocation of programs). It supports what is known as *discretionary access control* (DAC), since the access matrix can be changed at the discretion of authorizers. Other models—discussed later—support *mandatory access control* (MAC), which constrains what authorizers can do.

For a useful system, the access matrix is not static. Subjects and objects come and go, and so do rights. This means that the model must include operations to change the access matrix—to create or destroy subjects and objects, and to enter or delete rights. It is crucial to understand what a change to the access matrix implies and what rights subjects potentially can gain.

HRU model and safety. Harrison, Ruzzo, and Ullman (1976) formalized the access matrix model and proved that it cannot provide this crucial understanding, in the general case. In other words, the model is weak in relation to safety.

The *HRU* model defines a *protection system* as consisting of a set of *generic rights R* and a set of *commands C*. A command is like a very simple procedure (with parameters) that has a condition portion and a main portion. The condition portion tests for the presence of certain rights in the access matrix. If the tests succeed, the main portion is executed, carrying out a series of *primitive operations* that change the *protection configuration* (often called the *protection state*). The configuration is a triple (*S,O,AM*), where *S* is the current set of subjects, *O* the current set of objects, and *AM* the access matrix. The primitive operations create and destroy subjects and objects, enter rights in the access matrix, and delete rights. For example, **create object** is a primitive operation. Each operation is defined as a specific change to the access matrix.

Consider, for example, a system where a process may create a file and where the process then becomes the owner of that file and may confer rights to other subjects. This protection system has commands CREATE and CONFER-READ, as follows:

```
command CREATE(process,file)
      create object (file)
      enter own into (process,file)
end
command CONFER-READ(owner,subject,file)
      if own in (owner,file)
      then enter read into (subject,file)
end
```

The HRU model handles many realistic protection systems, such as the original UNIX protection scheme.

Executing a command transforms the protection configuration into a new configuration. HRU notation is

- $Q \vdash_{\alpha(x_1,\ldots,x_k)} Q'$. That is, configuration Q yields Q' when command α is run with the parameters given.
- $Q \vdash_{\alpha} Q'$ if there exist parameters $x_1,\ldots,x_k$ such that $Q \vdash_{\alpha(x_1,\ldots,x_k)} Q'$. That is, Q' can be reached from Q by application of command α.
- $Q \vdash Q'$ if there exists any command α such that $Q \vdash_{\alpha} Q'$. Informally, Q' is reachable from Q.

- $Q \vdash^* Q'$ is also used; $\vdash^*$ represents zero or more applications of $\vdash$.

Returning now to safety, the question is whether a contemplated change to the access matrix can result (indirectly) in *leakage* of rights to unauthorized subjects. HRU defines leakage as follows: A command α leaks a right r from protection configuration Q if, when α is run on Q, it can execute a primitive operation that enters r into some cell of the access matrix that did not previously contain r. (Some subject now has right r on some object; previously the subject did not have that right.) "...the initial configuration Q_0 is *unsafe* for r (or *leaks* r) if there is a configuration Q and a command α such that (1) $Q_0 \vdash^* Q$ and (2) α leaks r from Q" (Harrison, Ruzzo, and Ullman 1976: 467). That is, Q_0 is unsafe for a right (**write,** for example) if we can reach from Q_0 another configuration Q that leaks the right. If a configuration is not unsafe, it is safe.

The important result of HRU is that it is undecidable whether a given configuration is safe for a given right. (The proof involves making a correspondence between (1) leakage of a right and (2) an arbitrary Turing machine entering a final state, which is known to be undecidable.) Although this result about the access matrix model is fundamental, it applies only to a general and unrestricted protection system. For a more restricted *monooperational* system (where each command is a single primitive operation), safety is decidable, but the decision procedure is so computationally complex that it is probably impractical.

The HRU results have led researchers to devise more restricted protection systems, in the hopes of finding useful ones with better safety properties. One such attempt is the *monotonic* system, where rights can only be given and not taken away. This may not sound very practical, but many practical systems can be reduced to monotonic systems for the purpose of safety analysis. Even monotonic systems have quite poor safety properties, however. *Take-Grant* models (described later in this chapter) have better safety properties. Entirely new frameworks for protection have been developed, as well.

In spite of the safety results, the unrestricted access matrix is probably the most widely used security model. On the whole it is successful. Leakage of rights is constrained by controls within the protection system (how the commands are defined) and outside the protection system (the good judgment of users).

Other features of the access matrix model. HRU is a bare-bones model designed to answer fundamental questions. Other features appear in other versions of the access matrix model.

Transfer of rights. In some systems subjects can receive rights that are transferable. That is, the subject may transfer the right to another subject. This transferability of a right is sometimes described as a *copy flag,* following the usage of Lampson. A copy flag attached to a right in $AM[s,o]$ means that subject s can copy that right to another cell in column o, choosing whether or not to copy the flag as well.

The reference monitor. Implied by the access matrix model is some mechanism that monitors all access attempts. The mechanism is sometimes viewed as associated with the object, more often as part of the general protection system. G. Scott Graham and Peter Denning (1972) used the term *monitor* for the mechanism that validates access to each object *type.* James Anderson (1972) introduced the term *reference monitor* for the general mechanism that ensures that each access is authorized by the access matrix (see Fig. 4.4).

Access request and decision. An *access request,* specified by the triple (s,o,r) is the event that the reference monitor mediates. Subject s requests access of type r to object o. The *access decision* may allow or deny the request, or modify it into a different request.

Access validation rules specify how the reference monitor decides the fate of a request—how it makes the access decision.

Authorization rules specify how the access matrix itself can be modified. (Authorization rules would be represented in HRU by the condition portions of the commands.)

Capabilities and the Take-Grant model

A row of the access matrix can be viewed as a capability list specifying all the rights of the subject associated with that row. The two main ways of implementing access control are access control lists

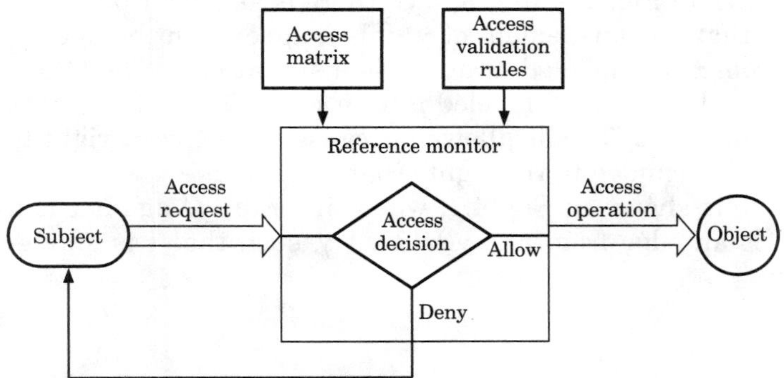

Figure 4.4 Access request mediated by the reference monitor.

(attached to objects and corresponding to columns of the access matrix) and capabilities. A *capability* is held by a subject and is defined as

$$(object, rights, random)$$

where the third component is a random number generated to prevent forgery. A capability is something like a ticket that the holder can present to obtain access to some object. Since capabilities cannot be forged, they can be passed around without intervention by any monitor. This property of capabilities makes for a great deal of flexibility in system design; operating systems and hardware architectures have been designed around capabilities. This same flexibility also makes it impossible to guarantee certain properties in a pure capability system. For example, a classic capability system cannot enforce the *-property.

Closely identified with capability systems are *Take-Grant* models, which represent the protection state by a directed graph. In Fig. 4.5, vertex b (solid) represents a subject and vertex c (open) represents an object. The directed edge from b to c (labeled α) represents a set of rights that subject b has for object c. The edge then represents a capability for c owned by b. The rights α must be a subset of a fixed set of rights R. For example, R = {**read, write, take, grant**}, or {**r, w, t, g**}. A vertex that represents either a subject or an object is shown as $\otimes$.

A Take-Grant model specifies a set of rules for transforming protection graphs. These rules control how rights can be passed. By varying the rules, one can define different Take-Grant models. One example model includes rules *Create, Remove, Grant,* and *Take,* where the first two govern how vertices are added and removed, and Grant and Take govern how one subject can grant rights to another or take rights from another. The Grant rule defines a new graph G' formed from graph G, as shown in Fig. 4.6. In graph G, there is an edge from x to y labeled γ, such that **g** is an element of γ (only **g** appears in the figure), and an edge from x to z labeled α, and β is a subset of α. The Grant rule adds a new edge (dashed) labeled β from y to z. That is, x grants y the ability to do β to z. This is allowed because x has **grant** right to y and because β is included in the rights that x has to z.

The Take rule is shown in Fig. 4.7, where in graph G again x is a subject, there is an edge from x to y labeled γ, such that **t** is an ele-

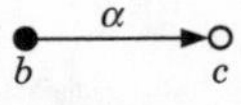

$b \bullet \xrightarrow{\alpha} \circ c$

Figure 4.5 Simple protection graph.

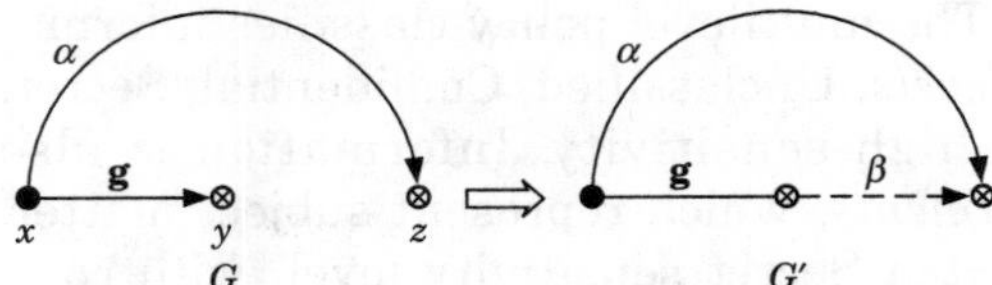

Figure 4.6 Grant rule of Take-Grant model.

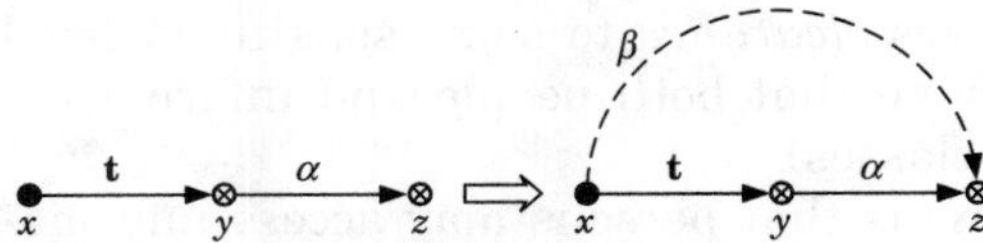

Figure 4.7 Take rule of Take-Grant model.

ment of γ (only **t** appears in the figure), and an edge from y to z labeled α, and β is a subset of α. The Take rule adds an edge from x to z labeled β. That is, x takes from y the ability to do β to z.

Compared to the HRU model (which can also be represented graphically) the Take-Grant model is more restrictive, because it has particular rules for transforming the protection graph. Since the model is more restrictive, safety decisions are possible.

Limitations of discretionary access control

One limitation of traditional DAC approaches is the safety problem. Even more serious is the vulnerability of DAC to Trojan horse attacks. A *Trojan horse* is an apparently useful program containing hidden functions that can exploit the rights of the subject, and so violate security policy. For example, the Trojan horse could leak confidential information to an accomplice or could destroy the user's files. Since a Trojan horse executes with the rights of the user who has unwittingly invoked it, DAC is powerless to protect against it. The next section describes a mandatory access control model intended to solve this problem.

The Bell-LaPadula model

The *Bell-LaPadula* (*BLP*) *model* formalizes the multilevel security policy. The model, developed by D. E. Bell and L. J. LaPadula (1976), is treated here as an access control model, since it is expressed in terms of access control. The goal of the policy, though, is information flow control. The BLP model has played a key role in the efforts to build systems whose security can be verified.

The multilevel security policy. The multilevel policy classifies information at one of four *sensitivity levels:* Unclassified, Confidential, Secret, or Top Secret—from low to high sensitivity. Information is also described in terms of *compartments,* which represent subject matter. A document might be designated Secret sensitivity level, with compartments Artillery and Nuclear. The *security level* or *access class* of the document is the combination of its sensitivity level and its set of compartments. A person receives *clearance* to some sensitivity level and to a set of compartments, so that both people and information have security levels (or access classes).

The policy (mandated by law) is that persons may access information only up to their clearance level. For example, a person cleared for Secret can access Secret, Confidential, and Unclassified, but not Top Secret. Further, access is allowed only if a person has clearance for all the compartments of the information. A person who has a classified document must exercise *discretion* about giving it to other properly cleared persons.

When a new document is created, it typically contains portions at various levels; the document is classified at the highest level of any of its parts.

Early computing systems separated the security levels, using a different computer or different period of time for processing each level. This scheme was inefficient and limited in function. An important goal, then, was to build *multilevel secure* systems that could work on different levels concurrently.

State machine models. BLP is a *state machine model,* as are many computer security models. A state machine model views a system as a triple (*S, I, F*), where *S* is a set of states, *I* is a set of possible inputs, and *F* is a *transition function* that takes the system from one state to another. There may also be other sets of entities, such as outputs, and other functions. A model of security also has axioms giving conditions for security. The axioms may restrict the system state, the state transitions, or the outputs. Proofs of security use an inductive method. They show that the initial state is secure and that all transitions from a secure state lead to a secure state.

Sets and properties. The BLP model includes the following sets:

S	*subjects*
O	*objects*
A	*access modes* such as **read** (**r**) and **write** (**w**)
L	*security levels*

A *secure state* is defined by three properties that are intended to express the multilevel policy: the *simple security* (*ss-*) *property,* the **-property* (pronounced star-property), and the *discretionary security property.* The ss-property expresses clearance-classification policy. The *-property represents the policy of no unauthorized flow of information from a higher level to a lower one. These two properties represent mandatory access control. The discretionary security property reflects the principle of authorization and is expressed in an access matrix. Only the mandatory properties are described here.

System, states, and state transitions. A system is a state machine with states V. Each state v is an element of the set of possible states $V = (B \times F)$, where:

B is the set of all possible *current access sets.* The current access set b represents the accesses that are currently held—that have been requested and approved, and not released. An element of b is a triple (s, o, a)—subject, object, access mode.

F is a subset of $L^S \times L^O$. Each element f is a pair of functions (f_S, f_O), where f_S gives the security level associated with each subject, and f_O gives the security level associated with each object. One security level f_1 *dominates* another f_2 if the classification of f_1 is greater than or equal to that of f_2 and the category set of f_1 includes the category set of f_2.

The inputs to the system are a set of *requests R,* and the outputs are *decisions D.* A *rule* is a function that associates a pair (request, state) with a pair (decision, state). An *action* of the system is described as (r, d, v^*, v). That is, a request r made in state v yields a decision d and moves the system from state v to state v^*. The term *request-response* is sometimes applied to this paradigm. When BLP is interpreted for the Multics operating system, the rules correspond to system operations, such as **get-read** (which alters the current access set), **give-access** (which alters the access matrix) and **change-object-security-level.** Some versions of BLP assume that objects do not change security level; this is called the *tranquility* principle. Rules of operation are important for guiding system design, but are often omitted from abstract models.

The security properties. A state satisfies the ss-property if and only if, for each element of the current access set b, the security level of the subject dominates the security level of the object. This property is also called *no read up.* (A formal statement appears below.)

The *-property is satisfied if and only if (1) for each **write** access in the current access set b, the level of the object equals the current level of the subject, and (2) for each **read** access in b, the level of the subject dominates the level of the object. The *-property ensures that, if a subject has read access to one object and write access to another, then the level of the first is dominated by the level of the second. The *-property is sometimes called *no write down,* or the *confinement* property.

The *-property represents the policy that a subject cannot copy higher level information into a lower level object. The actual specification of the property is stronger than that, since the model deals with access to whole objects and does not delve into what information is being transferred.

Trusted subjects. A system that enforced the model as described so far would be unworkable. For example, the *-property would prohibit moving a paragraph about unclassified topics from a Confidential document to an Unclassified document. It would prevent the downgrading of information by a security officer. To address this problem, the model includes the concept of *trusted subjects,* who are allowed to violate the *-property but are trusted not to violate its intent (as in the examples). Set S', a subset of S, represents the untrusted subjects—those to whom the *-property applies.

Formal statements of properties. Formally, a state $v = (b, f)$ satisfies the ss-property if and only if:

$$s \in S \Rightarrow [(o \in b(s\text{: }\mathbf{r,w})) \Rightarrow (f_S(s) \text{ dominates } f_O(o))]$$

where $b(s\text{: }\mathbf{r,w})$ stands for $\{o\text{: }(s,o,\mathbf{r}) \in b \text{ or } (s,o,\mathbf{w}) \in b\}$. A state satisfies the *-property relative to S' if and only if

$$s \in S' \Rightarrow [(o \in b(s:\mathbf{w})) \Rightarrow (f_O(o) = f_S(s))]$$

and

$$[(o \in b(s:\mathbf{r})) \Rightarrow (f_S(s) \text{ dominates } f_O(o))].$$

Secure system. The simple security and *-properties define a secure *state.* The model must also define a secure *system.* A system is defined as all sequences of actions with some initial state that satisfy a relation W on the successive states. The relation W defines how the security properties are preserved. Some additional notation:

W	$W \subset R{\times}D{\times}V{\times}V$; subset of actions
X	Request sequences
Y	Decision sequences

T 1,2,…,t,…; t is an index to a state sequence
Z State sequences; z_t is the tth state in the sequence z
z_0 Initial state of the system

The system $\Sigma(R,D,W,z_0) \subset X \times Y \times Z$ is defined as follows:

$(x,y,z) \in \Sigma(R,D,W,z_0)$ if and only if, for each t in T,

$(x_t, y_t, z_t, z_{t-1}) \in W$

That is, a system is defined by its initial state and its possible actions under the conditions.

A state sequence z is secure if and only if each state in the sequence is secure. An element (x,y,z) of the system is called an *appearance* of the system; it is a *secure appearance* if and only if z is a secure sequence. Finally, a system is secure if and only if each appearance of the system is a secure appearance. The notion of appearance is used in proving the BLP theorems.

Theorems. BLP proves a theorem for each security property, stating that the system satisfies the property, for any initial state z_0 that satisfies the property, if and only if W satisfies certain conditions for each action.

For simple security, the conditions are (1) each element of the new current access set b^* satisfies the ss-property relative to the new security levels f^* and (2) any element of the old current access set b that does not satisfy the ss-property relative to f^* is not in b^*. Similarly, for the *-property, (1) for each new element of b^* specifying **write,** the level f^* of the object equals the level f^* of the subject, and for **read,** f^* of the subject dominates f^* of the object, and (2) each element of b not satisfying the *-property in relation to f^* is not in b^*.

The main result of the model is the *basic security theorem,* a corollary of the theorems about the properties. It states that a system is secure if its initial state is secure and W satisfies the conditions of the separate theorems for each action. This result is important because it shows that preserving security from one state to the next guarantees system security.

Bell-LaPadula as a base for concrete models. Bell-LaPadula has been used as the base for many concrete system models. The concrete model must be a *valid interpretation* of the abstract BLP model. It must satisfy the axioms of BLP. If it does, the same theorems are true and the security properties of BLP carry over. The concrete model will be stated in terms of entities such as users, processes, and files, rather than subjects and objects. The entities and relations of the concrete model must be mapped to the corresponding entities of BLP.

Bell-LaPadula issues. Although BLP has long been the leading abstract model, issues remain about its concepts and about what role it should play.

Limitations of access control models. One problem is that an access control model can only roughly express the multilevel policy. *Information flow* models (described in the next section) do that more precisely. The *-property of access control has to be stronger, more restrictive, than the policy. Another problem is that important real-world policies (such as n-person control or originator controlled) cannot be expressed. Access control models have the advantage, however, of being closer to the way systems are implemented than information flow models and thus providing a better base for concrete models and more guidance for building systems.

Restrictiveness of the *-property. BLP prohibits information flow from high to low. The assumption is that such flow is equivalent to disclosing secrets. However, systems that enforce BLP cannot support activities that are routine in the paper-based world. "In all practical systems information flow from high to low is unavoidable, and, in some systems, it is the main required activity" (Nelson 1994: 76).

Trusted subjects. Because the *-property is so restrictive, the model introduces trusted subjects. Since the model places no constraints on how trusted processes may violate the *-property, each system that is developed makes its own rules about what trusted subjects can do. It is therefore unclear just what security rules a system does enforce, and any proof of security based on the BLP axioms being enforced does not apply to the whole system including trusted processes.

Incompleteness of the model. The BLP model deals with the current access set; it does not explicitly model actual reads and writes. The complexity of current systems (with buffering, file servers, and file sharing as a few examples) means that supplementary models must be used for assurance that reads and writes are consistent with the current access set. (These supplementary policies have been called *entelechy policies.*)

Covert channels. Access control models such as BLP deal with attempts to gain and pass information through normal "overt" access requests, modeled as inputs to the state machine. The model does not deal with information that is passed in more indirect ways known as *covert channels.* One subject can pass information to another through any resource that they share. For example, a Secret process could leak information to an Unclassified process by placing a lock on an Unclassified file. The information being leaked could be coded in the length of time the lock is held.

Secure state transition. The BLP notion of a secure system has been criticized because it has no independent definition of a secure state transition; it has only the Basic Security Theorem statement that a secure transition leads to a secure state. A system can be secure according to BLP, but still exhibit nonsecure transitions. This becomes clear for the imaginary System Z described by John McLean. In System Z, on any request whatsoever, all subjects and objects are downgraded to the lowest possible level, and the requested access is added to the current access set. Although the new state does not violate the security properties, anyone can access anything—clearly not the intent of the policy. This problem could be corrected by adding to the model necessary conditions for secure state transitions.

Policy issues. Finally, the multilevel policy embodied in BLP is far from meeting all policy needs, even for military systems. An example given earlier is ORCON, which is only one form of dissemination control policy. Also mentioned earlier was the Chinese Wall policy, whose support requires extending or reinterpreting BLP. And BLP does not incorporate mandatory integrity for the content of data—only for its classification. (A companion model of mandatory integrity is described later in this chapter.)

Application-oriented models

One appeal of Bell-LaPadula is its abstractness, but that same quality makes it difficult to apply. It has no place for application-dependent security rules. A different approach is taken by Carl Landwehr, Constance Heitmeyer, and John McLean (1984), who begin with the functional and security requirements of a specific application—a military message system. From these requirements they develop a set of security assertions that the system must enforce. Their model distinguishes between single-level objects and *containers,* which are multilevel information structures containing objects and other containers. Examples of assertions are

- The classification of any container is always at least as high as the maximum of the classifications of the entities it contains.

- Any entity viewed by a user must be labeled with its classification.

With this approach there is no discrepancy between an abstract model (such as BLP) and the model of what is actually built. The assertions of the model are enforced by all the software. Further, since the entities of the model are meaningful to users, the model is more understandable.

Authorization

Discretionary access control has two parts: (1) people specify the security policy to the system and (2) the system enforces that specification. The first part is *authorization.* It might seem easy—just make entries in the access matrix—but it is not. A security policy or model for a system should take into account the meaning of:

- *Groups* of subjects and objects
- *Roles* with respect to applications
- *Roles* with respect to authorization
- *Denial* of access
- *Transformation* of rights
- *Access modes* and their ordering or other structure
- *Context-dependent* and *content-dependent* control
- *Object hierarchies* or other structures

Groups and application-specific roles. For access control to be practical, both subjects and objects must be treated as groups. Otherwise the authorizer's task would be immense. A subject (think of a process) operates on behalf of a user, who may belong to more than one group. One possible policy is for the subject to have the union of the rights of these groups. An alternative is for the user to choose one group identity for a session. The user then takes on a specific application-defined role.

A more elegant approach is to group rights rather than people. A role then becomes simply a named group of rights, and a person is given the right to act in that role. This approach corresponds more closely to how the business world works, with a role corresponding to a job responsibility. The system must know both the role and the individual identity of the user, to support the principle of individual accountability.

Authorization roles. Real-world policies involve roles such as originator, authorizer, classifier, and user. Access control policies typically distinguish rights that affect the protection state and restrict who may gain those rights. For example, only certain users may add new users, or create certain types of objects. In one common policy the creator of an object (a file, for example) automatically becomes its *owner,* with the sole right to grant access to the object. This may be appropriate for systems supporting programmers or researchers, but it is wrong for most operational systems. There, ownership reflects the structure of the organization and the way authority is exercised.

Authorization must be decentralized in a way that corresponds to the organizational structure. The authorizer has two domains of authority. The *organizational domain* defines the people to whom the authorizer can grant rights, and the *resource domain* defines what operations on what resources can be granted. Distributed systems entail decentralization of the authorizer's role on a geographic basis (which sometimes corresponds to an organizational basis).

Transformation of rights. Access rights can be transformed in many ways. They can be granted to additional subjects, as allowed by the copy flag of the access matrix model, or as in the Take-Grant model. Rights can be automatically *amplified,* as when a program's rights amplify the user's rights, or *restricted,* as when the program's rights place a ceiling on what the user may do. For example, the bank teller can write to the account record when using the Deposit transaction, but not when using the Inquiry transaction. (Another way to look at amplification and restriction is to associate rights with a user-program pair. For business transactions this is highly appropriate.) Access rights may be viewed as ordered, so that one right implies another. For example, it is reasonable for **write** to imply **append.** The right to grant access to an object may imply the right to access the object. Such a right may be *attenuated* when it is passed to another subject, the new subject receiving only the right to access, not the right to grant. Alternatively (and usually better) the right to grant is completely separate from the right to access.

Ravi Sandhu and his colleagues have tried to unify these various cases in the concept of *transformation.* With *internal transformation* a subject who has certain rights for an object obtains additional rights, possibly losing existing rights. With *grant transformation* a subject who has a right to an object can grant some rights for the object to another subject. The *Transformation Model* (TRM) focuses on the *authorization scheme* that governs how the protection state gets changed. A scheme for a system is defined by:

1. A set of access rights
2. Sets of subject types and object types

3. State-changing commands, where each command specifies the authorization for its execution and its effect on the protection state

All subjects and objects have types that never change. This means that TRM can enforce nondiscretionary policies, including (it seems) BLP. The propagation of rights in the transformation model is based entirely on existing rights for the object (and not on other rights of the subject or other subjects' rights). This makes it appropriate for distributed systems, since a location that controls some objects can make access decisions based solely on its own authorization scheme and protection state.

Denial of access. Only positive access rights have been described so far. Explicit denial of rights also is used in some systems, and the TCSEC requires (for discretionary access control) the ability to specify individuals and groups who cannot be given access to some object. Denial may be interpreted in alternative ways. According to the *most-specific* rule, grants or denials to an individual take precedence over those for groups. Assume User 1 belongs to Group A, and Group A is denied **read** on File 1. Then, under the most-specific rule, if User 1 has been given **read** rights to File 1, User 1 may read File 1. An alternative rule is that denial takes precedence, whether group or individual. Under this rule User 1 would not be able to read File 1.

Hierarchies of objects. Hierarchical structures of objects are ubiquitous. Many file systems have hierarchical directory structures, and access to a file may require the right to all directories above it in the hierarchy. In a structural hierarchy, one object is part of another. In a relational database system, for example, a relation is part of a database. A reasonable policy then is that access to the relation requires the corresponding right for the database.

Context-dependent and content-dependent access control. An access decision may use information about the context in which the decision is made. This may be environment information (time of day, for example), subject attributes (such as location, job responsibilities, or history of other accesses), and object attributes (such as file size or creation date). Access control using such information is called *context-dependent. Content-dependent* control uses information in the object being accessed. Content-dependent control is especially relevant for database systems, where the data is structured enough to be used in access decisions. For example, a personnel clerk might have read access to the Salary field of some relation if the Department field shows a department that he handles.

A model of authorization

The many policy issues show that it is important to model the abstract semantics of access control, separate from the mechanisms. This separation is achieved in a model of authorization proposed by Thomas Woo and Simon Lam (1992). The term *authorization* here covers both how access rights are *specified* or *represented* and how they are *evaluated.* The specification is given a precise semantics, so that it is computable; thus evaluation is reduced to computation of the semantics of the specification. Authorization is represented in a declarative language as rules, which are like first-order formulas in logic, but with restrictions to ensure computable semantics. A set of these rules can be translated into an extended form of logic program. (A logic program, written in a logic programming language such as Prolog, can execute mathematic logic.)

A request for access goes to an *authorization module,* which is an interpreter that takes as input the authorization requirements—the set of rules—and the system state (because rules may refer to state information such as the history of access or the time of day). The authorization module tries to verify, for *request*(s, o, r), that either *grant*(s, o, r) or *deny*(s, o, r) logically follows from the inputs. If neither *grant* nor *deny* follows, the decision is *fail*(s, o, r).

A rule has the form $(f : f')/g$, representing three formulas called the *prerequisite, assumption,* and *consequent* of the rule. The rules can express many useful access control policies. For example, a simple rule (g) can say that users must be able to read and write their home directories:

$$\mathbf{read}^{+}(\text{User},\text{User.home}) \wedge \mathbf{write}^{+}(\text{User},\text{User.home})$$

A rule with a prerequisite can say that a user x who may execute a program P.exe is also authorized to read the associated documentation P.doc:

$$\mathbf{execute}^{+}(x,\text{P.exe}) \Rightarrow \mathbf{read}^{+}(x,\text{P.doc})$$

Example. Woo and Lam express a simplified Bell-LaPadula model (only the ss-property and *-property, with levels High and Low) as follows:

$$BLP = R^{-} \cup W^{-} \cup R^{+} \cup W^{+}$$

where
$$\begin{aligned} R^{-} &= \{s \in \text{Low} \wedge o \in \text{High} \Rightarrow \mathbf{read}^{-}(s,o)\} \\ W^{-} &= \{s \in \text{High} \wedge o \in \text{Low} \Rightarrow \mathbf{write}^{-}(s,o)\} \\ R^{+} &= \{o \in \text{Low} \Rightarrow \mathbf{read}^{+}(s,o)\} \\ W^{+} &= \{s \in \text{Low} \Rightarrow \mathbf{write}^{+}(s,o)\} \end{aligned}$$

Information Flow Models

A goal of most security policy is to protect information. Access control models approach this goal indirectly, dealing not with information but with objects (such as files) that contain information. Another type of model deals directly with *information flow*. But what *is* information? What is information flow?

Information theory

Information theory, which was developed by Claude Shannon for dealing with communication, provides a systematic view of information. Information theory has been used in information flow models and is relevant to other computer security problems and methods, notably cryptography. This is not surprising, since both communication and computer security are concerned with the transmission of information.

Information theory defines information in terms of uncertainty. Giving information is the same as removing uncertainty. Some uncertain situations are clearly more uncertain than others. A race for mayor among three equally ranked candidates is more uncertain than a race between two. The concept of *entropy* captures this idea.

Entropy. A random variable, such as the result of throwing a die, has a set of possible values, such as 1, 2, 3, 4, 5, and 6. The entropy of a random variable depends on the probabilities of its values. Let X be a random variable that takes a finite set of values with probabilities $p_1, \ldots, p_k, \ldots, p_n$. The entropy H of X is defined as

$$H(X) = -\sum_k p_k \log_2 p_k$$

or

$$H(X) = \sum_k p_k \log_2\left(\frac{1}{p_k}\right)$$

(It is customary in information theory to use logarithms to the base 2; from now on the base is omitted.)

Example. A mayoral race has two candidates, A and B, equally likely to win, so $p_A = .5$ and $p_B = .5$. The log of 1/.5 (the log of 2) is 1.

$$H = .5 \times 1 + .5 \times 1 = 1$$

Entropy is always a positive quantity. An upper bound for H is given by log n. H is equal to log n (is greatest) when all the probabilities are equal, as in the example. The unit of entropy is a *bit*. When we learn who wins the mayoral race we gain one bit of information, which could be represented in a computer by a one-bit field.

Example. A third candidate C enters the race, and the new polls show probabilities of .5 for A, .25 for B, and .25 for C.

$$\log(1/.25) = \log(4) = 2$$
$$H = .5 \times 1 + .25 \times 2 + .25 \times 2 = 1.5$$

We gain 1.5 bits of information by learning the winner of this race.

Conditional entropy. An important concept for information flow models (and also for cryptography) is *conditional entropy.* The conditional entropy of X given Y is a measure of the uncertainty of X given side knowledge about Y. For each value y_j of Y, there is a conditional entropy of X given y_j.

$$H(X \mid y_j) = -\sum_k p(x_k \mid y_j) \log p(x_k \mid y_j)$$
$$= \sum_k p(x_k \mid y_j) \log \frac{1}{p(x_k \mid y_j)}$$

where $p(x_k \mid y_j)$ is the conditional probability that $X = x_k$ given that $Y = y_j$. The conditional entropy of X given Y is defined as:

$$H(X \mid Y) = \sum_j H(X \mid y_j) p(y_j)$$

That is, $H(X \mid Y)$ is the entropy of X given a particular value of Y, averaged over the possible values of Y.

Conditional entropy measures how much information about X can be gained through knowledge about Y. If X and Y are independent, knowing Y has no effect on the entropy of X. That is, the conditional entropy of X given Y is equal to the entropy of X. The conditional entropy can never be greater than the entropy.

Example. Assume that Hawaii women are 75% Democrat and 25% Republican, and the men are 70% Democrat. Also, 80% of Republican women are married to Democratic men. How much information about a husband's party is conveyed by the wife's party? The conditional probabilities are as follows:

$$p(\mathrm{R} \mid \mathrm{D}) = .333$$
$$p(\mathrm{D} \mid \mathrm{D}) = .667$$
$$p(\mathrm{R} \mid \mathrm{R}) = .2$$
$$p(\mathrm{D} \mid \mathrm{R}) = .8$$

The conditional entropy of a husband's party given a Democratic wife:

$$H(PTY_{\mathrm{H}} \mid PTY_{\mathrm{W}} = \mathrm{D}) = .333 \log(1/.333) + .667 \log(1/.667)$$
$$= .333 \times 1.585 + .667 \times .585 = .918$$

Given a Republican wife:

$$H(PTY_{\mathrm{H}} \mid PTY_{\mathrm{W}} = \mathrm{R}) = .2 \log(1/.2) + .8 \log(1/.8)$$
$$= .2 \times 2.322 + .8 \times .322 = .722$$

The conditional entropy of a husband's party given his wife's party is

$$H(PTY_H \mid PTY_W = H(PTY_H \mid PTY_W = \mathrm{D})\, p\, (PTY_W = \mathrm{D})$$

$$+ H(PTY_H \mid PTY_W = \mathrm{R})\, p\, (PTY_W = \mathrm{R})$$

$$= .918 \times .75 + .722 \times .25 = .869$$

The entropy of a husband's party (not knowing his wife's party) is

$$H(PTY_H) = .7 \log 1/.7 + .3 \log 1/.3$$

$$= .360 + .521 = .881$$

So knowing the wife's party reduces the entropy of the husband's party from .881 bits to .869 bits; it provides .012 bits of information.

Channels. A *channel* is a black box that accepts strings of *symbols* from some *input alphabet* and emits strings of symbols from some *output alphabet.* Information theory defines different kinds of channels. A *discrete channel* can transmit only symbols from a finite input alphabet. In a *memoryless* channel the output is independent of any previous input or output. A *discrete memoryless channel* emits a string the same length as the input string. This channel is defined by its input and output alphabets and by a matrix containing the conditional probability of each output symbol given each input symbol. One kind of discrete memoryless channel is the *binary symmetric channel.* It has input and output alphabets {0,1} and a fixed probability q of an output symbol being the same as the input symbol; $q = 1-p$, where p is the probability of error. The channel matrix is shown in Fig. 4.8.

Channel capacity is a measure of the channel's ability to transmit information. It is expressed (depending on the context) as bits per second or bits per symbol and can be computed from the channel matrix. For example, the capacity of the binary symmetric channel is

$$C = 1 + p \log p + q \log q$$

A lattice model of information flow

An information flow policy defines the classes of information that a system can have and how information may flow between these class-

$$\boldsymbol{P} = \begin{bmatrix} 1-p & p \\ p & 1-p \end{bmatrix}$$

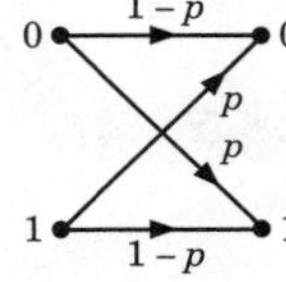

Figure 4.8 Channel matrix for a discrete memoryless channel.

es. An information flow model developed by Dorothy Denning (1976, 1982) can express the multilevel policy in terms of information flow rather than access control (as in Bell-LaPadula). It can also express other useful policies. The flow policy is defined by a *lattice.*

Lattice structure. A lattice is a mathematical structure that neatly represents the meaning of security levels. A lattice consists of a partially ordered set plus a *least upper bound* operator $\oplus$ and a *greatest lower bound operator* $\otimes$. In an information flow model, the lattice $(SC, \leq, \oplus, \otimes)$ represents a set of security classes *SC* and an ordering relation $\leq$ on the classes. The least upper bound operator $\oplus$ yields the highest security class of the classes it is applied to, and the greatest lower bound operator $\otimes$ yields the lowest security class. The ordering relation $\leq$ is transitive. That is, for classes *A, B,* and *C*

$$A \leq B \text{ and } B \leq C \text{ implies } A \leq C$$

Many useful policies can be expressed in lattice form. The U.S. government multilevel policy is often called the *lattice policy,* even when no information flow model is used. For the multilevel policy, if *L* and *L´* are sensitivity-level classes, and *C* and *C´* are sets of compartments, *dominates* is expressed as

1. $(L, C) \leq (L', C')$ if and only if $L \leq L'$ and $C \subseteq C'$

and (interpreting the least upper bound operator as a class-combining operator)

2. $(L, C) \oplus (L', C) = (\max(L, L'), C \cup C')$

Example. A company's policy forms a lattice with levels *Public* and *Company Confidential* (*CC*) and categories *Engineering* (*E*) and *Marketing* (*M*). The lattice is shown in Fig. 4.9, where an arrow indicates that information may flow along that path.

$$SC = \{Public, CC, E, M\}$$

$$Public \leq CC$$

$$(Public, E) \oplus CC = (CC, E)$$

and

$$(Public, E) \otimes (CC, E, M) = (Public, E)$$

An information flow system. A information flow system is defined as a set of objects, a flow policy (lattice), states, and state transitions. Note that objects here represent all potential holders of information,

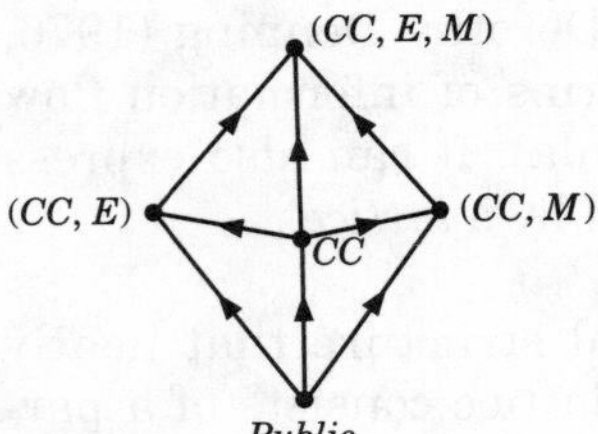

Figure 4.9 Lattice for a company's security policy.

including users. The information state of the system is described by the value and security class of each object. The security class of an object x, written as $\underline{x}$, may be either fixed or variable. A flow from object x to object y (written as $x \to y$) is permitted if and only if $\underline{x} \le \underline{y}$, where $\underline{y}$ is the class of y after the flow. If the class $\underline{y}$ is variable, it can change to make the flow permissible. For the multilevel policy without the tranquility principle, the new class $\underline{y}$ would be determined according to 2 above.

State transitions are modeled by operations to create or delete objects, change their values, or change their security class. Only operations that change values can be associated with information flow.

Measuring information flow. An operation causes information to flow from x to y if it reduces the conditional entropy of x given y. That is, new information about x can be obtained from y. The amount of information that flows is measured by the reduction in the conditional entropy $H(x \mid y)$. A potential flow is a channel whose capacity is the maximum information that can be transferred by that flow.

Example. Variable x represents which of four possible locations has been chosen for a military attack. If the locations are equally likely, and the value of x is not known, the flow $x \to y$ can transfer two bits to y.

Examining a program statically (for example, when it is compiled) reveals its potential information flows, even though the path at execution time is not known. An assignment statement, such as $x := y$, indicates an explicit flow. Conditional statements may indicate implicit flow.

Example. A program contains the statement

```
if x=1 then y :=1
```

where x is 0 or 1 with probability .5 each, and y is initially 0. The entropy of x is one. Before the statement is executed, nothing can be learned about x by examining y. That is, $H(x \mid y) = H(x) = 1$. After the statement is executed, $H(x \mid y) = 0$, since the value of x can be learned with certainty by examining y. One bit of information has been transferred.

In practice, information flow analysis has been applied to formal specifications of programs much more than to programs themselves. Most often it is used to find covert channels.

High water marks and confinement. In the lattice model, the security class of an object can change. When information flows from a higher class into the object, its class rises. The current class of an object is thus a kind of *high water mark* showing the highest class of information that it has "sunk." Simon Foley extends the Denning model by associating a pair of security classes with each entity (subject or object). Each entity x is confined by two classes—a low class $\underline{x}_L$ and a high class $\underline{x}_H$—where

Information in x can flow to class a only if $\underline{x}_L \leq a$

Information at class a can flow into x only if $a \leq \underline{x}_H$

For information to flow from x to y it must hold that $\underline{x}_L \leq \underline{y}_H$.

This confinement flow model can represent flow policies with nontransitive orderings. For example, objects x, y, and z might be confined as follows:

$$confine(x) = [\text{unclassified,unclassified}]$$

$$confine(y) = [\text{unclassified,top-secret}]$$

$$confine(z) = [\text{secret,top-secret}]$$

Information may flow from z to y and from y to x, but not from z to x.

Noninterference

A precise definition of information flow restriction is found in the concept of *noninterference.* One group of users is noninterfering with another group if the actions of the first group using certain commands have no effect on what the second group can see. Noninterference was introduced by Joseph Goguen and José Meseguer (1982, 1984).

The system model. A system is modeled as the following sets:

U users

C state-changing commands

R read commands

O outputs

S internal states, with initial state s_0

along with a transition function *do* and an output function *out.*

do: $S \times U \times C \rightarrow S$, where $do(s,u,c)$ gives the next state after user u executes command c in state s

out: $S \times U \times R \rightarrow O$ where $out(s,u,r)$ gives the result of user u executing a read command r in state s

It is assumed that output commands do not affect the state and that state-changing commands produce no output.

A key concept of the model is the *history* of a system, which is the sequence w of all (*user,command*) pairs since the initial start-up.

$$w = (u_1,c_1)\ldots(u_n, c_n)$$

The state after executing a sequence of state commands, starting from initial state *s,* is given by function *do**:

$$do^* : S \times (U \times C)^* \rightarrow S$$

The state $[[w]]$ is the state after execution of the sequence w. That is,

$$[[w]] = do^* (s_0,w)$$

Noninterference assertions. Security policies are specified by using noninterference assertions. An assertion is expressed as

$$G, A : \mid G', B$$

meaning that user group G executing set A of state commands does not interfere with user group G' executing set B of output commands. That is, any A commands by G users are completely invisible to G' users. The notation :| can be thought of as a one-way mirror, where : indicates the "open" side and | the closed side.

The assertion holds if any sequence of commands, given by any users, produces the same effect for users in G' as the corresponding sequence purged of all commands in A given by users in G. That is, for each sequence w, each user v in G', and each output command r in B,

$$out([[w]], v, r) = out([[p_{G,A}(w)]], v, r)$$

where $p_{G,A}(w)$ is the sequence obtained by deleting from w all pairs (u,c) with u in G and c in A. The view of anyone in group G' excludes effects from anything done by anyone in G using A commands. This is expressed as a system history purged of any such actions. The commands that are removed are known as *purgeable.*

Example. Assume that $G = \{u_1,u_2\}$ and $A = \{c_1,c_2\}$. If the sequence

$$w = (u_3,c_1)\,(u_1,c_3)\,(u_1,c_2)\,(u_4,c_1)$$

then the sequence

$$p_{G,A}(w) = (u_3,c_1)\,(u_1,c_3)\,(u_4,c_1)$$

Noninterference assertions must often be conditional. For example, to express the policy that user u can communicate with user v only through commands from set A,

$$u :| \; v \text{ unless } Q_A$$

where Q_A is a predicate expressing that condition. Conditional assertions can also express policies based on past history or the current protection state. They are needed to express the multilevel policy.

Unwinding. Noninterference assertions express security policy as abstract requirements. Useful application requires moving from the assertions to conditions that can be placed on a system's transition function. If those conditions hold, the policy holds. Reaching the conditions from the assertions is known as *unwinding.* Goguen and Meseguer (1984) state assumptions for a multilevel secure system and define multilevel security as noninterference $u{:}|\,v$ for all pairs of users (u,v) except those with $level(u) \leq level(v)$. The definition is not very useful in this form, however, since it must hold for all sequences of (*user,command*) pairs. What is needed is a condition to be applied to state transitions—something like the Bell-LaPadula Basic Security Theorem. Goguen and Meseguer prove such an *unwinding theorem* for multilevel security.

Issues in information flow security

Noninterference is a clear and appealing approach to policies that restrict information flow. Researchers have found problems with it, however, and have suggested new models to correct these problems. One problem is that Goguen and Meseguer modeled systems as deterministic state machines, although systems often are designed with nondeterminism. Scheduling and encryption algorithms, for example, may use randomness. Second, some practical problems cannot be handled, such as the policy that information can flow to a lower level by passing through a trusted downgrader. A third problem is that noninterference does not allow for the generation of high-level data from low-level inputs. This would happen whenever the computer processing itself, not the inputs, determined the security level of the output. For example, a system might take public stock market data as inputs, apply massive computing using public algorithms, and produce private trading decisions. A final and fundamental problem is that noninterference is too strong a requirement. Real systems must settle for some interference, accept some risk. Models must be able to express a quantified amount of interference.

Some progress has been made on these problems. Several theories address nondeterministic systems. Using a model based on logical deduction, Sutherland (1986) defined a property called nondeducibility. Entities at low level should not be able to deduce anything about the activities of high-level entities. Daryl McCullough (1988) defined restrictiveness, which is a composable property. These models still did not handle probabilistic interference, where a higher level event can affect the probability of a lower level event. James Gray introduced P-restrictiveness, which does take into account probabilistic channels. There is also a version of noninterference that accommodates known potential interference.

We have seen that different models use different information-flow confidentiality properties. The models also differ in their models of computation, and that makes them hard to compare. Jeremy Jacob (1991) unifies these different interpretations in a single framework that assumes no specific model of computation. A shared system is treated as a relation. A *window* is a place on the boundary of the system that information can flow from and to. Interactions with the system are made through windows. A system with n windows is modeled as an n-place relation, where the ith place represents interactions through the ith window. Using this framework, Jacob represents, among other properties, noninterference and nondeducibility.

It is important to recognize that researchers do not fully understand confidentiality, let alone integrity and availability.

Composition

Theories of *composition* tell us what security properties result when components or systems are combined in various ways. Since networks and large systems are built by composition, such theories could have great practical value. The main topic studied has been whether a security property is preserved under composition of two systems with that same property.

John McLean (1994) presents a general theory of composition for several security properties called "possibilistic." The most general form of composition of two systems is *hookup,* where each component can communicate with the other component and also with the outside world. With *cascading,* the output of one system is passed as input to the other. With *feedback* composition, one system serves as front end to a second, which provides feedback to the first. These are *external* composition constructs. *Internal* composition constructs include set union, intersection, and difference. The union of two component systems, for example, accepts any input acceptable to either system and behaves as the relevant system would behave. (The relevant system is the one for which the input is acceptable). If the input is acceptable to both, the composite's output could be the output of either one.

Under cascading, the security properties are preserved when composed with themselves or with stronger properties. Their survival under feedback or internal composition depends on the functions of the systems.

Integrity Models

Integrity means that information is not modified in unauthorized ways, that it is internally consistent and consistent with the real-world objects that it represents, and that the system performs correctly.

Definitions and goals

The definition just given is a good working definition, but it may not include enough. Perhaps a single definition cannot encompass all the properties that have been called *integrity.* It seems that, in order to maintain the constraint

$$\text{Security} = \text{confidentiality} + \text{integrity} + \text{availability}$$

integrity is being defined as all of security except confidentiality and availability. In general, integrity has to do with meeting expectations. *Systems integrity* has to do with a system behaving according to expectations even in the face of attack. *Data integrity* includes two kinds of *consistency.* Data must be internally consistent. For example, the total budget amount must equal the sum of the department budgets. Data must also be consistent with the real-world entities that they represent. For example, the inventory records for the linen department must be consistent with the count of real sheets and towels. A broader concept of data integrity is data *quality*; quality includes such attributes as timeliness, completeness, and pedigree. Robert Courtney and Willis Ware (1994) urge using integrity "to mean that an object has integrity if its quality meets expectations which were determined before the fact."

The following are goals for data integrity:

- Prevent unauthorized modifications
- Maintain *internal* and *external consistency*
- Maintain other data quality attributes
- Prevent authorized but improper modifications

This last goal has to do with those aspects of "proper" that cannot be expressed as consistency requirements. Fraud threatens integrity even if it leaves the data consistent.

For systems integrity the goals are similar, but they apply to the integrity of the computing system itself, rather than its data. Systems integrity is discussed in Chaps. 6 and 7.

All of the security principles discussed in this chapter apply to integrity. The models of discretionary access control also apply to integrity, specifically to the goal of preventing unauthorized modifications. Noninterference can also be interpreted as an integrity model. The Bell-LaPadula model of mandatory access control does not deal with integrity; a companion model was developed to do that.

Biba model

The integrity model of K. J. Biba (1977) assumes a lattice of integrity levels (analogous to security levels) with ordering relation *leq* (less than or equal). Objects are assigned integrity classes according to how damaging it would be if they were improperly modified. Users are assigned integrity classes based on their trustworthiness. Integrity compartments are interpreted like confidentiality compartments. The integrity level of a subject is based on the integrity level of the user it represents and on its needs according to the least privilege principle.

Biba presents several models, all based on the same entities, but representing different integrity policies. The model described here represents the *strict integrity* policy, which is intended as a dual of the Bell-LaPadula confidentiality policy. The entities of the model are

S, O, I	the sets of subjects, objects, and integrity levels
il	a function defining the integrity level of each subject and object
leq	partial ordering relation on integrity levels, *less than or equal*
min	a function returning the greatest lower bound of the subset of *I* specified
o, m	relations defining the ability of a subject *s* to observe (***o***) or modify (***m***) an object *o*

$\boldsymbol{i}$ a relation defining the ability of subject s_1 to invoke another subject s_2.

The strict integrity policy is characterized by three axioms:

1. $s\ \boldsymbol{o}\ o$ implies $il(s)\ leq\ il(o)$
2. $s\ \boldsymbol{m}\ o$ implies $il(o)\ leq\ il(s)$
3. $s_1\ \boldsymbol{i}\ s_2$ implies $il(s_2)\ leq\ il(s_1)$

According to the first two axioms, a subject may not observe an object of lower integrity and may not modify an object of higher integrity. Axiom 3 states that a subject may not invoke another subject of higher integrity. (The intent here is to prevent the invoking subject from indirectly modifying objects of higher integrity.)

An *information transfer path* is defined as a sequence of objects $o_1,\ldots,o_n$ and a corresponding sequence of subjects $s_1,\ldots,s_{n+1}$ such that, for any $i \in 1,\ldots,n$,

$$s_i\ \boldsymbol{o}\ o_i \text{ and } s_i\ \boldsymbol{m}\ o_{i+1}$$

That is, somewhere in the sequence, some subject reads one object and subsequently modifies another. (Like BLP and unlike information flow models, this model defines information transfer indirectly, in terms of access to objects.) Biba proves that, under the strict integrity axioms, if there is a transfer path from object o_1 to object o_{n+1}, then,

$$il(o_{n+1})\ leq\ il(o_1)$$

That is, information is not transferred to a higher integrity level.

The Biba model has not been used much, perhaps because it does not correspond to an established real-world policy.

Conflict with confidentiality

Integrity sometimes conflicts with confidentiality. For example, protecting against viruses means preserving the integrity of executable modules. This is awkward at best in a system that enforces the Bell-LaPadula model. Using the *- property (no write down) for protection would require classifying a highly sensitive module at the lowest level. If it were classified at the highest level, any subject could write to it. Further, a module classified at the lowest level could be copied and run by a high-level user, who would then risk infection. In these examples the confidentiality policy works against providing integrity. Integrity measures can also work against confidentiality. For example, synchronization methods used to preserve integrity (such as locking) introduce information flow channels. Confidentiality is also threatened when activity is monitored or data examined to detect or diagnose system problems.

Clark-Wilson model

The integrity model of David Clark and David Wilson (1987, 1989) started a revolution in computer security research. It is not a highly formal model, but rather a framework for describing integrity requirements.

Clark and Wilson point out that, for most computing concerned with business operations and the control of assets, integrity is far more important than confidentiality. Yet most of the effort to provide secure systems, prompted by military needs, addresses only confidentiality. They argue that integrity policies demand different models from confidentiality models, and different mechanisms as well. They focus on two controls that are central in the commercial world: the well-formed transaction and separation of duty (both defined earlier in this chapter.)

Entities of the model. The data items whose integrity is to be preserved are called *constrained data items* (CDIs). The CDIs are manipulated by *transformation procedures* (TPs). The TP of the model represents the well-formed transaction; the purpose of a TP is to transform the set of CDIs from one valid state to another. An *integrity verification procedure* (IVP) has the purpose of confirming that (when it is executed) all of the CDIs are in a valid state; that is, they meet the integrity requirements. The IVP checks for both internal consistency and for consistency with external reality, according to some view of that reality. The particular view of reality is called an *integrity domain.* The role played by the IVP is analogous to the audit function in accounting.

The system must ensure that only TPs can manipulate the CDIs. The TPs and IVPs must be certified with respect to a specific integrity policy. A TP must meet its specifications, and its specifications must be correct. *Unconstrained data items* (UDIs), such as input data, also are relevant because they could be transformed into CDIs.

Rules of the model. The rules of the model define an integrity-enforcing system. *Enforcement rules* (E), which are application-independent, are amenable to being implemented by the system. *Certification rules* (C) involve primarily human analysis and decision making, although some automation is possible. The following rules relate to internal and external consistency:

C1 All IVPs must properly ensure that all CDIs are in a valid state at the time the IVP is run.

C2 All TPs must be certified to be valid. That is, they transform a CDI to a valid final state, if the CDI is in a valid state to start. Each TP must be certified for a specific set of CDIs, as expressed in the relation

$$(TP_i, CDI-list)$$

E1 The system must maintain a list of the relations of rule C2 and must ensure that any manipulation of a CDI is by a TP and is "authorized" by some relation.

Additional rules are needed for separation of duty:

E2 The system must maintain a list of relations of the form

$$(UserId, TP_i, CDI-list)$$

which relate a user, a TP, and the CDIs that the TP may manipulate on behalf of that user.

C3 The list of relations of E2 must be certified to meet the separation of duty requirement.

The relation of E2, known as the *access triple,* is at the heart of this model. It sums up how the model differs from traditional access control, where subjects gain access to objects directly, rather than through certified programs.

Four other rules complete the model. They specify that:

E3 Users who invoke TPs must be authenticated.

C4 All TPs must be certified to do logging.

C5 TPs that transform UDIs to CDIs must be certified.

E4 Only certain designated users may specify the relations.

These rules enforce a mandatory integrity policy, at least as seen by users. A great deal of human discretion is involved, however, as for example in the certification of TPs.

Implications for computer security. This framework for integrity leads to a set of requirements for computer security services (Clark and Wilson 1989):

Change logs and integrity labels. Authorship must be securely recorded with the data itself (to support the policy of attribution of change). The integrity label records that the data was certified by an IVP, and what integrity domain was used.

Support of the access triple. To enforce the policy of constrained change, the access control triple binds together user, program, and data. Support for it is crucial for this model.

Enhanced user authentication. Although authentication is needed for confidentiality, it takes on special importance for integrity, particularly in relation to the policy of separation of duty. Passwords are inadequate. They can be given away or observed, allowing someone to act as two different persons, thus violating separation of duty rules.

Control of privileged users. Separation of duty must be enforced for the people who maintain the access triples, or who certify TPs. For example, people who can add new users to a system should not be able to change the access triples for those users.

Application program control. A system needs automated tools for managing application software and ensuring its integrity.

Dynamic separation of duty related to TPs. Separation of duty often requires that different steps in a sequence be carried out by different people. Although a static assignment can meet this requirement, a more flexible approach is for the system to keep track of who has executed each step and to enforce separation of duty at each step. This is closer to what happens in the real world. Dynamic separation of duty could be enforced by applications, but mandatory enforcement by the operating system would be better.

Modeling external consistency

One study of integrity elaborated the Clark-Wilson integrity objective into four requirements: external consistency, separation of duty, internal consistency, and error recovery. External consistency is perhaps the most elusive of these, because of its complex relations with the world outside the computing system. The external consistency objective is stated as: "certain users have specified responsibilities for maintaining accurate correspondence between external situations and corresponding information stored in, and available from, the computer. These assigned responsibilities define user roles" (Abrams et al. 1993: 681). An organization must authorize some persons to define roles and others to assign roles to users. The system must ensure that users' authorizations are consistent with their assigned roles. An explicit policy on I/O devices is needed, so that inputs are not forged and outputs not misused.

Taking off from this work, James Williams and Leonard LaPadula (1993) propose two models of external consistency, a simpler one dealing only with correct user inputs, and a more realistic one that allows for user errors.

A system's external interface is modeled as propositions called *sentences*. The "author" of a sentence can be either the system (output) or a user (input). The three kinds of sentences are

- *Assertion:* the author claims that a proposition is true.
- *Question:* the author wants to know whether or not a proposition is true.
- *Request:* the author wants a proposition to become true.

Each user input is associated with a *direct observation* that documents it; the direct observation (but not the input sentence) is assumed to be correct.

The *external-consistency objective* is that each output assertion or request is correct. That is, assertions are true and requests are legitimate according to criteria of the organization or application. However, for efficiency, not all outputs are required to meet this objective; those that do are marked *warranted.* For example, output to a check-writing device would be warranted. A warranted output has an associated *I/O basis* consisting of previous inputs and outputs used in the computation of that output.

The *output-warranty requirement* is for the system's vendor to be able to guarantee that every output marked as warranted is *warrantable,* in that

1. Its I/O basis is warrantable.
2. It is correct provided each sentence in its I/O basis is correct.

An I/O basis is recursively defined to be *warrantable* if and only if all of its outputs are warrantable.

That is, the vendor guarantees that, if the user inputs on which the output is based are correct, then the output is correct. This means the system must be able to perform deductions to show that the output is a consequence of the inputs. The other requirement on systems is that each direct observation is a correct assertion. The responsibility of users (in the first model) is that all their assertions and requests must be correct. These include the software that they install.

Finally, a proof is given of the following result: "If the above system requirements and user responsibility are met, then the external-consistency objectives are satisfied for warranted outputs; in fact, every warrantable sentence is correct."

Williams and LaPadula caution that real systems could only approximate their model, which assumes certified correct software.

Denial of Service

Little has been done to model the third security property—availability—and its inverse, denial of service. One reason is that the requirements are not clearly defined. Jonathan Millen (1992) views a denial of service policy as a guarantee that the system will behave as specified in the face of certain kinds of attack. The policy is enforced by a *Denial-of-Service Protection Base* (DPB), analogous to the reference monitor. The DPB is tamperproof, it cannot be prevented from operating, and it guarantees the availability of the resources under its control. Those resources are a limited subset whose unavailability would be a serious problem.

The model focuses on allocation of shared resources, such as processor time, memory, and files. Since a long delay in service amounts to denial, *waiting time* is used to measure denial. The DPB is characterized by:

- A resource allocation system, which allocates resources to processes. It is modeled as a state machine, with states described by resource allocations, processes' requirements for time and space resources, and the progress of processes.
- A resource monitor algorithm, governing state transitions.
- A waiting time policy, such as fixed maximum waiting time, or finite waiting time.
- *User agreements*—constraints respected by *benign* (as opposed to malicious) processes. For example, benign processes acquire multiple resources in a specified order, to prevent deadlock.

The DPB has to satisfy the conditions that

> (1) Each benign process will make progress in accordance with the waiting time policy.
> (2) No non-CPU resource is revoked from a benign process until its time requirement is zero. (Millen 1992: 146)

These conditions are shown to be satisfied for a simple example DPB with a maximum-waiting-time policy. This model makes a good start, but only a start, toward a realistic model for denial of service.

Security Policy in Practice

This section first describes the role of security policy and models in building trusted systems. Then it introduces the topic of how organizations can set and implement policy. (Chapter 12 returns to this topic.)

Policies, models, and the criteria

The TCSEC specify a methodology for assuring that systems support their security policy (usually BLP). The methodology relies heavily on formal models. For the highest assurance level, there must be a formal model of the policy. The criteria require a formal top-level specification of the *Trusted Computing Base* (TCB), the portion of the system that is trusted to enforce the policy. This specification must be shown to be consistent with the model—by formal methods if possible.

The TCSEC specify one policy. A system certified to meet these criteria may not be able to support other security policies. The European Information Technology Security Evaluation Criteria (ITSEC) also demand that a specific policy be chosen, although they do not restrict what that policy is. It has been argued that the criteria take the wrong approach. For one thing, the approach is inflexible; any change in policy means a complete recertification. Second, cooperation is needed between systems belonging to different organizations, even different nations, and supporting different policies. Third, even one organization needs different policies for its different applications. It would be better (if it could be done) to build systems that can support multiple policies and still be certifiable.

Establishing and carrying out security policy

The computer security policy of an organization must advance the organization's goals and must faithfully represent its real-world security policy. The policy must be practical and usable. It must be cost-effective—addressing the most important threats and accepting some risk where that is appropriate. It should set concrete standards for enforcing security and spell out the response to misuse. The policy must be understandable for users. It must be enforceable technically and must have management behind it. It should aim for the right balance between security and convenient use—a balance that will certainly differ among organizations.

Top management is responsible for setting overall policy, and further responsibility corresponds to the organization's way of distributing authority. Those with authority over people make policy about what rights those people may have. Those responsible for resources make policy about how those resources are used and how they are protected. This pattern applies both to the resources that are available through computers and to the computing resources themselves.

Different roles entail different responsibilities. One generic set of roles in relation to resources is: *owner, user,* and *supplier of services.* The owner of resources is responsible for determining their value, assigning them the right classification, authorizing access to them, and ensuring that they are properly protected. The owner must also make sure that the policy and controls are clearly understood. People must know what is expected of them.

Users are responsible for understanding and respecting the security policy. They must comply with the controls, using resources only for the approved purposes of the organization, and only in the authorized ways. Users have these responsibilities independent of any security mechanisms that may or may not be available. They must use the mechanisms that are provided and must carry out specific obligations, such as selecting a good password and changing it when the policy specifies. The supplier of computing services is responsible for carrying out the controls specified by owners, as well as for controls that apply to computing resources in general. Everyone, regardless of role, is responsible for alerting management to any security exposures or misuse. Management is responsible for making sure that everyone understands his or her role and its responsibilities.

These generic roles are not the only ones that policy must consider. Some systems have built-in roles, such as the *system administrator* of UNIX. The policy must consider the responsibilities of this role, who may take it on, and who they are accountable to. Is the role centralized, so that, for example, all new accounts are opened at a central place, or is the administration distributed to geographic sites and organizational units? A system administrator is responsible for applying security mechanisms, advising management about security weaknesses and possible improvements, auditing security, and responding appropriately to misuse.

Summary

Long before computers there was a need to protect secrets and control fraud and error. Real-world security policies reflect organizations' goals and situations, as well as principles that apply broadly: individual accountability, authorization, least privilege, separation of duty, auditing, redundancy, and risk reduction.

For confidentiality, documents are often classified and people are given clearances. Access is allowed only if the clearance is at least as high as the classification. Organizations also describe categories; the categories of the person have to include all the categories of the document. For integrity, people can take only those actions they are authorized for. Dividing a task into parts that are performed by different people helps prevent fraud, as does rotating duties. Usually, data should be changed only in prescribed and structured ways. Data must be internally consistent and also consistent with external reality.

Some policy elements—such as role—are common to many application-specific policies.

The scope of security policy broadens for computer security. The real-world security policy must be automated, and policy choices must be made about the computing situation itself.

Models of computer security provide a framework that aids understanding, and an unambiguous representation of policy. A security model should: validly and precisely represent security policy; aid understanding through focused and exact expression and proofs of properties; support safety analysis; support system building and system verification; allow systems to be modeled in parts that are then put together.

Access control is the process of ensuring that all access to resources is authorized access. The access matrix model is simple and intuitive, and it can express many protection policies. The access matrix has a row for each subject and a column for each object. In the access matrix *AM,* cell *AM*[*s,o*] specifies the rights that subject *s* has to object *o.* A row of the access matrix corresponds to a capability list—the list of all the rights of a subject. A column corresponds to an access control list—the list of all the rights held by subjects to some object. The access matrix supports discretionary access control (DAC), and other models support mandatory access control (MAC). A security model should support decisions about safety—whether there is some state of the modeled system in which some security property is not preserved. Harrison, Ruzzo, and Ullman showed that it is undecidable whether a given access matrix configuration is safe for a given right.

DAC is vulnerable to Trojan horse attacks. The Bell-LaPadula (BLP) model formalizes a MAC security policy. It has played a key role in relation to the TCSEC. BLP is a state machine model. A secure state is defined by three properties that are intended to express the multilevel policy: the simple security (ss-) property, the *-property, and the discretionary security property. The ss-property expresses clearance-classification policy. The *-property represents the policy of no unauthorized flow of information from a higher level to a lower one. The model includes trusted subjects, who may violate the *-property but are trusted not to violate its intent. The basic security theorem says that preserving security from one state to the next guarantees system security.

BLP has limitations. An access control model cannot express the multilevel policy as precisely as information flow models. The *-property is too restrictive. BLP does not model covert channels or constrain the behavior of trusted processes. The BLP notion of a secure system has been criticized. The multilevel policy does not meet all policy needs.

An important aspect of DAC is *authorization*—specifying the security policy to the system. Models of authorization should take into account: groups of subjects and objects, application roles, authorization roles, denial of access, transformation of rights, access modes and their structure, context-dependent and content-dependent control, and hierarchies of objects.

A goal of most security policy is to protect information. Information flow models approach this goal more directly than access control models. Information theory defines information in terms of uncertainty. Giving information is the same as removing uncertainty. The conditional entropy of x given y is a measure of the uncertainty of x given side knowledge about y. The lattice model of information flow can express the multilevel policy and others. An operation causes information to flow from x to y if it reduces the conditional entropy of x given y.

Noninterference provides a precise definition of information flow restriction. One group of users is noninterfering with another group if the actions of the first group using certain commands have no effect on what the second group can see. Security policies are specified by using noninterference assertions, but useful application requires placing conditions on a system's transition function. Reaching the conditions from the assertions is known as *unwinding*. Noninterference and related concepts are an active research area, but researchers do not fully understand confidentiality, let alone integrity and availability. Theories of composition tell us what security properties result when components or systems are combined.

Integrity means that information is not modified in unauthorized ways, that it is internally consistent and consistent with the real-world objects that it represents, and that the system performs correctly. More generally, integrity has to do with meeting expectations. Goals for data integrity include: prevent unauthorized modifications, maintain internal and external consistency and other data quality attributes, prevent authorized but improper modifications. Integrity sometimes conflicts with confidentiality.

The Clark-Wilson integrity model takes off from two important business controls: the well-formed transaction and separation of duty. Data items whose integrity is to be preserved [constrained data items (CDIs)] are manipulated by transformation procedures (TPs). An integrity verification procedure (IVP) has the purpose of confirming that the CDIs meet the integrity requirements. The system must ensure that only TPs can manipulate the CDIs. The TPs and IVPs must be certified with respect to a specific integrity policy. The model includes enforcement rules, which are application-independent and amenable to automation, and certification rules, which involve primarily human analysis and decision. The access triple controls access to CDIs on the basis of both user ID and TP. This framework leads to requirements for computer security services

Security policy and models are an essential part of building trusted systems. The TCSEC require a formal top-level TCB specification that must be shown to be consistent with the model. An organization's security policy should set concrete standards for enforcing security and spell out the response to misuse. It should aim for the right balance between security and convenient use.

Bibliographic Notes

The definition of security policy is still evolving. The current criteria are inconsistent with one another and even with themselves. Good discussions of the issues are provided by Sterne (1991) and Chizmadia (1992). The ITSEC criteria (European Community—Commission 1991) use the terms *corporate security policy, system security policy* (for a specific installation), and *technical security policy* (for the hardware and software of a system or product). The principles underlying computer security policy are discussed in Chap. 1. Landwehr (1981) describes the multilevel policy. Fernandez, Summers, and Wood (1981) describe maximized sharing. Our discussion of integrity policies draws on Roskos et al. (1990), Clark and Wilson (1987, 1989), Sterne et al. (1991), and NCSC (1991 a and b). The Chinese Wall policy is described by Brewer and Nash (1989). Graubart (1989) discusses the ORCON policy.

Sterne (1991) uses the term *automated security policy.* Delaney et al. (1991) describe generally accepted accounting principles.

Williams and Abrams (1995) give an overview of the use of formal models in developing trusted systems, and Gasser (1988) treats the subject in depth. The process of going from model to implemented system is discussed in Chap. 6.

Sandhu and Samarati (1994) provide an overview of access control. Early versions of the access matrix model were developed by Lampson (1971), Graham and Denning (1972), and Conway, Maxwell, and Morgan (1972). A Typed Access Matrix Model was developed by Sandhu (1992a) and an extension is proposed by Dacier and Deswarte (1994). James Anderson (1972) introduced the term *reference monitor.*

Millen and Cerniglia (1984) discuss concrete models as interpretations of the abstract BLP model. ORCON and dissemination control policy are discussed by McCollum, Messing, and Notargiacomo (1990). Supporting the Chinese Wall policy with BLP is described by Sandhu (1992b, 1993). McLean (1987, 1990b) presents a critique of BLP. Lindgreen and Herschberg (1994) warn of the false (but widely held) impression that providing a secure computer system is equivalent to providing BLP-like access control. Entelechy policies are discussed by Fellows (1992). Covert channels are discussed in Chap. 6.

Roles are considered by Sterne et al. (1991), Baldwin (1990), Ferraiolo and Kuhn (1992), Sandhu et al. (1996) and in Chaps. 8 and 9. Transformation and transformation models are described by Sandhu (1989, 1992a) and Sandhu and Ganta (1994a, 1994b). Sandhu (1988) describes an earlier Schematic Protection Model. Capabilities are described further in Chap. 7. The Take-Grant model is described by Snyder (1981). Lunt (1989) discusses denial of access. Moffett and Sloman (1988) discuss the right to grant as separate from the right to access. Hierarchies of objects and implied authorization more generally are discussed in Chap. 9. This book simplifies the model of Woo and Lam (1992) by omitting their consideration of multiple sets of independently specified rules.

Information theory is described by Shannon and Weaver (1949). A clear mathematical treatment can be found in Welsh (1988). Another good source is Blahut (1987). Entropy is defined more precisely as a number associated with a probability distribution. The entropy of a random variable X is the entropy of the probability distribution of X. The example about Hawaii women is based on Welsh (1988: 12). Denning (1982) applies information theory to information flow and cryptography and gives many examples and exercises. The lattice model is described by Denning (1976, 1982). Compile-time analysis of programs to reveal information flows is treated by Denning and Denning (1977). Information flow analysis for detecting covert channels is discussed in Chap. 6. The term *high water mark* was used for the ADEPT system (Weissman 1969), where the security level of a process reflects the highest level of data that it has read.

Our discussion of issues in noninterference models draws from Gray (1990) and McLean (1990a). The term *traces* is often used rather than *history.* It comes from *Communicating Sequential Processes* (CSP), a mathematical framework for proving properties of processes (Hoare 1985). A trace represents a sequence of events in the life of a process. *Event-based* traces, while useful for abstract models like noninterference, are not appropriate for specifying and verifying systems. Approaches based on allowable sequences of procedure calls are proposed for that purpose (Meadows 1992). Murphy, Crocker, and Redmond (1992) deal with known potential interference. Shi, McDermid, and Moffett (1993) apply noninterference to composition. Other work on composition is reported by Dinolt, Benzinger, and Yatabe (1994) and Millen (1994). Chapter 9, “Database Security,” discusses the problem of inference.

According to U.S. government classification policy (Clinton 1995) integrity means “the state that exists when information is unchanged from its source and has not been accidentally or intentionally modified, altered, or destroyed." Principles of integrity are discussed in Sandhu and Jajodia (1990) and NCSC (1991a,b). This chapter draws heavily from NCSC (1991a), but sums things up differently. The dual custody policy is described by McLean (1990b). Appearance of the Clark and Wilson model led to two integrity workshops (Katzke and Ruthberg 1989, Ruthberg and Polk 1989). Data quality is defined in Ruthberg and Polk. Dynamic separation of duty is discussed by Nash and Poland (1990). Abrams et al. (1993) elaborate on the Clark-Wilson objectives. Limoges et al. (1994) describe a model that supports the access triple. Lipner (1982) shows how the Biba model could be applied in a commercial environment. A system that enforces the Biba model is described in Chap. 9. Motro (1989) considers integrity definitions and theory. Applying the BLP model to protecting against viruses is discussed by Cohen (1987, 1990).

Millen's work on denial of service (1992) builds on work of Yu and Gligor (1990).

The process of developing systems to meet the TCSEC criteria is described in Chap. 6. Multipolicy approaches are described by Abrams et al. (1990), LaPadula (1995), Hosmer (1992), and Bell (1994).

Our discussion of establishing and carrying out security policy draws from Fites, Kratz, and Brebner (1989), the report of the National Research Council (1991), guidelines for Internet site security (Holbrook and Reynolds 1991), and a study of security policy for the National Research and Education Network (Oldehoeft 1992). More about this topic can be found in Chap. 12.

Exercises

4.1 What are the parts to computer security policy? Give three additional examples of each part.

4.2 Discuss the principles of least privilege and separation of duty. How do they support the principle of authorization?

4.3 Why is composability an important quality for models?

4.4 What is the significance of the HRU access matrix model?

4.5 Describe precisely the main result obtained by Harrison, Ruzzo, and Ullman.

4.6 The Typed Access Matrix Model of Sandhu can be used for the ORCON policy. The problem is to prevent a person p_1 granted read access to an ORCON document from copying the information into another document and granting p_2 access to that copy. The solution involves the special access rights confined read and parent, and the security types confined subject and confined object. The originator grants p_1 confined read access to the confined object. How would you define the command use-confined-read? Hint: create a temporary subject of type "confined subject"; define the type confined subject with appropriate limitations.

4.7 Discuss the advantages and limitations of discretionary access control. Which limitation is the most serious?

4.8 Describe the purpose of the *-property. Describe precisely in words its specification in the Bell-LaPadula model. What is the relationship between the purpose and the specification?

4.9 Define and draw a lattice representing a security policy for a company with three separate areas of product development and two levels of information sensitivity.

4.10 Can a virus spread between the levels of a multilevel system? Explain.

4.11 Describe the concept of noninterference.

4.12 Assume a noninterference assertion

$$G, A: G', B$$

Group $G = \{u_1,u_2\}$ and command set $A = \{c_1,c_2\}$. The sequence $w = (u_3,c_1)(u_1,c_3)(u_2,c_1)(u_1,c_2)(u_4,c_1)$. List the purgeable commands of the sequence.

4.13 List three types of constraints that are placed on the Constrained Data Items of the Clark-Wilson model.

4.14 What is the significance of the access triple of the Clark-Wilson model? Give an example of a business situation where this type of control is needed.

4.15 The TCSEC and ITSEC both assume that a system will enforce a specific security policy. Discuss the pros and cons of this approach.

4.16 Write a computer security policy for a large public library. Assume the computing system is used for acquisitions and cataloging, records about library card holders, and circulation. The on-line catalog is available to all patrons. Access is through PCs, many of them in public areas.

References

Abrams, Marshall D., Edward G. Amoroso, Leonard J. LaPadula, Teresa F. Lunt, and James G. Williams. 1993. Report of an integrity research study group. *Computers & Security* **12**(7): 679–689.

Abrams, Marshall D., Leonard J. LaPadula, Kenneth W. Eggers, and Ingrid M. Olson. 1990. A generalized framework for access control: An informal description. *Proceedings of the 13th National Computer Security Conference,* 135–143. NIST/NCSC.

Anderson, James P. 1972. *Computer Security Technology Planning Study.* Report ESD-TR-73-51, Vol. I. AD 758206. Bedford, Mass.: U.S. Air Force Electronic Systems Division.

Baldwin, Robert W. 1990. Naming and grouping privileges to simplify security management in large databases. *Proceedings of the 1990 IEEE Computer Society Symposium on Research in Security and Privacy,* 116–132. Los Alamitos, Calif.: IEEE Computer Society Press.

Bell, D. Elliott. 1994. Modeling the "Multipolicy Machine." *Proceedings of the 1994 ACM SIGSAC New Security Paradigms Workshop,* 2–9. Los Alamitos, Calif.: IEEE Computer Society.

Bell, D. E. and L. J. LaPadula. 1976. *Secure Computer System: Unified Exposition and Multics Interpretation.* Report MTR-2997 Rev. 1. AD A023 588. Bedford, Mass.: The Mitre Corporation.

Biba, K. J. 1977. Integrity Considerations for Secure Computer Systems. Report ESD-TR-76-372, AD A039324. Bedford, Mass.: U.S. Air Force Electronic Systems Division.

Blahut, Richard E. 1987. *Principles and Practice of Information Theory.* Reading, Mass.: Addison-Wesley.

Brewer, David F. C. and Michael J. Nash. 1989. The Chinese Wall security policy. *Proceedings of the 1989 IEEE Computer Society Symposium on Research in Security and Privacy,* 206–214. Los Alamitos, Calif.: IEEE Computer Society Press.

Chizmadia, David M. 1992. Some more thoughts on the buzzword "security policy." *Proceedings of the 15th National Computer Security Conference,* Vol. II, 651–660. NIST/NCSC.

Clark, David D., and David R. Wilson. 1987. A comparison of commercial and military computer security policies. *Proceedings of the 1987 IEEE Computer Society Symposium on Research in Security and Privacy,* 184–194. Los Alamitos, Calif.: IEEE Computer Society Press.

Clark, David D. and David R. Wilson. 1989. Evolution of a model for computer integrity. *Report of the Invitational Workshop on Data Integrity,* A.2-1–A.2-13. NIST Special Publication 500-168.

Clinton, William J. 1995. *Classified National Security Information.* Executive Order, April 17. Washington, D.C.: The White House.

Cohen, Fred. 1987. Computer viruses: Theory and experiments. *Computers & Security* **6**(1): 22-35.

Cohen, Fred. 1990. Implications of computer viruses and current methods of defense. In *Computers under Attack: Intruders, Worms, and Viruses,* Peter J. Denning, ed., 381–406. New York: ACM Press.

Conway, R. W., W. L. Maxwell, and H. L. Morgan. 1972. On the implementation of security measures in information systems. *Communications of the ACM* **15**(4): 211–220.

Courtney, Robert H., and Willis H. Ware. 1994. What do we mean by integrity? *Computers & Security* **13**(3): 206–208.

Dacier, Marc, and Yves Deswarte. 1994. Privilege graph: An extension to the Typed Access Matrix model. *Computer Security—ESORICS 94. Proceedings of the Third European Symposium on Research in Computer Security,* 319–334. Berlin: Springer-Verlag.

Delaney, Patrick R., James R. Adler, Barry J. Epstein, and Michael F. Foran. 1991. *GAAP: Interpretation and Application of Generally Accepted Accounting Principles.* New York: John Wiley & Sons.

Denning, Dorothy E. 1976. A lattice model of secure information flow. *Communications of the ACM* **19**(5): 236–243.

———. 1982. *Cryptography and Data Security.* Reading, Mass.: Addison-Wesley.

Denning, D. E., and P. J. Denning. 1977. Certification of programs for secure information flow. *Communications of the ACM* **20**(7): 504–513.

Dinolt, G. W., L. A. Benzinger, and M. G. Yatabe. 1994. Combining components and policies. *Proceedings of the Computer Security Foundations Workshop VII,* 22–33. Los Alamitos, Calif.: IEEE Computer Society.

European Communities—Commission. 1991. ITSEC: Information Technology Security Evaluation Criteria: Provisional Harmonised Criteria. Luxembourg: Office for Official Publications of the EC.

Fellows, Jonathan. 1992. Mandatory policy issues of high assurance composite systems. *Proceedings of the 15th National Computer Security Conference,* Vol. I, 350–358. NIST/NCSC.

Fernandez, Eduardo B., Rita C. Summers, and Christopher Wood. 1981. *Database Security and Integrity.* Reading, Mass.: Addison-Wesley.

Ferraiolo, David and Richard Kuhn. 1992. Role-based access controls. *Proceedings of the 15th National Computer Security Conference,* 554–563. NIST/NCSC.

Fites, Philip E., Martin P. J. Kratz, and Alan F. Brebner. 1989. *Control and Security of Computer Information Systems.* Rockville, Md.: Computer Science Press.

Foley, Simon N. 1989. A model for secure information flow. *Proceedings of the 1989 IEEE Computer Society Symposium on Research in Security and Privacy,* 248–258. Los Alamitos, Calif.: IEEE Computer Society Press.

Gasser, Morrie. 1988. *Building a Secure Computer System.* New York: Van Nostrand Reinhold.

Goguen, J. A., and J. Meseguer. 1982. Security policies and security models. *Proceedings of the 1982 Symposium on Security and Privacy,* 11–20. Los Alamitos, Calif.: IEEE Computer Society Press.

Goguen, Joseph A., and José Meseguer. 1984. Unwinding and inference control. *Proceedings of the 1984 Symposium on Security and Privacy,* 75–86. Los Alamitos, Calif.: IEEE Computer Society Press.

Graham, G. Scott, and Peter J. Denning. 1972. Protection—principles and practice. *Proceedings of the 1972 Spring Joint Computer Conference,* 417–429. Montvale, N.J.: AFIPS Press.

Graubart, Richard. 1989. On the need for a third form of access control. *Proceedings of the 12th National Computer Security Conference,* 296–304. NIST/NCSC.

Gray, James W. III. 1990. Probabilistic interference. *Proceedings of the 1990 IEEE Computer Society Symposium on Research in Security and Privacy,* 170–179. Los Alamitos, Calif.: IEEE Computer Society Press.

Harrison, M. A., W. L. Ruzzo, and J. D. Ullman. 1976. Protection in operating systems. *Communications of the ACM* **19**(8): 461–471.

Hoare, C. A. R. 1985. *Communicating Sequential Processes.* Englewood Cliffs, N.J.: Prentice-Hall.

Holbrook, J. Paul, and Joyce K. Reynolds. 1991. *Site Security Handbook.* Internet Site Security Policy Handbook Working Group. RFC 1244.

Hosmer, Hilary H. 1992. The multipolicy paradigm. *Proceedings of the 15th National Computer Security Conference,* vol. II, 409–422. NIST/NCSC.

Jacob, Jeremy. 1991. A uniform presentation of confidentiality properties. *IEEE Transactions on Software Engineering* **17**(11): 1186–1194.

Katzke, Stuart W., and Zella G. Ruthberg, eds. 1989. *Report of the Invitational Workshop on Integrity Policy in Computer Information Systems* (*WIPCIS*). NIST Special Publication 500-160.

Lampson, Butler W. 1971. Protection. *Proceedings of the 5th Annual Princeton Conference on Information Sciences and Systems,* 437–443. Reprinted in *Operating Systems Review* **8**(1): 18–24, January 1974.

Landwehr, Carl E. 1981. Formal models for computer security. *Computing Surveys* **13**(3): 247–278.

Landwehr, Carl E., Constance L. Heitmeyer, and John McLean. 1984. A security model for military message systems. *ACM Transactions on Computer Systems* **2**(3): 198–222.

LaPadula, Leonard J. 1995. Rule-set modeling of a trusted computer system. In *Information Security: An Integrated Collection of Essays,* 187–241. Los Alamitos, Calif.: IEEE Computer Society.

Limoges, Charles G., Ruth R. Nelson, John H. Heimann, and David S. Becker. 1994. Versatile integrity and security environment (VISE) for computer systems.

Proceedings of the 1994 ACM SIGSAC New Security Paradigms Workshop, 109–118. Los Alamitos, Calif.: IEEE Computer Society.

Lindgreen, E. Roos, and I. S. Herschberg. 1994. On the validity of the Bell-LaPadula model. *Computers & Security* **13**(4): 317–333.

Lipner, Steven B. 1982. Non-discretionary controls for commercial applications. *Proceedings of the 1982 Symposium on Security and Privacy,* 2–10. Los Alamitos, Calif.: IEEE Computer Society Press.

Lunt, Teresa F. 1989. Access control policies: Some unanswered questions. *Computers & Security* **8**(1): 43–54.

McCollum, Catherine J., Judith R. Messing, and LouAnna Notargiacomo. 1990. Beyond the pale of MAC and DAC—defining new forms of access control. *Proceedings of the 1990 IEEE Computer Society Symposium on Research in Security and Privacy,* 190–200. Los Alamitos, Calif.: IEEE Computer Society Press.

McCullough, Daryl. 1988. Noninterference and the composability of security properties. *Proceedings of the 1988 IEEE Computer Society Symposium on Research in Security and Privacy,* 177–186. Washington, D.C.: IEEE Computer Society Press.

McLean, John. 1987. Reasoning about security models. *Proceedings of the 1987 IEEE Computer Society Symposium on Research in Security and Privacy,* 123–131. Los Alamitos, Calif.: IEEE Computer Society Press.

______. 1990a. Security models and information flow. *Proceedings of the 1990 IEEE Computer Society Symposium on Research in Security and Privacy,* 180–187. Los Alamitos, Calif.: IEEE Computer Society Press.

______. 1990b. The specification and modeling of computer security. *Computer* **23**(1): 9–16.

———. 1994. A general theory of composition for trace sets closed under selective interleaving functions. *Proceedings of the 1994 IEEE Computer Society Symposium on Research in Security and Privacy,* 79–93. Los Alamitos, Calif.: IEEE Computer Society.

Meadows, Catherine. 1992. Using traces based on procedure calls to reason about composability. *Proceedings of the 1992 IEEE Computer Society Symposium on Research in Security and Privacy,* 177–188. Los Alamitos, Calif.: IEEE Computer Society Press.

Millen, Jonathan K. 1992. A resource allocation model for denial of service. *Proceedings of the 1992 IEEE Computer Society Symposium on Research in Security and Privacy,* 137–147. Los Alamitos, Calif.: IEEE Computer Society Press.

______. 1994. Unwinding forward correctability. *Proceedings of the Computer Security Foundations Workshop VII,* 2–10. Los Alamitos, Calif.: IEEE Computer Society.

Millen, J. K., and C. M. Cerniglia. 1984. *Computer Security Models.* Report MTR9531. AD A166 920. Bedford, Mass.: The MITRE Corporation.

Moffett, Jonathan D., and Sloman, Morris S. 1988. The source of authority for commercial access control. *Computer* **21**(2): 59–69.

Motro, Amihai. 1989. Integrity = validity + completeness. *ACM Transactions on Database Systems* **14**(4): 480–502.

Murphy, Sandra R., Stephen Crocker, and Timothy Redmond. 1992. Unwinding and the LOCK proof referees study. *Proceedings of the Computer Security Foundations Workshop V,* 9–21. Los Alamitos, Calif.: IEEE Computer Society Press.

Nash, Michael J., and Keith R. Poland. 1990. Some conundrums concerning separation of duty. *Proceedings of the 1990 IEEE Computer Society Symposium on Research in Security and Privacy,* 201–207. Los Alamitos, Calif.: IEEE Computer Society Press.

National Research Council. 1991. *Computers at Risk: Safe Computing in the Information Age.* Washington, D.C.: National Academy Press.

NCSC. 1988. *Glossary of Computer Security Terms.* Report NCSC-TG-004. Fort Meade, Md.: NCSC.

______. 1991a. *Integrity in Automated Information Systems.* Prepared by Terry Mayfield et al. C Technical Report 79-91. Fort Meade, Md.: NCSC.

______. 1991b. *Integrity-Oriented Control Objectives: Proposed Revisions to the Trusted Computer System Evaluation Criteria (TCSEC).* Prepared by Terry Mayfield et al. C Technical Report 111-91. Fort Meade, Md.: NCSC.

Nelson, Ruth. 1994. What is a Secret—and—What does that have to do with Computer

Security? *Proceedings of the 1994 ACM SIGSAC New Security Paradigms Workshop,* 74–79. Los Alamitos, Calif.: IEEE Computer Society.

Oldehoeft, Arthur E. 1992. *Foundations of a Security Policy for Use of the National Research and Educational Network.* Report NISTIR 4734. Gaithersburg, Md.: NIST.

Roskos, J. Eric, Stephen R. Welke, John M. Boone, and Terry Mayfield. 1990. A taxonomy of integrity models, implementations and mechanisms. *Proceedings of the 13th National Computer Security Conference,* 541–551. NIST/NCSC.

Ruthberg, Zella G., and William T. Polk, eds. 1989. *Report of the Invitational Workshop on Data Integrity.* NIST Special Publication 500-168. Gaithersburg, Md.: NIST.

Sandhu, Ravinderpal Singh. 1988. The Schematic Protection Model: Its definition and analysis for acyclic attenuating schemes. *Journal of the Association for Computing Machinery* **35**(2): 404–432.

Sandhu, Ravi. 1989. Transformation of access rights. *Proceedings of the 1989 IEEE Computer Society Symposium on Research in Security and Privacy,* 259–268. Los Alamitos, Calif.: IEEE Computer Society Press.

———. 1992a. The typed access matrix model. *Proceedings of the 1992 IEEE Computer Society Symposium on Research in Security and Privacy,* 122–136. Los Alamitos, Calif.: IEEE Computer Society Press.

———. 1992b. A lattice interpretation of the Chinese wall policy. *Proceedings of the 15th National Computer Security Conference,* Vol. I, 329–339. NIST/NCSC.

———. 1993. Lattice-based access control models. *Computer* **26**(11): 9–19.

Sandhu, Ravi S., Edward J. Coyne, Hal L. Feinstein, and Charles E. Youman. 1996. Role-based access control models. *Computer* **29**(2): 38–47.

Sandhu, Ravi S., and Srinivas Ganta. 1994a. On the expressive power of the unary transformation model. *Computer Security—ESORICS 94. Proceedings of the Third European Symposium on Research in Computer Security,* 301–318. Berlin: Springer-Verlag.

———. 1994b. On the minimality of testing for rights in transformation models. *Proceedings of the 1994 IEEE Computer Society Symposium on Research in Security and Privacy,* 230–241. Los Alamitos, Calif.: IEEE Computer Society.

Sandhu, Ravi, and Sushil Jajodia. 1990. Integrity mechanisms in database management systems. *Proceedings of the 13th National Computer Security Conference,* Vol. II, 526–540. Washington, D.C.: NIST/NCSC.

Sandhu, Ravi S., and Pierangela Samarati. 1994. Access control: Principles and practice. *IEEE Communications Magazine* **32**(9): 40–48.

Shannon, Claude E., and Warren Weaver. 1949. *The Mathematical Theory of Communication.* Urbana, Ill.: The University of Illinois Press.

Shi, Qi, J. A. McDermid, and J. D. Moffett. 1993. Applying noninterference to composition of systems: A more practical approach. *Proceedings of the Ninth Annual Computer Security Applications Conference,* 210–220. Los Alamitos, Calif.: IEEE Computer Society.

Snyder, Lawrence. 1981. Formal models of capability-based protection systems. *IEEE Transactions on Computers* **C-30**(3): 172–181.

Sterne, Daniel F. 1991. On the buzzword "security policy." *Proceedings of the 1991 IEEE Computer Society Symposium on Research in Security and Privacy,* 219–230. Los Alamitos, Calif.: IEEE Computer Society Press.

Sterne, Daniel F., Martha A. Branstad, Brian S. Hubbard, Barbara A. Mayer, and Dawn M. Wolcott. 1991. An analysis of application-specific security policies. In *Proceedings of the 14th National Computer Security Conference,* Vol. I, 25–36. NIST/NCSC.

Sutherland, D. 1986. A model of information. *Proceedings of the 9th National Computer Security Conference,* 175–183. NIST/NCSC.

Weissman, C. 1969. Security controls in the ADEPT-50 time-sharing system. *AFIPS Conference Proceedings, 1969 FJCC,* 119–133. Montvale, N.J.: AFIPS Press.

Welsh, Dominic. 1988. *Codes and Cryptography.* Oxford: Clarendon Press.

Williams, James G., and Marshall D. Abrams. 1995. Formal methods and models. In *Information Security: An Integrated Collection of Essays,* 170–186. Los Alamitos, Calif.: IEEE Computer Society.

Williams, James G., and Leonard J. LaPadula. 1993. Automated support for external consistency. *Proceedings of the Computer Security Foundations Workshop VI,* 71–81. Los Alamitos, Calif.: IEEE Computer Society.

Woo, Thomas Y. C., and Simon S. Lam. 1992. Authorization in distributed systems: A formal approach. *Proceedings of the 1992 IEEE Computer Society Symposium on Research in Security and Privacy,* 33–50. Los Alamitos, Calif.: IEEE Computer Society Press.

Yu, Che-Fn, and Virgil D. Gligor. 1990. A specification and verification method for preventing denial of service. *IEEE Transactions on Software Engineering,* **16**(6): 581–592.

Part

2

Methods

Chapter

5

Cryptography

Cryptography is the art of transforming information to ensure its secrecy or authenticity or both. For thousands of years cryptography has been used for military and diplomatic secrecy. The traditional applications now are joined and perhaps overwhelmed by new ones. Electronic commerce creates urgent needs, while advances in cryptography and increases in computing power make it possible to fill those needs. Among many applications, cryptography is used to:

- Authenticate retail and banking transactions
- Authenticate transactions between businesses or between government and businesses
- Protect the integrity of electronic funds transfers
- Protect the secrecy of personal, military, and commercial communications
- Provide secrecy and integrity for Internet transactions
- Protect the integrity of software and of databases
- Authenticate the identity of network users and network entities

Cryptography can be applied in seemingly limitless ways to solve problems ranging from secrecy of voice communications to verification of international treaties. This chapter deals with cryptography as it applies to the security of computer-based information, systems, and actions.

First, we introduce concepts and terminology and the main types of cryptographic systems and applications. The theoretical foundations of cryptography are then reviewed. Cryptographic techniques are described, including classical methods, the Data Encryption Standard, stream ciphers, and public key methods. We consider threats to information integrity and methods to counter them, including digital signatures. We discuss the problem of managing cryptographic keys and describe key management schemes. The final section is about cryptographic protocols and how to make them secure.

Overview

This section provides an overview of concepts and terminology, and introduces the main types of cryptographic systems and applications.

Concepts and definitions

Cryptography is one branch of *cryptology*—a field that deals with secret communications. The word *cryptology* derives from the Greek for *hidden* and *word*. The other branch of cryptology—*cryptanalysis*—is concerned with breaking or defeating cryptography.

Cryptography is traditionally described in relation to messages. The original message is called the *plaintext,* and the message after cryptography has been applied is the *cryptogram* or *ciphertext*. The process that transforms the plaintext into the ciphertext is *enciphering* or *encryption*; the process that transforms the ciphertext into the original plaintext is *deciphering* or *decryption*. If M is the plaintext message, and E and D are the encryption and decryption transformations, it is required that

$$D(E(M)) = M$$

That is, decrypting the encrypted message results in the original plaintext message.

The transformation E is usually an algorithm with parameters called *keys,* K. If C is the ciphertext, we can write

$$C = E(M, K)$$

That is, ciphertext C is the result of applying the algorithm E, using the key K, to message M. The *cryptosystem* is the entire setup—messages, ciphertext, transformations, and keys, as shown in Fig. 5.1. The figure shows that an enemy *cryptanalyst* can eavesdrop on the channel that carries the ciphertext. For some cryptosystems the key is secret, and there must be a separate *secure channel* for delivering the secret key to the decrypter. *Ciphers* are cryptographic transformations that operate on characters or bits, while *codes* work at the level of words or phrases. One type of cipher is *simple substitution,* where each letter of the message is replaced by a fixed substitute. The key is

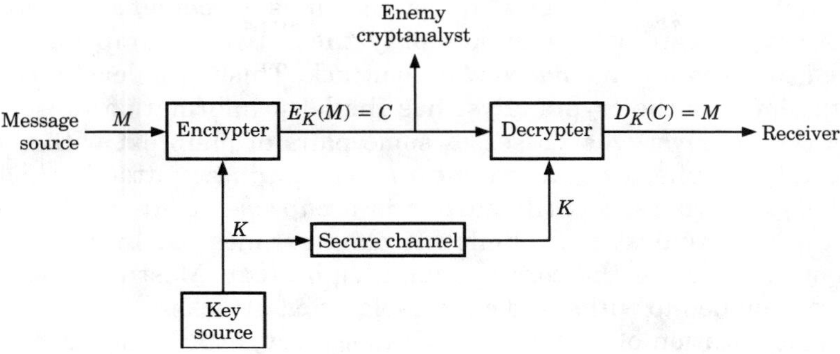

Figure 5.1 A cryptosystem.

a permutation of the alphabet, and each letter of the message is replaced by the letter of the key corresponding to its alphabetic position. If the key is

igfewqydsahxzbjrukoplvcnmt

the message "secure" becomes ciphertext "owflkw."

Cryptosystems provide the security properties *secrecy* and *authenticity,* which includes *integrity*; they can also provide *nonrepudiation.* Secrecy, the historical goal of cryptography, lines up with the confidentiality goal of computer security. Authenticity lines up with the integrity goal of computer security. Authenticity implies that the recipient of a message should be able to determine (1) its origin and (2) that it was not modified in transit. Although cryptographic methods also apply to stored information, the focus is on transmitted messages. Nonrepudiation applies strictly to messages; it is the inability of a sender to deny sending a message.

The first comprehensive theory of cryptography was developed by Shannon, who built on his work in information theory. Later cryptographic methods have depended on work in number theory and computational complexity. We might expect, with all this theoretical and mathematical underpinning, that the security of cryptosystems could be proved mathematically. This turns out to be true for only a few rather impractical cryptosystems. Instead, cryptographers gain confidence in a cryptosystem incrementally, as it survives *attacks* by cryptanalysts playing the role of enemy to the cryptographer. An attack seeks to either break the cryptosystem and recover the plaintext or key, or to forge a message without detection.

Attacks are classified according to how much information the cryptanalyst has. The cryptanalyst is always assumed to have the entire ciphertext. Usually it is assumed that the encryption algorithm is known; only the key is secret. (This is known as *Kerckhoff's assumption.*) A cryptosystem that makes only these two assumptions is designed to withstand a *ciphertext-only* attack. This is the least stringent standard, as the cryptanalyst has the least information to work with. A cryptanalyst who possesses some pairs of plaintext with the corresponding ciphertext can mount a *known-plaintext* attack, which is harder to withstand. Still harder is a *chosen-plaintext* attack, where the cryptanalyst can submit any plaintext message to the cryptosystem and receive the corresponding ciphertext. Most cryptosystems are designed to withstand chosen-plaintext attacks.

This classification of attacks applies to secrecy; attacks on authenticity are classified differently. In an *impersonation attack,* the adversary cryptanalyst creates a fraudulent ciphertext without knowledge of the authentic ciphertext. The attack succeeds if the decrypter accepts the fraudulent ciphertext as valid. In a *substitution attack* the cryptanalyst intercepts the authentic ciphertext and replaces it with a fraudulent one.

Although the classical theory deals mainly with ciphertext-only attacks, the best policy is to assume the cryptanalyst has every advantage. The structure and language of the messages (such as computer programs, or well-defined transactions) may give the cryptanalyst using ciphertext-only the equivalent of a stronger attack. In practice it is usually assumed that the cryptanalyst uses chosen-plaintext and also possesses part of the key.

A note on terminology and notation

The literature on cryptography uses several alternative notations. The symbol X is often used for the plaintext, with Y for the corresponding ciphertext, and Z for the key. Sometimes P is used for plaintext. This book uses M, C, and K, except where it is best to use an author's original notation. The participants in a cryptographic protocol are often called Alice and Bob, with Alice being the sender of a message or the first person described in a protocol. The person trying to break a cryptosystem is called the cryptanalyst or the *enemy, opponent,* or *attacker.*

Types of cryptosystems

There are two main types of cryptosystems: *conventional* and *public key.* Conventional cryptosystems are also called *classical, symmetric, single key,* or *secret key*; public key systems are also called *asymmetric* or *two-key.* In classical cryptography a single secret key, known to both the sender and receiver, is used for both encryption and decryption. Secret keys must be distributed securely. In public key cryptog-

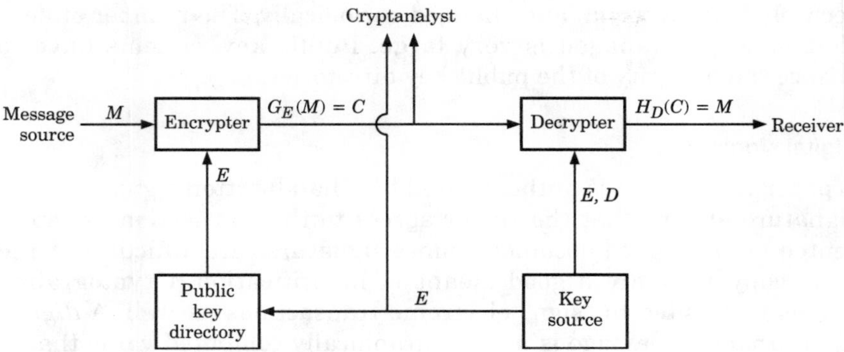

Figure 5.2 Public key cryptosystem.

raphy the receiver's encryption key E is published for all senders to use; the receiver decrypts with a private secret key D. The two kinds of cryptosystems are shown in Figs. 5.1 and 5.2.

Most conventional cryptosystems follow the *Data Encryption Standard* (DES), which was adopted as a U.S. government standard in 1977. The standard has been reviewed every 5 years since its adoption and has been reaffirmed through 1998. Although advances in computing speed and parallelism have made attacks possible, DES still provides good protection for many applications. Very fast DES implementations are available. The leading public key method is *RSA,* named for its inventors Ronald Rivest, Adi Shamir, and Leonard Adleman. Compared to DES, RSA is believed to be much more secure, and key distribution is simpler, but RSA is much slower.

Cryptographic protocols

There is much more to a cryptographic application than just the cryptosystem. The whole context and design of the application determine its success. A *protocol* is a set of rules or an algorithm by which parties cooperate to accomplish some task. A *cryptographic protocol* is a protocol that uses a cryptosystem or cryptographic algorithm. It is a *secure* protocol if the application's security needs are met. Designing sound protocols is just as important as designing secure algorithms, and at least as difficult. Since *cryptosystem* traditionally has a narrower definition, we use the term *cryptographic application* for an application that depends on cryptosystems and cryptographic protocols. Such an application can be very simple—file encryption on a PC—or enormously complex—an international financial transaction system.

Protocols must solve the problem of *key management.* Secret keys must be selected, securely delivered to the communicating parties, securely kept by them, and changed periodically. The number of keys that must be managed is very large. Public key systems have to ensure the integrity of the public key directories.

Digital signatures

A paper transaction is authenticated by a handwritten signature. The signature affirms that the signer agrees to the transaction as represented by the signed document. Since signatures are difficult to forge or to copy, they are a good means of identification. Cryptography makes it possible to "sign" electronic transactions as well. A *digital signature* on a message is a cryptographically computed value that is attached to the message. The digital signature serves more functions than a handwritten signature. Like a signature, it identifies the sender and prevents repudiation; unlike a signature it also confirms the integrity of the message—even after it is received. Digital signatures primarily use public key methods.

Evaluation of cryptosystems and protocols

The designer of a cryptographic application must decide what algorithms and protocols to use. Security is the first consideration. One measure of security for cryptosystems is the amount of work (measured in people time and computer time, for example) to break the system, using the best available cryptanalysis techniques. Confidence in a cryptographic application is gained through extensive analysis and trial of both the cryptosystem and the protocols, making pessimistic assumptions about the opponent's knowledge and capabilities. The analysis can be complete only if the cryptographic algorithms are open to study. Confidence is also enhanced if the cryptosystem is certified by standards organizations, but there is no guarantee. Even published standards have been flawed.

The next criterion is speed, which is especially critical for applications involving encryption of masses of data. Security is no advantage if it makes the entire application impractical. Encryption and decryption should be fast, and the ciphertext should not be much longer than the plaintext. Long keys also detract from efficiency, since they must be securely generated, distributed and maintained. (However, hardware encryption is slowed little by longer keys.)

Since cryptosystems support communications systems, error propagation must be considered. We want to avoid cryptosystems where a single error in transmission of the ciphertext causes many errors in the deciphered message.

Cost is crucial—both the initial cost and the operating cost. Much encryption is done by software, whose cost is low. Hardware devices are faster, but cost more. Standards are important here; if they are widely accepted they encourage (by broadening the market) the development of low-cost cryptographic hardware. The cost to end users should be low as well—they should not be greatly restricted or slowed in their work.

A cryptosystem should be versatile—capable of being used in different modes and for different applications. The DES, for example, can be used for both secrecy and authentication, in different modes for either goal.

Theoretical Foundations

Claude Shannon developed the first mathematical theory of cryptography. His paper "Communication theory of secrecy systems" appeared in 1949, soon after his introduction of information theory, and it builds on information theory (which came out of earlier work on cryptography). So the two theories are intimately related. More recent work is based less on information theory and more on the theory of computational complexity, number theory, and the study of protocols.

Classical cryptosystems

Shannon's work established the concepts that still shape cryptography. His theory is of classical cryptosystems.

Basic concepts. A classical cryptosystem transforms a message so that it can be read only by those possessing the secret key to the transformation. The function or algorithm that transforms the message is called the *encrypting* function E. The encryption is $E(M)$, where M is the message. If D represents the *decrypting* function, then the following relationship must hold:

$$D(E(M)) = M$$

That is, applying the decrypting function to the encrypted message gives back the original message. The encrypting function E has a parameter, called the *key,* K. The *ciphertext* C, then, is

$$C = E_K(M)$$

That is, the ciphertext results from applying the encrypting function to the *plaintext* message, using the key K. The ciphertext is also called the *cryptogram* or the *cipher.* And it must be true that

$$D_K(C) = M$$

That is, applying the decrypting function to the ciphertext, using the same key, results in the plaintext message. The encrypting transformation is invertible.

A *cryptosystem,* then, is defined as a set of transformations from a *message space* to a *ciphertext space.* A specific transformation of the set corresponds to encrypting with a specific key. Simple substitution using a permuted alphabet is a cryptosystem; a specific transformation uses a specific permutation, such as "igfewqydsahxzbjrukoplvcnmt," which is the key.

Cryptanalysis. Cryptology assumes that an enemy will try to break the cryptosystem. The enemy (or someone playing the role of enemy in order to be friendly) is a *cryptanalyst.* The situation is represented in Fig. 5.1. The system is considered *broken* when there is a unique solution to the ciphertext. That is, only one message could correspond to the ciphertext, with probability close to one. In Shannon's theory the cryptanalyst is assumed to have unlimited time and computing power, and to possess only the ciphertext.

Entropy and equivocation. The concept of entropy (introduced in Chap. 4 in relation to information flow) measures uncertainty. The entropy of a message M (which can have various values) is given by

$$H(M) = -\sum p_i \log p_i$$

where p_i is the probability that $M = M_i$. Similarly, entropies $H(K)$ and $H(C)$ are defined for the possible keys and possible ciphertexts.

In Chap. 4 the concept of conditional entropy or *equivocation* was introduced; equivocation measures the uncertainty of one variable given knowledge about another. For cryptosystems the key equivocation, $H(K \mid C)$, is a critical measure. It is the uncertainty about the key when the ciphertext is known. The *message equivocation,* $H(M \mid C)$, measures the uncertainty about the plaintext message if the ciphertext is known. Zero equivocation corresponds to complete knowledge, where one message or key has probability of one. The key equivocation is at least as great as the message equivocation.

Perfect secrecy. A cryptosystem is said to have *perfect secrecy* if

$$P(M \mid C) = P(M)$$

That is, the probability of message M if ciphertext C is intercepted equals the a priori probability of M, for all M and all C. Knowing the ciphertext is no help at all in determining the message. A necessary condition for perfect secrecy is that the cryptosystem have as many keys as messages. This means the key must be as long as the message, and it must not be used for another message. As might be expected, very few cryptosystems provide perfect secrecy, and those few have very limited application.

Redundancy and unicity. Given that few cryptosystems offer perfect secrecy, what can be said about the difficulty of breaking imperfect systems? One approach involves the concept of *unicity distance,* which relates closely to the concept of *redundancy.*

Natural languages are highly redundant. Redundancy allows us to understand speech when the room is noisy, or to read unclear handwriting. Redundancy similarly is valuable to the cryptanalyst. Shannon gave a mathematical definition to the familiar notion of redundancy. First, the *rate* of a language is defined as the average amount of information conveyed per character. So for messages of length n the rate r is given by

$$r = H(M) / n$$

where $H(M)$ is the entropy of the language. For English, the rate has been estimated at 1 to 1.3 bits per letter. This can be compared with the *absolute rate,* which is the maximum information per character assuming all sequences of characters are equally likely. With this assumption, the absolute rate R is the maximum entropy for the characters, so that

$$R = \log_2 L$$

where L is the number of characters in the language. For English L is 26 (not counting spaces and punctuation) and R is log 26 or 4.7. The redundancy D is defined as $R-r$. Redundancy is the difference in information per character between (1) a message that carries the maximum possible information and (2) a message of the same length that is meaningful in the language. If we assume that English has a rate of 1.2, then its redundancy is

$$D = R - r = 4.7 - 1.2 = 3.5$$

The *percentage redundancy, D/R,* would be 3.5/4.7 or 74 percent. (The redundancy of a natural language is far more complex to determine than this example indicates.)

The *key equivocation function* $f(n)$ measures the uncertainty about the key after the first n symbols of the ciphertext have been examined.

$$f(n) = H(K \mid C_1, C_2, \ldots, C_n)$$

(Recall that *equivocation* is another word for conditional entropy. Here the concern is the entropy of the key as it depends on the amount of ciphertext available to the cryptanalyst.) The *unicity distance u* is defined as the smallest n such that the key equivocation function approaches zero. That is, only after examining u symbols of the ciphertext can the cryptanalyst know the value of the key. For a ciphertext of length u there is only one key that could have produced those u symbols. For a class of cryptosystems analyzed by Shannon,

$$u \approx \frac{H(K)}{D}$$

That is, the unicity distance approximates the key entropy divided by the redundancy. For a simple substitution cipher with randomly chosen key, $H(K)$ is log 26!, or 88.4, and D is about 3.5, so the unicity distance is 88.4/3.5, or about 25. After examining 25 ciphertext letters, the cryptanalyst knows the key. Shannon's approximation for unicity holds not just for the cryptosystems he analyzed, but also for many conventional cryptosystems that others have analyzed.

Since unicity distance is directly related to the entropy of the key, it follows that the larger the key set (and the longer the key), the harder it is to break the cryptosystem. In fact, if the number of possible keys is as large as the number of meaningful messages, the system cannot be broken. This relationship holds for the *one-time pad,* or *Vernam cipher,* where the key is a randomly chosen series of letters, of the same length as the message. The key is never reused. The one-time pad has perfect secrecy. It is highly impractical for most applications, but it was used at one time for the hot line between Moscow and Washington.

Since unicity distance is inversely related to redundancy, reducing redundancy enhances secrecy. Shannon suggested doing this by compressing messages before encryption. Modern compression techniques can increase unicity distance for English text by a factor of 3 to 6. If a language has no redundancy at all, the unicity distance is infinite; there is no length of ciphertext that will allow the cryptanalyst to succeed.

Work characteristic. A concept introduced by Shannon, and still used, is the *work characteristic* $W(n)$ of a cryptosystem, which is defined as the average amount of work (in man-hours originally, in computer time now) to find the key, given a ciphertext of size n. It is assumed that the work uses the best possible cryptanalytic attack. The work needed to *break* the cryptosystem is described by $W(\infty)$, the work characteristic as n approaches infinity. What the cryptographer wants to know is the lower bound of $W(\infty)$, but that is not known for most practical systems. There is no way to compute it without knowing what the best possible attack is. Cryptographers have to be content with the *historical work characteristic,* based on the best attacks that are known.

Diffusion and confusion. Cryptanalytic attacks can exploit redundancy and statistical properties of messages in general. Shannon suggested two principles of cipher design to make such attacks more difficult. *Diffusion* spreads the influence of a plaintext character over many ciphertext characters. *Confusion* hides the way that the ciphertext statistics depend on the plaintext statistics. The DES very successfully uses diffusion and confusion.

A good way to create diffusion and confusion is to combine several different cryptosystems. Shannon suggested two kinds of combination—the *weighted sum* and the *product.* The weighted sum involves determining, with some probability, which system to use for each message. The product involves first applying one system to the message, then applying the next system to the ciphertext produced by the first, and so on. Product ciphers are effective and widely used.

Many of the classical concepts still apply to modern cryptography. New developments, however, often depend not on information theory, but on the theory of computational complexity.

Computational complexity

Inventing a new cryptosystem, especially a public key system, means inventing or exploiting problems that are hard to solve. For example, factoring a large number is hard. The theory of computational complexity is relevant here, since it classifies algorithms according to their difficulty. Various measures of difficulty could be used, such as elapsed time, the amount of memory needed, or the complexity of the hardware circuits needed. Elapsed time clearly has practical importance; if a message cannot be deciphered quickly, it loses its value for the attacker.

Time complexity and polynomial time. The most commonly used measure is related to time; it is the number of basic steps or operations (such as additions or comparisons of bits) in the algorithm that solves the problem. This measure has the advantage of being independent of hardware speed. The *time complexity* of an algorithm is a function of the size n of the input to the algorithm. For example, n might be the number of bits of a key. An algorithm A has *polynomial time complexity* if there exists some polynomial $p(x)$ such that $t_A(n) \leq p(n)$ for each n, where $t_A(n)$ is the maximum time taken by the algorithm, over all inputs of size n. Time complexity is based on the worst possible case. The "big O" notation describes time or space estimates as orders of magnitude. It is said that $f(n) = O(g(n))$ if there exists a constant C such that $f(n)$ is always less than $Cg(n)$. For a polynomial time algorithm, $t(n) = O(n^k)$ for some constant k. The important thing is not the value of k, but that it is constant.

If some problem can be solved by an algorithm with polynomial time complexity, the problem *belongs to the class P*. Problems in P are called *computationally tractable,* and problems not in P are *intractable.* (The formal definition of P is based on a Turing machine—see Fig. 5.3.) An example of a problem in P is sorting, which can be done in time $O(n)$—*order* of n—where n is the number of items being sorted. Computing a factorial is not in P. It is not known if factoring an integer is in P.

Nondeterministic polynomial time. The problems in class P are solved by *deterministic* algorithms: at each step of the computation there is a unique next step. Many important algorithms are *nondeterministic:* some step of the computation involves a decision, such as "choose a number between 1 and 1000." This means that the same input can generate multiple different computations. Problems solved by nondeterministic algorithms are in the *class NP.* For problems in NP, it is tractable to check the correctness of a guess for the solution. For example, factoring an integer is in NP, because we can guess the factors and compute their product to see if the guess is right. P clearly is

A *Turing machine* has a tape divided into squares that can each hold one letter. A read-write head scans the tape one letter at a time. At any moment the machine is in one of a finite number of possible states, q. The machine's action a is determined by its current state and the letter currently scanned. Thus every pair (q, a) determines a triple (q_1, a_1, m), where the value of m can be "left," "right," or "no move." The machine goes to state q_1, writes a_1 in place of a, and moves the read-write head according to m. This constitutes a *step.* The tape can be extended indefinitely. A *computation* starts when the machine, in its initial state, is presented with an input string of n letters, placed on the first n squares of the tape. The machine scans square 1 and continues with its basic operation. The computation ends when the machine halts in its final state. The output is the content of the tape when the machine halts. Then the time complexity of a Turing machine M is defined as a function of n:

$$t_M(n) = \max\{t \mid M \text{ halts after } t \text{ steps for an input } x \text{ with } |x| = n\}$$

That is, the time complexity of machine M is the maximum number of steps taken by M for inputs of length n.

Figure 5.3 Turing machine.

included in NP. It is not known if P equals NP; theorists conjecture (from experience) that P is *not* equal to NP.

Some NP problems have a property called *NP-hard.* If a problem is NP-hard, *every* problem in NP can be reduced to that problem in polynomial time. A problem is *NP-complete* if it is in P and is also NP-hard. All NP-complete problems are computationally equivalent, and they are generally considered to be intractable.

Limitations of complexity theory for cryptography. Complexity theory deals mainly with worst-case complexity—the very hardest cases, and to a lesser extent average complexity. For cryptosystems, we need to know how many cases are very easy. The systems need to be secure "almost always." A few easy cases are acceptable if an opponent cannot easily find them.

Number theory

Cryptosystems have always depended on the properties of numbers. This section introduces some number theory concepts and terminology.

Cryptosystems often use *finite arithmetic,* an arithmetic that works on finite sets of numbers. For example, a cipher based on the alphabet uses the set {0 ... 25}. Arithmetic on the numbers $\{0, 1, \ldots, m\}$ is called *modulo m* arithmetic, and m is called the *modulus.* Counting starts over after m, as with "24, 25, 0, 1." Addition, $a + b$, starts at a and counts b times, so that $24+ 3 = 1$. A normal integer x (which may be greater than m) is brought in range by dividing it by m. The result is x modulo m, also written $x \bmod m$ or $x \pmod{m}$. The remainder from the division is called the *residue* of x modulo m. Cryptographic algorithms often use modulo 2 arithmetic, which is efficiently implemented by bitwise exclusive-OR (written as XOR or $\oplus$). The exclusive-OR of two bits is 1 if they are different, 0 if they are the same.

For the integers a, b, and m, a is *congruent* to b modulo m if $a-b$ is divisible by m. This is written $a \equiv b \bmod m$. For example, 26 is congruent to 10 modulo 8, $26 \equiv 10 \bmod 8$. Congruences with the same modulus can be added, subtracted or multiplied. For example, if $a \equiv b \bmod m$ and $c \equiv d \bmod m$ then $a + c \equiv b + d \bmod m$.

Prime numbers are important in cryptography. A prime number p is one whose only factors are 1 and p. In finite arithmetic, division is not always possible. If the modulus is a prime, however, it is possible to divide by any nonzero number.

The *greatest common divisor* (*gcd*) of two integers a and b is the largest integer dividing both a and b. The *Euclidean algorithm* finds the gcd without factoring the integers. The algorithm uses a series of divisions and its time is $O(\log^3(a))$, where a is the larger of the two integers. Two integers are *relatively prime* if their gcd is 1. If a and m are relatively prime, there exists b such that $ab \equiv 1 \bmod m$, and b is called the *inverse of* a mod m, or $a^{-1} \bmod m$.

A *field* is a set along with addition and multiplication operations that satisfy certain requirements: associative, commutative, and distributive laws; identities 0 (for addition) and 1 (for multiplication); inverses for addition and multiplication except for 0. The real numbers constitute a field. A *finite field* $F(q)$ has a fixed number q of elements. A prime number p is the *characteristic* of the field, and q is a power of p. A finite field is also called a *Galois field*, $GF(q)$. The nonzero elements of $F(q)$ form a *finite group*, $F^*(q)$. A number α is a *primitive element* of $F(q)$ if any element y can be generated as $\alpha^x = y$. The integer x is called the *discrete logarithm* of y to the base α.

Interactive proof systems

Many cryptographic problems involve interactions between two parties. *Interactive proof* systems formalize two-player games where a *prover* tries to convince a *verifier* that some assertion is true. This paradigm fits user authentication, for example, where a user tries to prove her identity to an operating system. Research on interactive proof systems tries to answer questions about how much interaction is needed to convince the verifier, or how much knowledge is imparted to the verifier. For an important class of proofs—called *zero-knowledge*—no information at all is imparted to the verifier.

Cryptographic Techniques

This section describes some basic cryptographic techniques and cryptosystems.

Classical cryptosystems and techniques

The early systems provide simple illustrations of principles and methods that are still important.

Substitution. A simple substitution cipher replaces each letter of the message with a fixed substitute. The key is a permutation of the alphabet, for example

TREWQYUIOPGFDSAHJKLVCXZBNM

Each message letter is replaced by the key letter that is in the message letter's alphabetic position. For example, the message "INSECURE" becomes ciphertext "OSLQECKQ." Simple substitution is easy to break by statistical analysis. For example, E is a good candidate plaintext for Q, since Q appears twice. If the alphabet were much larger (for example, all possible 32-bit words) frequency analysis would be far more difficult, but the key would become impractically large.

The substitution of this example is *monoalphabetic:* the same permutation applies to the whole message. A *polyalphabetic* cipher uses several different permuted alphabets as keys, in a periodic way. With four alphabets, for example, the first alphabet enciphers letters 1, 5, 9, and 13 of the message; the second alphabet enciphers letters 2, 6, 10, and 14, and so on. Polyalphabetic ciphers were solved in the nineteenth century by a method for discovering the period. A cryptanalyst who knows the period can solve the cipher as several monoalphabetic ciphers.

Transposition. Transposition divides the message into fixed-size blocks and arranges the letters within each block (including spaces) according to some permutation.

Example If the block size is 5 and the permutation is (3 2 4 5 1), the message

```
THIS |IS IN|SECUR|E TOO
```

becomes

```
IHS T| SINI|CEURS|T OOE
```

Transposition hides the statistical properties of letter pairs (such as IS), triples (such as TOO), and longer combinations. Attacks on transposition ciphers use frequency tables for the combinations and find permutations that restore the hidden combinations.

Vigenère ciphers. The key for a Vigenère cipher is a sequence of d letters. The message and repetitions of the key are added modulo 26, considering the alphabet as numbered from 0 to 25. For example, with $d = 4$ and key = FBAC,

```
THINK CIPHERS
FBACF BACFBAC
YIIPP DIRMFRU
```

The case where $d = 1$ (the key is a single letter) is the *Caesar cipher* used by Julius Caesar. The Caesar cipher can be described by a linear equation

$$C = M + b \bmod N$$

where b is a fixed integer, and N is the size of the alphabet. This is a special case of an *affine cryptosystem*

$$C = aM + b \bmod N$$

where a and b together make up the key. Contemporary cryptosystems avoid affine transformations, which are relatively easy to break with frequency-analysis attacks.

Running-key ciphers. A *running-key cipher* improves on the polyalphabetic cipher by doing away with any periodicity. The key is a long sequence that does not repeat. A classical method for generating running keys is to use the text of a book. The sender and receiver know the secret—the name of the book and where to find the text that is the key. Attacks can break running-key ciphers by exploiting the redundancy in the key.

Vernam cipher. The Vernam cipher, which was invented for the encryption of telegraph messages, used a random sequence of numbers as a running key. The numbers were punched into a paper tape, which was then read and combined with the plaintext stream (also on tape) by modulo 2 addition. The essence of this cipher is that no part of the key is used more than once. It is called the *one-time tape* or *one-time pad.* ("One-time tape" refers to the paper tape. "One-time pad" refers to a manual form of the cipher where sender and receiver had identical pads of paper containing the keys.) The one-time pad has perfect secrecy, from an information theory viewpoint. Although one-time pads are impractical, the concepts of the Vernam cipher are still very much alive.

Block and stream ciphers

Cryptosystems often are classified as block or stream ciphers. A *block cipher* divides the plaintext into blocks and applies the same encryption algorithm (with the same key) to each block. If the blocks of M are $M_1, M_2, \ldots$,

$$E_K(M) = E_K(M_1)\, E_K(M_2) \cdots$$

That is, the ciphertext is a concatenation of the ciphertexts of the individual blocks, and the same encryption transformation is used for each block. A substitution cipher is a block cipher with a block length of one character.

A *stream cipher* applies encryption to the individual plaintext digits. Encryption uses a sequence of digits called the *keystream,* which is produced by a device or algorithm called a *keystream generator.* Most stream ciphers are *binary additive* stream ciphers, where the ciphertext bits are formed by modulo 2 addition of the plaintext bits and keystream bits. Each bit C_n of the ciphertext is formed as $C_n = M_n \oplus K'_n$, where M_n is the nth bit of the plaintext and K'_n is the nth bit of the keystream that is generated from the secret key K. Decryption consists of the same modulo 2 addition, $M_n = C_n \oplus K'_n$. Binary additive stream ciphers thus have the great advantage that encryption and decryption can be performed by identical and very simple devices. In their simplest form these ciphers have no diffusion at all, since the entire operation is bit by bit. The design challenge for stream ciphers is keystream generation.

Cipher feedback. One way to provide diffusion is to make each ciphertext character depend on previously generated ciphertext. This method is called *cipher feedback*. Think of a feedback shift register as in Fig. 5.4, which shows an 8-character, 64-bit register. Each plaintext character P_i is added modulo 2 to one character of the encryption algorithm output, where the input to the algorithm is the current contents of the register. The result of the addition is the current ciphertext character C_i. For feedback C_i is shifted into one end of the register, and the character at the other end is discarded. The process repeats for the next plaintext character. A similar shift register is used at the receiving end. If there are transmission errors the two shift registers will differ and decryption will be disrupted—but only for the number of characters of the shift register.

Cipher block chaining. One problem with block ciphers is that two identical blocks of plaintext produce the same ciphertext. A ciphertext searching attack can exploit this to look for patterns in the ciphertext.

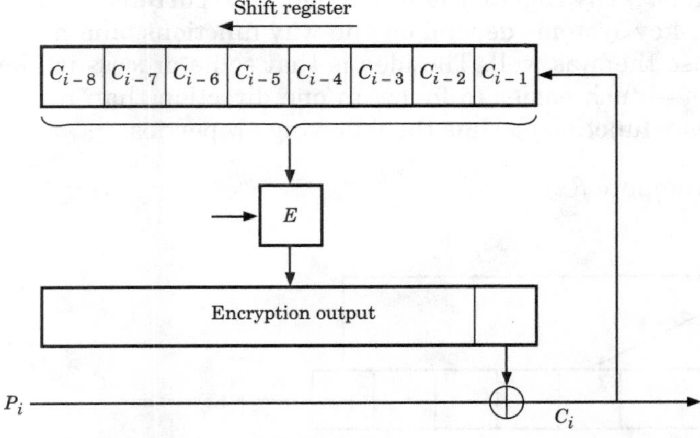

Figure 5.4 Shift register with feedback.

The technique of *cipher block chaining* (CBC) removes this exposure and also protects message integrity. Each block of ciphertext is fed back and added modulo 2 to the next block of plaintext. The resulting block is then encrypted. This method provides good diffusion, since each block of ciphertext depends on all preceding blocks of plaintext. Since the last block of ciphertext depends on all previous blocks, it constitutes a checksum that protects against transmission errors and tampering.

Cipher feedback and cipher block chaining both are used with the DES.

Linear-feedback shift registers. A *linear-feedback shift register* (LFSR) can transform a relatively short key into a very long pseudo-random keystream that approximates a one-time pad. As shown in Fig. 5.5, each keystream bit produced is added modulo 2 to some of the bits of the register (defined by the *tap sequence*—1,0,0,1,0,0,0,1 in the figure) to form the new leftmost bit of the register. With an appropriate tap sequence, an LFSR of length n can generate a stream with a period of 2^n-1. (A keystream with *period* d repeats itself after d digits.) Although an attack described by Whitfield Diffie and Martin Hellman (1979) breaks this system quite easily, LFSRs remain very important for both implementing and analyzing stream ciphers. Useful ciphers are obtained by filtering the output from an LFSR or by combining several LFSRs—both methods introducing nonlinearity. Unfortunately, many LFSR-based schemes turn out to have subtle regularities that make them insecure.

One-way functions

The concept of a *one-way function* is fundamental to current cryptography. All public-key systems depend on one-way functions, and many other systems use them as well. The idea is that some process is like a one-way street—much easier to follow in one direction than in the reverse. A one-way function $f(x)$ has the following properties:

1. It is easy to compute $f(x)$

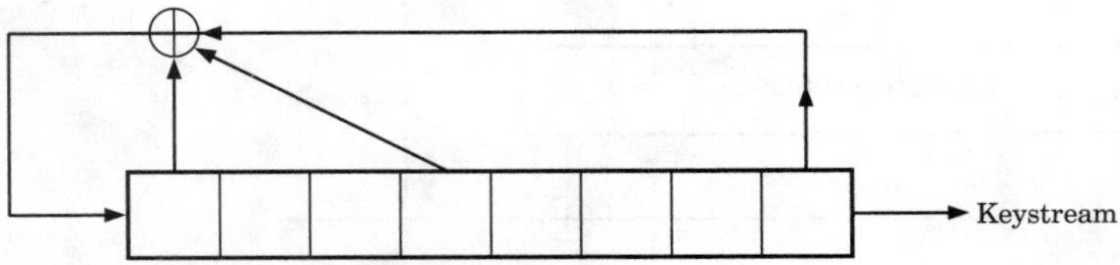

Figure 5.5 Linear-feedback shift register.

2. It is computationally infeasible to compute x from $f(x)$—at least for most values of $f(x)$

An example of a one-way function is a telephone book for a large city. Given a name x we can easily find the corresponding telephone number $f(x)$; given only the number we would have a hard time finding the name.

For public key cryptography, the one-way function is the encryption function and its reverse is decryption.

$$f\colon \boldsymbol{M} \rightarrow \boldsymbol{C}$$

$$f^{-1}\colon \boldsymbol{C} \rightarrow \boldsymbol{M}$$

Clearly a one-way function by itself is not very useful for encryption. Neither the cryptanalyst nor the legitimate receiver can recover the plaintext. There must also be a *trapdoor* that makes decryption easy. For a *trapdoor one-way function* it is computationally infeasible to compute the inverse function unless one knows certain information that was used in designing the function.

The properties of the one-way function are rather informal. "Easy" can be interpreted as efficient enough for the intended purpose. For the one-way functions used in cryptography, the infeasibility of computing x from $f(x)$ cannot be proved. One major cryptosystem (RSA) uses multiplication of primes as the one-way function. The reverse process (factoring) is believed to be infeasible, but there is no proof. Modular arithmetic is important for cryptography because it turns continuous functions into discontinuous ones whose inverses are harder to compute.

One-way functions are also used as *hash functions.* A one-way hash function produces a shorter fixed-length digest of a longer message. A hash function should be collision-free; that is, two messages should not have the same digest.

The Data Encryption Standard

The *Data Encryption Standard* (DES) is an encryption algorithm that was adopted as a standard.

History. During the 1970s it was recognized that a standard for the commercial application of encryption would be useful. For one thing, a standard would encourage mass production of encryption devices. This availability, coupled with confidence in an endorsed technique, would lead to wider use of encryption. In 1977 the National Bureau of Standards adopted a scheme based on the LUCIFER system developed at IBM. The DES did result in wide availability of encryption hardware and software, and wide use. Although the DES was criticized from the first—for weakness and for improper adoption procedures—it has proved to be a strong cryptosystem.

Techniques and algorithm. The DES uses the techniques that were suggested by Shannon:

- *Confusion.* The DES creates confusion by substitution, using nonlinear substitution devices called *S-boxes.*
- *Diffusion.* Diffusion in DES is based on permutation, using *P-boxes* that define the permutations.
- *Product ciphers.* The DES is a product cipher, with encryption applied 16 times.
- *Mixing transformations.* Mixing transformations are those that spread high-probability messages of a message space uniformly through the space. The DES follows Shannon's suggestion of alternating encryption with mixing transformations in a product cipher.

The DES is a block cipher with 64-bit blocks. The key is 56 bits long. An overview of the algorithm is shown in Fig. 5.6. After an initial permutation (using a fixed table) the input block goes through 16 *rounds* of encryption and substitution. The output of each round is the input to the next round. Each round consists of the following steps:

1. The 64-bit block is divided into 32-bit left and right halves (L and R in the figure). The right block is viewed as eight 4-bit blocks. These are expanded into 6-bit blocks by copying some of the bits. Now there are 48 bits.
2. A 48-bit key for the round is added modulo 2 to the result of Step 1. (How this key is obtained is described below.)
3. Each 6-bit block forms the input to one of 8 S-boxes. The substitutions of each S-box are defined in a 4×16 table; the 6 bits of the input block select the row and column to be used. Each S-box returns a 4-bit block, and the eight 4-bit blocks are concatenated.
4. The 32-bit result of Step 3 undergoes another permutation by a P-box.
5. The result of Step 4 is added modulo 2 to the left half of the 64-bit block, and the two halves are interchanged.

The ith round can be described as follows:

$$L_i = R_{i-1} \qquad R_i = L_{i-1} \oplus f(R_{i-1}, K_i)$$

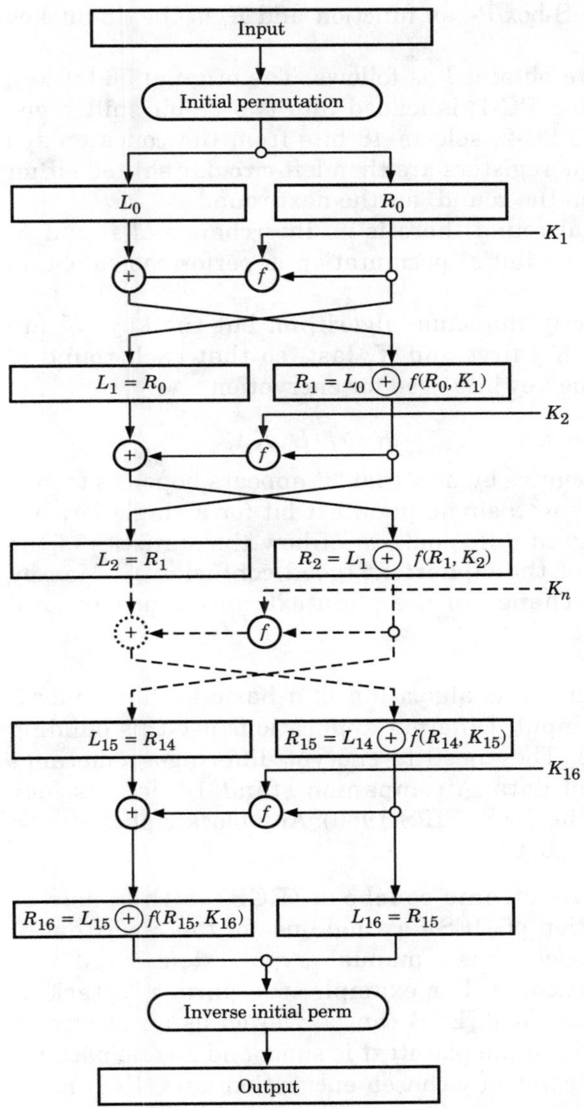

Figure 5.6 Overview of the DES algorithm.

where f represents the S-box/P-box function and K_i is the 48-bit key used for the round.

The 48-bit keys K_i are obtained as follows. The original 56-bit key, after a fixed permutation PC-1, is loaded into two 28-bit shift registers. A subset function, PC-2, selects 48 bits from the concatenated registers for each K_i. The registers are then left-circular shifted either 1 or 2 bits (depending on the round) for the next round.

On the 16th and final round there is no interchange of L and R. Finally, the inverse of the initial permutation is performed to obtain the 64-bit ciphertext.

Decryption uses exactly the same algorithm, but the keys K_i are used in reverse order, K_{16} first and K_1 last, so that each round of decryption uses the same key bits used for encryption.

$$R_{i-1} = L_i \qquad L_{i-1} = R_i \oplus f(L_i, K_i)$$

The reader probably agrees by now that "it appears hopeless to give a useful description of how a single plaintext bit (or a single key bit) affects the ciphertext (good diffusion!), or of how the statistics of the plaintext affect those of the ciphertext (good confusion!)" (Massey 1992: 21). A single-bit change in the plaintext causes nearly total change in the ciphertext.

Modes of operation. The DES algorithm is a basic building block, operating on 64 bits of input. Different applications use this building block in different ways. They need to encrypt differing—sometimes very great—amounts of data. A companion standard defines four *modes of operation* for the DES (FIPS 1980). Any block cipher can be used in these modes, not just DES.

Electronic codebook. Electronic codebook (ECB) is the basic or "native" mode of operation of DES—a single use of the algorithm to encrypt one block. [A *codebook* is a manual cryptosystem based on a book of pairs (plaintext,code). For example, the phrase "attack at dawn" might be coded as 7356. ECB can be viewed as an electronic version.] ECB is used where the plaintext is short and has no pattern, for example, to encrypt randomly chosen encryption keys. ECB mode is not used for encrypting longer messages (one block at a time) because the mode is weak for typical messages. Most messages have repetitive patterns that will occasionally show in the ciphertext, giving clues to the cryptanalyst. This is especially true for the structured messages used in electronic transactions. Other modes overcome this weakness by not treating each block separately.

Cipher block chaining. Cipher block chaining (CBC) mode uses the DES algorithm repeatedly, exclusive-ORing the ciphertext of one

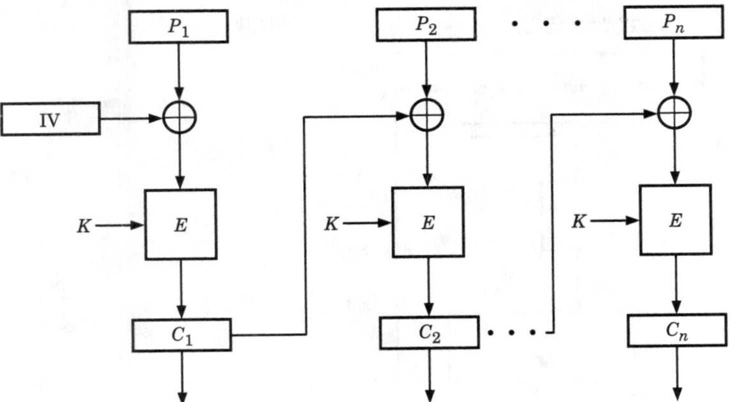

Figure 5.7 Cipher block chaining mode.

block with the plaintext of the next block (see Fig. 5.7). This chaining eliminates the weakness shown by ECB. CBC is the primary method used to encrypt long messages with DES. To handle the first block, when there is no "previous" ciphertext, a pseudo-random *initialization vector* (IV) starts the process off. The same IV must be used for encryption and decryption, and its integrity must be preserved. Sending the IV in encrypted form prevents attacks that purposefully change the first block by changing the IV. When the same key and IV are reused, equal plaintext blocks of different messages will produce the same ciphertext, but (in contrast to ECB mode) only up to the first unequal blocks. Starting each message with a unique identifier easily corrects this problem.

A transmission error in one block affects the next two blocks (only). However, an attacker could use an error in one block to cause controlled changes to the next block. For this reason, error recovery procedures should discard and retransmit the entire chain in which an error occurs.

Cipher feedback. Cipher feedback (CFB) mode encrypts one character at a time. This is useful, for example, for characters generated one at a time at a terminal. The "character" is any small unit, even a bit, although 8-bit characters are most common. With a character length of m the mode is called m-bit cipher feedback. As shown in Fig. 5.8, the input to the DES algorithm comes from a 64-bit shift register that holds the most recent 64 bits of ciphertext. Only the leftmost 8 bits of the DES output are used. They are exclusive-ORed with the plaintext to form the 8-bit ciphertext, which also feeds back into the right end of the shift register. With CFB mode, the receiver also uses the encryption algorithm.

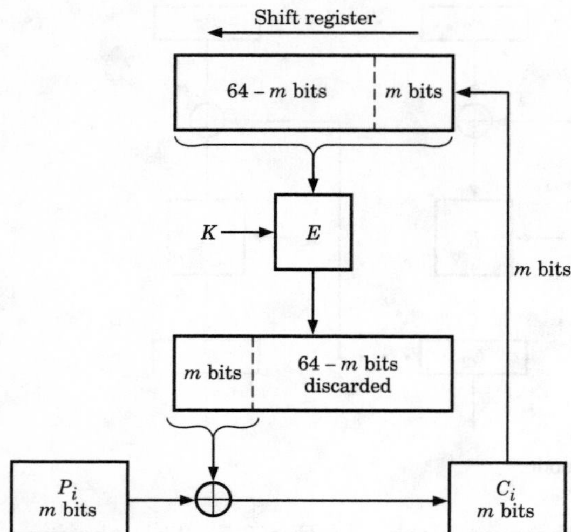

Figure 5.8 Cipher feedback mode.

Output feedback. Output feedback (OFB) mode is very much like CFB, but the feedback comes from the DES output *before* it is exclusive-ORed with the plaintext. A modified OFB is used for applications (such as digital speech or video) where the error properties of the other methods are unacceptable.

Implementations of the DES. Software and hardware implementations provide the DES at a range of speeds and prices. Many provide not only the basic algorithm but also various modes of operation. The National Institute of Standards and Technology (NIST) validates implementations of DES; by 1993, about 50 different implementations had been validated. In 1994, a typical commercial DES chip could encrypt at 15 megabits per second. In 1992, a prototype DES chip reached a throughput of 1 gigabit per second. Besides being faster than software, hardware implementations are more secure. Encryption software could be modified by an intruder, whereas hardware can be tamper-resistant. For example, a tamper-evident coating would have to be broken to get access to cryptographic keys or other critical information. Software encryption is easier to integrate into everyday applications, like word processing and email.

Fast Data Encryption Algorithm. An algorithm that is similar to DES is *Fast Data Encryption Algorithm* (FEAL). Since FEAL does not use any table lookups, it is simpler to implement than DES, and it is faster. The number of rounds is variable, with eight rounds the usual choice for CBC mode. Cryptanalysis has shown, however, that FEAL with four or eight rounds is not strong.

Exportable encryption. Because of restrictions on export of DES from the United States, exportable alternatives have been developed. Ronald Rivest developed two variable-key-length algorithms—RC2 (a block cipher) and RC4 (a stream cipher). RC2 and RC4 are proprietary algorithms. For another Rivest block cipher, RC5, the block size and number of rounds are parameters, as well as the key length. Products using RC2 and RC4 can be exported if the key size is limited to 40 bits (versus the DES 56 bits). Of course encryption is weaker with a 40-bit key. Lotus was able to export 64-bit encryption after giving the NSA access to 24 of the bits. Another problem is that RC2 and RC4 are not compatible with DES, so that products using them cannot communicate with products using DES. The Commercial Data Masking Facility weakens the DEA itself by generating keys that have an effective 40-bit length.

Security of the DES. From its inception the DES was criticized as vulnerable to attack by exhaustive search and possibly by other methods. The main criticisms have been:

1. The key is too short, permitting exhaustive search
2. The S-boxes contain trapdoors

Also, the choice of 16 rounds was questioned. Why not fewer or more? The answer to that question is given later.

Some of the advantage of a longer key can be had by encrypting multiple times, with different keys, preferably in complex ways. For example, a method proposed by IBM uses two keys, enciphering with the first key, then deciphering with the second, and finally enciphering with the first. Key management standards for wholesale banking also specify triple encryption with a double-length key (encipher with left half of the key, decipher with right half, encipher with left half). In 1981, Ralph Merkle and Martin Hellman showed potential weakness in this method and recommended triple encryption with three independent keys; this method is widely used. A group of experts concluded (Blaze et al. 1996) that symmetric systems need at least 75-bit keys, and that 90-bit keys are needed to protect information for 20 years.

Since the S-boxes are the only nonlinear part of DES, its security depends totally on their design. How the S-boxes were designed was classified, and this secrecy led to years of suspicion and controversy. Martin Hellman and others showed that it would be possible to design S-boxes with trapdoors. The suspicion was that trapdoors were inserted at the behest of the National Security Agency (NSA), to allow intelligence organizations to monitor communications. A Congressional investigation concluded in 1979 that NSA influenced the key length decision but did not tamper with the DES design. Eventually some of the design criteria were published. No trapdoors have been found by academic researchers, despite much investigation. DES has been reviewed every 5 years since it became a standard and has been reaffirmed until 1998. Although few people expect that DES will be reaffirmed again, triple DES encryption with three keys remains strong protection.

Cryptanalysis of the DES. Many researchers have long believed that successful cryptanalysis of the DES was inevitable. The first experimental cryptanalysis was done in 1994 by Mitsuru Matsui, using a method called *linear cryptanalysis.* Before describing this milestone, we review two other methods of DES cryptanalysis.

Exhaustive search or *brute force* attack presumes that the attacker has somehow obtained sample plaintext-ciphertext pairs. The attack then tests each possible key in turn, by encrypting a plaintext sample to see if the key produces the corresponding ciphertext sample. With the fastest conceivable implementation, this straightforward method would take thousands of years. If the search could be performed in parallel, however, by a million DES devices, the attack would indeed threaten DES security. Diffie and Hellman (1977) considered a hypothetical machine of a million LSI chips, each capable of checking one key per microsecond, and estimated it could do an exhaustive search in 20 hours. Since on average the key is found after testing half the possible keys, the average time for the successful attack is 10 hours. Diffie and Hellman felt such a machine would be practical by 1990. But no such attack had succeeded by 1990, as far as was publicly known.

Cryptanalysts have looked for approaches that might be more efficient than exhaustive search. One approach is *differential cryptanalysis,* developed by Eli Biham and Adi Shamir. It applies to any DES-like cipher, including FEAL. Differential cryptanalysis is a chosen plaintext attack. It works with *pairs* of plaintext and the corresponding pairs of ciphertext. Assume that P and P' are a plaintext pair; their exclusive-OR is called the *differential plaintext.* P and P' encipher to C and C'. If the differential plaintext is chosen carefully, the exclusive-OR of C and C' has some useful probability of taking on a specific value called the *characteristic.* For example, Biham and Shamir found a differential plaintext that produced a specific characteristic with a probability of about one in 10,000. This characteristic repeated portions of the differential plaintext. The attack then involves deciphering portions of the ciphertext to determine whether the characteristic has occurred. If so, some bits of the key can be derived. The procedure must be repeated many times to derive the full key. This attack is theoretically able to break the full 16-round DES with 2^{47} chosen plaintexts. The method can also be applied in a known-plaintext attack, if very many plaintexts are available. Because it takes so many plaintexts, differential cryptanalysis is not considered a practical threat to DES.

Returning to the question of why DES has 16 rounds: after Biham and Shamir's work, it was learned that the IBM cryptographers designed the S-boxes and number of rounds to resist differential cryptanalysis. Changing a single S-box entry makes the algorithm significantly less resistant to differential cryptanalysis.

In 1994, *linear cryptanalysis* was used in the first successful experimental attack on 16-round DES. Mitsuru Matsui carried out the experiment, which took 50 days on 12 computers (99-MHz RISC) to find one key. Of the 50 days, 40 were spent generating plaintexts and ciphertexts, 10 on the actual key search. Linear cryptanalysis is more dangerous than differential cryptanalysis because it uses known plaintext rather than chosen plaintext. That is, any available plaintext-ciphertext pairs can be used.

Linear cryptanalysis involves finding a linear approximation expression relating bits of the plaintext and ciphertext to bits of the key.

$$P[i_1, i_2, \dots, i_a] \oplus C[j_1, j_2, \dots, j_b] = K[k_1, k_2, \dots, k_c]$$

where $\oplus$ is exclusive-OR, $P[i_1, i_2, \dots, i_a]$ represents the exclusive-OR of specific bit positions of the plaintext, and similarly for the ciphertext and key. Each side of the equation represents one bit. There is some probability that the equation holds; the further this probability is from 1/2, the more effective the expression in finding the key bit. The expression gives a guess for a key-bit, and each plaintext/ciphertext pair confirms or does not confirm that guess. The more effective the expression, the fewer the samples of text needed for confidence about the guess. Matsui first found linear approximations for the individual S-boxes, then extended these to the entire algorithm. He found two equations for 14-round DES that hold with probability $1/2-1.19\times2^{-21}$. He found 26 key bits by linear cryptanalysis and the remaining 30 by exhaustive search. This cryptanalysis of the DES was a milestone, but it does not represent a significant near-term threat.

IDEA

IDEA (International Data Encryption Algorithm) was developed by Huejia Lai and James Massey. It is designed to be more secure than DES against brute-force attacks and differential cryptanalysis. The key is 128 bits, so exhaustive search is far harder than for the DES 56-bit key. The 128-bit key is used to generate 16-bit subkeys. As with DES, input is 64-bit blocks, which get broken into 16-bit subblocks. There are eight rounds, plus a final transformation. Each round operates on four subblocks of plaintext and six subkeys, and the final transformation uses four subkeys. Like DES, IDEA makes good use of confusion and diffusion. DES uses only exclusive-OR operations, relying on the S-boxes for confusion. IDEA mixes three different operations:

1. Exclusive-OR
2. Addition modulo 2^{16}
3. Multiplication modulo $2^{16}+1$

Mixing these three operations makes the transformation much more complex.

IDEA is designed to be more secure than DES, but it has undergone much less cryptanalysis. Although IDEA is patented in Europe, it can be used noncommercially without fee. It is widely used as part of the Pretty Good Privacy system (described in Chap. 10).

SKIPJACK

SKIPJACK is the encryption algorithm used in the Escrowed Encryption Standard. It was designed by the NSA. Since SKIPJACK is classified Secret, little is known about it publicly. We do know that it uses an 80-bit key. This means that exhaustive search would take 16 million times longer than for DES. Like DES, SKIPJACK works on a 64-bit block. It uses 32 rounds of processing. It can be used in all four operating modes defined for DES. The security of SKIPJACK was studied by outside experts who were given access to the classified information. "The review group concluded that there was no significant risk that the algorithm had 'trapdoors' or could be broken by any known method of attack" (Denning and Smid 1994: 59).

Stream ciphers

A stream cipher operates on individual plaintext digits, using a long keystream that both sender and receiver generate from the key. The way the cipher operates on each digit depends on the system state, which changes after each digit operation. A stream encryptor can be described as

$$s_{i+1} = F(K, s_i, M_i)$$

$$C_i = f(K, s_i, M_i)$$

where s_i is the current state, F is the next state function, and f is the output function that determines the next ciphertext digit. (K is the key, M_i is the plaintext digit, and C_i is the ciphertext digit.) The keystream is a sequence:

$$\{K_i' = f(K, s_i) : i \geq 1\}$$

The keystream segment K_i', which is used to encrypt the ith plaintext digit, depends on the original key K and on the system state s_i.

Types of stream ciphers. In some stream ciphers, called *synchronous,* the next state depends *only* on the previous state and the base key and not on the input. When the system is used in *counter mode,* its state does not even depend on the key. For example, the keystream might be generated by encrypting with DES the integers 1, 2,...; the next-state function F simply adds 1, and the key K is used only by the output function f. In output feedback mode, the reverse is true: the state depends on the key, but the output function does not. A valuable property of a synchronous stream cipher is that errors do not propagate at all. The sender and receiver must be perfectly synchronized, however.

Other stream ciphers are called *self-synchronizing.* When used in cipher feedback mode (as in the DES mode CFB)

$$s_i = F(C_{i-1}, C_{i-2}, \ldots, C_{i-N})$$

$$K_i' = f(K, s_i)$$

That is, the state depends on the last N ciphertext digits. With self-synchronizing ciphers, errors propagate, but for only N digits.

Approaches to stream cipher design. Rainer Rueppel distinguishes four approaches to designing stream ciphers: information-theoretic, system-theoretic, complexity-theoretic, and *randomized stream ciphers.* All the approaches focus on the keystream generator, whose task is to transform a relatively short key into a much longer pseudo-random keystream.

Information-theoretic approach. The unicity distance (introduced earlier in the chapter) is the amount of ciphertext the cryptanalyst needs to be able to find the key. For many cryptosystems, unicity is approximately equal to the entropy of the key, divided by the redundancy of the plaintext:

$$u \approx \frac{H(K)}{D}$$

The concept of unicity can be adapted for a stream cipher. The unicity distance of a keystream generator is the amount of keystream needed to determine the key. For a known plaintext attack the denominator becomes 1, and the unicity distance equals the key entropy.

System-theoretic approach. Cryptographers following this approach—the most widely used one—have developed a set of design criteria. The criteria come from studying principles of cryptanalysis to find rules for preventing attacks based on those principles. Of course a cipher that meets these criteria is not guaranteed to be secure, since there is no general theory of cryptanalysis. The main criteria include our old friends diffusion and confusion, as well as:

- Long period—as long as the message. (A keystream with *period d* repeats itself after *d* digits.)
- Linear complexity criteria. The *linear complexity* of a key sequence is defined as the length of the shortest LFSR that could produce the sequence. Unless the linear complexity of a stream cipher is large, the cipher is vulnerable to known methods of attack.
- Statistical criteria, such as the distributions of digraphs and triples.
- Nonlinearity criteria.

The system-theoretic approach is not limited to stream ciphers. The DES is a block cipher that was designed according to system-theoretic principles. The approach has the advantage that each new system poses a new challenge to the cryptanalyst. That is not true for other approaches to cryptosystem design. The keystream generators designed with this approach include:

- *Filter generators,* which use a nonlinear transformation of the state of an LFSR.
- *Combination generators,* which combine the output sequences from several LFSRs.
- *Clock-controlled shift registers,* which use irregular clocking to introduce nonlinearity. For example, the output of one register could be used as input to the clock of another.

Correlation attacks analyze combination generators to determine if they leak information about the output sequences that are combined. Good combining functions are called *correlation-immune.* Correlation attacks can also be applied to filter generators, by simulating them as combination generators. The history of broken keystream generator designs shows that the criteria of large periods and large linear complexity alone are inadequate.

Complexity-theoretic approach. With this approach the enemy is assumed to be limited to polynomial-time attacks. Cryptanalysis succeeds if it predicts a digit of the keystream or if it can distinguish the keystream sequence from a truly random sequence.

Randomized stream ciphers. This approach focuses on the size of the cryptanalysis problem, in particular the number of bits the cryptanalyst must examine. (The complexity-theoretic approach focuses on the difficulty rather than the size.) The idea is to use a very large, public random string for encryption and decryption. The role of the secret key here is to select which part of the public string is used. An attacker, not knowing the key, would have to examine very large amounts of potential keystream. The work characteristic can be computed for such ciphers; this means they can be provably secure.

One randomized stream cipher sends bits of the encrypted message alternately with bits of another stream. That stream consists of a random "preamble" of K bits, followed by the keystream. (The value of K is the secret key.) The receiver simply waits until the preamble has passed to start decrypting. It can be proved about the work characteristic (measured in bit operations) that

$$W(\infty) \approx 2^{K/2}$$

That is, the work for the attacker is an exponential function of the preamble length. The only problem is that the legitimate receiver must wait until about 2^K bits have arrived to start decrypting. That is why this cipher is named *Rip van Winkle.*

A potentially more practical randomized stream cipher was developed by Ueli Maurer (1992). This cipher too is provably secure, according to a slightly relaxed version of Shannon's notion of perfect secrecy.

Advantages and disadvantages of stream ciphers. Stream ciphers have important advantages for some uses. They are relatively easy to design, and the implementation can be very fast using LFSRs. The same device is used for both encryption and decryption. Since encryption is bit by bit there is no error propagation. This property is especially valuable for military applications, where communication channels are noisy, and for voice communications. Finally, progress in the theory of stream ciphers gives cryptographers trust in their security. One disadvantage is that the sender and receiver must stay exactly synchronized; they must be using the same keystream bits for the same text. In practice extra information is sent just for synchronization, thus increasing communication overhead.

Public Key Cryptography

In conventional cryptosystems the sender and receiver share secret information, namely a single key. Public key systems take a radically different approach, where the key material has both secret and public components. Public key systems were devised originally for key distribution, which is a serious problem when the keys must be kept secret. Public key systems are still used for that purpose, but perhaps even more important is their use for message authentication.

Diffie-Hellman concepts

The idea of public key cryptography was introduced by Diffie and Hellman (1976), who proposed using it for distribution of secret encryption keys.

Public key cryptosystem. Diffie and Hellman defined a public key cryptosystem in terms of families of transformations E_K and D_K. (For now, think of them as enciphering and deciphering transformations.) The cryptosystem has some interesting properties:

1. For every key K,

   $$D_K(E_K(M)) = M$$

   That is, decrypting the encrypted form yields the message M.
2. The transformations E_K and D_K are easy to compute.
3. For "almost every" K, it is computationally infeasible to derive D_K from E_K.
4. It is also true that $E_K(D_K(M)) = M$. Encrypting the decrypted form yields the original message.
5. For every key K, it is feasible to compute inverse pairs E_K and D_K from K.

Since D cannot be computed from E (Property 3), it is perfectly secure for E to be public. Property 1 supports secrecy, and Property 4 supports authentication.

A public key system is used in the following way for transmitting secret messages. Alice generates a pair of inverse transformations, E_A and D_A. The deciphering transformation D is kept secret, and the enciphering transformation E is published, to be used by anyone who wants to communicate with Alice in secrecy. E_A is Alice's *public key.* Anyone can encrypt with E_A, but only Alice can decrypt, because only she has the secret key D_A.

Bob, to send a secret message to Alice,

1. Looks up in the public directory Alice's public key E_A.
2. Uses that key to generate the ciphertext $C = E_A(M)$ and sends the ciphertext.

On receiving the ciphertext, Alice applies the secret transformation to obtain the plaintext message: $M = D_A(C)$.

A metaphor for this public key scheme is a strongbox whose locks have two combinations: one for locking and another for unlocking. Anyone can lock information in the box, but only its owner has the combination to unlock it.

Exponential key exchange. Diffie and Hellman went on to propose a way of finding the transformations E and D. The method is based on a difficult problem in the arithmetic of finite fields or Galois fields—the *discrete logarithm* problem—one of several famous hard problems that public key systems rely on. The one-way function here is exponentiation. If $GF(q)$ is a finite field with a prime number q of elements, and α is a fixed primitive element of $GF(q)$, the one-way function is

$$y = \alpha^x \bmod q$$

This calculation of y from x is easy, taking at most $2 \log_2 q$ multiplications. The inverse function takes the logarithm of y to the base α

$$x = \log_\alpha y \bmod q$$

The discrete logarithm is computationally infeasible, as far as anyone knows, except for certain values of the prime q.

Key exchange works as follows. Suppose Alice and Bob want to agree on a secret key. Each of them generates a random number x between 1 and $q-1$. Alice keeps x_A secret, but publishes

$$y_A = \alpha^{x_A} \bmod q$$

Bob similarly publishes y_B. The agreed secret key for Alice and Bob is

$$K_{AB} = \alpha^{x_A x_B} \bmod q$$

Alice computes this key by obtaining y_B from the public directory and then computing

$$K_{AB} = y_B^{\,x_A} \bmod q$$

$$= (\alpha^{x_B})^{x_A} \bmod q$$

$$= \alpha^{x_B x_A} = \alpha^{x_A x_B} \bmod q$$

And Bob obtains the secret key similarly.

An attacker must compute K_{AB} from y_A and y_B. No way to do this is known other than computing the discrete log and finding x_A or x_B. For q about 1000 bits long, computing y takes a few thousand multiplications, whereas taking the logarithm would take 10^{30} operations (Diffie 1992). The Diffie-Hellman method is still used for key exchange.

Digital signatures. Written signatures, which authenticate documents such as checks and purchase contracts and tax returns, are essential to commercial and government transactions. A written signature is easy to recognize and very hard to forge. A *digital signature* plays a similar role for electronic transactions. It assures the receiver that a message is authentic, and it can be kept as evidence that a particular message was sent by the signer. A digital signature guards against fraud such as forging of the signature (by the receiver or someone else) or repudiation of the message by the sender. Digital signatures use public key cryptography.

The digital signature proposed by Diffie and Hellman uses the same transformations D and E of the public key system, but in the reverse order from their use for secrecy. When Alice wants to send an authenticated message to Bob, she applies her secret key and sends $D_A(M)$. Bob "encrypts" the message with Alice's public key E_A. This makes the message readable and assures Bob that the message really came from Alice. Bob keeps $D_A(M)$ as evidence that he received the message from Alice.

Digital signatures are as important as any cryptographic method for the security of computer-based activities. They are described in more detail later in the chapter.

Trapdoor cryptosystems. Diffie and Hellman had the insight that trapdoor one-way functions are powerful tools for constructing cryptosystems. All contemporary public key systems are trapdoor systems whose security is based on problems in finite arithmetic, such as factoring, or computing logarithms. Since little has been proved about how hard these problems are, confidence in their difficulty is based on years of attempts to solve them.

How to build a public key cryptosystem

Arto Salomaa (1990) gives a recipe for building a public key cryptosystem in five steps.

1. Pick a difficult problem *P*. It should be intractable according to complexity theory.
2. Pick an easy subproblem of *P* and call it P_{easy}.
3. "Shuffle" P_{easy} into a problem $P_{shuffle}$ that does not look like P_{easy} but instead resembles *P*.
4. Publish $P_{shuffle}$ and keep secret how to recover P_{easy} from $P_{shuffle}$. This information is the trapdoor.
5. Set up the cryptosystem so that the legitimate receiver can use the trapdoor and solve P_{easy}, whereas an attacker must solve $P_{shuffle}$.

An example of this approach is found in the *trapdoor knapsack* system.

Trapdoor knapsacks

Using *puzzles* for public key systems was proposed by Ralph Merkle in 1978. The idea is for the sender to construct a puzzle that the receiver must solve in order to recover the plaintext. One such puzzle is the *knapsack* problem, so-called because it corresponds to the problem of packing assorted items into a knapsack. The solver of the puzzle is given a set of weights (the *knapsack vector* or *cargo vector*) and a total weight. The problem is to find the subset of weights which add up to the total. A variation of the problem is known to be NP complete in its general case, but certain instances are easy. This fact was the basis of a knapsack cryptosystem introduced by Merkle and Hellman (1978), but broken by Adi Shamir (1984) and also by others. Knapsacks are probably dead.

The RSA system

A system that so far remains unbroken is called *RSA,* after its inventors Rivest, Shamir, and Adleman (1978). Of all the public key systems, RSA has seen by far the most use. It supports both secrecy and authentication, and it is practical to implement. RSA is based on a simple idea: it is easy to multiply two large prime numbers, but exceedingly difficult to factor large composite numbers. Thus multiplication is the one-way function for RSA.

How RSA works. Encryption raises the message M to a power e, modulo n. Decryption raises the ciphertext to another power d also modulo n. Thus (e,n) is the public encryption key and d is the private decryption key.

The keys are computed as follows. Alice chooses randomly two very large prime numbers p and q (keeping them secret). She then computes $n = pq$ and $\phi(n) = (p-1)(q-1)$. Next she randomly chooses an integer e, between 1 and $\phi(n)-1$, that is relatively prime to $\phi(n)$, and computes its inverse d such that $ed \equiv 1 \bmod \phi(n)$. Knowing $\phi(n)$ makes it easy to compute d. To encrypt a message block M

$$E(M) = M^e \bmod n$$

The corresponding decryption is

$$D(C) = C^d \bmod n$$

A proof that this does indeed recover the plaintext can be found in the original article.

Example A tiny example gives an idea of the computations. The primes are $p = 17$ and $q = 31$. Then $n = pq = 527$, and $\phi(n) = (p-1)(q-1) = 480$. The value 7 is chosen for e. Then $d = 343$. $(7 \times 343 = 2401 = 1 \bmod 480.)$ Encrypting the message $M = 2$,

$$\begin{aligned} C &= M^e \bmod n \\ &= 2^7 \bmod 527 \\ &= 128 \end{aligned}$$

The decryption, using the secret value d, is

$$\begin{aligned} M &= C^d \bmod n \\ &= 128^{343} \bmod 527 \\ &= 128^{256} \times 128^{64} \times 128^{16} \times 128^{4} \times 128^{2} \times 128^{1} \bmod 527 \\ &= 35 \times 256 \times 35 \times 101 \times 47 \times 128 \bmod 527 \\ &= 2 \bmod 527 \end{aligned}$$

This example is from Diffie and Hellman (© 1979 IEEE).

Security of RSA. The security of RSA depends on the difficulty of factoring large numbers (although there is no proof that factoring is the best attack on RSA). If the modulus n is large enough, and if p and q are suitably chosen, attacks on RSA are not feasible. In 1994, the largest number factored by the best algorithm (a form of the quadratic sieve) was 129 decimal digits, and that took 5000 MIPS-years on a worldwide network of computers. Most experts believe that 220-digit numbers will be secure for many years—barring some breakthrough in factoring methods. Certain numbers are dramatically easier to factor than the average, but this has not yet given cryptanalysis any advantage. It is important for p and q to be roughly equal in size, to prevent the use of certain algorithms. Also (and this goes for all cryptosystems) we cannot predict how rapidly computing power will increase, or how much more efficiently parallelism will be used. It makes sense to allow a variable modulus size that can be increased without changing software and hardware (Beth, Frisch, and Simmons 1992).

For the *timing attack* against RSA (and other cryptosystems) the attacker eavesdrops on the cryptographic operations. Their time varies with the value of the encryption key, so the key can be recovered from timing measurements of multiple operations that use the same secret key. Possible safeguards are (1) forcing all operations to take the maximum time, and (2) *blinding*—introducing random components into the operations, making their timing independent of key values.

Implementation of RSA. Many custom RSA chips are marketed, and standard digital signal processors have been microprogrammed for RSA. Most chips use a 512-bit modulus, which has advantages for implementation. (A modulus of 1024 bits is recommended for information that must be kept for many years.) In 1991, with 512-bit exponentiation, the highest RSA encryption rate was about 50,000 bits per second. This compared with 45 megabits per second for DES with custom VLSI chips. In 1994, a typical commercial RSA chip could achieve a throughput of 10 kilobits per second, compared with about 15 megabits per second for DES chips. So RSA is appropriate for key management and digital signatures, but not for bulk encryption.

Since the exponent e is public and arbitrary, some people have suggested using a fixed value for all implementations. The value 3 was proposed, but it has been shown that low values of e are less secure. A more secure proposed fixed value is 65,537.

ElGamal scheme

In 1985, Taher ElGamal introduced a public key scheme that (like Diffie-Hellman) is based on exponentiation and the difficulty of computing discrete logarithms. Since interest in ElGamal has focused on its use for digital signatures, we describe it in that context later in this chapter.

Authentication of Information

Authentication means making sure that some entity is what it purports to be. Two main types of authentication are needed for secure computing. One is the authentication of users and of entities (such as processes) that represent users. This *identity authentication* is described in later chapters. Here we describe how cryptography supports the second type, *message authentication,* or the authentication of information. Message authenticity and message secrecy are separable goals that can be implemented either separately or together.

Threats to message integrity

A message event is modeled as having four potential participants: authorized sender, legitimate receiver, opponent, and referee. It is assumed that the sender and receiver may cheat (for commercial transactions the insiders are the very parties most likely to cheat) and that the referee can be trusted to arbitrate disputes between them. The model assumes that the opponent understands the authentication scheme and can eavesdrop, compute, and alter messages. The threats include:

- *Impersonating the sender, or masquerading.* The opponent sends a fraudulent message.
- *Substitution.* The opponent eavesdrops on a series of messages and then sends her own message, either substituting for a legitimate one or inserting in the legitimate sequence. The substituted message may be an alteration of a legitimate one.
- *Forgery.* The opponent fabricates a message and claims to have received it from the sender.
- *Disavowal or reneging.* The sender sends a message and later claims not to have sent it.
- *Replay.* A previously sent message is sent again.

This list shows that message authentication includes both guaranteeing the authenticity of the parties and protecting the integrity of the message contents. Some of the methods developed to protect message integrity can also protect the integrity of stored data.

Cryptographic methods for message authentication

The methods used for message authentication can be classified according to whether or not (1) they use secret parameters (analogous to encryption keys) and (2) they combine integrity protection with encryption for secrecy. *Message authentication codes* (MACs) use secret information and protect integrity separately. Most *hash functions* use no key; hash functions are used mainly in combination with encryption or digital signatures, but they can be used independently. Digital signatures use public key cryptography, with public and private keys; they are used either with or without encryption for secrecy. All the methods add information to messages for the purpose of protecting their integrity.

Message authentication codes. One method of authenticating a message is to compute a value, called the *authenticator*, that is a function of the message and a secret key shared by the sender and receiver. That is, $A = f(K, M)$, where f is a public function and K is a secret key. The authenticator should be a function of every bit of the message. The authenticator A is sent along with the original message M. The receiver, knowing f and K, can also compute the authenticator and compare it with the received one. If f is a good authenticator algorithm, only a sender who knows K could have sent the message. The authenticator here is also called a message authentication code.

Two *MAC* methods use the DES, one in cipher block chaining (CBC) mode, the other in cipher feedback mode (CFB). The CBC method enciphers the entire message, using as authenticator the most significant m bits of the last block of ciphertext. No other ciphertext is sent. The CFB method is similar, but the last block of ciphertext is fed into the DES once more, and m bits of that output become the authenticator.

The longer the authenticator, the less chance there is of a match for a fraudulent message. A 1993 standard uses 160 bits.

Hash functions and message digests. *One-way hash functions* were introduced in order to solve some problems of implementing digital signatures. A digital signature must be a function of the entire message, but messages can be very long, and the public key algorithms used are relatively slow. Also, certain attacks are possible if messages are broken into blocks before signing, and other attacks if signatures are simply used without hashing. The solution is to build a shorter fixed-length digest of the message. Message digests can also be used outside of a signature scheme to protect the integrity of messages or stored data. Instead of being a function of the message and a key, the authenticator here is a function only of the message: $A = h(M)$.

A one-way hash function is a public function, preferably simple and fast, with the following properties:

- It converts a message M of arbitrary length into a *message digest* $h(M)$ of a fixed length. The message digest is also called a *cryptographic checksum* or a *manipulation detection code* (MDC).
- It is one-way. That is, given a digest value, it is computationally infeasible to find the corresponding message.
- It is *collision-free*. That is, it is computationally infeasible to construct two different messages with the same digest—messages M and M' such that $h(M) = h(M')$.

This last property is needed to prevent the following situation. M' is a message that Alice would like Bob to sign (but that he would not want to sign) and M is a message that Bob *would* want to sign. If Alice can construct two messages M and M' with the same digest, and persuade Bob to sign M, she can obtain a signature that she can attach to M'. It turns out that a hash function must produce quite a large message digest to guard against a *birthday attack.*

A birthday attack (see Fig. 5.9) finds the collision (the fraudulent and legitimate messages with the same digest) by trying many variations. If the number of possible digest values is 2^n, a birthday attack has a reasonable chance of succeeding with $2^{n/2}$ variations of each message. For example, with a digest 32 bits long, the 50 percent chance corresponds to 216 variations, not an infeasible number. A digest of 160 bits is specified in current standards. Including timestamps or sequence numbers in messages makes it still harder for an opponent to find a useful collision.

Designing practical and secure one-way hash functions is difficult. Many of the proposed ones have severe weaknesses. For example, the MAC using cipher block chaining could be viewed as a *keyed hash function,* but it is not one-way. Also, using the DES, the message digest would be only 64 bits long—too small when used for digital signatures. Another method, called *DM,* also uses a block cipher, and exploits the fact that $E_K(M)$ is a one-way function of K (but not of M, or of K and M jointly). The method splits the message into blocks of 56 bits (the DES key length); each block is enciphered and then XOR-

The birthday attack is named after the well-known "birthday paradox" about how large a group must be to make it likely that two people have the same birthday. The answer is 23, which seems too small. The paradox is removed by considering that we are not looking for a specific birthday, but only for a match between any two birthdays. This corresponds to the match between possible fraudulent and legitimate messages.

Figure 5.9 The birthday attack.

ed with the previous output block. This function can be proved to be one-way, but it is not collision-free unless the block size is much larger than that of DES. Several hash functions based on modular arithmetic have not stood up well under scrutiny. Weaknesses were shown in the *MD4* algorithm of Rivest, which relies on complex linear functions that are usually hard to invert. Two improved algorithms based on MD4 are *MD5* and the *Secure Hash Algorithm* (SHA), which was developed by the NSA and adopted as a U.S. federal standard. The SHA accepts a message of any length up to 2^{64} bits and produces a 160-bit message digest.

Digital signatures. Message authentication using a secret key is a good solution if the parties are confident in the key's secrecy and if no disputes can arise, but such methods can never prove to a referee that a message came from the sender. Since both the sender and the receiver know the key, either one could have sent the message. Verifying the sender's identity and resolving disputes require digital signatures.

Digital signatures

Digital signatures authenticate electronic transactions much as handwritten signatures authenticate paper transactions. A digital signature on a message must guarantee the sender's identity to the receiver or referee. It must also vouch for the integrity of the message—that it was not altered since signing. Each party must be able to produce his digital signature easily and efficiently, and the method must guarantee that only he could have produced it. Unlike a handwritten signature, a person's digital signature is different for each message; it is a function that depends on every bit of the message. If the signature were not message-dependent, the message could be modified, or the signature could be attached to a different message entirely. Also unlike a handwritten signature, which a forger may learn to reproduce by studying many examples, many examples of a digital signature should not teach a forger anything.

Signing and verifying. Since a digital signature must prove identity, the signing process must use secret information that only the sender has. The verification process, in contrast, must use public information about the sender. If S_A is the signing transformation for Alice, then $S = S_A(M)$ is the signature of message M by Alice. The signature is concatenated to the message to form the *signed version* (M, S). The process V_A verifies the authenticity of messages sent by Alice; $V_A(M, S) = \text{True}$ if the verification succeeds. The verification must succeed, of course, only if Alice sent the message. That is, (1) $V_A(M, S)$ = True if and only if $S = S_A(M)$. This requirement is not enough, though. Alice must be assured that verification will not succeed for a forgery. No one but Alice, using her secret information, should be able to construct a message and signature that will be verified as sent by Alice. That is, (2) it must not be computationally feasible for anyone except Alice, using S_A, to construct (M, S) such that $V_A(M, S)$ = True.

Disputes. The cryptographic transformations must fit into a total digital signature scheme that includes agreements among the parties (sender, receiver, referee) about how messages will be verified and how disputes will be resolved. As digital signatures come into wider use, more standards and legislation surely will govern their use.

A scheme that allows resolution of disputes must have the following properties:

- The transformations S and V meet requirements (1) and (2) above. Since proof is often lacking, trust in a scheme comes from its resistance to cryptanalysis over the years.
- The verifying transformation is authentic. The referee must make sure that V_A is the same one Alice has agreed to, and that it has not been modified. (This can involve a trusted registry and protection by digital signatures; the verifying transformation of the registry itself can be widely published.)
- The referee is trustworthy.
- The secret signing transformation is secure. If it is not, signatures can be forged. The solution is many-faceted, involving measures like physical security and user identity authentication. If Alice discovers that the secret has been compromised, a protocol must be followed to allow her to repudiate signatures—but not earlier ones, or she could deliberately reveal the secret in order to renege on a transaction. Or, the secret could be kept from Alice herself by sealing it in hardware.

Digital signature based on RSA. The most important digital signature schemes are based on public key cryptography, primarily RSA and ElGamal.

Recall that encryption in RSA uses a one-way function

$$E(M) = M^e \bmod n$$

where e is public, and decryption uses a private value d:

$$D(C) = C^d \bmod n$$

The encryption and decryption exponents e and d are inverses of one another.

As originally proposed, the RSA signature scheme includes secrecy. To send a message to Alice, Bob first computes his signature S using his decryption algorithm. He then encrypts S using Alice's public encryption algorithm. The signed version of the message is simply S; Bob does not need to send M, since Alice can compute it from S by applying her decryption algorithm.

More commonly, RSA signatures are used without encryption, or separately from encryption, which is more efficient with DES or IDEA. (But RSA encryption and signatures can use the same public key, a definite advantage for key management.) Bob computes the signature $S = M^d \bmod n$, using his private exponent d. The signed version of the message is (M,S). Alice verifies the signature using Bob's public exponent e. Raising both sides to the eth power, we have $S^e = M^{de} \bmod n$ and, since d and e are inverses, $S^e = M \bmod n$. Alice can verify Bob's signature by computing $S^e \bmod n$ and comparing it with the received message M.

ElGamal scheme. The ElGamal public key cryptosystem was proposed for digital signatures and for secrecy. Secrecy is described first.

Public key cryptosystem. Like Diffie-Hellman, this system is based on the difficulty of discrete logarithms. For the whole system there is a fixed primitive element α of the finite field $GF(p)$, where p is a large prime. Alice chooses for her secret deciphering key an integer $x = x_A$. Her public enciphering key is $y = \alpha^x \bmod p$. To send a message to Alice, Bob chooses randomly an integer k, between 0 and $p-1$. Bob computes $\alpha^k \bmod p$ and $y^k \bmod p$. He sends to Alice the pair of integers

$$(\alpha^k \bmod p, My^k \bmod p)$$

Alice computes $y^k \bmod p$ by raising the first element of the message, $\alpha^k \bmod p$, to the power x. Only someone who knows x can do this. She then recovers the plaintext M by dividing the second element by $y^k \bmod p$.

The security of ElGamal is believed to depend on the difficulty of finding the secret key x given the public key $\alpha^x \bmod p$. This is the discrete logarithm problem.

Signature scheme. To sign a message Alice chooses randomly an integer k, between 0 and $p-1$, and relatively prime to $p-1$. It must not have been used for a previous message. She then computes two integers r and s, which together make up the signature.

$$r \equiv \alpha^k \bmod p$$

Alice finds s such that

$$M \equiv xr + ks \bmod (p-1)$$

The calculation for s first uses the Euclidean algorithm to find the inverse I such that

$$kI = 1 \bmod (p-1)$$

Then s can be computed as

$$s = I(M-xr) \bmod (p-1)$$

The signed version of the message is (M, r, s).

The recipient, Bob, uses Alice's public key, $y \equiv \alpha^x \bmod p$, to verify the signature. Verification succeeds if

$$\alpha^M \equiv y^r r^s \bmod p$$

Note that to make the scheme secure for all messages, the signature must be computed from a hash function of M:

$$s = I(h\,(M)-xr) \bmod (p-1)$$

Other methods for digital signatures. Fiat and Shamir developed a method for authenticating identity and then extended it for signatures. The scheme is based on the difficulty of taking square roots in modular arithmetic. The signing process is much faster than for RSA, but secret key sizes are greater.

Digital signatures could use conventional cryptosystems such as DES. One such scheme, known as Lamport-Diffie, uses up secret and public keys each time a signature is used; it is a "one-time" signature scheme. Merkle (1990) extended the idea to allow any number of signatures, with the size of the signature increasing as more signatures are generated. A scheme developed by Michael Rabin (1978) has security equivalent to that of an underlying block cipher (such as DES). The sender participates in the verification process by revealing part of the secret signing information. The full information is revealed only if a dispute arises, and then only to a referee. The drawback for this scheme is that the sender and receiver must exchange large numbers of secret keys (in encoded form). So far, digital signatures based on conventional ciphers have not seen practical use.

Digital Signature Standard. Amid much controversy (see Chap. 2), a standard for signatures was adopted in 1994. The *Digital Signature*

Standard (DSS) uses the *Digital Signature Algorithm* (DSA), which is based on the ElGamal method. In announcing the standard, NIST reviewed the arguments against it: "the selection process for the Digital Signature Algorithm (DSA) was not public; time provided for analysis of the DSA was not sufficient; the DSA may infringe on other patents; the DSA does not provide for secret key distribution; the DSA is incomplete because no hash algorithm is specified; the DSA is not compatible with international standards; the DSA is not secure; the DSA is not efficient." Some of these problems disappeared. More time was allowed; the Secure Hash Algorithm was specified; security was improved by allowing for a flexible key size, from 512 to 1024 bits. Remaining obstacles were the possible patent infringement, the lack of a public key infrastructure, and difficulty of interoperating with the widely used RSA digital signature.

Blind signatures. David Chaum introduced an extension to digital signatures called *blind signatures.* These signatures are blind in that the signer knows nothing about the content of the message. If the signer is a bank, a message carrying the bank's signature could be used as digital cash without the bank being able to trace the payments. The protocol is as follows, where n is the modulus:

1. Alice chooses a random *blinding factor* r, and she presents to the bank $Mr^e \pmod{n}$, where M is the note to be signed and e is the bank's public key.
2. The bank signs, using its private key d, obtaining $(Mr^e)^d$. Since d and e are inverses,

$$(Mr^e)^d = rM^d \pmod{n}$$

3. Alice divides out the blinding factor that she earlier multiplied in

$$(rM^d)/r = M^d \pmod{n}$$

and stores M^d to use as the signed note.

The secrecy of the blinded note depends completely on the unpredictability of Alice's random number.

Key Management

Key management is the whole process of handling cryptographic keys. It includes generating keys, distributing them, protecting them, and eventually destroying them. Key secrecy is essential because "...encipherment concentrates the risk of discovery on the key in order that the data can be handled more easily" (Davies and Price 1989). And key integrity is just as important. Key management is probably the main design problem for all applications of cryptography.

The simple cryptosystem diagram at the beginning of this chapter shows a "secure channel" for transmitting a secret key between the sender and receiver. Traditionally, the secure channel was a trusted courier, or certified mail; with these manual methods, the key management problem explodes for a large network. There are very many possible pairs of senders and receivers. Keys must be changed frequently. Key authenticity and (usually) secrecy must be assured. Expired keys must be destroyed. And of course any key management scheme must meet constraints on performance and storage. The threats to keys are disclosure, modification, substitution, insertion, and deletion.

Most key management schemes distinguish between *master keys* and *session keys.* A master key is used to encrypt other keys; it has a relatively long life or *cryptoperiod.* Session keys are used for just one communication session. Other terms for much the same distinction are *key encrypting key* and *data encrypting key.* Clearly the two kinds of keys need different management.

Key generation

For conventional secret key systems, a user must select a key or instruct hardware or software to generate a key. (At issue here is the initial secret key, and not the keystream that is generated for stream ciphers.) For simple protection an arbitrary selection of digits is workable. For a higher level of security the key should be as good as possible.

Randomness for keys. The ideal key is a truly random selection from the keyspace. (We qualify this statement later on.) The aspect of randomness that is most needed is unpredictability; an attacker should not be able to predict a key from information about previously used keys. Truly random methods exist, but they are practical only for keys that change rarely. Surprisingly, this highly technical problem has a manual solution: coin tosses or throws of the dice. Another solution is a random bit generator—a device that uses electrical noise as the truly random source. Other methods approximate randomness. One method measures—in microseconds—a human response time. Ciphers themselves can help generate random numbers; for example, one method encrypts (with a master key) a number representing the date and time.

Most data encrypting keys come from algorithms that generate sequences of pseudo-random numbers. The random number generator must start with a *seed* that is randomly selected by a truly random method, and the seed must be changed periodically.

Good and bad choices for keys. The ideal key is randomly selected, but with measures to avoid "bad" keys. The two most important encryption algorithms are both vulnerable if certain keys are chosen.

For the DES, four *weak keys* have been identified; encrypting twice with a weak key yields the plaintext without deciphering. Since there are only four such keys, key generation software can easily avoid them, and so can manual methods. Six pairs of *semiweak keys* are also bad choices. Encryption with one member of a pair followed by encryption with the other member yields the plaintext without decryption. Again, these bad keys are few and easily avoided.

For RSA, the prime numbers p and q must be chosen carefully. They should be random primes, selected by generating a random number and then testing if it is prime (as opposed to selecting from a table of primes). Primality testing can be done in polynomial time with probabilistic algorithms that have very small possibility of error. The two primes should not be extremely close in value, for that makes factoring easier. Their lengths should be similar, but not exactly the same. They should be at least 75 (decimal) digits long—100 if the encrypted material needs long-term protection. Other criteria relate to $\phi(n)$, which is $(p-1)\ (q-1)$. Problems in relation to $\phi(n)$ can be avoided by choosing *safe* primes; a prime p is safe if $(p-1)/2$ is also prime.

The exponents d and e also require careful choice. Small values reduce the time for encryption or decryption; for a given modulus pq, the time is roughly proportional to the exponent length. For small devices (such as smart cards) communicating with large systems, one would like the device to have a short secret exponent d and the large system a short public exponent e. Unfortunately, small exponents reduce security. If d is too small it can be found by exhaustive testing. If e is small, other attacks are possible. For greatest security, both d and e should be large, but for speed they should be small. Most RSA implementations adopt a compromise.

Key distribution

Key distribution gets encryption keys to where they will be used. Distribution must be secure, protecting key integrity and confidentiality, and also efficient.

Distribution by secure channel. Encryption keys are still distributed over secure channels, manually or with partial automation. When keys are changed, the new keys are written on paper or portable media and carried or mailed to their destination. Then they are entered into the equipment manually. The principle of separation of duty can be used to good advantage here: the key can be divided into two parts that are carried and entered separately. Manual distribution works where the volume is low, the couriers can be trusted, and the key entry cannot be spied on. The method is slow and costly, and for many environments it is not secure. A semiautomatic alternative is the *key gun* or *key transport module,* a portable module into which encryption keys are stored for later loading into devices such as automatic teller machines (ATMs) or point-of-sale terminals. These modules are tamper-resistant, and there are safeguards to ensure that each device gets the right key.

Manual distribution breaks down as volume grows. An authentication system formerly used by banks involved secret data analogous to encryption keys, and these data were mailed in two separate registered mailings. The new key was used only when the recipient's return receipts came back. For large mailings this method was slow, unreliable, and insecure; distributing new keys was riskier than not changing keys.

For cryptographic keys, a natural solution is to distribute them over the insecure channel, protecting them by encryption.

Concepts and techniques for key distribution. Since keys distributed over insecure channels need protection, they are encrypted with other keys. Some schemes use two levels of keys—those used to encrypt data and those used to encrypt keys. Other schemes have a *key hierarchy* of three or more levels, with all but the lowest level used for key encryption.

The simplest key distribution protocols are *point-to-point:* two communicators agree on a key for their communications. This is fine for some applications, but unworkable for the general problem of communicating over a network. If a network has n users or communicating entities, potentially $n(n-1)$ keys must be agreed on, distributed, and stored. A more practical approach uses a *key distribution center* (KDC) that specializes in providing keys at the request of communicating parties. Key distribution can be centralized—for example, at one node of a network—or the key distribution service can be distributed over various nodes of the network. A related entity is the *key translation center,* which does not generate keys, but receives a session key chosen by one party and changes its encryption for use by both parties. Ideally, each network entity has a secure *key management facility* for the cryptographic equipment and operations and for *keying material.* (Keying material includes the cryptographic keys and all the other material used to manage them.) This facility could be, for example, a secure room containing a cryptographic server, or a special hardware unit of a mainframe computer. For a small device it could be a tamper-resistant enclosure.

Key notarization helps ensure that keys intended for one purpose are not intercepted and used for another purpose. The purpose (sender and receiver) of a session key is stamped into a master key before it is used to encrypt the session key. To guard against reuse of keys, *key offset* is used: the master key is modified with a counter that is incremented for each use of the master key.

A key management standard. Two of the most complete key management designs are the IBM key management scheme and the ANSI standard for wholesale banking (ANSI 1985), which we describe here. The ANSI standard was also adopted with some modifications as an ISO standard (ISO 1988) and as a U.S. standard for government use (NIST 1992). The standard covers messages between banks, and between banks and governments or corporate customers.

The standard allows either a two-level or three-level key hierarchy. The three-level hierarchy consists of data keys (KDs), key encrypting keys (KKs) at the optional level, and highest-level key encrypting keys (KKMs). Data keys are used to encrypt or authenticate data, and also to authenticate messages used in key distribution protocols. If two banks, or a bank and a key distribution center, share KKMs, they can exchange keys over the network. The KKMs are generated, distributed, and entered manually according to guidelines of the standard, including dual-control measures. KKs are distributed over the network. Notarization and offset are specified by the standard. The standard addresses three key distribution environments: point-to-point, key distribution center, and key translation center. We describe a protocol using a key distribution center (see Fig. 5.10).

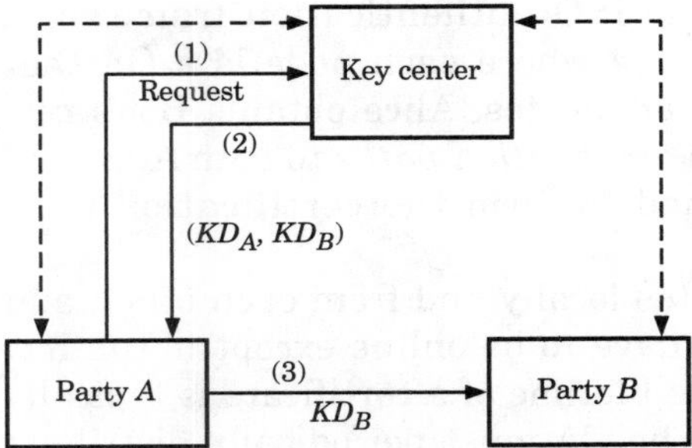

Figure 5.10 Key distribution with a key distribution center.

Before two banks A and B can communicate, each must share a KKM pair with the center. ("Pair" because KKMs are double-length keys, used for triple encryption as described in the section on DES.) Bank A sends to the center a request indicating the types of keys needed. The KDC response to A includes two sets of keys. The keys in the two sets are identical, but they are notarized and encrypted differently: one with a KKM shared by the KDC and Bank A and the other with a KKM shared by the KDC and Bank B. Bank A then sends B's encrypted keys to B.

Key management for public key systems

Public keys are sometimes considered simpler to manage because secrecy is not a concern, so that keys can be distributed over insecure channels. Integrity is a concern, however. When Alice wishes to communicate with Bob she must be assured that she is using Bob's correct and authentic public key. If she receives a signed message she must be assured that the signature is authentic and still valid.

Certificates and certification authorities. The usual solution for public key and digital signature systems is for users to register their public keys with a trusted registry or *certification authority* (CA). The CA distributes *certificates,* which are public keys carrying the digital signature of the CA. To verify a certificate, a user needs only the public key of the CA; that key can be published in many ways and places. Since certificates are protected (by the CA signature) against tampering, they can be stored in local directory servers with lower levels of security than the CA. Certificates can also be passed among users and stored by them. Alice can ask Bob for his certificate. Registering a new public key must follow an authentication protocol and should include a delay to allow the user to make sure the registration is correct before it takes effect.

The CA itself can be distributed; in fact it normally would be distributed. The X.509 standard, the ISO authentication framework, specifies a *directory information tree* where each node is a CA that maintains and distributes some certificates. Alice obtains Bob's certificate by finding a node that has *certification paths* to both Alice and Bob. These paths are then joined to form the certification path between Alice and Bob.

Since users can obtain certificates locally and from each other, and can cache them, the CA does not have to be online except to confirm that a certificate is still valid. (The lifetime of a certificate is typically a few months to a year or two.) The CA must periodically distribute lists of certificates that have become invalid, so that servers and users can update their caches. If each revocation list carries the date of the next issue, users can determine if they are looking at the latest list. An attacker who compromises the CA can forge bogus certificates. This compromise is less dangerous than compromise of a conventional key distribution center, because the attacker must use active wiretaps that are likely to be detected rapidly.

A certificate contains more than just the public key. The key is combined with other significant information before signing. The following information is specified for the X.509 certificate:

- Identifier of the digital signature algorithm—for example, RSA or DSA
- Name of issuer of certificate
- Validity period (start and finish dates)
- Name of user
- Public key of user
- Identifier of the public key algorithm

All this information is bound together by the signature.

Securing private and public keys. Users must securely store their public and private keys, and they must keep the private keys secret. If Alice's private key is revealed (or if she so claims) she could repudiate messages she has signed. Most of the protocols proposed for preventing fraudulent repudiation are inconvenient or insecure, and only partly effective. A better solution is to keep the key secret from Alice herself. This can be done by a hardware device such as a smart card.

Key escrow

A controversial issue (see Chap. 2) has been how to arrange for law enforcement agencies to wiretap encrypted communications. Rivest (1992a) suggested *escrowed secret keys*—a scheme where users deposit their keys with a trusted third party. More generally, a *key escrow system* is any system "that will allow an authorized third party to eavesdrop, while continuing to protect the information from all other third parties" (Ganesan 1996: 33). Since encrypted data may become unavailable because users lose (or withhold) secret keys, organizations need safeguards that allow for key recovery. Key escrow provides controlled protection against this risk.

The Escrowed Encryption Standard. A key escrow scheme and the *Escrowed Encryption Standard* (EES) were developed by the U.S. government to provide strong encryption for confidentiality while also allowing wiretap by law enforcement officials. The scheme allows law enforcement agents (once they obtain a secret key) to understand encrypted telephone calls. The standard also pertains to fax and data transmission. It specifies how encryption is to be implemented in hardware devices that go into secure telephones or security products for PCs.

An EES device implements the SKIPJACK encryption/decryption algorithm, and it identifies itself by transmitting a *Law Enforcement Access Field* (LEAF). If the LEAF is intercepted and used with the secret key, a conversation can be decrypted. At the factory, each secret key is split into two pieces; then, each piece is placed with a different escrow agent. The agents are to release keys only to law enforcement officials who present appropriate authorization. The SKIPJACK and LEAF algorithms are secret and can be implemented only in tamper-resistant hardware.

An EES device implements SKIPJACK and a LEAF Creation Method. The device holds a Device Unique ID (UID), an 80-bit secret Device Unique Key (KU), and an 80-bit secret Family Key that is common to all EES devices. For each conversation, two devices agree on an 80-bit session key, KS. The 128-bit LEAF is constructed from KS (encrypted under KU), UID, and an authenticator, all encrypted under the Family Key. Thus the session key is encrypted twice. The LEAF is transmitted with each communication. The same session key encrypts transmitted data and decrypts received data. (If Alice's line is tapped, and she calls Bob, agents can understand what Bob says.)

Law enforcement agents use a Decrypt Processor, which decrypts the LEAF, revealing the UID. The UID is presented, along with evidence of legal authorization, to the two escrow agents, who release their KU components. The two components are loaded into the Decrypt Processor, which then decrypts the session key and uses it to decrypt the conversation.

The Clipper chip implements the EES and is used in the AT&T 3600 secure telephone. The Capstone chip implements the EES, the DSS, a public key algorithm, random number generation, and other features. Capstone is embedded in the Fortezza card. In 1995, Fortezza cost $98, and the DoD was ordering large quantities for users of the Defense Message System.

In 1994, Matt Blaze pointed out software techniques that allow EES devices to communicate without transmitting valid LEAFs. The attacks rely on trying many LEAFs until one is found that the device accepts as valid. Some techniques would allow communication only between two rogue parties. Others would allow a rogue to interoperate with legitimate EES users. This is more significant because such a rogue would have all the function and secrecy advantages of the

EES without the wiretap potential. The attacks are impractical for voice communications, but they could get around law-enforcement decryption of email. Devices could defend against the attacks by making it more time-consuming to check a LEAF, limiting the number of tries, or (a much more fundamental change) increasing the length of the LEAF authenticator.

Cryptographic Protocols

Cryptographic applications rely on secure protocols. A cryptographic protocol is an algorithm that the parties to a cryptographic application jointly execute. New applications of cryptography demand new protocols, which must be both secure and efficient. Often the protocols are subtle, complex, and multilayered. Simpler protocols for message secrecy and authenticity are building blocks for more complex protocols.

"What is not obvious,...and indeed often comes as a shock to the protocol designer or user, is that a protocol can be completely subverted without impeaching, or even eroding, the security of the underlying cryptoalgorithm" (Simmons 1994: 56). The security of a cryptographic application depends on a whole framework that includes:

- The strength of the cryptographic algorithms or cryptosystems, such as RSA or DES. (The application cannot be more secure than these, and it may be less secure.)
- The correctness of the protocol and its adequacy for the application
- The implementations of algorithms and protocol
- The entire context, including physical security, hardware and software security, and user behavior

A simple cryptographic protocol

A protocol for distributing secret keys is a simple example. The protocol, which involves a trusted key distribution center, is

1. The KDC delivers a randomly chosen secret key to each user, using a secure channel. Alice receives K_A.
2. When Alice wishes to communicate with Bob she sends the KDC a request for a key to use for the communication.
3. The KDC randomly chooses a key K_{AB} and builds a message containing a header and K_{AB}. The KDC encrypts the message with Alice's key and sends the ciphertext to Alice. It encrypts the same message with Bob's key K_B and sends that ciphertext to Bob.

4. Alice and Bob each decrypt their messages from the KDC and they now have a secret key for subsequent communication.

Even this very simple protocol illustrates a common hazard. The protocol is less secure against a ciphertext-only attack than the underlying cryptosystem because an eavesdropper could obtain the same plaintext encrypted with two different keys.

Arbitrated and nonarbitrated protocols

Many transactions involve parties who do not trust each other completely. When we send an important document we use certified mail with return receipt so that the recipient cannot later deny receiving the document. Documents may also be delivered by a process server, a third party who vouches for the document's receipt. The parties to electronic transactions also need protection against cheating. An *arbitrated protocol* involves a trusted system component called an *arbitrator.* An arbitrator participates in the steps of the protocol, in contrast to an *adjudicator* (such as a human judge), who resolves later disputes. The arbitrator is on-line. [This useful terminology, suggested by DeMillo and Merritt (1983), is not standard. The terms *arbitrator* and *referee* are both used for the third party, on-line or not. *Referee* here means arbitrator *or* adjudicator.] Using an arbitrator can make a protocol simpler. But setting up the arbitrator may be difficult and costly, the parties may not trust the same arbitrator, and the arbitrated protocol is usually less efficient.

The digital signature protocol that has been described is a *true signature* protocol, with the sender transmitting the signature directly to the receiver. To review, the protocol is

1. Alice, using her signing transformation S_A, forms a signature $S = S_A(M)$ and sends to Bob the signed version (M, S).
2. Bob applies Alice's public verifying transformation V_A to the signed version to verify the authenticity of the message. He retains the signed version for use in case of disputes.

This protocol has two serious problems. The first is that Alice could publicize her secret transformation and disown the message. The second problem is that the verifying transformation must be a trapdoor one-way function. Cryptography relies on a very few of these, and future research could break them.

An *arbitrated signature* protocol solves these two problems. Every signed message goes through an arbitrator that verifies its origin and integrity, timestamps it, and forwards it to the receiver. A message cannot be disowned, because the arbitrator has validated it. Trapdoor one-way functions are not needed; any encryption method can authenticate the sender to the arbitrator.

The following is one example of an arbitrated signature protocol. Each user shares a secret key with the arbitrator. Bob shares K_B with the arbitrator.

1. Bob wants to send a signed message to Carol. He signs message M by encrypting it with K_B so that $S_B(M) = E_{K_B}(M)$ and sends the signed version S to the arbitrator.
2. The arbitrator decrypts M and, if it is a valid message for Bob to have sent, forms the new message (Bob, M, S), encrypts that with K_C, and sends it to Carol.
3. Carol decrypts the message from the arbitrator and, if message M from Bob is acceptable to her, accepts S as Bob's signature of M. Since she cannot verify the signature directly, she must rely on the arbitrator. She can produce the signature to settle a dispute.

Although arbitrated signatures solve the problems of true signatures, they introduce other problems. The arbitrator must be trusted to behave correctly and to ensure the secrecy of keys and the integrity of all its information. Using an arbitrator makes the protocol less efficient and may introduce a bottleneck.

Some protocols

Researchers have designed intriguing protocols. For example, "mental poker" allows the parties to play poker without cards and without cheating. Coin flipping "by telephone" allows the parties to jointly generate a random number, without completely trusting each other and without using an arbitrator. Research protocols have applications such as verifying treaty compliance or authenticating users. Perhaps even more important, the research leads to better understanding about protocols in general.

Secret sharing. Protocols for *sharing secrets* seek to ensure that users do not lose their secret keys, and at the same time to protect key secrecy. The idea is to divide a secret (such as a cryptographic key) into a number of pieces and to give each piece to a different party. The secret is put together again by combining some of these pieces; not all of them are needed. If the secret is divided into ten pieces, and eight pieces are needed to reconstitute it, two parties can lose their pieces and the secret will not be lost. This use of redundancy generalizes to protect against any unreliability or lack of trustworthiness. Some encryption products, for example, allow emergency decryption authority to be split among a number of trustees; some threshold number of the trustees must agree.

Shared secrets can also mean *shared control* over actions, or separation of responsibility. This is seen clearly in the military dual control of weapons, where two persons each have secret information and both pieces are needed to authorize use. Either piece of information alone gives no control at all.

It is said that l parties *k-share* a secret c if:

1. Each party knows some information a_i that none of the other parties knows.
2. The secret c can be computed easily from any k of the a_i's.
3. The secret c cannot be determined from any $k-1$ of the a_i's.

[This is also called a k-out-of-l secret scheme, or a (k,l) *threshold* scheme.] The schemes that have been developed are unconditionally secure; even infinite computing power gives an attacker no advantage over a guess. Simmons (1992c) and Salomaa (1990) describe the mathematics behind shared secret schemes. Here we give an idea of their properties and uses.

Shared control schemes must identify which subsets (or *concurrences*) of the parties may control the actions. The scheme could require unanimous consent (k out of k), for example. In a multilevel scheme, the parties have differing control capabilities. For example, two bank vice-presidents or one vice-president and two senior tellers could approve a large funds transfer. Treaty verification would use a compartmented scheme, where two parties from each country have to agree on an action.

When the parties do not completely trust each other or any central arbitrator or authority, they can jointly set up a shared control scheme. Each party contributes to determining the secret (but keeps her contribution secret), and each party distributes her secret contribution among the other parties, setting up only the concurrences that she trusts.

Oblivious transfer. Many protocols are concerned with transferring information securely to accomplish a goal. The goal may include keeping some party in the dark about just what information was transferred.

Suppose that Alice wants to transfer a secret to Bob in such a way that she will not know whether Bob got the secret, but Bob will know. Or, Alice has several secrets and wants to transfer one of them so that only Bob knows which one. These properties might be needed, for example, in negotiations between countries where one country (Bob's) does not want to disclose its ignorance about a matter. The countries may not be able to agree on a trusted arbitrator. A nonarbitrated protocol was invented by Rabin for such *oblivious transfer.* The mathematical basis for the protocol is the fact that if we know two square roots mod n of the same number we can factor n.

1. Alice selects two large primes p and q and sends to Bob their product $n = pq$.
2. Bob randomly chooses a number x between 1 and n and sends Alice $y = x^2 \bmod n$.
3. Alice computes the four square roots of y mod n. (She can do this because she knows the factors of n.) Two of the roots are x and $-x$, but Alice does not know which two, since she only knows x^2. Alice sends one of the roots to Bob, with .5 probability that it is x or $-x$, and .5 probability that it is not.
4. If Bob receives x or $-x$ he gets no new information. Otherwise he now has two square roots of the same number y mod n, and he can factor n.

The information being transferred (or not) here is the factorization, which could represent any information encrypted by using RSA. Extensions of oblivious transfer have been applied to sending certified mail and signing contracts. This protocol and many others use randomness to achieve their objectives.

Zero-knowledge proofs. Alice may wish to prove something to Bob without revealing any other information. For example, she may want to prove that she is Alice, but if she sent Bob identifying information (such as her password) Bob could use that information to impersonate her. Perhaps she trusts Bob, but an eavesdropper who obtained the password could also impersonate Alice. She wants to prove to Bob that she has the password, but without revealing it. This is an application of *zero-knowledge proofs,* from the theory of interactive proof systems.

An interactive proof system assumes a *prover P* and a *verifier V.* The prover tries to convince the verifier that some assertion is true or that he possesses some information (such as the password). Interactive proof systems often involve multiple rounds of a protocol—as many as needed to convince the verifier with the desired certainty.

Zero-knowledge proofs of identity allow a community of users to authenticate themselves to one another. The scheme relies on the infeasibility of computing square roots modulo a large composite integer without knowing its factors. Each user has a pair (I, S) where I is the user's public identification and S is his secret key. The goal is for a user (the prover) to convince another user (the verifier) that he knows S, without revealing anything else about S. We give here a general idea of the protocol.

A trusted center starts things off by generating two large primes p and q that satisfy a certain congruence. The center keeps p and q secret but publishes their product m. Each user randomly generates I and S, which are vectors of numbers of length t, so that the product of an element of I and the square of the corresponding element of S satisfy a certain congruence. The prover and verifier then interact in four protocol steps for each of t rounds of the protocol. A random number generated by the prover in Step 1 masks the values sent so that the verifier cannot learn S. In Step 4 the verifier tries to confirm a congruence that would hold only if the right S was used. If this confirmation fails on any round, the verifier rejects. Otherwise another round is performed.

Zero-knowledge proofs of identity apply well to authentication of smart cards, since little computation is done by the prover (the card). The length of the key S can be chosen to provide the amount of security desired, with a longer key requiring more rounds of the protocol.

Design and analysis of protocols

Cryptographers have no sure formula for designing secure protocols. Failures can come from many sources. The protocol logic can be flawed, or the protocol just may not consider all the relevant factors in the applications's environment. For example, the simplest protocols for public key systems do not consider the possibility of an attack on the public key directory. An opponent capable of such an attack can substitute another public key for Bob's, preventing Bob from getting the messages Alice intended for him.

Protocol failures and lessons learned. Moore (1992) has collected telling examples of well-known protocols that turned out to be faulty. An authentication protocol for manipulation detection codes was even proposed as a U.S. standard before the realization that it failed to detect important possible manipulations. This method takes an exclusive-OR sum of the blocks of a message before they are encrypted with DES. The receiver checks this authenticator after decrypting. The blocks of the message could be rearranged without affecting the authenticator at all. Any number of blocks could be inserted, as long as they were in identical pairs. An attacker could perform any kind of manipulation that did not affect the exclusive-OR sum. The point is that, although such exposures are acceptable for many applications, a widely used or standard protocol should be clear about what attacks it can and cannot withstand.

A second example pertains to RSA used with a common modulus. Generating keys in RSA involves picking two large primes and calculating their product, the modulus. Some proposed key distribution schemes use a common modulus for the whole system. Moore describes three attacks on this scheme. If the same message is sent to two users whose public exponents are relatively prime, an eavesdropper who knows the modulus can recover the plaintext from the two ciphertexts. This is serious, but does not break the cryptosystem. The other two attacks do. Anyone who has one pair (public exponent, secret exponent) can factor the modulus and thus break the cryptosystem. Since every user has such a pair, the system is totally insecure. Finally, a user can use his own public and private exponents, along with the public exponent of another user, to compute the private exponent of the other user.

These and other examples exhibit three types of weaknesses:

1. Weakness in the cryptoalgorithm when used according to the protocol. Examples are the MDC or RSA with a common modulus.
2. Failure to consider some broad principle. For example, public key encryption should not be used when the message space has very low entropy.
3. Failure to clarify limits on the security that the protocol can provide.

Gustavus Simmons (1994) has listed three rules for cryptanalysis of protocols:

- Enumerate all the properties of the quantities involved, including those implicitly assumed in the use of the protocol. For example, a party is supposed to construct a number as a product of two primes. What if the number is not of that form?
- Take nothing for granted. For each possible violation of a property, examine the protocol to see if this affects the outcome.
- If violating a property can affect the outcome, determine if this can be exploited to advance a meaningful deception.

These rules reflect the general principle: "Never assume anything you can't enforce or verify."

Designers should also consider how the protocol stands up to attacks using ciphertext collections where the keys are related in some way, or the plaintexts are related in some way. Specifically, an opponent may have collections of ciphertext where:

1. Various keys are used to encrypt the same message.

2. The same key is used to encrypt different messages that are related in a known way.
3. Various keys are used to encrypt known variations of the same message.

Formal approaches. The maxims of Moore and Simmons extend and refine the system-theoretic approach. More formal approaches take off from the methods used to verify the correctness of computer systems (including secure operating systems). A system is specified in a formal specification language, then theorems are proved about it. Both the specification itself and the theorems contribute to better understanding of the system. Cryptographers can build a formal model of the security to be provided by a cryptographic application, a model that tries to capture the real-world needs of the application. Potentially, the security of the application protocols can be proved with respect to the model. Specialized logics are used for analyzing the protocols, and automated tools can uncover vulnerabilities or help prove that a protocol is secure.

Summary

Cryptography is the art of transforming information to ensure its secrecy or authenticity or both. *Cryptanalysis* is concerned with breaking or defeating cryptography. A message before transformation is called the *plaintext,* and after transformation the *ciphertext.* Transforming plaintext into ciphertext is *encryption,* and transforming the ciphertext into the original plaintext is *decryption.* The transformation algorithm has parameters called *keys,* which are often secret.

Cryptography theory was first developed by Claude Shannon, building on information theory. Later cryptographic methods have depended on work in number theory and computational complexity.

Attacks are classified according to how much information the cryptanalyst has. The cryptanalyst always is assumed to have the entire ciphertext and to know the encryption algorithm; only the key is secret. The easiest to defend against is a ciphertext-only attack. Harder is a known-plaintext attack, and still harder is a chosen-plaintext attack, where the cryptanalyst can obtain the ciphertext corresponding to any plaintext.

There are two main types of cryptosystems: conventional and public key. In conventional systems a single secret key, known to both the sender and receiver, is used for both encryption and decryption. In public key cryptography the receiver's encryption key is published for all senders to use; the receiver decrypts with a private secret key.

In classical cryptography, a cryptosystem is defined as a set of transformations from a message space to a ciphertext space. The key equivocation measures the uncertainty about the key when the ciphertext is known. The message equivocation measures the uncertainty about the plaintext message if the ciphertext is known. A cryptosystem has perfect secrecy if the probability of a message M if ciphertext C is intercepted equals the a priori probability of M. Very few cryptosystems provide perfect secrecy.

Cryptanalytic attacks can exploit redundancy and other statistical properties of messages. Shannon suggested two principles of cipher design to make such attacks more difficult. Diffusion spreads the influence of a plaintext character over many ciphertext characters. Confusion hides the way that the ciphertext statistics depend on the plaintext statistics.

Inventing a new cryptosystem, especially a public key system, means inventing or exploiting problems that are hard to solve. For example, factoring a large number is hard. The theory of computational complexity classifies algorithms according to their difficulty.

Cryptosystems are classified as block or stream ciphers. A *block cipher* divides the plaintext into blocks and applies the same encryption algorithm (with the same key) to each block. A *stream cipher* applies encryption to the individual plaintext digits, using a sequence of digits called the *keystream*.

All public-key systems depend on one-way functions, and many other systems use them as well. For a one-way function $f(x)$, it is easy to compute $f(x)$, but computationally infeasible to compute x from $f(x)$.

The *Data Encryption Standard* (DES) is a block cipher with 64-bit blocks. The key is 56 bits long. After an initial permutation, the input block goes through 16 rounds of encryption and substitution. The DES algorithm is a basic building block that different applications use in different ways. A companion standard defines four modes of operation for the DES. An experimental attack on DES succeeded in 1994, using linear cryptanalysis. Another attack uses differential cryptanalysis. Exhaustive search is expected to become practical before long. However, triple DES encryption with three keys remains strong protection.

IDEA (International Data Encryption Algorithm) is designed to be more secure than DES against brute-force attacks and differential cryptanalysis. The key is 128 bits. SKIPJACK is the encryption algorithm used in the Escrowed Encryption Standard. It uses an 80-bit key and has 32 rounds of processing.

The idea of public key cryptography was introduced by Diffie and Hellman (1976). A public key system is used in the following way for transmitting secret messages. Alice generates a pair of inverse transformations, E_A and D_A. The deciphering transformation D is kept secret, and the enciphering transformation E is published, to be used by anyone who wants to communicate with Alice in secrecy. E_A is Alice's public key. Anyone can encrypt with E_A, but only Alice can decrypt, because only she has the secret key D_A.

The most widely used public key system is RSA, which uses multiplication as the one-way function. RSA is much slower than DES, so it is used for key management and digital signatures, but not for bulk encryption.

Authentication means making sure that some entity is what it purports to be. Threats include: impersonating the sender, substitution or insertion of messages, forgery, reneging, and replay of a previously sent message. The authenticity of the parties must be guaranteed, and the integrity of the message contents must be protected. One authentication method computes a value that is a function of the message and a secret key. Another uses a message digest produced by a one-way hash function.

A *digital signature* is a cryptographically computed value that is attached to a message. Like a handwritten signature, a digital signature identifies the sender and prevents repudiation. It also confirms the integrity of the message. The signing process uses secret information that only the sender has, and the verification process uses public information about the sender. The most important schemes are based on public key cryptography, primarily RSA and ElGamal, whose security is based on the difficulty of the discrete logarithm problem. The Digital Signature Standard is based on the ElGamal method.

Key management is the whole process of handling cryptographic keys, including generating keys, distributing them, protecting them, and eventually destroying them. A master key is used to encrypt other keys. A session key is used for just one communication session. The ideal secret key is a truly random selection from the keyspace. DES and RSA are both vulnerable if certain keys are chosen. Keys are distributed over insecure channels, encrypted with other keys. A key distribution center (KDC) specializes in providing keys to communicating parties. For public key systems, users register their public keys with a certification authority. The CA distributes certificates, which are public keys carrying the digital signature of the CA.

A key escrow scheme and the Escrowed Encryption Standard (EES) were developed by the U.S. government to provide strong encryption for confidentiality while also allowing wiretapping by law enforcement officials. The scheme allows law enforcement agents (once they obtain a secret key) to understand encrypted telephone calls. At the factory, each secret key is split into two pieces; then, each piece is placed with a different escrow agent. The agents are to release keys only to law enforcement officials who present appropriate authorization.

Cryptographic applications rely on secure protocols. A cryptographic protocol is an algorithm that the parties to a cryptographic application jointly execute. The security of a cryptographic application depends on a whole framework that includes: the strength of the cryptographic algorithms, the correctness and adequacy of the protocol, the implementations of algorithms and protocol, and the entire application context. An arbitrated protocol involves a trusted system component called an *arbitrator.* Protocols for sharing secrets divide a secret into a number of pieces and give each piece to a different party. The secret is put together again by combining some of these pieces. Zero-knowledge proofs prove something without revealing any other information. Experience with protocol failures has led to the design principle: Never assume anything you can't enforce or verify. Researchers are developing more formal approaches to protocol design and analysis.

Bibliographic Notes

General cryptography

Davies and Price (1989) is an excellent single source on implementing and using cryptography. Schneier (1996) is a comprehensive reference aimed at the implementor of cryptographic algorithms. The book edited by Simmons (1992a) provides overview articles by experts in the different subfields of cryptography. Rhee (1994) is a textbook and reference with many diagrams and examples. Brassard (1988) provides a highly readable overview. Stallings (1995) is mainly about cryptography. Kaliski (1993) surveys encryption standards. Welsh (1988) provides a mathematical introduction to cryptography, with proofs and exercises. Denning (1982) is an excellent source for the older material, with many examples and exercises. Another cryptography textbook is by Seberry and Pieprzyk (1989). The surveys by Diffie and Hellman (1979) and Simmons (1979) are still valuable. Current research appears in the proceedings of two annual conferences—CRYPTO and EUROCRYPT, in the *Journal of Cryptology* and *Cryptologia,* and in computing journals. Frequently asked questions are answered clearly in Sci.crypt (1994). Alice and Bob were introduced (to cryptography) by Rivest, Shamir, and Adleman (1978).

Theoretical foundations

Koblitz (1987) covers the number theory behind cryptography; a second edition was published in 1994. A brief tutorial on number theory can be found in Salomaa (1990). See Feigenbaum (1992) for an overview and formal definitions of interactive proof systems and zero-knowledge. Massey (1992) describes the historical work characteristic.

Cryptographic techniques

Boyd (1991) gives the effect of compression on unicity distance. See Hellman (1979) for examples and insight into the use of one-way functions. DES is described in NIST (1993). Our description of the steps for DES rounds follows Konheim (1981). Davies and Price (1989) describe the modes of operation and give guidelines for implementing and using them. Our description of IDEA is based on Stallings (1995) and Schneier (1994). Much of our discussion of stream ciphers follows Rueppel (1992), but with different notation. Rueppel gives a detailed survey of keystream generators. Zeng et al. (1991) discuss the difficulties of designing good ones. The cited encryption rates for DES and RSA are from Beth, Frisch, and Simmons (1992), Landau et al.(1994), and Schneier (1994). RC5 is described by Rivest (1995). The Commercial Data Masking Facility is described by Johnson et al. (1994). See Brickell and Odlyzko (1992) for a review of DES cryptanalysis results and Denning (1990) for a history of studies of DES security. Linear cryptanalysis is described by Matsui (1994a, 1994b). Langford and Hellman (1994) describe an attack that uses techniques from both differential and linear cryptanalysis, but uses fewer plaintexts.

Public key cryptography

For a recapitulation of the first decade of public key cryptography see Diffie (1992). A 1991 workshop report (Beth, Frisch, and Simmons 1992) compactly summarizes the status and issues in public key cryptography. More complete sources are Nechvatal (1992) and Salomaa (1990). The fascinating patent history of public key systems is reviewed by Landau et al. (1994) and Garfinkel (1995). In 1996, Security Dynamics agreed to acquire RSA Data Security, holder of the RSA patents. For more on exponents and other RSA considerations, see Nechvatal (1992), Salomaa (1990), and Wiener (1990). Factoring of the 129-digit number was done over 8 months by a worldwide team coordinated by Arjen Lenstra. Lenstra and other team members received a $100 prize that had been offered by *Scientific American* magazine in 1977. Lin, Chang, and Lee (1995) propose a public-key system based on a different mathematical problem. Timing attacks were first described by Kocher (1995).

Authentication of information

Our description of threats to message integrity follows the model of Simmons (1992b). Criteria for authenticator algorithms are described by Davies and Price (1989). More on the birthday paradox can be found in Davies and Price (1989), Mitchell, Piper, and Wild (1992), and Nechvatal (1992). A 1991 workshop concluded that "construction of a 'good' cryptographic hash function still is an unsolved problem" (Beth, Frisch, and Simmons 1992: 31). The MD5 Message-Digest Algorithm is described in Rivest (1992b). The Secure Hash Algorithm was adopted as a standard in 1993. A flaw was found, and a revised standard was issued (NIST 1995). A message authentication standard for financial institutions is described in ANSI (1986). Use of the DES for message authentication codes is described in NIST (1985). Lomas and Christianson (1995) describe a use for hash functions that are designed to be collision-rich rather than collision-free. Our discussion of digital signatures is based mainly on the survey by Mitchell, Piper, and Wild (1992). Fiat and Shamir's signature method is described in their 1987 paper and in Davies and Price (1989). Lamport-Diffie is described by Davies and Price (1989) and Diffie and Hellman (1976). The DSA is described in NIST (1994a). For solutions to the deliberate-compromise problem, see Denning (1983) and Mitchell, Piper, and Wild (1992) Sec. 2.7. The use of blind signatures is described by Chaum (1985, 1992) and in Chap. 10. Blind signature protocols are described by Schneier (1994).

Key management

See Matyas and Meyer (1978) for randomness by coin toss. The IBM key management scheme is described by Ehrsam et al. (1978) and Matyas and Meyer (1978). Our description of the ANSI key management protocol is highly simplified. More detailed descriptions of the ANSI and ISO standards are given by Balenson (1985) and Davies and Price (1989). Fumy and Landrock (1993) provide a systematic overview of key management principles. See Nechvatal (1992) for nonrepudiation protocols, and Davies and Price (1989) for hardware protection of keys. Kapidzic and Davidson (1995) describe a complete certificate management system. Bahreman (1995) describes a toolkit for building a certification hierarchy "from the bottom up." Chokhani (1994) describes concepts for a public key infrastructure for the U.S. government. Denning and Branstad (1996) place key escrow systems in a taxonomy. Commercial schemes are described by Walker et al. (1996) and Maher (1996). Our description of the EES is based on the standard (NIST 1994b) and on Denning and Smid (1994). The EES also is described by Denning (1995). Lomas and Roe (1994) describe how a law enforcement officer could forge a call from a tapped EES device. Cryptography policy, including the EES, is discussed in Chap. 2. FIPS Publication 140-1 (NIST 1994c) sets out requirements for incorporating cryptographic algorithms (DES, EES, and DSS) into hardware and software modules. It considers physical security, software security, authentication of operators, and key management.

Cryptographic protocols

Syverson (1994) provides a taxonomy of replay attacks on protocols. Kailar (1995) proposes a framework for analyzing protocols that require *accountability*—the ability to prove to a third party the unique originator of an object or action. Our discussion of secret sharing is based on Simmons (1992c). Oblivious transfer protocols are described in more detail by Salomaa (1990). The idea of zero-knowledge was introduced by Goldwasser, Micali, and Rackoff (1989). The protocol for zero-knowledge proof of identity is due to Feige, Fiat, and Shamir (1988) and is summarized by Feigenbaum (1992) and Salomaa (1990). Another zero-knowledge proof protocol for smart cards is described by Guillou, Ugon, and Quisquater (1992). It requires more computation but fewer interactions, probably a good tradeoff. Burrows, Abadi, and Needham (1990) and Syverson (1992) describe specialized logics for analyzing protocols. Kemmerer, Meadows, and Millen (1994) describe formal approaches to cryptographic protocol analysis and three experimental systems. Stubblebine and Gligor (1992) identify protocol vulnerabilities by using a model of message integrity, and Meadows (1991) identifies flaws in key management protocols using formal specification and verification, aided by automated tools.

Exercises

5.1 Using Shannon's definition of redundancy, show how the percentage redundancy of English can be computed.

5.2 What is the greatest common divisor (gcd) of 22 and 24?

5.3 Give two integers that are relatively prime.

5.4 What is the relationship between the Vernam cipher and a stream cipher?

5.5 What is the main purpose of cipher feedback? Of cipher block chaining?

5.6 Why are one-way functions important for cryptography?

5.7 List all the methods described in the chapter for creating confusion or diffusion.

5.8 How does the DES create confusion and diffusion?

5.9 Define unicity distance. How does it apply to stream ciphers?

5.10 Extend the system-theoretic approach, applying it to cryptographic applications rather than just cipher design. What additional criteria are needed? What are the advantages and disadvantages of this approach compared with the more formal approaches now being tried?

5.11 Encrypt the plaintext "secrecy and authentication" using as running key the second sentence of this chapter.

5.12 Describe the Diffie-Hellman key exchange protocol.

5.13 List the ways that digital signatures are *not* analogous to handwritten signatures.

5.14 For an RSA cryptosystem, the following values have been selected: $p = 47$, $q = 59$, and $e = 17$. Which of the following is correct for the value of the secret exponent d: 131, 149, or 157? Why are all the selections bad?

5.15 What is the difference between forgery and impersonating the sender?

5.16 Why should a hash function be a one-way function?

5.17 What is the most serious limitation of message authentication codes?

5.18 Why should a digital signature be computed on a message digest?

5.19 What are some drawbacks to using arbitrated protocols?

5.20 How can shared secret schemes be used to enforce separation of responsibility?

5.21 Why is it insecure to use a "common modulus" for RSA?

References

ANSI. 1985. *ANSI X9.17-1985: Financial Institution Key Management (Wholesale)*. New York: American National Standards Institute.

______. 1986. *ANSI X9.9-1986: Financial Institution Message Authentication (Wholesale)*. Washington, D.C.: American Bankers Association.

Bahreman, Alireza. 1995. PEMToolKit: Building a top-down certification hierarchy for PEM from the bottom up. *Proceedings of the Symposium on Network and Distributed System Security,* 161–171. Los Alamitos, Calif.: IEEE Computer Society.

Balenson, David M. 1985. Automated distribution of cryptographic keys using the financial institution key management standard. *IEEE Communications Magazine* (September): 41–46. Reprinted in Abrams, Marshall D., and Harold J. Podell, eds. 1987. *Tutorial: Computer and Network Security,* 387–392. Washington, D.C.: IEEE Computer Society Press.

Beth, Thomas, Markus Frisch, and Gustavus J. Simmons, eds. 1992. *Public-Key Cryptography: State of the Art and Future Directions.* Berlin: Springer-Verlag.

Biham, Eli and Adi Shamir. 1993. *Differential Cryptanalysis of the Data Encryption Standard.* New York: Springer-Verlag.

Blaze, Matt, Whitfield Diffie, Ronald L. Rivest, Bruce Schneier, Tsutomu Shimomura,

Eric Thompson, and Michael Wiener. 1996. *Minimal Key Lengths for Symmetric Ciphers to Provide Adequate Commercial Security.* A report by an ad hoc group of cryptographers and computer scientists. World Wide Web document, January 1996.

Boyd, Colin. 1991. Enhancing secrecy by data compression: Theoretical and practical aspects. *Advances in Cryptology—EUROCRYPT '91,* 266–280. Berlin: Springer-Verlag.

Brassard, Gilles. 1988. *Modern Cryptology: A Tutorial.* New York: Springer-Verlag.

Brickell, E. F. and A. M. Odlyzko. 1992. Cryptanalysis: A survey of recent results. In Simmons, Gustavus J., ed. *Contemporary Cryptology: The Science of Information Integrity,* 501–540. Piscataway, N.J.: IEEE Press.

Burrows, Michael, Martín Abadi, and Roger Needham. 1990. A logic of authentication. *ACM Transactions on Computer Systems* **8**(1): 18–36.

Chaum, David. 1985. Security without identification: Transaction systems to make big brother obsolete. *Communications of the ACM* **28**(10): 1030–1044.

______. 1992. Achieving electronic privacy. *Scientific American,* August: 96–101.

Chokhani, Santosh. 1994. Toward a national Public Key Infrastructure. *IEEE Communications Magazine* **32**(9): 70–74.

Davies, D. W. and W. L. Price. 1989. *Security for Computer Networks: An Introduction to Data Security in Teleprocessing and Electronics Funds Transfer.* 2d ed. Chichester, U.K.: Wiley.

DeMillo, Richard, and Michael Merritt. 1983. Protocols for data security. *Computer* **16**(2): 39–51.

Denning, Dorothy E. 1982. *Cryptography and Data Security.* Reading, Mass.: Addison-Wesley.

______. 1983. Protecting public keys and signature keys. *Computer* **16**(2): 27–35.

______. 1990. The Data Encryption Standard: Fifteen years of public scrutiny. *Proceedings of 6th Annual Computer Security Applications Conference,* x–xv. Los Alamitos, Calif.: IEEE Computer Society Press.

______. 1995. Key escrow encryption: The third paradigm. *Computer Security Journal* **XI**(1): 43–52.

Denning, Dorothy E., and Dennis K. Branstad. 1996. A taxonomy for key escrow encryption systems. *Communications of the ACM* **39**(3): 34–40.

Denning, Dorothy E., and Miles Smid. 1994. Key escrowing today. *IEEE Communications Magazine,* September: 58–68.

Diffie, Whitfield. 1992. The first ten years of public key cryptology. In Simmons, Gustavus J., ed. *Contemporary Cryptology: The Science of Information Integrity,* 137–175. Piscataway, N.J.: IEEE Press. See also IEEE 1988, 560–577.

Diffie, Whitfield and Martin E. Hellman. 1976. New directions in cryptography. *IEEE Transactions on Information Theory* **IT-22**(6): 644–654.

______. 1977. Exhaustive cryptanalysis of the NBS data encryption standard. *Computer* **10**(6): 74–84.

______. 1979. Privacy and authentication: An introduction to cryptography. *Proceedings of the IEEE* **67**(3): 397–427.

ElGamal, Taher. 1985. A public key cryptosystem and a signature scheme based on discrete logarithms. *IEEE Transactions on Information Theory* **IT-31**(4): 469–472.

Ehrsam, W. F., S. M. Matyas, C. H. Meyer, and W. L. Tuchman. 1978. A cryptographic key management scheme for implementing the Data Encryption Standard. *IBM Systems Journal* **17**(2): 106–125.

Feige, U., A. Fiat, and A. Shamir. 1988. Zero knowledge proofs of identity. *Journal of Cryptology* **1**(2): 77–94.

Feigenbaum, J. 1992. Overview of interactive proof systems and zero-knowledge. In Simmons, Gustavus J., ed. *Contemporary Cryptology: The Science of Information Integrity,* 423–439. Piscataway, N.J.: IEEE Press.

Fiat, Amos, and Adi Shamir. 1987. How to prove yourself: Practical solutions to identification and signature problems. *Advances in Cryptology—CRYPTO '86,* 186–194. Berlin: Springer-Verlag.

FIPS. 1980. *DES Modes of Operation.* FIPS PUB 81. Washington: National Bureau of Standards.

Fumy, Walter, and Peter Landrock. 1993. Principles of key management. *IEEE Journal on Selected Areas in Communications,* **11**(5): 785–795.

Ganesan, Ravi. 1996. How to use key escrow. *Communications of the ACM* **39**(3): 33.

Garfinkel, Simson L. 1995. Patented secrecy. *Forbes* **155**(5): 122–124.

Goldwasser, S., S. Micali, and C. Rackoff. 1989. The knowledge complexity of interactive proof systems. *SIAM Journal on Computing* **18**(1): 186–208.

Guillou, Louis Claude, Michel Ugon, and Jean-Jacques Quisquater. 1992. The smart card: A standardized security device dedicated to public cryptology. In Simmons, Gustavus J., ed. *Contemporary Cryptology: The Science of Information Integrity,* 561–613. Piscataway, N.J.: IEEE Press.

Hellman, Martin E. 1979. The mathematics of public-key cryptography. *Scientific American* (August): 146–157.

IEEE. 1988. Special section on cryptology. *Proceedings of the IEEE* **76**(5).

ISO. 1988. *Banking—Key Management (Wholesale), International Standard ISO 8732.* Geneva: International Organization for Standardization.

Johnson, D. B., S. M. Matyas, A. V. Le, and J. D. Wilkins. 1994. The Commercial Data Masking Facility (CDMF) data privacy algorithm. *IBM Journal of Research and Development* **38**(2): 217–226.

Kailar, Rajashekar. 1995. Reasoning about accountability in protocols for electronic commerce. *Proceedings of the 1995 IEEE Symposium on Security and Privacy,* 236–250. Los Alamitos, Calif.: IEEE Computer Society.

Kaliski, Burt. 1993. A survey of encryption standards. *IEEE Micro* (December): 74–81.

Kapidzic, Nada, and Alan Davidson. 1995. A certificate management system: Structure, functions, and protocols. *Proceedings of the Symposium on Network and Distributed System Security,* 153–160. Los Alamitos, Calif.: IEEE Computer Society.

Kemmerer, R., C. Meadows, and J. Millen. 1994. Three systems for cryptographic protocol analysis. *Journal of Cryptology* **7**(2): 79–130.

Koblitz, Neal. 1987. *A Course in Number Theory and Cryptography.* New York: Springer-Verlag.

Kocher, Paul C. 1995. Cryptanalysis of Diffie-Hellman, RSA, DSS, and Other Systems Using Timing Attacks. Extended Abstract, December 7, 1995. World Wide Web document.

Konheim, Alan G. 1981. *Cryptography: A Primer.* New York: John Wiley & Sons.

Landau, Susan, Stephen Kent, Clint Brooks, Scott Charney, Dorothy Denning, Whitfield Diffie, Anthony Lauck, Doug Miller, Peter Neumann, and David Sobel. 1994. *Issues in U.S. Crypto Policy.* Report of a Special Panel of the ACM U.S. Public Policy Committee (USACM), June 1994. New York: Association for Computing Machinery.

Langford, Susan K., and Martin E. Hellman. 1994. Differential-linear cryptanalysis. *Advances in Cryptology—Crypto '94,* 17–25. Berlin: Springer-Verlag.

Lin, C. H., C. C. Chang, and R. C. T. Lee. 1995. A new public-key cipher system based upon the Diophantine equations. *IEEE Transactions on Computers* **44**(1): 13–19.

Lomas, Mark, and Bruce Christianson. 1995. Remote booting in a hostile world: To whom am I speaking? *Computer* **28**(1): 50–54.

Lomas, Mark, and Michael Roe. 1994. Forging a Clipper message (letter to the editor). *Communications of the ACM* **37**(12): 12.

Maher, David Paul. 1996. Crypto backup and key escrow. *Communications of the ACM* **39**(3): 48–53.

Massey, James L. 1992. Contemporary Cryptology: An introduction. In Simmons, Gustavus J., ed. *Contemporary Cryptology: The Science of Information Integrity,* 1–39. Piscataway, N.J.: IEEE Press.

Matsui, Mitsuru. 1994a. The first experimental cryptanalysis of the Data Encryption Standard. *Advances in Cryptology—Crypto '94,* 1–11. Berlin: Springer-Verlag.

______. 1994b. Linear cryptanalysis method for DES cipher. *Advances in Cryptology—Eurocrypt '93,* 386–397. Berlin: Springer-Verlag.

Matyas, S. M., and C. H. Meyer. 1978. Generation, distribution, and installation of cryptographic keys. *IBM Systems Journal* **17**(2): 126–137.

Maurer, Ueli M. 1992. Conditionally-perfect secrecy and a provably-secure randomized cipher. *Journal of Cryptology* **5:** 53–66.

Meadows, Catherine. 1991. A system for the specification and analysis of key management protocols. *Proceedings of the 1991 IEEE Computer Society Symposium on Research in Security and Privacy,* 182–195. Los Alamitos, Calif.: IEEE Computer Society Press.

Merkle, Ralph C. 1978. Secure communication over insecure channels. *Communications of the ACM* **21**(4): 294–299.

______. 1990. A certified digital signature. *Advances in Cryptology—CRYPTO '89,* 218–238. Berlin: Springer-Verlag.

Merkle, Ralph C. and Martin E. Hellman. 1978. Hiding information and signatures in trapdoor knapsacks. *IEEE Transactions on Information Theory* **IT-24**(5): 525–530.

______. 1981. On the security of multiple encryption. *Communications of the ACM* **24**(7): 465–467.

Millen, Jonathan K. 1995. The Interrogator model. *Proceedings of the 1995 IEEE Symposium on Security and Privacy,* 251–260. Los Alamitos, Calif.: IEEE Computer Society.

Mitchell, C. J., F. Piper, and P. Wild. 1992. Digital signatures. In Simmons, Gustavus J., ed. *Contemporary Cryptology: The Science of Information Integrity,* 325–378. Piscataway, N.J.: IEEE Press.

Moore, J. H. 1992. Protocol failures in cryptosystems. In Simmons, Gustavus J., ed. *Contemporary Cryptology: The Science of Information Integrity,* 541–558. Piscataway, N.J.: IEEE Press. See also IEEE 1988, 594–602.

Nechvatal, James. 1992. Public key cryptography. In Simmons, Gustavus J., ed. *Contemporary Cryptology: The Science of Information Integrity,* 177–288. Piscataway, N.J.: IEEE Press. See also *Public-key Cryptography.* 1991. NIST Special Publication 800-2. Gaithersburg, Md.: National Institute of Standards and Technology.

NIST. 1985. *Standard on Computer Data Authentication*. FIPS PUB 113, May 1985. Gaithersburg, Md.: National Institute of Standards and Technology.

______. 1992. *Key Management Using ANSI X9.17.* FIPS PUB 171. Gaithersburg, Md.: National Institute of Standards and Technology.

______. 1993. *Data Encryption Standard* (*DES*). FIPS PUB 46-2. Gaithersburg, Md.: National Institute of Standards and Technology.

______. 1994a. *Digital Signature Standard* (*DSS*). FIPS PUB 186, May 1994. Gaithersburg, Md.: National Institute of Standards and Technology.

______. 1994b. *Escrowed Encryption Standard.* FIPS PUB 185, February 1994. Gaithersburg, Md.: National Institute of Standards and Technology.

______. 1994c. *Specifications for the Security Requirements for Cryptographic Modules.* FIPS PUB 140-1, January 1994. Gaithersburg, Md.: National Institute of Standards and Technology.

______. 1995. *Secure Hash Standard.* FIPS PUB 180-1, April 1995. Gaithersburg, Md.: National Institute of Standards and Technology.

Rabin, Michael O. 1978. Digitalized signatures. In Richard A. DeMillo, David P. Dobkin, Anita K. Jones, and Richard J. Lipton, eds. *Foundations of Secure Computation,* 155–166. New York: Academic Press.

Rhee, Man Young. 1994. *Cryptography and Secure Communications.* Singapore: McGraw-Hill.

Rivest, Ronald L. 1992a. Response to NIST's proposal. *Communications of the ACM* **35**(7): 41–47.

______. 1992b. *The MD5 Message-Digest Algorithm.* Internet Request for Comments RFC 1321, April 1992. Internet Activities Board.

______. 1995. The RC5 encryption algorithm. *Dr. Dobb's Journal* **20**(1): 146, 148.

Rivest, R. L., A. Shamir, and L. Adleman. 1978. A method for obtaining digital signatures and public-key cryptosystems. *Communications of the ACM* **21**(2): 120–126.

Rueppel, Rainer A. 1992. Stream ciphers. In Simmons, Gustavus J., ed. *Contemporary Cryptology: The Science of Information Integrity,* 65–134. Piscataway, N.J.: IEEE Press.

Salomaa, Arto. 1990. *Public-Key Cryptography.* Berlin: Springer-Verlag.

Schneier, Bruce. 1994. *Applied Cryptography: Protocols, Algorithms and Source Code in C.* New York: John Wiley & Sons.

______. 1996. *Applied Cryptography: Protocols, Algorithms and Source Code in C.* 2d ed. New York: John Wiley & Sons.

Sci.crypt. 1994. *FAQ.* Internet news group sci.crypt FAQ, 4/94.

Seberry, Jennifer and Josef Pieprzyk. 1989. *Cryptography: An Introduction to Computer Security.* New York: Prentice-Hall.

Shamir, Adi. 1984. A polynomial-time algorithm for breaking the basic Merkle-Hellman cryptosystem. *IEEE Transactions on Information Theory* **IT-30**(5): 699–704.

Shannon, C. E. 1949. Communication theory of secrecy systems. *Bell System Technical Journal* **28**(Oct): 656–715.

Simmons, Gustavus J. 1979. Symmetric and asymmetric encryption. *ACM Computing Surveys* **11**(4): 305–330.

Simmons, Gustavus J., ed. 1992a. *Contemporary Cryptology: The Science of Information Integrity.* Piscataway, N. J.: IEEE Press.

______. 1992b. A survey of information authentication. In Simmons, Gustavus J., ed. *Contemporary Cryptology: The Science of Information Integrity,* 379–419. Piscataway, N.J.: IEEE Press. See also IEEE 1988, 603–620.

______. 1992c. An introduction to shared secret and/or shared control schemes and their application. In Simmons, Gustavus J., ed. *Contemporary Cryptology: The Science of Information Integrity,* 441–497. Piscataway, N.J.: IEEE Press.

______. 1994. Cryptanalysis and protocol failures. *Communications of the ACM* **37**(11): 56–65.

Stallings, William. 1995. *Network and Internetwork Security: Principles and Practice.* Englewood Cliffs, N.J.: Prentice-Hall.

Stubblebine, Stuart G. and Virgil D. Gligor. 1992. On message integrity in cryptographic protocols. *Proceedings of the 1992 IEEE Computer Society Symposium on Research in Security and Privacy,* 85–104. Los Alamitos, Calif.: IEEE Computer Society Press.

Syverson, Paul. 1992. The use of logic in the analysis of cryptographic protocols. *Proceedings of the 1992 IEEE Computer Society Symposium on Research in Security and Privacy,* 156–170. Los Alamitos, Calif.: IEEE Computer Society Press.

______. 1994. A taxonomy of replay attacks. *Proceedings of the Computer Security Foundations Workshop VII,* 187–191. Los Alamitos, Calif.: IEEE Computer Society.

Walker, Stephen T., Steven B. Lipner, Carl M. Ellison, and David M. Balenson. 1996. Commercial key recovery. *Communications of the ACM* **39**(3): 41–47.

Welsh, Dominic. 1988. *Codes and Cryptography.* Oxford: Clarendon Press.

Wiener, Michael J. 1990. Cryptanalysis of short RSA secret exponents. *IEEE Transactions on Information Theory* **36**(3): 553–558.

Zeng, Kancheng, Chung-Huang Yang, Dah-Yea Wei, and T. R. N. Rao. 1991. Pseudorandom bit generators in stream-cipher cryptography. *Computer* **24**(2): 8–17.

Chapter

6

Designing and Building Secure Systems

This chapter is about designing and building systems to meet their security requirements. There are two distinct but overlapping problems: (1) the development of products and (2) the development of operational systems that include people and nonautomated procedures, as well as products. The security of operating system products is fundamental, and it has received the most study and attention. However, since secure products do not guarantee a secure operational system, a broad information systems perspective is essential.

This chapter describes problems, principles, approaches, criteria, and development methods; the next two chapters describe mechanisms and services. The rest of this section briefly discusses concepts: trustworthiness, quality, safety, and assurance. The next section is about software engineering in general, surveying concepts and methods that are relevant to security. The following section describes security flaws in software. Principles of secure design are then discussed. Next, the main architectural approaches are presented. Criteria for evaluating security are described; they include the U.S. Trusted Computer System Evaluation Criteria (TCSEC), European Information Technology Security Evaluation Criteria (ITSEC), and Canadian criteria. Problems and new criteria efforts are discussed. The final section is about the process of developing secure systems. It deals with security requirements specification, formal methods, testing, documentation, and configuration management.

Security is a property of trustworthy systems, along with quality and safety. When security is viewed broadly (as in this book), the properties overlap. *High-quality* software is suitable for its intended use, meets its technical specifications, and satisfies its users; its failures have limited effects. Software for *safety-critical* systems (such as air traffic control) aims at reducing the risk of harm due to system failures. Software for highly secure systems must have high quality. Poor quality in software for security functions directly lessens security. Poor quality in other software indirectly lessens security. For example, a bad user interface leads to user errors.

An important concept for secure system development is *assurance*—the amount of confidence that some system meets its security requirements. Assurance derives from many sources, including the architecture and design of the system, the process used in developing it, the thoroughness of analysis and testing, the past performance of the developers and vendor, and the results of independent evaluations.

Software Engineering

The term *software engineering* has been given many definitions. According to Bruce Blum (1992), "...software engineering is the application of tools, methods, and disciplines to produce and maintain an automated solution to a real-world problem."

The software life cycle

Figure 6.1 shows a classic model of software development stages, often called the *systems development life cycle* (SDLC). Each stage produces some document that serves as input to the next stage. The "waterfall" of Fig. 6.1 suggests an orderly top-down sequence of stages. In reality, there is much iteration and interaction of stages, as captured by the "spiral" model of Fig. 6.2, where the outward spiral represents cumulative cost (the radial dimension) and progress in each cycle (the angular dimension). Simplifying the waterfall model, system development can be seen as a transformation from a real-world problem to a system. A statement of the problem (a *specification*) is developed and then transformed into an *implementation* statement that includes design descriptions, source code, and testing materials. The problem statement may involve several levels of modeling, starting with a model in application-domain terms and moving toward a model of the software product. Specifications can be written in words, diagrams, formal specification languages, high-level code or pseudocode, or combinations of these forms.

The goal of the whole software process is for the completed system to meet the real-world needs. *Validation* is concerned with predicting how well the system will meet that goal. *Verification* is concerned with determining if the implementation is consistent with the specification. In principle, if the specification is precise enough, verification

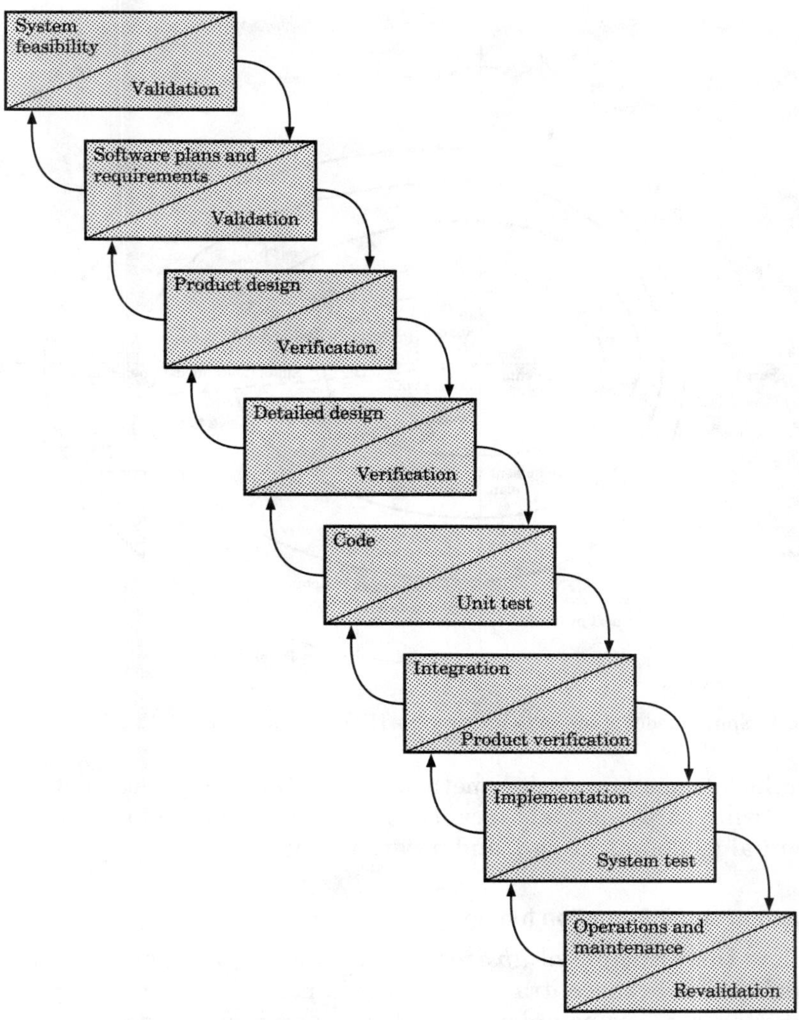

Figure 6.1 The waterfall model of the software life cycle. [*From Boehm, © 1988 (IEEE)*]

can be completely objective, but validation is always partly subjective. Barry Boehm has said that "verification is doing the job right and validation is doing the right job." Verification and validation are applied throughout the life cycle. They are often treated as a single process called *V&V.*

Most organizations that build large software systems select a methodology that provides structure and discipline. Although it might seem simpler to apply the same methodology in all stages of the life cycle, this is not usually practical or even desirable. There are analy-

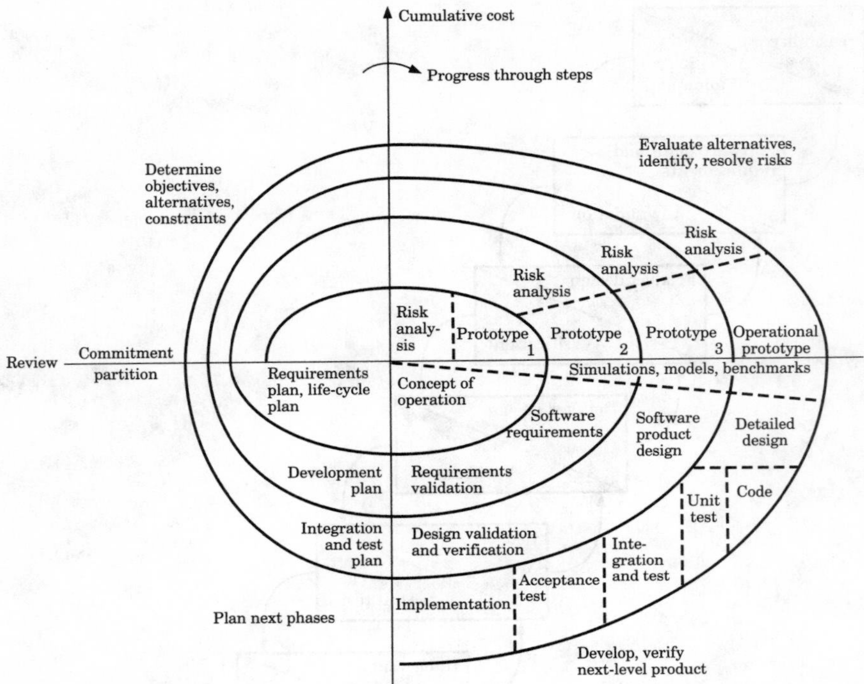

Figure 6.2 Spiral model of the software process. [*From Boehm, © 1988 (IEEE)*]

sis methodologies and design methodologies. *Object-oriented* methodologies (which are relatively recent) do hold the promise of supporting conceptual modeling, design, and programming.

Abstraction and information hiding

To follow the principle of *abstraction* means to ignore or segregate details in order to concentrate on what is important for some purpose. Abstraction reduces complexity, making specifications and designs easier to understand. An entity that results from applying the abstraction principle is also called an *abstraction*. There can be procedural abstractions, data abstractions, or *objects* that combine procedures and data. An operating system, for example, may provide a *process* object.

Ideally, each component reveals to other components only its external properties. Its implementation and data are hidden. This is known as *information hiding*. The term *encapsulation* is also used, emphasizing the barriers that prevent access to the procedures and data of the component. Abstraction and information hiding apply to requirements analysis, design, and programming. Structured methodologies and automated tools can support or enforce appropriate structure at all stages of the life cycle. At the code stage, the programming language is the main support.

Operating systems have always provided abstractions. For example, real printers with all their heterogeneity and complexity can be treated uniformly as output streams. Components of the operating system can be viewed as *virtual machines* that turn the real resources of a computing system into virtual resources that are far easier to use. These virtual machine abstractions may form a layered structure, where each layer uses abstractions provided by the layer below to create its own abstractions, which in turn are used by the layer above.

In the design phase of the life cycle, the software *architecture* is developed. It identifies the software components or modules and determines how they are structured. For example, the software structure may be hierarchical, as in Fig. 6.3. In a good design, each component represents some abstraction from the viewpoint of other components that interact with it. Certain aspects of the software architecture are relevant to security; these form the *security architecture.*

Operating system models

Contemporary operating system designs follow the *object model,* where the system is organized as abstractions that encompass both data and procedure. (The term *object* here has a richer and more specific meaning than in the access matrix model.) Examples of operating system objects are queues or memory segments. Operations are associated with each object; they provide the only way to use the object. Associated with a segment object, for example, are such operations as **create** or **destroy** or **set security.** There is no direct way to get at the data structures or code that represents the segment. **Create** is a generic operation that applies to many or all objects. Other operations are object-specific; for example, a file object has the

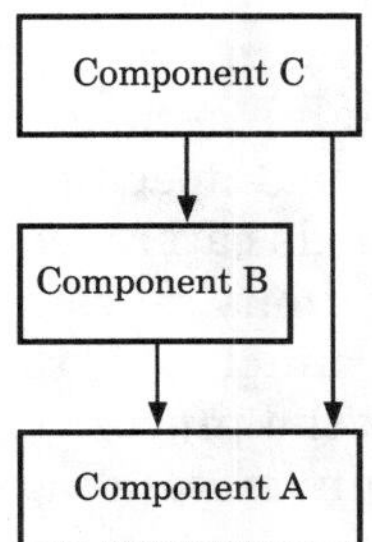

Figure 6.3 Hierarchical software structure.

operation **read.** Each type of object is implemented by an object manager, and a type manager implements the basic object system itself. The object model supports abstraction and information hiding. It is appropriate for distributed systems, since an object is used in the same way, whatever its location.

The object model has security advantages. It puts an intermediary—the object manager—between the object's implementation and its users. The object system itself provides a common access-control mechanism, and where this is not enough, the object manager can implement additional controls. For example, it can do specialized auditing or data-dependent access control. Chapters 7 and 8 describe operating systems that are designed according to the object model.

The *client-server model* extends the object model in a way that is suited to both distributed systems and single systems. The object is a *service* that can be requested by *clients.* At the lowest level, a client makes a request by sending a message to a *port* owned by the service. A *server* process handles the message and performs the service. The service-request messages may not be visible directly to application programs, being hidden under procedure calls. A *remote procedure call* is the typical program interface to services.

Object-oriented systems

Object-oriented systems go beyond the object model in several respects, and they are built with object-oriented programming languages. Object-oriented analysis and design methods also are used. Object-oriented programming languages support the concept of a *class,* which is a collection of objects with common features. Classes can have structured relationships, and a class *inherits* the features of its parent class. The characteristics of object-oriented systems are summarized in Fig. 6.4.

Formal methods

A *formal* method for system development is grounded in mathematics. It permits a precise description of system properties. Formal methods are used increasingly, and they are prominent in security standards and practices. They apply to all stages of the life cycle and are especially valuable in the earlier stages, to catch bad specifications before they are further transformed. Formal methods can reveal ambiguity, incompleteness, or inconsistency of specifications. Formal specification is done with a specification language—much as programming is done with a programming language. Just the process of developing a formal specification can greatly improve understanding.

An *object-oriented system* models all real-world entities as *objects*. An object has both a state and a behavior. Each object has a unique identifier, which is fixed for the life of the object. Associated with each object is a set of *attributes*; the value of an attribute can be an object or set of objects. Attributes are also called *variables*. The behavior of the object is represented by a set of *methods,* which can be invoked from outside the object. The state of the object is the set of values for its attributes; these values are modified and revealed only by the methods. A method is invoked by sending a message to its object specifying the method and passing objects as parameters. A method may do three kinds of things: (1) read and write the attribute values of its object, (2) invoke the methods of other objects or its own object, and (3) return a value to the invoker.

All the objects with the same attributes and methods form a *class*; an object is an *instance* of one class. A new class can be defined as a *subclass* of another class. The subclass *inherits* all the attributes and methods of its superclass and also may have its own attributes and methods. The subclass is a *specialization* of the superclass. A class is represented by a class object.

Figure 6.4 Object-oriented systems.

However, the unique advantage of a formal specification is that it can be analyzed by machine. This analysis can be used to uncover problems, to prove new properties, or to demonstrate that one level of specification is consistent with another level. That is, *formal verification* can be done.

Formal verification is used much less than formal specification, but security methodologies emphasize verification. Formal verification typically involves a logical inference system that can prove new properties about the specification—properties not explicitly stated in the specification. Mechanical theorem provers and proof checkers are used; formal verification is too big a job to do without them.

A disadvantage of formal, as compared with informal, specifications is that fewer people have the training and experience to understand them. In fact, the implementers of the system may have difficulty understanding what the specifiers wrote.

Verification and validation

Verification and validation methods include formal and informal analyses, formal verification (discussed more later), inspection, and testing.

Inspection is a highly structured review aimed at finding errors. It can be applied to specifications, design documents, and code. A code inspection is carried out in meetings by a team of people with well-defined roles. A moderator chairs the meeting and records the errors found. The author of the code observes only. The inspectors are knowledgeable peers of the author who have studied the design documents and code. They proceed by paraphrasing lines of code, describing them in words. Inspection has proved to be a cost-effective way to find errors before testing.

There are many reasons for testing. Testing can find errors, demonstrate that requirements have been satisfied, and measure reliability. Also, well-documented testing is evidence of due care in developing a product. Testing methods are categorized as *black box* (*functional*) or *white box* (*structural*). Black box testing looks only at the functional specifications to determine which tests to perform. White box testing uses test cases that are constructed from the code, without considering the functional specifications. The test cases are designed to provide good coverage, according to various structural properties of the code. Coverage criteria include the following:

- Exercise all statements.
- Exercise each outcome of every decision and all the ways each decision can be reached.
- Test all control flow paths.
- Test all exception conditions.

The customary stages or modes of testing are unit testing (mainly white box); package testing, in which units are tested together; integration testing, where a skeleton complete system is tested and then gradually populated with more and more units; system testing; and acceptance testing. Modified code goes through regression testing to verify that the modifications work properly and that unmodified code still works as before. Testing should be done by a separate team, not by the designers and programmers. (It is hard for people to test their own designs and programs in an unbiased way.) Often an independent contractor is used.

Security Flaws

A *security flaw* in a system is a part of the system that can cause it to violate its security requirements. Flaws can be introduced at any stage of the life cycle. If they are aware of generic types of flaws, developers can avoid introducing flaws of those types. Figure 6.5 shows a program flaw taxonomy developed by Carl E. Landwehr and colleagues. This figure categorizes the flaws by genesis, which can be either intentional or inadvertent. The taxonomy also characterizes flaws according to when they are introduced (development, maintenance, or operation) and where they are located (hardware, operating

<table>
<tr><td rowspan="13">Genesis</td><td rowspan="7">Intentional</td><td rowspan="4">Malicious</td><td rowspan="2">Trojan horse</td><td>Non-replicating</td></tr>
<tr><td>Replicating (virus)</td></tr>
<tr><td colspan="2">Trapdoor</td></tr>
<tr><td colspan="2">Logic/time bomb</td></tr>
<tr><td rowspan="3">Nonmalicious</td><td rowspan="2">Covert channel</td><td>Storage</td></tr>
<tr><td>Timing</td></tr>
<tr><td colspan="2">Other</td></tr>
<tr><td rowspan="6">Inadvertent</td><td colspan="3">Validation error (incomplete/inconsistent)</td></tr>
<tr><td colspan="3">Domain error (including object reuse, residuals, and exposed representation errors)</td></tr>
<tr><td colspan="3">Serialization/aliasing (including TOCTTOU errors)</td></tr>
<tr><td colspan="3">Identification/authentication inadequate</td></tr>
<tr><td colspan="3">Boundary condition violation (including resource exhaustion and violable constraint errors)</td></tr>
<tr><td colspan="3">Other exploitable logic error</td></tr>
</table>

Figure 6.5 Security flaw taxonomy. [*From Landwehr et al. (1994). Copyright © Association for Computing Machinery, Inc. (ACM). Reprinted with permission.*]

system, utilities, or application). Here, inadvertent flaws are discussed; deliberate threats are described in Chap. 3.

Validation flaws

A *validation flaw* occurs when a program component does not adequately check information that is supplied to it. For example, it may not check an input buffer for exceeding the expected maximum length. This type of validation flaw was exploited by the 1988 Internet worm. A different validation flaw was found in a UNIX support program that allowed remote execution of a limited set of commands. When the program scanned the input command line for commands, it used an incomplete set of delimiters, so some commands were never detected or checked. Any command could be executed remotely if it followed one of the ignored delimiters.

Domain flaws

A *domain flaw* is a weakness in the boundaries between protection environments. One kind of domain flaw is *object reuse*; for example, data from a file opened by one user remains in memory that is reallocated for another user. Another type is *exposed representation,* where a lower-level representation of some object is exposed. This type of flaw, in the TENEX operating system for the DEC PDP-10, made it much easier for a user to guess a password (used to control access to files). The system retrieved the password a character at a time from user memory, stopping when it found an incorrect character. A user's program could place the password so that the first unknown character was at the end of a page of virtual storage. If this character was correct and the next page was not in memory, a page fault would occur, and the user would learn that the character was correct. This scheme worked because the system provided page-fault counts and information about which pages were in memory.

Serialization errors

Some of the hardest flaws to avoid are *serialization errors,* which exploit asynchronous operation of different system components. For example, a component carefully validates all its parameters, but then the parameters are changed before they are used. This is called the *time-of-check-to-time-of-use* (TOCTTOU) *problem.* The OS/360 operating system had such a flaw in its checking of file passwords. A user could run a separate process that modified the file name after the system retrieved it for checking. The user originally supplied the name of a file whose password was known and then changed the name to that of the desired file. In general, systems can avoid TOCTTOU problems by moving parameters to protected storage before checking and using them.

Boundary-condition flaws

Boundary-condition flaws allow programs to exceed limits on consumption of resources, causing denial of service. For example, when a Multics user created an extremely deep directory tree, a fundamental system table would overflow, causing a crash.

Covert channels

A *covert channel* is an unintended communication path that can be used to violate a system's security policy. *Storage channels* use changes to stored information, and *timing channels* use the timing of events. Many covert channels include aspects of both storage and timing channels. Butler Lampson (1973) first called attention to covert channels as one form of the *confinement problem:* how to prevent a program from leaking data that its "customer" gives it. Covert channels are extremely important for systems that implement a mandatory security policy such as Bell-LaPadula. In fact, for these systems, any communication path that can violate policy is a covert channel. A Trojan horse could use a covert channel to subvert the *-property.

One example of a storage channel is the exhaustion of memory used by operating system tables. Suppose that the operating system has a fixed amount of memory available for process tables. To receive information on this covert channel, a process R creates processes until no more table space is available and then synchronizes with a sending process S. Process S then either deletes a process or does not. Process R tries again to create a process and, depending on the success of this attempt, records a 0 or 1. One bit has been transmitted from S to R. The sequence is repeated until all the information has been transmitted.

An example of a timing channel is the *bus-contention channel,* which may exist in any multiprocessor system where the processors share a common bus. One processor can saturate the bus, and another processor can detect this condition, since its own requests are delayed. To send a 1, the sender executes a sequence of instructions that generates bus traffic; to send a 0, it executes instructions that generate no bus traffic. The receiver generates bus requests at a constant rate and measures the time for them to complete.

The danger of a covert channel depends on its *bandwidth*—the rate at which it transmits information, in bits per second. The bandwidth of a storage channel depends on how much information it contains and how rapidly modifications can be made by a sender and detected by a receiver. The bandwidth of covert channels is reduced by noise. In the table-exhaustion channel, for example, other processes running concurrently with the sender and receiver also would create and destroy processes. Channels that use hardware events generally have a higher bandwidth than channels that use software events, such as creating processes. From the operating system designer's viewpoint, hardware channels are also much harder to control; software channels often can be eliminated by careful design.

There are many potential storage channels. Some operating systems allow users to see the names and other attributes (such as size and time stamp) of files that they cannot read. The sender can modify these attributes systematically. Even the fact that a file exists conveys one bit of information. The sender can deliberately fill up a printer queue; a receiver that tries to print easily detects this. Other potential channels are blocks of memory or of disk storage and shared devices such as tapes or plotters. In fact, any shared resource is a possible covert channel.

A timing channel requires some kind of clock, such as an interval timer or time of day. Even if the operating system does not provide a clock, a program can build its own clock from I/O operations or other asynchronous events.

Identifying covert channels. A few systematic methods for identifying storage channels have been developed.

The *shared-resource matrix* methodology developed by Richard Kemmerer (1983) is based on the following criteria for a storage channel:

- The sending and receiving processes must have access to the same attribute of a shared resource. For example, both have access to a file lock.
- The sender has a way to force the attribute to change.
- The receiver has a way to detect the change.
- The two have a way to synchronize. This could be another covert channel with smaller bandwidth.

The methodology tries to identify when the first three criteria are met. It can be used with natural language requirements, formal specifications, or source code. It involves building a matrix, where the columns represent primitive operations of the system, the rows represent attributes of objects, and a cell contains R if the operation references the attribute, M if it writes the attribute, or is blank. With informal requirements, the analyst studies them to identify the objects and attributes. Then, for each operation, the analyst looks for words such as *checks* or *reads* or *if* that indicate reference and words such as *change* or *set* that indicate modification. The matrix is filled out accordingly. At this point the matrix does not include indirect references, where an attribute referenced by one operation is modified by another operation, which references other attributes. The next step is to trace these indirect references systematically and add them to the matrix. Any row containing both an R and an M represents a potentially troublesome attribute; each such attribute is analyzed for the types of information flows that it allows. Some are legal, some convey no useful information, and others are potential storage channels.

Another method for identifying covert channels uses information flow analysis. Automated tools analyze code or formal specifications to identify all information flows and determine if they violate policy. (These methods extend the information flow analysis discussed in Chap. 4.) Unlike the shared-resource matrix method, information flow analysis cannot be applied to informal specifications, but it does reliably find all potential covert channels. The main problem is that it identifies flow violations that are not real. Rather, these *formal flow violations* arise from the treatment of variables (such as machine registers) that are not considered objects in the security model. The flow analysis must consider them in order to find all illegal flows, but in so doing, it enforces too restrictive a policy. People must then examine each potential flow violation and decide if it is real. For example, there may be no system functions that could exploit the flow. (However, if such a function were added to the specification, the flow would become real.) Automated tools could better distinguish real flow violations if the specifications contained additional semantic information.

Countermeasures. Once a covert channel has been uncovered, the system designers can choose to

- Eliminate the channel.
- Reduce its bandwidth by introducing noise.
- For a timing channel, reduce the bandwidth by hiding the exact timing of events.
- Leave the channel and audit for its use.
- Ignore the channel because its bandwidth is very low.

Eliminating channels. The usual way to eliminate covert channels is to eliminate shared resources. This is done by preallocating resources, either to individual users or processes or to security levels. For example, use separate pools of table space for Secret and Confidential processes. Of course, there is usually some performance penalty, since resources are used less effectively. It is also possible to change a system's external interface to eliminate features that provide covert channels.

Reducing bandwidth. A covert channel is not a serious threat if its bandwidth is very low. The bandwidth can be reduced by introducing noise into the channel or by slowing down the channel. For example, to make the bus-contention channel noisy, the operating system could make unpredictable bus references (with a performance penalty). To slow down a resource-exhaustion channel, the operating system could delay responding to a failed resource request.

Fuzzy time. Using a timing channel means using a clock. A possible control is to remove the clock by allowing a process to see only virtual time, which depends only on the activity of the process. However, virtual time is correlated with real time, so it still provides a channel. This correlation can be reduced, however, by introducing randomness into the relation between virtual time and all the possible clocks. For example, random delays can be added to I/O completions. This approach is called *fuzzy time*.

Auditing. Auditing for the use of known covert channels requires recording all events that possibly use covert channels and then analyzing them to determine if they actually did. If so, it is necessary to identify which channel was used and which processes were sending and receiving. Users of covert channels must not be able to circumvent the auditing.

Ignoring. A covert channel whose bandwidth is too low for practical use can be ignored.

The unsolved problem. Despite the methods that have been described and many other efforts, it has not been possible to control the covert channels in trusted operating systems. The problem grows worse as processor and I/O speeds increase, thus increasing the bandwidth of the covert channels.

Principles of Design for Security

This section discusses principles derived from experience in building secure systems. The principles apply to both the architecture and the external interface. A system designed according to these principles is more likely to meet its security goals. Also, a well-designed system encourages users to behave in ways that enhance security. A good design can still be compromised by a poor implementation, but a good design is essential.

The principles are best applied from the very beginning of a project. "Adding security" to an existing system is much harder to do and achieves far less. However, designers are constrained by history and economics. Often a new design must support old external interfaces and must use much old code.

Saltzer and Schroeder principles

In 1975, Jerome Saltzer and Michael Schroeder, summing up the state of the art and their experience with the Multics operating system, articulated principles of system design for security. These principles remain highly relevant. (My comments appear in brackets; other text describes the original principles.)

Economy of mechanism. "Keep the design as simple and small as possible." This is particularly important because security errors are not revealed in normal use, so special methods of study are needed to evaluate the mechanism. [This principle is the foundation of important design approaches. Keeping the security mechanism small and simple is a design challenge, since security touches so many aspects of a system.]

Fail-safe defaults. "Base access decisions on permission rather than exclusion." Omitting a parameter from an operating system call, or failing to make a call, should cause the system to take the more secure alternative. A new file should be accessible only to its creator, unless permission is explicitly given. This principle applies the *closed-system policy*—that access is based on permissions, not implied. [This principle must be tempered, however. Uncompromising fail-safe defaults are not always appropriate. For example, they could cause paralysis when access control is first added to an operational system.]

Complete mediation. Every access to every object must be validated. There must be no path to the object that bypasses validation. This principle corresponds to the reference monitor concept of the access-matrix model. Not only normal operation but also special processes such as initialization and recovery must be subject to this mediation.

Open design. The design itself should not be secret. An open design can be reviewed by many experts and by potential users. Any errors or deficiencies are thus more likely to be found, made known, and corrected. Secrecy is needed for passwords and encryption keys but not for designs. [As Chap. 2 indicates, this principle is widely but not universally accepted; organizations such as the National Security Agency (NSA) often keep designs secret.]

Separation of privilege. Much as separation of duty applies to people's responsibilities, separation of privilege applies to system design. Security is enhanced if two or more keys are needed to unlock a protection mechanism or if two independent mechanisms must agree before an action is allowed.

Least privilege. Every program or system component must operate with the minimum set of privileges it needs to accomplish its task. For example, the command processor of an operating system provides many services that need no special privilege. Under the principle of least privilege, these would run with only the privileges of application programs.

Another example concerns the external interface. The system operator should not be able to perform security administration tasks.

Least-common mechanism. Minimize the amount of mechanism that operates on behalf of many users and that could compromise security if it operated incorrectly. [The point seems to be: Do not threaten the simplicity and correctness of the basic mechanisms by handling special requirements that could be handled by application-level code.]

Psychological acceptability. Security facilities must be easy to understand and use. [Only then will they be installed widely and used routinely and correctly.]

Other principles

Many other principles have been articulated. The following few seem especially important.

Consideration of environment. It is essential to consider the total environment of a system—including its users, its management, and other systems that interact with it.

Separation of policy and mechanism. A general-purpose system should be designed to clearly separate security policies from the mechanisms that implement them. It should be possible for the same mechanisms to support multiple policies.

Invisible database. A user should not be able to distinguish lack of access to some object from nonexistence of that object. (This principle was first described in the context of database security, but it applies equally to files or other objects.)

Explicitness. The design should make explicit the required system properties, and the implementation should check that they hold.

Auditability. A system should produce evidence that can be reviewed to determine how effectively it enforces its security policy.

Anticipation of future requirements. Morrie Gasser points out that security design should take into account future security features, even if they are not in the current plan. This can cost far less than ignoring such features until it is time to build them.

Proper weight to other goals. Security is one of many design goals, and it often conflicts with ease of use, function, performance, and cost. Even where security is the highest concern, these other goals cannot be shortchanged.

Architectural Approaches

Most of the design principles apply broadly, whatever the system architecture. Some of the principles also underlie specific approaches to structuring systems for security.

A goal of some approaches is to support *multilevel secure systems,* which hold information of different classification levels and support users at different clearance levels. Multilevel secure operation is more effective and convenient than the alternative of *system-high operation,* where a system operates at the level of the highest information classification, and all users are cleared for that level.

Kernel approach

Chapter 4 described the concept of the reference monitor—the mechanism that ensures that all access is authorized. The influential report prepared by James Anderson in 1972 used the term *reference validation mechanism* for the hardware and software that implement the reference monitor. The requirements are that

a. The reference validation mechanism must be tamperproof. That is, it must not be possible for any of its components (hardware, firmware, or software) to be modified.

b. The reference validation mechanism *always* must be invoked. There must be no path to protected objects that bypasses reference validation.

c. The reference validation mechanism must be small enough to be subject to analysis and tests, whose completeness can be ensured.

The short terms for these requirements are *isolation, completeness,* and *verifiability.*

The reference validation mechanism often is built as a *security kernel.* The idea is that isolating this mechanism, and keeping it relatively small, gives a better chance of meeting the reference monitor requirements. Roger Schell first articulated the idea of a security kernel as a compact portion of the operating system and hardware such that an antagonist could supply the rest of the system without compromising security. Early kernel-based systems provided UNIX functionality, reworking the UNIX kernel to enforce multilevel security. Much of the security-relevant mechanism was built as kernel calls, but some of it involved nonkernel components called *trusted processes* (they were indeed processes). A trusted process can violate the security policy selectively, but it is trusted to enforce the intent of the policy; for example, it can downgrade the security level of a file.

The TCSEC use the term *Trusted Computing Base* (TCB) for "the totality of protection mechanisms within a computer system—including hardware, firmware, and software—the combination of which is responsible for enforcing a security policy." For a general-purpose operating system based on a kernel design, the TCB includes the kernel and trusted processes. For a special-purpose system, the TCB might include parts of the applications or even the entire system. The *security perimeter* is the boundary separating the TCB from the rest of the system (see Fig. 6.6). There must be a *trusted path* between the user and the TCB so that nontrusted components cannot subvert the user's intent or spoof the user.

The kernel approach has taken different forms:

1. A software kernel that uses standard protection hardware and runs in its own hardware protection domain. This is the traditional approach.
2. A separate attached hardware unit that does most or all of the reference validation.
3. A *virtual machine monitor,* which implements a set of virtual machines on a single real machine. Each virtual machine behaves (except for performance) exactly like the real machine. Different virtual machines support users at different security levels, and the

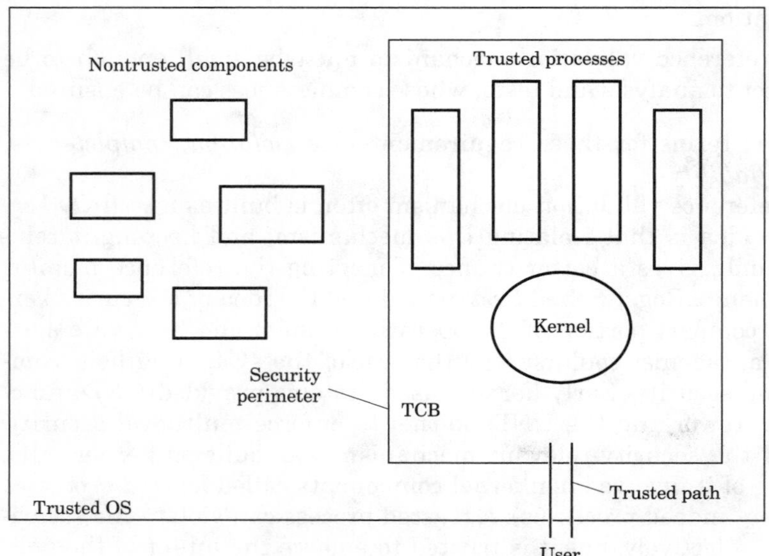

Figure 6.6 Trusted operating system with TCB.

virtual machines are totally isolated from one another except as mediated by the kernel. The kernel is much simpler than in the traditional approach, but data cannot be shared without relaxing the strict isolation. The virtual machine monitor provides some services (other than security) for the virtual machines.

4. A separation kernel. A *separation kernel* is a virtual machine monitor carried to the extreme: there is absolutely no sharing. The separation kernel enforces an extremely simple security policy—isolation. The subject is always strictly equal in level to the object. A variation of this approach uses physically separated real machines and mediates all communication between them.

The traditional kernel approach is open to serious criticisms. It just may not be possible to isolate all security-critical functions in a small and simple portion of the system. Trusted processes are security-critical but tend to be less thoroughly analyzed or verified. Kernel-based systems may perform poorly, and the nonkernel parts may become extremely complex. Covert channels cannot be eliminated. Malicious software can subvert accountability. Building one policy into a kernel does not satisfy the needs for varied confidentiality and integrity policies. Finally, the high development and maintenance costs and the limited market have discouraged vendors from developing kernel-based systems.

Hierarchical layers of abstraction

The TCB concept is generalized in the approach called *hierarchical layers of abstraction.* The idea of hierarchical or layered operating systems has a long history. For example, Edsger Dijkstra's THE system had an "onion" structure, where each layer rested on and hid the next inner layer. Such strict and detailed layering is hard to achieve for today's complex operating systems, but the hierarchical approach remains valid. Peter Neumann (1986, 1990) has applied it for systems that must satisfy critical requirements—including security. This approach envisions a hierarchy of TCBs.

The hierarchical approach builds on abstraction and information hiding, adding a requirement for downward-only dependence. (*Depends on* here means "depends on for its correctness.") In Fig. 6.3, for example, layer C depends on layer B, but B cannot depend on C or any higher layer. The more fundamental abstractions (representing the more critical requirements) are in the lower layers. If lower layers implement the multilevel security policy, errors or attacks in upper layers cannot cause violation of that policy. Associated with each layer are models of the requirements and specifications for that layer. It is possible, then, to prove or convincingly demonstrate that a layer's specifications satisfy its requirements.

This approach applies the principle of information hiding in that each layer reveals to others only what they need, hiding its internal implementation and its private state information. This, of course, helps to enforce the principle of least privilege for the layers. It also helps separate policy from mechanism, since mechanisms within a layer are not visible to the layer's users. This approach leads us to add another design principle: *preserve hierarchical orderings*.

The hierarchical approach has not been used much for complete operating systems; perhaps it is too hard to find the right hierarchical decomposition. However, strictly layered security kernels have been built. Fortunately, some of the same benefits are provided by modular systems that are not strictly hierarchical. There each component (rather than layer) must defend itself against compromise by other components. For example, it validates all parameters and ensures that certain conditions hold when it is invoked. Each component also detects its own errors and prevents them from compromising other components. For example, it checks the consistency of its own data structures.

TCB subsets

After the TCB approach was developed, computing systems changed radically in their structure and in the way they were acquired and configured. These changes affected the use of criteria (such as the TCSEC) to evaluate systems. It became essential to consider not only operating systems but also database management systems, networking software, user interface systems, word processing, spreadsheets, standard application systems (such as accounting and payroll), industry-specific standard applications, and local applications. The typical computing system is a custom brew of products provided by different vendors, yet the system must be evaluated as a whole. Products that have been evaluated once need to be reevaluated when they undergo improvements. There are product families that users customize for their own needs. These factors all point to the need to evaluate systems built in parts. This need is recognized in the idea of *TCB subsets*.

A *TCB subset* is a reference validation mechanism with a difference: It can depend on other, more primitive (and privileged) TCB subsets. A TCB subset is a TCB that is built on other TCB subsets rather than only directly on hardware. Thus a trusted database management system (DBMS) could depend on an operating system, and a trusted logistics system could depend on a DBMS and an operating system. Alternatively, TCB subsets could cooperate in a distributed system. Each object is mediated by just one TCB subset, and each TCB subset enforces its own policy. It may rely, though, on more primitive TCB subsets to enforce their policies on more primitive objects. The lowest-level TCB subset (the reference monitor) implements the least restrictive policy, and other TCB subsets implement additional, more restrictive policies.

The TCB subset approach tries to make assurance a realistic objective, even though systems are composed of separately developed products. It tries to preserve the relevance of TCSEC methodology for systems that support policies other than the multilevel policy and multiple policies on one system.

Security guards

When information must pass between systems that operate at different security levels, a "trusted transfer" can be done through a *security guard.* For example, users of an Unclassified system submit queries to a Secret system, using the guard as intermediary. The guard is used because the Secret system is not trusted to protect itself or its data against threats from the Unclassified system. The guard passes on the queries unchanged but reviews the results to make sure they contain no Secret information. Another example is a mail guard, which transfers email between networks that operate at different levels. A guard usually is implemented on a separate trusted computing system that is connected to all the varied-level systems. The guard system may support a human reviewer, or the review may be automated. Guards are widely used in Department of Defense (DoD) systems, most of which operate in system-high mode.

Controlled application sets

The kernel approach draws the security perimeter around a portion of the operating system. This approach is essentially built into the TCSEC. Many researchers have concluded that the TCSEC TCB cannot by itself guarantee security. For example, Daniel F. Sterne, Glenn S. Benson, and Homayoon Tajalli (1994) point out that the TCB cannot prevent leakage through covert channels or subversion of accountability by malicious software. It cannot keep applications from modifying information so as to harm integrity. Therefore, applications must be trusted. These authors propose the following principle:

> Any application that can manipulate sensitive information must be trusted not to behave maliciously and therefore requires some assurance.

They advocate redrawing the security perimeter to include both a TCB and a *Controlled Application Set* (CAS) that would include database management systems as well as applications for which there is some assurance of benign behavior. Assurance can be less rigorous than for the TCB, since the TCB constrains the CAS. New requirements are imposed on the TCB to protect the CAS and control its use.

Security Evaluation Criteria

Chapter 2 introduced the many standards and criteria that affect computer security directly or indirectly. They include software quality standards, networking standards, and standards for applications such as banking. This section considers security criteria, touching on the OSI standards and describing the U.S., European, and Canadian criteria, as well as newer criteria efforts.

There are compelling reasons to have criteria for evaluating the security of computer systems and products. Criteria provide a common terminology for describing security services and degrees of security. Vendors are guided by criteria in deciding what features to develop and what development practices to follow. Users rely on criteria and evaluations in selecting and acquiring products.

The OSI security standards

Chapter 2 introduced the Open Systems Interconnection (OSI) architecture and reference model. Although the OSI focuses on communication *between* systems, it also defines an architecture for the communication functions *within* systems. This architecture is in fact strictly layered, following the approach of hierarchical layers of abstraction. Each of the seven layers provides services to the layer above it and uses services of the layer below it. The lowest layer is the most physical, and the highest layer is closest to the application. The term *service* is used for the capability or function provided by a layer. The active elements within a layer are called *entities*. An entity on one system interacts with its *peer entities* in the same layer on other systems, using the protocols defined for that layer.

OSI security standards pertain to communications and not to the security within each system, so these standards are covered in Chap. 10 on network security. It is noted here only that a set of basic security services has been specified, along with a set of security mechanisms that may be used to provide those services.

Trusted Computer System Evaluation Criteria (TCSEC)

The *Trusted Computer System Evaluation Criteria* (NCSC 1985)—also called the TCSEC and the "Orange Book"—were developed as part of a broader program for the security of DoD computing systems. The DoD encourages vendors to develop products that satisfy the criteria. It evaluates the products and puts those which qualify on an *Evaluated Products List.* The criteria are oriented primarily to operating systems. They are intended to provide

- A standard as to what security features vendors should build into commercial products.
- A metric that DoD units can use to evaluate systems' trustworthiness for secure processing of sensitive information.
- A basis for specifying security requirements in acquisition specifications.

The Orange Book

- Establishes a set of fundamental requirements that derive from basic *control objectives.*
- Defines major divisions of systems and classes within the divisions. The divisions are ordered, with higher divisions providing more comprehensive security and warranting more confidence.

The three basic control objectives are security policy, accountability, and assurance. Each gives rise to several requirements.

Security policy objective. Since "a given system can only be said to be secure with respect to its enforcement of some specific policy," each system must define and implement a security policy that accurately reflects the relevant laws, regulations, and general policies.

Requirement 1: Security policy. The system must enforce an explicit and well-defined security policy. More specifically, a mandatory security policy must be enforced, and discretionary controls are also required.

Requirement 2: Marking. Access control labels must be associated with objects, reliably identifying the objects' classifications and/or the access modes allowed to subjects.

Accountability objective. Systems must ensure individual accountability.

Requirement 3: Identification. "Individual subjects must be identified. Each access to information must be mediated based on who is accessing the information and what classes of information they are authorized to deal with." The computer system must securely maintain the identification and authorization information.

Requirement 4: Accountability. If individuals are to be held accountable, the system must record security-relevant events in an audit log so that actions affecting security can be traced. The audit data must be protected from modification or destruction.

Assurance objective. Systems "must be designed to guarantee correct and accurate interpretation of the security policy and must not distort the intent of that policy." Two types of assurance are needed. *Life-cycle assurance* pertains to the way the system is designed, developed, and maintained. *Operational assurance* pertains to how the security features enforce security policy during operation.

Requirement 5: Assurance. The system must include mechanisms that can be evaluated independently to provide assurance that the four requirements listed above are indeed enforced. The mechanisms that do the enforcement (typically in the operating system but also including hardware) must be identified explicitly. The basis for trusting them must be documented clearly to allow for the independent evaluation.

Requirement 6: Continuous protection. The enforcement mechanisms themselves must be protected against tampering or unauthorized modification, and this protection must be continuous.

Classes of systems. The Orange Book identifies four main divisions of its criteria, labeled D through A from least to most stringent. (Division D is for systems that do not qualify for any higher division.) Divisions B and C each have further subdivisions called *classes.* Figures 6.7 and 6.8 show the requirements for each class. Mandatory protection is required only for divisions A and B. The security feature requirements are the same for class A1 and class B3, but the assurance requirements are different. Class A1 systems must have a formally verified design.

The requirement for the TCB architecture of A1 systems summarizes key security design principles. It calls for well-defined, largely independent modules, designed according to the principle of least privilege. The TCB must use layering, abstraction, and data hiding. It must be simple, excluding modules that are not critical for security. The Orange Book also calls for hardware protection to provide a separate domain for TCB execution, to support separate address spaces for processes, and to give separate access attributes to distinct storage objects.

The Orange Book requires searching for all covert storage channels (storage and timing for A1 systems) and estimating the bandwidth of

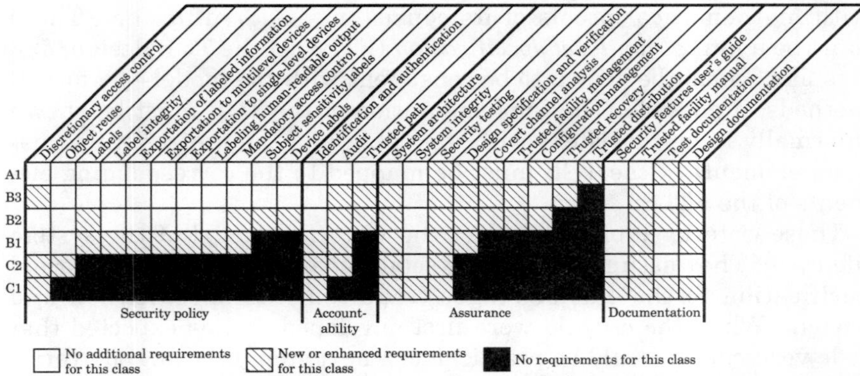

Figure 6.7 Trusted Computer System Evaluation Criteria: summary chart. (*From NCSC, 1985.*)

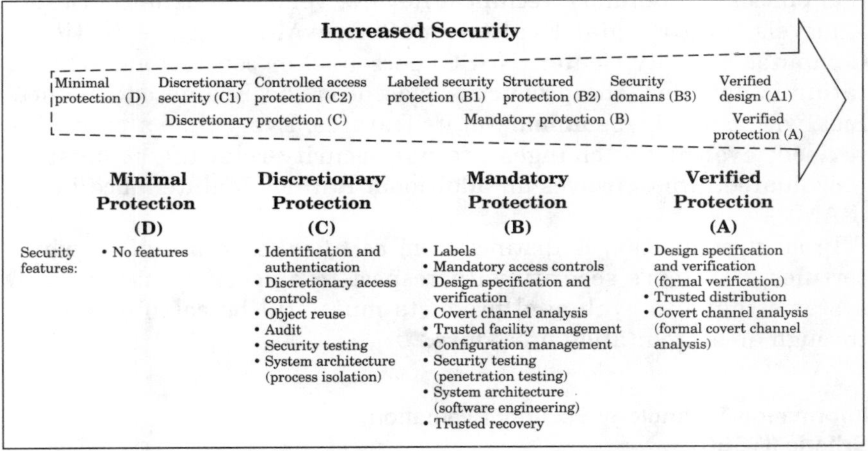

Figure 6.8 Trusted Computer System Evaluation Criteria: rating scale. [*From Chokhani (1992). Copyright (©) 1992 Association for Computing Machinery, Inc. (ACM). Reprinted by permission.*]

each one. It mandates eliminating high-bandwidth channels and suggests auditing medium-bandwidth channels. Orange Book guidelines interpret *high* as 100 bits/second—a figure based on 1980s rates of terminals—and suggest an acceptable bandwidth of 1 bit per 10 seconds. A later guide (NCSC 1993a) points out that the danger from a specific rate depends on the nature of the application, the possible threats, and the characteristics of each covert channel.

Formal verification. Design verification (class A1 only) starts from a formal model of the security policy. The model must be documented with mathematical proofs of its consistency and sufficiency. There must be a *formal top-level specification* (FTLS) of the TCB design, and this FTLS must be shown to be consistent with the model—by formal methods, if possible. The implementation of the TCB must be shown informally to be consistent with its FTLS, and the protection mechanism elements of the TCB must be mapped to the corresponding elements of the FTLS.

These criteria implicitly reflect the waterfall model of the system life cycle. They assume an orderly sequence of stages and add formal verification to the earlier stages (requirements specification and design). When the criteria were first developed, it was expected that code verification would be practical as a next step. Indeed, code verification was the real goal, design verification being only a first step.

The TCSEC in practice. Products to be rated go through four evaluation phases: Preliminary Technical Review, Vendor Assistance, Design Analysis, and Formal Evaluation. The evaluators are National Computer Security Center (NCSC) personnel or contractors. When a rating is awarded, the product is placed on the Evaluated Products List, with a detailed summary of its features. Every time a product is revised, even if the changes are not security-relevant, it must be reevaluated. This involves an additional Ratings Maintenance Phase (RAMP).

Product evaluation is distinct from *certification evaluation,* which certifies a system's security with respect to a specific mission. DoD systems that use evaluated products must still be certified and go through an accreditation procedure.

Information Technology Security Evaluation Criteria (ITSEC)

France, Germany, the Netherlands, and the United Kingdom cooperated in developing *Information Technology Security Evaluation Criteria* (ITSEC 1991). In contrast to the TCSEC, the ITSEC address both commercial and government requirements, and they consider goals other than secrecy. They more clearly separate functionality from assurance. For functionality, security features are viewed at three levels: security objectives, *security-enforcing functions,* and security mechanisms. (These correspond roughly to *policies, services,* and *mechanisms* in this book's terminology.) The criteria also distinguish between products and systems. "An *IT system* is a specific IT installation with a particular purpose and known operational environment. An *IT product* is a hardware and/or software package that can be bought off the shelf and incorporated into a variety of systems." The criteria apply to both products and systems. A system or product to be evaluated is called a *target of evaluation* (TOE). Unlike the TCSEC, the ITSEC do not require an identifiable TCB. However, architectural and design constraints are imposed at the higher evaluation levels.

Security functions. The recommended grouping of functions is

- Identification and authentication
- Access control
- Accountability
- Audit
- Object reuse
- Accuracy
- Reliability of service
- Data exchange (functions to ensure the security of data during transmission)

Ten examples of functionality classes are included in the ITSEC document. Classes F-C1 to F-B3 are hierarchically ordered and correspond closely to the TCSEC classes (Table 6.1). The other example classes address specific needs, such as high availability or high integrity for data and programs. The security functions may be specified in informal, semiformal, or formal style, depending on the target evaluation level. Semiformal specifications use a notation that is less ambiguous than natural language but not mathematically defined.

Assurance. There are two kinds of assurance: *correctness* (of the implementation of the security functions) and *effectiveness* (of the TOE in operation). Correctness evaluation deals primarily with the

TABLE 6.1 Correspondence between ITSEC and TCSEC Classes

ITSEC	TCSEC class
EO	D
F-C1,E1	C1
F-C2,E2	C2
F-B1,E3	B1
F-B2,E4	B2
F-B3,E5	B3
F-B3,E6	A1

Source: From ITSEC (1991).

development process, operational procedures, and documentation. Once the TOE has been deemed correct at the targeted class level, it must be evaluated for effectiveness in its intended use. Six aspects of effectiveness are considered. The first four aspects concern the construction of the TOE.

1. Are the security functions provided suitable to counter the threats?
2. Do the individual functions and mechanisms work together to provide an effective whole?
3. How well can the security mechanisms withstand direct attack? This aspect is called *strength of mechanisms.* It recognizes that "even if a security enforcing mechanism cannot be bypassed, deactivated, corrupted, or circumvented, it may still be possible to defeat it by a direct attack based on deficiencies in its underlying algorithms, principles or properties." Mechanisms are rated basic, medium, or high, depending on the expertise, resources, and opportunity that an attacker would need.
4. Will it be possible in practice to exploit any design or implementation weaknesses found during evaluation?

The other two aspects pertain to effectiveness in operation.

5. Will it be possible in practice to exploit operational vulnerabilities found during evaluation?
6. How easy to use are the security functions? Is the TOE prone to be configured or used in an insecure way?

A TOE must have a defined *security target,* which specifies

- A system security policy or a product rationale
- Security-enforcing functions
- Security mechanisms
- The minimum strength-of-mechanisms rating
- The target evaluation level

Comparison with TCSEC. One major difference from the TCSEC is that the ITSEC include integrity and availability as security goals along with confidentiality. They also give some attention to networking. Another major difference is the unbundling of functionality and assurance. Bundled ratings may be simpler to understand and apply, but they are less flexible. For example, a user may need a high degree of assurance but not all the security function. A less costly product would suffice if assurance could be obtained with fewer features.

Each country evaluates products according to the criteria. In the United Kingdom, evaluations are done by nongovernment Certified Licensed Evaluation Facilities (CLEFs). The evaluators start their work during the development process. Product sponsors (not necessarily the developers) determine the security target and pay for the evaluations. Vendors whose products were evaluated in both the United States and the United Kingdom found the U.K. evaluation faster and less costly.

Canadian Trusted Computer Product Evaluation Criteria (CTCPEC)

In the early 1990s, the government of Canada developed the *Canadian Trusted Computer Product Evaluation Criteria* (Canadian System Security Centre 1993). Like the ITSEC, the CTCPEC clearly separate functionality and assurance. They target not only operating systems but also databases, networked systems, object-oriented systems, and other products (not systems). A product is viewed as a collection of functionality services, and it receives a global level of assurance. There are functionality criteria for Confidentiality, Integrity, Availability, and Accountability, with services defined for each, as shown in Table 6.2. For example, Availability services are Containment, Fault Tolerance, Robustness, and Recovery. A service can be provided at different levels, with a higher level providing better defense against a specific set of threats. A product is expected to enforce some security policy. (No specific policy is built into the criteria.) The product's policy must define, for each service, what objects the service applies to.

The CTCPEC use a TCB concept similar to that of the TCSEC. For the higher assurance levels, the TCB must use modularity, abstraction, and data hiding, and each module must enforce the least-privilege principle. At these levels, the TCB should include only protection-critical components, and its complexity should be minimized. Everything under the control of the TCB is considered an object, where objects can be both active and passive (both subjects and objects in access-matrix terminology). Anything to be protected is defined as an object. A trusted product is supposed to isolate objects and to guarantee that access requests are mediated and that information flows are auditable. All security functionality is considered to be encompassed by isolation, mediation, and audit.

Assurance is based on the development process as well as the evaluation process. The rating from an evaluation includes all the service

TABLE 6.2 Criteria and Services

Criteria	Services
Confidentiality	Covert channels
	Discretionary confidentiality
	Mandatory confidentiality
	Object reuse
Integrity	Domain integrity (TCB)
	Discretionary integrity
	Mandatory integrity
	Physical integrity
	Rollback
	Separation of duties
	Self-testing
Availability	Containment
	Fault tolerance
	Robustness
	Recovery
Accountability	Audit
	Identification and authentication
	Trusted path

Source: From Canadian System Security Centre (1993). Copyright © The Government of Canada.

levels and a single assurance level, which applies to all the services. Levels range from zero to some maximum for each service. For example, there are four levels of mandatory confidentiality and five levels of audit. There are seven assurance levels.

The CTCPEC are flexible and extensible. They represent a practical way to rate functionality and assurance independently and without an explosion of rating categories. Subsequent criteria efforts have drawn on this work.

Problems and directions

Although they have definitely furthered the development and application of security technology, the criteria are far from ideal.

Problems with the TCSEC. The TCSEC are lacking in many respects. They give no attention to integrity or availability. A product with features to support Clark-Wilson integrity receives no higher rating than a product without those features. The TCB concept is inadequate for contemporary systems. Many interpretations and guides have been published, but much remains nebulous. The bundled ratings are inflexible and hard to extend. Long and costly evaluations are a problem for all the criteria, especially for the TCSEC. Products are obsolete by the time evaluation is completed. A trusted version of a product tends to lag behind the standard product in function.

Trying to remedy some of these problems, the NIST and NSA cooperated in developing new *Federal Criteria.* In addition to enhancing the TCSEC, this work sought to address private-sector needs, take into account the international market and international standards, and consider distributed systems. Canada participated, and the ITSEC also was used. A draft was published in 1993, but the Federal Criteria were never completed, since it was decided to work with the Europeans on common criteria.

Common criteria. There is a need for common criteria for at least Canada, Europe, and the United States. Without common criteria or mutual recognition of evaluations, vendors who want to sell their products in all the markets must obtain evaluations under the CTCPEC, ITSEC, and TCSEC. Of course, this greatly increases their costs. Non-U.S. vendors have not been able to get TCSEC evaluations. In 1993, the European Commission and the governments of Canada and the United States began to develop the *Common Criteria* (Common Criteria Editorial Board 1996), intending to resolve the differences among the three sets of criteria. The ultimate goal was an ISO standard. The Federal Criteria served as input to the project. At this writing, it is not known if the Common Criteria will be adopted any time soon. A possible interim step is mutual recognition of evaluations; for the lower assurance levels (CTCPEC T3, ITSEC E2, TCSEC C2), there is considerable equivalence.

The Development Process and Security

Security needs affect the entire development life cycle. They apply to the system being developed as well as to the development process and its tools and intermediate products.

Security requirements specification

The requirements specification must include a statement of the security policy that the system will support. Sometimes the policy is quite general and open-ended. For example, an operating system intended for commercial use must provide services that can support a variety of policies. The requirements specification also describes the security-related functions—the security services. For an existing system that is being enhanced for security, the new commands and system calls are described. Performance and resource requirements for the security services also may be specified. Security requirements add to the memory and computing capacity needed. Security requirements also mean budgeting more time and money for development. Not only

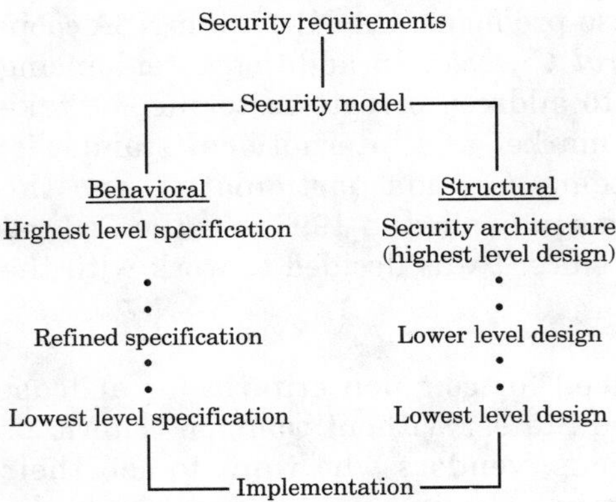

Figure 6.9 Levels of specification.

must the security services be developed, but unusually thorough review and analysis are needed at each stage and especially at the earlier stages.

Figure 6.9 shows a series of increasingly detailed specifications for the security-relevant behavior and structure of a system. Each level must be shown (either formally or informally) to correctly implement the level above it. Paralleling the behavioral specifications is the *security architecture*—a description of how a system is structured to satisfy the security requirements. The security architecture is the highest-level design. It identifies and describes all the components that are relevant for security. It also shows how the system conforms to the architectural approach chosen—such as the kernel approach. Each level of specification and each stage of design need the right amount of detail. Making too many design decisions at early stages complicates the higher levels and constrains them unnecessarily.

Formal methods for security

Formal methods allow security requirements to be expressed more precisely and unambiguously. They help to keep each stage of elaboration consistent with the preceding stage. They support formal verification, which demonstrates consistency between system descriptions at different levels. Formal methods are required for systems targeted at high TCSEC assurance levels. More generally, formal methods are one path to quality.

Steps in formal specification and verification. The steps in formal specification and verification are

1. State the security requirements in mathematical terms—as a formal security model. Informally, confirm that the model corresponds to the original requirements for the system. (There is no formal way to show that the model captures the true intent of the framers of the requirements.)
2. Produce a highest-level formal specification (the FTLS in Orange Book terminology) that gives a mathematical description of the system's behavior, leaving out many details. Prove that it corresponds to the formal requirements.
3. Produce a series of refinements. Each refinement implements the next-higher-level specification, but with more detail. Prove that each *level of refinement* is consistent with the one above it.
4. Code the system. Show that the implementation is consistent with the lowest-level formal specification.

This is an idealized sequence. For one thing, most formal specification and verification have been conducted after the fact for systems that were already designed and implemented. For another, code verification is enormously difficult for programs of significant size, and few projects attempt it. Rather, formal verification is used at higher levels and informal verification at lower levels.

Formal methodologies. The methodologies that have been used for security include Gypsy, the Hierarchical Development Method, and the Formal Development Method (FDM). Here FDM is described briefly, and an example of its use is given.

Much of the formal work in security uses state machine modeling. FDM is in this tradition. Its specification language (called *Ina Jo*) treats a system and its data as a state machine. A specification in Ina Jo includes declarations of types, constants, and variables; initial conditions; *transforms*; and *assertions*. Assertions describe properties the machine must satisfy; FDM involves proving that these properties are satisfied. *Criteria* are assertions describing individual states, and *constraints* are assertions describing pairs of consecutive states. The possible state transitions for a machine are given in transform specifications, each consisting of a *reference condition* and an *effect*. The reference condition describes the set of states in which the transform may legitimately be invoked. The effect describes all possible relations between the state at the start of the invocation and the state at the end.

The transforms and the variables express the function of the system. Eventually they will be implemented by procedures and variables of a programming language. The criteria and constraints express the desired security properties (based on the security model). It must be proved that the initial condition satisfies the criteria and that each transform preserves the criteria and satisfies the constraints.

FDM uses levels of refinement; a higher-level machine is implemented by a lower-level machine. The Ina Jo language supports this with facilities for mapping between levels. Types, constants, variables, and transforms of the higher-level specification are mapped to their counterparts in the lower-level specification. (Unfortunately, the word *level* has at least three different uses in this chapter: security level, as in Top Secret, level of assurance, as in the CTCPEC, and level of refinement.)

Example of formal specification. A small example of formal specification is the Secure Release Terminal (SRT) described by Kemmerer (© 1990 IEEE). The purpose of the terminal is to move classified documents from a higher-level host system to a lower-level system. The terminal is used by a security officer, who reviews a document and removes any higher-level information. At any moment the terminal is at a specific security level; the user can change that level. This project used FDM.

Security requirements. Five security properties were to be preserved. Two of these were

- "The SRT can be connected only to a host at the same level."
- "For an SRT to change levels, its text buffer must first be sanitized or else the data it contains must be reviewed and accepted for a level change before the change can take place."

Highest-level formal specification. The Ina Jo types included

```
Level = (High,Low,Sanitized),
Connect_Level = T"L:Level(L = High | L = Low),
Buffer
```

(T″ defines a subtype.) Note that the type Buffer has no structure, since its structure was not considered relevant for this highest-level specification. The Ina Jo variables included

```
Terminal_level:Level,
Reviewed:Boolean,
Active_Host:Connect_Level,
Terminal_Buffer:Buffer
```

The initial state is described as follows:

```
Terminal_Level = Sanitized
& ~Connected
```

```
& ~Reviewed
& ~Accepted
& Terminal_Buffer = Sanitized_Buffer
```

The state changes as a result of actions initiated by the user. For example, the action **Connect_To**(Lev:Connect_Level) connects the terminal to the level Lev host. The following is the Ina Jo transform for that action (N″ means "new value of"):

```
Transform
Connect_To(Lev:Connect_Level)
Refcond
      ~Connected
      & (Terminal_Level = Lev | Terminal_Level = Sanitized)
Effect
N"Connected
& N"Terminal_Level = Lev
& N"Active_Host = Lev
& ~N"Reviewed
& ~N"Accepted
```

The **Refcond** section expresses that for this transition to occur, the terminal must not be connected, and it must be either sanitized or at the same level as the specified host. The **Effect** section expresses the state after the transform fires. For example, the terminal has the level of the host it is connected to. Any variables not appearing in the **Effect** section are assumed not to change.

Verification. From these highest-level specifications the Ina Jo processor produced the proof obligations (additional assumptions to be proved) needed to guarantee that the transforms satisfied the formal requirements. The processor generated an Initial Conditions Theorem, and for each transform it generated a transform theorem:

$$CR \;\&\; R \;\&\; E \rightarrow N''CR \;\&\; CO$$

where CR is the Criterion, R and E are the Reference Condition and Effect, and CO is the Constraint. These theorems were proved using the Interactive Theorem Prover of FDM.

Detailed specifications. The specification was next carried to a more detailed level. For example, a buffer was further defined as a list of lines, and the display screen was introduced. Mappings also were introduced. For example,

```
Connect_To(Lev)  ==
      (Lev = High & Connect_to_High | Lev = Low & Connect_To_Low)
```

Part of the detailed specification appears in Kemmerer's article (1990).

The value of formal verification. Formal verification has its limits and its difficulties. Errors in proofs are possible at all levels, and automated provers can have errors. Despite automated tools, verification remains enormously laborious. One kernel design verification resulted in proof documentation equivalent to more than 7000 pages. In a comprehensive critique, Marvin Schaefer (1989) questions the value of all this effort. Too few people are capable of doing verification, and the tools are not production quality or user-friendly. To be simple enough for verification, the specification has to be very abstract, so it may lose crucial detail. The code, since it must correspond closely to the specification, is likely to be inefficient. Very few successful A1 systems have been produced. They are too much work to develop in relation to the payoff. Even if verification were practical, there are limits to what it can prove. One can never prove that the highest-level formal description fully captures the real-world requirements. TCB verification cannot guarantee a secure system; some systems undergoing evaluation have been able to totally bypass the TCB.

Security of a program depends on many things beyond the program itself, such as the compiler, the run-time library, the computer, and the peripheral devices. Security of an operational system depends on its whole context, including management and users.

Perhaps the greatest danger is that formal verification diverts resources and attention away from rigorous informal analysis and testing. However, there is value in formally stating the security policy and specifying how it is implemented, even if verification is not done.

Methodologies and languages

The design methods described in this chapter, which have their roots in the TCSEC approach, have been used for relatively few systems. Structured methodologies are increasingly important for system development in general, but they have not been integrated with security design methods. Designers often consider security separately, using risk analysis. (One reason is that security often is an add-on.) A few approaches that link the two design problems are described in Chap. 13.

The choice of programming language can make a real difference in a program's security. A higher-level language means less code and thus less chance for error. The programs are far easier to review and analyze. Strong typing is invaluable in detecting programming errors, and many other kinds of error checking are possible. Some languages allow for assertions that are checked at compile time or at run time. However, compilers and run-time libraries themselves may be faulty (as shown by the Internet worm), and they introduce the possibility of tunneling attacks.

Traditionally, operating systems were written either in assembly language or in high-level languages such as C that are "unsafe." These languages do not enforce or promote good program design (such as information hiding) or prevent common errors. They were used because they permit access to all machine resources and do not interfere with programming for performance. The code in these languages is so hard to read and understand that ensuring its security is nearly impossible. Major applications that were written long ago also remain in assembly language. The situation is changing with the advent of languages that promote quality and security without imposing unworkable constraints. Languages such as Ada support modularity, abstraction, and information hiding. Object-oriented languages such as C++ support inheritance as well. Inheritance promotes good structure and (by making it easier to reuse existing code) correctness. In addition to features that support security, a compiler or other tool should have stability and a good track record.

Methodologies and languages are only one part of the picture. Peter Neumann puts it well: "The bottom line is that requirements specifiers, system designers, implementers, operators, and users need to be experienced, intelligent, disciplined, far-sighted, realistic, wary, and even a little lucky at times" (1993: 114).

Using existing software

Many security efforts are enhancements to existing products. Operating system vendors often add security services and fix vulnerabilities when they introduce new versions. Building an entirely new system is a very large task compared with enhancing an old one, with far more opportunity to introduce error. Trust can grow out of experience and evolution. Similarly, it can be more secure to "buy not build"—if an appropriate component already exists and if its security function and assurance meet the new needs. Since the vulnerabilities of an older and widely used product are better known, operational procedures often can compensate for them. A related issue, mainly for application systems, is development by outside contractors. An organization that contracts for development must assess the security of the developer's process and write process security requirements into the specifications.

Testing for security

Assurance that a system is secure derives from three types of sources, all necessary:

- Specifications (preferably formal), systematic design verification through analysis, and inspection

- Qualified developers and a rational development process
- Testing

Testing remains the main way to gain assurance that a system provides its specified services and enforces its security policy. Only testing can find security flaws in any aspect of the system, including policy, assumptions, user interfaces, and documentation. Only testing can reveal discrepancies between the security model and the real-world requirements. Only testing can catch the coding errors that survive inspections.

However, like analysis, testing can achieve only so much. It is expensive and time-consuming, so usually it is limited by time and money constraints, not by exhausting the security flaws. Testing cannot in general demonstrate that a system is secure; it can only fail to find security flaws. "...the designer must search out every way to penetrate security and correct all; the penetrator is really interested in finding and using only one. This is an unbalanced 'game of wits' in which the attacker has a substantial advantage" (Brinkley and Schell 1995: 82). Theoretical results about testing reveal its limitations. These results are framed in terms of sets of test cases for a specific program. Ideally, there would be a *reliable test set*—one that implies that the program is correct for all inputs. If the program has errors, the reliable test set will show that. However, a further result is that "there is no effective procedure for generating reliable test sets of *finite* size" (DeMillo and Offutt 1991). Testing cannot in general show correctness.

Testing specifically for security must supplement more general testing methods. Security testing includes

1. *Functional testing,* which demonstrates that the security services and mechanisms are complete and correct and consistent with the documentation.
2. *Penetration testing,* which stresses a system to expose security flaws.

Functional testing for TCSEC evaluations. TCSEC evaluations include rigorous security testing, especially for the higher classes. Both functional testing and penetration testing are done by NCSC evaluation teams, and functional testing is also done by vendors before submitting their products for evaluation. Special techniques are used for testing the TCB of a secure operating system, because standard testing methods can be impractical. For example, the entire system environment has to be initialized for each test of a primitive operation of the TCB. This is so time-consuming that testing must be automated.

Also, it is necessary to weed out tests that are redundant or not security-relevant.

A *test plan* defines, by means of *test conditions,* how the testing covers the security mechanisms. A test condition is a security-relevant constraint that a TCB primitive must satisfy. For example, the **read** primitive must satisfy, for each object type that it applies to (such as files and devices), the condition "that **read** fails, if neither **open** nor **creat** call has been performed before the **read** call." Test conditions are developed from the security model or requirements. The test plan also specifies the *test data* used to demonstrate that a test condition is satisfied. The test conditions and test data together are intended to ensure coverage of the TCB primitives and the security model. The test plan also includes an explicit *coverage analysis.*

Flaw hypothesis methodology. The *flaw hypothesis methodology* (FHM) is a systematic approach to penetration analysis that includes testing and other activities for finding and eliminating flaws. FHM was developed by Clark Weissman and others in the 1970s and has been used for TCSEC assurance, especially for systems intended for class B2 or higher. However, as commercial systems become more exposed (through networks) to hostile attacks, the methodology becomes more broadly appropriate. A penetration analysis must define the security threats to be considered and the capabilities of the attacker. In *open-box testing,* as opposed to *closed-box testing,* the testing team has access to internal code. Open-box testing is appropriate for general-purpose systems such as UNIX or MVS, and closed-box testing is appropriate for specialized products that never run user code. A testing team is small and includes expertise in both the tested system and security testing.

FHM has four stages:

1. *Flaw generation* develops an inventory of suspected flaws.
2. *Flaw confirmation* assesses each flaw hypothesis as true, false, or untested.
3. *Flaw generalization* analyzes the generality of the underlying security weakness represented by each confirmed flaw.
4. *Flaw elimination* recommends flaw repair or the use of external controls to manage risks associated with residual flaws. [List is from Weissman (1995: 277).]

Flaw generation. The team develops flaw hypotheses by studying the system documentation and conducting intensive brainstorming sessions. Design considerations that are the leading flaw generators are shown in Fig. 6.10.

1. Past experience with flaws in similar systems
2. Ambiguous architecture and design
3. Circumvention of critical security controls
4. Incomplete design of interfaces and implicit sharing
5. Deviations from the security policy and model
6. Deviations from initial conditions and assumptions
7. System anomalies, limits, and prohibitions
8. Operational practices, spoofs, and initialization flaws
9. Development practices and environment
10. Implementation errors

Figure 6.10 Most productive flaw hypothesis generators. [*From Weissman (© 1995 IEEE).*]

Flaw confirmation. For each area of the system design, the hypothesized flaws are sorted by priority, based on probability of existence, potential damage, and work to confirm. The potential flaws are confirmed primarily by desk checking, which is far less costly than live testing. Live testing is most useful for confirming complex or time-dependent flaws.

Flaw generalization. Each confirmed flaw is examined to see if it belongs to a larger class of flaws. If so, the flaw may generate new flaw hypotheses. If the flaw can be exploited in combination with other flaws, the damage potential may become very high, so priorities change.

Flaw elimination. Ways to repair the flaws are recommended, such as fixing an error or using a known countermeasure for a generic design flaw. Some flaws may not be practical to repair but can be controlled by operational procedures.

Documentation

Documentation is a crucial aspect of the development process; it is the only product for much of that process. Development methodologies often are document-driven. For a system's customers—prospective and current—documentation tells what the security services are and how to use them. It provides assurance that the system meets their security needs.

The TCSEC require four types of documentation. A Security Features Users Guide tells how to use the TCB features. A Trusted Facility Manual describes security-related operator and administrator functions, gives guidelines for system operation, tells how to generate a new TCB, and describes the audit procedures. Test Documentation describes the test plan, procedures, and results. Design Documentation describes the security policy and security model and explains how the model is sufficient to enforce the policy. It identifies the TCB mechanisms and shows that they satisfy the model.

Design Documentation, which is intended to guide the building of the system, is key to life-cycle assurance. It covers not only the final design but also the design history. It must be kept current, changing when the system changes. It serves to educate new project members and the people who will eventually maintain the system. The Orange Book requires only TCB documentation but strongly recommends documentation of the whole system. The documentation must describe the security policy, the protection mechanisms, and the covert channel analysis. The amount of required documentation increases with the security class. Hardware, firmware, and software are all included.

Configuration management and trusted distribution

The purpose of *configuration management* is to preserve a system's integrity through all the changes that occur as the system is developed, distributed, and operated. Any software project involving more than a handful of people needs configuration management, which includes

- Identifying the *configuration items*
- Controlling changes to the configuration
- Status accounting
- Auditing

The configuration items include software modules (source and object), hardware and firmware, documentation, development tools (such as editors and compilers), and configuration management tools. Each configuration item has a unique identifier. A system is viewed as a collection of configuration items. From the complete *library* of items, a specific *configuration* of the system is built.

A *baseline* is the set of configuration items at some significant point in the life cycle. One example is the version turned over to a testing group. The current baseline is the reference point against which all changes must be approved. Changes to a baseline module often are stored as *deltas*—files containing the changes. Some standards identify specific baselines:

1. Functional baseline that includes functional requirements
2. Allocated baseline that allocates requirements to specific configuration items
3. Product baseline, including design documentation and code

Most organizations define other baselines.

Configuration management must support sharing of items while preventing problems such as two people independently changing the same module. Proposed additions or changes to libraries must be authorized. Often, final approval on changes is the responsibility of a board whose members come from different parts of the organization. Auditors must be able to examine the history of a program—what changes were made, when, and by whom. The libraries must be secure, protected by integrity measures, access control, and audit. Configuration management helps ensure that security reviews are conducted on the latest documentation.

A configuration management system includes both procedural controls and automated tools. The UNIX Source Code Control System (SCCS) is one widely used tool. It maintains baselines and supports multiple revisions and variations of modules. An authorized user can *charge-out* a module and *charge-in* a new version. The UNIX **make** facility ensures that all the components used to build an executable module are current. (It is guided by a user-prepared file describing the dependencies of the module.)

Much more can be done in configuration management. A system can maintain relationships between items (such as mappings between specification items and code items). It can check for completeness and conformance to standards. It can be part of an integrated development environment.

For distributing a system, procedures are needed to ensure that the right system is received. The distribution process must answer the questions: "(*a*) Did the product received come from the organization who was supposed to have sent it? and (*b*) Did the recipient receive exactly what the sender intended?" (NCSC 1988: 20). Procedures for *trusted distribution* are a TCSEC requirement for class A1, but the need is far broader. Every organization has a continuing need to distribute the right software to all its computing systems, including PCs. Now that vendors distribute software over networks, trust is a critical issue for all software users. For software distributed in hard form, safeguards include tamper-resistant packaging, couriers, registered mail, and cryptographic authentication. For network distribution, certificate-based authentication schemes have been developed (but are not widely used). Vendors have an additional problem—how to alert users to security vulnerabilities without making them known publicly.

Summary

Developing secure systems includes (1) developing secure products and (2) developing secure operational systems that include people and nonautomated procedures as well as products. Software for secure systems must be high-quality software. Assurance—confidence that a system meets its security requirements—derives from the system design, the development process, analysis and testing, past performance of the developers and vendor, and independent evaluations.

"...Software engineering is the application of tools, methods, and disciplines to produce and maintain an automated solution to a real-world problem." The systems development life cycle consists of a sequence of stages in which a statement of the problem (a specification) is developed and transformed into an implementation statement that includes design descriptions, code, and testing materials. Verification determines if the implementation is consistent with the specification. Validation predicts how well a system will meet the real-world needs.

In the design stage, the software architecture is developed, determining the components and their structure. Each component should represent some abstraction. The principle of abstraction means ignoring some aspects of a subject in order to concentrate on the most relevant aspects. Each component should reveal to other components only its external properties, hiding its implementation and data. This is known as information hiding.

Contemporary operating system designs follow the object model, where the system is organized as abstractions that encompass both data and procedure. Operations associated with each object provide the only way to use the object. The object model has security advantages. It puts an intermediary—the object manager—between the object's implementation and its users. The object system provides a common access-control mechanism, and the object manager can implement additional controls. The client-server model interprets the object model in a way that is suited for distributed systems. A service is an object that can be requested by clients. Object-oriented systems have additional properties that support security.

Formal methods grounded in mathematics are prominent in security standards and practices. A formal specification can be analyzed by machine to uncover problems, prove new properties, or demonstrate that one level of specification is consistent with another level (do formal verification).

Verification and validation methods include formal and informal analysis, formal verification, inspection, and testing. Inspection is a highly structured review aimed at finding errors in specifications, designs, and code. Testing can find errors, demonstrate that requirements have been satisfied, measure reliability, and serve as evidence of due care.

A security flaw is a part of the system that can cause it to violate its security requirements. Generic types of flaws are worth studying. A validation flaw occurs when a program component does not adequately check information that is supplied to it. A domain flaw is a weakness in the boundaries between protection environments. Domain flaws include object reuse and exposing a lower-level representation of some object. Boundary-condition flaws allow programs to exceed resource limits, causing denial of service.

A covert channel is an unintended communication path that can be used to violate a system's security policy. Storage channels use changes to stored information, and timing channels use the timing of events. The danger of a covert channel depends on its bandwidth—the rate at which it transmits information. Methods for identifying storage channels include the shared resource matrix methodology, where the columns of a matrix represent primitive operations of the system, the rows represent attributes of objects, and a cell contains R if the operation references the attribute and M if it writes the attribute. Both direct and indirect references are included. Any row containing both an R and an M may represent a potential storage channel. Another method analyzes information flow, using automated tools to analyze code or formal specifications. However, this method identifies "formal flow violations" that are not real.

Once a covert channel has been uncovered, the system designers can choose to eliminate it, reduce its bandwidth by introducing noise or by hiding the exact timing of events, leave it and audit for its use, or ignore it because its bandwidth is very low. A way to eliminate some covert channels is to eliminate sharing by preallocating resources, either to individual users or processes or to security levels. Despite much effort, it has not been possible to control the covert channels in trusted operating systems. The problem grows worse as processor and I/O speeds increase.

Basic design principles for security include economy of mechanism, fail-safe defaults, complete mediation, open design, least privilege, psychological acceptability, explicitness, invisible database, separation of policy and mechanism, auditability, anticipation of future requirements, and proper weight to other goals. The total environment must be considered, including the system's users and management and other systems that interact with it.

Several architectural approaches have been developed for security, some of them primarily for multilevel secure systems. The kernel architecture tries to isolate and minimize the reference validation mechanism (which implements the reference monitor concept). The TCSEC use the term Trusted Computing Base or TCB. The security perimeter separates the TCB from the rest of the system. There must be a trusted path between the user and the TCB. The kernel approach has been influential but has deficiencies. Other approaches—hierarchical levels of abstraction and TCB subsets—generalize the TCB. A TCB subset is a TCB that is built on other TCB subsets. A security guard transfers data between systems that operate at different security levels. The guard is usually implemented on a separate trusted computing system. Some researchers believe that security requires trusting applications. The security perimeter then would include both a TCB and a Controlled Application Set of database management systems and trustworthy applications.

There are compelling reasons to have security criteria. Criteria provide a common terminology, guide vendors, and help users select and acquire products. The U.S. Trusted Computer System Evaluation Criteria establish requirements that derive from basic control objectives—security policy, accountability, and assurance. There are two kinds of requirements: security function and assurance. Divisions of systems are defined, as are classes within the divisions. The divisions are ordered, with higher divisions providing more function and greater assurance. A system must enforce an explicit security policy, including mandatory and discretionary controls. Objects must be labeled, subjects' identities must be authenticated, and each access must be mediated. The system must record security-relevant events. Two types of assurance are needed: life-cycle assurance for development and maintenance and operational assurance for security policy enforcement during operation. Of the four divisions (labeled D through A), mandatory security is required only of divisions A and B. Class A1 systems must have a formally verified design.

The European Information Technology Security Evaluation Criteria address both commercial and government requirements and consider policies other than secrecy. They separate functionality ratings from assurance ratings. Functionality is viewed at three levels: security objectives, security-enforcing functions, and security mechanisms. The criteria also distinguish between products and systems; they apply to both types of "targets of evaluation." Ten examples of functionality classes are provided; five of them correspond to the TCSEC classes. Assurance includes correctness (of the implementation of the security functions) and effectiveness (of the target of evaluation in operation).

The Canadian Trusted Computer Product Evaluation Criteria also separate functionality and assurance. A product is viewed as a collection of functionality services, and it receives a global level of assurance. There are functionality criteria for Confidentiality, Integrity, Availability, and Accountability, with services defined for each. A service can be provided at different levels, with a higher level providing better defense. The CTCPEC use a TCB concept similar to that of the TCSEC. A rating includes all the service levels and a single assurance level.

The criteria are lacking in many respects. The TCSEC give no attention to integrity or availability. The TCB concept is inadequate for contemporary systems. The bundled ratings are inflexible and hard to extend. Long and costly evaluations are a problem for all the criteria. There is a need for common criteria to facilitate an international market. Draft Common Criteria have been published.

Security needs affect the entire development life cycle, applying to both the system being developed and the development process. The requirements specification should describe the security policy, services, and mechanisms. The security architecture describes how a system is structured to satisfy the security requirements. It identifies and describes all the security-relevant components. Security requirements add to the memory and computing capacity needed. More time and money must be budgeted for development.

Formal methods are a path to quality software and are required for TCSEC A1 systems. The steps in formal specification and verification are to develop a formal security model and show informally that it corresponds to the original requirements produce a highest-level formal specification and prove that it corresponds to the security model, and produce a series of more detailed specifications and prove that each is consistent with the one above it. A formal methodology involves a specification language and a logical inference system, with mechanical theorem provers and proof checkers. The FDM methodology was used for a simple example given in the chapter. Formal verification is costly and hard to complete correctly. It provides imperfect assurance about real systems, and it diverts resources and attention from rigorous informal validation.

Only testing can find security flaws in any aspect of the system. However, testing is costly, and it cannot in general demonstrate that a system is secure; it can only fail to find security flaws. Functional testing demonstrates that the security services and mechanisms are complete and correct, and penetration testing stresses a system to expose security flaws. The flaw hypothesis methodology is used for penetration analysis and testing.

Documentation is a necessary part of a secure system. The TCSEC, for example, require documentation of security features; operator, administrator, system programmer, and auditor functions; testing; and design. Configuration management keeps track of a system and preserves its integrity. Trusted distribution ensures that the right system is received.

Bibliographic Notes

Gasser (1988) is a good source for designers and students. This book is highly readable and expresses clear views based on experience, primarily with systems designed for TCSEC requirements. Baskerville (1988) provides an information systems view of security design. *Computers at Risk* (National Research Council 1991) reviews secure system development and discusses problems and issues. Silberschatz et al. (1991) is a text on operating system concepts. Issues of software for safety-critical systems are discussed by Abbott (1990), Leveson (1991, 1995), and Parnas et al. (1990). Everyone, in the software field or not, should read the story of the Therac-25 radiation therapy machine (Leveson and Turner 1993).

Software engineering

Books on software engineering include Sommerville (1992) and Blum (1992); I use Blum's view of the simplified waterfall model. Davis (1993) is a comprehensive source on software requirements. The verification and validation quote is from Barry Boehm, quoted in Dunn and Ullman (1994); they provide a management-oriented view of the entire development process, with focus on quality. Blum (1994) surveys software development methods and presents a taxonomy. He points out that emphasis has shifted from the life cycle to the software process.

Wegner (1990) describes object-oriented programming concepts. Coad and Yourdon (1991a, 1991b) and Korson and McGregor (1990) describe object-oriented analysis and design. Fichman and Kemerer (1992) compare object-oriented and conventional analysis and design methodologies.

A good introduction to formal methods is provided by Wing (1990). Bowen and Hinchey (1995) give guidelines for using formal methods successfully. The Vienna Development Method (VDM) and Z are widely used methodologies for formal specification. Spivey (1990) provides an example of formal specification used without verification.

Inspection was developed at IBM by Michael Fagan. Experiences with it are described by Russell (1991) and Weller (1993). Books on testing include those by Beizer (1990) and Myers (1979).

The discussion of security flaws draws on Landwehr et al. (1994). Flaws found in penetration testing are described by Weissman (1995).

NCSC (1993a) is a detailed examination of issues in covert channel analysis for trusted systems. Haigh et al. (1987) report on analyzing the same specifications using both the shared resource matrix method and an approach based on noninterference. Flow analysis methods are discussed by Gasser (1988), Fine (1992), Eckmann (1994), Kemmerer and Porras (1991), and Tsai et al. (1987, 1990). Better understanding of covert channels came out of trusted system projects, such as VAX VMM (described in Chap. 7); several papers appear in the *Proceedings of the 1991 IEEE Computer Society Symposium on Research in Security and Privacy.* The shared-bus contention channel and fuzzy time are described by Hu (1991). Karger and Wray (1991) describe covert channels arising from disk I/O optimization. Wray

(1991) argues that a conventional clock is not needed for a timing channel, only two independent sequences of events whose timings can be compared. To use a shared-disk device as a timing channel, for example, the receiver issues two seeks and observes which completes first, as determined by a seek issued by the sender. Levin and Tao (1990) provide an example of a covert storage channel analysis. Browne (1994) proposes partitioning systems so that no resources are shared but periodically repartitioning. Covert channels then can arise only when repartitioning occurs.

Principles of design for security

The Saltzer and Schroeder article (1975) remains well worth studying. The principle of explicitness is discussed by Anderson (1994). Apropos of the principle of "proper attention to other goals," Gasser (1988) warns the security architect against losing influence by acting like a security fanatic. The relation between policy and mechanism is discussed by Fernandez et al. (1981).

Architectural approaches

Ames et al. (1983) provide an authoritative introduction to security kernels. A longer, highly readable introduction is provided by Brinkley and Schell (1995). Kernel design and implementation are described in Chap. 7. John Rushby introduced the separation kernel concept; it is discussed by Abrams and Joyce (1995a, 1995b). An extension is described by Kelem and Feiertag (1991), and a system that uses a separation kernel is described by Rushby and Randell (1983). Karger et al. (1990) describe the VAX VMM security kernel, which uses a strict level of abstraction approach. Landwehr (1983) surveys secure operating system projects, including kernel-based designs.

The concept of TCB subsets was introduced by Shockley and Schell (1987). TCB subsets are the main topic of the Trusted Database Management System Interpretation (NCSC 1991). Sterne (1992) describes a project that uses TCB subsets to support the Clark-Wilson policy. Trusted DBMSs using the approach are described in Chap. 9. King (1994a, 1994b) points out that products need to be designed to be composable and describes some practical U.S. government initiatives. Theoretical approaches to the composition problem are described in Chap. 4. NCSC (1994b) suggests a methodology for putting together multiple evaluated products into a trusted system. NCSC (1994c) considers problems of procurement and accreditation for existing and evolving systems, which typically differ in policy and degree of trust. Interconnecting them can result in the "cascading" of risk.

Security guards are discussed by Neugent (1989). Gosselin (1991) describes a guard that allows low-system users to update a high-system database but allows no transfer of data from high to low.

Abrams and Joyce (1995c) describe *policy-enforcing applications,* which manage and control access to their objects, as operating systems do for their objects. Like CASs, these applications must be trusted.

Security evaluation criteria

The Open Systems Interconnection (OSI) architecture and security standards are described in Chap. 10.

The TCSEC are published in NCSC (1985). Chokhani (1992) provides an overview of the TCSEC and the trusted product evaluation process, which is also described in NCSC (1990). DoD Directive 5200.28 (DoD 1988) states security requirements for DoD systems handling all classes of information. The Trusted Network Interpretation is discussed in Chap. 10. Ware (1995) provides an interesting history of the criteria, based on involvement and close observation over 20 years. Dinkel (1992) reviews and compares the TCSEC and ITSEC from the viewpoint of the NIST. Bačić and Robison (1993) discuss the Canadian criteria.

Critiques of the TCSEC are given by Parker (1992) and Schaefer (1993). Dobry and Schanken (1994) discuss, from an NCSC viewpoint, what new criteria should have for evaluating distributed systems. Certification and accreditation are discussed in NCSC (1994a).

Industry groups are working on other criteria, such as the GSSP, described in Chap. 2. Standards for open systems—such as UNIX—serve as security criteria because they define security services. Distributed system standards as they affect security are discussed in Chap. 10. Quality standards are discussed by Dunn and Ullman (1994), Coallier (1994), Paulk (1995), and Saiedian and Kuzara (1995).

The development process and security

Formal methods are discussed by Williams and Abrams (1995). Cheheyl et al. (1981) provide an excellent introduction to security verification and describe the important tools. Gerhart et al. (1994) consider several case studies of using formal methods, including a secure gateway. Stages of elaboration of security requirements are described in LaPadula and Williams (1991) and LaPadula (1993). NCSC (1992) provides guidance on TCSEC security modeling requirements. My description of the steps in formal specification and verification is based on Kemmerer (1990) and Berry (1987). Di Vito et al. (1990) describe the specification and verification of an operating system kernel.

Baskerville (1993) surveys IS security design methods, especially risk analysis. He points out that they lag behind general development methodologies and suggests integrating security considerations into the general methods. Risk analysis is covered in Chap. 13. Meadows and Landwehr (1992) describe potential advantages of using an object-oriented data model for designing a trusted application. Talvitie (1993) describes an object model for authorization for business applications. In both these efforts, the object-oriented method is useful for incorporating role-based access control. Gupta (1994) describes the use of object-oriented design and the C^{++} language for a trusted operating system.

Theoretical results about testing are reviewed by DeMillo and Offutt (1991). NCSC (1993b) is a detailed guide to testing for TCSEC evaluation. It considers both software and hardware security testing. My description of the flaw hypothesis methodology is based on Weissman (1995). Attanasio et al. (1976) describe a penetration analysis of IBM's VM/370 operating system. Gupta and Gligor (1991, 1992) criticize FHM flaw hypotheses generation as ad hoc. They present a model of penetration resistance and describe an automated tool for penetration analysis.

Testing can be made more efficient by *slicing*. A slice is an executable part of a program that behaves the same as the full program with respect to some criterion. Fink and Levitt (1994) describe using security specifications as criteria for slicing and also to determine the correct results of tests.

NCSC (1988b) is a guide to design documentation for trusted systems. Other types of documentation are discussed in Chap. 8.

Sources on configuration management include Babich (1986) and NCSC (1988a). Buckley (1994) considers requirements for a configuration management environment and briefly describes configuration management standards. Bersoff and Davis (1991) describe changes to the discipline of configuration management that are needed because of newer software development processes. SCCS is described by Rochkind (1975). Another configuration management system is DEC's CMS. Rubin (1995) describes a cryptography-based scheme for trusted distribution over the Internet. Bianco (1992) describes a tamper-resistant container for trusted distribution.

Exercises

6.1 Define the principle of abstraction. If you know two programming languages, describe how each one supports abstraction.

6.2 Relate the principles of abstraction and information hiding to the concepts of security service and security mechanism.

6.3 Which of the security flaws described is most likely to allow the tunneling attack described in Chap. 3?

6.4 Think of two potential covert channels that were not described in the chapter. Give a scenario of how each could be used to violate the multilevel policy. Which one do you think has the greater bandwidth?

6.5 Give an example of fail-safe defaults (for confidentiality or integrity) in an operating system or other software system that you have used.

6.6 Which of the Saltzer and Schroeder principles are evident in the kernel approach?

6.7 Various criticisms of the kernel approach have been presented. Which of these (or other) criticisms is the most serious, and why? Are all the criticisms valid?

6.8 What changes in computing led to the TCB subset approach?

6.9 Compare the two approaches—hierarchical levels of abstraction and TCB subsets. In what ways are they alike? In what ways are they different?

6.10 In the TCSEC, what is the distinction between security function requirements and assurance requirements?

6.11 Compare the basic approaches of the CTCPEC, ITSEC, and TCSEC. Do you think these approaches can be reconciled in Common Criteria?

6.12 In system design, what role is played by the security architecture?

6.13 State the security requirements for a very simple badge-reading system that controls doors. The system controls all the outside doors and some inside doors of a small building. Another system maintains the database used by this system. Sketch an informal security model, the highest-level behavioral specifications, and the security architecture.

6.14 Describe how levels of refinement are used in formal specification and verification.

6.15 Why are testing and verification through analysis both important? List some advantages and disadvantages of each method.

6.16 What are the main security threats to the development process and its products? Consider integrity, confidentiality, and availability.

6.17 Penetration analysis using the flaw hypothesis method has been effective but costly. This methodology was developed in the 1970s. What factors in the current environment might make penetration analysis of operating systems more cost-effective?

References

Abbott, Russell J. 1990. Resourceful systems for fault tolerance, reliability, and safety. *ACM Computing Surveys* **22**(1): 35–68.

Abrams, Marshall D., and Michael V. Joyce. 1995a. New thinking about information technology security. *Computers & Security* **14**(1): 69–81.

______. 1995b. Trusted computing update. *Computers & Security* **14**(1): 57–68.

______. 1995c. Trusted system concepts. *Computers & Security* **14**(1): 45–56.

Ames, Stanley R., Jr., Morrie Gasser, and Roger R. Schell. 1983. Security kernel design and implementation: An introduction. *Computer* **16**(7): 14–22.

Anderson, James P. 1972. *Computer Security Technology Planning Study.* Report ESD-TR-73-51. Bedford, Mass.: Electronic Systems Division, AFSC, October 1972.

Anderson, Ross J. 1994. Why cryptosystems fail. *Communications of the ACM* **37**(11): 32–40.

Attanasio, C. R., P. W. Markstein, and R. J. Phillips. 1976. Penetrating an operating system: A study of VM/370 integrity. *IBM Systems Journal* **15**(1): 102–116.

Babich, Wayne A. 1986. *Software Configuration Management.* Reading, Mass.: Addison-Wesley.

Bačić, Eugen Mate, and Andrew Robison. 1993. The rationale behind the Canadian criteria. *Proceedings of the Ninth Annual Computer Security Applications Conference,* 170–179. Los Alamitos, Calif.: IEEE Computer Society.

Baskerville, Richard. 1988. *Designing Information Systems Security.* Chichester, U.K.: Wiley.

______. 1993. Information systems security design methods: Implications for information systems development. *ACM Computing Surveys* **25**(4): 375–414.

Beizer, Boris. 1990. *Software Testing Techniques,* 2d ed. New York: Van Nostrand Reinhold.

Berry, Daniel M. 1987. Towards a formal basis for the formal development method and the Ina Jo specification language. *IEEE Transactions on Software Engineering* **13**(2): 184–201.

Bersoff, Edward H., and Alan M. Davis. 1991. Impacts of life cycle models on software configuration management. *Communications of the ACM* **34**(8): 104–118.

Bianco, Mark. 1992. A tamper-resistant seal for trusted distribution and life-cycle integrity assurance. *Proceedings of the 15th National Computer Security Conference,* 670–679. NIST/NCSC.

Blum, Bruce I. 1992. *Software Engineering: A Holistic View.* New York: Oxford University Press.

______. 1994. A taxonomy of software development methods. *Communications of the ACM* **37**(11): 82–94.

Boehm, Barry W. 1988. A spiral model of software development and enhancement. *Computer* **21**(5): 61–72.

Bowen, Jonathan P., and Michael G. Hinchey. 1995. Ten commandments of formal methods. *Computer* **28**(4): 56–63.

Brinkley, Donald L., and Roger R. Schell. 1995. Concepts and terminology for computer security. In Marshall D. Abrams, Sushil Jajodia, and Harold J. Podell, eds., *Information Security: An Integrated Collection of Essays,* 40–97. Los Alamitos, Calif.: IEEE Computer Society.

Browne, Randy. 1994. Mode security: An infrastructure for covert channel suppression. *Proceedings of the 1994 IEEE Computer Society Symposium on Research in Security and Privacy,* 39–55. Los Alamitos, Calif.: IEEE Computer Society.

Buckley, Fletcher J. 1994. Implementing a software configuration management environment. *Computer* **27**(2): 56–61.

Canadian System Security Centre. 1993. *The Canadian Trusted Computer Product Evaluation Criteria,* version 3.0e. Ottawa: Communications Security Establishment, Government of Canada.

Cheheyl, Maureen Harris, Morrie Gasser, George A. Huff, and Jonathan K. Millen. 1981. Verifying security. *ACM Computing Surveys* **13**(3): 279–339.

Chokhani, Santosh. 1992. Trusted products evaluation. *Communications of the ACM* **35**(7): 64–76.

Coad, Peter, and Edward Yourdon. 1991a. *Object-Oriented Analysis,* 2d ed. Englewood Cliffs, N.J.: Yourdon Press.

______. 1991b. *Object-Oriented Design.* Englewood Cliffs, N.J.: Yourdon Press.

Coallier, François. 1994. How ISO 9001 fits into the software world. *IEEE Software* **11**(1): 98–100.

Common Criteria Editorial Board. 1996. *Common Criteria for Information Technology Security Evaluation,* version 1.0. January 1996. Available from NIST.

Davis, Alan M. 1993. *Software Requirements: Objects, Functions, and States.* Englewood Cliffs, N.J.: PTR Prentice-Hall.

DeMillo, Richard A., and A. Jefferson Offutt. 1991. Constraint-based automatic test data generation. *IEEE Transactions on Software Engineering* **17**(9): 900–910.

Dinkel, Charles R. 1992. *A Review of U.S. and European Security Evaluation Criteria.* NISTIR 4774. Gaithersburg, Md.: National Institute of Standards and Technology.

Di Vito, Ben L., Paul H. Palmquist, Eric R. Anderson, and Michael L. Johnston. 1990. Specification and verification of the ASOS kernel. *Proceedings of the 1990 IEEE Computer Society Symposium on Research in Security and Privacy,* 61–74. Los Alamitos, Calif.: IEEE Computer Society.

Dobry, Rob, and Mary D. Schanken. 1994. Security concerns for distributed systems. *Proceedings of the Tenth Annual Computer Security Applications Conference,* 12–20. Los Alamitos, Calif.: IEEE Computer Society.

DoD. 1988. *Security Requirements for Automated Information Systems.* DoD Directive 5200.28. Washington, D.C.: Department of Defense.

Dunn, Robert H., and Richard S. Ullman. 1994. *TQM for Computer Software,* 2d ed. New York: McGraw-Hill.

Eckmann, Steven T. 1994. Eliminating formal flows in automated information flow analysis. *Proceedings of the 1994 IEEE Computer Society Symposium on Research in Security and Privacy,* 30–38. Los Alamitos, Calif.: IEEE Computer Society.

Fernandez, Eduardo B., Rita C. Summers, and Christopher Wood. 1981. *Database Security and Integrity.* Reading, Mass.: Addison-Wesley.

Fichman, Robert G., and Chris F. Kemerer. 1992. Object-oriented and conventional analysis and design methodologies. *Computer* **25**(10): 22–39.

Fine, Todd. 1992. A foundation for covert channel analysis. *Proceedings of the 15th National Computer Security Conference,* 204–212. NIST/NCSC.

Fink, George, and Karl Levitt. 1994. Property-based testing of privileged programs. *Proceedings of the Tenth Annual Computer Security Applications Conference,* 154–163. Los Alamitos, Calif.: IEEE Computer Society.

Gasser, Morrie. 1988. *Building a Secure Computer System.* New York: Van Nostrand Reinhold.

Gerhart, Susan, Dan Craigen, and Ted Ralston. 1994. Case study: Multinet Gateway System. *IEEE Software* **11**(1): 37–39.

Gosselin, Michelle J. 1991. The development of a low-to-high guard. *Proceedings of the 14th National Computer Security Conference,* 157–166. NIST/NCSC.

Gupta, Sarbari. 1994. Object-oriented security in the Trusted Mach operating system. *Security for Object-Oriented Systems. Proceedings of the OOPSLA-93 Conference Workshop on Security for Object-Oriented Systems,* 90–95. London: Springer-Verlag.

Gupta, Sarbari, and Virgil D. Gligor. 1991. Towards a theory of penetration-resistant systems and its applications. *The Computer Security Foundations Workshop IV,* 62–78. Los Alamitos, Calif.: IEEE Computer Society.

______. 1992. Experience with a penetration analysis method and tool. *Proceedings of the 15th National Computer Security Conference,* 165–183. NIST/NCSC.

Haigh, J. Thomas, Richard A. Kemmerer, John McHugh, and William D. Young. 1987. An experience using two covert channel analysis techniques on a real system design. *IEEE Transactions on Software Engineering* **13**(2): 157–168.

Hu, Wei-Ming. 1991. Reducing timing channels with fuzzy time. *Proceedings of the 1991 IEEE Computer Society Symposium on Research in Security and Privacy,* 8–19. Los Alamitos, Calif.: IEEE Computer Society.

ITSEC. 1991. *ITSEC: Information Technology Security Evaluation Criteria.* Luxembourg: European Communities—Commission.

Karger, Paul A., and John C. Wray. 1991. Storage channels in disk arm optimization. *Proceedings of the 1991 IEEE Computer Society Symposium on Research in Security and Privacy,* 52–61. Los Alamitos, Calif.: IEEE Computer Society.

Karger, Paul A., Mary Ellen Zurko, Douglas W. Bonin, Andrew H. Mason, and Clifford E. Kahn. 1990. A VMM security kernel for the VAX architecture. *Proceedings of the 1990 IEEE Computer Society Symposium on Research in Security and Privacy,* 2–19. Los Alamitos, Calif.: IEEE Computer Society.

Kelem, Nancy L., and Richard J. Feiertag. 1991. A separation model for virtual machine monitors. *Proceedings of the 1991 IEEE Computer Society Symposium on Research in Security and Privacy,* 78–86. Los Alamitos, Calif.: IEEE Computer Society.

Kemmerer, Richard A. 1983. Shared resource matrix methodology: An approach to identifying storage and timing channels. *ACM Transactions on Computer Systems* **1**(3): 256–277.

______. 1990. Integrating formal methods into the development process. *IEEE Software* **7**(5): 37–50.

Kemmerer, Richard A., and Phillip A. Porras. 1991. Covert flow trees: A visual approach to analyzing covert storage channels. *IEEE Transactions on Software Engineering* **17**(11): 1166–1185.

King, Guy. 1994a. The composition problem: An analysis. *Proceedings of the 17th National Computer Security Conference,* 292–298. NIST/NCSC.

______. 1994b. Secure system composition: Five practical initiatives. *Proceedings of the Tenth Annual Computer Security Applications Conference,* 67–73. Los Alamitos, Calif.: IEEE Computer Society.

Korson, Tim, and John D. McGregor. 1990. Understanding object-oriented: A unifying paradigm. *Communications of the ACM* **33**(9): 40–60.

Lampson, Butler W. 1973. A note on the confinement problem. *Communications of the ACM* **16**(10): 613–615.

Landwehr, Carl E. 1983. The best available technologies for computer security. *Computer* **16**(7): 86–100.

Landwehr, Carl E., Alan R. Bull, John P. McDermott, and William S. Choi. 1994. A taxonomy of computer program security flaws. *ACM Computing Surveys* **26**(3): 211–254.

LaPadula, Leonard J. 1993. Prospect on security paradigms. *Proceedings of the 1992–1993 ACM SIGSAC New Security Paradigms Workshop,* 62–68. Los Alamitos, Calif.: IEEE Computer Society.

LaPadula, Leonard J., and James G. Williams. 1991. Toward a universal integrity model. *Proceedings of the Computer Security Foundations Workshop IV,* 216–218. Los Alamitos, Calif.: IEEE Computer Society.

Leveson, Nancy G. 1991. Software safety in embedded computer systems. *Communications of the ACM* **34**(2): 34–46.

______. 1995. *Safeware: System Safety and Computers.* Reading, Mass.: Addison-Wesley.

Leveson, Nancy G., and Clark S. Turner. 1993. An investigation of the Therac-25 accidents. *Computer* **26**(7): 18–41.

Levin, Timothy E., and Albert Tao. 1990. Covert storage channel analysis: A worked example. *Proceedings of the 13th National Computer Security Conference,* 10–19. NIST/NCSC.

Meadows, Catherine, and Carl Landwehr. 1992. Designing a trusted application using an object-oriented data model. In Teresa F. Lunt, ed., *Research Directions in Database Security,* 191–198. New York: Springer-Verlag.

Myers, Glenford J. 1979. *The Art of Software Testing.* New York: Wiley.

National Research Council. 1991. *Computers at Risk: Safe Computing in the Information Age.* Washington, D.C.: National Academy Press.

NCSC. 1985. *Department of Defense Trusted Computer System Evaluation Criteria.* Report DOD 5200.28-STD. Fort Meade, Md.: National Computer Security Center.

______. 1988a. *A Guide to Understanding Configuration Management in Trusted Systems.* NCSC-TG-006. Fort Meade, Md.: National Computer Security Center.

______. 1988b. *A Guide to Understanding Design Documentation in Trusted Systems.* NCSC-TG-007. Ft. Meade, Md.: National Computer Security Center.

______. 1990. *Trusted Product Evaluations: A Guide for Vendors.* NCSC-TG-002. Ft. Meade, Md.: National Computer Security Center.

______. 1991. *Trusted Database Management System Interpretation of the Trusted Computer System Evaluation Criteria.* NCSC-TG-021. Fort Meade, Md.: National Computer Security Center.

______. 1992. *A Guide to Understanding Security Modeling in Trusted Systems.* NCSC-TG-010. Fort Meade, Md.: National Computer Security Center.

______. 1993a. *A Guide to Understanding Covert Channel Analysis of Trusted Systems.* NCSC-TG-030. Fort Meade, Md.: National Computer Security Center.

______. 1993b. *A Guide to Understanding Security Testing and Test Documentation in Trusted Systems.* NCSC-TG-023. Fort Meade, Md.: National Computer Security Center.

______. 1994a. *Introduction to Certification and Accreditation.* NCSC-TG-029. Fort Meade, Md.: National Computer Security Center.

______. 1994b. *Turning Multiple Evaluated Products into Trusted Systems.* Technical report-003, library no. S-241,353. Fort Meade, Md.: National Computer Security Center.

______. 1994c. *Use of the Trusted Computer System Evaluation Criteria (TCSEC) for Complex, Evolving, Multipolicy Systems.* Technical report-002, library no. S-241,321. Fort Meade, Md.: National Computer Security Center.

Neugent, William. 1989. Guidelines for specifying security guards. *Proceedings of the 12th National Computer Security Conference,* 320–338. NIST/NCSC.

Neumann, Peter G. 1986. On hierarchical design of computer systems for critical applications. *IEEE Transactions on Software Engineering* **12**(9): 905–920.

______. 1990. *On the Design of Dependable Computer Systems for Critical Applications.* CSL technical report. Menlo Park, Calif.: SRI International.

______. 1993. The role of software engineering. *Communications of the ACM* **36**(5): 114.

Parker, Donn B. 1992. Restating the foundation of information security. In *IT Security: The Need for International Cooperation. Proceedings of the IFIP TC11 Eighth International Conference on Information Security, IFIP/Sec '92,* 139–151. Amsterdam: North-Holland.

Parnas, David L., A. John van Schouwen, and Shu Po Kwan. 1990. Evaluation of safety-critical software. *Communications of the ACM* **33**(6): 636–648.

Paulk, Mark C. 1995. How ISO 9001 compares with the CMM. *IEEE Software* **12**(1): 74–83.

Rochkind, M. J. 1975. The Source Code Control System. *IEEE Transactions on Software Engineering* **1**(4): 364–370.

Rubin, Aviel D. 1995. Trusted distribution of software over the Internet. *Proceedings of the Symposium on Network and Distributed System Security,* 47–53. Los Alamitos, Calif.: IEEE Computer Society.

Rushby, John, and Brian Randell. 1983. A distributed secure system. *Computer* **16**(7): 55–66.

Russell, Glen W. 1991. Experience with inspection in ultralarge-scale developments. *IEEE Software* **8**(1): 25–31.

Saiedian, Hossein, and Richard Kuzara. 1995. SEI Capability Maturity Model's impact on contractors. *Computer* **28**(1): 16–26.

Saltzer, Jerome H., and Michael D. Schroeder. 1975. The protection of information in computer systems. *Proceedings of the IEEE* **63**(9): 1278–1308.

Schaefer, Marvin. 1989. Symbol security condition considered harmful. *Proceedings of the 1989 IEEE Computer Society Symposium on Security and Privacy,* 20–46. Los Alamitos, Calif.: IEEE Computer Society.

______. 1993. We need to think about the foundations of computer security. *Proceedings of the 1992–1993 ACM SIGSAC New Security Paradigms Workshop,* 120–125. Los Alamitos, Calif.: IEEE Computer Society.

Shockley, William R., and Roger R. Schell. 1987. TCB subsets for incremental evaluation. *AIAA/ASIS/IEEE Third Aerospace Computer Security Conference: Applying Technology to Systems,* 131–139. Washington, D.C.: American Institute of Aeronautics and Astronautics.

Silberschatz, Abraham, James L. Peterson, and Peter B. Galvin. 1991. *Operating System Concepts,* 3d ed. Reading, Mass.: Addison-Wesley.

Sommerville, Ian. 1992. *Software Engineering,* 4th ed. Wokingham, England: Addison-Wesley.

Spivey, J. Michael. 1990. Specifying a real-time kernel. *IEEE Software* **7**(5): 21–28.

Sterne, Daniel F. 1992. A TCB subset for integrity and role-based access control. *Proceedings of the 15th National Computer Security Conference,* 680–696. NIST/NCSC.

Sterne, Daniel F., Glenn S. Benson, and Homayoon Tajalli. 1994. Redrawing the security perimeter of a trusted system. *Proceedings of the Computer Security Foundations Workshop VII,* 162–174. Los Alamitos, Calif.: IEEE Computer Society.

Talvitie, James Alan. 1993. An object-oriented application security framework. *Security for Object-Oriented Systems. Proceedings of the OOPSLA-93 Conference Workshop on Security for Object-Oriented Systems,* 55–75. London: Springer-Verlag.

Tsai, Chii-Ren, Virgil D. Gligor, and C. Sekar Chandersekaran. 1987. A formal method for the identification of covert storage channels in source code. *Proceedings of the 1987 IEEE Symposium on Security and Privacy,* 74–86. Washington, D.C.: IEEE Computer Society.

______. 1990. On the identification of covert storage channels in secure systems. *IEEE Transactions on Software Engineering* **16**(6): 569–580.

Ware, Willis H. 1995. A retrospective on the criteria movement. *Proceedings of the 18th National Information Systems Security Conference,* 582–588. NIST/NCSC.

Wegner, Peter. 1990. Concepts and paradigms of object-oriented programming. *OOPS Messenger* **1**(1): 7–87.

Weissman, Clark. 1995. Penetration testing. In Marshall D. Abrams, Sushil Jajodia, and Harold J. Podell, eds., *Information Security: An Integrated Collection of Essays,* 269–296. Los Alamitos, Calif.: IEEE Computer Society.

Weller, Edward F. 1993. Lessons from three years of inspection data. *IEEE Software* **10**(5): 38–45.

Williams, James G., and Marshall D. Abrams. 1995. Formal methods and models. In Marshall D. Abrams, Sushil Jajodia, and Harold J. Podell, eds., *Information Security: An Integrated Collection of Essays,* 170–186. Los Alamitos, Calif.: IEEE Computer Society.

Wing, Jeannette M. 1990. A specifier's introduction to formal methods. *Computer* **23**(9): 8–24.

Wray, John C. 1991. An analysis of covert timing channels. *Proceedings of the 1991 IEEE Computer Society Symposium on Research in Security and Privacy,* 2–7. Los Alamitos, Calif.: IEEE Computer Society.

Chapter

7

Protection Mechanisms in Hardware Architecture and Operating Systems

Computing services are provided by complex systems that include products built by many companies and that may span the globe. Although security depends on the entire system, each product also must be considered on its own—by its designers and builders, standards groups, potential customers, and users. This chapter deals with the security mechanisms of units such as microprocessors and operating systems. It is these mechanisms that underlie security services and security policies. The term *protection* traditionally refers to security mechanisms in hardware and lower levels of operating systems. This chapter is about protection mechanisms, and the next chapter is about security services in operating systems, as shown in Fig. 7.1.

This chapter begins with a brief overview of the concepts and mechanisms, providing a framework for the material that follows. Then come problems that protection must solve and a review of the history of protection. The next section gets to the heart of the topic, describing five basic types of mechanisms and giving brief examples of their use. There follow more extended examples of protection systems. The chapter then turns to an important protection approach—capabilities. Three capability-based systems are described. The next section is devoted to security kernels—goals, alternative forms, and mechanisms. Four examples of kernel-based systems are described. There follow sections on object reuse and debugging features.

Operating system	Security services (Chapter 8)	Identification Authentication Access control Audit User facilities
	Protection mechanisms (Chapter 7)	Processes Interprocess communication Rings Access control lists Capabilities Memory protection Security kernels Object reuse protection
Hardware architecture		

Figure 7.1 Topics of Chaps. 7 and 8.

Overview of Concepts and Mechanisms

According to the access-matrix model, active entities called *subjects* have specified rights to objects. A computer concurrently runs multiple active entities called *processes* or *tasks*. A process is often defined as a "virtual processor" because it behaves much like a processor, although it shares the processor hardware with other processes. A process has registers, an instruction counter, and other state information. There is a way to associate a process with a user whose work it is doing.

At any moment a process has certain access rights. It can execute some machine instructions and not others. It can fetch instructions from certain areas of memory and can read or write in other areas. These rights form the *protection domain* of the process. The domain can change; after executing a supervisor call, for example, the process can execute additional instructions. The set of objects the process can write, for example, is called its *write domain*.

From a protection viewpoint, the objects of the access-matrix model include pieces of memory, files, I/O devices, and programs. *Memory protection* is a key mechanism that often protects files and I/O devices as well as memory. Memory protection is closely tied to virtual memory, which provides virtual address spaces larger than the real memory. In many systems each process has its own address space. Checking of access rights to memory is often combined with the translation of virtual addresses to real addresses. Access control for memory applies most importantly at the level of *segments*. A segment is a contiguous section of memory that corresponds to some program entity, such as a procedure, a stack, or a collection of data items. A *segment descriptor* serves as an identifier and specifies access rights to the segment. Access rights also reside in *access control lists* for objects or in *capability lists* for processes. *Capability systems* are designed around capabilities and use special hardware. A *security kernel* concentrates all security-relevant functions in a relatively small part of a system.

This brief overview shows that protection is closely intertwined with mechanisms for parallelism and memory access.

Protection Problems

A *protection problem* is a description of some class of restricted behaviors. The problem is "solved" if the protection mechanisms can guarantee that the behavior is properly restricted. For example, the *object-reuse problem* describes accessing information by way of discarded containers of objects. Alternatively, we can view a protection problem as solved if some security property is guaranteed. What problems must a protection system solve?

First, it must protect itself and the operating system against modification and improper use. It must isolate the processes from one another and provide confidentiality for their private objects. Complete isolation is rarely the desired policy, however, so processes must be able to communicate and to share objects in controlled ways. There must be a guarantee that certain objects cannot be modified at all in normal operation—objects such as kernel code, for example. The information of an object must not become accessible through reuse of the object's physical container. It should be possible to dynamically change rights—to give them out and revoke them—and to place limits on how they may propagate. Controlled passages from one domain to another are needed. These are called *gates,* because they are like gates in the walls surrounding domains.

The protection system should support the protection needs of *subsystems,* such as database management systems, and should allow *protected subsystems* to be constructed. A protected subsystem encapsulates objects or object types so that all access to them is through the subsystem; it acts as an intermediary between subject and object. The protected subsystem can then implement security policies not supported directly by the basic mechanisms, making protection more flexible and extensible. For example, it can enforce data-dependent or context-dependent controls or restrict access to parts of an object. The subsystem's protection domain includes both its inherent rights and those passed to it when it is invoked to operate on a specific object. For example, an investment adviser may have the right to use a proprietary portfolio analyzer program but no right to the proprietary market data that the program uses. The analyzer, for its part, has no rights to the portfolio data until it gets those rights upon invocation.

Since the investment adviser must give the analyzer access to confidential portfolio data, the concern arises that the analyzer may leak these data. *Confinement* is the problem of preventing a program from leaking information to anyone but its caller. This problem is not solved by the usual protection mechanisms. As discussed in Chap. 6, multilevel secure systems try to prevent leakage by controlling covert channels. The problem of *mutually suspicious subsystems* arises when a computation involves multiple subsystems that do not fully trust one another, as when the portfolio analyzer invokes an asset-allocation analyzer. An invoking program must be assured that an invoked program gets access only to explicitly passed data.

Finally, the Trojan horse threat can be countered by protection measures that restrict the domains of editors, compilers, and other system programs, as well as applications.

History and Trends

The earliest computers had no protection mechanisms at all. When computers began to run concurrent jobs and to support time sharing, confidentiality was of little concern, and integrity features were rudimentary.

Nearly all of today's protection mechanisms were in use by the early 1970s, having been invented in a few short years. Many of them came out of MIT's Multics—a time-shared operating system that used specially designed protection hardware. The virtual machine concept was developed by IBM. Interest in capability machines peaked in the 1970s, but it has continued and may revive. Progress in protection during the next two decades was small compared with the revolution in hardware and in operating system function over the same period. This is a tribute to the early work in protection, but it is also a result of the priorities of the times. The marketplace did not value security highly compared with function, performance, and cost. Operating systems researchers turned to other areas, and the protection research that was done (often military-sponsored) was not applied widely.

Earlier operating systems, such as Multics, were usually intended for specific hardware. The developers could choose whether to implement a mechanism in hardware or in software. A hardware mechanism performs better and can be protected more readily. A software mechanism is cheaper to produce and more flexible, and software can enable a simple hardware mechanism to support different policies.

The trend, however, is toward operating systems (such as UNIX and Windows NT) that can run on many hardware platforms.

Reinforcing the trend are *microkernel* architectures, which introduce a layer between the hardware and the traditional operating system. The microkernel provides the lowest-level functions, such as process management, interprocess communication, low-level memory management, and I/O. Everything else is done by servers running on top of the microkernel. The same microkernel can support different operating system "personalities," even on the same machine at once. Microkernels are well suited for distributed systems, whose servers may be on different machines. The *remote procedure call* of distributed systems can be used efficiently on a single machine in a "lightweight" version. Microkernel designs are potentially very secure and reliable, since there is little "common mechanism," and since each server runs in its own protection domain. Some microkernels do not even include protection, but most do.

Another trend is toward *RISCs* (Reduced Instruction Set Computers). RISCs have extremely simple instruction sets, and they leave vastly more responsibility to compilers. Finally, enormous address spaces are possible, and that affects protection designs.

Basic Protection Mechanisms

The basic mechanisms of protection include processes, domains, and memory protection. Protection information is represented in access control lists and capability lists.

Processes

A *process* is variously defined as, for example, (1) a virtual processor, (2) a program in execution, or (3) "the active system entity through which programs run. The entity in a computer system to which authorizations are granted; thus the unit of accountability in a computer system...." Any of these definitions is fine for our purposes. Definition 3 makes clear that accountability for computing actions depends on the process concept. The process acts on behalf of a user or some other entity, such as a user playing a specific role. The *principal* is the person or entity that is accountable for what a process does.

An operating system, with hardware support, maintains the state of each process and allows the processes to share the hardware. The state typically includes an instruction counter, registers, a stack or activation record and stack pointer, and domain information such as descriptors of accessible memory. The state also includes accounting information. The shared hardware includes processors, memory, and registers (although some machines provide multiple sets of registers). Each process has its own stack in nonshared memory, as well as private data memory. Memory containing code, especially system code, is often shared. A *context switch,* when a processor switches from working on one process to working on another, saves the state of one process and loads the state of another.

Processes can create other processes, which execute (at least initially) in the same domain as their creator. Recent operating systems, designed to exploit multiple processors, provide simpler units of parallelism—*threads.* A thread has much lower overhead for maintaining state and context switching. Multiple threads run in the protection domain of a task or process, sharing a single address space. Threads are sometimes called *lightweight processes.*

Interprocess communication

Processes interact by sharing memory and by sending messages. Sending messages works even when the processes run on different machines that do not share memory. Interprocess communication must be controlled both because it involves information flow and because it is a way to access objects. In systems based on message passing, accessing an object means sending a message to a *port*—a one-way communication channel that represents the object. By controlling rights to use ports, an operating system controls access to objects.

Protection domains and rings

A *domain* is a set of rights to objects. The subject of the access-matrix model corresponds to the pair (process, domain). When a process enters a different domain, the subject changes, and a different row of the access matrix specifies the rights of the process. A *domain* is also an object that can be accessed by entering it. A system supports the principle of least privilege by providing many small domains. Fine granularity of domain is important for both confidentiality and integrity.

Hardware supports the domain concept with *execution domains.* Some architectures have only two domains or *modes: supervisor* and *user*; the mode determines which instructions can be executed. I/O instructions, for example, can be issued only in supervisor mode; they are *privileged instructions.* To perform I/O operations, a program issues a *Supervisor Call* or *SVC,* which moves it into supervisor mode, and the supervisor issues the actual I/O instruction. SVCs are software-invoked or synchronous interrupts; asynchronous interrupts also cause supervisor mode to be entered. After an interrupt, the process executes at a point specified by an interrupt vector stored in protected memory. The process thus cannot misuse supervisor privileges by executing arbitrary sections of supervisor code.

Supervisor/user protection, with only two modes, is quite coarse. It can be generalized to a more precise domain scheme called *protection rings.* Figure 7.2 shows four concentric rings with the most privileged ring at the center and the least privileged at the periphery. Ring 0, the most privileged, is appropriate for the operating system kernel. The outermost ring is the least privileged, to be used by application programs. Nonkernel system code might use ring 1 and subsystems ring 2. Protection-ring schemes are hierarchical; each ring's rights include the rights of all higher-numbered rings. The rights of ring 0 include the rights of rings 1, 2, and 3. Supervisor/user mode is a two-ring scheme.

A process moves to a lower (more privileged) ring through a *gate.* The gate mechanism, used on a **call** to a different segment, ensures that the called segment is accessible to the ring of the caller. The gate also forces the process to begin its execution at a specific point—a *protected entry point* (Fig. 7.3). If a process could enter a more privileged procedure at an arbitrary point, it might trick the code into unauthorized behavior. Gates protect against this threat.

Developers of operating systems and subsystems must decide where in the ring structure to place components. The principle of least privilege provides the best guidance—each component should get the minimum privilege it needs to do its work. Another guiding principle is that more trustworthy components warrant more privilege. These principles might lead designers to use many rings, but that can be costly. Ring crossing substantially increases execution

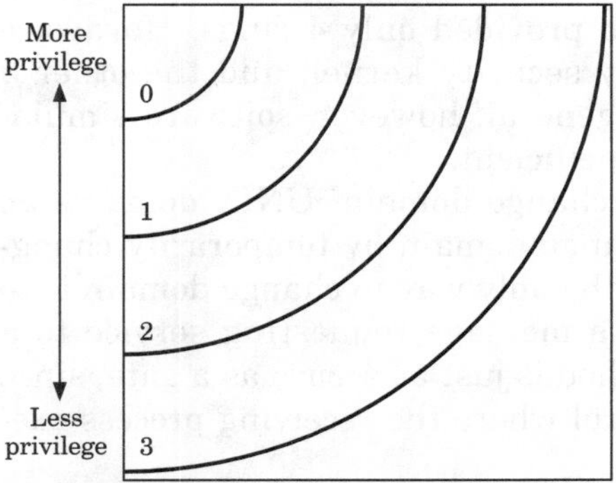

Figure 7.2 Protection rings.

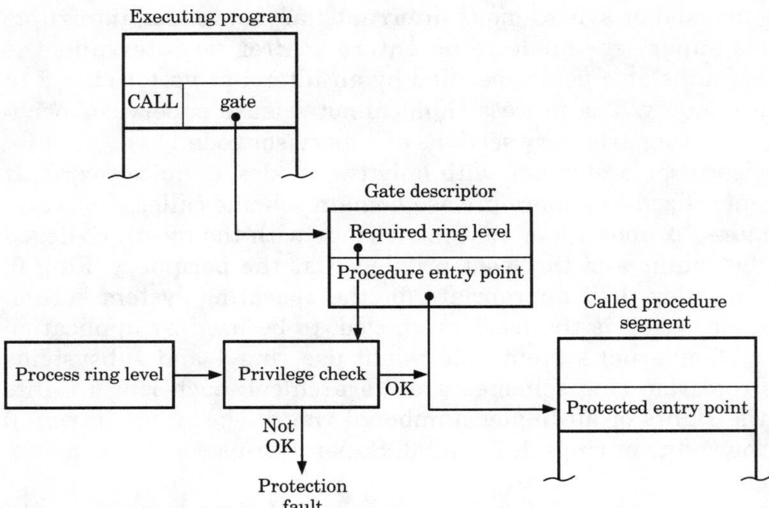

Figure 7.3 Gate mechanism.

time for a call. The code that runs at different privilege levels must reside in different segments, and a process needs a stack segment for each level. A program's "working set" of memory could thus be larger.

Hardware support for rings is practical and efficient because of the simple hierarchical ordering of privilege. A strict hierarchy does not best support least privilege, however, because any object accessible to ring r also must be accessible to ring $r-1$. Another difficulty is that the number of rings provided by the hardware rarely matches the number needed. The original Multics design provided 64 rings, but only 8 were used. If the hardware provides too few rings, software can simulate more. For example, the GEMSOS project built an 8-ring system on the Intel IAPX286, which provided only 4 rings. Hardware ring 0 was used for a mandatory security kernel, and the other 3 hardware rings were shared. In general, however, software simulation of rings is both complex and inefficient.

Gates are not the only way to change domain. UNIX domains go with users, and a process can change domain by temporarily changing the user ID. In other systems the only way to change domain is to change process; a process sends a message requesting service to a more privileged process. This method is just as secure as a gate, since the sending process does not control where the receiving process executes after receiving the message.

Representing access control information

A crucial issue in protection system design is how to represent the access control information—the information of the access matrix. A matrix representation is inefficient because the matrix is sparse and can be very large. Instead, most systems use access control lists, capabilities, or *permission bits*—or combinations of these mechanisms. Each method has its good and bad points, and the balance shifts as technology changes.

An *access control list* (ACL) is associated with an object and specifies all the subjects that can access the object, along with their rights to the object. That is, each entry in the list is a pair (subject, set of rights). An ACL corresponds to a column of the access matrix. Figure 7.4 shows an access control list for a file named PAYROLL.EXE. A file descriptor points to the ACL, which contains an entry for each user who has access to PAYROLL.EXE.

A *capability list* (*C-list*) is associated with a subject and specifies all its rights. Each entry in the list is a *capability*—a pair (object, set of rights). A capability list corresponds to a row of the access matrix. Since presenting the appropriate capability guarantees access, capabilities are like tickets. Unlike tickets, capabilities can be copied; the possessor of a capability can give a copy to someone else. Clearly, the protection system must ensure that capabilities are not forged or improperly changed and must control how they propagate. Capability-based systems often use special capability architecture.

The rights that are specified in ACLs and capabilities include **read, write,** and **execute.** Some protection systems enforce a much expanded set of generic rights and also support checking rights specific to a type of object. Windows NT, for example, defines (in addition to **read, write,** and **execute**) other standard access types that apply to all kinds of objects. They include rights to delete the object and to read or change its control information.

Access control lists have several advantages over C-lists. They are a better cognitive match to the task of specifying rights. ACLs provide a ready answer to the question, "Who has access to this object?" They

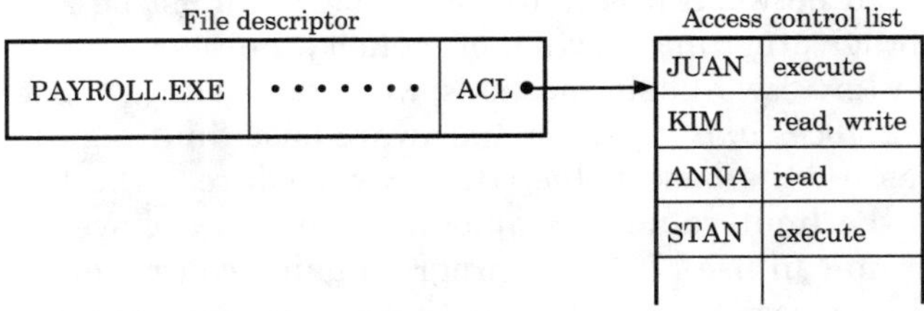

Figure 7.4 Access control list.

carry over well to distributed systems, since the ACL can be located with the object. ACLs are inefficient, however, for checking rights on each access; the check may involve searching a long list and performing a complex rights evaluation. ACLs work well if rights are checked only on first access—such as when a process opens a file or adds a segment to its virtual memory. For this reason, many systems use a combination of ACLs and capabilities. When a process opens a file for read access, for example, the ACL is searched, and if read access is allowed, a read capability is set up for the process. When a **read** or **write** is attempted, only these capabilities need be checked. Another way to improve ACL performance is to cache for each process the results of recently used ACL evaluations.

A third mechanism is a string of bits representing permissions—the access rights of built-in user categories, such as the object's owner or group. Permissions, which are used by UNIX, are efficient but inflexible.

Access control can be refined and strengthened by *type enforcement,* where each subject and each object has a security type. A subject's rights to an object then depend on the rights of its type to the object type. In the LOCK system, for example, each object has a type and each subject is associated with a domain. Examples of types are *DBMS data, DBMS code,* and *Trusted Program 1 Code.* Examples of domains are *DBMS* and *Trusted Program 1.* A Domain Definition Table relates domains (rows) and object types (columns) in an access matrix. The table might show that only a subject of type *DBMS* can **execute** *DBMS code.* A Domain Interaction Table defines the rights (such as **signal** or **create**) that each domain has to other domains. Type enforcement can ensure least privilege for operating system components and also constrain subsystems and applications.

Memory protection

Since most of the objects managed by operating systems are represented in memory, nothing is more central to protection than memory protection.

If memory is shared between programs, one program must be kept from modifying another program's portion of memory. For early multiprogrammed computers, two basic methods were devised: (1) *base-limit registers* and (2) *locks and keys.* The hardware base-limit register contains two addresses: the base value (the lowest address the program can use) and the limit value (the amount of memory above the base that the program can use). When a program gains control of the processor, the hardware register is loaded with the base and limit values for that program. Each memory reference is then checked by hardware to ensure that it falls within the range of the base and limit.

The lock-and-key method associates a lock value with each unit of memory. Access is allowed only if the processor is currently executing with a matching key. The IBM System/360, for example, assigns a 4-bit storage key to each memory block, while the processor status includes a 4-bit protection key. Access may occur only if the storage and protection keys match.

The lock-and-key method is no longer useful because memories are too large and processes too numerous. Base-limit registers do survive as descriptors in virtual memory systems.

Virtual memory and segments. Virtual memory allows programs to be larger than the real physical memory and to execute while only partly in real memory. Virtual memory is a natural place to implement memory protection.

The simplest type of virtual memory is a single virtual address space that is shared by multiple programs. (The programs can be loaded anywhere in memory, either because they contain no absolute addresses or because the loading process modifies them appropriately.) Single-address-space virtual memory was soon abandoned for *multiple virtual address spaces,* which provide much more total address space.

Multiple virtual address spaces provide powerful protection. Each process has its own virtual memory that other processes cannot even address. Processes also can share parts of their virtual memories. For example, a portion of every address space can be dedicated to shared system code. Real memory is allocated in fixed-size units called *pages,* often 4 kbytes. Some systems offer protection at the page level, but segment-level protection is more common.

Systems differ in their virtual memory architecture. For example, segment size can be fixed or variable. First, a simplified fictional system is described, and later, two specific architectures are presented. In the fictional system, as shown in Fig. 7.5, each process has a table

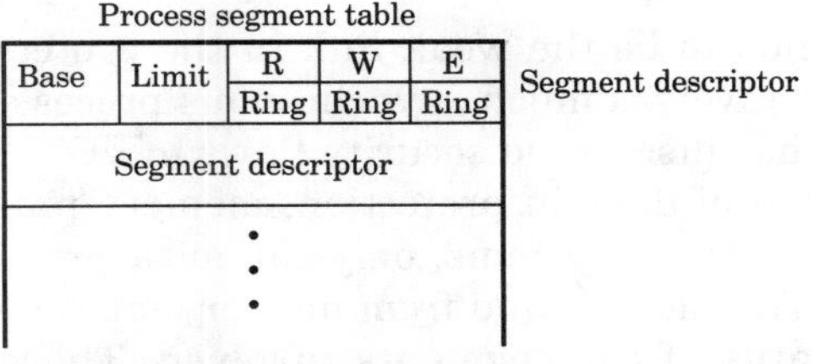

Figure 7.5 Process segment table.

describing all the segments that it can use. Each entry in the table is a *segment descriptor,* which contains the real-memory base and the limit. It also contains access control information—the highest ring that can access the segment in each of the modes **read, write,** and **execute.** The operating system provides functions to create and destroy segments and to change their access control information. When a process is in execution, some of its segment descriptors are loaded into hardware *segment registers.*

The virtual address used in a memory reference is interpreted as a segment number and an offset within the segment. The segment number is used as an index to select a descriptor in the segment table. The base address from the descriptor is then used to translate the virtual address into a real address that is the base plus offset. On most memory references, translation does not need to use the segment descriptor table; instead, it uses a *translation lookaside buffer* (TLB), which has associative hardware for fast lookup. The TLB contains only the most recently used addresses. If the virtual address is not found in the TLB, the segment descriptor table is used. (For simplicity, this description ignores two things: paging and segments that are not in real memory.)

Protection and virtual memory. Where does protection fit into this scheme? Assume that a new process with a new virtual memory is created when a user logs on. Call the user Kim and the process P_K. In order to access a segment S_1, process P_K must add S_1 to its virtual memory. At P_K's first reference to S_1, a segment descriptor for S_1 is added to the segment table, and the protection bits in the descriptor are set, based on (1) S_1's protection characteristics and (2) Kim's ACL rights for S_1. The process of another user might have different rights, or no rights, to S_1. The limit value in the descriptor prevents references outside the segment, which could result from out-of-range subscripts or bad pointers. Once software has set up the segment descriptor, the hardware takes over. That is, the software maintains the protection information for active segments, and the hardware interprets that information and enforces protection.

I/O protection. Input/output tends to be the weak link in the protection chain. It is complex, and it involves much asynchronous processing. Penetration analysis often has discovered security flaws in I/O.

I/O protection is a combination of domain protection, memory protection, and device protection. In many systems, only the most privileged domain can perform I/O. Transfers to and from memory must be governed by the protection status of the segments involved. These include not only I/O buffers but also locations that contain I/O commands or that will receive status information. And access to specific devices must be controlled.

I/O instructions either can perform I/O directly and synchronously, or they can start an I/O operation that proceeds in parallel, using *direct memory access* (DMA), where the device "directly" accesses memory. No special instructions are used with *memory-mapped I/O,* where a portion of the address space represents I/O ports, and I/O can be done by any instruction that references memory. Some systems provide both methods. Memory-mapped I/O undergoes exactly the same protection checks as any other memory references.

Some systems use I/O *channels,* which are (at least conceptually) separate processors that execute their own *channel programs* asynchronously with the main processors. Privileged I/O instructions start up the channel programs. If the hardware architecture provides no I/O memory protection, each address in a channel program must be checked for accessibility before I/O starts. Other safeguards are needed. For example, the operating system can move the channel program into protected system memory to prevent its being modified after I/O starts. Alternatively, it can validate each address when it is used. Completion of I/O generates an interrupt, and interrupts also can occur during the progress of a channel program. These interrupts are tricky because although the interrupt-handling software includes nonkernel device-specific code, it must execute with high privilege (to restart I/O, for example).

Some systems have device protection. The Intelx86 has an I/O permission bit map for a task, and the task can do I/O on a port only if the bits representing the port are clear. Unfortunately, no processor mechanism can protect against devices that do not carry out their commands properly.

File security. File security may or may not be included in a system's basic protection mechanisms. There are two main ways that files (and file security) can relate to memory (and memory protection). In the more elegant approach, files *are* segments, and exactly the same protection applies to files and memory. When a file is opened, it becomes an active, accessible segment. Multics takes this approach. With the more common approach, the file system is a subsystem with its own security. The advantages of this approach are that the basic protection mechanisms stay simple and that they can support different file systems.

Examples of Protection Systems

So far this chapter has described the basic protection mechanisms separately in a fairly abstract way. This section describes how they work in three specific systems—Multics, the Mach kernel, and Intelx86 (386, 486, Pentium) systems.

Memory protection and rings in Multics

The Multics project developed both an operating system and its hardware support, with protection strongly influencing the whole design. Multics is a good example of a unified, coherent protection scheme. This discussion begins with the segmented virtual memory and then describes memory protection and domains (rings). How Multics controls domain changes is illustrated.

Each Multics process has its own segmented virtual memory; the process and its memory are created when a user logs on. Before a process can use segments, it must add them to its memory. Certain segments have well-defined functions, such as procedure segments, data segments, and stack segments. Using separate segments for each function is important for integrity. It prevents the harm caused, for example, when the stack overflows into data or procedures. Other segments are part of the supervisor, shared by all processes. (The supervisor is the part of the operating system that manages processes and memory; the supervisor itself operates in a virtual memory.)

Virtual addresses have the form (*s,o*), where *s* is the segment number and *o* is the offset within the segment. Access to memory is through a *segment descriptor word* (SDW) in a table called the *descriptor segment* (DS). Each process has its own DS, and the SDW for segment *s* is the *s*th entry in the DS. Segments are physically scattered through real memory in pages of 1024 words whose locations and status are kept in a page table for each segment. Translation from virtual to real addresses uses an associative memory containing the most recently used page table entries and SDWs.

Segments (files) have symbolic names that appear in the Multics directory structure. It is in this directory entry that access control information for a segment is kept: the IDs and rights of the authorized users appear in an access control list. (The file's creator initially specifies this information.) When a symbolic name is first used by a process, a segment number *s* is assigned and an SDW is built. At first reference to the segment number, the access control information from the directory goes into the SDW. This information consists of a flag plus a number for each of the access modes (**read, execute, write,** and **append**). If the flag is OFF, the process has no access in that mode. If the flag is ON, the number gives the highest ring for access in that mode. For example, if the write flag is on and the corresponding number is 2, the process can write the segment only if the process ring is 0, 1, or 2. This range is called the *write bracket* of the segment for the process. Hardware interprets the mode flags and brackets, and it generates a protection fault on an access violation. Execute brackets, which are used for procedure segments, get special treatment. The other brackets always have zero as a lower limit, but an execute bracket has an arbitrary lower limit. This supports least privilege; a procedure can be designed to execute at no greater privilege than ring 2, and that intent will be enforced. Execute protection is checked on each instruction fetch.

Multics uses both access control lists and capabilities. Access control lists carry the permanent information, in the directory, but checking at the moment of access uses the SDW. The SDW is (like a capability) a protected descriptor that is associated with a subject and that determines the subject's access rights. The descriptor segment is the capability list.

It has not yet been described how a process crosses from one ring to another and how ring crossing is constrained. A segment may have a list of gate locations, and its execute bracket may have a "gate extension" that specifies the highest ring that can transfer to a gate of the segment. (The gate list and gate extension come from the access control list and go into the SDW.) When a process changes ring, its stack segment also must change. A process has a stack segment for each ring used, and higher rings cannot access the stacks of lower rings. A cross-ring call leaves the caller's ring number in a register, and return to a lower ring is prevented.

The called procedure can make use of the caller's ring number. An access can be validated against a higher ring than the current execution ring under program control. This feature allows a more privileged service procedure to assume the ring of its caller when validating parameters or doing work for the caller—and so to guard against Trojan horse threats.

Rings were used by the Multics software as follows. The "kernel" of the operating system ran in ring 0, and other portions (such as accounting) ran in ring 1. Subsystems could use rings 2 and 3. User programs were at ring 4, and the higher rings could be used to test new versions or try out borrowed programs.

The Mach kernel and interprocess communication

Mach is a distributed operating system kernel that follows the object model. It provides a very few basic abstractions: task, thread, message, port, and memory object. It provides device support and supports distributed hardware. All other operating system functions, including the file system and user-level memory management, are outside the kernel. This means that the kernel can support functionally different operating systems. (The first Mach goal was to support UNIX 4.3BSD.) The Mach communication mechanism, which mediates all object access, is also the protection mechanism. Protection consists of controlling and enforcing port rights, which act much like capabilities.

Tasks hold resources, such as memory and port rights, and threads are the active elements of a task. Threads of different tasks communicate by sending messages to ports. A sending task must have *send rights* to the port, and a receiving task must have *receive rights* to the port. Only one task may have receive rights to a port, but multiple tasks can have send rights. An operation on any object results in a message to a port. Tasks and threads communicate with the kernel through special ports; every task is the receiver for a "task-notify" port and the sender for a "task-self" port. Kernel commands result in messages to the task-self port, for which the kernel is the receiver. (Threads have thread-self ports.) Messages can contain data and data pointers, as well as port rights. That is, rights are transferred via messages. A task loses receive rights when it transfers them (since a port has only one receiver). The kernel holds transferred rights until the message is received; then the receiver gets them. The kernel keeps tight control over rights; it knows who holds rights for each port and what rights each task holds.

Intelx86 protection

Intelx86 microprocessors are everywhere, as the engines for personal computers and many other products. Their hardware protection architecture includes rings, segment-level memory protection, and gates, as well as types and other mechanisms. First, the protection information is described and then how the processor checks protection.

The Intelx86 provides four rings, called *privilege levels*; the processor at any moment has a *current privilege level* (CPL). Each segment has a privilege level and also a type that determines what access is permitted, regardless of privilege level. Segments are typed as either system or application and either code or data. An application code segment can be "execute-only" or "execute/read," and a data segment is "read-only" or "read/write." Code segments are *conforming* or not; a conforming segment executes at the privilege level of its caller. A segment's privilege level, which is kept in a segment descriptor, is called the *descriptor privilege level* (DPL). The CPL is the privilege level of the currently executing code segment. A *requester privilege level* (RPL) can override the CPL, allowing a privileged program to access memory with less privilege. For example, a device driver can use its caller's level for reading into memory. The term *effective privilege level* (EPL) is used here for the maximum (least privileged) of the CPL and RPL. (Intel does not use this term, but it simplifies the description.)

Protection information resides in segment descriptors and segment registers. The descriptors needed by a task are in a *local descriptor table* for that task. A segment descriptor contains the base and limit values, the type, and the DPL. Each segment register holds a *segment selector* that includes a segment descriptor index and the RPL. There are six segment registers, used for code, stack, and four data segments. Loading a segment register determines how a segment will be used, so protection is checked on loading. Can the segment, given its type, be used as a data segment? As a code segment? Does the process have the privilege needed to use the segment?

The x86 supports several kinds of gates; the call gate is described here. A call gate descriptor specifies an entry point and the privilege level (called the *gate DPL*) the caller must have. Since the same segment can have multiple gates (for different procedures or entry points), gates control transfers at a finer granularity than the segment.

For a "far call" (a call to a different segment), the hardware can recognize when a gate is involved because the segment selector for the destination points to a gate descriptor rather than to a segment descriptor. Two conditions must be satisfied for the call to proceed:

1. The EPL must not exceed the gate DPL.
2. The DPL of the destination segment must not exceed the CPL.

The gate DPL specifies what level a procedure is intended for, and Condition 1 says that the level used for the call cannot be greater. Condition 2 prevents transfer through a gate to a higher (less-privileged) level. Parameters for the call are automatically copied to a stack used at the new privilege level.

Now x86 protection checking can be summarized. Since all segment references depend on segment registers, checking occurs when a register is loaded. Segment registers have invisible fields containing protection information: base, limit, type, and privilege level. Once the registers are loaded, protection checks occur on each memory reference, in parallel with address translation. The main protection checks are

- *Type checking.* The segment register must be compatible with the segment type. For example, the stack segment register can be loaded only with the selector of a writable data segment. All references to a segment must observe the type constraints. For example, no instruction can write into a data segment that is not read/write.

- *Limit checking.* References must be within the segment, as defined by the limit.
- *Privilege-level checking for data.* For a data segment to be used, its segment selector (containing the descriptor index and RPL) must first be loaded into a data-segment register. Checking occurs at that time; the DPL must not be lower than the EPL. If the CPL and RPL are 1, for example, the EPL is 1, and data segments at levels 1, 2, and 3 are accessible. If the CPL is 1 and the RPL is 3, the EPL is 3, and only level 3 segments are accessible.
- *Privilege-level checking for control transfers.* All far calls are checked. If the call does not use a gate, either the called segment has privilege equal to the CPL or the called segment is conforming and more privileged (so it will execute at the CPL). As described earlier, if the transfer does use a call gate, the gate DPL must exceed the EPL; this check ensures that the gate is used only from the intended levels. Further, a call destination DPL cannot exceed the CPL.
- *Privileged and sensitive instructions.* Certain privileged instructions can be executed only when the CPL is 0. Other "sensitive" I/O instructions can be performed only when the CPL is lower than an I/O privilege level set by the operating system.

The security of the Intelx86 architecture was analyzed by Olin Sibert, Phillip A. Porras, and Robert Lindell (1995). Their goal was to evaluate the suitability of x86-based products for high-assurance trusted products. Several security "pitfalls" were found, most of them providing covert channels. For example, a Task Switch flag is set whenever a task switch occurs and is cleared when a floating-point instruction is executed. This flag is visible through unprivileged instructions and can be used for signaling. From published reports of implementation errors, the analysis identified 17 security-related flaws. In the 486, for example, several instructions that are designated privileged could be executed from a nonprivileged state. (These instructions invalidate TLB entries and cache.) The study concluded (based only on public reports) that later x86 processors could be used for trusted systems.

This study did not count integrity flaws that would not directly affect a trusted system. One example is a bug in the Pentium floating-point arithmetic that generated much customer outrage and led to Intel replacing many Pentiums. Most contemporary processors are extremely complex, and it is reasonable to believe that flaws remain undiscovered. If critical computations cannot be checked independently for validity, a good safeguard is to perform them on two different hardware architectures. The same principle applies to compilers.

Protection and translation: examples

Protection checking and address translation relate to each other differently in different processors. Here are a few examples from RISC processors. Since most of them aim to support multiple operating systems, their unit of protection is a page or a set of pages rather than a segment. The TLB is used for both translation and protection.

In Advanced Micro Devices' Am29000, each TLB entry refers to a page (which is associated with a user) and contains the access permissions for that page. Protection checks take into account the processor mode and the user ID. The Digital Alpha AXP architecture protects and translates a unit that is either a page or a set of contiguous pages with the same protection. The larger unit uses the translation buffer more effectively, since one entry can represent many pages; still the smaller unit is available when fine-grained protection is needed.

The Hewlett-Packard PA-RISC also allows sets of pages to share some protection information. A *protection set* is a set of pages accessible to the same list of processes. Each page has a protection-set identifier (essentially the name of an access control list) as well as information specifying what type of access is allowed and from what privilege level. The protection domain of a process is the protection sets it can access; identifiers for four sets can be in fast control registers. Protection and translation information for a page gets loaded into the TLB. Then a memory reference is allowed only if the page's protection-set identifier matches one in a control register and if the access-type and privilege-level criteria are also met.

A project at the University of Washington takes a different approach. The work assumes a 64-bit virtual address, so there is plenty of address space with a single virtual memory for all processes. Protection then uses finely honed protection domains rather than address-space separation. Protection and translation are decoupled. Protection information is kept in a *protection lookaside buffer* (PLB), where each entry specifies the access rights of one protection domain for one virtual page. The TLB becomes much simpler.

Capability Systems

The systems described in this section not only use capabilities, they are designed around them. Capabilities are an integral part of their addressing schemes. First, some properties of these systems are summarized, and, then the discussion considers how to protect the integrity of capabilities and how to control their propagation. Two "classic" but quite different capability systems are described, as is a later system that adapts capabilities for a distributed environment. Capabilities are then considered in relation to multilevel security.

Capability systems: advantages and disadvantages

Classic capability systems have some good protection properties:

- The granularity of protection can be very fine. Small objects can be protected, and the domain of a process can change with each procedure that it calls. Protection domains are flexible, in contrast to the fixed structure imposed by rings. These properties support the least-privilege principle.
- In a sense, protection is prior to addressing. A capability is both an address and a proof of rights, and all references must be made through capabilities.
- Capabilities cannot be forged, so user programs can pass them around and store them in files. This makes sharing of objects simple and flexible.
- Capabilities are well suited for implementing protected subsystems or object-model designs. They are also well suited for distributed systems because they can be checked anywhere, not just at the site of an access control list. This is good for both efficiency and availability.

Capability systems also have some disadvantages:

- The propagation of capabilities is hard to control.
- Traceability of access and revocation of access are far more difficult than with access control lists.
- The multilevel model cannot be supported by a pure capability system.

A capability names an object that a process can access and describes the process's rights to the object, as in Fig. 7.6. An object might be, for

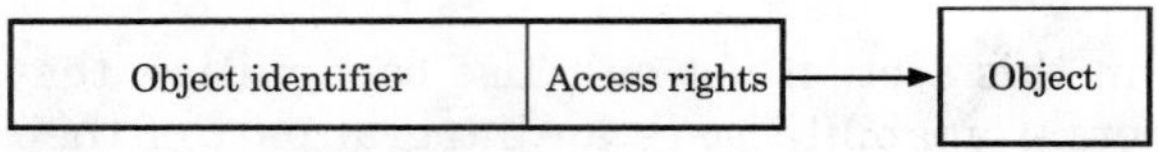

Figure 7.6 Capability.

example, a segment or a set of pages. The process presents the capability in order to use the object. The protection domain of the process is defined by the capabilities it can use.

Capabilities have a context-independent meaning; no matter what process is using the capability, it refers to the same object. Also, no matter when the capability is used, it refers to the same object, because each object of a system has a unique capability identifier that is never reused. This means, of course, that capabilities must be quite large. The same capability naming scheme applies to objects in both memory and permanent storage, providing a "single-level store." Some systems, however, use different capability identifiers internally and externally. The capabilities that a process can use at some moment are in *capability registers,* which act as a capability cache.

When a process creates an object, the system typically creates and returns a capability for the object. Alternatively, the process later presents the symbolic name of the object to obtain a capability. The process prepares to use the capability by loading it into a capability register. When the process generates an address using the capability register, access succeeds or fails. It would fail, for example, on a write operation if the capability in the register does not include write access. Most systems allow the process to alter the rights in a capability in the direction of less privilege. A process can pass a capability as a parameter when it calls a procedure. It can copy a capability or send one to another process.

Protecting capabilities

The integrity of capabilities must be guaranteed. If capabilities were not inviolate, the whole scheme would fall apart. For example, a process holding a capability for read access to an object could modify the rights field to give itself write access. Two classic approaches to capability integrity—*tagged* and *partitioned*—use hardware to prevent direct modification of capabilities. Two other approaches (often used together)—*sparse capabilities* and *capability authenticators*—detect forged capabilities and prevent their use. With any approach, only the protection system can create capabilities.

With the tagged approach, each word in memory and each register is tagged as containing either a capability or an ordinary word. A program cannot simply load or store a capability. In other ways, however, programs can treat capabilities just like any data. For example, capabilities can reside anywhere in data structures. One disadvantage of the approach is the need for tag bits in memory. Another disadvantage is that capabilities and other words must be the same length, although capabilities may need to be very long.

The partitioned approach reserves some segments of memory and some registers exclusively for capabilities. Memory protection can then apply to capability segments, allowing modification only by the protection system. Additional checks ensure that capabilities are stored only in capability segments and registers. Programming is less convenient than with the tagged method, since a capability cannot be stored in just any data structure. The usual way around this is to store a pointer to the capability instead. The partitioned approach makes it easier for the operating system to find capabilities. A capability in one capability segment can provide access to another capability segment, so hierarchical or other structures of capabilities are possible.

The classic methods of partitioning and tagging are useless when capabilities are passed around a distributed system. The sparse-capability approach uses an enormous capability address space (such as 2^{256}) to guard against forgery. Capabilities are secret. Anyone who knows a capability can use it, but guessing the right value is computationally unfeasible. Only a tiny portion of the address space is used, hence the term *sparse*. In addition, a one-way function can be applied to a capability value to compute a check-field value. An object manager checks the capability's validity by computing the same one-way function and comparing the result to the check field.

Controlling propagation of capabilities

One of the best things about capabilities is also one of the worst. It is easy to pass capabilities around, but it is hard to find them and take them back. One would like to take them back when an object's protection status changes. Because *revocation* is complex, most capability systems have not supported it. In the IBM System/38, objects can have revocable capabilities, but these are weak capabilities. When such an "unauthorized pointer" is used, an access control list is checked to determine if access is currently allowed.

The Cambridge CAP computer

The CAP computer and its operating system were developed at Cambridge University in the 1970s. CAP has a segmented memory that is accessed only through capabilities. CAP uses the partitioned approach, with up to 16 capability segments per process. The architecture and operating system conventions determine the use of some *capability segments*. The address of a memory word consists of a *capability specifier* (capability segment identifier and offset) plus the word's offset within its segment. The protection architecture is implemented by a microprogram that evaluates capabilities and a hardware *capability unit* that holds 64 evaluated capabilities. A design goal for the microprogram is that its safe operation does not depend on the correctness of the operating system.

CAP processes have a hierarchical structure; one process can create another and give it some of its own resources. All the segments potentially available to a process are in its *process resource list* (PRL), whose entries are pointers to capabilities owned by the parent process. Capabilities are of different types: for entry to protected procedures, for capabilities, and for data. A data-type capability contains a PRL index (to identify the segment) plus base, limit, and access fields. These fields make it possible to *refine* access rights when copying a capability. If the original capability allows read/write access to the whole segment, for example, the refined copy can allow read access to the first half of the segment.

Protected procedures play a major role in CAP. In fact, the operating system consists entirely of sets of protected procedures, and each user program is a protected procedure. Operating system procedures are executed by the caller's process, but with a different protection domain.

In implementing protected objects, a system must solve a tricky problem. It must ensure that only the object manager (a protected procedure in CAP) has access to an object's representation. Also, an instance of the object manager must get access only to the object instance for which it is invoked. Suppose, for example, that process *p* owns a directory that is represented in segment *s*. The directory manager must get its rights to *s* from *p*—which should not have them! CAP solves this problem by using different capabilities for objects (protected procedures) and their representations and by *sealing* these capabilities in an *enter capability* so that they are unsealed only when the protected procedure is entered.

When an **enter** instruction is executed, five of the process's capability segments change. The caller must possess an enter capability, pointing to an *enter* PRL entry that specifies the new capability segments 4, 5, and 6. These contain, respectively,

- P capabilities for the code of the called procedure
- I capabilities for the execution of the procedure by this process
- R capabilities for the representation of the object instance being operated on

Each instance of a directory object would use the same P segment but a different R segment. To create a new directory, the directory manager creates a new R segment. To build a protected procedure, a user requests creation of an enter capability, supplying capabilities for the P, I, and R capability segments. Capability segments 2 and 3 also have defined roles: 2 contains capabilities for the arguments passed to a protected procedure, and 3 is used to prepare arguments for a call. **Enter** causes the old 2 to become inaccessible, the old 3 to become the new 2, and the new 3 to become undefined.

The CAP system gives up some of the simplicity and freedom possible with capabilities in order to achieve more structure and control. Its capabilities are not unique identifiers but are process-specific, with an indirect form that limits protection domains and makes them easier to keep track of.

Hydra and rights amplification

The Hydra system was developed at Carnegie-Mellon University in the 1970s. Hydra gave high priority to protection, using capabilities and the object model with inventive elegance.

Hydra is a kernel. It supports the building of new objects, and its protection mechanisms apply uniformly to all objects. All objects have types, and all objects, whatever their type, have the same structure. The same generic operations apply to all objects, and all objects can have capability lists. An object can be described as (name, type, representation), where the representation consists of a C-list and a *Data-part.* The C-list includes capabilities for the procedures that implement the operations of the object; these procedures form a *subsystem.*

Hydra extends the concept of access rights beyond the usual **read, write,** and **execute.** Twenty-four rights can be associated with any object. Some of the rights correspond to generic operations and apply to all objects—rights such as "get data from Data-part" or "copy object"—and other rights are type-specific. For every attempted operation, the kernel ensures that a capability contains the required rights.

The protection domain of an executing program is defined by the C-list of a *local name space* (LNS) object. The protection domain includes both the objects in that C-list and (since those objects also may have capabilities) all the objects reachable by some path of capabilities. Rights in each capability along the path can limit access. A procedure is an object with its own C-list, and so is a process. Every procedure call creates a new LNS that gets pushed onto a stack belonging to the process, and so the protection domain changes with each call. The way it changes depends on the called procedure's C-list and on the capabilities passed as arguments.

A mechanism called *templates* supports the secure creation of objects. Templates also solve (through a method called *rights amplification*) the problem of giving an object manager access to an object's representation. A template serves as a prototype capability for all objects of a specific type. A creation template for a type determines what rights go in a capability for a new object of that type. Parameter and amplification templates appear in a procedure's C-list and get matched with call parameters. A parameter template specifies the "required rights" for a capability for that parameter. An amplification template specifies both required rights and "new rights." Each call parameter consists of a capability plus a mask that allows a caller to pass only some of its rights. The call fails if the required rights are not passed. An amplification template in a procedure's C-list results in a capability with the new rights. That is, if the caller has the required rights, the new rights go into the C-list of the LNS. Amplification can give an object manager access to the representation—but only when it receives a capability with the required rights.

Although the Hydra implementation was not a success (partly because, using no special hardware, it performed badly), the ideas had a lasting influence.

Capabilities in the Amoeba distributed operating system

Amoeba is a research distributed operating system developed in Amsterdam. Like most distributed operating systems, Amoeba implements the object model through clients and servers. When an application operates on an object, a message gets sent to the port of a *service.* The service manages the object, using one or more server threads. The object identifier consists of the service port plus the object number. A file identifier, for example, consists of the file service port plus the number of the specific file. A capability for the file contains these two values, along with the access rights and a check field computed on the other fields. A capability is created by the server when it creates the object; the capability is returned to the client and also stored in the server's tables. When the capability is used, the server recomputes the check field to assure itself that the capability has not been modified. Capabilities authenticated in this way can be handled and passed around by any program.

Capabilities and multilevel systems

Capability-based approaches must be modified to meet the needs of multilevel systems. A system cannot enforce the *–property if capabilities can propagate like any other data. For example, a process could copy a capability *C* from one segment to another, making *C* available to all processes that can read capabilities from the second segment. Suppose that C is copied from a Confidential segment to a Top Secret segment and that C conveys append-access to a Secret segment. A Top Secret process could then use C to "write down" into a Secret segment, violating the *-property.

One solution to this problem lets capabilities be copied freely but checks access rights against the multilevel rules when the capability is prepared for access; at that time the levels of the process and segment are known. With this solution, capabilities lose their absolute power.

An alternative solution checks access against the rules (or an access control list) when a capability is propagated. This makes sense if propagation is much less frequent than access. One such proposal, for an "identity-based capability system," uses extended capabilities that carry their owners' identities. If a capability is like a ticket, the extended capability is like a ticket with the holder's picture. An extended capability propagates only with monitoring by an access control server (either a kernel or an object manager). Since the access control server can keep records of propagation, revocation is also supported with this scheme. The LOCK project (for a multilevel secure system) also designed a propagation-monitoring scheme. The scheme uses "touch-limited capabilities" that contain additional information such as security level and type. When a capability is copied, the reference monitor adjusts the rights in the copy so as to preserve the *-property. This approach was eventually rejected for LOCK because it made revocation too costly.

Security Kernels

A *security kernel* was defined originally as that part of the software and hardware that ensured security, even if an antagonist provided the rest of the system. An NCSC glossary defines the security kernel as "the hardware, firmware, and software elements of a Trusted Computing Base that implement the reference monitor concept" (NCSC 1988a: 115). These definitions imply both an architecture and a set of protection mechanisms. The architecture separates the reference-validation mechanism from the rest of the system, arriving at a smaller, more verifiable "kernel." The protection mechanisms of the kernel support its functions, protect it from the untrusted components, and support the rest of the TCB.

Although the kernel concept makes sense for almost any security policy, it has been intimately associated with the multilevel policy and the TCSEC.

Goals of kernel-based systems

Kernel-based systems vary in their functional goals. One goal is to mimic the function of an existing operating system—to provide a "multilevel secure UNIX" or "trusted VAX VMS." Such a system is broadly useful, and it can run preexisting applications (unless they violate policy). A different goal is to support some intended applications without trying for compatibility with existing interfaces. Kernel-based systems also differ in their policy goals. Most support one policy—multilevel confidentiality, as formalized in the Bell-LaPadula model—and some also support Biba integrity. More recent kernel work reflects the need to support other policies and multiple policies, for both confidentiality and integrity.

Forms of the kernel approach

Several forms of kernel-based systems have been used.

Traditional kernels. The traditional method takes the kernel of an untrusted operating system, extracts the security-relevant functions, and reimplements them using the methods prescribed by the TCSEC. The kernel uses standard protection hardware, so software carries much of the burden of reference validation. Security kernel code is executed by all processes (as kernel calls), and the kernel must be protected against nonkernel code (system or application).

Experience with this approach has been disappointing. Reimplementing all the security-critical functions is complex and costly. If the original operating system changes, the trusted version must change as well, and it lags behind. Performance without special hardware has been poor. Modeling and verification are extremely complex.

Virtual machine monitors. The second approach avoids some of these difficulties. The kernel supports a set of virtual machines, and each virtual machine supports users and objects at a single security level. The kernel here is a *virtual machine monitor* (VMM). The VMM causes a single real machine to act like multiple virtual machines, each virtual machine behaving exactly like the real machine except for performance. Although virtual machine architectures were first designed for time sharing, they soon proved valuable for security and integrity. User programs are isolated from one another and from the VMM. Since errors in the operating system of one virtual machine do not affect the other machines, new versions of operating systems can be tested conveniently. Each virtual machine's I/O devices and file storage are virtualized and segregated, providing protection against I/O errors and penetration attempts.

A computer needs certain hardware features to be "virtualizable." It needs a privileged mode, to be used by the VMM. It needs to trap all privileged instructions and all references to sensitive data that are issued outside privileged mode. (Sensitive data reveal or modify the privileged state.) One successful VMM is IBM's VM/370, which is the base for a security kernel system called *KVM/370.*

It is not obvious exactly what policy a VMM kernel should enforce. A possible choice is the *separation property*—a strong form of noninterference. A *separation virtual machine monitor* enforces such a policy, with no sharing at all, allowing access only if the subject and object are exactly equal in level. Separation is a relatively simple policy to implement and to verify. Most security VMMs are much more complex (although still simpler than traditional kernels); they enforce the Bell-LaPadula model, allowing controlled communication between levels (Fig. 7.7).

In a variation on the VMM approach, the virtual machines become real. Each processor of a distributed system supports one access class. (An *access class* is a combination of levels and categories.) There are no multilevel processors, but multilevel work is supported through multilevel disks and through network connections.

Reference-validation processors. The third approach uses special hardware to speed up reference validation. The Scomp system, for example, adds to a standard minicomputer an additional hardware unit that does both address translation and reference validation.

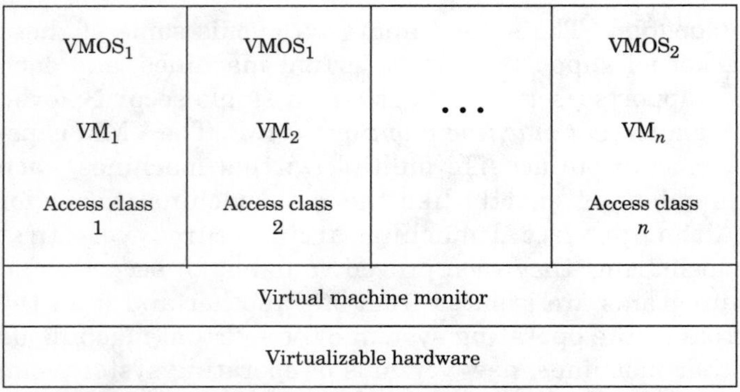

$VMOS_1$ VM_1 Access class 1	$VMOS_1$ VM_2 Access class 2	. . .	$VMOS_2$ VM_n Access class n
Virtual machine monitor			
Virtualizable hardware			

Figure 7.7 Virtual machine monitor.

Mechanisms for security kernels

The general mechanism of the security kernel includes specific hardware and software protection mechanisms.

Kernel hardware. An NCSC report (1988b) lists the hardware that is considered part of the TCSEC reference monitor. The list includes the components responsible for address translation, isolating processes from one another, fault handling, I/O control, and hardware diagnostics. The design of other components, not strictly part of the reference monitor, must be documented to meet TCSEC requirements. These components include the CPU, memory-management hardware, I/O processors, and any other processors.

Basic kernel protection mechanisms. Hardware or software, kernel protection mechanisms do not differ greatly from protection mechanisms in general. There must be processes—representing subjects—and the kernel must mediate all interprocess communication. Memory segments—representing objects—should be variable in size, and a process should be able to access many different segments. Segment access should be through descriptors that distinguish modes of access—at least **read** and **write.** For efficiency, access validation should be done along with address translation, using a translation lookaside buffer or other hardware assist. To protect the kernel, and to protect memory protection, a kernel system needs domains or rings of privilege. One domain must be reserved for the kernel and another for nonkernel operating system components, so a processor needs three domains. An efficient gate mechanism should provide, at the least, multiple entry points into the kernel. Kernel procedures should be able to assume the caller's domain for accessing arguments.

I/O devices and I/O processes (such as channel programs) must be treated as untrusted subjects. I/O is one of the most troublesome areas for a kernel system. With some I/O architectures, for example, I/O must be started in kernel mode using absolute addresses; this means that potential violations must be detected by careful prechecking. One kernel system, SCOMP, provides descriptor-controlled hardware mediation of I/O, as do other processors.

Although hardware support is needed for security and performance, much of the responsibility falls on kernel software. It must maintain the descriptors and tables that the hardware uses for validation. It must attach to each object and each subject a *sensitivity label* specifying its access class and must maintain the integrity of the labels. The entities that are subjects and objects will vary depending on the architecture. Subjects are users and processes, (process, domain) pairs, or virtual machines. Objects include segments, files, devices, and ports.

Although discretionary access control may reside outside the kernel, kernel calls must support it. For example, kernel calls are needed for modifying the access matrix. Kernel functions—software and hardware—also must enforce DAC requirements on each access.

Some kernels include a significant portion of the file system, maintaining the directory structure and ensuring the integrity of labels. Since the same external media may contain files at different levels or access classes, each file must be securely labeled with its level and category set. File access must obey the system security policy.

The kernel must support auditing. It needs, for example, calls that turn auditing on and off (generally per process) and that write audit records. (Other TCB software actually may do the writing to media.) Other functions the kernel must perform or support are secure backup and restore and secure restart after failures.

Trusted processes. For a traditional kernel system, the nonkernel TCB consists of trusted processes that do not run in kernel mode. Their main uses are for login, to support the system operator, for audit, and for administrative functions such as modifying the security levels of users or objects. Trusted processes are a conceptual weak spot in the kernel approach. Reducing the kernel to a verifiable size leaves out a lot of function that is security-relevant and that must go somewhere. That somewhere is the trusted processes. In principle, they should receive the same rigorous design, analysis, testing, and verification as the kernel; if they did, though, the superkernel might no longer be "small enough to be subject to analysis and tests, whose completeness can be assured."

A trusted process can behave in ways not allowed for an untrusted one. The term *privilege* is used to describe a specific exemption from the general security policy. For example, a trusted process could have the privilege of downgrading a file. One kernel-based system, ASOS, defines about 20 such privileges and associates them with trusted processes when the system is generated. The kernel must recognize trusted processes and their privileges and perform its access validation accordingly. Some trusted processes do not need to violate policy; they just perform security-critical functions outside the kernel.

Trusted path. Consider a user working at Secret level and interacting with, say, a database application. The user needs to be sure that the application is also Secret level; otherwise, by entering data the user could be "writing down" in violation of policy. The same caution applies to category sets. The user gets assurance by communicating directly with the TCB, which verifies the access class of the application. For purposes such as this, the kernel must provide a *trusted path* from the user to the TCB. The user activates the trusted path by using a dedicated key sequence to generate a *secure attention signal.* The system designers must show that this signal cannot be subverted. This demonstration may be relatively simple for a dumb terminal. For a PC or workstation, either it too must be a trusted system, or the user must have an independent trusted path.

Covert channel protection. Satisfying the completeness principle means eliminating covert channels—as discussed in Chap. 6.

Examples of kernel-based systems

This section describes four kernel-based systems: SCOMP and LOCK, which use separate security processors; VAX VMM, based on a virtual machine monitor; and Trusted Mach.

SCOMP. SCOMP (Honeywell Secure Communications Processor) was probably the most successful system based on the kernel concept. Not only did it receive the first A1 rating from the NCSC, it also became a commercial product with good performance. One reason for its success was its functional goal of providing an efficient application interface—easier to achieve than emulating another operating system. Another reason was its use of special hardware to make reference validation efficient. SCOMP supports multilevel confidentiality and integrity; its objects are segments, devices, and processes.

The SCOMP hardware structure is shown in Fig. 7.8. A standard 16-bit bus-structured minicomputer is configured with a *Security Protection Module* (SPM), an additional element that does reference validation. The SPM resides on the bus between the (modified) CPU and the other system components—memory and I/O controllers. With this structure, all access requests for memory or I/O are captured and mediated by the SPM. The SPM bases its mediation on the values in Multics-like descriptors maintained by software. The kernel consists of the SPM and the kernel software.

SCOMP provides four rings of protection and a gate mechanism. The kernel uses ring 0. An "argument-addressing mode" allows a procedure to access its caller's arguments using the caller's ring level. A descriptor cache is part of the SPM, which performs both address translation and access validation. An important feature is that the SPM mediates all I/O access. I/O uses virtual device names and virtual addresses, and I/O instructions do not require ring 0. This scheme reduces the number of kernel calls and simplifies the kernel software,

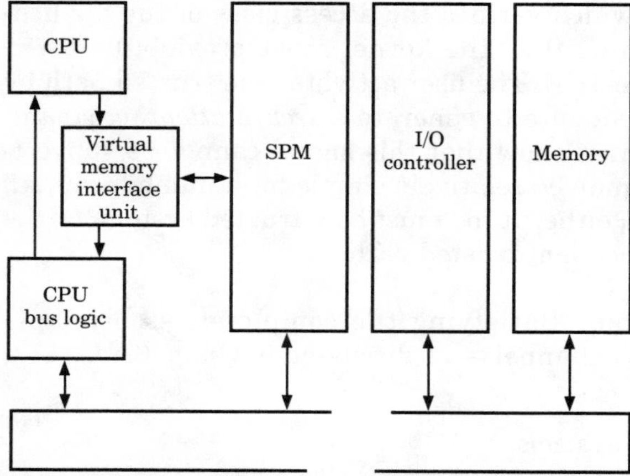

Figure 7.8 Structure of the SCOMP system. [*From Fraim (© 1983 IEEE).*]

since device drivers are outside the kernel, and I/O memory access does not have to be checked by software.

LOCK. Logical Coprocessing Kernel (LOCK) also uses a separate processor—called *SIDEARM*—for reference validation. SIDEARM attaches to a host processor so as to mediate all the host's memory references. In addition to the type enforcement discussed earlier, SIDEARM enforces mandatory and discretionary access control. An access must satisfy all three types of control. In addition to SIDEARM, the LOCK TCB includes host software: a low-level supervisor and "kernel extensions." The kernel extensions run on top of the supervisor and are constrained by SIDEARM. They implement application-specific security policies. The operating system that supports applications runs on top of the LOCK TCB. For example, a version of UNIX called LOCKix can be used. Using type and domain enforcement, LOCK provides a mechanism called *assured pipelines*. Each pipeline is composed of a group of subjects that are constrained in domain, security level, and discretionary attributes. Pipelines can guarantee that data pass between domains only through trusted import and export filters. LOCK supports roles through domain enforcement and a Role Authorization Table. A role is represented by a set of domains, and the table specifies which users can have subjects in those domains (and thus can operate in that role). LOCK has been used as the base for a network file service, a mail guard, and a multilevel secure database system.

VAX VMM. The VAX VMM system virtualizes DEC's VAX computer to provide multilevel security and integrity and discretionary access control, aiming at class A1. Each virtual machine (VM) is assigned a single *access class,* which consists of a *secrecy class* and an *integrity class* (each consisting of a level and category set). That is, all subjects and objects on a VM have the same level and the same category set, for both confidentiality and integrity. The main subjects are virtual machines, and the objects are virtual disks (isolated sections of real disks). This is a much coarser granularity than processes and files but is still highly useful. The functional goal was to support existing operating systems; a virtual machine runs one of these VMOSs.

One challenge was to virtualize protection rings, since the VMS operating system used all four rings of the VAX. VAX VMM hides the real ring numbers from the VMOS, which sees the two most privileged rings compressed into one. Because of the way VMS used rings, this caused no loss of security within the virtual machine.

VAX VMM uses no trusted processes in the usual sense. Entities called *servers* perform trusted-process functions, such as login, but they execute trusted code within the kernel, with rights derived from their users. A user communicates either with a server over a trusted path or with a VM. Most privileges (such as downgrading) can be held only by users and not by VMs.

Although VAX VMM reached its technical goals, the project was canceled by DEC—mainly for market reasons.

TMach. The Trusted Mach (TMach) kernel, developed by Trusted Information Systems, is traditional in one sense. It is a modification of an existing kernel, and it supports a modification of an existing operating system (UNIX). In another sense, TMach is quite unconventional. Since it builds on a message-passing kernel, its access mediation is quite different from systems (such as SCOMP or Multics) where the main objects are segments and memory references are mediated. In TMach, the objects are ports, and message passing is mediated. TMach enforces Bell-LaPadula security, aiming at meeting TCSEC requirements for class B3. The TMach TCB consists of a kernel and trusted servers.

The subject for TMach is a task, which is essentially an environment for a set of threads. The only objects are ports, which represent all the other kinds of Mach abstractions. Each task is labeled with a maximum read level (*T.R*) and a minimum write level (*T.W*), and each port has a single security label (*P.L*). Since Mach port rights act like capabilities, access mediation is done by TMach when a port right is received. At that time, TMach ensures that the new state of rights satisfies security invariants that are the TMach interpretation of Bell-LaPadula. For example, for each task *T*, *T.R* dominates *T.L.*; if task *T* has send rights to port *P*, *P.L* dominates *T.R*.

Message-passing systems have a generic covert channel problem that is illustrated by Mach and TMach. A Mach port has a maximum capacity, and sending a message can result in the sender being notified that the port is full. In TMach, if the task level is lower than the port level, this feedback provides a covert channel. TMach simply discards the message to a full port without notifying the sender. A similar potential covert channel is the notification a sender gets when the port has been destroyed. TMach does not actually delete a "destroyed" port while tasks hold send rights to it, but it discards any messages.

While it was straightforward to modify the Mach kernel for mandatory access control, Mach's capability-based discretionary access control was harder to reconcile with the TCSEC view of DAC. To support DAC by the kernel and by servers (including the Name Server that supports the file system), TMach had to add quite a few features. TMach associates a user ID with a task; each message is tagged with the sender's user ID, and this tag is available to the receiver. TMach also limits the transferability of port rights and defines privileges that allow tasks to selectively violate the general policies.

Object Reuse

Objects often are built out of lower-level objects. For example, a segment is built of pages and segment descriptors; a port is built of descriptors and queue entries. The same applies to subjects. A process is built of control blocks, stacks, registers, and so on. The lower-level objects *contain the information* of the higher-level object. *Object reuse* occurs when the containers are reassigned for other uses. The protection system must ensure that no information residue is available to the new subject.

Object reuse was a gross vulnerability in early operating systems, leaving them open to browsing attacks. PCs remained vulnerable long after the problem was addressed in larger systems. For example, early users of Prodigy network services complained that Prodigy was tapping their personal data. Prodigy software ran on DOS on the user's PC, sending data over telephone lines from PC memory to the Prodigy system. Since DOS did not purge memory on allocation or deallocation, memory allocated to Prodigy contained samples of the user's own data. (Malicious software running similarly could have read or modified anything!) More sophisticated systems are vulnerable in subtler ways. Memory from pools used for stacks or heaps or I/O buffers could be reallocated containing old data. A process could free a piece of memory that its child process still has access to. The system could fail to clear the registers of a vector processor before assigning it to a different process.

The TCSEC requirements on object reuse recognize two types of errors: access residue and content residue. The access requirement is that all authorizations to the information contained within a storage object must be revoked before the object is assigned, allocated, or reallocated from the TCBs free storage pool. (A *storage object* is one that supports both read and write access.) Clearly, if this requirement were not met, subjects could access storage belonging to other subjects, violating security policy and also integrity. The content requirement is that no information produced by a prior subject's actions be available to a subject that gets access to a formerly released object. Object reuse applies, of course, to storage on disks or other media as well as to memory. It also applies to registers, cache memory, and math coprocessors.

Mechanisms to guard against the object-reuse problem can operate at three possible times: when free pools are initialized or extended, when objects are deallocated, and when objects are allocated. Allocation time is the last chance to comply with the requirements before a new subject gets the storage component. There are alternative ways to comply. For example, the container can be set to zeroes or a fixed pattern, or it can be filled with the new subject's initial data (appropriate especially for page frames).

Support for Debugging

Hardware and operating systems can contribute greatly to security by supporting debugging. Operating systems, networking software, and other systems components are notoriously difficult to debug, and hardware support is invaluable for assurance. Debugging for RISC computers is especially hard; the programs have more instructions, and the compiler-generated order of instructions is hard to understand.

The most common hardware support is for *breakpoints. Control breakpoints* allow a user to specify events that will be traced or will stop execution. For example, the user could set breakpoints on all **call** and **return** instructions. The hardware generates traps, and software maintains a trace buffer. *Data breakpoints* are triggered by reference to specific memory locations. The Intel486, for example, has four debug address registers, for four breakpoints, and a control register specifying the kind of access for each breakpoint (execute, write, or read/write). Four breakpoints is a very limited number, however. All-software approaches are more flexible, at a performance cost, and external debugging devices are also used. Many processors support single-stepping under software control. With *software breakpoints,* the programmer can insert instructions that cause debug interrupts; the interrupts can be enabled or disabled under program control.

Debug facilities also represent a potential penetration path, so they must be closely controlled by a TCB and by operational procedures.

Summary

The term *protection* refers to security mechanisms in hardware or lower levels of operating systems. Protection forms the basis for all higher-level security mechanisms and services. In general, the subjects are processes, and the objects are pieces of memory. The basic mechanisms of protection include processes, domains, and memory protection.

A protection system must protect itself and the operating system. It must isolate processes from one another but also allow them to communicate and to share objects. At any moment a process has certain access rights that form its protection domain. Controlled passages from one protection domain to another are needed; these are called gates. The system should support the construction of protected subsystems that encapsulate objects. Interprocess communication must be controlled both because it involves information flow and because, in some systems, accessing an object means sending a message.

A domain is a set of rights to objects, and least privilege is supported by many small domains. Execution domains determine which instructions may be executed. Protection rings provide hierarchical domains; each ring's rights include the rights of all higher-numbered rings. Ring 0 is the most privileged, appropriate for the operating system kernel. A process moves to a more privileged ring through a gate, which ensures that a called segment is accessible to the ring of the caller and causes execution to begin at a protected entry point.

Access control information can be represented as access control lists (ACLs), capabilities, or permission bits. An ACL is associated with an object, and each entry in the list is a pair (subject, set of rights). A capability list (C-list) is associated with a subject, and each entry in the list is a capability—a pair (object, set of rights). The possessor of a capability can give a copy to someone else, so the protection system must ensure that capabilities are not forged or improperly changed. Capability-based systems often use special capability architecture. The rights that are specified in ACLs and capabilities include **read, write,** and **execute.** Some protection systems enforce a larger set of generic rights and also support checking rights specific to a type of object. Compared with C-lists, ACLs are a better cognitive match to the task of specifying rights, and they make it easy to determine who has access to an object. However, ACLs are inefficient for checking rights on each access, so many systems use a combination of ACLs and capabilities. Permission bits are associated with an object and represent the access rights of user categories such as the object's owner or group. Permission bits are efficient but inflexible.

Since operating system objects are represented in memory, memory protection is crucial. Many systems implement memory protection through virtual memory. Usually, each process has its own virtual memory that other processes cannot address. Each process has a table describing all the memory segments that it can use. Each entry in the table is a segment descriptor, which contains the real-memory limits, along with access control information. When a process first references a segment, a descriptor for that segment is added to the segment table, and the protection field is set, based on the segment's protection characteristics and the user's rights. The software maintains the protection information for active segments, and the hardware interprets that information and enforces protection.

I/O protection includes domain protection, memory protection, and device protection. In many systems, only the most privileged domain can perform I/O. Transfers to and from memory are constrained by the protection status of the segments involved. Access to specific devices must be controlled.

The Multics project developed both an operating system and its hardware support, with protection strongly influencing the whole design. Multics uses both access control lists and capabilities. Access control lists carry the permanent information, in the directory, but checking at the moment of access uses the segment descriptor, which acts like a capability.

Mach is a distributed operating system kernel that provides a very few basic abstractions: task, thread, message, port, and memory object. (Threads are the active elements of a task.) Most operating system functions are outside the kernel. An operation on any object results in a message to a port. Protection consists of controlling and enforcing port rights. Tasks hold resources, such as memory and port rights. A sending task must have send rights to the port, and a receiving task must have receive rights. Rights are transferred via messages. The kernel keeps tight control over rights; it knows who holds rights for each port and what rights each task holds.

The protection architecture of Intelx86 microprocessors includes rings, segment-level memory protection, and gates, as well as types and other mechanisms. There are four rings, called privilege levels. Segments are typed as either system or application and as either code or data. A privileged program can access memory with reduced privilege. For a call gate, a descriptor specifies an entry point and the privilege level the caller must have. Protection information resides in segment descriptors and segment registers. Loading a segment register determines how a segment will be used, so protection is checked on loading. Once registers are loaded, protection checks occur on each memory reference, in parallel with address translation. The main protection checks are type—the segment register must be compatible with the segment type; limit—references must be within the segment; privilege-level for data and for control transfers; and execution of privileged and sensitive instructions. An analysis of the x86 architecture revealed several security problems, mainly covert channels.

Capability systems have some good protection properties: The granularity of protection can be very fine; protection domains are flexible; capabilities can be passed around and stored in files, simplifying sharing of objects; and capabilities provide good support for protected subsystems or object-model designs. Capability systems also have some disadvantages: Propagation is hard to control; it is hard to trace access and revocation of access; and the multilevel model cannot be supported by a pure capability system.

When a process creates an object, the system typically creates and returns a capability for the object. The process prepares to use the capability by loading it into a capability register. When the process generates an address using the capability register, access succeeds or fails.

If capabilities were not inviolate, the whole scheme would fall apart. Two classic approaches to capability integrity—tagged and partitioned—use hardware to prevent direct modification of capabilities. Two other approaches—sparse capabilities and capability authenticators—detect forged capabilities. With any approach, only the protection system can create capabilities.

Capability systems include CAP, Hydra, and Amoeba. The Cambridge CAP computer uses the partitioned approach. It gives up some of the simplicity and freedom possible with capabilities in order to achieve more structure and control.

The Hydra kernel uses capabilities and the object model elegantly. All objects have types, and all objects have the same structure. The same generic operations apply to all objects, and all objects can have capability lists. Hydra ideas have had a lasting influence.

Amoeba is a distributed operating system that implements the object model through clients and servers. A capability (which includes a check field) is created by a server when it creates an object; the capability is returned to the client and also stored in the server's tables. When the capability is used, the server recomputes the check field to assure itself that the capability has not been modified.

Capability-based approaches must be modified to meet the needs of multilevel systems.

A security kernel concentrates all security-relevant functions in a relatively small part of a system. A kernel-based system may try to provide the function of an existing operating system, or it may support an intended application without trying for compatibility. A traditional kernel system reimplements the security-critical functions of an untrusted operating system so as to meet trusted system requirements. A virtual machine monitor supports a set of virtual machines, and each virtual machine supports users and objects at a single security level. In a variation on the VMM approach, each processor of a distributed system supports one access class. Another form of kernel uses special hardware to speed up reference validation.

For a traditional kernel system, the nonkernel TCB consists of trusted processes that do not run in kernel mode. Their main uses are for login, audit, and administrative functions. A trusted process has privileges, which are specific exemptions from the general security policy. Trusted processes are a conceptual weak spot in the kernel approach.

Examples of kernel-based systems are Scomp, LOCK, VAX VMM, and Trusted Mach. In Scomp, all access requests for memory or I/O are captured and mediated by a separate Security Protection Module. LOCK also uses a separate processor for reference validation, and it provides type enforcement. VAX VMM is based on a virtual machine monitor; it virtualizes DEC's VAX computer to provide multilevel security and integrity. Trusted Mach, in contrast to systems that mediate memory references, mediates message passing. The only objects are ports, which represent everything else. Message-passing systems, including TMach, must solve a covert channel problem that arises when a message is sent to a full or destroyed port.

In all systems, lower-level objects contain the information of higher-level objects. Object reuse occurs when containers are reassigned for other uses. The protection system must ensure that no information residue is available to the new subject.

Debug facilities contribute to security but also represent a potential penetration path.

Bibliographic Notes

Excellent early surveys of protection are provided by Saltzer and Schroeder (1975) and Linden (1976). Lampson (1971) relates the basic concepts and mechanisms to the access-matrix model. Cohen and Jefferson (1975) define and describe protection problems. Lampson (1973) characterizes the confinement problem. Landwehr and Carroll (1984) develop a useful framework for hardware requirements. Myers

(1990) categorizes processor protection mechanisms. Singhal and Shivaratri (1994) provide an overview of operating system protection.

Of the definitions of *process,* 1 is from Saltzer and Schroeder (1975), 2 is from Silberschatz et al. (1991), and 2 and 3 are from a NIST glossary (1991: 113).

Karger and Herbert (1984) compare capabilities and access control lists and propose ways to get the best of both. Kelter (1991) describes cached ACL evaluations. The typed access-matrix model of Sandhu (1992) includes type enforcement. Types and domains in LOCK are described by O'Brien and Rogers (1991). Badger et al. (1995) describe applying domain and type enforcement to UNIX.

Multics protection is described by Saltzer (1974), Organick (1972), Bensoussan et al. (1972), and Schroeder and Saltzer (1972). Patterson (1985) gives a readable introduction to RISCs. Microkernel design and lightweight RPC are described by Bershad et al. (1990). Interprocess communication in Mach is described by Branstad et al. (1989) and by Silberschatz et al. (1991). The Mach architecture is described in Black et al. (1992).

The description of Intelx86 protection is based on the Intel486 Reference Manual (Intel 1992), which includes many features not described here. The Pentium has additional integrity features. Smith (1982) describes TLBs. Translation and protection in the Am29000 are described by Mann (1992). The Digital Alpha AXP architecture is described by Sites (1993) and by Kronenberg et al. (1993). Koldinger et al. (1992) propose a protection lookaside buffer. Wilkes and Sears (1992) discuss this proposal and the PA-RISC protection architecture. Okamoto et al. (1992) describe another protection design for a large single virtual address space.

Capabilities and capability lists were introduced by Dennis and Van Horn (1966), who credited the Burroughs B5000 system. The book by Levy (1984) is an excellent source on all the capability systems that existed when it was published. Fabry (1974) discusses capability-based addressing and compares the tagged and partitioned approaches. Linden (1976) discusses many capability system issues. Protection in the CAP computer is described by Needham and Walker (1977). Hydra protection is described by Cohen and Jefferson (1975) and by Wulf et al. (1974). Amoeba is described by Mullender and Tanenbaum (1984, 1986), Tanenbaum et al. (1986), Mullender et al. (1990), and Tanenbaum and Kaashoek (1994). Two techniques for efficient revocation of capabilities are proposed by Karger (1989).

Karger (1988) proposes a capability-based method of enforcing the Clark-Wilson integrity model. Capability systems in support of the multilevel model are treated by Karger and Herbert (1984), Saydjari et al. on LOCK (1989), and Gong (1989). Kain and Landwehr (1987) provide a taxonomy of capability-system designs.

Ames et al. (1983) give an overview of the security kernel concept. More about kernels is found in Gasser (1988) and in Chap. 6 of this book. "Virtualizable" architectures are characterized by Popek and Goldberg (1974).

Examples of traditional kernel architecture are ASOS (Waldhart 1990), KSOS (McCauley and Drongowski 1979), and Trusted Xenix (Gligor et al. 1987). GEMSOS (Schell et al. 1985) extends kernel architecture for a multiprocessor computer. LOCK is described by Saydjari et al. (1989) and O'Brien and Rogers (1991). Subsystems based on LOCK are described by Smith (1993, 1994) and in Chap. 9. SCOMP is described by Fraim (1983). Virtual machine monitors are used in KVM/370 (Gold et al. 1984) and VAX VMM (Karger et al. 1991). Russell and Schaefer (1989) describe a separation kernel for the IBM ES/3090. Distributed approaches are proposed by Rushby and Randall (1983) and by Proctor and Neumann (1992). The TMach kernel is described by Branstad et al. (1989). Gupta (1994) describes the implementation of the TMach trusted servers using C++. Bernstein and Kim (1994) describe a real-time operating system in which access mediation is performed at system build time.

For more about object reuse, see NCSC (1992) and Wichers (1990). For more on debugging support, see Wahbe (1992).

Exercises

7.1 Design a data structure for the Multics access control list.

7.2 Describe the fields of the Multics segment descriptor word.

7.3 List all the protection mechanisms that can be used to support protected subsystems.

7.4 Name three mechanisms that can support secure domain change. Explain how each one works.

7.5 Assume that you are designing a portfolio-analysis procedure to run on Hydra. The caller passes portfolio data plus parameters describing what analysis to do. What Hydra facilities are used for the data and the procedure? Design an amplification template, and explain what it accomplishes.

7.6 This chapter describes alternative goals and architectures for kernel-based systems. Which architectures best suit which goals, and why?

7.7 Explain why and how access control lists are used in conjunction with capabilities; give two examples from systems described in this chapter.

7.8 Explain the meaning of the term *write bracket* in Multics.

7.9 Why does a Multics process need a separate stack segment for each ring that it uses?

7.10 What is *requestor privilege level* in the Intel486? What is its purpose?

7.11 Try to design a way of implementing capabilities that would support efficient revocation.

7.12 Which architecture for multilevel systems do you think would be more secure: a virtual machine system with single-level virtual machines or a distributed system with interconnected single-level processors and a multilevel file store? Why? (Read the references on these approaches before answering.)

7.13 What is meant by the term *privilege* in relation to a trusted process?

7.14 Explain the covert channel exposure in TMach ports.

7.15 The TCSEC has two requirements regarding object reuse. Explain what they are and how they differ.

References

Ames, Stanley R., Jr., Morrie Gasser, and Roger R. Schell. 1983. Security kernel design and implementation: An introduction. *Computer* **16**(7): 14–22. Reprinted in Marshall D. Abrams and Harold J. Podell, eds., *Tutorial: Computer and Network Security,* 142–150. Washington, D.C.: IEEE Computer Society, 1987.

Badger, Lee, Daniel F. Sterne, David L. Sherman, Kenneth M. Walker, and Sheila A. Haghighat. 1995. Practical domain and type enforcement for UNIX. *Proceedings of the 1995 IEEE Symposium on Security and Privacy,* 66–77. Los Alamitos, Calif.: IEEE Computer Society.

Bensoussan, A., C. T. Clingen, and R. C. Daley. 1972. The Multics virtual memory: Concepts and design. *Communications of the ACM* **15**(5): 308–318.

Bernstein, Mary M., and Chulsoo Kim. 1994. AOS: An avionics operating system for multi-level secure real-time environments. *Proceedings of the Tenth Annual Computer Security Applications Conference,* 236–245. Los Alamitos, Calif.: IEEE Computer Society.

Bershad, Brian N., Thomas E. Anderson, Edward D. Lazowska, and Henry M. Levy. 1990. Lightweight Remote Procedure Call. *ACM Transactions on Computer Systems* **8**(1): 37–55.

Black, David L., David B. Golub, Daniel P. Julin, Richard F. Rashid, Richard P. Draves, Randall W. Dean, Alessandro Forin, Joseph Barrera, Hideyuki Tokuda, Gerald Malan, and David Bohman. 1992. Microkernel operating system architecture and Mach. *Proceedings of the USENIX Workshop on Micro-kernels and Other Kernel Architectures,* 11–30. Berkeley, Calif.: USENIX Association.

Branstad, Martha, Homayoon Tajalli, Frank Mayer, and David Dalva. 1989. Access mediation in a message passing kernel. *Proceedings of the 1989 IEEE Computer*

Society Symposium on Security and Privacy, 66–72. Washington, D.C.: IEEE Computer Society.

Cohen, Ellis, and David Jefferson. 1975. Protection in the Hydra Operating System. *ACM Operating Systems Review* **9**(5): 141–160.

Dennis, Jack B., and Earl C. Van Horn. 1966. Programming semantics for multiprogrammed computations. *Communications of the ACM* **9**(3): 143–155.

Fabry, R. S. 1974. Capability-based addressing. *Communications of the ACM* **17**(7): 403–412.

Fraim, Lester J. 1983. SCOMP: A solution to the multilevel security problem. *Computer* **16**(7): 26–34. Reprinted in Marshall D. Abrams and Harold J. Podell, eds., *Tutorial: Computer and Network Security,* 220–227. Washington, D.C.: IEEE Computer Society, 1987.

Gasser, Morrie. 1988. *Building a Secure Computer System.* New York: Van Nostrand Reinhold.

Gligor, Virgil D., C. S. Chandersekaran, Robert S. Chapman, Leslie J. Dotterer, Matthew S. Hecht, Wen-Der Jiang, Abhai Johri, Gary L. Luckenbaugh, and N. Vasudevan. 1987. Design and implementation of Secure Xenix. *IEEE Transactions on Software Engineering* **SE-13**(2): 208–221.

Gold, B. D., R. R. Linde, and P. F. Cudney. 1984. KVM/370 in retrospect. *Proceedings of the 1984 Symposium on Security and Privacy,* 13–23. Silver Spring, Md.: IEEE Computer Society.

Gong, Li. 1989. A secure identity-based capability system. *Proceedings of the 1989 IEEE Computer Society Symposium on Security and Privacy,* 56–63. Washington, D.C.: IEEE Computer Society.

Gupta, Sarbari. 1994. Object-oriented security in the Trusted Mach operating system. *Proceedings of the OOPSLA-93 Conference Workshop on Security for Object-Oriented Systems,* 90–95. London: Springer-Verlag.

Intel. 1992. *Intel486 Microprocessor Family Programmer's Reference Manual.* Mt. Prospect, Ill.: Intel Corporation.

Kain, Richard Y., and Carl E. Landwehr. 1987. On access checking in capability-based systems. *IEEE Transactions on Software Engineering* **SE-13**(2): 202–207.

Karger, Paul A. 1988. Implementing commercial data integrity with secure capabilities. *Proceedings of the 1988 IEEE Symposium on Security and Privacy,* 130–139. Washington, D.C.: IEEE Computer Society.

______. 1989. New methods for immediate revocation. *Proceedings of the 1989 IEEE Computer Society Symposium on Security and Privacy,* 48–55. Washington, D.C.: IEEE Computer Society.

Karger, Paul A., and Andrew J. Herbert. 1984. An augmented capability architecture to support lattice security and traceability of access. *Proceedings of the 1984 Symposium on Security and Privacy,* 2–12. Silver Spring, Md.: IEEE Computer Society.

Karger, Paul A., Mary Ellen Zurko, Douglas W. Bonin, Andrew H. Mason, and Clifford E. Kahn. 1991. A retrospective on the VAX VMM security kernel. *IEEE Transactions on Software Engineering* **17**(11): 1147–1165.

Kelter, Udo. 1991. Discretionary access controls in a high-performance object management system. *Proceedings of the 1991 IEEE Computer Society Symposium on Research in Security and Privacy,* 288–299. Los Alamitos, Calif.: IEEE Computer Society.

Koldinger, Eric J., Jeffrey S. Chase, and Susan J. Eggers. 1992. Architectural support for single address space operating systems. *Proceedings of the Fifth International Conference on Architectural Support for Programming Languages and Operating Systems,* 175–186. New York: ACM Press.

Kronenberg, Nancy, Thomas R. Benson, Wayne M. Cardoza, Ravindran Jagannathan, and Benjamin J. Thomas. 1993. Porting OpenVMS from VAX to Alpha AXP. *Communications of the ACM* **36**(2): 45–53.

Lampson, Butler W. 1971. Protection. *Proceedings of the 5th Annual Princeton Conference on Information Sciences and Systems,* 437–443. Reprinted in *Operating Systems Review* **8**(1): 18–24, January 1974.

______. 1973. A note on the confinement problem. *Communications of the ACM* **16**(10): 613–615.

Landwehr, C. E., and J. M. Carroll. 1984. Hardware requirements for secure computer systems: a framework. *Proceedings of the 1984 Symposium on Security and Privacy,* 34–40. Silver Spring, Md.: IEEE Computer Society.

Levy, Henry M. 1984. *Capability-Based Computer Systems.* Bedford, Mass.: Digital Press.

Linden, Theodore A. 1976. Operating system structures to support security and reliable software. *ACM Computing Surveys* **8**(4): 409–445.

Mann, Daniel. 1992. Unix and the Am29000 microprocessor. *IEEE Micro* **12**(2): 23–31.

McCauley, E. J., and P. L. Drongowski. 1979. KSOS—The design of a secure operating system. *AFIPS Conference Proceedings, 1979 NCC,* 345–353. Reprinted in Rein Turn, ed., *Advances in Computer System Security,* 145–161. Dedham, Mass.: Artech House, 1981.

Mullender, Sape J., and Andrew S. Tanenbaum. 1984. Protection and resource control in distributed operating systems. *Computer Networks* **8:** 421–432.

______. 1986. The design of a capability-based distributed operating system. *The Computer Journal* **29**(4): 289–299.

Mullender, Sape J., Guido van Rossum, Andrew S. Tanenbaum, Robbert van Renesse, and Hans van Staveren. 1990. Amoeba: A distributed operating system for the 1990s. *Computer* **23**(5): 44–53.

Myers, Eugene D. 1990. A categorization of processor protection mechanisms. *Proceedings of the 13th National Computer Security Conference,* 728–737. NIST/NCSC.

NCSC. 1988a. *Glossary of Computer Security Terms.* NCSC-TG-004. Fort Meade, Md.: National Computer Security Center.

______. 1988b. *A Guide to Understanding Design Documentation in Trusted Systems.* NCSC-TG-007 Fort Meade, Md.: National Computer Security Center.

______. 1992. *A Guide to Understanding Object Reuse in Trusted Systems.* NCSC-TG-018. Fort Meade, Md.: National Computer Security Center.

Needham, R. M., and R. D. H. Walker. 1977. The Cambridge CAP computer and its protection system. *Proceedings of the Sixth ACM Symposium on Operating Systems Principles, ACM Operating Systems Review* **11**(5): 1–10.

NIST. 1991. *Glossary of Computer Security Terminology.* NISTIR 4659, PB92-112259. Gaithersburg, Md.: National Institute of Standards and Technology.

O'Brien, Richard, and Clyde Rogers. 1991. Developing applications on LOCK. *Proceedings of the 14th National Computer Security Conference,* 147–156. NIST/NCSC.

Okamoto, Toshio, Hideo Segawa, Sung Ho Shin, Hiroshi Nozue, Kenichi Maeda, and Mitsuo Saito. 1992. A micro kernel architecture for next generation processors. *Proceedings of the USENIX Workshop on Micro-kernels and Other Kernel Architectures,* 83–94. Berkeley, Calif.: USENIX Association.

Organick, Elliott I. 1972. *The Multics System: An Examination of Its Structure.* Cambridge, Mass.: The MIT Press.

Patterson, David A. 1985. Reduced instruction set computers. *Communications of the ACM* **28**(1): 8–21.

Popek, Gerald J., and Robert P. Goldberg. 1974. Formal requirements for virtualizable third generation architectures. *Communications of the ACM* **17**(7): 412–421.

Proctor, Norman E., and Peter G. Neumann. 1992. Architectural implications of covert channels. *Proceedings of the 15th National Computer Security Conference,* vol. I, 28–43. NIST/NCSC.

Rushby, John, and Brian Randall. 1983. A distributed secure system. *Computer* **16**(7): 55–67.

Russell, Thomas T., and Marvin Schaefer. 1989. Toward a high B level security architecture for the IBM ES/3090 Processor Resource/Systems Manager (PR/SM). *Proceedings of the 12th National Computer Security Conference,* 184–196. NIST/NCSC.

Saltzer, Jerome H. 1974. Protection and the control of information sharing in Multics. *Communications of the ACM* **17**(7): 388–402.

Saltzer, Jerome H., and Michael D. Schroeder. 1975. The protection of information in computer systems. *Proceedings of the IEEE* **63**(9): 1278–1308.

Sandhu, Ravi. 1992. The typed access matrix model. *Proceedings of the 1992 IEEE Computer Society Symposium on Research in Security and Privacy,* 122–136. Los Alamitos, Calif.: IEEE Computer Society.

Saydjari, O. Sami, Joseph M. Beckman, and Jeffrey R. Leaman. 1989. LOCK trek: Navigating uncharted space. *Proceedings of the 1989 IEEE Computer Society Symposium on Security and Privacy,* 167–175. Washington, D.C.: IEEE Computer Society.

Schell, Roger R., Tien F. Tao, and Mark Heckman. 1985. Designing the GEMSOS security kernel for security and performance. *Proceedings of the 8th National Computer Security Conference,* 108–119. NIST/NCSC. Reprinted in Marshall D. Abrams and Harold J. Podell, eds., *Tutorial: Computer and Network Security,* 255–266. Washington, D.C.: IEEE Computer Society, 1987.

Schroeder, Michael D., and Jerome H. Saltzer. 1972. A hardware architecture for implementing protection rings. *Communications of the ACM* **15**(3): 157–170.

Sibert, Olin, Phillip A. Porras, and Robert Lindell. 1995. The Intel 80x86 processor architecture: Pitfalls for secure systems. *Proceedings of the 1995 IEEE Symposium on Security and Privacy,* 211–222. Los Alamitos, Calif.: IEEE Computer Society.

Silberschatz, Abraham, James L. Peterson, and Peter B. Galvin. 1991. *Operating System Concepts.* 3d ed. Reading, Mass: Addison-Wesley.

Singhal, Mukesh, and Niranjan G. Shivaratri. 1994. *Advanced Concepts in Operating Systems: Distributed, Database, and Multiprocessor Operating Systems.* New York: McGraw-Hill.

Sites, Richard L. 1993. Alpha AXP architecture. *Communications of the ACM* **36**(2): 33–44.

Smith, Alan Jay. 1982. Cache memories. *Computing Surveys* **14**(3): 473–530.

Smith, Richard E. 1993. MLS file service for network data sharing. *Proceedings of the Ninth Annual Computer Security Applications Conference,* 94–99. Los Alamitos, Calif.: IEEE Computer Society.

______. 1994. Constructing a high assurance mail guard. *Proceedings of the 17th National Computer Security Conference,* 247–253. NIST/NCSC.

Tanenbaum, Andrew S., and M. Frans Kaashoek. 1994. The Amoeba microkernel. In *Distributed Open Systems,* 11–30. Los Alamitos, Calif.: IEEE Computer Society.

Tanenbaum, Andrew S., Sape J. Mullender, and Robbert van Renesse. 1986. Using sparse capabilities in a distributed operating system. *Proceedings of the 6th International Conference on Distributed Computing Systems,* 558–563. Washington, D.C.: IEEE Computer Society.

Wahbe, Robert. 1992. Efficient data breakpoints. *ASPLOS-V Proceedings of the Fifth International Conference on Architectural Support for Programming Languages and Operating Systems,* 200–212. New York: ACM Press.

Waldhart, Neil A. 1990. The Army Secure Operating System. *Proceedings of the 1990 IEEE Computer Society Symposium on Research in Security and Privacy,* 50–60. Los Alamitos, Calif.: IEEE Computer Society.

Wichers, David R. 1990. Conducting an object reuse study. *Proceedings of the 13th National Computer Security Conference,* vol. II, 738–747. NIST/NCSC.

Wilkes, John, and Bart Sears. 1992. *A Comparison of "Protection Lookaside Buffers" and the PA-RISC Protection Architecture.* Technical report HPL-92-55. HP Laboratories.

Wulf, W., E. Cohen, W. Corwin, A. Jones, R. Levin, C. Pierson, and F. Pollack. 1974. HYDRA: The kernel of a multiprocessor operating system. *Communications of the ACM* **17**(6): 337–345.

Chapter

8

Security Services in Operating Systems

This chapter is about operating system security services. It describes what the services accomplish, how they are implemented, and how people use or abuse them. The chapter also describes add-on software that fills the security gaps left by operating systems.

Overview

Access control, audit, and other services depend on correct identification of users, and a user's identity must be *authenticated.* This chapter describes authentication methods that use passwords, token devices, and biometrics. Once a system verifies a user's identity and right to enter the system, it must control the user's access to resources. Access control services are described, with special attention to file access control. Then services that support system availability and data integrity are described. Audit services are described next; they record information about security-relevant actions and make that information available to auditors. The chapter then describes security facilities for people who use, operate, administer, and audit operating systems. Security of windowing systems is discussed. Finally, examples are given of security in four operating systems: UNIX, MVS, OpenVMS, and Windows NT.

Identification and Authentication

One of the key security principles is *accountability*—someone is responsible for each action. A process is associated with a user, who is accountable for its actions. Rights to resources are granted to users. Accountability and access control depend on knowing the user's identity. A user is assigned an identifier and claims that identifier when logging on. The user ID is not secret, but the user must prove his or her claim to it by presenting evidence that no one else can present. The system evaluates the evidence to verify the user's claim. This process is *authentication.* It makes use of *authentication information* kept by the system, such as a password. The participants in the authentication process are the user (sometimes assisted by a device), a login component, and an *authentication server* (AS). Figure 8.1 shows an overview of authentication.

Authentication methods

Authentication can be based on

- Something the user *knows.*
- Something the user *has.*
- Something the user *is* or *does.*

The user knows a password, has an ATM card, and "is" a fingerprint. In other words, authentication uses knowledge, possession, or characteristic—or a combination of methods. For example, the user of an ATM must have the ATM card and also must know a password (the PIN).

Authentication by knowledge has many advantages. It is inexpensive to implement, and users can easily protect the knowledge and carry it wherever they go. The knowledge is easy to change if compromise is suspected. The main disadvantage is that the knowledge can be guessed—by brute-force attacks or by using side knowledge. For exam-

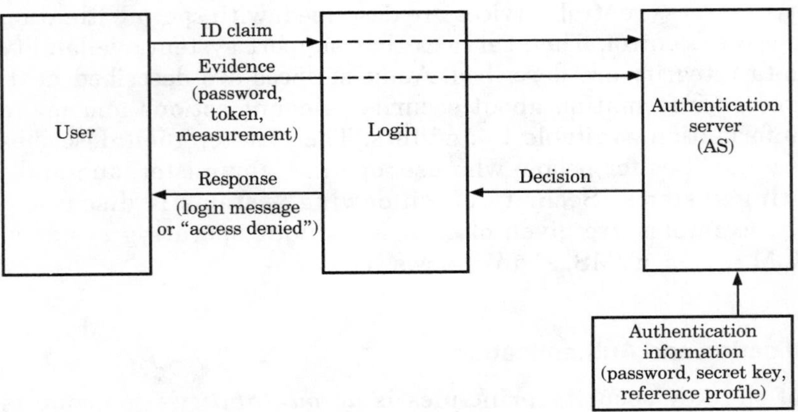

Figure 8.1 Overview of authentication.

ple, attackers who know user IDs can guess 30 percent of passwords. Authentication by possession avoids this weakness, but possessions can be lost or stolen, and the user must remember to carry them. Authentication by characteristic is the most closely tied to identity, but it can be costly and intrusive. Each method has its vulnerabilities.

The predominant "knows" method uses a *password*—a short secret shared by the user and the system. "Has" methods include memory cards (such as ATM cards) and smart cards. "Is" methods use measures of patterns in the retina, hand geometry, fingerprints, or voice qualities. "Does" methods use the dynamics of keystrokes or handwritten signatures.

Passwords

Passwords control access to most computer-based resources. Often, despite exhortation and monitoring, people use passwords carelessly. Also, operating systems have been tardy with facilities to promote good usage and protect password secrecy. Still, passwords are familiar and inexpensive, and some of their problems can be solved.

Good passwords. A good password is easy to remember and hard to guess. If passwords are hard to remember, people write them down, making disclosure more likely, or they forget them and have to gain system entry in a special and vulnerable way. Remembering passwords is an unwanted burden for users, especially those who use multiple systems. The two criteria—easy to remember and hard to guess—work against one another. Something is easy to remember if it is meaningfully related to other things one knows. These same relationships make it easy to guess. Many passwords are cracked because they are names of children, spouses, or pets, or because they are simple transformations of the user's name, user ID, or previous password.

Vulnerabilities. The vulnerability of passwords is well known, especially as implemented in UNIX. For example, Robert Morris and Ken Thompson published in 1979 the general method of attack that worked in the Internet worm of 1988 and (apparently) in the Wily Hacker's intrusions. Traditional UNIX keeps passwords in a file accessible to everyone. They are encrypted, but that safeguard is inadequate. Using the system's encryption method, the attacker encrypts many candidate passwords, looking for matches with the password file. Where a match occurs, the corresponding plaintext is the password. Such attacks often copy the password file and analyze it away from the target computer, avoiding detection. The main types of attacks using the password file are as follows:

- *Exhaustive search,* encrypting all possible passwords of the minimum length. This attack is most effective if many passwords are short and contain only letters.
- *Dictionary attack,* encrypting each word in a dictionary to see if it matches an encrypted password. This attack is more efficient than exhaustive search because only meaningful words are tried, and passwords tend to be meaningful. A standard dictionary can be enhanced with words commonly chosen for passwords, such as first names and street and city names.

Morris and Thompson found that 86 percent of a large sample of passwords could be found using a dictionary and a few other lists.

An attacker who knows something about the password's owner does not even need the password file. A university department of economics and commerce (ECON/COM for short) used an account name of ECON and a password of...you guessed it. Good guesses are repetitions of the user's initials, permutations of the user ID, names of family members or pets, or the user's make of car or license plate number. Another easy target is a built-in account that comes with an operating system or subsystem. Many installations have never changed the well-known original passwords for these accounts.

All these attacks aim at guessing passwords—by brute force or more intelligently. They are especially effective for a hacker seeking to break into *any* account on a system, because some users are likely to have weak passwords.

Guessing is not the only way to find passwords. An attacker can see and hear keying of the password. Passwords are found on scraps of paper in offices or in the trash. A PIN is sometimes written on the ATM card itself—the least secure place. An attacker can tap the line between the user's station and the authentication server. A spoofing attack (where attack software impersonates login) can capture the password. More generally, the user must trust the authentication server not to misuse or reveal the secret.

Achieving strong passwords. Guessing attacks exploit weak passwords and poor password protection. Each vulnerability can be reduced dramatically.

Password generators. One way to ensure strong passwords is for the system to generate random strings. One problem, however, is that some password generators are vulnerable to an attack whose goal is to compromise any account on a system. Another problem is that generated passwords, even pronounceable ones, are hard to remember. A user who must accept a system-generated password can try memory tactics. For example, invent a phrase whose initial letters come from the password, as in password *w4lo2tcp* and the phrase "We four live only to try cracking passwords." It helps if the user can select from several generated passwords.

Guidelines. Users can be guided to select stronger passwords. For example, guessing attacks are harder if passwords contain special characters and numbers as well as letters. The password will not appear in a dictionary, and exhaustive search is also harder because the password space is larger. However, special characters make passwords harder to remember, and their position on the keyboard makes these characters easier to observe. Other ways to protect against dictionary attacks are to misspell words, combine two words, and insert punctuation. A minimum length (such as eight characters) should be enforced. A new password should differ from any recent password, and it should differ substantially from the most recent one. There also may be a list of passwords to avoid (essentially the cracker's list). Systems can enforce password guidelines by checking passwords when they are selected, spotting easy-to-guess passwords by attempting to crack them. Password checking is a common feature of add-on security software.

Password monitoring. Many installations regularly audit passwords for conformance with the guidelines.

Passphrases. Fortunately, a motivated user can take advantage of many good ideas for selecting strong, easy-to-remember passwords. For example, select a meaningful phrase and then use its initial letters in the password. Selecting the book title *The Complete Plays and Poems of William Shakespeare,* I get the password *TCP+POWS*. Or the system can generate easy-to-remember passphrases. Stanley Kurzban (1985) suggested randomly selecting a phrase consisting of a sequence such as adjective, noun, and verb. Such a sequence seems meaningful even when it is nonsense.

User-friendly selection. Ben and Marthalee Barton (1984) applied theories of memory and cognition to password selection. They suggest choosing an expression based on either general knowledge (such as song or movie titles) or personal information (such as childhood disliked foods). The user then transforms the expression to disguise its relationship to ordinary experience or to himself or herself. For example, the disliked fried eggplant becomes *FRIEGGPLA*. The system could help by prompting for the general or personal information and suggesting possible transformations. L. G. Lawrence (1993) suggests transforming meaningful strings into passwords by applying simple algorithms that use keys. With this method, the user can write down the key. Suppose the key "4,6" means "start with character 4 and take 6 characters." The string "GoneWithTheWind" then yields the password *ewitht.*

Protecting passwords. Passwords must be protected against compromise and loss.

Keeping the secret. Password mechanisms work only if passwords are kept secret at all stages. Secrecy can be lost when passwords are entered, when they are transmitted, and when they are stored. (And when they are displayed or printed, but there is no reason to do that.) Secrecy is lost, of course, if passwords are shared. Nearly always, a password should belong to a single person, for accountability. Sometimes it is necessary to temporarily reveal a password. For example, someone watched a login, or a system programmer told her password to a colleague who called at night about an emergency. When the password has been revealed, the owner should change it as soon as possible. Writing down passwords is bad practice, but notes that jog the owner's memory are useless to others.

A user may telephone an administrator and claim to have forgotten her password. The claim could be valid, or the user could be an intruder. Administrators need clear guidelines on assuring themselves of the user's identity. A commercial service may mail a new password to the address of record. There is no reason for administrators to have access to passwords, except very temporarily for new accounts.

Systems should not display passwords. A new password must be entered twice to ensure correctness, since the user cannot check it visually. Although operating systems do not display them, passwords do get displayed. A login script that is used to access a remote system may contain cleartext passwords that get displayed when the profile is used. (The script files are also vulnerable.)

As much as possible, the system should respond in the same way to valid and invalid passwords. An observer or eavesdropper should get no cue from response time or displays. Rather than responding with "invalid password," the system should collect all login information and then respond with "access denied."

Secrecy in transmission. If a password is transmitted in cleartext, an eavesdropper can learn it. Even without eavesdropping on transmission, transmitted passwords are vulnerable to *sniffer* attacks by system intruders (see Chap. 10).

Protecting stored passwords. Attacks using password files have succeeded dramatically, as in the 1988 Internet worm. No user or component, except for the authentication server, needs to access passwords. However, the UNIX password file originally was accessible to all, and since many commands used it, it had to remain accessible. Some UNIX systems then made it possible to keep the passwords in a *shadow* file not generally accessible. Access control can protect passwords against unprivileged users; encryption provides another layer of protection and protects the passwords against privileged users such as systems programmers or operators who may see system dumps. However, Trojan horse attacks remain a great danger.

Password aging. Since only the cracker may know that a password has been cracked, it is standard practice to change passwords regularly. The longevity of a password has to strike a balance. Frequent changes lead people to pick weak passwords or to write down passwords, whereas infrequent changes can allow break-ins using compromised passwords. Many installations use 60 days. The system should give a user time to pick a strong new password—notifying a week in advance or allowing a short grace period. Password aging is taken to an extreme with the *one-time password.* For example, the user receives a new password at each login, for use at the next login. One-time passwords (as opposed to reusable passwords) are needed to counter threats from networking.

Lost or unavailable passwords. A single human memory cannot be relied on for some critical passwords, such as a LAN administrator's password. A critical password can be told to another trusted person or locked in a safe. Each part of a multipart password can be given to a different person so that all must agree to its use.

Multiple passwords. Applications often require further authentication using *secondary passwords.* Some systems also use secondary passwords to control access to resources such as files or databases, but such an approach is not recommended. Resource passwords just increase the user's memory burden. They are not needed if the primary authentication and access control services are doing their jobs. A better use of secondary passwords is for more protection at login—but at a cost of user time and patience.

Many users regularly log on to multiple systems; ten or fifteen is not unusual. The traditional guidelines about remembering and not recording passwords become obsolete. If we have trouble remembering one, ten is probably hopeless. What most users and organizations would like is a *single sign-on* for an entire work session. Ways to accomplish this are discussed in Chap. 11.

Pass algorithms and challenge-response. Rather than a secret string of characters (a pass *word*), a user can know a secret algorithm—a *pass* *algorithm.* Or the user can know one or more passwords plus an algorithm that works on them. Pass algorithms are a form of *challenge-response:* The system presents a challenge, and the user responds. If the algorithm is "add one to each character and insert nonsense," *UAJ!NMF* would be a valid response to the challenge *TIME*. The secret algorithm can be selected from a large library and changed frequently. Another possible challenge is a series of questions for which the user's answers have been recorded. Or the user could set up a list of word pairs, each a cue and a response. The challenge then is a randomly chosen subset of the cues.

Authentication using token devices

In methods based on "something the user has," the user presents an object—a *token*—as evidence of identity. Usually, an organization issues tokens as evidence of both identity and the right to use a system or application. ATM cards and telephone credit cards are familiar examples. A token is a unique object that cannot be "guessed." This and ease of use are its main advantages. The main disadvantages are that (1) the user must always have it, (2) it can be lost or stolen, and (3) it is relatively costly.

Memory cards. The simplest token devices are cards that contain magnetically recorded information. A *memory card* used for authentication stores (for example) the issuer's identity, the user ID, and an expiration date. Although a memory card is inexpensive, it must be inserted in a special card-reading device, so the total cost is significant. To guard against theft or counterfeiting, memory cards are used with *personal identification numbers* (PINs)—usually four-digit numbers. One might expect these short PINs to be vulnerable to brute-force attacks, but usually they are not. The keyed PIN goes directly to the authentication server, which, after a few bad tries, terminates authentication and may even cause the card to be seized. There is no opportunity for an unobserved brute-force attack.

Although memory cards work well for some applications, they cannot provide strong authentication for computing system access. Lacking processing power, the card cannot check a password or PIN or encrypt it for transmission. With ATM cards, these functions can be performed by the ATM; for login from a workstation, there is no trusted counterpart.

See-through devices. Another class of token devices has processing power but no connection to the authentication server. The device helps the user with the authentication process. These *see-through devices* have displays and keypads, like pocket calculators. Each user gets a device with a unique secret built-in key. Authentication requires both the device and a "PIN" that is permanently associated with the device.

Some see-through products use a challenge-response scheme called *Polonius,* based on a variation of the one-time pad cryptosystem (where sender and receiver have identical lists of secret keys, and each key is used for only one message). Polonius pad entries are generated rather than stored and are used in any order. The authentication server generates a seven-digit challenge that names a pad entry. The user reads this number from the workstation display and enters it into the device, which applies a cryptographic algorithm to the secret key, PIN, and challenge. The user reads the response from the device display and enters it at the workstation. Some devices read the challenge directly from the workstation screen.

Another type of see-through card is time-based. The card contains a clock and has a display but no keypad. Each device has a secret key and a PIN. Once a minute the card enciphers the clock reading with the secret key and displays the result. This pseudo-random number serves as a one-time or *dynamic* password. The user enters this number and the card's PIN at the workstation. The authentication server is a companion module that plugs into the target system and that knows the secret keys of all the cards. Since it is synchronized with the card and knows its secret key, it can verify that the specific card produced the dynamic password.

We think of token devices as belonging to users. It is possible, however, for an impersonal device to participate in authentication by providing a secure channel between the user and the authentication server. In one proposed scheme, a simple card can be shared by users, and the user performs some of the computations for the authentication protocol.

See-through devices protect against password interception. They achieve one-time passwords simply and without special workstation hardware. The user must do more than just enter a password but does not have to choose or memorize passwords.

Smart cards. A *smart card* has processing power and also directly connects to a system. The card is built to prevent unauthorized access to the CPU, bus, or memory. It is used with a password or PIN. Smart cards are used widely for applications such as retail sales, billed telephone calls, and parking. The smart card itself can verify the user's PIN or password. Then, in a common protocol, it builds a message containing the user's name and password and the date and time. It enciphers this message using a built-in secret key known to the authentication server (AS) and sends the ciphertext to the AS. If the AS can decipher the message properly, authentication succeeds. No secret information is transmitted in the clear. (The workstation, however, has learned the password from the user, so this scheme is not appropriate for shared or public workstations.)

Smart cards are used to control access to PCs or workstations. A hardware security unit that attaches to a PC requires the smart card to be inserted before the PC can start. The smart card also can store the user's security profile for purposes other than authentication. For example, it can describe the user's access rights to drives or directories.

The unique advantage of smart cards for authentication is their ability to use public key cryptographic methods. These methods involve very long keys, so they cannot be used with see-through devices, which rely on small displays and human copying. The alternative of secret key encryption has two serious problems. First, the authentication server must be trusted with the secret. Especially in distributed systems, users may not trust all the services they use. Second, the management of secret keys is very difficult. With public key methods, key distribution is much simpler, and identity can be proved without trusting the AS. With *zero-knowledge proofs of identity* (see Chap. 5) a user proves knowledge of a secret key to the AS without revealing the key. Some zero-knowledge protocols require relatively little computation by the prover, so they are suitable for smart cards.

Threats to token devices. A person who finds or steals a token device could (1) use the device directly to gain system access, (2) attack the hardware components to obtain a stored PIN or secret key or to alter data, or (3) carry out a brute-force attack off-line to obtain a PIN.

Requiring a PIN protects effectively against the first threat, if the AS restricts bad tries. Unfortunately, however, a thief has a fair chance of finding the PIN recorded on the card. The threat of hardware penetration is lessened by making token devices *tamper-resistant.* For example, the key-storage memory and encryption circuitry of an IBM smart card are wrapped in a membrane that contains a conductive ink pattern. When a break is detected, the secret data are erased. An off-line brute-force attack makes sense only for cards that verify the PIN themselves, and these cards can be programmed to delay after a few unsuccessful tries.

Authentication using biometric methods

Authentication based on physical or behavioral characteristics—something the person is or does—is called *biometric*. The main use of biometric methods has been to control physical access to high-security facilities, such as nuclear plants. They also have been used to identify crime suspects and prisoners. Use for computer system access control is rare because of cost, intrusiveness, and lack of precision. Each of these barriers is coming down, and we can expect more use of biometric methods.

Phases in biometric authentication. All the methods follow a common pattern. In an *enrollment* phase, the characteristic is measured. The person gives a fingerprint or signs his or her name with a special pen. Several examples are taken. The data are analyzed, and a *reference profile* or *template* is built. When the person claims an identity, the characteristic is measured again, and the measurements are compared with the template. The method then either accepts or rejects the claim. Decisions about passwords are exact: The keyed password matches the stored one, or it does not. Biometric methods, in contrast, must base their decision on how closely the test measurement matches the reference profile. There are two possible errors: accepting a false claim or rejecting a true claim. The tolerance level can be adjusted to lower one error rate, but then the other will rise. A very low false acceptance rate is secure, but the rejections may infuriate authorized users.

Criteria. The first criterion for a biometric authentication method is its rate of false acceptances. For commercial use, a rate of 1 percent may be acceptable, depending on the application. Many products claim much lower rates, such as 0.0001 percent. The rate of true rejection can be higher. Just as important as the error rates is the effect on people. The method must not harm them, and it must be acceptable to them.

The biometric methods need templates of quite different sizes, ranging from about 80 bytes for retinal blood vessel patterns to 20,000 bytes or so for voice recognition. With a small template, access and comparison are faster, and the template can be stored in a token device. (Template size and processing time become less important as token devices become very powerful.) Finally, the cost of the measurement device should be low.

To sum up, a good biometric authentication method has very few false acceptances and true rejections. The measurement process does not harm or bother people. The template size is small, and the comparison can be made rapidly. Cost is low.

Devices using physical measurements. Each person has a different pattern of blood vessels in the retina. For authentication, a *retinal scanner* uses a beam of infrared light. Since blood vessels absorb more light than the other tissue, the intensity of reflected light varies for different points on the retina. The template is based on these intensity measurements. The main concerns are about possible harm from the infrared beam or infection from a device that is brought close to the eyes. The method is one of the most accurate.

Other highly accurate methods are based on hand geometry. Hand scanners seem less intrusive than retinal scanners. They have been used experimentally with international travelers to verify that the person goes with the passport. Fingerprint recognition is highly developed and accurate and can be done by microprocessor-based devices. The main disadvantage is that people hesitate—rightly—to give up personal information whose most prominent use is for tracking down criminals. Some devices address this concern by extracting only key features of a fingerprint so that the fingerprint cannot be reconstructed from the template data. Palmprint readers also are very accurate. Fingerprints and palmprints require people to touch a surface that many other people touch, but this is also true of public doors and public telephones.

Two biometric techniques that are being developed are quite nonintrusive. In one, an infrared scanner collects data about the pattern of veins on the back of the hand. The other is the method used for identification in everyday life—face recognition.

Devices using behavioral measurements. Behavioral methods tend to be less accurate than physical ones, because behavior varies more from day to day or hour to hour. Their advantage is that they can be less intrusive.

A seemingly ideal authentication method for financial transactions uses handwritten signatures, which traditionally authenticate paper transactions. Current products use signature dynamics, taking measurements when the person writes with a special pen. The measures include acceleration and change in pressure. Considerable computation is needed to compare a new signature with the reference; an IBM product uses a signal processor for this work. Since a person's signature may change gradually over time, signature verification devices are designed to adapt to these changes. The signature dynamics method is quite accurate, and the dynamics are very hard to forge.

Voice recognition, also called *speaker verification,* has had some success, and several devices are marketed.

Another method uses the times between keystrokes of a person typing. Typing rhythms are quite recognizable, even for unskilled typists. Keystroke dynamics can be measured either on a designated sequence (such as user ID, password, or first and last names) or on typing during a whole session. This means that authentication can be repeated throughout a session at the system's will (and without the user's knowledge). This repeated authentication can guard against a change of user after authentication. It also is a form of workplace monitoring, which has been criticized as intrusive. An obvious advantage of keystroke dynamics is that no special hardware is needed.

Security of biometric authentication. Biometric methods are evaluated on the basis of error rates, costs, and acceptability to users. Equally important are how a method or device fits into the total authentication scheme and what attacks are possible. One type of attack presents a person's physical characteristic in the absence of the person. We can imagine, for example, a glove that simulates another person's fingerprint. Another type of attack targets the path between the device and the AS. A replay attack is possible, where the attacker intercepts biometric data and uses them later. In software-based methods, such as keystroke dynamics, the software must be trusted. This is also true for any software components of hardware-based methods.

Biometric methods have been used too little for computer access control to permit evaluating them against passwords and nonbiometric token devices. Progress is rapid, and we can expect smart card and biometric methods to be used together.

Mutual authentication

Users need to be assured that they are indeed logged on to their intended systems. Spoofing attacks could steal crucial data, including passwords or other authentication information. With client-server computing, the user's programs request services from servers. The client must be assured that the right server is handling its request, and the server must be assured that the client system properly identified the user. Both need to be assured that their authentication communications are secure. These problems have led to the development of *authentication protocols* for distributed systems, described in Chap. 11.

Operating system requirements

In its work on the Federal Criteria, NIST developed minimum security requirements for operating systems for general commercial or government use (Ferraiolo et al. 1993). Here are some of the requirements pertaining to identification and authentication.

The operating system must assign identifiers to users and keep user profiles. It must associate the identifiers with processes. It also must support identifiers for groups and be able to associate individuals with groups. Administrators must be able to disable and reenable user IDs and to check on their status. A process must have only a strictly limited ability to increase its privileges by changing user ID.

Login must be initiated through the trusted path. The operating system must authenticate all users before any other interactions can occur. The authentication process must not reveal any authentication information. There must be a secure way for an installation to replace the system-supplied authentication mechanism with a different one (biometric, for example), and there must be an application program interface to authentication. Access to authentication information must require special privilege. Passwords must be stored one-way encrypted, and there must be no access by anyone to cleartext passwords.

Users must be required to change their passwords after an installation-specified time, and they must be notified in advance or allowed a grace period. The system must ensure the complexity of user-chosen passwords. It should reject passwords that appear on lists of excluded ones. If the system generates passwords, they must be easy to remember and hard to crack, and the user should have a choice of passwords. There must be a way to force a direct connection (the trusted path) between the user's device and the authentication mechanism. The password must not be displayed. A few (default three) unsuccessful attempts must terminate login, generate an alarm, and temporarily disallow login from the device. Password changes and login attempts must be audited.

Control of System Entry

Other services, in addition to identification and authentication, ensure that all access to a computing system is authorized. Once the system verifies a user's identity, it must make other checks. Does the user have an account? Is it active, or has it been temporarily disabled? Environmental criteria also must be checked. For example, dial-up or network access may be denied, the user may be restricted to a specific set of terminals, and access may be allowed only during the user's normal work shift. A multilevel system controls entry based on the security levels of the user and the terminal and the level the user now wants to work at. The system then applies its policy to determine if entry is allowed and, if so, the level of the session. For example, entry is denied if the system's minimum level dominates the user's maximum level; the session level is the minimum of the system level, user level, terminal level, and requested session level.

Operating systems need to prevent someone (other than the identified user) from walking up to a terminal and taking over an ongoing session. *Session locking,* which prevents any interaction except authorized unlocking, can be initiated by the user and by the system. The user locks the session before temporarily leaving the terminal; the system locks the session after some interval (such as 15 minutes) with no interaction. The system overwrites the locked display to wipe out any session information. To unlock the session, the user must be authenticated again. Some systems terminate sessions rather than just locking them. There must be no way for a dial-up user to connect to the previous session for the same port.

The system can use the initial screen to tell users about system access policy. The NIST report suggests the unfriendly default of "NOTICE: This is a private computer system. Unauthorized access or use is prohibited and may lead to prosecution"(Ferraiolo et al. 1993: 3–9). Such a notice is needed for successful prosecution of intruders. After successful login, the system should inform users about recent activity on their accounts, which might be misuse: date and time of the last login and the source of entry (which network host, dial-in line or terminal) and any unsuccessful attempts on their accounts since the last entry.

For access to stand-alone PCs or workstations, the controls lie mainly outside the operating system, because intruders can boot up PCs using their own software. The most common protection is physical security of the location. Add-on software can provide *boot protection,* which prevents access to the hard disk until a password is supplied. Since most software-only protection is not secure against hacker-intruders, *bootlock protection* using special hardware has been developed. One product relies on encryption of the hard disk boot sector and a special boot "diskette" that is really a smart card. Booting from the smart diskette causes password checking and decryption of the hard disk boot sector.

Access Control

Access control is the process of ensuring that all access to resources is authorized access. External barriers and administrative procedures provide *physical access control*; software and hardware provide *logical access control.* Although applications, subsystems, and gateways also perform access control, the operating system has the basic responsibility. This section discusses the logical access control services of operating systems. It begins with the entities of the access control model: subjects, objects, access rights, and access validation.

Subjects

After a user has been identified and authenticated, the operating system creates processes, tasks, or jobs that are tagged with the user's identity. A process acts on behalf of a user, with the rights of that user. Good access control supports granting rights to individuals; that is, the granularity of access control is the individual user. An operating system provides facilities to add new users, to revoke users' rights to use the system, and to specify security information about users. Access control depends on this *user security profile* information. If mandatory access control is used, the information includes the user's clearance and category set. The profile also specifies what actions of the user should be audited. The profile may contain restrictions; for example, the user can enter the system only from a locally attached terminal and only during the hours 4 P.M. to midnight. Figure 8.2 shows user security information for a hypothetical system. The operating system must enforce any entry restrictions and must securely attach the user's security attributes to the subjects that it creates.

Although fine-grained access control is needed, it would be unworkable to grant all access rights individually. A tiny corps of administrators may be responsible for tens of thousands of users. They must be able to define groups of users and assign rights to the groups or to delegate administrative responsibility for a group. The group profile is a user profile that also includes a list of group members. Systems have different policies about what group rights apply to a session. For some systems, the user specifies one group; for others, the subject gets the rights of all the user's groups. Individual rights generally should take precedence over group rights. Say that Lisa belongs to the Advertising group, which has read access to the Accounts file. If Lisa herself has read and write access, she can modify the Accounts file. If Lisa is both granted and *denied* read and write access, she cannot read the Accounts file.

User ID
User name and user data
Password
Password history
Group memberships
Privileges
Logon restrictions
Default protections for new objects
Audit specifications
[Sensitivity label]

Figure 8.2 Security attributes of users.

Objects

What objects are protected. A system should control access to all objects. Of course, an organization may not need to protect absolutely everything, but that should be a conscious choice. Systems are moving toward fail-safe default protection.

Access control services apply mainly to files and devices, as well as to higher-level organizations of files, such as directories and libraries. Directories are crucial in access control. Files often inherit access control specifications from their directories, and special rights apply to creating or deleting files in a directory. Access to transactions also must be controlled, either by a transaction-processing subsystem or by the operating system.

Object security information. An object has an *owner*—an individual or a group, or both. Only the owner can specify other security information about the object. Figure 8.3 shows security information for objects of a hypothetical system. The information includes ownership and what access rights apply to the object (especially important for systems that allow users to define new object types.) There is an access control list or a list of permissions. Access control information for a directory includes the default specifications for files created in that directory. There may be restrictions based on time, location, or mode of system entry. Suppose that BioWidget's product plans are too sensitive to display where visitors might see them. Access to the product-plan files could be restricted to terminals in controlled locations. Systems often deny execution of certain commands to users logged on through networks.

Authorized access. Associated with each object is some specification of who can access it and how. This specification can take the form of a password, permission bits, or access control lists. Passwords are a bad

Owner
Group
Allowable access modes
Access restrictions
Access control list
Audit specifications
Default protections for new objects
[Sensitivity label]
[Integrity label]

Figure 8.3 Security attributes of objects.

way to control access to objects; since many passwords are needed, users' password problems are multiplied. Permission bits specify what access rights are granted to built-in user categories: owner, group or project, and everyone else. Permission bits (used in UNIX) are simple and efficient, and they do the job if the built-in categories fit the organization's needs. However, they cannot provide fine-grained access control, such as granting write access to one person. Too much policy is built into the mechanism.

Access control lists (ACLs) are the method of choice. An access control list entry specifies a user ID or group ID, a set of rights, and whether the rights are allowed or denied. ACLs usually have no limit on their length, but very long ACLs may take too long to search.

Access rights

A system must be able to let users access information without letting them modify it. The basic rights are **read, write,** and **execute.** These access modes can be recognized by hardware, and they meet most access control needs. Other rights apply to operating system objects, such as the right to **wait** on an event or to **send** to a port. At a higher level are rights to user-defined objects.

There are also special rights, such as the right to create files in a directory. A user with a **control** right can modify the object's access control information. Usually this right goes to the object's creator, who automatically becomes its owner. It is more flexible, though, to separate ownership from control.

Special rights called *privileges* are associated with privileged roles, such as operator and security administrator. Some privileges override the normal access control policy. The UNIX *superuser,* for example, has all rights to everything. It is better to set up real-world roles and define each role as a set of privileges—only the privileges that the role needs. A person then gets access to the role.

Because of their power, privileges must be controlled more closely than ordinary access rights. The privilege for granting privileges should be separate from all others. There should be no way to disable auditing of privilege use; that is, every use of privilege should be audited. A privileged subject should be able to set its privileges dynamically—so that it always runs with the least privilege it needs.

Subjects, objects, and mandatory access control

For mandatory access control, each subject and each object carries a *sensitivity label* that includes its level and category set. There also may be an integrity label. The labels need to be maintained both within the computing system and outside it. Displayed and printed output must be labeled. The TCSEC require *secure export* for class B1. Export devices (such as communications channels and I/O devices) can be either single-level or multilevel. Printers, tape drives, and communication ports are typically designated as single-level. A multilevel device (such as a disk or communication channel) can accept data within a range of security levels. If objects are exported to a multilevel device, their labels must go with them; if they are exported outside the system, the labels should have a form that receiving systems can interpret.

Users need to know the level at which they are working. A session level may differ from the user's clearance level, and it can change. The session level must be displayed whenever it changes.

Access validation

The access control information associated with subjects and objects is used to determine if an access is allowed. Putting it abstractly, given an *access request* (subject, object, requested access), the operating system uses *access validation rules* to reach an *access decision.* Operating system users do not get a list of access validation rules. What they may get (if they probe) is a description of the algorithm for searching the access control list. A hypothetical example:

> All "denial" entries appear first. The ACL is searched in order, starting at the top, until an entry is found that matches the user ID and access mode. The decision is based on the first entry found.

The algorithm must implement the system's policy about individual and group access rights. The system must protect all the information used by access validation, including subject and object security profiles and environment information such as time of day.

Mandatory access control follows well-defined validation rules that interpret the Bell-LaPadula model. Access is permitted only if allowed by both the mandatory rules and the discretionary rights. In principle, operating systems could support other mandatory policies or even allow customers to select from alternative sets of access validation rules that implement different policies. Use of mandatory access control (MAC) is rare in commercial systems, but this may change as intensified interest in commercial security coincides with the availability of MAC in operating systems.

Most systems validate file access against the access control list only when the file is opened, because checking each access would be too expensive. A process opens a file (or other object) for a specific access type, such as **read** or **execute,** and gets back a "capability" for that type of access. Subsequent access uses this capability. In Windows NT, for example, a program supplies a bitmask describing the desired accesses to an object. The system returns an object handle, and the allowed accesses are recorded in an object table for the process.

Attributes for new objects

Objects get their initial access control attributes from create-time parameters, from default settings, or from a combination of the two. Defaults can be system-wide or inherited from a higher-level object (usually a directory), or they can apply to the user or session. For example, a UNIX user can set a mask that constrains the rights specified by any programs running on his or her behalf. The original setting of the mask comes, in turn, from a system-wide default.

Operating systems arrive with "system-supplied" default settings. All too often these settings are not reconsidered when the system is installed. Thus it is important for the system-supplied defaults to be fail-safe.

Constrained environments

One way to limit users' rights is to constrain their interface to the operating system. For example, a *restricted shell* may deny a UNIX user sensitive commands, such as changing the working directory. In other ways the restricted shell works like an ordinary shell. This approach works only if the constraints are securely implemented so that users cannot break out. Restricted shells are often insecure in the face of abnormal terminations or applications with "shell escapes" that allow arbitrary command execution. Users also can be limited to a graphic interface that presents only certain applications. Again, there must be no way to escape. Another method sets up a totally separate directory system for constrained users, giving them their own limited object universe.

Availability and Integrity

A computing system has good *availability* if its authorized users can get at system resources when they need them. *High-availability* systems are needed for telephone networks, air traffic control, hospitals, and many other applications. Although high availability is outside the scope of this book, some aspects are relevant here. One is how systems restart after failure and preserve security. Another is how they protect the integrity of system and user objects against failure.

Integrity has to do with meeting expectations. A *system* has integrity if it behaves according to expectations even in the face of attack. *Data* have integrity if they are internally consistent and also consistent with the real-world entities that they represent. The goals for data integrity are to

- Prevent unauthorized modifications
- Maintain internal and external consistency
- Maintain other data quality attributes
- Prevent authorized but improper modifications

The goals for systems integrity are similar, but they apply to the integrity of the computing system and its own objects.

The way that a system is designed, built, and distributed determines how likely it is to crash or otherwise deny service. This section focuses on the services that most specifically pertain to availability and integrity.

Why and how systems fail

In *fault-tolerance* terminology, a *failure* occurs when a module (or the whole system) fails to behave as specified. A failure is due to an *error* in some module that in turn is caused by a defect or *fault* in the module. Many system failures are due to software faults, and the most common response is to simply restart the system. Faults can be categorized as hardware, design (mostly software), operations (such as an operator error), and environmental (such as power outage or high temperature).

An operating system can detect many errors, and it can correct some. For example, it can retry a disk read. It also can detect its own errors and, if not correct them, at least localize the damage. For example, it can kill an executing process if the error affects no other state. For some detected errors (such as inconsistencies is its own tables), no correction is possible. An operating system also can be designed to prevent damage if failure occurs. For example, it can update system tables so as to minimize the interval during which values are inconsistent.

A system can crash, or it can fail in an orderly and controlled way. For example, it may shut itself down because a critical resource (such as swap space) is exhausted. The operator may take it down because response has slowed inexplicably. Users then would have a chance to shut down their sessions gracefully. An administrator-controlled failure is called a *discontinuity.*

Recovery

After a system crash or discontinuity, *recovery procedures* restore the system's ability to operate and restore any affected objects. An operating system provides some automatic procedures for recovery and restart, and subsystems and applications have their own recovery procedures. People do the rest. The system must restart in a secure state, and recovery must not provide an opportunity for misuse.

Recovery procedures. A system needs to start up in a *maintenance mode,* which allows only privileged users from privileged terminals. If the start-up follows a system failure, it is necessary to restore the system state, including its security state, as well as the user objects. Automated recovery procedures are better than administrative ones because they are faster, meaning less denial of service, and because errors are less likely. Since recovery operates at least partly outside the normal protection, errors can be deadly. An example of an automated recovery tool is the UNIX **fsck** command, which checks file systems for inconsistency and repairs them, either on its own or interacting with an administrator. When damaged objects are found but cannot be repaired, the operating system should automatically notify the owners.

Trusted recovery. The TCSEC for class B3 require *trusted recovery*—mechanisms and procedures for bringing the system to a secure state after a failure. A state is secure if the *security invariants, integrity invariants,* and *security constraints* hold. The security invariants are both formal—from the system's interpretation of its security model—and informal, such as: In each access control list, all entries for denied access precede any entries for allowed access. Integrity invariants concern the TCB's own variables. For example, a disk sector is either free or allocated. Constraints pertain to state transitions. For example, when the security level of an object is changed, the new level must dominate the original security level of the object. Unless the invariants and constraints are specified, it cannot be known if the restored state is secure, and so trusted recovery cannot occur. The TCB must be designed to allow the constraints to be verified during recovery.

To support recovery, it might be possible to write TCB primitives as *transactions.* Recoverable transactions were developed for database systems, but they have properties that are important for recovery in general:

- *Atomicity.* Either all the actions of a transaction are done (it commits) or none are done.

- *Consistency.* A transaction preserves the invariants that characterize a correct state.
- *Durability.* If a transaction commits, its changes to the database will survive subsequent failures.

It is mainly transaction-processing subsystems and database systems that support these good properties, using highly sophisticated techniques. Implementing TCB primitives as transactions is too costly to do for all operations, but it makes sense for some, such as changing a security level.

Redundancy

The most important way to prepare for recovery and protect data integrity is through redundancy. If one copy of a file is destroyed or damaged, another copy may survive. Redundancy is also needed to support recoverable transactions. The services that an operating system can provide include backup, checkpoints, mirroring, and recovery logs.

Backup. Backup makes copies that can be used for recovery. Facilities for backup include commands for users and administrators, as well as automatic facilities. Users of multiuser systems are often unaware of backup until disaster strikes. Then they may happily learn that their data were backed up the previous night. Users of stand-alone workstations are on their own, so they have the greatest need for easy-to-use backup. Some backup services come with operating systems, and some are add-ons.

Backup needs to be fast, flexible, and secure. Large installations typically back up to tape and individuals to diskettes, a second hard drive, or a small tape drive. LAN users can back up to servers, as can clustered large systems. As hard disks become larger, speed becomes crucial. Flexibility promotes speed, because users can specify precisely what needs to be backed up.

Users need a way to identify sets of files to back up, with a granularity of individual files. For example, I might use a set named BOOK for all the files of this book. A *full backup* copies the contents of an entire set or entire drive. The amount of data can be reduced by *incremental backup,* which copies only files modified since the last backup, or *differential backup,* which copies only files modified since the last full backup. Or users can specify a date range. For each backup set, a catalog details what was backed up and when. The catalog is stored redundantly—on both the hard disk and the backup volume. Some software tries to completely automate backup, after interacting with the user to set up a strategy.

The backup copy must be correct. Error-correction codes can be added to the backup data, to support recovery even if some data are lost. Another option is to read back the copied data and compare them with the original. This can be done either during backup or when backup completes. For confidentiality, backups can be encrypted. For access control, backup tapes can be labeled with a password based on the creator's ID. Since backup violates normal access control, it needs to be a privileged action. Of course, backup data need to be protected with physical security; a good strategy is to store some copies offsite.

Restoring data is an error-prone operation. Good menus help users specify what to restore, and warnings force them to think twice about their actions. On systems with operators and administrators, restoring from backups is an opening for misuse. The restored data may not be the backed-up data. For example, files could be restored with altered access control lists that give access to an attacker, data values could be changed, or subverted operating system modules could be "restored." Systems can guard against misuse by privileged users by labeling tapes with passwords and by administrative procedures, authentication, audit, and careful assignment of privileges. For trusted systems, backup and restore must be trusted functions, since untrusted code could alter labels or other security-critical information.

Mirroring. With *mirroring,* every write operation is done a second time, to a different disk or different network node, so that two copies of the data are maintained. Mirroring can be done at the file level or at the disk level. Every write to a master disk or file is automatically written to its mirror (or shadow) disk or file. Mirroring is often provided with LANs, either as an operating system function or by a combination of software and special redundant hardware. File and database servers use special hardware that provides transparent disk redundancy and dedicated high-performance links between primary and secondary servers.

Checkpoints. A *system checkpoint* is a complete picture of the state of a system—all the information needed to restart the system where it was at the time of the checkpoint. Then, if failure occurs, the system can be restored to its checkpoint status. It used to be fairly simple to take a static snapshot of an entire system. Checkpoint logic has become very complicated because systems cannot be stopped to take a checkpoint and because transactions span many "systems." Checkpoints of data and transactions are used in connection with recovery logs.

Recovery logs. A *recovery log* or *journal* is a record of all changes to a database or file system. It can be used after system failure to bring the database to a consistent state and to minimize lost work. Although most associated with databases, recovery logs can be used for any data. If data are lost or damaged, they are restored from the most recent backup, and the log is processed forward from that point, redoing all the changes. If there is no media failure, it is faster to recover from the most recent checkpoint. At a checkpoint, all updates are completed and logged, and a checkpoint record is written. With this log information, recovery can restore a consistent state.

In a *log-structured file system, all* the data are stored in the form of a log. Although the main goal of these systems is fast updates, recovery is also faster.

Data integrity

An operating system can protect the integrity of stored data by preventing, tracking, and detecting changes that are unauthorized or improper.

File encryption. Encrypting files can support integrity as well as confidentiality. An intruder who cannot look at file contents does not know which files contain the target data. Even knowing the right file, the attacker cannot make precise fraudulent changes. Of course, destruction or random corruption is still possible.

Many operating systems provide encryption facilities at the user level. Because of U.S. export restrictions, some vendors provide no encryption or use proprietary algorithms rather than DES. PC utility and security packages also offer encryption. A PC user can specify sets of files that will be encrypted and decrypted automatically. Some products allow emergency decryption authority to be split among many people, some number of whom must agree to the decryption.

Protection against errors. A slip of the finger or mind can easily destroy or corrupt information. Most operating systems optionally warn users before files are deleted. It is also possible to *undelete* files. For example, an option of Norton Utilities causes "deleted" files to be moved to a special TrashCan directory. A fixed amount of disk space is allocated for the deleted files and the TrashCan directory, and the oldest files are purged as space is needed. Users can prevent unintended changes or deletions by marking directories or files as read-only. With *file wipe,* a user can cause a deleted file to be overwritten to make its recovery more difficult.

Checking and fixing data integrity. The **fsck** command of UNIX (mentioned earlier) checks file system consistency and repairs problems.

Similar services are provided by other operating systems and utilities. The logical structure of disks can be checked and repaired. Norton Utilities can repair some damage to files of word-processing programs and spread sheets. Utilities also monitor the physical "health" of disks and can warn of impending failures. Self-checking is built into the storage systems for mainframes.

A more complex problem is detecting changes in files, as would be caused by a virus or other malicious software. Add-on file integrity checkers are available. Tripwire for UNIX, for example, creates a reference database that contains a "signature" for each file to be checked. MD5, SHA, or some other algorithm is used to generate the signature. When invoked, Tripwire reports on changed, added, or deleted files. Administrators specify what directories or files will be checked and what file attributes will be ignored for each file. The Tripwire database is accessible to all, but it must be protected against alteration—by placing it on a secure server, for example.

Mandatory integrity. Some of the operating systems that provide mandatory access control also support the Biba model for mandatory integrity.

Clark-Wilson integrity

The Clark-Wilson model of integrity lays a foundation for automating two important real-world controls: separation of duty and the well-formed transaction. Chapter 4 describes the model and its implications for security services. Here, some of those implications are revisited.

Change logs and integrity labels. Since the source of data may be the best assurance of their integrity, authorship should be recorded with the data. It may be necessary to keep an entire change log, stored with the data. (Audit logs, in contrast, are kept separate from user data.) A constrained data item (CDI) also must be labeled with its integrity certification—an indication that an integrity verification procedure certified the CDI for a specific integrity domain.

Support for the access triple. Traditional access control enforces authorized access by subjects to objects. Clark-Wilson controls access to CDIs based on both user and transformation procedure (TP). An access triple gives a user access to some objects through some TP; viewed differently, it gives the TP access to some objects when working on behalf of some user. One suggestion (NCSC 1991e) for achieving the goals of the access triple is to bind together operations and objects into *duties*; a duty is an operation on some object or class of objects. A *role* is a privilege to perform a set of duties. The operating system would need to support the definition of domains and of roles within domains. It would provide the functions of a domain role administrator, and it would enforce separation of duty by constraining role assignment. Finally, the system would restrict a subject to what its role allows.

Audit

The audit services of an operating system provide a chronological record of events, called an *audit trail*. Audit supports the principle of individual accountability by recording individuals' actions and providing auditors with timely access to the records. Audit is a safety net for access control. If access control fails to block misuse, audit detects it. If authorized persons misuse their rights, audit can detect that. In addition to detecting misuse, audit may deter it. A would-be attacker who learns that actions will be recorded may think twice. If misuse does occur, audit helps to assess the damage—to pinpoint what data were divulged or corrupted or lost. Audit can help identify who did it and how. The audit trail is potential evidence for legal or administrative actions, as in the Burleson case described in Chap. 3. Audit also serves as an assurance tool, revealing how well the security mechanisms are working.

Both existing audit services and audit requirements are described in the following subsections.

Recording audit data

Figure 8.4 gives an overview of audit. Trusted components of the operating system call an audit facility, providing information about an event to be recorded. For example, the login component reports successful login, or the access validation component reports an unauthorized **open** attempt. The audit facility decides (based on dynamic criteria) whether the event should be recorded. If so, it writes the event to an *audit log* file. Some types of events are always recorded. Like access validation, audit should be tamperproof and always invoked. The audit facility is either part of the operating system or a tightly integrated add-on (sometimes called an *audit subsystem*).

The operating system must be able to audit all security-relevant events, as well as to selectively disable auditing. Login—successful or unsuccessful—is always recorded, and so is password change. So are all the actions that require privilege, such as authorizing users to the system, changing the security level of an object, or changing the set of audited events. There must be no way to disable auditing of privi-

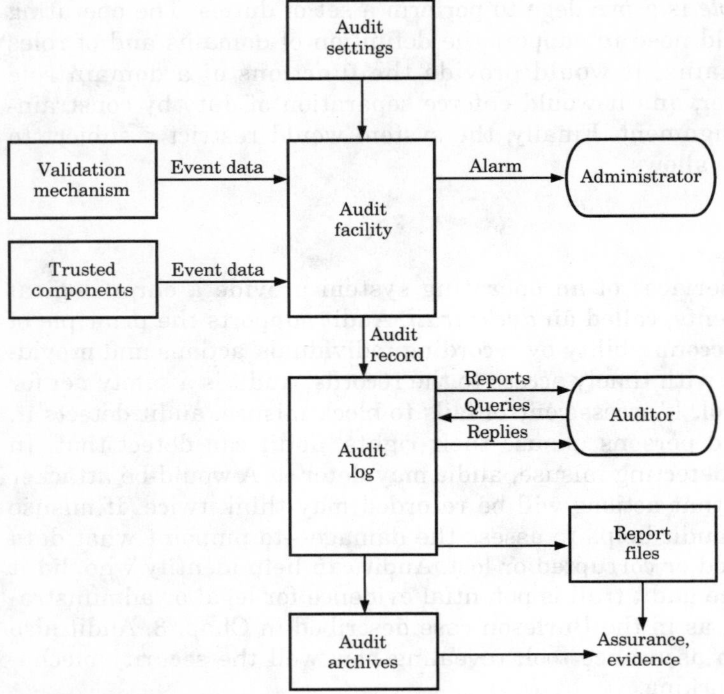

Figure 8.4 Overview of audit.

leged actions. Every new access of an object is auditable—opening or creating a file, executing a program, deleting a file. A change of working directory should be audited. TCSEC class B2 systems must audit the events that can exploit known covert channels.

The amount of data generated by auditing all events is massive. For analysis to be timely or even feasible, the data need to be reduced. Also, if auditing affects performance too much, administrators may disable it entirely. Thus it must be possible to record selectively. Systems may provide for selective auditing based on user or object attributes. For class B1 systems, it must be possible to audit, for example, all actions of user Lisa or all accesses to Top Secret objects.

Certain information is recorded for all types of events. This includes the date and time, user ID, type of event, and the result of the event (such as succeed or fail). Records for object access include the object name, and records for privileged commands include the command parameters. For multilevel systems, the object's access class is included. Login records include the terminal but *not* the supplied password.

Protecting audit data

Both secrecy and integrity of audit data must be maintained, with integrity the more critical requirement. If attackers could remove or alter the records of their actions, the audit trail would be worthless. An organization that uses the audit trail as legal evidence must be able to demonstrate its integrity.

Protection of the audit log uses both privilege and standard access rights. Only the auditor role should have the privileges needed for the commands that manage auditing. Only an auditor should have read access to the audit files. Cryptographic methods are also valuable. Encryption for secrecy is less important than authentication. An authenticator, such as a cryptographic checksum, can be part of each event record. To guard against event deletion, checksums also can be taken on series of records.

The parameters that control auditing must be protected. A perpetrator who knows which events are not being audited has an advantage; one who can turn off auditing has a greater advantage. The display and modification of these settings require privilege.

The goal is to audit without interruption and to lose no data. Systems often use two or more preallocated files for the audit log data; when one is filled, recording automatically switches to the other. The filled file then is archived by the auditor. There needs to be some procedure for disposing of archived audit data. For example, the archive may carry an expiration date, after which the auditor may delete it. The audit data must survive a system crash and restart. If audit events are buffered in memory before being written to the audit log, data can be lost in a crash. Accepting some risk of lost data is probably best, since the alternative of writing out each record immediately is very costly.

On a multilevel system, the audit log must be at the highest level so that all levels of data can be written to it. This means the auditor must be cleared to the highest level.

Reporting and analysis

Audit facilities typically generate several types of reports. *Exception* reports list the suspicious events, such as failed logins and failed opens. A summary report gives a quick overview of numbers of events by type and result. Reports of privileged actions are needed. Detailed reports can include all the audited events. An installation should be able to tailor the content and form of these reports. Auditors also need selective reports in order to monitor suspected threats or to keep close watch over especially sensitive resources. An auditor must be able to request all actions of a specified user or all actions on a specified resource. The reporting and analysis tools should run during normal system operation.

Audit data usually are analyzed after the fact in order to detect misuse. Auditing also can be *preventive*—detecting an accumulation of events that may be leading to misuse and taking defensive action. The accumulation might consist of repeated password failures, for example. For class B3, the TCSEC require real-time alarms when *thresholds* are exceeded. If the events continue, action must be taken to terminate them. For password failures or repeated access failures, the user ID and terminal might be disabled. For other types of events, it might be necessary to shut down the system. Thresholds can be based on type of event, number of repetitions in some period of time (e.g., five unauthorized opens in 5 minutes), and result of the event.

Auditors' work is difficult and time-consuming. The sea of paper can be overwhelming. The market has responded to this problem with add-on analysis and reduction tools. Chapter 13 describes more sophisticated analysis methods, most of them still in the research stage.

Security Facilities for Users

Users need to deal with access control, audit, and other security services. Ordinary users need commands or menus for granting rights to their files and for changing passwords. Privileged users need specialized facilities.

Privileged roles

An operating system must support at least one privileged administrative role, and the principle of least privilege calls for a finer separation of duties. The TCSEC, for example, require separate roles of administrator and operator for class B2. For class B3, security-relevant functions must be separated from other administrative functions (because their need for trust is greater). This section considers four privileged roles: security administrator, operator, auditor, and system programmer. Specific systems choose different cuts, assigning these duties to fewer roles or dividing them among more roles.

Facilities should be easy to use, or people will use them wrong or try to avoid them. Most of the interfaces use commands or menus. They rarely take advantage of graphics or other visual aids.

Security administrators

Administrators authorize users to access the system, and they revoke the authorizations. They set and modify security attributes of users, such as security level and group membership. They specify any limits on how and when a user may log in. They must be able to list all authorized users. They define groups and their memberships. They set the system criteria for session locking and the limit for unsuccessful login tries. They must be able to temporarily disable user IDs and to reenable them, as well as to query the status of a user ID. They need to list user groups and their membership. They must be able to set group quotas for resources such as disk space.

If the system has more than one authentication method, administrators specify which one to use for specific users or groups. They set up the password-checking and password-aging criteria and install any programs that are used for challenge-response authentication. They must be able to initialize or change passwords.

Administrators maintain the file system hierarchy. They must be able to change the ownership of objects and to modify access control lists (in case of owner error or suspected intrusion). They must be able to list all resources a user owns and all the user can access, along with the access rights. They need a way to deny specific rights. They assign privileges to users. For systems with mandatory access control, administrators set security levels for devices and file systems. They label imported data and reclassify objects.

Administrators need to set the system's security characteristics. For a multilevel system, for example, they would specify the system-high level, and for an MVS system with RACF, they would specify whether unprotected data sets could be created. Status reports must be available that clearly show all these security-relevant settings. Tools are needed to do consistency checks on security profiles, on the operating system, and on the system configuration. Administrators receive real-time alarms. They must be able to kill processes.

Auditors

Auditors maintain and manage the audit log files—setting their sizes, taking care of full audit logs, and archiving logs. They control which events are recorded. They run tools to format, compress, and analyze data. They call up audit reports. They must be able to review all the actions of a specified user or all the activity on a specified object.

Operators

Operators start up the system securely, put it into normal operating mode, and shut it down. They set the time and date. They enable and disable devices and network connections, mount file systems, and load external media such as tapes. They need cataloging facilities for off-line media. They handle printed output according to its security characteristics. They run system diagnostics and test the operation of devices. They back up system and user files. After a system failure, they run the restart procedures, including identifying damaged files and disks.

System programmers

The system programmer role is the most privileged of all, because its functions are performed largely without the normal system protection. For the same reason, operating systems can do only so much to control system programmer actions. They can, however, simplify system generation and maintenance and so prevent error. The system should provide tools for keeping track of the system configuration, analyzing system dumps, updating the system, and repairing damaged data. Use of these tools should produce an audit trail, which could go to a system printer.

Users

Every user must deal with security, and object owners are responsible for security of their objects. System facilities can help users adopt good password strategies and get the right default protection for new objects. The system can provide information that allows users to detect misuse of their data. Where security administration is decentralized, many domain administrators are not professional administrators. Good user interfaces are especially important for these users.

Documentation

Each role recognized by the system must be documented, either in a separate security manual or as portions of the user's guide and reference manual. On-line help and documentation also should be provided.

Documentation for general users explains the security policy and the approach taken to enforcing it, with attention to the user's responsibilities. The documentation describes all the security services that affect general users and gives guidelines on using them. It also explains what services are reserved for privileged users. It emphasizes the importance of identification and authentication, giving guidance on choosing and protecting passwords. It explains why and how to use the trusted path. It describes the basic concepts of access control and explains how objects get their initial protection. Documentation for multilevel systems also explains sensitivity labels, how a session level is set, and how MAC constrains user actions. It describes why and how output is labeled. For trusted systems, this documentation is called a *Security Features User's Guide.* The guide can be organized by security features or by tasks. Figure 8.5 shows an example outline for a task-oriented guide.

Privileged users get both the user's guide and their own documentation. For the TCSEC, this is called the *Trusted Facility Manual* (TFM) (NCSC 1992b). Its describes how to configure and install a secure system, operate it securely, control access to administrative functions and information, and avoid compromise of TCB and user security. Although the TFM is specified as a single manual, separate manuals for auditors or operators are appropriate for some systems. Figure 8.6 shows a suggested outline for a TFM for class B2.

Windowing System Security

Users interact with applications through multiple windows on their displays. Each window may open onto a different application, and each application may run on a different machine. The *X Window System* (X) is widely used for display management, especially for UNIX and for multivendor networks. X was designed for performance and openness, not for security. This section discusses why X is important, why its security is weak, and what trusted versions have done. Many X security issues apply to windowing systems in general.

The X Window System

The X Window System uses a client-server architecture. The server, at the user's workstation, manages display resources such as win-

1. Introduction to the Security Features User's Guide
2. System security overview
   - 2.1 System philosophy of protection
   - 2.2 Definition of terms and services
   - 2.3 The system security officer
   - 2.4 User security responsibilities
3. Security-related commands for users
   - 3.1 System access
     - 3.1.1 Session initiation
     - 3.1.2 Changing the session profile
     - 3.1.3 Changing the user profile
     - 3.1.4 Potential access problems and solutions
   - 3.2 Access control facilities
   - 3.3 Protecting removable objects
   - 3.4 Logging security-relevant events

Figure 8.5 Example outline for a Security Features User's Guide. (*From NCSC 1991c.*)

1. TFM introduction
   1.1 Scope of the manual
   1.2 Recommended use of the manual
   1.3 TFM contents
2. System security overview
   2.1 Threats to system security
   2.2 Countermeasures based on security and accountability policies and procedures
   2.3 Explicit physical security assumptions
   2.4 Protection mechanisms available to administrative users
   2.5 Security vulnerabilities of administrative users and warnings
   2.6 Separation of administrative roles (for classes B2–A1)
3. Security policy
   3.1 Discretionary access control
   3.2 Mandatory access control
   3.3 Management of user accounts
   3.4 Commands, system calls, and functions
   3.5 Warnings of specific vulnerabilities
4. Accountability
   4.1 Identification and authentication
   4.2 Definition and change of system parameters for login
   4.3 Audit mechanisms
   4.4 Commands, system calls, and functions
   4.5 Warnings of specific vulnerabilities
5. Routine operations
   5.1 Security-relevant procedures and operations
   5.2 Security-irrelevant procedures and operations
   5.3 Commands, system calls, and functions
   5.4 Warnings of specific vulnerabilities
6. Security of the TCB
   6.1 Generation of the TCB source code
   6.2 Configuration management policy
   6.3 Ratings-maintenance plan
   6.4 TCB installation procedure
   6.5 TCB maintenance procedure
   6.6 Trusted distribution of the TCB
   6.7 Commands, system calls, and functions
   6.8 Warnings of specific vulnerabilities

Figure 8.6 Suggested outline for a Trusted Facility Manual for class B2. (*Based on NCSC 1992b.*)

dows and cursors. It handles requests from multiple clients, which are applications that need to interact with the user. The server collects user inputs for all the clients and sends the right input to the right client. Only the server is concerned with hardware specifics, since clients operate on abstractions such as windows. The client and server can run on different machines that can have different architectures or different operating systems. Thus X provides applications with three kinds of independence: location independence, hardware independence, and operating system independence. Location independence is essential for distributed computing. Hardware independence and operating system independence let vendors write applications once for multiple platforms.

Security weaknesses

X is weak in controlling access to the server and in authentication. The server restricts only the computers from which it will accept connections, not which clients at those computers. The system is vulnerable to various kinds of spoofing. A client could spoof the server, causing display of information that did not come from the user's application. Clients also could be spoofed; they could receive input that did not come from their users, and their output could be modified or could fail to reach the user at all. X has no concept of privilege and no access control; once a computer is connected to the server, any client at that computer can make any request. It can even turn off authentication for future clients. Clients can, if they violate protocol, kill other clients. Some versions of X allow per-user authentication, using *Kerberos* (see Chap. 10), or authentication by means of a "magic cookie" that the client must send to the server.

Compartmented Mode Workstation and trusted X Window

More problems arise where the multilevel security policy applies. The U.S. Defense Intelligence Agency wanted its analysts to use windowing workstations for *compartmented mode* work, where the analysts concurrently deal with information at different security levels. This need led to a set of requirements called *Compartmented Mode Workstation* (CMW). The CMW requirements, which go well beyond trusted windowing, are consistent with the TCSEC for class B1. (The TCSEC do not consider windowing systems.)

Users of the CMW work with multiple windows, each labeled with its security level. Operations such as moving data from one window to another must obey the mandatory access control policy. CMW introduces a second type of label. In addition to sensitivity labels that represent the classification and category set, there are *information labels* that reflect the flow of data during processing. The information label of a file or process can float upward as it receives higher-level data. (Floating labels can help prevent overclassification of data.) The information label also includes markings that DoD policy requires on human-readable output, such as restrictions on who may see it. The sensitivity label governs access control, and the information label governs the display of output. Windows carry both types of labels. The user opens a trusted path menu (in some CMW implementations) by selecting an item on a dedicated area of the screen. A special symbol is displayed while the trusted path is being used. In other systems a keystroke sequence invokes the trusted path, since untrusted code may control the position of the cursor. Trusted-path functions include login, changing password, changing the active security level, downgrading information, and locking sessions.

The challenge for CMW systems and "trusted X" systems is to honor the requirements while retaining enough X function to run off-the-shelf software. The versions from different vendors must be able to work with one another in heterogeneous networks.

In the SunOS CMW, certain clients are part of the TCB—for example, the window manager and the component that mediates data moves between windows. Each trusted client must be given the privileges it needs for its work, and the trusted clients must be protected from untrusted clients. The SunOS CMW also controls access to the server. Clients must appear in an access list provided by the user, and the session clearance must dominate the client's security level.

UNIX Security

UNIX is *open* in many senses of the word. This is its appeal but also its vulnerability. The source code has been available for many years, spawning different systems offered by different vendors. The original security features were minimal, designed to interfere the least with getting work done. UNIX facilities make it easy to develop programs but also easy to get in trouble. Networking, too, is easy but risky. UNIX users, often programmers, have had an open tradition. System managers often are programmers or users who take on the added responsibility part time. The 1990s saw UNIX propelled onto a commercial scene that is a world away from its traditional culture. A significant proportion of new business applications are now developed for UNIX.

UNIX was developed at AT&T Bell Laboratories, mainly by Ken Thompson and Dennis Ritchie. The source code became available and was modified substantially by the University of California at Berkeley, which distributed its own source. These two versions (System V for AT&T and 4.3BSD for Berkeley) diverged and had divergent offspring. The many UNIX vendors have tried to agree on a common version, but with little success. The greatest influence on UNIX security has been the Orange Book.

There have been trusted UNIX projects for many years and more general enhanced-security versions recently. The descriptions that follow use the term *traditional UNIX* for either System V or BSD without security enhancements.

Identification and authentication

A user supplies a *login name* and a password. Associated with the name is a user ID or *uid* number that an administrator assigned when adding the user. This number is used internally to identify who starts processes and who owns files. User IDs are supposed to be unique, but traditional UNIX does not ensure this. The supplied password is compared with the password associated with the user name in the password file. If the password is correct, the login process invokes the command (normally a shell) whose name appears in the password file.

A user can temporarily assume another user's identity by executing a program designated as *set user ID* (SUID). The program then executes with its owner's user ID and privilege rather than those of the user. When the program terminates, the original user ID is reinstated. The SUID feature simplifies the writing of system programs and seems to make them more secure, but in fact it is a great vulnerability. If the SUID program is not coded meticulously, its privilege can be exploited for misuse.

UNIX supports identifications for groups of users. System V and 4.3BSD treat groups differently. In 4.3BSD, a process is in all the groups the user belongs to. In System V, the user chooses one group at a time, using a **newgrp** command. Programs can be specified as *set group id* (SGID), analogous to SUID. Groups are very important in traditional UNIX access control, since UNIX does not have access control lists.

Traditional UNIX recognizes a superuser who has all privileges and is totally unconstrained by access control. The superuser has an account name of *root* and a user ID of zero. Other administrative accounts also may have zero user IDs, and the SUID feature can be used to temporarily change the user ID to zero. The command for changing passwords works that way. The password program is SUID, owned by root. Any process can execute the program and alter the password file.

As we have seen, traditional UNIX passwords are vulnerable. Password crackers target the encrypted passwords kept in password file */etc/passwd*. With some UNIX systems, administrators can split this file into two files: */etc/passwd* without any passwords and */etc/shadow* containing encrypted passwords. The shadow file is readable only by its owner, the root. The password file entry for a user also contains a comment field. By convention, BSD systems interpret this field as containing the user's name, office location, and telephone numbers. The **finger** command retrieves this information, making it easy for an intruder to learn personal information that helps in password cracking.

Access control

UNIX has a tree-structured file system, with a hierarchy of directories. The top-level directory is designated as /, and there are conventions for the second level. For example, */bin* contains system commands and */etc* contains control information such as the password and group files. Users and programs refer to files by path names that include the names of directories traversed to reach the files. Each directory or file contains a descriptive record called an *inode*; it is the inode that holds access control information. When a file or directory is opened, the inode is brought into memory. I/O devices, memory, and terminals are also treated as files for access control purposes.

Permissions. Access control is based on *permissions.* The scheme can be modeled as an access matrix with only three subjects: the file's owner, the file's group, and everyone else (the *world*). There are three access rights: **read, write,** and **execute.** A column of the matrix (corresponding to a file) is represented by nine *permission bits,* three each for owner, group, and other (Fig. 8.7). If the owner has **read** and **write** rights, the group has **read** and others have none, the permissions are 110100000, written as *rw-r-----*.

	Owner	Group	Other
General form	r w x	r w x	r w x

Examples

	Owner	Group	Other
File 1	r w –	– – –	– – –
File 2	r – x	r – x	r – x

Access matrix

	File 1	File 2
Owner	r w –	r – x
Group	– – –	r – x
Other	– – –	r – x

Figure 8.7 UNIX file permissions.

Permissions also appear in commands and documentation as octal digits—640 for the example.

Ownership and permissions for new files. The owner of a file is its creator. In System V, a new file's group is the group of the creating process; in BSD, a new file's group is inherited from its directory. System V users can give away file ownership with the **chown** command. The permissions for a new file are based on two sources: parameters of the system call that creates the file and a variable called the *user mask* or *umask*. Programs such as linkers and word processors typically specify very permissive permissions, which are constrained by the umask. The umask has the same bits as the permissions, and each umask bit turns *off* the corresponding permission for the new file. The user can change the default umask with the **umask** command. For example, *umask 077* denies access to all but the owner. The owner can change the permissions using the **chmod** command.

Access validation. Each set of permissions is checked independently in the order owner, group, and other. If the current user is the owner, the access request is checked against the owner permissions only. If the user belongs to the file's group, the request is checked against the group permissions only. If the user matches neither owner nor group, the request is checked against "other" permissions. This method can have surprising results; for example, the owner of a file may be the only member of the group with no access. Superuser requests are not checked at all.

Directories and permissions. Directories are special files that contain names of files and the corresponding inode numbers. Multiple names can correspond to the same inode; that is, there are multiple *links* to the same inode. Since the permissions are in the inode, all the links have the same permissions. Directories have the same permission bits as ordinary files, but with different meaning. Since execute permission is meaningless for a directory, the execute bits are used for *search* permission. Read permission allows reading the file names and inode numbers in the directory; it does not permit reading the inodes themselves. Write permission allows adding, changing, or deleting directory entries. Search permission allows reading both the directory entries and the inodes they refer to.

The relation between directory permissions and file permissions is tricky. A user with write and search permission for a directory can remove any filename in the directory. When the last link for an inode is removed, the inode itself is cleared. This can be done by a user with no permission to the file itself.

Security limitations of traditional UNIX

Unfortunately, the original UNIX design did too little about security. Although many specific holes have been plugged, these corrections cannot remove the basic limitations. System administrators and users must compensate as best they can, while UNIX vendors enhance security as best *they* can without sacrificing compatibility and usefulness.

UNIX and security principles. UNIX violates the principle of least privilege in several ways. Most fundamental is that access control is coarse and inflexible. UNIX has no access control lists, so access cannot be granted to individual users. The only way to selectively grant access is through groups. It is not possible to grant one group member read access and another write access. Further, users who grant group access may not be aware of changes in group membership. UNIX access control also violates the design principle of separating policy from mechanism. One view of how people work is built into the access control mechanisms. The design principle of fail-safe defaults is also violated. Systems are often distributed with unsafe defaults—for permissions on new files, for example—leaving it to system administrators and users to change them.

Another violation of least privilege is the superuser role. This single role has all possible privileges. Exempting the superuser from access control violates the principle of complete mediation. The ability to change user ID violates the principle of accountability.

Vulnerabilities. Most of the vulnerabilities described in this section result from combinations of the basic design deficiencies.

Superuser and SUID attacks. Anyone who attains superuser identity has taken over the entire system. Although there are safeguards against the most obvious ways, more subtle vulnerabilities remain. Suppose, for example, that a privileged user copies a program designated as SUID (becoming the owner of the copy) and inadvertently leaves on "others" write permission for the file or directory. An attacker can then modify the SUID program to carry out the attack (under superuser identity) whenever the program is invoked. For example, file permissions could be changed, allowing the attacker to read or modify any files. An attack may not even have to modify the SUID program; it can exploit the poor checking of some SUID programs, feeding them devious inputs. For example, some versions of the **mail** command could be caused to add entries to the password file. SUID programs should be used only when there is no alternative. They should be simple and thoroughly checked.

An administrator can obtain superuser status by the **su** command if he or she can supply the root password. The **su** command is a fine target for a spoofing attack. An attacker who gets an administrator to execute a bogus version of **su** learns the root password and can take over the system at will. The PATH vulnerability allows such an attack.

PATH and Trojan horse attacks. UNIX searches for a requested file in the directories and in the order specified by the *PATH* environment variable. The PATH variable for a session comes from a system default profile, which the user can override with a *.profile* file. In addition to the basic system directories, such as */bin,* the path will contain other directories that the user needs searched. Suppose user Gil often works with a directory */usr/gil,* that Gil's directory is writable by others, and that his path begins with */usr/gil*. An attacker needs only to place in */usr/gil* a fake version of a common command, such as **ls** (which lists files). When Gil issues **ls,** this Trojan horse executes with Gil's rights. Of course, the attack is especially dangerous if Gil is an administrator. The same attack can target the **su** command, with deadly results. The safeguards are to put the working directory last in the path and to make it nonwritable by others. Also, full path names can be used, at least for sensitive commands such as **su.**

Directory permissions. Administrators often make directories public so that users can move around them freely. However, write access to a directory effectively gives write access to all its files. Some applications or system components need publicly writable directories, but they are the exception. For most public directories, public access should be search only. A user's personal directories should have no permissions for others. The directory structure is also important; its design should reflect the installation's policies about ownership and security.

Booting. A UNIX system starts up in *single-user* mode, with the console user assumed to be root. This means that anyone with access to the console has full access to the system, as superuser. Typically, no login password is needed.

Audit. Traditional UNIX lacks real security auditing. Various logs can be kept, however. The process accounting records summarize what each process has done—who the user was and what commands were issued at what time. Reports produced from these records can help spot password-cracking attempts, unused accounts, and other anomalies. However, many installations turn off process accounting because of its heavy resource use. (There is no way to select events or users to record.) BSD systems log messages sent to the console, including all uses of the **su** command. System V keeps a separate log of **su** attempts. Some commands are also good audit tools. The **who** command displays user names, ports, and login times, and **ps** displays information about current processes. Sun Microsystems has offered auditing for some time, and other vendors now do as well.

Securing traditional UNIX

UNIX administrators and users must carry much of the security responsibility.

What administrators can do. Traditional UNIX does not distinguish a role of security administrator; rather, security administration is wrapped up with other administrative functions. There is no tailored user interface; administrators work mainly by modifying critical files. Here are some of the safeguards they can implement.

Educate users about security. Install shadow password files with no public access. Remove personal information from password file comments. Install an enhanced password program that checks for easy-to-guess passwords. Use password aging. Install programs to automatically log out, or at least lock, inactive sessions.

Look for SUID/SGID programs in writable directories, and try to eliminate them. If possible, disable the entire mechanism and provide a substitute mechanism that can be called. Make sure that PATH variables for administrators list system directories first and working directories last. Modify the **su** command so that it must be invoked with a full path name. Avoid publicly writable directories. Modify single-user start-up to require a password. Audit accounting records, **su** logs, and console logs.

Administrators can choose from packages of software tools to help with security tasks; many are available at no cost from on-line sources, and some are listed in books on UNIX security. Comprehensive add-on software products are also available.

Information that helps administrators also can help attackers. For example, the log of **su** activity provides just what an attacker needs: the names of promising targets for Trojan horse attacks. A record of unsuccessful login attempts will likely contain some passwords (because users entered their passwords instead of their names). These helpful sources should not be publicly readable.

What users can do. Users can do their part to compensate for UNIX frailties. Observe good password practices. Set file permissions not to allow writing by group or others. Use a umask that sets restrictive permissions on new files. Use encryption to further protect file secrecy—even from the superuser. (The UNIX **crypt** command is breakable; compress the file before encrypting to make the method stronger.) Pick a secret encryption key that is hard to guess. Make sure the PATH variable is safe. Log off or lock the workstation when leaving it.

System V Enhanced Security

Several vendors have enhanced UNIX to meet Orange Book requirements. Release 4.1 of UNIX System V had enhancements designed to meet class B2 requirements. It seems that "B2 represents what is likely the highest assurance level attainable by a UNIX system (barring a complete system rewrite) while having it still retain the classic UNIX system look and feel and maintain backward compatibility for existing applications" (Clark 1992: 335). The enhancements include a new approach to privilege, mandatory access control, access control lists, a trusted path, and auditing.

Privilege. The single superuser role is divided into an extensible set of roles, and the total privilege of the superuser is divided into a set of task-oriented privileges. A database defines what commands a role can execute and what privileges it needs for each command. For example, the *secadmin* role needs the *sysops* privilege to set the system date and time. A *secadmin* user issues the command **tfadmin date** (**tfadmin** for *trusted facility administration*). The database is then searched for a *secadmin* entry for **date.** The entry specifies the full path name for **date** (to prevent path attacks) and the *sysops* privilege. That privilege is given to the process that executes **date.**

A process has a *maximum* set of privileges—all that it can ever obtain—and a *working* set—what it needs for the work at hand. Executable files have two kinds of privilege: *inheritable* and *fixed.* When a process executes a file, it receives (as both maximum and working sets) the intersection of (1) the maximum privileges of the invoking process and (2) the inheritable privileges of the file. That is, it gets only what the program needs, and even that is limited by the maximum of the parent process. System commands turn off all working-set privileges before issuing **exec,** so the new process must explicitly set the privileges it needs.

This scheme clearly improves on SUID in supporting the least-privilege principle. Fixed privileges of files provide compatibility with SUID. They are added to the maximum set of the invoking process to form both sets for the new process.

Discretionary access control. Access control lists allow file owners to explicitly grant or deny access to single users or to groups. Traditional permissions are also supported, and the concepts of user ownership and group ownership are retained. A directory file has a *default* entry, which specifies the ACL entries for new files created in the directory.

Trusted path. A user must start login with the Secure Attention Key. This invokes the trusted path and causes the "TCB" to terminate any current login session and temporarily disable interaction. The login sequence then starts, and the prompt appears. If login does not complete within a time limit, interaction is disabled until the Secure Attention Key is used.

Audit. SVR4.1ES supports selective auditing. Administrators select classes of events to record as well as events within each class. Selection is both system-wide and for each user. The **useradd** command specifies what events will be audited for that user. Some "fixed events" are always audited because they are considered critical for system integrity. Applications can use the auditing facility to add their own records to the log file. With the **auditrpt** command, administrators can produce reports from the audit records.

Mandatory access control. SVR4.1ES implements a modified Bell-LaPadula policy of "read equal or down, write equal." Subjects are processes, and objects are files and interprocess communication objects. Administrators assign security classifications and categories to users and objects. An access class, or combination of classification and categories, is called a *fully qualified label*. An example is *Secret:Amazon,RioGrande,Snake,* where the categories are project code names. The label can be assigned a shorthand alias, such as *SR* for "secret rivers." A user specifies a label when logging on. A terminal line has a range of login levels; the user's login label must dominate the line's low level and be dominated by its high level.

Each different fully qualified label is represented internally (in inodes for files) by a *level identifier* (LID). Access checking on writes need only compare the LIDs for equality. Read checking must check for dominance, using the entire fully qualified labels. For speed, a cache of these values is used.

MVS Security

Since 1974, IBM's MVS has been a prominent mainframe operating system. The enhancement of its security over the years parallels concern about security—from casual to intense. Many critical applications run on MVS.

MVS runs on the S/370 and S/390 computers, whose protection facilities include two states (supervisor and problem), protection keys that MVS uses to designate privilege level, and multiple virtual memories. A special type of address space is the *data space,* which cannot be used for instructions. Transition from problem state to supervisor state is through a *supervisor call* (SVC) instruction. Sensitive supervisor data are protected by a storage key of zero. MVS components can assume the key of their caller to reduce their privilege to the least needed.

MVS alone provides only minimal support for authentication, access control, and audit. Many MVS installations use add-on *security subsystems* offered by IBM, Computer Associates, and other vendors. MVS has received B1 ratings with IBM's *Resource Access Control Facility* (RACF) and with *CA-ACF2* from Computer Associates. Here, MVS with RACF is described.

Identification and authentication

RACF maintains profiles for users and groups of users. The profiles include security levels and categories, passwords, and password history. Passwords are stored DES-encrypted, and the RACF database is not generally accessible. An installation can specify password criteria, including length, what special characters must be used, and when the password expires. Selection of recently used passwords can be prevented, and a maximum number of bad tries can be specified. Installations can provide their own password-checking programs. An administrator at one system can update passwords on other systems. A new password for a user can be applied automatically to all the user's IDs on multiple systems. Authentication can use, instead of a password, a *passticket* that was generated by another system; passtickets support single sign-on.

Access control

With RACF, MVS controls access to resources such as datasets (files) and transactions and to groups of resources. Each resource has an owner. Resource profiles include access control lists. Administrators can choose the default protection on new resources, ranging from none to the fail-safe option called *ProtectAll.* A command interface is provided for administrators, auditors, and owners of resources.

The multilevel security policy is supported. Users and resources can be assigned levels and categories, and a shorthand name can be assigned to a sensitivity label (including levels and categories). The simple security and *-properties are enforced. Output is labeled.

Privilege

MVS has three privilege mechanisms that can involve security exposures: supervisor calls (SVCs), operating system exits, and the Authorized Program Facility (APF). A program is authorized if (1) the link-editor flags its object code as authorized and (2) the program is in a designated APF library. That is, both the program module and the library must be authorized. A job step that starts with an authorized program gets flagged as authorized, which means it can put itself in supervisor state or in key zero. The job step is not allowed to execute an unauthorized program.

An SVC receives control in supervisor state and can essentially do anything. While this might pose no problem if only MVS components were invoked by SVCs, subsystems and applications involve many user-defined SVCs. An SVC can be defined so that only authorized programs may execute it. An operating system exit is used to modify the normal processing of an MVS component. Some exits receive control in supervisor state or with a privileged key.

RACF defines three privileged roles. A person with *special* privilege can create and modify profiles and set system defaults; *operations* users can control RACF; and *auditors* can access the audit trail and use a RACF reporting tool.

Audit

Audit records are written through the MVS systems management facility (SMF). MVS ensures the integrity and backup of the SMF log. RACF writes records on the SMF log about security-relevant events, as controlled by RACF *special* users. The events logged include failed login attempts, RACF commands, and unauthorized attempts to access resources. The RACF Report Writer prints tailored reports from the audit trail. RACF also can notify a dataset owner of invalid access attempts on the dataset.

IBM and other vendors offer packages that statically audit MVS security—ensuring, for example, that APF libraries and critical program libraries are protected by RACF and that user-defined SVCs are documented and authorized.

OpenVMS Security

The OpenVMS operating system (successor to VAX VMS) runs on DEC's VAX and Alpha AXP computers. Although the two computer architectures differ, they provide compatible protection features. Protection rings provide four access modes: User, Supervisor, Executive, and Kernel. Memory protection is on a per-page basis, and

OpenVMS provides a separate address space for each process. Access to the memory-mapped I/O registers is controlled through memory protection.

OpenVMS security includes privileges, permissions, access control lists, protected subsystems, audit, and alarms. A great deal of flexibility is provided. The user identification code (UIC) has one part that uniquely identifies the user and another part that identifies the user's group. A user may have other *identifiers,* which are assigned by the security administrator and also by the system, based on the user's mode of system entry. Login is controlled on the basis of UIC and also the time and mode of access. Users may be granted privileges, such as the right to start a network connection or to perform security administration. A program also can be assigned privileges, which are gained by a process that executes the program.

For objects such as files, both protection masks and access control lists are used. For each access mode, the protection mask specifies whether access is granted for the system, the file owner, other members of the owner's group, and all others (world). Unlike in UNIX, the owner's rights include the group's, which include the world's. "System" specifies the rights of a privileged owner. Access control list entries can either grant or deny access. If an access request is not explicitly granted or denied by the ACL, the protection masks are used. An ACL entry can specify either a UIC or identifiers. For example, a FINANCIAL identifier might include several groups. Then the ACL entry could specify FINANCIAL + LOCAL.

Protected subsystems, for OpenVMS, are applications with rights to objects. A user who invokes a protected subsystem is temporarily granted a new identifier, but only while in that application. Auditing facilities are very flexible; for example, ACL entries can request alarms or audit records.

Windows NT Security

The ancestors of Microsoft's Windows NT—DOS and Windows—gave hardly a nod to security. Windows NT, which is oriented to a network environment, provides a rich array of security facilities. It runs on multiple hardware platforms and supports multiple functional interfaces, including OS/2 and POSIX. Microsoft has stated that Windows NT aims at Orange Book class C2 and that its design reflects a further goal of B2 security.

Windows NT structure

A "hardware abstraction layer" isolates most of the operating system from hardware dependencies. Above that layer is the Windows NT kernel, called the *executive*. Most of the work is done by *protected subsystems* that run as servers. Only two protection domains are assumed: kernel and user. The executive runs in kernel mode, and the protected subsystems run in user mode. *Environment* protected subsystems implement OS/2 and POSIX function and the native *Win32* function. *Integral* protected subsystems include networking components and the security subsystem, which maintains a security database, authenticates users, and controls auditing. A *security reference monitor* is part of the kernel.

Objects and object security

Data that need to be shared and protected are kept in *objects*. Examples of executive objects are processes, threads, ports, and sections of memory. Examples of Win32 objects are windows and menus. Files are objects. All objects are treated uniformly for security, but there are also hooks for type-specific security. *Generic services* that apply to all object types include **Query security** and **Set security.** *Object methods* are generic services (such as **Open** or **Delete**) that different types of objects provide in different ways. The **security** method is called to read or change the protection of an object.

Identification and authentication

A person's *security identifier* (SID) is tied to a network domain. A person can operate in more than one domain but needs a different SID for each. This scheme supports a role-based policy, where rights go with the job. For example, a person from Advertising who fills in temporarily in Publications would get a new SID in the Publications domain for the duration of the stint. The SID includes numbers that identify (1) the "authenticating authority" (Windows NT), (2) the user's primary domain, and (3) the user within the domain. The SID is thus unique across a Windows NT network. An SID can belong to a group.

A user logs on either directly or through a network request. This subsection considers direct logon. Each domain keeps a *Security Account Manager* (SAM) database for the users who have accounts in that domain. The logon process checks the logon name and password against the SAM database, where passwords are stored in a doubly encrypted form. If logon succeeds, an *access token* is built and attached to the initial process. The access token contains all the security information about the user: SID, SIDs of all the groups the user belongs to, default access control list for objects the user creates, and privileges. The privileges convey access to functions that affect system integrity and security, such as loading device drivers or generating audit-log entries. Any child process inherits a copy of the access token and can change its copy without affecting the parent process or any other children.

Access control

When a process creates a new object, the object manager builds a *security descriptor* for it and returns a *handle,* which is an index into the process object table. The process always refers to the object by its handle. The security descriptor includes pointers to the owner's SID, a *discretionary access control list* (DACL), and a *system access control list* (SACL), which specifies which operations on the objects are audited. The owner SID for a new object comes from the access token of the creating process. The owner can change the ownership to any SID in the access token; this means that ownership can be given to any of the owner's groups. Only the owner can change the DACL. Each entry in the DACL either grants or denies some rights to an SID. The DACL for a new object usually is inherited from the object's directory, but the creating call also can specify a DACL. If the directory has no "inheritable" DACL entries and no DACL is specified, the default DACL of the access token is used.

A set of standard access rights applies to all objects, and other rights apply to specific object types. For example, **delete** is a standard right, and **suspend** is a right that applies to threads. An *access mask* in the DACL entry specifies the rights granted or denied. Ten bits of the mask represent standard rights, and 16 bits represent specific rights. The mask also represents *generic* rights **read, write, execute,** and **all.** Generic rights map to different specific rights for each object type. For a file object, **generic-read** maps to two standard rights and three specific rights.

A call that opens an object must specify the *desired access rights.* A process opens a file for read access, execute access, or read and write. The desired rights are expressed in the same form of access mask that appears in a DACL entry. If a process requests MAXIMUM_ALLOWED access, it receives all the rights to the object granted to it by DACL entries. The desired rights are passed to the reference monitor, which returns the granted rights; these are stored in the process object table. The process gets a handle (an index into the table) to use for all operations on the object. The DACL is checked only at first access, and the rights in the table entry govern all subsequent access. Kernel-mode code, which uses pointers rather than handles, is not subject to this checking.

Summary

Operating systems provide security services that include authentication, access control, integrity support, and audit. In the authentication process, a user claims an ID and proves the claim by presenting evidence that no one else can present; the system evaluates the evidence to verify the claim. Authentication participants are the user, a login component, and an authentication server. Authentication can be based on something the user *knows,* something the user *has,* or something the user *is* or *does.*

Passwords control access to most computer-based resources. A good password is easy to remember and hard to guess. Password mechanisms are vulnerable. For example, UNIX stored passwords, although encrypted, are vulnerable to exhaustive search attacks and dictionary attacks. Stronger passwords are possible through system generation of random strings and through guidance of users' selections. Passwords must be protected against compromise and loss. A transmitted password is vulnerable to eavesdropping and sniffer attacks. With challenge-response, the system presents a challenge and the user responds.

A user can present an object—a *token*—as evidence of identity. A token cannot be "guessed," and it is easy to use. However, the user must always have it, it can be lost or stolen, and it is relatively costly. The simplest token devices are memory cards. See-through devices have processing power but no connection to the system; they help the user. A smart card has processing power and also directly connects to a system. Smart cards can use public key cryptographic methods, simplifying key distribution and enabling identity to be proved without trusting the AS.

Biometric authentication is based on physical or behavioral characteristics. With each method, the characteristic is measured and a template is built. When the person claims an identity, the characteristic is measured again, and the measurements are compared with the template. The method then accepts or rejects the claim. A good method has few false acceptances and true rejections, does not harm or bother people, does rapid comparison, and is inexpensive. Physical measurement methods include retinal scanning, hand scanning, and fingerprint and palmprint recognition. Behavioral methods include recognition of handwritten signatures, voices, and typing rhythms.

Access control ensures that all access to resources is authorized access. External barriers and administrative procedures provide physical access control; software and hardware provide logical access control.

An OS process acts on behalf of a user, with the rights of that user. Good access control supports granting rights to individuals as well as to groups. An access control list is associated with an object to specify who can access it and how. An ACL entry specifies a user ID or group ID, a set of rights, and whether the rights are allowed or denied. Special rights called privileges are associated with privileged roles. For mandatory access control, each subject and each object carries a sensitivity label that includes its level and category set. The access control information associated with subjects and objects is used to determine if an access is allowed. Objects get their initial access control attributes from create-time parameters, default settings, or a combination of the two.

A computing system has good availability if its authorized users can get at system resources when they need them. The goals for data integrity are to prevent unauthorized modifications and to maintain data quality. After a system crash or discontinuity, recovery procedures restore the system's ability to operate and restore any affected objects. Recovery and restart involve services of the OS, applications, and people. The system must restart in a secure state, and recovery must not provide an opportunity for misuse. Transactions have properties that are important for recovery: atomicity, consistency, and durability.

The main way to prepare for recovery and protect data integrity is through redundancy, which is supported by backup, mirroring, checkpoints, and recovery logs. Backup must be correct, fast, flexible, and secure. With mirroring, every write operation is done to two different places. A system checkpoint is a complete snapshot that can be used to restart the system. Recovery logs, which record all changes to a database or file system, are used after a failure to bring data to a consistent state and to minimize lost work. An OS can protect data integrity by encrypting files and by preventing, tracking, and detecting changes that are unauthorized or improper. OSs and utilities can check consistency of file system data and repair problems.

An OS provides an audit trail, which helps in detecting and deterring misuse. If misuse occurs, audit helps to assess the damage and to identify the perpetrator and methods. The audit trail can serve as evidence for legal or administrative actions. It reveals how well the security mechanisms are working. Information recorded includes date and time, user ID, type of event, and result. Audit should be continuous, and both secrecy and integrity of audit data must be maintained. Audit facilities typically generate summaries plus reports of exceptions and privileged actions.

Every user must deal with security, and object owners are responsible for security of their objects. An OS must support at least one privileged administrative role; finer separation of duties is more secure. Privileged roles include security administrator, operator, auditor, and system programmer.

The X Window System, which is widely used for display management, has weak security. The need for analysts to work with information at different security levels led to the Compartmented Mode Workstation (CMW) requirements and products. Each CMW window is labeled with its security level. Operations such as moving data from one window to another must obey the mandatory access control policy.

Traditional UNIX has many vulnerabilities. When a user executes a program designated as set user ID (SUID), the program executes with the user ID and privilege of the program's owner. This privilege can be exploited for misuse. A superuser has all privileges and is totally unconstrained by access control. Passwords are vulnerable.

UNIX access control is based on permissions—equivalent to an access matrix with only three subjects (the file's owner, the file's group, and everyone else) and three access rights (**read, write,** and **execute**). Each set of permissions is checked independently in the order owner, group, and other, sometimes with surprising results. Superuser requests are not checked at all. The relation between directory permissions and file permissions is tricky. UNIX violates the principle of least privilege in several ways; most important, access control is coarse and inflexible. Traditional UNIX lacks real security auditing.

UNIX administrators and users must work on securing traditional UNIX. Several vendors have enhanced UNIX to meet Orange Book requirements. Release 4.1 of UNIX System V offers mandatory access control, access control lists, a trusted path, and auditing. The superuser role is divided into an extensible set of roles, and the superuser privilege is divided into a set of task-oriented privileges.

The MVS operating system alone provides minimal support for authentication, access control, and audit. Many MVS installations use add-on security subsystems, such as RACF. With RACF, MVS controls access to resources such as datasets and transactions, as well as to groups of resources. Resource profiles include access control lists. The multilevel security policy is supported.

OpenVMS security includes privileges, permissions, access control lists, protected subsystems, audit, and alarms. A great deal of flexibility is provided.

Windows NT provides rich security facilities. All protected objects are treated uniformly for security. A user's security identifier (SID) is tied to a network domain. Each domain keeps a security database for its users. At logon, an access token is built that contains all the security information about the user. When a new object is created, a security descriptor is built that includes an access control list. A set of standard rights applies to all objects, and other rights apply to specific object types. A call that opens an object specifies desired access rights.

Bibliographic Notes

National and international criteria for operating systems are discussed in Chap. 6. Ferraiolo et al. (1993) present the results of a NIST study on operating system requirements for commercial systems. NCSC (1988) interprets the TCSEC for add-on subsystems.

Surveys of authentication are provided by Davies and Price (1989) and Janson and Molva (1991). NIST (1994) is a comprehensive guideline. Identification and authentication for trusted systems are discussed in NCSC (1991a). Authentication for networks and distributed systems is described in Chaps. 10 and 11. Denning (1992) discusses password technology and issues. Jobusch and Oldehoeft (1989) survey password vulnerabilities and suggest ways to fix them, with particular reference to UNIX 4.3BSD. Spafford (1989) and Seeley (1989) describe how password attacks worked in the Internet worm of 1988. De Alvaré (1990) and Klein (1990) report on studies of password cracking. Haskett (1984) shows how pass-algorithms could be used without modifying operating systems. Barton and Barton (1984) suggest ways to select meaningful expressions and transform them into hard-to-guess passwords. Zviran and Haga (1993) report on experiments that compared types of passwords for memorability and users' preference. A standard algorithm for password generation (NIST 1993) was found to be vulnerable to attack (Ganesan and Davies 1994). King (1991) proposes remembering generated passwords by associating pictures with their syllables. Bishop (1991) describes a tool for checking user-selected passwords.

Wong et al. (1985) describe the Polonius scheme for see-through authentication. Smart cards are described by Guillou et al. (1992) and Königs (1991). NIST (1995) describes public key authentication methods. The one-time pad and zero-knowledge protocols are discussed in Chap. 5. IBM's Transaction Security System (for financial transactions) is described by Abraham et al. (1991). This system uses dynamic signature verification and smart cards. ISO Standard 7811 covers financial memory cards, and ISO Standard 7816 covers smart cards.

Conn et al. (1990) compare biometric authentication with other methods and conclude that it falls short, especially for remote authentication. Parks (1991) surveys biometric methods and lists names and addresses of companies that market devices. Joyce and Gupta (1990) describe methods using keystroke dynamics. Clark and Hoffman (1994) describe a prototype smart card–based system for controlling system entry and providing boot integrity (protecting against boot viruses, for example).

Chapter 4 describes access control policies and models, and Chap. 7 describes protection mechanisms that support access control.

Documents about access control for trusted systems include NCSC (1987b, 1992a). Role-based access control is discussed in Chaps. 4 and 9. Chapter 7 of Fernandez et al. (1981) discusses alternative interpretations of groups of subjects and objects. Farrow (1991) discusses constrained environments for UNIX.

Gray and Siewiorek (1991) describe high-availability systems and recovery. Gray and Reuter (1993) describe recovery in transaction-processing systems. Trusted recovery is described in NCSC (1991b). Backup strategies are described in Chap. 12. Schneier (1993) reviews add-on security packages for the Macintosh, reporting weakness in most of the protections. Phillips (1993) reviews PC add-ons, both software and hardware. Blaze (1993) describes a prototype UNIX system with encryption integrated into the file system.

Virus threats and safeguards are described in Chap. 3, which also lists books on viruses. Antivirus tools are discussed by Polk and Bassham (1992). With an antivirus scheme proposed by Davida et al. (1989), vendors cryptographically authenticate software. Tripwire is described by Kim and Spafford (1994).

Chapter 4 describes the Clark-Wilson integrity model. Possible services to support Clark-Wilson integrity are described by Bačić (1989, 1990), Clark and Wilson (1989), Jueneman (1989), Williams and LaPadula (1993), and NCSC reports (1991d, 1991e). Chapter 9 considers integrity services of database management systems. Government standards for audit are described in the ITSEC report (1991) and in NCSC reports (1985, 1987a, 1989). Schaen and McKenney (1991) provide an overview of auditing issues, especially for networks. Seiden and Melanson (1990) describe the auditing facility for the VAX/VMM kernel. Shieh and Gligor (1990) discuss auditing for covert storage channels. Intrusion detection and EDP audit are covered in Chap. 13.

Facilities and documentation for users and administrators are described in NIST (1993) and NCSC (1989, 1991c, 1992b). Heydon et al. (1990) describe visual languages for specifying security policy and access rights.

Epstein and Picciotto (1991) survey issues in trusted windowing systems. Huber (1994) gives the history and status of the CMW program. Woodward (1987) discusses the need for two kinds of labels. Picciotto (1991) discusses trusted cut and paste. The SunOS CMW implementation is described by Faden (1991). The X Window System is described by Scheifler and Gettys (1986). Reichard and Johnson (1995) describe security measures for X Window stations. Epstein et al. (1992) and Epstein and Pascale (1993) describe a prototype trusted X Window System based on Trusted Mach and aimed at class B3. A bibliography on secure windowing systems can be found in Epstein (1992). Spoofing is described in Chap. 3.

Landwehr (1983) surveys early trusted system projects. Graubart (1992) describes ways that trusted operating systems could better support trusted applications. Irvine (1995) discusses the design of file systems for trusted systems, and Benson (1992) describes the file system for Trusted Mach and how it solves the *secure reader-writer problem*—providing synchronization without using locks or other mechanisms that allow a low-level process to signal a high-level process. Chapter 7 describes the trusted path and secure attention key.

Quarterman and Wilhelm (1993) describe UNIX standards. The USENIX Association publishes proceedings of workshops on UNIX security (USENIX 1995). Grampp and Morris (1984) first sounded the alert on UNIX security. Books providing practical advice on UNIX security include Arnold (1993), Curry (1992), Farrow (1991), and Garfinkel and Spafford (1991). Dichter (1993) describes some publicly available tools. Baran et al. (1990) describe how UNIX administrators at Columbia University responded to a series of break-ins. Bishop (1990) describes an implementation of roles on UNIX.

Bunch (1992) gives commercial customers some background on UNIX security issues. Clark (1992) and Brady (1993) describe UNIX System V Release 4.1 Enhanced Security. The Brady article includes examples of using mandatory access control for system integrity. McIlroy and Reeds (1992) describe another implementation of UNIX multilevel security. Mandatory access control and the Bell-LaPadula model are described in Chap. 4. Multilevel-secure versions of UNIX are surveyed by Wong (1990). Levin et al. (1989) describe a model of SETUID developed for a trusted system. Badger et al. (1995) describe a prototype UNIX system that provides domain and type enforcement. Fine and Minear (1993) describe the design of DTMACH—a trusted, distributed version of Mach. Chapter 11 deals with UNIX network security.

Paans (1991) surveys MVS security and its history. Schramm (1993) describes exposures opened by the relation between MVS and RACF. Cavender (1992) and Villegas (1992) give guidance on secure use of APF and SVCs. OpenVMS security is described by Holden (1993) and Leichter (1994).

Custer (1993) provides an overview of the design and function of Windows NT, including its security features. Windows NT security is described by Reichel (1993). Ruley et al. (1994) discuss Windows NT administrative domains and interdomain trust. Chapter 11 describes network security aspects of Windows NT.

Exercises

8.1 Explain the difference between identification and authentication.

8.2 Describe a dictionary attack on passwords. What characteristics of passwords make dictionary attacks feasible?

8.3 A user can generate a password by transforming a meaningful phrase using a key. Suggest a way to use (without a computer) some cryptosystem from Chap. 5 to produce a strong password for which mnemonic aids can be written down.

8.4 What is a shadow password file?

8.5 What is the defining characteristic of see-through devices for authentication as compared with other kinds of token devices? Why is their potential limited as compared with smart cards?

8.6 Discuss the reasons that biometric authentication is not used widely to control computer system access.

8.7 A user with Top Secret clearance tries to log on to a system that supports levels Confidential and Secret from a terminal of level Confidential. She asks to work at Secret level. Is she allowed to log on? If so, what is the level of her session?

8.8 Considering the mechanisms, services, and systems described in this chapter and in Chap. 7, list all the ways that the protection of a new file can be determined.

8.9 Why does trusted recovery need explicit constraints and invariants?

8.10 The audit-log file for a multilevel system should be at the system-high level. Why?

8.11 Some operating systems enforce a modified multilevel policy that substitutes "write-equal" for "no write down." In such a system, how should the audit log be implemented?

8.12 Describe how UNIX interprets the permissions for user, owner, and other when it validates access to a file. Compare the UNIX method with the OpenVMS method.

8.13 Discuss the security significance of the UNIX PATH variable.

8.14 Describe how an organization might take advantage of OpenVMS identifiers to simplify access control.

8.15 Describe the ways that Windows NT is like a capability system. What Windows NT data structure corresponds to a capability list?

8.16 What disadvantages might there be to requesting the Windows NT MAXIMUM_ALLOWED access right?

References

Abraham, D. G., G. M. Dolan, G. P. Double, and J. V. Stevens. 1991. Transaction Security System. *IBM Systems Journal* **30**(2): 206–229.

Arnold, N. Derek. 1993. *UNIX Security: A Practical Tutorial.* New York: McGraw-Hill.

Bačić, Eugen M. 1989. Process execution controls as a method of ensuring integrity. In *Report of the Invitational Workshop on Data Integrity,* B.2-1–B.2-8. Gaithersburg, Md.: National Institute of Standards and Technology.

______. 1990. Process execution controls: Revisited. *Proceedings of the Sixth Annual Computer Security Applications Conference,* 334–339. Los Alamitos, Calif.: IEEE Computer Society.

Badger, Lee, Daniel F. Sterne, David L. Sherman, Kenneth M. Walker, and Sheila A. Haghighat. 1995. A domain and type enforcement UNIX prototype. *Proceedings of the Fifth USENIX UNIX Security Symposium,* 127–140. Berkeley, Calif.: USENIX Association.

Baran, Fuat, Howard Kaye, and Margarita Suarez. 1990. Security breaches: Five recent incidents at Columbia University. In *Unix Security Workshop II,* 151–167. Berkeley, Calif.: USENIX Association.

Barton, Ben F., and Marthalee S. Barton. 1984. User-friendly password methods for computer-mediated information systems. *Computers & Security* **3**(3): 186–195.

Benson, Glenn. 1992. An optimal solution to the secure reader-writer problem. *Proceedings of the 1992 IEEE Computer Society Symposium on Research in Security and Privacy,* 251–258. Los Alamitos, Calif.: IEEE Computer Society.

Bishop, Matt. 1990. Collaboration using roles. *Software Practice and Experience* **20**(5): 485–497.

______. 1991. A proactive password checker. *Proceedings of the IFIP TC11 Seventh International Conference on Information Security, IFIP/Sec '91,* 169–180. Amsterdam: North-Holland.

Blaze, Matt. 1993. A cryptographic file system for Unix. *Proceedings of the 1st ACM Conference on Computer and Communications Security,* 9–16. New York: ACM Press.

Brady, Kevin. 1992. Integrating B2 security into a UNIX system. *Proceedings of the IFIP TC11 Eighth International Conference on Information Security, IFIP/Sec'92,* 395–404.

______. 1993. SVR4.1ES: Making UNIX airtight. *UNIX Review* **11**(4): Amsterdam: North-Holland. 30 (7).

Bunch, Steve. 1992. UNIX security issues in the 1990s. *Computer Security Journal* **8**(1): 81–89.

Cavender, Terry. 1992. Understanding IBM's Authorized Program Facility. *EDPACS,* July: 11–17.

Clark, David D., and David R. Wilson. 1989. Evolution of a model for computer integrity. In Zella G. Ruthberg and William T. Polk, eds., *Report of the Invitational Workshop on Data Integrity,* A.2-1–A.2-13. Gaithersburg, Md.: National Institute of Standards and Technology.

Clark, James L. 1992. UNIX operating system security. In Guy G. Gable and William J. Caelli, eds., *IT Security: The Need for International Cooperation. Proceedings of the IFIP TC11 Eighth International Conference on Information Security, IFIP/Sec'92,* 335–343. Amsterdam: North-Holland.

Clark, Paul C., and Lance J. Hoffman. 1994. BITS: A smartcard protected operating system. *Communications of the ACM* **37**(11): 66–70, 94.

Conn, Alex P., John H. Parodi, and Michael Taylor. 1990. The place of biometrics in a user authentication taxonomy. *Proceedings of the 13th National Computer Security Conference,* vol. I, 72–79. NIST/NCSC.

Curry, David A. 1992. *UNIX System Security: A Guide for Users and System Administrators.* Reading, Mass.: Addison-Wesley.

Custer, Helen. 1993. *Inside Windows NT.* Redmond, Wash.: Microsoft Press.

Davida, George I., Yvo G. Desmedt, and Brian J. Matt. 1989. Defending systems against viruses through cryptographic authentication. *Proceedings of the 1989 IEEE Computer Society Symposium on Security and Privacy,* 312–318. Los Alamitos, Calif.: IEEE Computer Society.

Davies, D. W., and W. L. Price. 1989. *Security for Computer Networks: An Introduction to Data Security in Teleprocessing and Electronic Funds Transfer.* Chichester, England: Wiley.

De Alvaré, Ana Maria. 1990. How crackers crack passwords or what passwords to avoid. *USENIX Workshop Proceedings: UNIX Security II,* 103–107. Berkeley, Calif.: USENIX Association.

Denning, Peter J., ed. 1990. *Computers under Attack: Intruders, Worms, and Viruses.* New York: ACM Press.

Denning, Peter J. 1992. Passwords. *American Scientist* **80**(March–April): 117–120.

Dichter, Carl. 1993. Easy UNIX security. *UNIX Review* **11**(April): 43–49.

Epstein, Jeremy. 1992. A bibliography of windowing systems and security. *Security Audit & Control Review* **10**(4): 7–11.

Epstein, Jeremy, and Rita Pascale. 1993. User interface for a high assurance windowing system. *Proceedings of the Ninth Annual Computer Security Applications Conference,* 256–264. Los Alamitos, Calif.: IEEE Computer Society.

Epstein, Jeremy, and Jeffrey Picciotto. 1991. Trusting X: Issues in building trusted X Window systems—or—What's not trusted about X? *Proceedings of the 14th National Computer Security Conference,* vol. II, 619–629. NIST/NCSC.

Epstein, Jeremy, John McHugh, Rita Pascale, Charles Martin, Douglas Rothnie, Hilarie Orman, Ann Marmor-Squires, Martha Branstad, and Bonnie Danner. 1992. Evolution of a trusted B3 window system prototype. *Proceedings of the 1992 IEEE Computer Society Symposium on Research in Security and Privacy,* 226–239. Los Alamitos, Calif.: IEEE Computer Society.

Faden, Glenn. 1991. Reconciling CMW requirements with those of X11 applications. *Proceedings of the 14th National Computer Security Conference,* 472–479. NIST/NCSC.

Farrow, Rik. 1991. *UNIX System Security: How to Protect Your Data and Prevent Intruders.* Reading, Mass.: Addison-Wesley.

Fernandez, Eduardo B., Rita C. Summers, and Christopher Wood. 1981. *Database Security and Integrity.* Reading, Mass.: Addison-Wesley.

Ferraiolo, David, Nickilyn Lynch, Patricia Toth, David Chizmadia, Michael Ressler, Roberta Medlock, and Sarah Weinberg. 1993. *Minimum Security Requirements for Multi-User Operating Systems.* Report NISTIR 5153. Gaithersburg, Md.: National Institute of Standards and Technology.

Fine, Todd, and Spencer E. Minear. 1993. Assuring Distributed Trusted Mach. *Proceedings of the 1993 IEEE Computer Society Symposium on Research in Security and Privacy,* 206–217. Los Alamitos, Calif.: IEEE Computer Society.

Ganesan, Ravi, and Chris Davies. 1994. A new attack on random pronounceable password generators. *Proceedings of the 17th National Computer Security Conference,* 184–197. NIST/NCSC.

Garfinkel, Simson, and Gene Spafford. 1991. *Practical UNIX Security.* Sebastopol, Calif.: O'Reilly and Associates.

Grampp, F. T., and R. H. Morris. 1984. UNIX operating system security. *AT&T Bell Laboratories Technical Journal* **63**(8): 1649–1672.

Gray, Jim, and Andreas Reuter. 1993. *Transaction Processing: Concepts and Techniques.* San Mateo, Calif.: Morgan Kaufmann.

Gray, Jim, and Daniel P. Siewiorek. 1991. High-availability computer systems. *Computer* **24**(9): 39–48.

Guillou, Louis Claude, Michel Ugon, and Jean-Jacques Quisquater. 1992. The smart card: A standardized security device dedicated to public cryptology. In Gustavus J. Simmons, ed., *Contemporary Cryptology: The Science of Information Integrity,* 561–613. Piscataway, N.J.: IEEE Press.

Haskett, James A. 1984. Pass-algorithms: A user validation scheme based on knowledge of secret algorithms. *Communications of the ACM* **27**(8): 777–781.

Heydon, Allan, Mark W. Maimone, J. D. Tygar, Jeannette M. Wing, and Amy Moormann Zaremski. 1990. Miro: Visual specification of security. *IEEE Transactions on Software Engineering* **16**(10): 1185(13).

Holden, Donald B. 1993. Open VMS VAX security architecture. *EDP Auditor Journal* **I:** 39–45.

Huber, Gary. 1994. CMW introduction. *Security Audit & Control Review* **12**(4): 6–10.

Irvine, Cynthia E. 1995. A multilevel file system for high assurance. *Proceedings of the 1995 IEEE Symposium on Security and Privacy,* 78–87. Los Alamitos, Calif.: IEEE Computer Society.

ITSEC. 1991. *ITSEC: Information Technology Security Evaluation Criteria.* Luxembourg: European Communities—Commission.

Janson, P., and R. Molva. 1991. Security in open networks and distributed systems. *Computer Networks and ISDN Systems* **22:** 323–346.

Jobusch, David L., and Arthur E. Oldehoeft. 1989. A survey of password mechanisms: Weaknesses and potential improvements. *Computers & Security* **8:** 587–604 (part 1) and 675–689 (part 2).

Joyce, Rick, and Gopal Gupta. 1990. Identity authentication based on keystroke latencies. *Communications of the ACM* **33**(2): 168–176.

Jueneman, Robert R. 1989. Integrity controls for military and commercial applications, II. In Zella G. Ruthberg and William T. Polk, eds., *Report of the Invitational Workshop on Data Integrity,* A.5-1–A.5-61. NIST Special Publication 500-168. Gaithersburg, Md.: National Institute of Standards and Technology.

Kim, Gene H., and Eugene H. Spafford. 1994. The design and implementation of Tripwire: A file system integrity checker. *2nd ACM Conference on Computer and Communications Security,* 18–29. New York: ACM Press.

King, Maria M. 1991. Rebus passwords. *Proceedings of the Seventh Annual Computer Security Applications Conference,* 239–243. Los Alamitos, Calif: IEEE Computer Society.

Klein, Daniel V. 1990. "Foiling the cracker": A survey of, and improvements to, password security. *USENIX Workshop Proceedings: UNIX Security II,* 5–14. Berkeley, Calif.: USENIX Association.

Königs, Hans-Peter. 1991. Cryptographic identification methods for smart cards in the process of standardization. *IEEE Communications Magazine,* June: 42–48.

Kurzban, Stanley A. 1985. *Easily Remembered Passphrases: A Better Approach.* IBM Corporation.

Landwehr, Carl E. 1983. The best available technologies for computer security. *Computer* **16**(7): 86–100.

Lawrence, L. G. 1993. Password control. *Computer Fraud & Security Bulletin,* July: 16–19.

Leichter, Jerrold. 1994. OpenVMS security components. *Digital Systems Journal* **16**(4): 32(4).

Levin, Tim, Steven J. Padilla, and Cynthia E. Irvine. 1989. A formal model for UNIX SETUID. In *Proceedings of the 1989 IEEE Computer Society Symposium on Security and Privacy,* 73–83. Washington, D.C.: IEEE Computer Society.

McIlroy, M. D., and J. A. Reeds. 1992. Multilevel security in the UNIX tradition. *Software—Practice and Experience* **22**(8): 673–694.

Morris, Robert, and Ken Thompson. 1979. Password security: A case history. *Communications of the ACM* **22**(11): 594–597.

NCSC. 1985. *Department of Defense Trusted Computer System Evaluation Criteria.* DOD 5200.28-STD. Fort Meade, Md.: National Computer Security Center.

______. 1987a. *A Guide to Understanding Audit in Trusted Systems.* NCSC-TG-001-87. Fort Meade, Md.: National Computer Security Center.

______. 1987b. *A Guide to Understanding Discretionary Access Control in Trusted Systems.* NCSC-TG-003. Fort Meade, Md.: National Computer Security Center.

______. 1988. *Computer Security Subsystem Interpretation of the Trusted Computer System Evaluation Criteria.* NCSC-TG-009. Fort Meade, Md.: National Computer Security Center.

______. 1989. *A Guide to Understanding Trusted Facility Management.* NCSC-TG-015. Fort Meade, Md.: National Computer Security Center.

______. 1991a. *A Guide to Understanding Identification and Authentication in Trusted Systems.* NCSC-TG-017. Fort Meade, Md.: National Computer Security Center.

______. 1991b. *A Guide to Understanding Trusted Recovery in Trusted Systems.* NCSC-TG-022. Fort Meade, Md.: National Computer Security Center.

______. 1991c. *A Guide to Writing the Security Features User's Guide for Trusted Systems.* NCSC-TG-026. Fort Meade, Md.: National Computer Security Center.

______. 1991d. *Integrity in Automated Information Systems.* C technical report 79-91. Fort Meade, Md.: National Computer Security Center.

______. 1991e. *Integrity-Oriented Control Objectives: Proposed Revisions to the Trusted Computer System Evaluation Criteria (TCSEC), DOD 5200.28-STD.* C technical report 111-91. Fort Meade, Md.: National Computer Security Center.

______. 1992a. *Assessing Controlled Access Protection.* NCSC-TG-028. Fort Meade, Md.: National Computer Security Center.

______. 1992b. *Guidelines for Writing Trusted Facility Manuals.* NCSC-TG-016. Fort Meade, Md.: National Computer Security Center.

NIST. 1993. *Automated Password Generator (APG).* FIPS pub. 181. Gaithersburg, Md.: National Institute of Standards and Technology.

______. 1994. *Guideline for the Use of Advanced Authentication Technology Alternatives.* FIPS pub. 190. Gaithersburg, Md.: National Institute of Standards and Technology.

______. 1995. *Draft Standard for Public Key Cryptographic Entity Authentication Mechanisms.* Draft FIPS pub. Gaithersburg, Md.: National Institute of Standards and Technology.

Paans, Ronald. 1991. With MVS/ESA security labels towards B1. *Computers & Security* **10:** 309–324.

Parks, John R. 1991. Personal identification: Biometrics. *Information Security: Proceedings of the IFIP TC11 Seventh International Conference on Information Security, IFIP/Sec '91,* 181–191. Amsterdam: North-Holland.

Phillips, Tim. 1993. Security software. *Which Computer?* **16**(2): 55–73.

Picciotto, Jeffrey. 1991. Towards trusted cut and paste in the X Window System. *Proceedings of the Seventh Annual Computer Security Applications Conference,* 34–43. Los Alamitos, Calif.: IEEE Computer Society.

Picciotto, Jeffrey, and Richard D. Graubart. 1994. Extended labeling policies for enhanced application support. *Computers & Security* **13**(7): 587–599.

Polk, W. Timothy, and Lawrence E. Bassham III. 1992. *A Guide to the Selection of Anti-Virus Tools and Techniques.* NIST special publication 800-5. Gaithersburg, Md.: National Institute of Standards and Technology.

Quarterman, John S., and Susanne Wilhelm. 1993. *UNIX, POSIX, and Open Systems: The Open Standards Puzzle.* Reading, Mass.: Addison-Wesley.

Reichard, Kevin, and Eric F. Johnson. 1995. Securing your X environment. *UNIX Review* **13**(2): 73–76.

Reichel, Rob. 1993. Inside Windows NT Security, part 1. *Windows/DOS Developer's Journal,* April: 6–19.

Ruley, John D., et al. 1994. *Networking Windows NT.* New York: Wiley.

Schaen, Samuel I., and Brian W. McKenney. 1991. Network auditing: Issues and recommendations. *Proceedings of the Seventh Annual Computer Security Applications Conference,* 66–79. Los Alamitos, Calif.: IEEE Computer Society.

Scheifler, R. W., and J. Gettys. 1986. The X Window System. *ACM Transactions on Graphics* **5**(2): 79–109.

Schneier, Bruce. 1993. Data guardians. *MacWorld,* February: 145–151.

Schramm, Christof. 1993. Added-on security for MVS: Weaknesses and measures. *Computers & Security* **12**(4): 379–388.

Seeley, Donn. 1989. Password cracking: A game of wits. *Communications of the ACM* **32**(6): 700–703. Reprinted in Denning (1990): 244–252.

Seiden, Kenneth F., and Jeffrey P. Melanson. 1990. The auditing facility for a VMM security kernel. *Proceedings of the 1990 IEEE Computer Society Symposium on*

Research in Security and Privacy, 262–277. Los Alamitos, Calif.: IEEE Computer Society.

Shieh, Shiuh-Pyng W., and Virgil D. Gligor. 1990. Auditing the use of covert storage channels in secure systems. *Proceedings of the 1990 IEEE Computer Society Symposium on Research in Security and Privacy,* 285–295. Los Alamitos, Calif.: IEEE Computer Society.

Spafford, Eugene H. 1989. The Internet worm: Crisis and aftermath. *Communications of the ACM* **32**(6): 678–687. Reprinted in Denning (1990): 223–243.

USENIX. 1995. *Proceedings of the Fifth USENIX UNIX Security Symposium.* Berkeley, Calif.: USENIX Association.

Villegas, Miguel. 1992. Audit and control of supervisor calls. *EDPACS,* January: 7–14.

Williams, James G., and Leonard J. LaPadula. 1993. Automated support for external consistency. *Proceedings of the Computer Security Foundations Workshop VI,* 71–81. Los Alamitos, Calif.: IEEE Computer Society.

Wong, Raymond M. 1990. A comparison of secure UNIX operating systems. *Proceedings of the Sixth Annual Computer Security Applications Conference,* 322–333. Los Alamitos, Calif.: IEEE Computer Society.

Wong, Raymond M., Thomas A. Berson, and Richard J. Feiertag. 1985. Polonius: An identity authentication system. *Proceedings of the 1985 Symposium on Security and Privacy,* 101–107. Silver Spring, Md.: IEEE Computer Society.

Woodward, John P. L. 1987. Exploiting the dual nature of sensitivity labels. *Proceedings of the 1987 IEEE Symposium on Security and Privacy,* 23–30. Washington, D.C.: IEEE Computer Society.

Zviran, M., and W. J. Haga. 1993. A comparison of password techniques for multilevel authentication mechanisms. *The Computer Journal* **36**(3): 227–237.

Chapter

9

Database Security

Database systems are at the heart of most organizations, representing the organizations' assets, activities, and structure. The databases of a manufacturing company, for example, represent the products made, suppliers and customers, orders, and the company's departments and employees. Relationships among these entities are also represented—between customers and products and between employees and departments. By using a common database, an organization can integrate different functions, such as inventory management and customer orders. These functions use the same database but in different ways. Because databases are central to so many business processes, their security is crucial. A database system is secure if it lives up to its security policy; usually, this means that it provides integrity, availability, and confidentiality.

Overview of the Chapter

This chapter begins with a survey of database concepts and terminology. The relational model of data is described, and object-oriented and statistical databases are introduced. Then the special security requirements of databases are discussed. The section that follows is about security services for databases, especially access control and integrity services. The chapter then turns to the problem of building database systems that provide multilevel secure operation. Models, approaches, and projects are described. The next section discusses research on security for object-oriented databases. The final section is about inference in two contexts: statistical databases and multilevel secure databases.

Database Concepts and Terminology

Databases and database management systems

A *database* is a persistent collection of interrelated data items. Persistence is provided by storage on nonvolatile media and by integrity measures. The data are interrelated in that they represent real-world entities and the relationships among them. A *database management system* (DBMS) is the software that maintains databases and provides access to them. The DBMS allows programs and users to manipulate data and query the database. Query facilities help users pose ad-hoc questions and build database applications. Users can query databases through forms-based interfaces; designing forms is a simple and increasingly popular way to build database applications. A DBMS has facilities for defining databases—called a *data description language* (DDL). The database description is called a *schema.* A *data manipulation language* (DML) is used for querying and manipulating the database. Security and other control functions are supported in a *data control language* (DCL). A DBMS includes or depends on a transaction-processing component.

DBMSs protect the database against application errors and unauthorized access; they help maintain its integrity with integrity constraints, concurrency control, and recovery. They shield users and application programs from the complexity and changing organization of stored data. A DBMS also allows different applications to view the same data differently. DBMSs are used in every kind of computing environment. A user's workstation may contain replicated parts of databases and also may access LAN or mainframe database servers.

It is useful to think of three levels of database description, with mappings between the levels. The *conceptual schema* is a high-level description of the real-world entities that the database represents. A database design process maps the conceptual schema to an *external schema* that describes how users and applications view the database; the external schema is tied to a specific *data model.* The *internal schema* is closer to the storage level, describing, for example, how relations are represented in files. Internal schemas vary widely among DBMSs, whereas external schemas usually conform to industry standards. A DBMS represents the external and internal schemas in data objects that collectively form a *data dictionary.* Schema data are also called *metadata.*

A *data model* defines the entity types of the database and their relationships, as well as the database operations (such as **insert** or **update**). The model also includes rules about which operations are valid. A DBMS implements some data model. Early DBMSs implemented a hierarchical model, and object-oriented models are gaining ground, but the clearly dominant model is the *relational model.*

The relational model of data

The relational model was developed by E. F. Codd of IBM, who described the model in a noted 1970 article. All the leading DBMSs are based on the relational model, and so is much of the research on database security.

Relations. The basic entity type of the relational model is the *relation,* shown as a *table* in Fig. 9.1. The columns of the table represent the *attributes* of the relation, and the rows represent its *tuples.* Figure 9.1 shows two relations: *customers* and *orders.* The attributes of *customers* are *customer-#, name, phone,* and *address.* Each tuple (row) represents a customer. The attributes of *orders* are *order-#* and *customer-#*; each row represents an order. An attribute is built on a *domain,* which is a pool of allowable values that the attribute can take. For example, the domain for *customer-#* is the integers. Each relation has a *primary key,* which is an attribute or combination of attributes that uniquely identifies the tuples of the relation. The attributes that qualify in this way are called *candidate keys.* One of the candidate keys is explicitly designated as the primary key. The primary key for *customers* is *customer-#*; no two customers have the same *customer-#.* The primary key for *orders* is *order-#.* The primary key of a relation *functionally determines* the value of each attribute. For example, *customer-#* functionally determines *phone* in the *customers* relation.

customers			
customer-#	*name*	*phone*	*address*
9012	A. Lee	xxx-xxx-xxxx	123 Pine St., Smalltown, CA 12345
4309	B. Kent	yyy-yyy-yyyy	446 Oak St., Bigtown, CA 16789

orders	
order-#	*customer-#*
10293847	4309
61029384	4309

Figure 9.1 *Customers* and *orders* relations.

The definition of a relation is called the *relation schema.* It can be written as $R(A_1, A_2,..., A_n)$, where the A's are the attributes. The set of tuples at any time is called the *relation instance.* A tuple can be written as $(a_1,a_2,...,a_n)$.

It must be possible to link different relations. Suppose, for example, the mail-order company wants to call a customer about the status of an order. *Orders* must be linked to *customers* to find the phone number. The linking is done by matching the values of some attributes in two relations. An attribute of one relation is called a *foreign key* if it is the primary key of some other relation. In *orders, customer-#* is a foreign key that refers to the *customers* relation.

Operations on relations. When any operation is performed on a relation, the result is also a relation. The relational model defines five primitive operations: *select, project, union, minus,* and *times.* From the primitives are built other operations, such as *join.*

Select. Forms a new relation consisting of tuples that satisfy some formula, e.g., all the tuples of *orders* where *customer-#* equals 1134.

Project. Forms a new relation by including only some attributes and removing duplicate tuples; e.g., we could project *customers* on *name* and *address* to obtain a mailing list.

Union. From two relations R and S, with compatible schemas, forms a new relation consisting of each tuple that is in either R or S or both.

Minus. From two relations R and S, with compatible schemas, forms a new relation whose tuples are in R but not in S.

Times. Forms the Cartesian product of two relations R and S. (Each tuple of S is appended to each tuple of R.)

Join. From the Cartesian product of R and S, the *equijoin* selects tuples that have equal values for some attributes; e.g., *customers* and *orders* can be joined on *customer-#.*

Relational integrity rules. The relational model imposes constraints on the values that tuples can have. (These constraints apply to *all* relations, as opposed to other integrity constraints that users specify for specific databases or specific relations.) The constraints are expressed in two integrity rules:

Entity integrity rule. No tuple may have a null value for any of the primary key attributes. This rule ensures that every tuple of the relation is uniquely identifiable.

Referential integrity rule. For any foreign key value, the referenced relation must have a tuple with the same value for its primary key. This rule ensures that if one relation refers to another, the target of the reference exists. For example, if *customer-#* 1134 appears in *orders,* where it is a foreign key value, 1134 also must appear in *customers,* where it is a primary key value.

Views. New relations, called *views,* can be defined using the basic operations of select, project, and join. Views are significant for security because they can hide attributes or implement content-dependent access restrictions. By providing windows into the database that are tailored to particular uses, views support the principle of least privilege.

The SQL language. *SQL* is a standard language for relational database data definition and data manipulation. It was developed as part of System R—an IBM research DBMS that led to IBM's DB2 and other relational DBMS products. SQL is used from within programs and directly as commands. The SQL data definition language supports the creation and deletion of relations (called *tables*) and views. Tables that are not views are called *base tables.* The main data manipulation commands are **insert, select, update,** and **delete. Select** retrieves data that satisfy criteria specified in the command. **Grant** and **revoke** commands support access control. A series of SQL standards has been developed. *SQL-92* was adopted by ANSI and ISO and is a U.S. government FIPS. *SQL3* is in the works.

Object-oriented databases

Object-oriented databases grew out of the same concepts as object-oriented design methods and programming languages (discussed in Chap. 6). For these databases, all entities are modeled as objects. Object-oriented databases are potentially more flexible than relational databases, and they integrate well with object-oriented programming languages. There are object-oriented DBMSs (OODBMSs), and relational DBMSs are adding support for objects. Extensions to SQL have been developed. Although security has not been a high priority for OODBMS products, researchers have studied security for the object-oriented model.

Statistical databases

Sometimes it is necessary to restrict database users to averages or other *aggregate statistics.* This is true where individual data values must be confidential for reasons of privacy—as in census data or medical research data. A *statistical database system* is one that allows its users to retrieve only aggregate statistics, such as counts or sums. However, a data spy may be able to infer private information from aggregates. Inference from statistical databases is an important security problem.

Database Security Requirements

For a database system, as for any system, it is necessary to formulate a security policy and to provide the services and mechanisms that implement that policy. The requirements differ in several ways from operating system security requirements. First, the data objects have a more complex structure than the data objects known to operating systems, and this affects both policy and services. The metadata that describe the structure must be protected. A DBMS usually is implemented on top of an operating system. The DBMS may support a model of authorization that differs from the operating system's. Authorization for database access exploits the complex data structure, which allows fine-grained authorization. The authorization model must take into account that one object may be a component of another or defined in terms of another. Enforcing the multilevel policy is more difficult for DBMSs than for operating systems. Because DBMSs more closely support applications, role-based access control is more important.

A DBMS supports application-specific data integrity. For example, the DBMS can ensure that all customer addresses include a valid ZIP code or that an order can be entered only if the customer is in the database. Transactions must be supported, either by the DBMS itself or by a separate transaction manager. Concurrency control and recovery are more complex than for files, because the data objects have complex relationships and because transaction properties must be ensured. The audit trail must provide more detailed information. The DBMS is the right place for Clark-Wilson integrity support.

Organizations that follow the multilevel policy need multilevel databases and therefore need multilevel DBMSs. As trusted operating systems become available, a multilevel DBMS can encourage multilevel operation by making it easier to develop or convert applications. Multilevel databases must guard against illegal information flow that is due to inference and aggregation.

Security Services for Databases

Identification and authentication

Every DBMS has a user identity construct, such as the *authorization identifier* of the SQL standards. For mainframe DBMSs, the operating system is responsible for identifying and authenticating users; when the DBMS is invoked, the OS passes it the user's identity. The DBMS can then determine if the user is authorized for the DBMS and can use the identifier for access control. The OS may reauthenticate the user when the DBMS is invoked—to verify that the same person still controls the session. Authentication differs when the DBMS is on a *database server* that is accessible through a network. Database servers maintain their own user accounts and may do their own authentication. Some DBMSs use SQL authorization statements to enroll users and assign user status and passwords. The SQL standards define the **connect** statement for connecting to a database server.

Access control

Access control for database systems follows the same principles as for operating systems, but it must take into account the data models and the needs of database applications.

Authorization models. Models of authorization describe how security policy is expressed as *authorization rules,* or *authorizations,* that represent the information of the access matrix model in another form. An authorization rule has the form

$$(s,o,a,p)$$

specifying that subject s has access of type a to those occurrences of o for which predicate p is true. System R and other relational systems maintain the authorization rules as *authorization relations.* System R uses the ownership model of authorization: The user who creates a table, or other object, becomes its owner and holds all rights for the object. These rights can be granted to others, and the grants can be revoked. Although other authorization models could be used with relational databases, the ownership model prevails.

Subjects, objects, and privileges. In the SQL interpretation of the authorization rule, the subject is the authorization ID. The objects include tables, columns, domains, and views. The access types (called *privileges*) are of two kinds. *Database object privileges* apply to most data objects. *System* (or *database*) *privileges* apply to schema operations, such as creating tables, and to system operations, such as creating new users and starting or stopping the DBMS. System privileges are intended for administrators and database developers. Only the table owner can perform the DDL operations on a table. SQL-92 provides no way to grant privileges for these operations to others, but

DBMS products have ways to transfer ownership of schema objects. The object privileges are **select, insert, update, delete, references,** and **usage.** DBMS products also support an **execute** privilege that allows execution of a procedure. The predicate of the authorization rule is supported indirectly, through views.

Figure 9.2 shows three tables from the database of the GreatStuff mail-order company. CUSTOMERS and ORDERS are similar to the relations of Fig. 9.1. CONSUMER-INFO contains information purchased from other sources: consumer names, phone numbers, addresses, and income levels.

Granting and revoking privileges. A comprehensive scheme for granting and revoking privileges was developed for System R. The goal was to avoid the bottleneck of a central administrator. The System R scheme allows any user to create a table; the creator receives all privileges for the table and may grant them to others. A grant recipient may in turn grant a privilege to another user, but only if the grant carries a *grant option.* (In terms of the access-matrix model, the grant option is the copy flag.) The meaning of revoking a granted privilege is that the authorization state after the revoke is the same as if the grant had never occurred. Sometimes, even though a grant is revoked, the grantee retains the privilege. The following sequence (with users *A, B,* and *X*) shows how this can happen.

```
A:  grant select, insert, update on customers to X
B:  grant select, update on customers to X
A:  revoke insert, update on customers from X
```

After this sequence, *X* retains **select** and **update** privileges on CUSTOMERS. After a revocation, privileges granted by an independent source are retained.

CUSTOMERS			
customer-#	name	phone	address

ORDERS			
order-#	customer-#	total	• • •

CONSUMER-INFO			
name	phone	address	income-level

Figure 9.2 Example database schema.

SQL largely follows the System R grant scheme. For example, the owner of CUSTOMERS can allow Craig (a manager in the order department) to see the CUSTOMERS table and to insert new rows:

```
grant select, insert
      on customers
      to craig
```

The grant option allows the grant recipient to pass on the privilege:

```
grant select, insert
      on customers
      to craig with grant option
```

Craig may then grant his privilege on CUSTOMERS to order clerks Lisa and John.

A user who creates a schema object automatically gets all privileges with the grant option. Privileges can be granted on tables, columns, views, and domains. (Not discussed here are other SQL-92 objects, such as character sets.) A privilege may be granted to PUBLIC. A grant on a table causes the same privileges to be granted on all columns of the table—the current columns and also any that might be added. Craig can see all columns of CUSTOMERS but cannot update any. To give Craig the ability to change customers' telephone numbers:

```
grant update (phone)
       on customers
       to craig
```

The **references** privilege controls the use of foreign keys. The ORDERS table was defined as `references customers`, since CUSTOMER-# is a foreign key that refers to the CUSTOMERS table. The creator of ORDERS needed a **references** privilege on the CUSTOMER-# column of CUSTOMERS. If the use of foreign keys were not controlled, anyone could create a table *T* that references CUSTOMERS. Then, by trying to insert rows in *T* and seeing which inserts succeeded, the owner of *T* could learn the customer numbers that are in CUSTOMERS. The **usage** privilege on a domain is needed in order to define a column based on the domain.

Privileges are withdrawn by a **revoke** statement:

```
revoke select
     on customers
     from lisa

revoke grant option for select
      on customers
      from craig
```

The keywords **restrict** and **cascade** govern how **revoke** operates. **Restrict** prevents the privilege from being revoked if other users' privileges depend on it. **Cascade** causes all the *dependent privileges* to be revoked. For example, to revoke Craig's privilege and all the dependent privileges such as John's:

```
revoke select
     on customers
     from craig cascade
```

This statement is intended to leave the privilege status just as if the privilege had never been granted to Craig. (The exact semantics are much more complicated.)

Privileges on views. Views and privileges are the two SQL mechanisms for access control. A view that is defined from a table *T* can hide data by omitting some of *T*'s columns and also some rows, based on their content. Views are created with the **select** statement. For example,

```
create view affluent
        as select name,income-level
                from customer-info
                where income = 'high'
```

Suppose that GreatStuff wants to send out a catalog of expensive items and that Amy is assigned to build a mailing list. By joining CUSTOMERS and CUSTOMER-INFO on name and selecting those rows where income level is high, Amy creates a RICH-LIST view that retains only the customer number, name, and address. To create the view, Amy needs **select** access to the underlying tables—CUSTOMERS and CUSTOMER-INFO for this example. She receives only **select** access to RICH-LIST, since privileges on a view are based on privileges for the underlying tables. Since John will handle the mailing, Amy gives him **select** access to RICH-LIST; he gets no access to the sensitive columns of CUSTOMER-INFO. (But John can infer quite a bit from the context.) Since views are dynamic windows, view privileges change when privileges to the underlying tables change.

Roles. With SQL-92, except for privileges granted to PUBLIC, each grant is to an individual user. This makes security administration for large organizations essentially unworkable. Some DBMSs allow administrators to assign users to a group and grant privileges to the group. With the Ingres DBMS, for example, a user can belong to multiple groups. Still better is to use roles. A *role* is a named group of rights, and a person is granted a privilege to the role. For example, GreatStuff can define roles for order clerks and order supervisors, giving each role exactly the privileges needed. Then Lisa and John would be granted the clerk role and Craig both roles. When Craig fills in for Lisa, he assumes the clerk role, deliberately limiting his privileges.

The authorization model of SQL-92 has the following problems:

- If a user—say, Craig—changes jobs, administrators must review all his privileges, as well as all the privileges he has granted. If his privileges are simply removed, the clerks will lose theirs as well.
- Since Craig fills in for order clerks and also for managers in the purchasing department, he has more privileges than he needs for any one task. There is the risk that he will accidentally or deliberately abuse his privileges.
- The same application program typically supports many tasks or transactions that need different authorizations. The only way to specify these with SQL-92 is through privileges to the objects used—a complicated method.
- Changing security administrators is difficult. Administrators typically own the basic schema objects and grant access to users or subadministrators. If any administrator loses access, all users lower in the grant chain lose access, with the possibility of great disruption. Since procedures to avoid such disruption are complex, many organizations use a shared user ID that never loses access—in violation of the accountability principle.
- There is no simple way to support different administrative roles, such as security administrator, operator, and auditor.
- Users have found cascading revoke hard to understand and administer.

An extension to SQL designed to remedy these defects is called *named protection domains* (NPDs). Most of this extension was implemented as the role facility of the Oracle7 DBMS, and SQL3 defines a similar role facility. An NPD is a grouping of privileges. An *object privilege* is the right to perform some operation on some object—such as **insert** on CUSTOMERS. An object privilege can be granted to an NPD, and NPDs can be granted to other NPDs and to users. The resulting authorization structure forms a *privilege graph* leading from object privileges to users, through NPDs, as shown in Fig. 9.3. The privilege graph makes clear *why* a user has a certain privilege. A user may have been granted several NPDs, but only one NPD is active at any time. For example, Craig is acting either in the role of

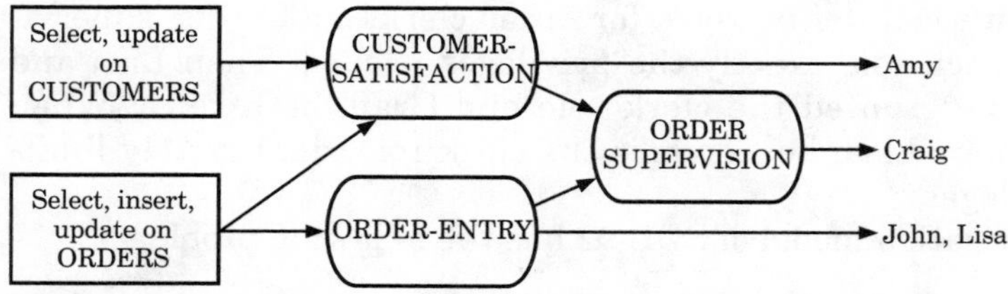

Figure 9.3 Privilege graph for named protection domains.

order supervisor or order clerk. However, the user has available all the privileges in the subtree rooted by the active NPD. For example, when Craig acts as order supervisor, the privileges of two NPDs are available: CUSTOMER-SATISFACTION and ORDER-ENTRY.

It is useful to create an NPD for each task of each application. In Fig. 9.3, GreatStuff has one NPD for ORDER-ENTRY and another for CUSTOMER-SATISFACTION. The same approach can be used to define security administration roles based on the tasks included in each role.

One way to use NPDs is to select the appropriate NPD at the time an application is invoked. Then access to an application's data can be restricted to users running the application; the same users could not access the data through a query language or another application. The SQL standard defines a **set role** statement that applications can use. The user must be authenticated for a role; Oracle7 does this either by password or via the operating system.

An NPD can be granted "with admin option," allowing the grantee to grant the NPD to someone else. The admin option differs from the grant option in what happens when the grantor's NPD grant is revoked: The granted NPDs remain in effect. There is no cascading revoke.

Integrity

The preceding two chapters described integrity services and mechanisms of operating systems. Ravi Sandhu and Sushil Jajodia (1995) argue that most integrity mechanisms belong in the DBMS rather than in the operating system or in applications. Operating systems provide no way to express most integrity policies, which are inherently application-oriented. It is both poor design and inappropriate to give the responsibility to applications. Sandhu and Jajodia argue that integrity mechanisms should be implemented at the lowest level where they make sense. Shared data should not be at the mercy of each application, since the developers of one application may not understand the consistency needs of the database as a whole. Also, application controls cannot protect the database from query-language users.

Sandhu and Jajodia list nine integrity principles (Table 9.1) that could be supported by various mechanisms—DBMS or other. The reader has seen most of these principles in earlier chapters; a few need explanation. The principle of *well-formed transactions* includes the policy of constrained change described in Chap. 4: Data should be changed only in prescribed and structured ways that protect their integrity. Data should be manipulated only by certified well-formed transactions. *Reconstruction of events* recognizes the need to deter and detect misuse through audit trails. *Delegation of authority* calls for flexible but constrained ways to acquire and distribute privileges. The *reality checks* principle calls for checking data against the real world. Table 9.1 shows where in this book each integrity mechanism is discussed.

Classes of database integrity safeguards. Database integrity safeguards can be grouped into three broad classes that protect against different threats:

- *Integrity constraints* protect against errors and misuse by users and applications. This class of safeguards is also called *semantic integrity.*
- *Concurrency control* guards against errors caused by the concurrent use of the database by multiple users and applications.

TABLE 9.1 Integrity principles

Integrity principles	DBMS mechanisms	Section or chapter
Well-formed transactions	Encapsulated updates Atomic transactions	Integrity, Chap. 8
	Consistency constraints	Integrity constraints
Continuity of operation	Redundancy Recovery	Chap. 11
Authenticated users	Authentication	Identification and authentication, Chaps. 8 and 10
Least privilege	Fine-grained access control	Access control
	Views	The relational model of data
Separation of duties	Transaction controls	Access control, integrity, object-oriented databases
	Layered updates	Bibliographic Notes
Reconstruction of events	Audit trail	Chap. 8
Delegation of authority	Dynamic authorization Propagation constraints *Roles*	Access control, object-oriented databases
Reality checks	Consistent snapshots	Chaps. 4 and 13
Ease of safe use	Fail-safe defaults Human factors	Chap. 6

SOURCE: Adapted from Sandhu and Jajodia 1995. (© 1995 IEEE).

- *Recovery* guards against errors due to system failures.

The *transaction* mechanism is important for all three classes of safeguards. Transactions, integrity constraints, and concurrency control are described here; references on database recovery can be found in the Bibliographic Notes.

Transactions. The transaction concept was first developed for database systems. A transaction groups database actions so that the transaction as a whole takes the database from one consistent state to another consistent state.

A *transaction* is a sequence of database *actions* that has the following properties:

- *Atomicity.* Either all the actions of a transaction are done (it *commits*) or none of them are done (it *aborts*).
- *Consistency.* A transaction preserves database consistency. For example, it does not violate the integrity rules and constraints.
- *Isolation.* Each transaction is isolated from the effects of concurrent transactions. Even if they read and write the same data, the effect will be the same as if the transactions ran one after another—*serially.*
- *Durability.* If a transaction commits, its changes to the database will survive subsequent failures.

These are called the *ACID properties.* SQL3 supports transactions with **start transaction, commit, rollback,** and other statements. Commits also occur automatically at certain points, such as after the creation of a table.

Integrity constraints. DBMS users express the consistency criteria for the database in the form of integrity constraints, which the DBMS then enforces. A database at time t_1 has a *state.* A database *transition* is a pair of database states—at time t_1 and the later time t_2. An integrity constraint may apply either to the state or to transitions. A correct database state satisfies all the *state constraints.* A correct database transition satisfies all the *transition constraints.* A state constraint might be that any telephone area code is in an enumerated list. A transition constraint might be that the count of orders placed during the month can never decrease. A general form for a constraint is

$$(t,c,a)$$

where

- *t* specifies the types of updates that may violate the constraint (e.g., a constraint might apply only when data are deleted)
- *c* is the predicate that must be satisfied by the database state or transition (alternatively, a constraint enforcement procedure may be specified)
- *a* is the *violation response action* (usually, the action is to abort the transaction). Sometimes, a *compensating update* is made to maintain consistency. For example, delete all the orders for a deleted customer.

This constraint form can be viewed as a special case of a *production rule:* (*event, conditions, actions*). When the event occurs, if the conditions are satisfied, the actions are performed. The event component is sometimes called a *trigger.* Some research DBMSs include generalized rule systems that support integrity, views, and application building.

From the definition of transaction, it seems that integrity constraints should be expected to hold only at the end of a transaction. However, not checking constraints until transaction end can waste the time and effort of users and systems. Some systems allow for *integrity checkpoints*—points during a transaction at which integrity constraints are enforced. If an integrity violation occurs later, the transaction is rolled back to the checkpoint rather than to the beginning. (SQL3 has *savepoints* that support rollback of portions of a transaction.) A related issue is whether the DBMS prevents integrity-violating updates or only detects them when the transaction commits. The latter is simpler, since integrity violations are easily detected at commit time, and the standard recovery techniques can undo the updates. One prevention mechanism is *query modification*—modifying the query before it executes so that it cannot violate constraints; this works for only some constraints. Research has been done on verifying that a transaction is *safe*—that it cannot violate integrity whatever the state of the database.

Describing the SQL standard, Chris Date and Hugh Darwen (1993) categorize integrity constraints as *domain constraints, general constraints,* and *base-table constraints.*

Domain constraints are associated with a domain and apply to every column defined on the domain. For example, birth dates might be constrained to the nineteenth, twentieth, or twenty-first centuries. Values might be non-null, within a range, or enumerated. Data types are much like domains with built-in constraints—not allowing, for example, a string to be inserted into a numeric column. Defining columns on domains protects integrity, and the **usage** privilege on domains strengthens this protection. SQL3 goes further by supporting abstract data types.

General constraints (created with **create assertion**) apply to any base tables in the database; they can express requirements for consistency between tables. For example, GreatStuff might require orders for Alaska customers to total at least $100. This constraint would refer to CUSTOMERS, ORDERS, and other tables that describe merchandise.

Base-table constraints are associated with specific tables but can refer to other tables. They include primary key and foreign key constraints and *check constraints.* A check constraint specifies a condition that must hold for any row created in the table. If a user defines a table T_1 with a check constraint that refers to table T_2, the user must have **select** access to T_2. This is so because evaluation of the constraint condition returns information about values in T_2. *Foreign key constraints* derive from the referential integrity rule of the relational model. Ensuring that they are enforced is the *referential integrity problem.* Enforcement can take different forms. The simplest is to reject an update that would violate referential integrity. However, the application may intend something different. For example, deleting a customer would violate referential integrity if the customer had outstanding orders. One way to maintain referential integrity is to delete all the orders for that customer. This is called *delete cascade.* SQL supports a choice of actions to support referential integrity.

Triggers. Some integrity constraints can be enforced directly by the DBMS. Another possibility is to invoke an application procedure to enforce the constraint. Most DBMSs allow *stored procedures* to be invoked by database applications. A trigger can be associated with operations on a table to cause a procedure invocation (or some other action) before, instead of, or after the normal action. Triggers have various integrity-maintaining uses. They can enforce constraints that are too complex to specify as assertions, and they can set off complex sequences of actions. An after-trigger is useful for creating specialized audit records. (The use of triggers is not limited to integrity. They can enforce complex access control requirements, and developers can use triggers to drive their applications.) Triggers are highly flexible, but they have problems. Unlike declarative constraints in SQL, their meaning is not apparent. They are more error-prone. It is not clear what protection domain triggered procedures should execute in.

Concurrency control. Suppose that two airline reservation agents are concurrently reserving seats on the same plane. Their transactions read and then update a seat-reservation data object. Suppose that both agents read the same version, each reserves a seat, and then each writes back a modified seat-reservation object. The update that occurred first would be overwritten by the other and would be lost. Other anomalies can occur, such as both agents reserving the same seat or an agent seeing tentative reservations that were never committed. If the actions of transactions are interleaved, some users may see an inconsistent state, and the database may be left in an inconsistent state. Preventing these inconsistencies is the *concurrency control problem.*

A transaction is modeled as a sequence of n steps:

$$a_1(d_1), a_2(d_2), \ldots, a_n(d_n)$$

where each step is an *action* a_i on an object d_i, and an action is either a read or a write. The set of objects that a transaction reads is called its *readset*; the set it writes is its *writeset.* Two transactions *conflict* if the readset of one intersects with the writeset of the other or if their writesets intersect. The seat-reservation transactions conflict in both ways. Consistency is preserved if the conflicting transactions are forced to execute *serially,* one transaction completing before the other begins. However, serial execution is bad for throughput and availability; it is intolerable for most applications. What is needed is an interleaving with the same effect as serial execution.

For models of concurrency control, a *schedule* or *history* records the sequence of steps of a set of transactions. Serial execution produces a *serial schedule.* A read operation $r(x)$ "reads from" a write operation $w(x)$ if $w(x)$ precedes $r(x)$ in the schedule and there is no intervening write. Two schedules are *equivalent* if every read action reads from the same write in both schedules and both schedules have the same final write actions. With equivalent schedules, each transaction sees the same values in both schedules, and the final state of the database is the same. An interleaved schedule that is equivalent to a serial schedule is a *serializable* schedule.

For some applications, lower levels of *isolation* than serializability are acceptable. The level of isolation corresponds to the integrity problems that do *not* occur. The defining problems are

- *Lost update.* This is what happens when one reservation transaction writes over another transaction's changes.
- *Dirty read.* Transaction T_1 reads data written by transaction T_2, and the value that T_1 reads is not the final committed value written by T_2. (T_2 might change the value or abort without committing.)
- *Unrepeatable read.* T_1 reads the same data item both before and after T_2 modifies it and commits.

- *Phantoms.* T_1 performs a **select,** then T_2 generates new rows that satisfy the selection criteria, and then T_1 repeats its **select** and sees a different result.

SQL standards define four isolation levels; the level can be set for a transaction. Level 3 guarantees serializability; it prevents all the listed problems. Phantoms can occur at level 2 and below, unrepeatable reads at level 1 and below, and dirty reads at level 0. The choice of levels is provided because it sometimes makes sense to trade isolation for availability and efficiency.

Concurrency control models call the DBMS component responsible for concurrency control the *scheduler.* The scheduler receives a stream of requests for the execution of database actions; it can grant, delay, or abort each request. Schedules are enforced primarily by locking. Besides consistency, a scheduler must provide high concurrency, availability, and recovery. Aborting transactions can badly affect availability, recovery, and what users observe. Also, although the database may be restored to internal consistency, the transaction may have acted on the real world irreversibly.

Schedules are enforced primarily by locking. With *two-phase locking,* each data element has an associated lock. When a transaction T tries to use element x, the scheduler tries to acquire the lock for x. If another transaction holds the lock, T is delayed until the lock is released. All of T's locks are acquired before any of them is released.

Multilevel Secure Database Systems

Most DBMSs were designed for commercial use and support only discretionary access control. However, the power and convenience of database systems are just as important for organizations that follow the multilevel security policy. A *multilevel secure* DBMS supports users who have different clearance levels and contains data at multiple sensitivity levels.

A multilevel secure DBMS must provide mandatory access control (MAC) supporting the multilevel policy. Data must be secure against both direct unauthorized access and indirect access through covert channels or inference. To support MAC, each data object must be labeled (perhaps indirectly) with its *access class,* which completely defines its MAC attributes. Discretionary access control also must be provided; for the higher evaluation classes it must include explicit denial of access. To support accountability, there must be user authentication and a protected audit log. Finally, the design and development of the DBMS must provide a basis for assurance. A great deal of research has aimed at meeting these goals. Most of the work assumes the relational model, which has been extended to support the multilevel policy.

Extending the relational model

In 1987, researchers on the SeaView project listed some requirements that an extended model must support:

- Mandatory security.
- Classification of atomic facts. The granularity of classification is an issue: What is the smallest object that has its own access class? Classification might apply to entire relations, to attributes, to tuples, or to *elements*—the individual attribute values of tuples.
- Multilevel views, where not all data in the view have the same classification. View classifications must be derived.
- Multilevel entry and updates—the ability to enter multilevel tuples and to update different-level elements within a single transaction.
- Consistency at each access class.
- Rule-based classification—integrity constraints on the access classes assigned to data.
- Retrievals based on access class.

The original SeaView model had four components: (1) multilevel relations, (2) multilevel relational integrity rules, (3) a method for decomposing multilevel relations into single-level relations and a corresponding recovery method, and (4) multilevel relational operators. The model to be described is a further development of the SeaView model.

Multilevel schema and instances. In the standard relational model, a relation schema has the form

$$R(A_1, A_2, \ldots, A_n)$$

For each *data attribute* A_i, the multilevel schema must add a *classification attribute* C_i that represents the access class of that attribute. For each tuple, the schema also includes a *tuple-class attribute* TC, representing the access class of the tuple. The schema, then, has the form

$$R(A_1, C_1, A_2, C_2, \ldots, A_n, C_n, TC)$$

where the domain of C_i is the set of allowed values for access classes. A subset of the attributes is the *apparent primary key AK.* For each schema R there is a collection of *relation instances,* one for each access class *c:*

$$R_c(A_1,C_1, A_2,C_2,\ldots, A_n,C_n,TC)$$

Each relation instance represents the view of the world that is appropriate for its access class. Each tuple of R_c has the form $(a_1,c_1,a_2,c_2,\ldots,a_n,c_n,tc)$, where the access class c of R_c dominates each classification attribute c_i. (A classification attribute cannot be null.) A *filter function* produces the relation instance $R_{c'}$, replacing by a null value each element of the multilevel relation R that is not visible in R_c and also maintaining multilevel integrity. The tuple-class attribute TC is used mainly for views.

Integrity properties. The entity integrity rule of the standard relational model states that no tuple may have a null value for any of the primary key attributes. This rule must be extended for the multilevel model, and three other properties are needed: null integrity, interinstance integrity, and polyinstantiation integrity.

Entity integrity. None of the AK attributes is null. In addition, all of them have the same classification c_{AK}, so the key is either entirely visible or entirely null. Finally, in any tuple the class of each nonkey attribute must dominate c_{AK}, to prevent a null primary key from occurring with non-null attributes.

Null integrity. Two properties are needed for null values. First, null values have the same classification as the apparent key. Second, a user must not see two tuples that differ only by null values. One tuple t *subsumes* another tuple s if, for every attribute, either t and s have the same value or s has a null value and t does not. The integrity property is that all relation instances must be subsumption free; they must not contain any two tuples where one subsumes the other.

Interinstance integrity. The multiple instances of a relation must be consistent. This consistency is defined in terms of the filter function that produces a lower-level instance ($R_{c'}$) from a higher-level instance (R_c):

1. For every tuple of R_c whose apparent key classification is dominated by c', there is a tuple of $R_{c'}$ with
   a. For each key attribute, the same data value and classification as in R_c.
   b. For each nonkey attribute with classification dominated by c', the same data value and classification as in R_c.
   c. For other attributes, null value and the same classification as the key.
2. There are no other tuples in $R_{c'}$.

Polyinstantiation integrity. This property, which defines the meaning of the primary key in a multilevel relation, is needed because a multilevel relation can have multiple tuples with the same apparent key. Polyinstantiation integrity is satisfied if and only if, for every relation instance, for all attributes, $AK, C_{AK}, C_i \rightarrow A_i$. That is, the apparent key, in conjunction with the classifications of the key and of the attribute, functionally determines the value of the attribute. The primary key (in the functional-dependence sense) is the union of the apparent key and the classification attributes.

Polyinstantiation. As seen in polyinstantiation integrity, a multilevel relation may contain several tuples for the same primary key value. These tuples have the same "name" but different access classes. This is *polyinstantiation.* Its purpose is to prevent low-level users from inferring the existence of higher-level data. This inference problem can arise when a person with low clearance assigns an identifier, not knowing that the same identifier has been used for another real-world entity. Suppose that GreatStuff supplies some military customers and that an Army-base tuple in *customers* is known only to high-level users. When Lisa (a low-level user) assigns the Army-base *customer-#* to a new customer, the system cannot inform Lisa of the conflict, since this would be an insecure information flow. Rather, a new tuple is added; it has the same *customer-#* but represents a different customer. This is called *entity polyinstantiation:* A relation has multiple tuples with the same apparent primary key but different classifications for that key. A similar problem occurs on update of attributes, but there the result is two tuples referring to the same real-world entity. This is called *attribute polyinstantiation.* Polyinstantiation can be used deliberately to provide *cover stories.* For example, low-clearance users may see "military exercises" as the reason for troop movements, while high-clearance users see "staging for invasion."

Different approaches to polyinstantiation may be appropriate for different organizations or applications. These approaches have been categorized as follows.

Propagation. New tuples are added to reflect all the combinations of attribute values. The SeaView prototype takes this approach.

Derived data. For any real-world entity there is only one tuple per access class, and all its attributes have the same classification. A Secret user who wants to modify an Unclassified tuple inserts a new tuple, specifying that some of its attributes are derived from the Unclassified tuple. The Lock Data Views project follows this approach.

Visible restrictions. Users are aware that data are restricted to certain levels; the database is more "honest." This approach has several variations, including letting users control what polyinstantiation they see. One possibility is to show users a special *restricted* value in place of high-level values.

Other aspects of the model. Extending the relational model for multilevel security is complex, and many problems are unresolved. Topics not covered here include alternatives to polyinstantiation, referential integrity, the semantics of update, and algorithms for decomposition and recovery. The Bibliographic Notes point out references on these topics.

Concurrency control

Concurrency control for standard database systems is fairly well understood, but the standard solutions do not apply for multilevel systems because schedulers may introduce covert channels. Suppose, for example, that a write action of an Unclassified transaction is delayed until a Secret transaction completes (to provide consistent reads for the Secret transaction). By varying the duration of the Secret transaction, the Secret subject can pass information to the Unclassified subject. This is a timing channel. Also, two different schedules can produce different read values. If a Secret subject can determine which value is seen by the Unclassified subject, there is a storage channel. Covert channels also may exist if one transaction can cause another to be rolled back. (Terms for security against these three types of problems are *delay-security, value-security,* and *recovery-security.*) Covert channels may arise from a scheduler's protocols, its implementation, or both.

One possible solution to these problems is to use *multiversion schedulers,* which allow multiple versions of data elements to exist in the database. The motivation is that covert channels arise from contention for shared resources, and multiple versions reduce contention. The *time-stamp ordering* (MVTO) algorithm for standard databases assigns a unique timestamp (the starting time) to a transaction and all its operations. Data items can exist in multiple versions, each with a *read timestamp* and a *write timestamp*. The read timestamp equals the timestamp of the most recent read operation. When a data item is written, a new version is created with a write timestamp equal to the write operation's timestamp. A read operation uses the *appropriate* version—the version with the most recent write timestamp earlier than the operation's timestamp. A write cannot proceed if its timestamp is later than the read timestamp of its appropriate version.

When an operation cannot proceed, the transaction is rolled back. Although the standard MVTO algorithm is not secure for multilevel systems, it can be modified for security.

The scheduler's security depends on both its algorithms and its architecture. If the scheduler runs as a trusted subject, high-level assurance may be difficult or impossible. Not only is a scheduler complex, but it works closely with other complex DBMS components such as buffer management and recovery. For this reason, some schedulers are implemented as multiple single-level subjects whose behavior is constrained by the underlying trusted operating system. The operating system's security policy limits communication of the single-level schedulers to one direction—from low to high. The multilevel input stream is broken down by access class, with each request going to the appropriate scheduler, which produces an output schedule for its access class. It must be shown that these single-level schedules together have the same effect as the multilevel schedule.

Architectures for multilevel secure database systems

A multilevel secure DBMS has to succeed on several fronts. It must provide both multilevel database access and the other functions that users expect from DBMSs. It must perform adequately. It must be practical to implement, without, for example, building an entire new DBMS. Finally, the design and implementation must provide a basis for assurance at the target evaluation class. With respect to assurance, the two main architectural approaches are called *TCB subset* and *trusted subject.* Each has several variations (Fig. 9.4).

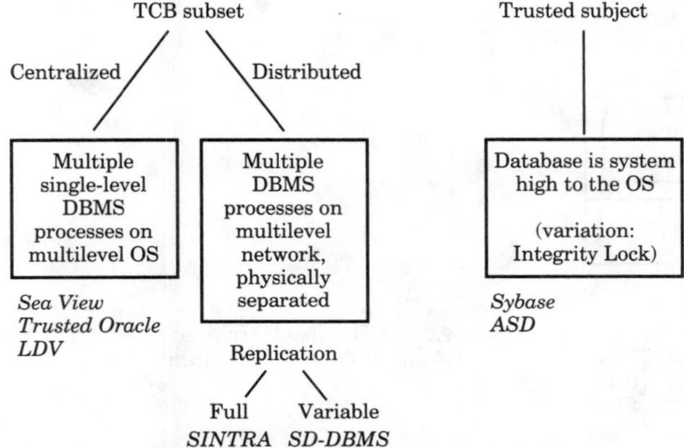

Figure 9.4 Architectures for multilevel secure DBMSs.

TCB subset architectures. The term *Trusted Computing Base* (TCB) refers to the totality of mechanisms in a system that are responsible for enforcing the security policy. A *TCB subset* is a TCB that is built on other TCBs or TCB subsets. Thus a multilevel DBMS might rely on a trusted multilevel file system, which in turn relies on a trusted multilevel microkernel. The idea of TCB subsets was used by Thomas Hinke and Marvin Schaefer (1975) in the first design for a multilevel secure DBMS—the Secure Data Management System. This system (never implemented) was designed to run on a secure Multics operating system. The design used the Multics directory structure in such a way that the DBMS had no security-relevant code; it relied entirely on secure Multics to enforce security.

The *Trusted Database Management System Interpretation* (TDI) emphasizes TCB subsets as a general approach for building and evaluating systems as components. The terms *strict* and *constrained* TCB subset refer to the pure form of the approach, where the DBMS TCB subset is constrained by the policies of the underlying operating system, and none of the DBMS operates as a trusted subject.

For DBMSs, the TCB subset approach can take a centralized or distributed form. With the centralized form, a trusted operating system enforces mandatory access control, and an untrusted DBMS does the database work. Multiple instances of the DBMS run as processes, each at a single access class, as shown in Fig. 9.5. The database is stored in single-level fragments, and each untrusted DBMS process works on single-level fragments. Additional code decomposes and recovers multilevel relations, so users work with their accustomed relational view of the database. The trusted OS enforces mandatory

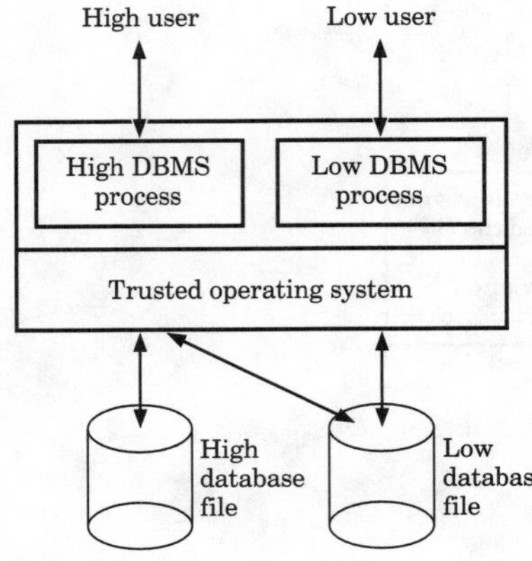

Figure 9.5 TCB subset architecture. (*From Polk and Bassham 1993.*)

access control on the stored data and on the DBMS instances. The untrusted DBMS enforces discretionary access control.

The great advantage of the TCB subset approach is its potential for high assurance—as high as the underlying operating system. The DBMS can be evaluated without having to reevaluate the OS, and the DBMS is more portable. Another advantage is that a commercial DBMS product can be used. There are disadvantages as well. Polyinstantiation is required, and the data model becomes highly complex. The DBMS instances cannot enforce any integrity constraints that involve data higher than their level. Implementing concurrency control in the DBMS without introducing covert channels is difficult. Assurance for discretionary access control is only as great as for the DBMS. Projects using the centralized TCB subset approach include SeaView, Trusted Oracle, and LOCK Data Views (LDV).

The distributed approach uses multiple untrusted "back-end" DBMSs, each running at a single level. In the *fully replicated* version of this architecture, each back-end DBMS contains replicated data from all lower classes. A trusted front-end processor sends each query to the appropriate back-end. There is no need to modify the query, since each DBMS has all the data it needs to handle the queries it receives. This approach has the assurance advantages of the centralized approach, with the additional protection of physical separation. The hard problem here is keeping the replicated data consistent without introducing insecure information flows. Since a separate machine is needed for each access class, the approach cannot handle a large number of classes. The SINTRA project uses this approach. The SD-DBMS project used a distributed *partially replicated* architecture.

Trusted subject architectures. With trusted subject architectures (Fig. 9.6), the DBMS runs at the system-high level on a trusted operating system. Either the entire database is stored as system-

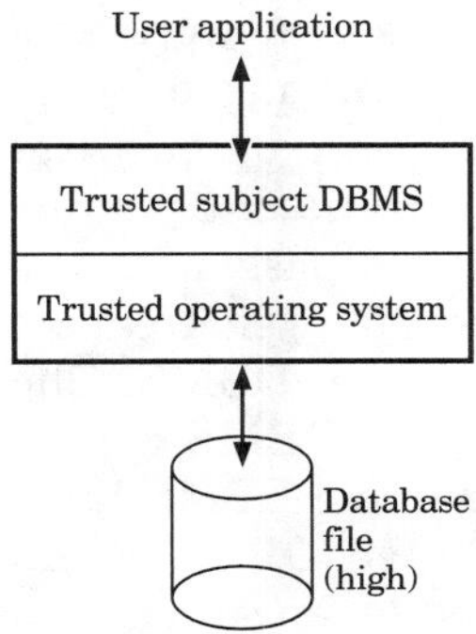

Figure 9.6 Trusted subject architecture. (*From Polk and Bassham 1993.*)

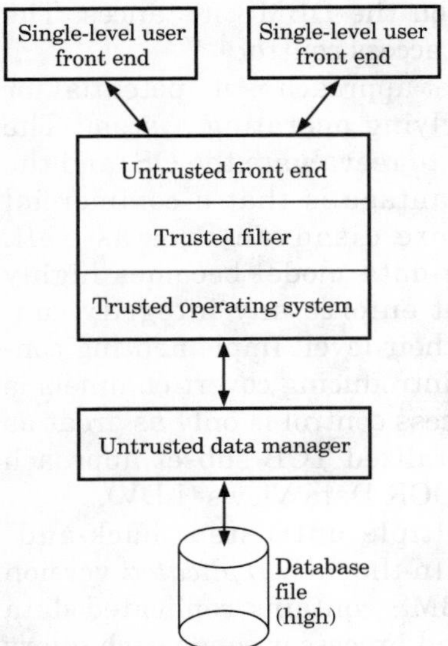

Figure 9.7 Integrity lock architecture. (*From Polk and Bassham 1993.*)

high files, or each multilevel relation is stored at its highest access class. The DBMS is completely responsible for enforcing security policy on the database. The main advantage of this architecture is that database function is not sacrificed; a standard DBMS can be enhanced with multilevel security without losing other functions. For example, interlevel integrity constraints can be enforced. The main disadvantage is that high assurance is very difficult. The products based on the trusted subject architecture have aimed at the B1 level rather than higher classes. They have provided tuple-level mandatory access control.

A trusted subject is used differently in the *integrity lock* architecture (Fig. 9.7)—as a trusted filter. An untrusted front-end communicates with the user and handles database operations that work at a single level. Database objects and their labels are managed by an untrusted DBMS that operates at system-high. The trusted filter attaches labels to data and generates cryptographic checksums (integrity locks). It also filters the results of selection, passing to the front-end only those tuples which are accessible to the user. Updates are done by the trusted filter and passed back to the DBMS. The main advantage of this approach is that a standard DBMS can be used, although the trusted filter also needs considerable DBMS function. The main disadvantage is that the untrusted DBMS could (albeit with difficulty) leak higher-level information by encoding it in lower-level data.

Multilevel secure DBMS products

Multilevel secure DBMS products have been developed by Informix (Online/Secure), Oracle (Trusted Oracle7), Sybase (Secure SQL Server 10), and Ingres (Ingres/Enhanced Security). Each of these has received the TCSEC B1 rating, and Ingres received the ITSEC E3/F-B1 rating. The following subsections describe the Oracle and Sybase products.

Trusted Oracle. *Trusted Oracle* is a version of Oracle that provides mandatory access control at the tuple or row level. Users see multilevel tables with labeled rows. Each relation has a special column, *rowlabel,* whose value is the access class of the row. SQL statements can refer to the *rowlabel* column as well as to the user's current access class.

Trusted Oracle has two alternative modes of operation, which correspond to the architectural alternatives of constrained TCB subset and trusted subject. In *OS MAC mode,* Trusted Oracle relies on the underlying secure OS to enforce the mandatory security policy. In *DBMS MAC mode,* Trusted Oracle itself enforces mandatory access control. In OS MAC mode, data are stored in single-level files at their access class; in DBMS MAC mode, multilevel data are stored in a file whose access class dominates all data in the file. In both modes, the DBMS handles discretionary access control. DBMS MAC mode provides *MAC privileges*—**writedown, writeup,** and **readup**—that allow users to violate security policy. Of course, these are not secure, but they facilitate applications such as reclassifying data. In OS MAC mode, there is an instance of Trusted Oracle for each access class.

For concurrency control, the default level of isolation allows unrepeatable reads, but users can structure transactions to achieve serializability. Each transaction has a single access class—the access class of the subject—and each action of the transaction has that same access class. Two classes of transactions are defined in order to achieve both security and high concurrency with a mixture of high-volume update transactions and long-running reporting transactions. Concurrency control for read-only transactions uses a modified MVTO. Read-write transactions use two-phase locking at their access class and modified MVTO to read lower access classes. The scheduler algorithms do not support a security model that allows writing up.

SYBASE Secure SQL Server. Like Trusted Oracle, the SYBASE Secure SQL Server enforces mandatory access control at the row level. Unlike Trusted Oracle, it follows the trusted subject architecture and does not rely on the operating system to enforce security policy—MAC or DAC. However, the OS must protect the files containing the DBMS data. This can be done by OS access control—giving access only to the DBMS process—or by dedicating a machine to the Secure SQL Server. System security officers can create and "certify" trusted stored procedures and triggers, which can be used to enforce multilevel integrity constraints or to downgrade information. Each table is assigned a range of labels that are permissible for its rows. Each trigger is also assigned a label or labels. Database functions can refer to labels.

Multilevel secure DBMS research projects

Several research designs and prototypes have been developed, some of them aimed at class A1 evaluation. Four systems are described here whose architectures are quite different.

SeaView. The SeaView project at SRI International developed a multilevel relational data model and implemented a prototype. SeaView users or their applications can create multilevel relations and perform queries on them, using an extended SQL called *MSQL.* A user obtains the results appropriate for his or her access class. When creating tables, users specify for each attribute or attribute-group a range of acceptable classifications. For example,

```
create table projects (
projno integer primary key check (label in (SECRET)),
group (proj-name char(20), budgets integer) not null
check (label in (SECRET, TOP-SECRET)),
);
```

For this table, the primary key must always be labeled SECRET, and the group of other columns must always be labeled either SECRET or TOP SECRET. Any new data from inserts and updates are assigned the current class of the user. (SeaView does not allow write up.) To preserve polyinstantiation integrity, updates may cause new tuples to be created. Selection operations can use classification level functions, as in

```
select * showlabel from projects where
class(projno) = class(proj-name);
```

Users also may select the highest, lowest, or most recent of polyinstantiated data. The **showlabel** keyword causes the access class labels to be displayed, and a predefined column named *rowlabel* returns the tuple class. However, the labels are "advisory" only, since there is no trusted path from the OS to the user. Integrity constraints involving multiple classes cannot be enforced, since they would introduce covert channels.

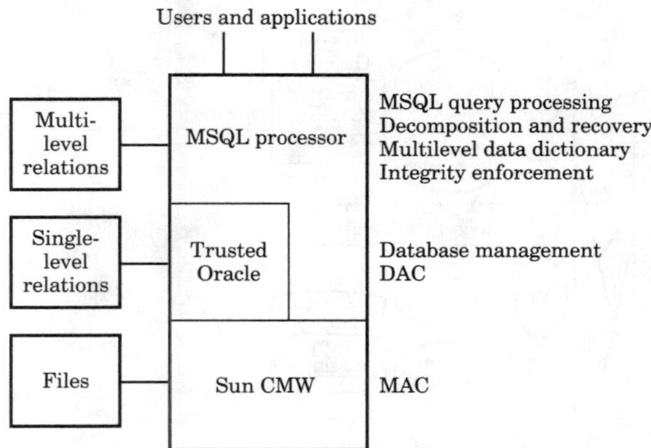

Figure 9.8 Architecture of the SeaView prototype.

SeaView uses a strict TCB subset design, as shown in Fig. 9.8. The bottom layer is a trusted operating system, Sun CMW. SeaView relies on the trusted OS to enforce mandatory access control. The next layer is the Trusted Oracle DBMS, which carries out SQL operations on single-level relations. Trusted Oracle was chosen because it provides multiple database servers, each operating at a single level and because (in OS-MAC mode) it runs untrusted. SeaView relies on Trusted Oracle for discretionary access control. Above these two layers is the SeaView MSQL processor, which creates multilevel relations and supports operations on them. All database processing is done by single-level processes, which are fully constrained by the trusted operating system.

When a user creates a multilevel table, SeaView creates a set of corresponding single-level Oracle tables. It also creates a view (a relation instance) for each access class at which the multilevel table is visible. All this is transparent to the user. The MSQL processor translates MSQL queries on multilevel relations into SQL queries on single-level relations. After DBMS processing, it assembles an appropriate result for the multilevel query. It enforces the multilevel integrity conditions, including referential integrity. Although Trusted Oracle provides only tuple-level MAC, SeaView stores its data in Oracle tables so as to achieve element-level MAC enforced by the trusted OS. An element's access class is derived from the class of the single-level relation (and thus the file) in which the element is stored. However, discretionary access control is at the tuple level only, and its assurance is that of Trusted Oracle.

SINTRA. The SINTRA prototype, developed by the Naval Research Laboratory, has a distributed replicated architecture. The system con-

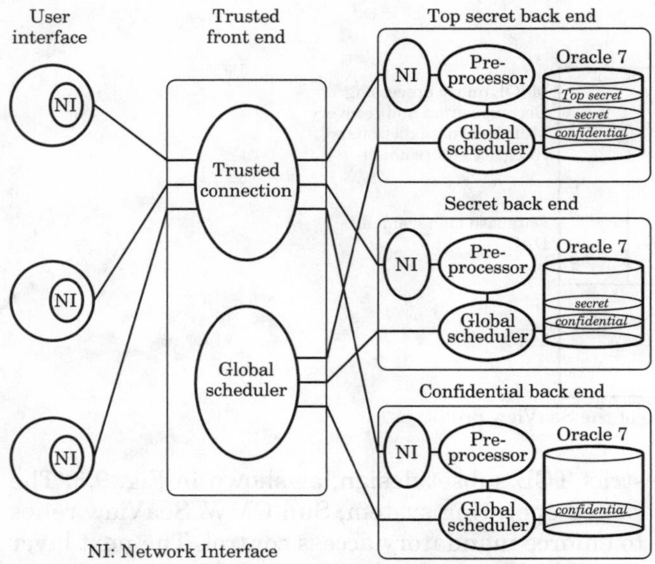

Figure 9.9 The SINTRA architecture. (*From Kang et al. 1994.*)

sists of a trusted front-end (TFE) that communicates with multiple untrusted back-end DBMSs (UBDs), one for each access class, as shown in Fig. 9.9. The TFE is trusted to connect a user only to the UBD at the user's access class. The UBDs are standard DBMS products (Oracle in the prototype). Each UBD holds all the data for its access class and all lower ones. For example, the Secret UBD holds Secret and Unclassified data. This means that any access request can be handled by a UBD in its usual manner. Physical separation and the trusted connection provided by the TFE enforce mandatory access control with very little trusted code. The UBDs enforce discretionary access control. The TFE changes the database state only through queries. A *query preprocessor* at each UBD (1) rejects or modifies queries to prevent a high-level user from modifying low-level data at the high-level UBD, (2) ensures the integrity of tuple labels and other system-maintained information, and (3) translates multilevel SQL queries into the SQL supported by the UBDs.

SINTRA must maintain the consistency of the replicated data without violating security policy. It does this with a *global scheduler,* which is implemented with components on the TFE and each UBD. Finding the usual transaction model inadequate for their needs, SINTRA researchers developed a three-layer model in which a transaction is a sequence of *queries,* and a query is a sequence of reads and writes. Two operations at the same layer conflict if they operate on the same data item and at least one of them is an update. The *update projection* of a transaction includes only its update queries—the only queries that need to be propagated to other UBDs. The TFE manages the propagation of updates.

Each UBD has a *local scheduler* (simply its normal scheduler) that deals with conflicts at the read-write layer. The global scheduler deals with conflicts at the query and transaction layers. The local scheduler imposes a transaction serialization order, and the global scheduler ensures that the same order is maintained at the higher-level UBDs. Otherwise, the database replicas could become inconsistent. The global-scheduler instance for access class *c* receives queries from the preprocessor and from lower-level global schedulers and sends them to UBD_c. When a transaction commits, the global scheduler sends an update projection to all higher-level UBDs.

Advanced Secure DBMS. *Advanced Secure DBMS* (ASD) is a research prototype developed at TRW that aimed at A1 evaluation. ASD provides tuple-level mandatory access control. Access denial as well as permission is supported, and each can be specified for an individual, a group, or the public. If a denial and a permission conflict, ASD uses the following rules: A more specific authorization takes precedence over a less specific one; at the same specificity, denial takes precedence over permission.

ASD is implemented as a network server, whose clients are at different access classes. It follows a trusted-subject architecture, with its TCB enforcing both discretionary and mandatory security. Much of the code is untrusted, however; it runs at the access class of the user's session. A trusted interface ensures that each query goes to the proper instance of the untrusted code. ASD relies on the underlying operating system for integrity of both the database and the ASD TCB. The database is stored (conceptually) as one big file, whose access class is the least upper bound of all the tuples. Since untrusted processes might be classified as high as this file, it must be protected against their modifying it. This protection comes from the operating system's enforcement of the Biba integrity policy (see Chap. 4). The database file is assigned an integrity compartment label; since the ASD TCB is the only subject with the same integrity compartment, only it can directly write the database file.

LOCK Data Views. The LOCK Data Views (LDV) design was developed at Secure Technology Computing Center of Honeywell. LDV uses the LOCK trusted operating system (see Chap. 7), whose mandatory security policy includes type enforcement. Each object has a type, and each subject is associated with a domain. Domains are limited in their rights to types. The Domain Definition Table might specify, for example, that only a subject in domain *exporter* can execute *trusted export code*. LOCK also provides assured pipelines, which guarantee that data pass between domains only through trusted import and export filters

LDV extends the LOCK security policy with a classification policy that supports three types of classification. *Name-dependent* classification rules (the usual type) refer to data items by name, at the granularity of relations and attributes. *Content-dependent* classification rules refer to data item values, providing granularity of tuples and elements. For example, salaries over $150,000 might be classified differently from other salaries. *Context-dependent* classification rules refer to combinations of items. For example, name and salary together might be classified higher than either alone. Context includes not just the current query but the user's history of queries. Since LDV uses multiple classification criteria, the results of a query may have a set of labels. Access is allowed only if the subject's access class dominates the dominant label of the set.

LDV enforces its policy with three assured pipelines. Each pipeline has both untrusted and trusted subjects—based on security needs. This architecture encapsulates and constrains the LDV components. Data are stored in single-level files at the level determined by name-dependent classification; they may have to be upgraded for the context-based access class. There is no replication of data at different levels. The query processor builds, for each base relation in a query, a partial relation representing the user's view; any remaining query processing uses these partial relations.

Security for Object-Oriented Databases

The object-oriented approach (summarized in Chap. 6) has an important place in computer security. Contemporary operating systems are based on the object model, and secure systems are developed using object-oriented modeling, design, and programming. Object-oriented concepts apply very well to databases and to database security.

Object-oriented database management systems

An object-oriented database management system (OODBMS) implements the object-oriented model. OODBMSs have advantages that make them increasingly popular. Although OODBMS products lag relational DBMSs in security, research has been done on both discretionary and mandatory access control and on integrity.

Authorization models for discretionary access control

Models of authorization describe how security policy is expressed as authorization rules or authorizations. An authorization rule has the form

$$(s,o,a,p)$$

specifying that subject s has access of type a to those occurrences of o for which predicate p is true. For o we use the term *authorization-object* to distinguish it from the object of the object model. The current set of authorizations is called the *authorization base*. Authorization models define how the authorization base is interpreted to validate access requests.

Authorization issues. Traditional authorization models do not address the special characteristics of object-oriented databases, such as methods, inheritance, and *composite objects*. Objects encompass both data and procedures. Since all information access and modification is through methods, and since methods are invoked by sending them messages, the flow of information is explicit. Since objects have relationships with one another, such as *component-of* or *subclass-of*, authorizations specified for one object might reasonably imply authorizations for another. One topic of research, then, is *implied authorization*. Implied authorization can save storage space and, more important, can make the authorizer's work simpler and more accurate. The case for implied authorization is stronger for object-oriented systems than for relational systems because OODBMSs often are used for component hierarchies, which provide a basis for implied authorization. Some researchers believe the class hierarchy does as well.

A defining characteristic of the object-oriented approach is that modelers and developers can work with application-level objects. This should be true for authorizers as well. Authorizing for methods is more appropriate than authorizing at the read-write level; it is closer to application needs and better implements the least-privilege principle. How to model authorization for methods is unclear, since they are both passive, like data objects, and active, like programs and subjects. One possibility is to treat methods as access types. Then the authorization model would require of each authorization for object o that the access type a is a method of o. Another possibility is to treat them as authorization-objects. The model must consider that one method m_1 may invoke another m_2 on the same object or a different one. Suppose that the user is not authorized to invoke m_2 directly, but only through m_1. If the invocation of m_2 is validated against the user's authorizations, it will fail. One proposed solution treats methods as subjects (with certain restrictions).

Relational DBMSs enforce conditional authorization (content-dependent, for example) through views or query modification. With an OODBMS, conditional access to method *m* might be accomplished by granting access to *m´*, which is derived from *m*. Method *m´* checks the conditions. The problem—as with all procedural enforcement of access control—is that the conditions are buried in the code. Also, method development becomes more complicated. Alternatively, a *guard* method could be associated with *m* and invoked when *m* is invoked. The guard method checks the conditions before invoking *m*. Finally, conditions could be specified in the predicate of the authorization rule, to be enforced by the OODBMS access control mechanism. OpenODB, an object-oriented DBMS, associates guards with authorization rules. When a user group is granted the privilege to call a function (the OpenODB equivalent of a method), the grant can specify a predicate. When the function is invoked, the invocation argument is used to evaluate the predicate. If the predicate returns *true,* the function is invoked with that argument. Suppose, for example, that we want to grant Supervisor the privilege to modify the salary for part-time employees. First, a function SalaryGuard is created that returns *true* if the employee is part-time. Then the privilege to call the salary-assignment function is granted to Supervisor "if SalaryGuard."

ORION model of authorization. The most complete model of authorization for object-oriented databases was developed for the ORION system at Microelectronics and Computer Technology Corporation. This work is based on implied authorization and two other concepts: (1) positive and negative authorization and (2) strong and weak authorization. A positive authorization states that a subject has access, and a negative authorization states that a subject has *no* access. (The TCSEC use the term *denial* for negative authorization.) A strong authorization cannot be overridden—nor can any of its implied authorizations. Weak authorizations can be overridden by other authorizations. Consider, for example, an inventory database with *Truck* and *Auto* classes. A user who is granted a strong write authorization on *Inventory* has implied write authorization on all objects in *Inventory.* If, instead, the user has a weak write authorization on *Inventory,* the situation is different. Then an explicit weak negative write authorization on *Truck* overrides what is implied for *Inventory.* If the user has a weak negative read authorization for class *Auto,* then an exception for one instance of *Auto* can be implemented by a strong positive read authorization for that instance.

To simplify the handling of subjects, authorization-objects, and access types, the model considers each in a lattice structure, where the directed arcs between nodes represent implication. Users are grouped according to role, and authorizations are granted to roles. The roles form a lattice, with each node representing a role and each role getting all the authorizations of all its descendants. Authorization types also form an implication lattice. For example, **write** implies **read,** which implies **read definition.** The lattice can be extended to associate the grant option with a type. (An ordering would be hard to define, however, if authorization types included methods.)

The model defines *authorization-objects.* Rather than just class *Auto,* for example, there are two authorization-objects: class *Auto* and its set of instances—*Auto-instances.* If this were not done, more authorization types would be needed—since updating the class definition has a very different meaning from updating the location of an auto. The authorization objects also form an implication lattice. For example, an arc from *Auto-instances* to *Instance-1* means that an authorization on *Auto-instances* implies the same authorization on *Instance-1.* Each node in the lattice belongs to one *authorization-object type,* and the types form an *authorization-object schema* (AOS), from which the lattice is derived. For each node of the AOS, only certain authorization types are meaningful or "correct," and only correct authorizations are stored in the authorization base. The AOS provides a flexible way to define how implied authorization works for a specific database.

Using the framework that has been sketched, rules of the model specify how to compute authorizations. The model has been applied to class hierarchies, composite objects, and versions. A key issue is how implied authorization should work for a class hierarchy. It is important not to discourage the reuse of existing classes to form new classes; this might be the result if authorization to a class implied authorization to a subclass. This model's default policy is that the creator of a class has no implied authorizations on instances of subclasses. The alternative policy is supported as a user option. Composite-object hierarchies are treated differently. Implied authorization allows a composite object to be a unit of authorization. The AOS can be designed so that a user who has an authorization for a composite class *C* has the same authorization for all instances of *C* and all their components.

Implied authorization and administration. Another model featuring implied authorization was developed by Eduardo Fernandez and colleagues (1994a). The following policies are proposed:

- P_1 (inherited authorization): A user who has access to a class C has the same access in subclasses of C to the attributes inherited from C.
- P_2 (class access): Access to a complete class implies access to both the attributes defined in that class and the inherited attributes.
- P_3 (visibility): An attribute defined for a class is not visible by accessing any of its superclasses.

(Policy P_1 differs from ORION's default policy that the class hierarchy does not imply authorization.) Authorization rules can have as their authorization-objects either the entire set of attributes of an object or individual attributes. The model distinguishes administrative access types from others and also distinguishes schema administration from security administration. Administration can be decentralized.

The model introduces the concept of a *security context*—a portion of the schema that is administered as a single unit with respect to security. A security context defines the set of classes that will be considered when a request is validated. An authorization rule is associated with a specific security context. The model includes policies about what happens when administrative units are defined, delegated, and revoked. One policy, for example, is that delegation of schema administration rights must be accompanied by delegation of security administration rights.

A method-based authorization model. Moving toward the goal of authorization for methods, the *method-based* model uses a data model that defines three types of associations between classes: generalization, aggregation, and relationships. The method-based model develops implied-authorization policies for each type of association. Authorization itself uses the same data model, treating subjects and data as objects and authorization as a relationship between them. The method-based model takes the position that authorization for a method implies authorization for all invoked methods.

Models for mandatory access control

Work on mandatory access control is less advanced for object-oriented than for relational databases. Several quite different models have been proposed.

The message filter model. The *message filter model* of Sushil Jajodia and Boris Kogan (1990) does not follow the customary Bell-LaPadula model but deals directly with information flow. Since all changes of state in an object-oriented system result (indirectly) from messages,

messages are the only means of information flow. A message filter acts as a kind of reference monitor, examining each message to determine if it conforms to the security policy and deciding what action is appropriate.

Jajodia and Kogan define an object-oriented model that includes special *User* objects, representing user sessions; user objects can invoke methods spontaneously, whereas ordinary objects invoke methods only in response to messages they receive. Access to internal attributes, invocation of internal methods, and object creation are all implemented by an object sending a message to itself. This means that all activities are explicit in messages.

Every object has a fixed security level, and information cannot legally flow down in level. Information transfer can occur when a message is passed from one object to another. The parameters of the message carry a *forward* flow, and the return value carries a *backward* flow. When an object is created, information flows from the creating to the created object. Flows can be direct or indirect through other objects. Classes and inheritance introduce implicit information flows. These implicit flows become explicit in the model because classification and inheritance are implemented by message passing. The message filter can check the flows.

In order to preserve the functionality of the system (its security is preserved by the message filter), two security-level constraints are needed: (1) an object's security level must dominate the level of its class object, and (2) a class security level must dominate the level of its parent class.

Depending on the type of message and the security levels of sender and receiver, the message filter either lets a message pass, blocks the message, or lets it pass but constrains the resulting method execution. The message filter may set a return value to null to prevent illegal backward flow.

The Millen-Lunt model. Jonathan Millen and Teresa Lunt (1992) propose a different model for a secure object-oriented system. Their object model is based on Smalltalk (an object-oriented programming language and system), and their security model is the multilevel model. Six security properties (to be described) are derived from the object and security models.

The object-system objects are also the security objects. Each object has a fixed security level, and its methods and variables have the same level. The *Hierarchy* property states that the level of an object must dominate the level of its class object. As with the message filter model, this property is necessary because the object must inherit methods and variables from its class object, and that involves reading.

A subject is the entity that executes methods and sends messages. A subject is created when a message is received by an object. That object is the *home* object of the subject. The subject is destroyed when the executed method terminates. *Subject Level* states that the security level of a subject dominates the level of the invoking subject and the level of the home object. This property allows the subject to read the message as well as the variables and methods in the home object. A subject can send messages to any objects, including those at higher levels. However, *Object Locality* states that a subject can execute methods or read or write variables only in its home object. The **-Property* states that a subject may write into its home object only if its security level is equal to that of the object. Subject Level and *-Property together prevent writing up and reading up, and *-Property prevents writing down. *Return Value* states that a subject can return a value to its invoking subject only if the two subjects are at the same security level. As in the message filter model, a null value sometimes must be returned. To avoid a timing channel, the system—not the invoked subject—determines when to return the null value. Also, to avoid covert channels, *Object Creation* states that the security level of a new object dominates the level of the creating subject.

The virtual view and MultiView models. With the *virtual view model,* a user works with a single-level virtual database that is derived from the real multilevel database. The user starts a transaction at a specific security level and performs database operations, which may include updates. If the transaction commits, any updates are propagated into the real multilevel database. This approach is quite simple, because all objects and attribute values in the virtual database have the same level (the current working level) and all processing for a transaction occurs at a single level. No access control is needed until commit time. Some simplifying assumptions are made, however. One such assumption is that the database schema is not protected; that is, every user has access to the classes.

The *MultiView model* shares many assumptions with the virtual view model. The MultiView model decomposes a multilevel database into single-level objects that are stored in different single-level databases, as is done for relational systems. There are *n* different single-level views of a multilevel database. Each view of an object is a single-level object, and there are dynamic links between these view-objects. This arrangement exploits the fact that several objects can share the same subobject. Consider, for example, two instances O_1 and O_2 of a class *person* with attribute *father* (also of class *person*). O_1 and O_2 share the same father, O_3. For O_1 the *father* value is (O_3,U), where U is Unclassified. But the identity of O_2's father is classified

Secret. The Unclassified-view value for O_2's *father* is "Secret"—the level value. The Confidential-view value is (O_2,U.*father*)—pointing to the Unclassified instance—and the Secret-view value is (O_3,U). Since O_1 and O_2 share O_3 as father, any updates to O_3 are reflected to both.

Clark-Wilson integrity interpretation

Although the properties of object-oriented database systems support integrity, it is usually left to designers of the databases and applications to take advantage of this support. Progress is needed in both systematic design approaches and DBMS function. A model developed by William Herndon (1994) interprets the Clark-Wilson model of integrity (described in Chap. 4) for object-oriented systems and suggests how database designers and DBMSs can support sophisticated integrity constraints. The model introduces the notion of a *restricted class* and identifies three integrity techniques to be used in constructing classes.

A restricted class is one whose methods all have been *certified* (in the Clark-Wilson sense) to preserve the integrity of the class instances; each method can be considered a well-formed transaction. The instances of a restricted class (called *restricted objects*) correspond to the Clark-Wilson *constrained data items* (CDIs). In addition to having certified methods, a restricted class must conform to three restrictions:

1. All methods not explicitly defined must be inherited from a restricted superclass.
2. No method may act on the return value from an instance of a nonrestricted class. This prevents certified methods from depending on results of uncertified methods.
3. No method of a nonrestricted superclass may be invoked.

Herndon identifies three *class construction techniques*—ways to design classes so that integrity constraints may be applied. The class construction techniques are

1. *Incremental constraints.* "Wherever possible, enforcement of superclass and subclass constraints should be decoupled." The idea here is to take advantage of the class hierarchy to enforce general and specific constraints in the appropriate place. Consider, for example, a class hierarchy from a database of the Bigtown city government. Class *Employee* is a subclass of class *Person.* The method *Person:setAddress* enforces general constraints about the format and values of addresses. The method *Employee:setAddress*

enforces an additional constraint that the employee's address is in Bigtown. *Employee:setAddress* checks the employee-specific constraint and then invokes its parent's *setAddress* to check the general constraints and set the address.

2. *Restricted class cloning.* It is useful to design a restricted class C_R that is a copy of its nonrestricted immediate superclass C. Then it is possible to add new subclasses of C for which the constraints of C_R are too stringent. This design also makes it easier to convert nonrestricted objects to restricted objects (UDIs to CDIs in Clark-Wilson terms).
3. *Constraint decoupling.* Constraint checks should be separated from state transformations and implemented within their own methods. For example, method *Person.setAddress* invokes method *checkAddress*. This decoupling clearly distinguishes constraints, and it allows an external integrity verification object (the Clark-Wilson IVP) to invoke all the constraint methods for an object.

Clark-Wilson integrity requires enforcing authorization (the access triple) and the relations between transformation procedures and CDIs. For these, Herndon suggests a mechanism similar to the message filter.

Inference

The *inference* problem arises when authorized information enables a user to infer something about information that is not authorized. The user combines information obtained from the database with outside knowledge or with the results of previous database queries. The inference problem is especially important for multilevel databases and for databases that protect privacy by revealing only statistics rather than specific values. This section first discusses security of statistical databases. It then describes research, in the context of multilevel secure databases, on inference and the related problem of aggregation. Although inference has been studied separately for statistical and multilevel databases, there is much commonality. For statistical databases, however, the goal is to give users the big picture without revealing the details, whereas for multilevel databases the goal often is to give users the details without revealing the big picture.

Statistical databases

Sometimes database access is limited to statistical measures, such as counts or sums. The motivation is to allow use of the database for information dissemination and research, while keeping individual data values confidential. Typically, the confidential data are about people whose privacy must be respected. This may be a matter of law or ethics, or the organization that collected the data may have pledged secrecy in order to obtain the data. Government census data and economic survey data, for example, are available only as macrostatistics (such as counts or sums) or as "deidentified" *microdata.* A more complex example is a medical database that supports both physicians and researchers. Physicians read and update the individual data, whereas researchers access only statistical measures. A statistical database that supports updating concurrently with research use is called *dynamic.*

Concepts and terminology. A *statistical database* (SDB) is a database whose users may retrieve only aggregate statistics. Statistical database security has its own terminology, which differs from other database and security terminology. A *query* is a statistical function (such as sum, count, or median) applied to a subset of records in the database; the subset of records is called the *query set.* The query set is specified by a *characteristic formula C,* such as

$$C = (\text{Age} = 35)\ \&\ (\text{Employer} = \text{BioWidget})\ \&\ (\text{Diagnosis} = \text{AIDS})$$

The characteristic formula is a logical formula over the attributes of some entity—hospital patients in this example. Some attributes of an entity—such as Diagnosis—are confidential. An example of a query is

Q1: COUNT (Age = 35) & (Employer = BioWidget)

The COUNT in query Q1 is a *two-order* statistic, because it involves two attributes.

The *user* of the SDB is authorized only to retrieve aggregate statistics. (Other persons may be authorized to directly read and update data, but they are outside the model used for SDBs.) A *database administrator* (DBA) is responsible for setting security policy and protecting the security of the database. The goal is to release no *sensitive* statistics that can be used to infer individual attribute values or other sensitive statistics. A user who tries to make improper use of authorized data is called a *snooper.* A snooper is assumed to have a priori or supplementary knowledge. Suppose that a snooper knows the age and employer of person *X.* After issuing query Q1 and getting an answer of one, the snooper knows how to retrieve information about *X.* For example, the snooper can issue the query

Q2: COUNT (Age = 35) & (Employer = BioWidget) &
(Diagnosis = AIDS)

After query Q2, the database has been *compromised.* That is, the snooper can infer the value of a confidential attribute—in this case that X does or does not have AIDS. A compromise (or disclosure) occurs if queries enable a snooper to infer the value of a confidential attribute. Compromise can be *exact* or *partial.*

A lattice model for statistical databases. The lattice model developed by Dorothy Denning and Jan Schlörer (1983) has been used to understand the statistical inference problem and evaluate its solutions. The model is influenced by the methods that government census bureaus use for publishing their data.

The SDB can be thought of as a set of relations, one for each entity, such as Patient. The tuples (called *records*) correspond to individuals. A relation has M attributes. Derived from the relations are *tables,* which partition the individuals in the database into categories by attribute values. Each table is associated with a statistic (such as count) and with m of the M attributes; the table is m-dimensional and is called an *m-table.* Each cell of a table represents a specific combination of attribute values—a *category*—and the cell contains a statistic computed over all the records in the category. From an m-table, it is possible to compute the statistics for all possible subsets of records over the m attributes.

This *tabular form* describes the information of the SDB at different levels of aggregation. For each statistic, there are 2^M tables, and these tables form a lattice, where table T1>T2 means that T1's attribute set is a subset of T2's. For example, a one-dimensional table partitioned by Employer is greater than a two-dimensional table partitioned by Age and Employer. Figure 9.10 shows a set of count tables for the patient database, and Figure 9.11 shows the corresponding lattice. For additive statistics, such as counts, the statistics in one table are the marginal sums of cell values in the table below it in the lattice. For example, table S shows a count of 163 for Male, which is the sum over all Employers in table SE. It is this relationship between tables that allows inferences to be made.

Overview of safeguards. Researchers have proposed criteria for evaluating security safeguards. These criteria include

1. *Security.* The level of protection against exact and partial disclosure.
2. *Robustness.* How well the method holds up under assumptions that snoopers have supplementary knowledge.
3. *Suitability for both numerical and categorical attributes.*

Table *All*
310

Table *A*			
Age			
0–20	21–45	46–65	>65
52	39	119	100

Table *S*	
Sex	
M	F
163	147

Table *E*		
Employer		
Unemployed	ABC-Co.	XYZ-Co.
162	26	122

Table *AS*				
	Age			
	0–20	21–45	46–65	>65
Sex				
M	25	23	66	49
F	27	16	53	51

Table *AE*				
	Age			
	0–20	21–45	46–65	>65
Employer				
Unemployed	50	2	10	100
ABC-Co.	0	17	9	0
XYZ-Co.	2	20	100	0

Table *SE*		
	Sex	
	M	F
Employer		
Unemployed	84	78
ABC-Co.	10	16
XYZ-Co.	69	53

Table *ASE*					
		Age			
		0–20	21–45	46–65	>65
Employer					
Unemployed	M	24	2	9	49
	F	26	0	1	51
ABC-Co.	M	0	1	9	0
	F	0	16	0	0
XYZ-Co.	M	1	20	48	0
	F	1	0	52	0

Figure 9.10 Tables at different levels of aggregation. [*Adapted from Adam and Wortmann. Copyright (©) 1989 Association for Computing Machinery, Inc. (ACM). Reprinted by permission.*]

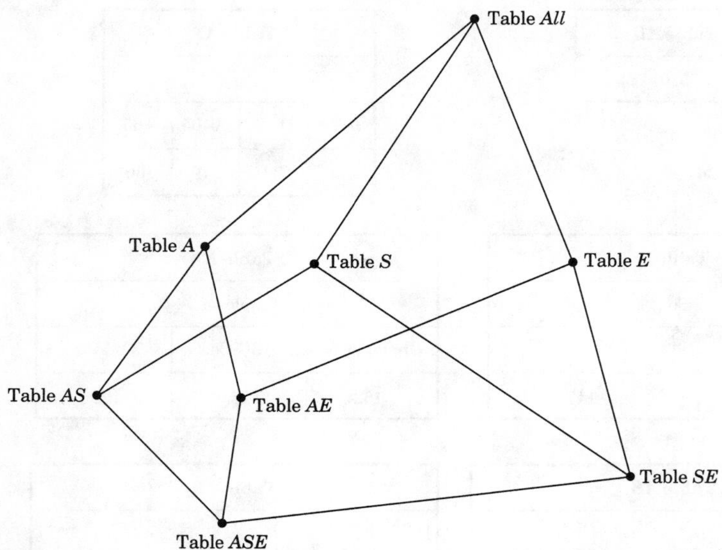

Figure 9.11 Lattice for the tables of Fig. 9.10. [*From Adam and Wortmann. Copyright (©) 1989 Association for Computing Machinery, Inc. (ACM). Reprinted by permission.*]

4. *Suitability to protect more than one confidential attribute.*
5. *Suitability for dynamic SDBs.* Those which are updated while being used for statistics.
6. *Richness of information revealed.* Users should get all relevant nonconfidential information. That is, a minimum of information should be lost, and the information revealed should be unbiased, precise, and consistent. *Consistency* means lacking contradictions (such as different responses to the same query) and paradoxes (such as a negative count value).
7. *Cost.* For implementing the security-control methods, processing overhead, and education of users.

These criteria often conflict, since higher security generally means less rich information and greater cost.

Techniques for protecting statistical database security take two main approaches. One approach restricts the queries that can be made or the data that can be published. Not only confidential values are restricted but also values that can be used to infer confidential values. The second approach introduces noise into either the query responses or the data used to compute statistics. This approach *perturbs* the data or the output. A few techniques are described from each main approach. Most of the techniques are only partial solutions. Some techniques can be combined to further reduce the risk of disclosure.

Restriction techniques

Query-set size control. Early research explored the control of releasing a statistic only if the size of the query set is neither very small or very large. (Large sizes are a problem because a formula *C* defines two query sets—*C* and NOT *C*. Suppose the count of unemployed patients is 2, and the total number of patients is 125. Then a query returning a count of 123 employed patients is just as dangerous as one that returns a count of 2 unemployed patients.) Query-set size control can be subverted easily by a query strategy called a *tracker.* A tracker attack pads small query sets to make them allowable and then subtracts out the results of the padding. Suppose that a snooper has a characteristic formula *C* that uniquely characterizes an individual but is not allowed to use *C* because the query-set size is only 1. The snooper can decompose *C* into two parts that are acceptable to the control and then combine their results. This example is an "individual tracker." A "general tracker" also can be found; it can bypass the query-set size control and can find any statistic with a few queries. Query-set size control remains useful, however, as a criterion for what data may be published, and it enhances the effectiveness of other techniques.

Auditing. The auditing approach keeps a log of all queries made by each user and checks for possible compromise when each new query is issued. The advantage is that restriction or perturbation is not necessary unless compromise is possible. The auditing approach does not, however, take into account possible collusion between users. This technique by itself is inadequate, but keeping a query log is useful in supporting other techniques.

Partitioning. The partitioning approach groups values of attributes and allows queries only within groups. For example, salaries might be partitioned into two or three groups. A group defines an *atomic population*—such as all the employees who earn less than $30,000. It has been shown that under certain conditions, inference is not possible for the protected attributes. The conditions are rather severe, however. One condition concerns the size of the atomic population. Populations of size 1 are not allowed, for example, and studies of real databases showed that such populations are common. Adding dummy records was considered, but such a method introduces bias in the statistics. Another condition limits updating, since that affects the population sizes. For some environments, this would unacceptably limit database usefulness.

Cell suppression. Cell suppression is used for published tables of census data. The technique suppresses (blanks out) all the cells of a table that contain sensitive statistics. These cells are called *primary suppressions.* Also suppressed are cells that could lead indirectly to disclosure of sensitive statistics; these are called *complementary suppressions.* Since interrelated tables are often published together, suppression techniques must take into account multiple tables.

A crucial part of this technique is the criterion for sensitivity. For count statistics, a query-set size criterion often is used. Sums may be considered sensitive if n or fewer values contribute more than k percent of the sum, where the values of n and k are set by the DBA and kept secret. Alternatively, the DBA may set an upper and lower protection level for each cell. These levels specify how precise an estimation of the cell value is permissible. For example, if the cell value is 100 and the upper and lower protection levels are each 15, then a user should be able to learn only that the value is between 85 and 115. It is also important to measure the amount of data suppression so that techniques can try to minimize it. One criterion is the sum of the values of the suppressed cells. Finding primary suppressions is straightforward, but finding complementary suppressions that try to minimize data suppression is an NP-hard computational problem. Linear programming methods have been used to find sets of primary and complementary suppressions that protect security.

Perturbation techniques

Data swapping. The data-swapping technique replaces a database D with another database D' that has completely different records but the same *t-order* statistics. (Recall that a *t-order statistic* is one computed over t attributes.) The database D' can be generated by swapping the attribute values of the records of D. The intent of the method is that any query involving a statistic of *t-order* or lower will get a correct answer. However, the technique introduces sizable error for some queries.

Rounding. Another possible control is to round the answer up or down to the nearest multiple of some base. Three types of rounding have been studied: systematic, random, and controlled. (Controlled rounding perturbs multiple cells of a table so as to preserve the true row and column sums.) Systematic rounding introduces bias and can be circumvented. Random rounding is subject to averaging attacks, where the snooper issues the same query multiple times and averages the results.

Random-sample queries. The random-sample query technique computes the answer to a query on a random sample of the query set. The probability *p* of a record being included in the sample is set by the DBA. The intent is for *p* to be fairly large, e.g., .8 or .9, and for users to know its value. The random-sample technique prevents a snooper from controlling the composition of the query set and thus protects against tracker attacks. The method is vulnerable to averaging attacks, however. If a user poses multiple queries specifying the same query set, a different random sample is used for each, and the user can average the results. This attack is practical if it is automated. A protection would be to detect the equivalence of these queries and use the same sample for each. Another type of averaging attack combines multiple queries whose query sets are disjoint subsets of the original query set.

Random-sample query with query-set size control. Random-sample query is vulnerable to attacks using small query-set sizes. When the two controls are combined, however, security is enhanced. The controls were analyzed using a probabilistic model. The model assumes a database of categorical data, and it analyzes the snooper's subjective probability that a particular individual is in a certain category. Before a query, the snooper has a *prior* probability that the individuals are distributed among categories in a specific way. After a query about any category, this probability is modified for all categories. The risk of disclosure depends on the snooper's *posterior* probabilities. This framework was used to analyze the combined control in the face of tracker attacks. The control was found to be effective unless very many repeated queries are used—a situation that could be detected by audit-trail analysis.

Inference in multilevel secure databases

Multilevel DBMSs must consider the threat from inference. An *inference problem* exists if a user, accessing low-level data, is able to draw conclusions about high-level information. A link or means that may allow inference is called an *inference channel.*

Types of inference channels. Inference is not a single, unified problem; there are different kinds of inference channels requiring different solutions. Channels have been characterized, for example, as deductive, abductive, and statistical. A *deductive* channel allows a formal deductive proof of the high data to be derived from the low data. An *abductive* channel exists if, through assuming certain low-level axioms, a deductive proof becomes possible. These axioms represent a user's knowledge that is not in the database. (Abductive reasoning, which is used in artificial intelligence, is appropriate for finding these additional assumptions that make high data provable from low data.) A *statistical* channel exists when the likelihood of the user's knowing these low-level axioms can be determined.

Another way to describe inference channels is to give specific examples that have been found. Some of these also have straightforward solutions.

Queries using unauthorized data. Consider a database with Unclassified relation *Employee*(*Employee-Name*,*Project-Name*) and Secret relation *Projects*(*Project-Name*,*Project-Type*). An uncleared user can issue a SQL query

```
select employee.employee-name
from employee,project
where employee.project-name = project.project-name
and project.project-type = 'covert-action'
```

Although only Unclassified data are returned, the user has learned which employees work on covert-action projects, thus learning a lot about the projects. The solution is to not allow unauthorized data to be used in query processing.

Integrity constraints. If an integrity constraint involves high data, a low user who knows about the constraint may be able to infer something about high data. One case (described earlier) occurs when a low user tries to add a new tuple with the same primary key as an existing high tuple. Adding the new tuple would violate entity integrity, but rejecting it would let the user know about the existing tuple. This problem can be solved with polyinstantiation. Another problem is a functional dependency that is known to users. Suppose that, for an employee database, *Salary* is considered sensitive and *Rank* is not. However, everyone knows that all employees of the same rank have the same salary. The solution here is to classify *Rank* as sensitive, i.e., assign security labels taking into account functional dependencies.

Integrity constraints may include predicates involving attribute values. If high data constrain updates to low data, the low user can infer something about the high data. For example, if a constraint requires the unclassified *Wage* to be less than the sensitive *WageLimit,* an unclassified payroll clerk can probe *WageLimit* by attempting updates to *Wage.* This is an example of a dynamic inference channel. A static inference channel exists if high data can be inferred from a combination of low data and integrity constraints. Suppose that the sum of all values of some attribute is constrained to be positive. If the sum of the low values is negative, then a low user can infer something about the high values.

Finally, a user who knows classification constraints can make inferences from the system's behavior in revealing or withholding information.

Detecting and eliminating inference channels. Since a user can make inferences based on any knowledge—whether represented in the database or not—it is not practical or even possible to eliminate all inference channels. The best that can be done is to find some channels and eliminate them. Several approaches can be used. One is for designers to follow inference-avoidance guidelines in designing databases. This could at least eliminate some of the inference channels that we have discussed. It would be better, though, if automated tools could detect potential channels by analyzing the database schema and still better if the tools also could take into account outside knowledge. Once inference channels are found, there are two possibilities: eliminate them by redesigning the database or activate mechanisms that monitor them at execution time.

Research at SRI International aims at detecting channels by analyzing the schema with an automated tool called *DISSECT.* The first target was a subclass of deductive channels called *compositional channels.* DISSECT finds potential inference channels by analyzing the relationships that link tables together. A database designer tells DISSECT which attributes could be matched on data value and security level. A linkage from table T_1 to table T_3 may be indirect, through T_2. If there is more than one sequence of relationships between T_1 and T_3 and accessing the different sequences requires different security levels, there may be a compositional channel.

For analysis, the schema is transformed into a graph, where nodes represent attributes and edges represent relationships between them. Foreign keys are represented by edges. Each node and edge is labeled with its security level. A compositional channel exists if two nodes are connected by a pair of paths that may have different security levels. Not all the channels detected reflect real inference problems, however. There is a problem only if the two paths represent the same relationship between the real-world entities. Database designers use the tool interactively, selecting those potential channels which have real significance. Once an inference channel has been identified, it can be eliminated by breaking the links between low and high data; this is done by upgrading some data.

Aggregation. The problem of *aggregation* is closely related to the inference problems. A user who retrieves many data items of the same type (such as tuples of a relation) can learn sensitive information not revealed by just a few of the items. The usual example is the telephone directory for a government agency that carries out secret projects. A user with unlimited access to the directory information could learn, for example, how many people were assigned to a project. On the other hand, classifying the whole directory could seriously hamper operation of the agency. The solution generally proposed is to maintain a history of access and to cut off access after some quota of records has been obtained.

Summary

Database security requirements differ from operating system security requirements. The data objects have a more complex structure, and metadata must be protected. The DBMS's model of authorization may differ from the operating system's model, allowing finer-grained authorization. One object may be a component of another or defined in terms of another. Enforcing the multilevel policy is more difficult. Role-based access control is more important. Transactions must be supported, and concurrency control and recovery are more complex. The audit trail must provide more detailed information. The DBMS can better support Clark-Wilson integrity. Inference must be controlled.

All the leading DBMSs and much security research are based on the relational model. New relations called views can be defined using the basic relational operations of select, project, and join. Views support the principle of least privilege because they can hide attributes or implement content-dependent access restrictions.

For models of authorization, security policy is expressed as authorization rules; a rule specifies that a subject has access of some type to those occurrences of an object for which a predicate is true. For the SQL language, the objects include tables, columns, domains, and views. Views and privileges are the two SQL mechanisms for access control. SQL follows the System R scheme for granting and revoking privileges, which allows any user to create a table. The creator receives all privileges for the table and may grant them to others. A grant recipient may in turn grant a privilege to another user, but only if the grant carries a grant option. The meaning of revoking a granted privilege is that the authorization state after the revoke is the same as if the grant had never occurred.

The SQL-92 standard does not support roles, making security administration difficult. For example, when users change jobs, administrators must review all their privileges and all the privileges they have granted. Extensions to SQL that remedy the problems have been used in some products.

Many integrity safeguards belong in the DBMS, rather than in the operating system or applications. Classes of database integrity safeguards are integrity constraints, concurrency control, and recovery. Transactions are important for all three classes. A transaction is a sequence of database actions that has the properties of atomicity, consistency, isolation, and durability. An integrity constraint may apply either to the database state or to transitions. A constraint specifies the types of updates that may violate the constraint, the predicate that must be satisfied, and the action to be taken on a violation. A trigger can be associated with operations on a table to cause some action before, instead of, or after the normal action.

If the actions of transactions are interleaved, some users may see an inconsistent state, and the database may be left in an inconsistent state. Preventing these inconsistencies is the concurrency-control problem. A schedule records the sequence of steps of a set of transactions. Serial execution produces a serial schedule. An interleaved schedule can be equivalent to a serial schedule. Such a schedule is called serializable. Schedules are enforced primarily by locking. For some applications, lower levels of isolation than serializability are acceptable; SQL standards define four isolation levels.

A multilevel secure DBMS supports users who have different clearance levels and contains data at multiple sensitivity levels. A multilevel relation schema must add a classification attribute for each data attribute and a tuple-class attribute for each tuple. A subset of the attributes is the apparent primary key. For each schema, there is a relation instance for each access class. The entity-integrity rule must be extended for the multilevel model, and other properties are needed. A multilevel relation may contain several tuples for the same primary key value; these tuples have different access classes. This is polyinstantiation, which prevents low-level users from inferring the existence of higher-level data.

The standard concurrency-control solutions do not apply for multilevel systems because schedulers may introduce covert channels. Schedulers that allow multiple versions of data elements reduce contention for shared resources and thus reduce covert channel potential. A scheduler's security depends on both its algorithms and its architecture. Some schedulers are implemented as multiple single-level subjects whose behavior is constrained by a trusted operating system.

A multilevel secure DBMS has to provide a basis for assurance. The two main architectural approaches are TCB subset and trusted subject. The TCB subset approach has the potential for high assurance. It can take a centralized or distributed form. The distributed approach uses multiple untrusted back-end DBMSs, each running at a single level. With trusted subject architectures, the DBMS runs at the system-high level on a trusted operating system and is completely responsible for enforcing security policy on the database. Database function is not sacrificed, but high assurance is very difficult. Multilevel secure DBMS products have been developed, as well as research designs and prototypes. Projects using the centralized TCB subset approach include SeaView and LOCK Data Views. SINTRA represents the distributed TCB subset approach. ASD uses the trusted subject approach. The Trusted Oracle product can use either approach.

Object-oriented DBMSs lag relational DBMSs in security, but much research has been done. Traditional authorization models do not address the special characteristics of object-oriented databases, such as methods, inheritance, and composite objects. Since objects have relationships, authorizations for one object can imply authorizations for another. The model of authorization for the ORION system is based on implied authorization, positive/negative authorization, and strong/weak authorization. Several models have been proposed for mandatory access control in object-oriented databases. For example, with the virtual view model, a user works with a single-level virtual database that is derived from the real multilevel database.

The inference problem arises when authorized information enables a user to infer something about information that is not authorized. The user combines information obtained from the database with outside knowledge or with the results of previous database queries. Some databases reveal only statistics rather than specific values. This allows use of the database for information dissemination and research, while keeping individual data values confidential. A query is a statistical function applied to a subset of database records called the query set; the query set is specified by a characteristic formula. A compromise occurs if queries enable a snooper to infer the value of a confidential attribute. The lattice model has been applied to the statistical inference problem and its solutions. Techniques for protecting statistical database security take two main approaches: restrict queries or perturb either the query responses or the data used to compute statistics. One restriction technique prevents very small or very large query sets. Another logs a user's queries and checks for possible compromise at each new query. The partitioning approach groups values of attributes and allows queries only within groups. Cell suppression blanks out all the cells of a table that contain sensitive statistics. Perturbation techniques include replacing a database with another that has completely different records but the same statistics. The answer can be rounded up or down or computed on a random sample of the query set.

For multilevel DBMSs, an inference problem exists if a user, accessing low-level data, is able to draw conclusions about high-level information. Different kinds of inference channels require different solutions. A query may return only authorized data but may reveal something about unauthorized data. An integrity constraint may allow a low user to infer something about high data. Designers can try to avoid inference channels in designing databases. Automated tools could detect potential channels by analyzing the database schema, possibly taking into account outside knowledge. Inference channels can be eliminated by redesigning the database or monitored at execution time. Closely related to the inference problem is aggregation: a user who retrieves many data items of the same type can learn sensitive information not revealed by just a few of the items.

Bibliographic Notes

Database concepts

Two books on database concepts are Ullman (1988) and Date (1995). The relational model of data was developed by Codd (1970). Books on database security are Castano et al. (1995) and Fernandez et al. (1981). Availability in general is discussed in Chap. 8 and (for distributed systems) Chap. 11. Gray and Reuter (1993) provide thorough treatment of database availability and recovery.

Security services for databases

The SQL standards are described by Melton and Simon (1993) and Date and Darwen (1993). They cover complexities of authorization that this chapter omits. Polk and Bassham (1993) discuss security features of SQL. System R is described by Chamberlin et al. (1981) and its authorization system by Griffiths and Wade (1976). Baldwin (1990) describes named protection domains. Bertino et al. (1993) describe a scheme for a noncascading revoke. For content-dependent access control, an alternative to views is query modification. Its use in the research version of INGRES is described by Fernandez et al. (1981). More on authorization models and access control services can be found in Chaps. 4 and 8. More on database security for distributed environments can be found in Chap. 11.

Definitions and models of integrity are discussed in Chap. 4. Principles of integrity are described by Sandhu and Jajodia (1995), who argue that most integrity mechanisms belong in the DBMS. They propose an approach to enforcing separation of duties that distinguishes between transient and persistent data. Grefen and Apers (1993) present a thorough survey of integrity constraint handling, covering both research and commercial systems. They conclude that there is a large gap between the two and that integrity research does not give enough importance to transactions as atomic units.

Stonebraker and Kemnitz (1991) describe a generalized rules system for the POSTGRES research DBMS. The rules are intended to support integrity constraints, authorization, and event-driven applications. Integrity constraints are expressed in a production-rule syntax. The implementation uses both query rewrite and record-level checking at run time. Lohman et al. (1991) describe the Starburst rule system. Stonebraker and Kemnitz (1991) describe POSTGRES. Well-formed transactions and the policy of constrained change are described in Chap. 4. Notargiacomo et al. (1994) interpret the Clark-Wilson policy in a way that could be enforced by a commercial trusted DBMS. Their model includes dynamic separation of duty. Abrams et al. (1993) discuss external consistency and how to support it. Lewis et al. (1992) describe a trigger mechanism and SQL extensions for writing triggers. Gray and Reuter (1993) describe theory and practice for transactions, concurrency control, and recovery. Berenson et al. (1995) criticize the definition of isolation levels in the SQL-92 standard.

Multilevel secure database systems

Multilevel policies and models are described in Chap. 4 and multilevel system design and assurance in Chap. 6. The description of the relational model for multilevel security follows Jajodia and Sandhu (1995), whose model was based on the SeaView model (Denning et al. 1987, Lunt et al. 1990). Chen and Sandhu (1995) describe a further refinement of the model. The term *polyinstantiation* was introduced by Denning et al. (1987) and the concept is discussed by Lunt (1992), Qian and Lunt (1993), and Jajodia et al. (1995). Referential integrity for the multilevel model is discussed by Doshi and Jajodia (1992) and by Meadows and Jajodia (1995).

The Secure Data Management System is described by Hinke and Schaefer (1975). The discussion of architectures for multilevel secure DBMSs is based mainly on Notargiacomo (1995). The TCB subset approach for incremental evaluation is described by Schaefer and Schell (1984), Shockley and Schell (1987), and in the Trusted Database Interpretation (NCSC 1991). The integrity-lock approach is described by Graubart (1984). Keefe et al. (1993) provide a theoretical framework for concurrency control in MLS systems and analyze standard textbook protocols for security—defined in terms of noninterference. Most of the protocols are not secure. Noninterference is described in Chap. 4. Trusted Oracle is described by Allen (1991) and Schultz and Ehrsam (1993). Its concurrency control is described by Maimone and Greenberg (1990) and by Atluri et al. (1993), who show how the methods can be extended for stricter correctness. SYBASE Secure SQL Server is described by Winkler-Parenty (1990). The

SeaView data model is described by Lunt et al. (1990). The prototype is described by Hsieh et al. (1993) and Lunt and Boucher (1994). SINTRA is described by Kang et al. (1994). Kang et al. (1993) describe its concurrency control. Costich and McDermott (1992) formalize multilevel transactions and correctness in the SINTRA context. Costich et al. (1994) formalize the SINTRA security policy. LOCK Data Views is described by Stachour and Thuraisingham (1990), Stachour (1992), and Hinke (1995). The description of ASD is based on Hinke (1995) and Hinke et al. (1992). The Biba integrity policy is described in Chap. 4. The SWORD prototype, developed at the U.K. Defence Research Agency, provides mandatory access control and a flexible trigger mechanism by which applications can implement all other security controls. SWORD is described by Lewis et al. (1992) and Wiseman (1993). SD-DBMS is described by McCollum and Notargiacomo (1992).

Security for object-oriented databases

There is no one standard model for object-oriented systems. The description is a composite. Object-oriented databases are described by Kim (1990) and Bertino and Martino (1991). An overview of security for these databases is provided by Castano et al. (1995). Authorization and authorization rules are described by Fernandez et al. (1981). Models of discretionary access control are described in Chap. 4. The special authorization needs of object-oriented systems are reviewed by Bertino and Samarati (1994). They describe approaches to conditional authorization, based on work by Rafiul Ahad and others at Hewlett Packard. The OpenODB system is described by Ahad and Cheng (1993). Implied authorization was first studied by Fernandez et al. (1975), who distinguished three forms of authorization rule: *stored, effective* (used to validate a matching request), and *defined* (specified by an authorizer). The ORION model is described by Rabitti et al. (1991). An extension and revision is presented by Bertino and Weigand (1994). The extension handles content-dependent authorization, with predicates expressed in a constraint language. The model of implied authorization and administration is described by Fernandez et al. (1994a). The method-based model is described by Fernandez et al. (1994b).

The message filter model is described by Jajodia and Kogan (1990). Two implementation schemes have been proposed for the message filter model, one using trusted subjects and the other not. These proposals are described by Sandhu et al. (1991) and Thomas and Sandhu (1993). Thomas and Sandhu (1994) apply the message filter model to a replicated-architecture DBMS. Millen and Lunt (1992) describe another model for mandatory access control. Bertino et al. (1994) show how, through composite objects, multilevel entities can be represented using single-level objects. The Virtual View model and MultiView models are described by Boulahia-Cuppens et al. (1993, 1994a, 1994b). The interpretation of Clark-Wilson integrity is described by Herndon (1994).

Inference

Surveys of research on statistical databases have been published by Denning and Schlörer (1983), Adam and Wortmann (1989), and Castano et al. (1995). The notation of Adam and Wortmann is used here. Lattice structures are introduced in Chap. 4. McLeish (1989) reviews partitioning and shows how to relax updating restrictions. Kumar (1994) describes cell suppression techniques for single and multiple tables. The study of random-sample query with query-set size control is described by Duncan and Mukherjee (1991). Duncan and Mukherjee (1993) suggest that responses to repeated queries should be modified with "autoregressive noise." This controls risk of disclosure from repeated queries while also preventing users from reaching an incorrect consensus. Duncan and Pearson (1991) discuss the problem of making microdata available for research while protecting individuals' privacy. For some types of research, such as longitudinal surveys, access to individual records is essential. Before such data are released, they are stripped of identifiers, such as name and Social Security number. Other "quasi-identifiers," such as race and sex, may be removed as well because their values are public. Transformations are applied to records and attributes, and noise is added.

The discussion of inference in multilevel secure databases draws on the overview by Jajodia and Meadows (1995). Garvey et al. (1991) distinguish types of inference channels and propose using abductive reasoning to model and detect them. Qian (1994) describes inference channels due to integrity constraints and shows how to avoid them. DISSECT is described by Qian et al. (1993), Lunt (1994), and Stickel (1994). Hinke and Delugach (1993) describe the AERIE model of inference detection. It involves detecting the real-world entities and activities that are represented in the database and identifying several classes of inference targets. Cuppens and Trouessin (1994) advocate modeling DBMS security as two subproblems: internal information flow controls and inference control. Binns (1993) proposes triggers that monitor potential inference paths at execution time. A trigger fires when a relation in such a path is modified. Aggregation is sometimes called *cardinality aggregation* or *quantity-based aggregation*. Lunt (1989) points out that aggregation problems like the directory are really a matter of protecting sensitive relations. She suggests a high classification for the aggregate, with individual data items being reviewed for release. Motro et al. (1994) propose ways to guard against aggregation without protecting the entire database (such as the whole telephone directory). Rather, sensitive concepts are defined; these can be disclosed, but only to a limited degree.

Exercises

9.1 Compare operating system security and database security. How are they alike? How do they differ?

9.2 Why are views significant for database security?

9.3 Consider the data and applications of an organization that you are familiar with; select a specific application task. Define a view of the data that is appropriate for the task. Decide who would get access to the view.

9.4 What is the effect of specifying **cascade** on a SQL **revoke** statement? What is the effect of specifying **restrict?** Why is it important to have this choice?

9.5 What are the advantages of granting privileges to roles rather than individuals?

9.6 Consider the organization of Exercise 3. Select several tasks and construct a privilege graph with NPDs. Decide what privileges are granted to each NPD and what NPDs to specific users.

9.7 Why are integrity checkpoints valuable?

9.8 Why must a user who defines a check constraint have **select** access to the tables referred to by the constraint?

9.9 Describe alternative ways of enforcing referential integrity.

9.10 Why does SQL provide different levels of isolation? How do the levels differ?

9.11 How does the multilevel relational model schema differ from the standard relational model schema?

9.12 What is the purpose of polyinstantiation?

9.13 In the SeaView prototype, multilevel relations are decomposed and reconstituted by untrusted code, yet the potential assurance level of SeaView is the assurance level of the operating system. Why is this so?

9.14 Suppose you were implementing an OODBMS on top of the Hydra operating system (described in Chap. 7). How would you solve the authorization problem for methods invoking methods?

9.15 Compare the use of NPDs with the use of roles in the ORION model.

9.16 Explain the class construction technique called "incremental constraints" in Herndon's interpretation of the Clark-Wilson model.

9.17 Describe the random-sample query technique for statistical database protection. How can it be modified to protect against averaging attacks?

References

Abrams, Marshall D., Edward G. Amoroso, Leonard J. LaPadula, Teresa F. Lunt, and James G. Williams. 1993. Report of an integrity research study group. *Computers & Security* **12:** 679–689.

Adam, Nabil R., and John C. Wortmann. 1989. Security-control methods for statistical databases: A comparative study. *ACM Computing Surveys* **21**(4): 515–556.

Ahad, Rafiul, and Tu-Ting Cheng. 1993. HP OpenODB: An object-oriented database management system for commercial applications. *Hewlett-Packard Journal* **4**(3): 20(11).

Allen, R. J. 1991. Trusted ORACLE: Multilevel secure data management for military computing. *Computers & Security* **10**(3): 271–275.

Atluri, Vijayalakshmi, Elisa Bertino, and Sushil Jajodia. 1993. Achieving stricter correctness requirements in multilevel secure databases. *Proceedings of the 1993 IEEE Computer Society Symposium on Research in Security and Privacy,* 135–147. Los Alamitos, Calif.: IEEE Computer Society.

Baldwin, Robert W. 1990. Naming and grouping privileges to simplify security management in large databases. *Proceedings of the 1990 IEEE Computer Society Symposium on Research in Security and Privacy,* 116–132. Los Alamitos, Calif.: IEEE Computer Society.

Berenson, Hal, Phil Bernstein, Jim Gray, Jim Melton, Elizabeth O'Neil, and Patrick O'Neil. 1995. A critique of ANSI SQL isolation levels. *SIGMOD RECORD* **24**(2): 1–10.

Bertino, Elisa, Sushil Jajodia, and Pierangela Samarati. 1994. Enforcing mandatory access control in object bases. *Security for Object-Oriented Systems. Proceedings of the OOPSLA-93 Conference Workshop on Security for Object-Oriented Systems,* 96–116. London: Springer-Verlag.

Bertino, Elisa, and Lorenzo Martino. 1991. Object-oriented database management systems: Concepts and issues. *Computer* **24**(4): 33–47.

Bertino, Elisa, and Pierangela Samarati. 1994. Research issues in discretionary authorizations for object bases. *Security for Object-Oriented Systems. Proceedings of the OOPSLA-93 Conference Workshop on Security for Object-Oriented Systems,* 183–199. London: Springer-Verlag.

Bertino, Elisa, Pierangela Samarati, and Sushil Jajodia. 1993. Authorizations in relational database management systems. *Proceedings of the 1st ACM Conference on Computer and Communications Security,* 130–139. New York: ACM Press.

Bertino, E., and H. Weigand. 1994. An approach to authorization modeling in object-oriented database systems. *Data & Knowledge Engineering* **12:** 1–29.

Binns, Leonard J. 1993. Inference through secondary path analysis. *Database Security: VI. Status and Prospects: Results of the IFIP WG 11.3 Workshop on Database Security,* 195–209. Amsterdam: North-Holland.

Boulahia-Cuppens, N., F. Cuppens, A. Gabillon, and K. Yazdanian. 1993. MultiView model for object-oriented database. *Proceedings of the Ninth Annual Computer Security Applications Conference,* 222–231. Los Alamitos, Calif.: IEEE Computer Society.

Boulahia-Cuppens, N., F. Cuppens, A. Gabillon, and K. Yazdanian. 1994a. Decomposition of multilevel objects in an object-oriented database. *Computer*

Security: ESORICS 94. Proceedings of the Third European Symposium on Research in Computer Security, 375–402. Berlin: Springer-Verlag.

Boulahia-Cuppens, N., F. Cuppens, A. Gabillon, and K. Yazdanian. 1994b. Virtual view model to design a secure object-oriented database. *Proceedings of the 17th National Computer Security Conference,* 66–76. NIST/NCSC.

Castano, Silvana, Maria Grazia Fugini, Giancarlo Martella, and Pierangela Samarati. 1995. *Database Security.* Wokingham, England: ACM Press/Addison-Wesley.

Chamberlin, Donald D., et al. 1981. A history and evaluation of System R. *Communications of the ACM* **24**(10): 632–646.

Codd, E. F. 1970. A relational model of data for large shared data banks. *Communications of the ACM* **13**(6): 377–387.

Costich, Oliver, and John McDermott. 1992. A multilevel transaction problem for multilevel secure database systems and its solution for the replicated architecture. *Proceedings of the 1992 IEEE Computer Society Symposium on Research in Security and Privacy,* 192–203. Los Alamitos, Calif.: IEEE Computer Society.

Costich, Oliver, John McLean, and John McDermott. 1994. Confidentiality in a replicated architecture trusted database system: A formal model. *Proceedings of the Computer Security Foundations Workshop VII,* 60–65. Los Alamitos, Calif.: IEEE Computer Society.

Cuppens, F., and G. Trouessin. 1994. Information flow controls vs inference controls: An integrated approach. *Computer Security: ESORICS 94. Proceedings of the Third European Symposium on Research in Computer Security,* 447–468. Berlin: Springer-Verlag.

Date, C. J. 1995. *An Introduction to Database Systems,* 6th ed. Reading, Mass.: Addison-Wesley.

Date, C. J., and Hugh Darwen. 1993. *A Guide to the SQL Standard: A User's Guide.* Reading, Mass.: Addison-Wesley.

Denning, Dorothy E., Teresa F. Lunt, Roger R. Schell, Mark Heckman, and William Shockley. 1987. A multilevel relational data model. *Proceedings of the 1987 IEEE Symposium on Security and Privacy,* 220–234. Los Alamitos, Calif.: IEEE Computer Society.

Denning, Dorothy E., and Jan Schlörer. 1983. Inference controls for statistical databases. *Computer* **16**(7): 69–82.

Doshi, Vinti M., and Sushil Jajodia. 1992. Enforcing entity and referential integrity in multilevel secure databases. *Proceedings of the 15th National Computer Security Conference,* 134–143. NIST/NCSC.

Duncan, George T., and Sumitra Mukherjee. 1991. Microdata disclosure limitation in statistical databases: Query size and random sample query control. *Proceedings of the 1991 IEEE Computer Society Symposium on Research in Security and Privacy,* 278–287. Los Alamitos, Calif.: IEEE Computer Society.

Duncan, George T., and Sumitra Mukherjee. 1993. Disclosure limitation using autocorrelated noise. *Database Security: VI. Status and Prospects: Results of the IFIP WG 11.3 Workshop on Database Security,* 211–224. Amsterdam: North-Holland.

Duncan, George T., and Robert W. Pearson. 1991. Enhancing access to microdata while protecting confidentiality: prospects for the future. *Statistical Science* **6**(3): 219–239.

Fernández, Eduardo B., Ehud Gudes, and Haiyan Song. 1994a. A model for evaluation and administration of security in object-oriented databases. *IEEE Transactions on Knowledge and Data Engineering* **6**(2): 275–292.

Fernández, Eduardo B., María M. Larrondo-Petrie, and Ehud Gudes. 1994b. A method-based authorization model for object-oriented databases. *Security for Object-Oriented Systems. Proceedings of the OOPSLA-93 Conference Workshop on Security for Object-Oriented Systems,* 135–150. London: Springer-Verlag.

Fernandez, Eduardo B., Rita C. Summers, and Tomas Lang. 1975. Definition and evaluation of access rules in data management systems. *Proceedings of the 1st International Conference on Very Large Databases,* 268–285. New York: ACM Press.

Fernandez, Eduardo B., Rita C. Summers, and Christopher Wood. 1981. *Database Security and Integrity.* Reading, Mass.: Addison-Wesley.

Garvey, Thomas D., Teresa F. Lunt, and Mark E. Stickel. 1991. Abductive and approximate reasoning models for characterizing inference channels. *Proceedings of the*

Computer Security Foundations Workshop IV, 118–126. Los Alamitos, Calif.: IEEE Computer Society.

Graubart, Richard. 1984. The integrity-lock approach to secure database management. *Proceedings of the 1984 IEEE Symposium on Security and Privacy,* 62–74. Silver Spring, Md.: IEEE Computer Society.

Gray, Jim, and Andreas Reuter. 1993. *Transaction Processing: Concepts and Techniques.* San Mateo, Calif.: Morgan Kaufmann.

Grefen, Paul W. P. J., and Peter M. G. Apers. 1993. Integrity control in relational database systems: An overview. *Data & Knowledge Engineering* **10**(2): 187–223.

Griffiths, Patricia P., and Bradford W. Wade. 1976. An authorization mechanism for a relational database system. *ACM Transactions on Database Systems* **1**(3): 242–255.

Herndon, William R. 1994. An interpretation of Clark-Wilson for object-oriented DBMSs. *Database Security: VII. Status and Prospects: Results of the IFIP WG 11.3 Workshop on Database Security,* 65–85. Amsterdam: North-Holland.

Hinke, Thomas H. 1995. Multilevel secure database management prototypes. In Marshall D. Abrams, Sushil Jajodia, and Harold J. Podell, eds., *Information Security: An Integrated Collection of Essays,* 542–569. Los Alamitos, Calif.: IEEE Computer Society.

Hinke, Thomas H., and Harry S. Delugach. 1993. AERIE: An inference modeling and detection approach for databases. *Database Security VI. Status and Prospects: Results of the IFIP WG 11.3 Workshop on Database Security.* 179–193. Amsterdam: North-Holland.

Hinke, Thomas H., Cristi Garvey, and Amy Wu. 1992. A1 Secure DBMS Architecture. In Teresa F. Lunt, ed., *Research Directions in Database Security,* 33–40. New York: Springer-Verlag.

Hinke, Thomas H., and Marvin Schaefer. 1975. *Secure Data Management System.* Report RADC-TR-75-266. Rome, NY: Rome Air Development Center.

Hsieh, Donovan, Teresa F. Lunt, and Peter K. Boucher. 1993. *The SeaView Prototype.* Report A012. Menlo Park, Calif.: SRI International.

Jajodia, Sushil, and Boris Kogan. 1990. Integrating an object-oriented data model with multilevel security. *Proceedings of the 1990 IEEE Computer Society Symposium on Research in Security and Privacy,* 76–85. Los Alamitos, Calif.: IEEE Computer Society.

Jajodia, Sushil, and Catherine Meadows. 1995. Inference problems in multilevel secure database management systems. In Marshall D. Abrams, Sushil Jajodia, and Harold J. Podell, eds., *Information Security: An Integrated Collection of Essays,* 570–584. Los Alamitos, Calif.: IEEE Computer Society.

Jajodia, Sushil, and Ravi S. Sandhu. 1995. Toward a multilevel secure relational data model. In Marshall D. Abrams, Sushil Jajodia, and Harold J. Podell, eds., *Information Security: An Integrated Collection of Essays,* 460–492. Los Alamitos, Calif.: IEEE Computer Society.

Jajodia, Sushil, Ravi S. Sandhu, and Barbara T. Blaustein. 1995. Solutions to the polyinstantiation problem. In Marshall D. Abrams, Sushil Jajodia, and Harold J. Podell, eds., *Information Security: An Integrated Collection of Essays,* 493–529. Los Alamitos, Calif.: IEEE Computer Society.

Kang, Myong H., Oliver Costich, and Judith N. Froscher. 1993. A practical transaction model and untrusted transaction manager for a multilevel-secure database system. In Bhavani M. Thuraisingham, and Carl E. Landwehr, eds., *Database Security: VI. Status and Prospects: Results of the IFIP WG 11.3 Workshop on Database Security,* 285–300. Amsterdam: North-Holland.

Kang, Myong H., Judith N. Froscher, John McDermott, Oliver Costich, and Rodney Peyton. 1994. Achieving database security through data replication: The SINTRA prototype. *Proceedings of the 17th National Computer Security Conference,* 77–87. NIST/NCSC.

Keefe, Thomas F., W. T. Tsai, and Jaideep Srivastava. 1993. Database concurrency control in multilevel secure database management systems. *IEEE Transactions on Knowledge and Data Engineering* **5**(6): 1039–1055.

Kim, Won. 1990. Object-oriented databases: Definition and research directions. *IEEE Transactions on Knowledge and Data Engineering* **2**(3): 327–341.

Kumar, Ram. 1994. Ensuring data security in interrelated tabular data. *Proceedings of the 1994 IEEE Computer Society Symposium on Research in Security and Privacy,* 96–105. Los Alamitos, Calif.: IEEE Computer Society.

Lewis, Sharon R., Simon R. Wiseman, and Neil D. Poulter. 1992. Providing security in a phone book database using triggers. *Proceedings of the Eighth Annual Computer Security Applications Conference,* 85–96. Los Alamitos, Calif.: IEEE Computer Society.

Lohman, Guy M., Bruce Lindsay, Hamid Pirahesh, and K. Bernhard Schiefer. 1991. Extensions to Starburst: Objects, types, functions, and rules. *Communications of the ACM* **34**(10): 95–109.

Lunt, Teresa F. 1989. Aggregation and inference: Facts and fallacies. *Proceedings of the 1989 IEEE Computer Society Symposium on Security and Privacy,* 102–109. Los Alamitos, Calif.: IEEE Computer Society.

Lunt, Teresa F. 1992. Security in database systems: A research perspective. *Computers & Security* **11:** 41–56.

Lunt, Teresa F., 1994. The inference problem: A practical solution. *Proceedings of the 17th National Computer Security Conference,* 507–509. NIST/NCSC.

Lunt, Teresa F., and Peter K. Boucher. 1994. The SeaView prototype: Project summary. *Proceedings of the 17th National Computer Security Conference,* 88–102. NIST/NCSC.

Lunt, Teresa F., Dorothy E. Denning, Roger R. Schell, Mark Heckman, and William R. Shockley. 1990. The SeaView security model. *IEEE Transactions on Software Engineering* **16**(6): 593–607.

Maimone, William T., and Ira B. Greenberg. 1990. Single-level multiversion schedulers for multilevel secure database systems. *Proceedings of the Sixth Annual Computer Security Applications Conference,* 137–147. Los Alamitos, Calif.: IEEE Computer Society.

McCollum, Catherine D., and LouAnna Notargiacomo. 1992. Distributed concurrency control with optional data replication. In Carl E. Landwehr and Sushil Jajodia, eds., *Database Security: V. Status and Prospects: Results of the IFIP WG 11.3 Workshop on Database Security,* 149–172. Amsterdam: North-Holland.

McLeish, Mary. 1989. Further results on the security of partitioned dynamic statistical databases. *ACM Transactions on Database Systems* **14**(1): 98–113.

Meadows, Catherine, and Sushil Jajodia. 1992. Integrity in multilevel secure database management systems. In Marshall D. Abrams, Sushil Jajodia, and Harold J. Podell, eds., *Information Security: An Integrated Collection of Essays,* 530–541. Los Alamitos, Calif.: IEEE Computer Society.

Melton, Jim, and Alan R. Simon. 1993. *Understanding the New SQL: A Complete Guide.* San Mateo, Calif.: Morgan Kaufmann.

Millen, Jonathan K., and Teresa F. Lunt. 1992. Security for object-oriented database systems. *Proceedings of the 1992 IEEE Computer Society Symposium on Research in Security and Privacy,* 260–272. Los Alamitos, Calif.: IEEE Computer Society.

Motro, Amihai, Donald G. Marks, and Sushil Jajodia. 1994. Aggregation in relational databases: Controlled disclosure of sensitive information. *Computer Security: ESORICS 94. Proceedings of the Third European Symposium on Research in Computer Security,* 431–445. Berlin: Springer-Verlag.

NCSC. 1991. *Trusted Database Management System Interpretation of the Trusted Computer System Evaluation Criteria.* NCSC-TG-021. Fort Meade, Md.: National Computer Security Center.

Notargiacomo, LouAnna. 1995. Architectures for MLS database management systems. In Marshall D. Abrams, Sushil Jajodia, and Harold J. Podell, eds., *Information Security: An Integrated Collection of Essays,* 439–459. Los Alamitos, Calif.: IEEE Computer Society.

Notargiacomo, LouAnna, Barbara T. Blaustein, and Catherine D. McCollum. 1994. A model of integrity and dynamic separation of duty for a trusted DBMS. *Database Security: VIII. Status and Prospects: IFIP WG 11.3 Workshop on Database Security,* 237–256. Amsterdam: North-Holland.

Polk, W. Timothy, and Lawrence E. Bassham. 1993. *Security Issues in the Database Language SQL.* NIST special publication 800-8. Gaithersburg, Md.: National Institute of Standards and Technology.

Qian, Xiaolei. 1994. Inference channel-free integrity constraints in multilevel relational databases. *Proceedings of the 1994 IEEE Computer Society Symposium on Research in Security and Privacy,* 158–167. Los Alamitos, Calif.: IEEE Computer Society.

Qian, Xiaolei, and Teresa F. Lunt. 1993. Tuple-level vs. element-level classification. In Bhavani M. Thuraisingham, and Carl E. Landwehr, eds., *Database Security: VI. Status and Prospects: Results of the IFIP WG 11.3 Workshop on Database Security,* 301–315. Amsterdam: North-Holland.

Qian, Xiaolei, Mark E. Stickel, Peter D. Karp, Teresa F. Lunt, and Thomas D. Garvey. 1993. Detection and elimination of inference channels in multilevel relational database systems. *Proceedings of the 1993 IEEE Computer Society Symposium on Research in Security and Privacy,* 196–205. Los Alamitos, Calif.: IEEE Computer Society.

Rabitti, Fausto, Elisa Bertino, Won Kim, and Darrell Woelk. 1991. A model of authorization for next-generation database systems. *ACM Transactions on Database Systems* **16**(1): 88–131.

Sandhu, Ravi S., and Sushil Jajodia. 1995. Integrity mechanisms in database management systems. In Marshall D. Abrams, Sushil Jajodia, and Harold J. Podell, eds., *Information Security: An Integrated Collection of Essays,* 617–634. Los Alamitos, Calif.: IEEE Computer Society.

Sandhu, Ravi, Roshan Thomas, and Sushil Jajodia. 1991. A secure kernelized architecture for multilevel object-oriented databases. *Proceedings of the Computer Security Foundations Workshop IV,* 139–152. Los Alamitos, Calif.: IEEE Computer Society.

Schaefer, Marvin, and Roger R. Schell. 1984. Toward an understanding of extensible architectures for evaluated trusted computer system products. *Proceedings of the 1984 Symposium on Security and Privacy,* 41–49. Silver Spring, Md.: IEEE Computer Society.

Schultz, Rick, and Tim Ehrsam. 1993. Migrating a commercial-off-the-shelf application to a multilevel secure environment. *Proceedings of the Ninth Annual Computer Security Applications Conference,* 21–28. Los Alamitos, Calif.: IEEE Computer Society.

Shockley, William R., and Roger R. Schell. 1987. TCB subsets for incremental evaluation. *AIAA/ASIS/IEEE Third Aerospace Computer Security Conference: Applying Technology to Systems,* 131–139. Washington, D.C.: American Institute of Aeronautics and Astronautics.

Stachour, Paul. 1992. LOCK Data Views. In Teresa F. Lunt, ed., *Research Directions in Database Security,* 63–80. New York: Springer-Verlag.

Stachour, Paul D., and Bhavani Thuraisingham. 1990. Design of LDV: A multilevel secure relational database management system. *IEEE Transactions on Knowledge and Data Engineering* **2**(2): 190–209.

Stickel, Mark E. 1994. Elimination of inference channels by optimal upgrading. *Proceedings of the 1994 IEEE Computer Society Symposium on Research in Security and Privacy,* 168–174. Los Alamitos, Calif.: IEEE Computer Society.

Stonebraker, Michael, and Greg Kemnitz. 1991. The POSTGRES next generation database management system. *Communications of the ACM* **34**(10): 79–92.

Thomas, Roshan K., and Ravi S. Sandhu. 1993. Implementing the message filter object-oriented security model without trusted subjects. *Database Security: VI. Status and Prospects: Results of the IFIP WG 11.3 Workshop on Database Security,* 15–34. Amsterdam: North-Holland.

Thomas, Roshan K., and Ravi S. Sandhu. 1994. Supporting object-based high-assurance write-up in multilevel databases for the replicated architecture. *Computer Security: ESORICS 94. Proceedings of the Third European Symposium on Research in Computer Security,* 403–428. Berlin: Springer-Verlag.

Ullman, Jeffrey D. 1988. *Principles of Database and Knowledge-Base Systems.* Rockville, Md.: Computer Science Press.

Winkler-Parenty, H. B. 1990. SYBASE: The trusted subject DBMS. *Proceedings of the 13th National Computer Security Conference,* 589–593. NIST/NCSC.

Wiseman, Simon R. 1993. Using SWORD for the Military Airlift Command Example database. *Database Security: VI. Status and Prospects: Results of the IFIP WG 11.3 Workshop on Database Security,* 73–89. Amsterdam: North-Holland.

Part

3

Security in Computer Networks

Chapter

10

Network Security

Introduction

"The network is the computer," the slogan goes. More and more of computing is done on networks. Computers provide access to networks, and networks provide access to them. The technologies for computing and for communications are irreversibly enmeshed, and so are the traditional applications. The physical network is the enabler, but it is new applications that fuel network growth. Increasingly, applications span organization boundaries. Companies deal with their suppliers and customers over networks, and value-added networks make a business of supporting these dealings. The Internet and the on-line services (such as America Online) are staples of everyday life. Local-area networks allow users to share files, use specialized services, update their software, schedule meetings, and work cooperatively.

As networking technology and applications sprint forward, network security struggles to catch up. Networking is the origin of many computer security threats, and it magnifies many others. Systems connected to the Internet have suffered attacks that compromised thousands of passwords. Mobile users communicate over unprotected broadcast media. There is no widely accepted architecture or model for network security. The providers of the international communications system are governed by differing laws and regulations about privacy and security.

The network is the computer, and network security is computer security. That is, computing is done on networks, and secure computing depends on secure networks. It is equally true that computers are the network, and computer security is network security. That is, networks are composed of computers, and secure networking depends on secure computing.

Concepts and definitions

A *computer network* is a collection of two or more computing systems that communicate with one another. The communicating systems are called *hosts* or *nodes.* The nodes communicate over *links* provided by *transmission media.* Some of the nodes are dedicated to switching or routing transmissions. Computer networks range in scope from tens of PCs to vast global *internetworks* that connect other networks. Networks can be classified according to how large an area they cover. *Local-area networks* (LANs) are limited to a few buildings and typically belong to one organization. *Metropolitan-area networks* (MANs) cover a metropolitan region and typically are shared by different organizations. *Wide-area networks* (WANs) cover long distances, and their communication facilities are provided by separate organizations called *common carriers.* For example, a WAN may connect all the computing facilities of a large corporation, using AT&T as common carrier. LANs are connected to one another and to MANs and WANs, and separate networks are connected to form an *internet* (see Fig. 10.1). The best-known internet is the *Internet.*

Most networks use *packet switching:* messages are broken into packets that each carry routing, sequencing, and integrity information, and that make their ways independently to their destination, where they are reassembled in the right order. The intermediate nodes that do routing are called *packet switches, routers,* or *bridges.* Networks can provide either *connectionless* service or *connection-oriented* service. A connection is like a conversation; it sets up a context within which data units are transmitted, and each party maintains some state information about the connection. Connectionless or *datagram* service simply sends packets from source to destination.

Information moves on cables and also by wireless or open transmission. Cables use copper wire, in the form of twisted pair or coaxial cable, and optical fiber. Open transmission (using microwaves for example) is increasingly important for satellite communications, portable computing, and wireless LANs. *Communications security* measures focus on protecting transmitted information—maintaining its integrity and confidentiality—and on providing availability of communications services. *Network security* includes communications security. It also includes measures, in the network services and in the hosts, that support secure computing in a network environment.

The term *distributed systems* refers to networks whose components cooperate on common tasks or applications, instead of simply exchanging data. This is sometimes called *distributed computing* or

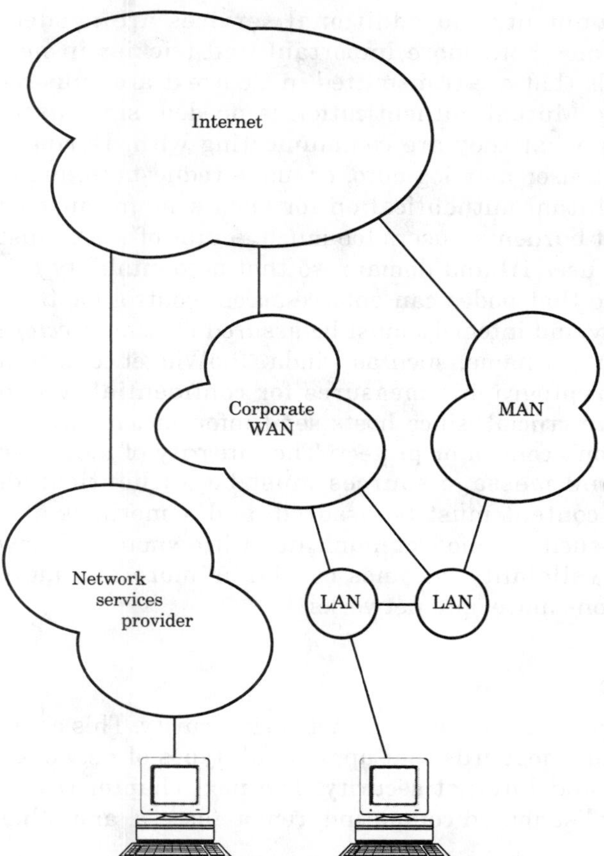

Figure 10.1 Networks and internet.

distributed processing. Since networks increasingly act as distributed systems, this chapter uses the briefer term "network" to include distributed systems. Some distributed systems are controlled by a common *distributed operating system,* so that the operating system entities such as processes and files are located on various nodes. When heterogeneous distributed systems follow common protocols for cooperation, they are called *interoperable.* Most distributed systems follow the *client-server* model: a client at one node requests a service, and a server somewhere in the network provides it.

Network security

The security services needed for operating systems (Chap. 8) are also needed for networks. These services must cope with harder problems in a network environment, and additional services are needed. Authentication becomes both more important and trickier in networks. Any passwords that are transmitted in cleartext are vulnerable to eavesdropping. Mutual authentication is needed, since users cannot know directly what they are communicating with. During a single work session, a user may log onto, or make requests to, many different systems. Mutual authentication for each system must be accomplished without burdening users too much. A unit of work must be associated with a user ID and domain, so that accountability can be maintained and so that nodes can enforce access control for their resources. Availability and integrity must be assured for the *directory* service, which converts a name, such as Linda@BioWidget.com, to a network address. Cryptographic measures for confidentiality and integrity become more crucial, since hosts send information through territory that they don't control or protect. The integrity of messages must be assured, and message sources must be authenticated. Secrecy of message content must be assured, and sometimes also secrecy of patterns—such as who communicates with whom and how often. Continuous availability becomes crucial as more and more operational applications move onto networks.

Overview of the chapter

Both this chapter and the next are about network security. This chapter covers threats and safeguards that apply to all types of networks. It also covers email and Internet security. The next chapter covers local-area networks, distributed computing, remote access, and other topics.

Standards are crucial for networks. The next section describes the role of network standards and introduces the dominant standards frameworks. The concepts of network architecture and network security architecture are discussed, along with the OSI and Internet architectures and their security architectures. Next, threats are described. Basic cryptography is reviewed, and the role of cryptography in network security is discussed.

Authentication is even more critical for networks than for operating systems. Types of authentication are described, as are issues in the design of authentication services. Specific authentication schemes are described. The next section covers other services, including access control, confidentiality, integrity, and nonrepudiation. The security role of network management is described.

We next consider Internet vulnerabilities and security efforts. Sometimes the only way to protect a network is to partially isolate it from the larger networking environment. This firewall approach is described. Security enhancements of the Internet protocols are described. Security of the World Wide Web is considered. The final section reviews work on network security architectures.

Architecture and Standards

Computer networks are enormously complex and heterogeneous. Suppose a user at Host *A* wants to retrieve a document from Host *B*. Some route from *A* to *B* must be found (taking into account links that are down and restrictions imposed by the user) and transmission errors must be handled. *A* and *B* may well have different operating systems and different file systems. *B*'s software must understand *A*'s request, and the received document must make sense to the user at *A*. All of this has to work on different transmission media, over a broad range of data rates and distances. A *network architecture* puts some order into this complexity.

Network architecture

A network architecture describes network functions and the protocols by which they are performed. The cooperating parties in network protocols are software and hardware entities within hosts. Network architectures are *layered.* The lowest layers concern physical aspects, middle layers deal with messages and connections, and the highest layers define how data is presented to users, as well as application protocols. Security services may reside at any or all layers. The network architecture consists of the layers, the interfaces between them, and the protocols. IBM's *System Network Architecture* (SNA) was one of the earliest network architectures; another proprietary architecture is *DECnet.* More important now are open systems architectures. The leading ones are (1) ISO/OSI (Open Systems Interconnection of the International Organization for Standardization) and (2) the layered protocols used for the Internet.

Network security architecture

A network architecture should be accompanied by a network security architecture. For trusted systems, the security architecture describes how a system is structured to satisfy its security requirements and identifies the security-relevant system components. Efforts in network security architecture take varied forms. For open systems, the focus is on what security services are provided and at what layer, and on general frameworks for specific services. The DoD develops security architectures for its own networks, and vendors have worked on security architecture for their product lines. In the main, however, the people who build and operate networks must develop their own security architectures.

Open Systems Interconnection

The OSI *Reference Model* provides a foundation for the OSI standards. Its concepts and terminology are widely used even for non-OSI networks.

The OSI Reference Model. Figure 10.2 shows the seven layers of the OSI model. Hardware and software *entities* at each layer carry out some part of the total network task. For each layer, protocols are carried out between *peer entities* at the same layer on different systems. For example, a transport layer entity of Host *A* carries out a protocol with a transport layer entity at Host *B*. The OSI model defines the responsibilities of each layer, and how the layers relate. Each layer (along with all the layers below it) provides a *service* to the layer immediately above; a layer depends on and uses the service of the next lower layer on its own system. The transmitted data flows down the layers on the way out and up the layers on the way in. The lower four layers deal with communications, while the upper three are more application-oriented.

The model does not define the protocols; alternative protocols can be—and are—used at each layer. Although a layer depends on the services of the layer beneath it, its protocols do *not* depend on the lower layer's protocols; each layer's protocols can change independently. The data items that entities at layer *n* exchange are called *n-protocol data units* (*n*-PDUs). Entities at the network layer, for exam-

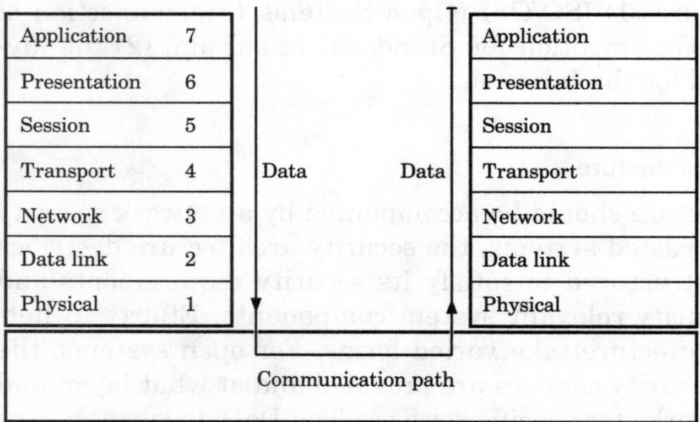

Figure 10.2 OSI Reference Model layers.

ple, exchange network PDUs. *Protocol control information* accompanies the PDUs. This takes the form of *headers*; each layer adds its header to the PDU that it receives from the layer above to form its own PDU. Entities at one layer do not look at the headers of other layers. The *physical* layer deals with mechanical and electrical specifications for transforming bits into signals for the cable or other medium. The *data link* layer provides reliable transmission of groups of bits (called *frames*) between two systems; it detects errors, usually by means of a checksum in the frame header. Either the error is corrected or the frame is retransmitted. [IEEE LAN standards define a *media access control* (MAC) layer within the physical and link layer.] The *network* layer provides safe routing of data packets between source and destination systems; this includes routing the packets through intermediate nodes or *intermediate systems.*

The *transport layer* (layer 4) offers reliable transport and connection. That is, it sets up connections, and sends and receives data units, hiding all network characteristics from the layers above. It ensures that all data units are delivered, without errors and in order, with no duplications.

The *session layer* sets up connections between pairs of *application processes* and coordinates their interaction. The *presentation layer* is responsible for transforming data to and from a common representation, so that processes on disparate systems can interact, even though they use different character sets and different displays. The application layers offer services such as directories, file transfer, and *message handling* (which includes electronic mail). OSI standards efforts also touch application areas, such as office document architecture and electronic data interchange (EDI).

Notes on ISO standards. ISO and its partners recognized that their full standards would be too complete for most implementations, so individual governments or other entities can define subsets. For example, the OSI Implementors Workshop (a North American group) developed Minimal OSI for the upper layers. *ASN.1—Abstract Syntax Notation One* is used in ISO standards and elsewhere for describing messages. ISO has standardized a formal language—LOTOS—for specifying protocols. LOTOS can be used for analyzing protocols and verifying their correctness.

OSI Security Architecture. Just as the Reference Model is a foundation for OSI networking standards, the OSI Security Architecture is a foundation for OSI security standards. It identifies the needed services and mechanisms, and positions them within the layers. *Frameworks* dealing with the specific services expand on the original architecture. (In addition to the frameworks, standards groups adopt security extensions to the various layer protocols and to applications, such as message handling and directory services.)

The security services identified are

- Authentication
- Access control
- Confidentiality
- Integrity
- Nonrepudiation

The same service (confidentiality, for example) can be provided at more than one layer, although some services make sense only at specific layers. The architecture includes some layering principles. For example: minimize the number of different ways a service is provided; avoid duplicating existing communications functionality; do not violate the independence of the layers; minimize the amount of trusted functionality; define services in a way that allows modular rather than all-or-none implementation.

The OSI security architecture also describes mechanisms that can be used to provide the services, as shown in Table 10.1—for example, the encryption mechanism for the data confidentiality service and digital signatures for peer entity authentication. Other mechanisms are traffic padding (which counters the traffic analysis threat), routing control (which routes data units over paths that meet some security requirement), and notarization (functions of a trusted third party,

TABLE 10.1 OSI Security Services and Mechanisms

Services
Authentication
Access control
Confidentiality
Integrity
Nonrepudiation

Mechanisms
Encipherment
Digital signature
Access control
Data integrity
Authentication exchange
Traffic padding
Routing control
Notarization

as in the arbitrated protocols described in Chap. 5). There are also *pervasive mechanisms* that do not specifically support services. These mechanisms provide properties or functions that were discussed in Chaps. 6 and 8: trusted functionality, security labels, event detection, audit trail, and secure recovery.

Internet architecture

The OSI Reference Model came out of a conscious top-down effort at architecture. The Internet architecture took shape gradually and less formally, tracking developments in the Internet itself. The Internet does have well-developed procedures for developing, reviewing, and approving its protocols. Anyone with access to the Internet has access to the standards and also the working documents.

Internet layered architecture. The Internet is viewed as heterogeneous networks connected by *routers,* which are nodes whose purpose is just that—connecting heterogeneous networks. The routers cooperate to find routes from source to destination. As with OSI, the Internet architecture is layered. Six layers are shown in Table 10.2; other representations use four or five. The lower three layers correspond well to the lower three layers of OSI. The *Internet* or *IP* layer provides a datagram service from one host to another. This is simple from the viewpoint of the IP user, but it involves highly complex routing protocols. Above IP, at the transport layer, is *TCP,* a connection-oriented protocol that provides a reliable communication path, or virtual circuit, between two processes. Processes have ports; the combination of port ID and host IP address is called a *socket,* and connections are set up between sockets. *User Datagram Protocol* (UDP) provides transport-layer datagram service. IP, TCP, UDP, and other protocols, along with some application protocols that use them, form the *TCP/IP protocol suite.*

Most of the Internet applications (the top layer) use TCP or UDP. A few of the applications and corresponding protocols are

TABLE 10.2 Internet Layers

Layer	Example protocol
Application	Telnet
Transport	TCP
Internet (network)	IP
Subnetwork	Ethernet
Link	HDLC
Physical	RS232

- Mail—*Simple Mail Transfer Protocol* (SMTP)
- File transfer—*File Transfer Protocol* (FTP)
- Remote access—*Telnet*
- Directory services, including the *Domain Name System*

Most of the applications follow a client-server model (although without that terminology) and use common conventions for requests and replies. Applications are associated with specific *well-known ports*; for example, a Telnet server uses Port 23. The Internet has no layer corresponding to the OSI presentation or session layers; those functions are handled by applications.

There has been much cross-fertilization between TCP/IP and OSI, and OSI security standards have strongly influenced TCP/IP security enhancements. Vendors have good reason to develop security products that will run on both kinds of networks; this motivates convergence.

Internet security architecture. There is not yet an Internet security architecture, but some work has been done on articulating a philosophy. For example, the architecture should seek a compromise between generality and specificity. It should encompass technologies that provide a broad range of strength of security. It should include security features that are mandatory although their use is optional.

Network security standards

Many standards address security. For layer 2 of the OSI model, IEEE standard 802.10 (IEEE 1993) specifies *Secure Data Exchange* (SDE) protocols to support confidentiality, connectionless integrity, data origin authentication, and access control. ISO has developed transport-layer and network-layer security protocols (*TLSP* and *NLSP*). A revised IP specification includes authentication of data origin, data integrity, and encryption for confidentiality.

The International Telecommunication Union (ITU) has developed *recommendations* for security of electronic mail (X.400 series) and for directory services (*The Directory*—X.500 series), including an authentication framework (X.509). X.500 Directory services have triple relevance for network security:

- The security of the network depends on the integrity of Directory information, and some Directory information must also be confidential.
- The Directory must authenticate itself to its users and they to it.

- The Directory supports the security needs of applications; it acts as repository for public key certificates.

The European Computer Manufacturers Association (ECMA) also has done work on security in open systems. And of course cryptography standards (discussed in Chaps. 2 and 5) have their main application in network security.

Threats to Network Security

Since they carry and hold information of enormous total value, computer networks are exceedingly attractive targets to attack. Networking brings more resources within reach of more potential attackers.

Like threats to computing systems, threats to networks can compromise confidentiality or integrity or can deny service. Attacks on confidentiality are called *passive,* because the intruder simply listens or *eavesdrops* without actively changing anything. A passive attack, if successful, results in *release of message contents.* A passive attack can threaten secrecy even if the contents are meaningless to the intruder (as they would be if encrypted). The intruder could interpret a message header (often in plaintext even if data are encrypted) to learn the message's source and destination. The intruder could observe the lengths and frequencies of messages transmitted between parties. This *traffic analysis* attack violates confidentiality without releasing message contents.

Attacks on integrity and availability are *active.* By actively modifying message traffic, the intruder can achieve various results. The most direct result is to modify the content of the *payload*—the actual transmitted data. Modifying the account number on a funds-transfer message could cause the transfer to be made into the intruder's account. This result could be achieved, for example, by substituting the intruder's message for the true message. An intruder might also *replay* a previously sent message, such as an authentic message that transfers into the intruder's account. An intruder might alter the apparent origin of a message. For example, Ed receives email that appears to be from his manager, Mac, but it was really sent by an intruder, Iris, who is plotting to undermine the company. Iris is *impersonating the sender* or *masquerading.* An active attack can cause a message to arrive at the wrong destination. Ed's email to Mac goes to Iris instead. A sender or receiver can *repudiate* a message. For example, a bank customer denies having carried out a transaction that debits her account.

An attack can result in unauthorized access to resources. By various means (such as masquerading, or taking advantage of flaws and poor access control) the attacker can get unauthorized access to files at some network host. The attacker may steal computing services or communications services. The attacker may seriously compromise a host's basic protection—perhaps without detection. Then all the hosts on the same network or internet are vulnerable to attack from the compromised host.

Denial of service can range from waylaying or delaying specific messages, through deliberate overloading, to total loss of service. Iris prevents Mac's email from reaching Ed; an attacker deliberately floods a node with packets; the 1988 Internet worm takes many hosts off line to repair and prevent damage.

Attacks over networks are hard to trace to their source. The attacker uses a complex path through a series of networks to reach the target. (This is called *network weaving.*) Host administrators find it difficult or impossible to learn the location of the attacker.

Networks also are threatened by accidents and errors. Earthquakes, floods, or fires can damage cables, hosts, and switches. Debris in space can damage satellites. Hardware, software, and human errors can take down hosts or switches.

Vulnerabilities of transmission media

Many different transmission media carry network traffic. Local-area networks use either twisted-pair or coaxial cable or wireless communication. Long-distance links use predominantly optical fiber, with satellite communications used for certain kinds of data. All types of cables are vulnerable to *wiretapping*—any unauthorized cutting in on a communications line. A *direct-connection* tap, which penetrates the cable and attaches a device, provides the best signal to the intruder. Common carriers have equipment that can detect possible taps, but the same symptoms can also have other causes. A *remote* or *passive* tap picks up emanations from cables. Twisted pair and coaxial cable are both quite vulnerable to direct-connection taps and remote taps. Fiber is much more secure. The cables contain extremely fine threads that carry pulses of light; the individual threads are hard to get at, and it is easier to detect taps. Still, a skilled attacker willing to spend enough can tap fiber.

Open transmission is open to eavesdropping. Anyone with an antenna can eavesdrop on satellite communications; anyone with the right radio receiver can listen in on cellular phone calls. Encryption protects against eavesdropping, but not against *jamming,* in which an attacker transmits signals that disrupt legitimate transmissions, or even replace them. (In 1986, a jammer caused a satellite to transmit his message in place of a cable movie channel's programming; the message protested encryption of cable signals.) There are measures that can greatly increase the cost to the jammer.

Certain points in a network are most vulnerable to attack—because they are physically accessible, or because an attack there is hard to detect, or because the payoff is greatest. Where cables cover large areas, periodic *repeaters* are needed to amplify the signal; these are a target for undetected taps. The cables of most LANs go through *wiring closets,* which are ideal places for wiretapping on a choice of lines. The *network interface unit* that connects a computer to a LAN can read (in popular LAN protocols) all the packets that travel the LAN, regardless of their destination. If the unit is well-behaved, it picks up only its own packets. If not, it can eavesdrop. Eavesdropping on long-distance lines is difficult, because many conversations or connections are interleaved on the same line, and any one connection is spread over many lines in an unpredictable way. It is more fruitful to eavesdrop on a local line.

Types of attacks

Victor Voydock and Stephen Kent (1985) have classified active attacks in terms of their effect on protocols and data units:

- *Message-stream modification,* which includes attacks on authenticity of origin, integrity, and ordering. Preserving ordering means that a data unit can be placed in the right order in the stream of data units for an *association* (a connection between peer entities).
- *Denial of message service* (such as deleting all the data units passing on the association for Mac's mail to Ed).
- *Spurious association initiation,* which sets up an association under a false identity.

Voydock and Kent also list five security goals that correspond to passive and active threats. For some threats, prevention is the goal; for others, only detection is possible. The goals are

- Preventing release of message contents
- Preventing traffic analysis
- Detecting message-stream modification
- Detecting denial of message service
- Detecting spurious association initiation

In practice, network security is most threatened by penetrated hosts. Both active and passive attacks help an intruder to penetrate a host. The following are examples of attack methods:

- *Doorknob attack.* A network attacker has a great advantage: it does not matter very much which system is penetrated first. Like a burglar trying many doorknobs, the attacker systematically probes many hosts, looking for weaknesses in configuration. Each system that is penetrated provides the attacker with more information (such as account names and passwords) and more possible penetration routes to other systems.
- *Exploiting trust relationships.* There are mechanisms that put one system's fate in the hands of another system. For example, some UNIX systems allow the specification of trusted hosts. A user at Host 2, which is trusted by Host 1, can log in to Host 1, or execute remote commands at Host 1, without entering a password. If Host 2 is penetrated, Host 1's security is affected.
- *Forged source addresses.* Hosts and routers base authentication and access control decisions on the origin of messages. (Trusted hosts are one example.) If the origin is forged, authentication and access control are subverted. Unfortunately, source addresses can be forged quite easily.
- *Eavesdropping on passwords.* When a user logs onto a remote system (via Telnet, for example) the password typically is transmitted in cleartext. The attacker can learn the password by eavesdropping on the link or by installing a Trojan horse that monitors network connections at the local or remote host. Using X Windows, a rogue remote application can learn a password by stealing keystrokes intended for another application's window.

Cryptography in Network Security

Cryptography is the indispensable mechanism for network security. It is the foundation for authentication, confidentiality, and integrity. We review here briefly (from Chap. 5) some terminology and results that are important for understanding network security services.

Cryptography review

In secret key cryptosystems, the sender and receiver use the same secret key for both encryption and decryption. Encryption is written as

$$C = E_K(M)$$

where the ciphertext C results from applying the encrypting function E to the plaintext message M, using the secret key K.

In public key systems, a receiver's encryption key is published for all senders to use, and the receiver decrypts with a private secret key. The most widely used public key system is *RSA,* which uses a one-way function

$$E(M) = M^e \bmod n$$

where e is public, and decryption uses a private value d:

$$D(C) = C^d \bmod n$$

The encryption and decryption exponents e and d are inverses of one another.

Public key methods are used for *digital signatures.* A digital signature securely identifies the sender and also confirms the integrity of the message. A signed message can be kept by the receiver to guard against repudiation. Digital signatures are often based on RSA. Bob signs a message using his private exponent d. Alice verifies the signature using Bob's public exponent e. Digital signatures are used for authentication. A message signed using the private key of a principal is taken as proof of identity.

Key management is the whole process of handling cryptographic keys. It includes generating keys, distributing them, protecting their secrecy and integrity, and eventually destroying them. Keys are managed differently, depending on their expected longevity. A *session key* is used for just one communication session. A *key distribution center* (KDC) specializes in providing keys at the request of communicating parties. Public keys are registered with a trusted *certification authority* (CA). The CA distributes *certificates,* which are public keys carrying the digital signature of the CA. Since certificates are protected (by the CA signature) against tampering, they can be stored in local directory servers and kept by users.

The place of cryptography

Although there is no question about the importance of cryptographic measures, there are questions about their place in the network security architecture. At what layer is encryption best performed? What network entities are responsible? How are keys managed?

A fundamental issue is where to do encryption. *Link encryption* is done at the data link layer (a very low layer) and is invisible to all higher layers. Link encryption occurs independently for each link; each connected pair of nodes shares a key that is known only to that pair. A data unit, on its path from source to destination, is encrypted each time it leaves a node and decrypted when it arrives at the next node (see Fig. 10.3). The entire message, including protocol headers, is encrypted.

In the alternative approach, called *end-to-end encryption,* or E^3, encryption is done at the source, and decryption occurs only at the destination (see Fig. 10.4). The term *end* has different possible interpretations. It can mean, for example, a host computer, or an application process, or the transport-layer entity of a host or node. So there are more than just two choices for architectural placement. With an end-to-end approach, only the data portion of the message is encrypted. The headers that contain addressing information must remain in cleartext so that intermediate nodes will be able to route the message properly. This addressing information must *bypass* the encryption process. One way to accomplish this is to *encapsulate* the entire encrypted message, including headers, in another message whose headers are in plaintext.

Each approach has its advantages. Link encryption service is easy to add to a protocol, and it can be added without affecting any higher-level protocols. Nothing additional is required from users or applications. Since the entire data unit including addresses is encrypted, link encryption can protect against traffic analysis attacks based on source-destination patterns. The key management problem is quite manageable, since a node only needs a key for each other node it is connected with. The most serious disadvantage is that every intermediate node must be trusted to preserve the security of the data, which

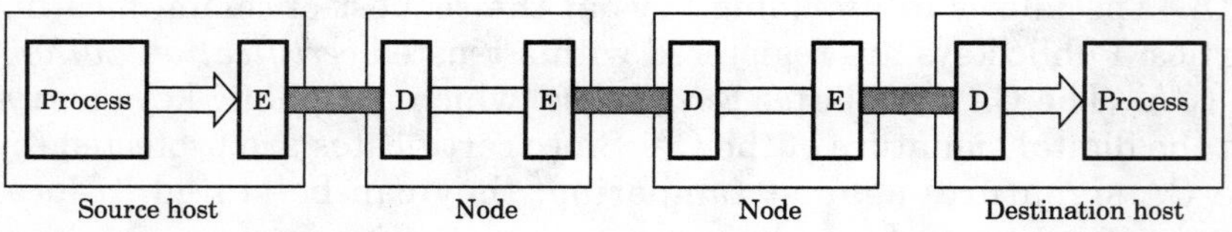

Figure 10.3 Link encryption.

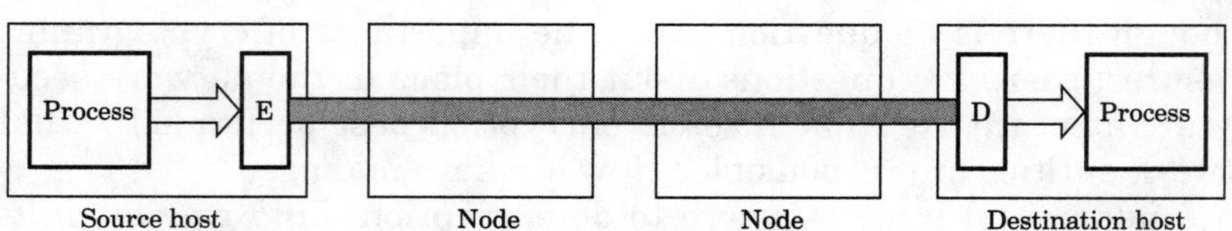

Figure 10.4 End-to-end encryption.

will reside at each node for a while in plaintext form. If any node has been penetrated, security cannot be assured. Users, or individual hosts, have no control over what cryptographic algorithms and key management methods are used.

End-to-end encryption is fundamentally more secure, in that no intermediate nodes need be trusted. Even lower layers in the source and destination nodes need not be trusted. This approach observes the design principles of least privilege and least common mechanism. (Although we can preserve confidentiality and detect integrity problems without trusting intermediate nodes, we must trust them to deliver the message.) Probably, end-to-end encryption is less costly to operate. The cost of encryption and decryption is incurred only once per message, rather than once per link. Since only the endpoints take special measures, the cost of security is borne by those who want it, and this is more equitable. The need for costly security measures at the intermediate nodes is reduced. However, end-to-end encryption devices can be complex and costly to build.

Key management is more complex with end-to-end encryption. If hosts are the endpoints, a host needs a key for every other host it may communicate with, instead of the many fewer nodes it is connected with. If processes are the endpoints, even more keys are needed. An end-to-end approach is feasible only with dynamic key distribution. End-to-end encryption does not protect against traffic analysis, since address information is in the clear. In some host-to-host E^3 systems, cleartext messages go into an E^3 unit that separates a trusted host from an untrusted network. With this architecture, the bypass mechanism is trusted to pass in cleartext nothing but protocol information. End-to-end encryption is incompatible with some useful processing techniques. For example, lower protocol layers cannot perform data compression that depends on text characteristics. End-to-end measures may also conflict with the firewall approach.

Clearly, both approaches have advantages. Both can be used in the same network or the same host, or for different needs of the same application.

Generic security services

It is useful to have a common application program interface for invoking cryptographic and other security services—an interface that can be implemented with different mechanisms and in different protocol environments, so that application programs are portable. That is the approach of Generic Security Service Application Program Interface (GSS-API). The "application" is a protocol entity that calls GSS-API to obtain security services: authentication, integrity, and confidentiality. The entity receives tokens from its local GSS-API and sends them to its peer entity, which passes them to *its* local GSS-API. Peer entity authentication is one operation; data origin authentication and integrity protection are others. An association called a *security context* is set up between peers. Although the services of GSS-API are based on ISO definitions, they can be provided in a TCP/IP environment as well.

Authentication

This section and the next discuss specific services, taking off from those described in the OSI security architecture.

Authentication in operating systems is mainly user authentication. A user claims an identity and presents evidence to back up the claim. The evidence is something the user knows, has, or does. The system evaluates the evidence, using stored authentication information. Authentication in networks must solve a broader problem under circumstances of greater threat. The problem is broader because:

- Not only users but also other entities need to be authenticated. Hosts must authenticate themselves to other hosts, and processes to processes. The OSI terminology is *peer entity authentication*; another term is *identity authentication*. The network entities that participate in authentication are *principals*. Principals include users, hosts, and processes.
- *Mutual authentication* is needed. The user needs to be assured that she is logging on to the right host. A server process must know what client is making a request, and the client needs to know that the intended server is handling it.
- Users must authenticate themselves to many different hosts and services. For convenience—and their sanity—users want *single sign-on,* where one login authenticates a user to all the network resources.
- Multiple domains of authority are involved. There are many authentication services, with different policies. The trust relationships among them are complex, yet they need to cooperate on authentication.
- Although the network is "broken" or partly broken most of the time, authentication service must be available when it is needed.

The circumstances hold more threat in that:

- Authentication information, such as passwords, is subject to eavesdropping.

- Authentication done at the beginning of a session or connection is at greater risk of becoming invalid during the connection.
- Attacks can modify messages, including those for authentication.
- Some links and nodes of the network may not be trusted by the source and destination hosts.
- Intruders are more remote and harder to trace.

The OSI security architecture specifies, in addition to peer identity authentication, other authentication services that are discussed later—data origin authentication and message content authentication.

Types of identity authentication

The simplest type of authentication is called just that—*simple authentication.* Simple authentication is one-way; a *claimant* (such as a user or a client process) authenticates itself to a *verifier* (such as an operating system or a server process) by providing some proof of identity, such as a password or token. Simple authentication is called *disclosing* because the proof of identity is disclosed to eavesdroppers. A commonly used proof of host identity is the network address in a packet. This *address-based authentication* is weak because network addresses can be impersonated quite easily. In an *authentication protocol,* the claimant and verifier carry out a sequence of steps, some involving messages and others involving computation. Nearly all authentication protocols are based on cryptography. Both secret key and public key methods are used. The steps for simple authentication might be

```
Claimant→Verifier:   userID
Verifier→Claimant:   Please enter password
Claimant→Verifier:   password
Verifier:            Looks up password, accepts or rejects
```

This protocol—familiar to all computer users—has fatal flaws in the network environment. One problem is that an eavesdropper can learn the password and later use it to impersonate the claimant. Further, passwords tend to be weak. Finally, the authentication is only one-way. It does not provide for a user authenticating a host, or a client authenticating a server.

We could prevent an eavesdropper from learning the password by using a one-way transformation *f*. The transformation *f* is publicly known. The verifier stores passwords transformed in the same way.

```
Claimant:            Compute q′ = f(password)
Claimant→Verifier:   (userID, q′)
Verifier:            Look up transformed password q corresponding to
                     userID; if q′ = q, accept
```

This *protected password* (or *protected simple authentication*) method prevents an easy grab of a password, but it is still vulnerable to eavesdropping and replay. A similar method uses cryptography; a secret key *k* is shared by the claimant (*C*) and verifier (*V*) and no one else:

```
C→V:    "I am C", Ek("I am C")
V:      Using k corresponding to C, decrypt encrypted "I am C". Compare
        result with "I am C". If equal, accept claim.
```

(This works because only a claimant who knows *k* could have produced a message that decrypts properly.) A replay attack is still possible; the eavesdropper can replay the entire message.

Replay can be prevented if the verifier can be sure that each message is *fresh.* One way to establish freshness is to include in the message either a time stamp or a *nonce*—a randomly generated identifier that is used only once. Nonces are used with challenge-response methods, as in the following improved protocol, where *n* is a nonce:

```
C→V:    "I am C"
V→C:    n
C:      Compute n' = Ek(n)
C→V:    n'
V:      If Ek(n) = n', accept
```

The verifier sends a nonce as a challenge; the correct response can be computed only by a claimant who knows the secret key *k*. Eavesdropping on previous exchanges would not help an intruder, who would never have seen this specific nonce.

These examples move toward *strong authentication,* in which the claimant does not risk disclosure of any secret. But strong one-way authentication is not enough. A distributed system needs *mutual authentication,* in which each principal verifies the other's claim of identity. A user who logs on to a remote host assumes that host will behave responsibly—take good care of his data, give correct answers, not perform transactions in his name that he did not authorize. The user trusts the host, based on his knowledge about it, and needs to be sure that some other host is not impersonating the one he trusts. Similarly, a client process needs assurance that the intended server is handling its request. Each principal must authenticate the other. With *strong mutual authentication,* neither principal risks disclosure of the secret information that it uses to prove its claim. No secret is disclosed to the other principal or to an eavesdropper.

Mutual authentication and authentication servers

Since two-way authentication is needed, it might seem reasonable to use two one-way protocols: principal *A* authenticates *B*, and then *B* authenticates A. This is not good practice, however, for two reasons. First, the two protocols in sequence can have vulnerabilities that each separately does not have. Second, a protocol specifically designed for mutual authentication is more efficient than two one-way protocols.

The following is a simple, but flawed, protocol (n_1 and n_2 are nonces, k is a key shared by A and B):

$A \rightarrow B$:	"I am A", n_1
$B \rightarrow A$:	$E_k(n_1)$, $E_k(n_2)$
A:	Decrypt n_1 and verify. Decrypt n_2.
$A \rightarrow B$:	n_2
B:	Verify n_2.

B demonstrates to A that it knows k by encrypting A's challenge, and A verifies by decrypting. A demonstrates to B that it knows k by decrypting B's challenge. Only three messages are needed, since message 2 combines response and challenge. Unfortunately, this protocol is vulnerable to attack; an intruder who intercepts the first message can pose as B and send the same challenge, n_1, to A, which will respond with the encrypted value. Designing secure mutual authentication protocols is extremely difficult.

The protocols above use secret key encryption, and other protocols use public key methods. For both kinds, key distribution becomes a serious problem. For this and other reasons, authentication often uses a trusted third party called an *authentication server* (AS). The server is typically implemented on a separate host dedicated to authentication and related functions such as key management and administering user IDs, resource names, and passwords. Using an authentication server is good security design, since the server can be carefully protected and managed.

An important design issue is whether the server acts *on line*—for example at the start of each client-server connection—or instead issues *credentials* that principals can save for later use. There are usually two kinds of credentials—long-lived ones that are issued when a principal is registered, and dynamically issued ones. An online AS may become a bottleneck. If multiple domains are involved, all the ASs must be available. For this reason, authentication servers often are replicated. Replication increases vulnerability, however, since compromising one AS compromises them all. Off-line servers and credentials have the disadvantage that it is difficult or impossible to revoke the credentials that have been given out. The usual solution is a time limit. Too short a limit does little to remove the bottleneck and does not provide for long-running jobs or batch jobs that run later; too long a limit allows the use of credentials that no longer correspond to security policy.

Issues in authentication service design

In addition to the on-line/off-line decision, issues in authentication service design include:

- What protocols are used, what attacks they must counter, and how they are designed and verified
- What cryptosystems are used
- How encryption keys are managed
- How much trust has to be placed in authentication servers
- How authentication works across multiple domains of authority

Like our last examples, real authentication protocols rely on challenge-response; the response usually requires decrypting the challenge. To prevent replay attacks, the challenge must change for every execution of the protocol. Most protocols use as challenge either time stamps or nonces. To use a time stamp, for example, *A* reads its own clock, encrypts the reading, and sends the result to *B*. *B* must verify that the time stamp is current, but it cannot do so directly. The message has taken some time to arrive, and *B*'s clock is sure not to be exactly synchronized with *A*'s clock. So "current" must be interpreted as within some time window. Further, everything depends on the security of the clock, or time service. And if only an authenticated time server can be trusted, the trust is circular. A nonce depends for its one-time property on good pseudo-random number generation.

In addition to the cryptosystem attacks—known plaintext and chosen ciphertext—there are attacks specific to authentication protocols. In an *oracle session attack,* an intruder uses a second execution of the protocol to trick one of the principals into behaving as an oracle—revealing critical information. In the flawed protocol previously described, an intruder can trick *A* into revealing the encrypted value of the original challenge. The generic flaw is that an attack can use one message of a protocol as the basis for later messages of the protocol. Attacks of this type have been called *interleaving attacks.*

A fair number of cryptographic protocols, even some adopted as standards, have turned out to be flawed, and authentication protocols are no exception. For now, the main safeguards are systematic design techniques and thorough examination by the cryptography community. Formal methods for analyzing and verifying security are being explored.

Authentication can use either secret key or public key cryptography. Secret key methods involve on-line servers, whereas public key methods use off-line certification of the public key. This is especially an advantage with multiple domains, since on-line authentication could involve authentication servers in several domains, and all would have to be available.

The Kerberos authentication system

The *Kerberos* authentication system was developed for Project Athena at MIT—an environment where users at anonymous (and untrusted) workstations requested services from larger computers. Kerberos has been implemented in many other environments; it is the most commonly used cryptographic method for authentication.

Overview of Kerberos. Kerberos provides both user authentication and mutual authentication of client and server. The protocols, which rely on secret key encryption, use a trusted third-party authentication server. (Kerberos is the three-headed dog that guards the entrance to the underworld of Greek myth.) The assumption is that hosts, including workstations and server machines, are not trusted and that network messages are vulnerable. A trusted *key distribution center* (KDC) maintains the secret keys of all the principals. The secret key of a user is computed from the user's password. The KDC also acts as an on-line authentication server. A logically distinct *ticket-granting server* (TGS) has access to the same keys. A client obtains from the KDC *credentials* for a server. The credentials include a secret session key and a *ticket* that, when accompanied by an *authenticator,* can authenticate the client to that server. A ticket expires after some interval, such as 10 hours. A client can also ask the server to authenticate itself. Once credentials are obtained, they can be used not only for authentication, but also for integrity and confidentiality of messages. Principals in separately administered *realms* can authenticate one another if the administrators have arranged for a shared secret or if the realms are part of a realm hierarchy.

Kerberos protocols. When a user logs in, a message exchange with the AS occurs, resulting in a ticket for the TGS. This is a *ticket-granting ticket* (TGT). To obtain a ticket for another server, a client process (on behalf of the user) exchanges messages with the TGS. Finally, the client presents the credentials to the server, as in Fig. 10.5. The message exchanges are described here in simplified form. The notation $\{m\}K_c$ is used for message m encrypted under the key of principal c.

The *authentication service exchange* is (where c identifies a client, s identifies a server, and n is a nonce):

Client→Kerberos:	c,s,n
Kerberos→Client:	$\{K_{c,s},\ s,\ n\}K_c,\ \{T_{c,s}\}K_s$

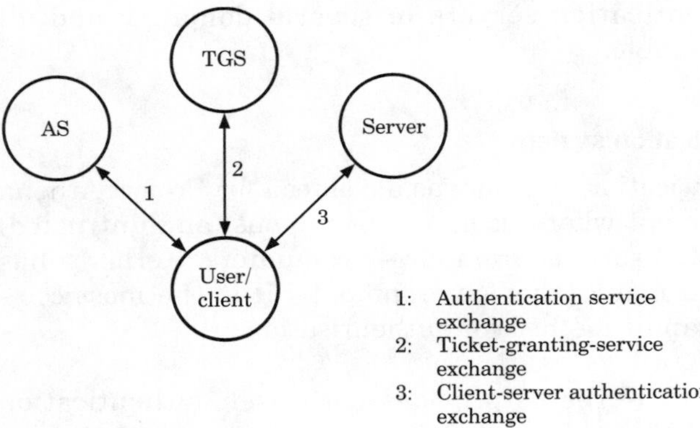

Figure 10.5 Kerberos message exchanges.

The client sends, in cleartext, its own identity and that of the target server, and a nonce. Kerberos randomly generates a session key, then creates a ticket T_{cs} containing the client ID, the session key K_{cs}, and start and expiration times. Since the ticket is encrypted by the key known only to the server, it is protected against reading or modification by any other party. The response from Kerberos also contains the session key, server ID, and original nonce, encrypted by the client's key K_c. The client decrypts the session key and nonce, and verifies that the nonce matches the one in its request. It saves the ticket and session key for later use.

The AS exchange is used mainly at login to obtain a ticket for the TGS; after that, tickets are obtained from the TGS. The AS exchange for the TGS is

Client→Kerberos: c, tgs, n
Kerberos→Client: $\{K_{c,tgs}, tgs, n\}K_c, \{T_{c,tgs}\}K_{tgs}$

One reason for using a TGS is to reduce exposure of the client's secret key. When the user's password is entered, it is converted to the secret key. This key needs to be kept in workstation memory only until the AS exchange completes.

The following messages are exchanged to obtain a ticket for a server:

Client→TGS: $\{A_c\}K_{c,tgs}, \{T_{c,tgs}\}K_{tgs}, s, n$
TGS→Client: $\{K_{c,s}, s, n\}K_{c,tgs}, \{\mathrm{T}_{c,s}\}K_s$

The client sends an authenticator A_c, along with the ticket-granting ticket obtained in the previous exchange, the server ID, and a nonce. The purpose of the authenticator is to foil replay attacks using a ticket obtained by eavesdropping. The authenticator includes a time stamp and is encrypted in the client-TGS session key, which never gets transmitted in cleartext. The authenticator proves that the message is recent and that the client knows the session key. The TGS sends back a ticket for the server, encrypted under the server's key, along with a client-server session key and the nonce, encrypted under the client-TGS session key. The client decrypts the session key to use in the next exchange.

To authenticate itself to the server, the client sends the message:

Client→Server: $\{A_c\}K_{c,s}, \{T_{c,s}\}K_s$

This message contains a freshly generated authenticator, encrypted by the session key obtained in the TGS exchange, and the ticket. The server decrypts the ticket and uses the session key in the ticket to decrypt the authenticator. The authenticator time stamp must agree within some window (such as 5 minutes) with the local server time. The server now knows the client's identity and can use it for access control, accounting, and auditing. It knows the session key, which it can use to encrypt later messages for secrecy.

The client has the option of requesting mutual authentication. If it does, the server returns to the client the time stamp from the authenticator, encrypted by the session key. Only the server could have decrypted the authenticator using the session key.

Other Kerberos services. Kerberos protocols support interrealm authentication: a principal in one realm is authenticated to a principal in another realm. Each realm has its own KDC. For realms *A* and *B* to interauthenticate, the administrators of realms exchange secret interrealm keys. The TGS of *A* then becomes a principal in realm *B*, where it can be used by *B* clients, and vice versa. Realms typically are organized in a hierarchy, and an authentication involves traversing the hierarchy up to a common node, and then down. (There also can be shortcut links across the tree.) The authentication path—all the realms consulted—is documented in the ticket. A ticket then could be rejected by a server that does not trust all the realms.

A client may need to allow a server to use its identity, but only for limited purposes. A client may, for example, allow a print server to access the file server on its behalf, but only for purposes of printing a file. Kerberos provides a *proxy* mechanism for this purpose. A ticket normally specifies the host addresses for which it is valid, so it cannot be simply passed to a server. Instead, the client uses a *proxiable* TGT to obtain a proxy ticket for the file service that is valid for a different host address (in this example the address of the print server.) The client passes this proxy to the print server. Since proxy tickets are flagged as such, the file server can perform additional authentication and authorization checking. A less restricted form of proxy supports *authentication forwarding,* which allows a user to be authenticated for remote login without reentering the password. This feature supports single sign-on.

The short life of a ticket precludes its use for a long-running job, or for a batch job that runs long after it is submitted. Long-lived tickets are a poor solution, since an intruder who stole one would gain a long period of access. Renewing tickets frequently is also bad, since the client would have to keep the secret key available (and vulnerable) or else bother the user, who may not even be present. Kerberos addresses these problems with renewable tickets and postdating. A renewable ticket has two expiration dates, and the KDC will renew an unexpired ticket up until the second expiration date. The KDC can check lists of stolen tickets before renewing. Postdating reduces the time valid tickets sit around in batch queues.

Kerberos weaknesses. The environment for which Kerberos was designed differs from the more general environments where it has been used. In the more general environment, autonomous processes carry out functions such as file transfer and email; many hosts are multiuser systems. A weakness for this environment is that, during the AS exchange, secret keys are stored briefly at the client machine. There they are vulnerable to intruders, especially other users of the same host. Session keys are vulnerable (at client and server machines) for a much longer period.

Another problem is that key management becomes very difficult as Kerberos is applied in large multirealm environments. Even within a single realm, there is the task of registering each application service as a Kerberos principal and maintaining a secret key for it.

The time-stamp approach for preventing replay of the authenticator may be inadequate. A replay could occur within the time window, and the time stamps rely on the hosts' clocks being roughly synchronized and on the trustworthiness of the time service. Password-guessing attacks are also possible for an intruder who records AS exchanges at login. The intruder can guess at a password, convert it to a guessed K_c, and try to decrypt the message from the AS. With weak passwords, such attacks are a significant threat; a countermeasure is to combine Kerberos with one-time passwords.

As in any system relying on secret keys, a compromise of the KDC would compromise all the keys it maintains. A dedicated machine should be used for the KDC. The KDC and its backup tapes must be protected with strong physical security. Kerberos depends on the availability of an on-line authentication server. The AS can be—and usually is—replicated, but this solution makes it more vulnerable to compromise. Client-server applications need to be modified—*Kerberized*—to take advantage of Kerberos.

The *SESAME* project in Europe has extended Kerberos to remove some of these weaknesses. The SESAME V2 extension distributes keys by using public key methods. There is a trusted authentication server at each host, which simplifies key management. Generalized support for access control is also provided.

X.509 Directory authentication

The X.509 protocols were specified to meet the authentication needs of the X.500 Directory services and of the applications that use them. X.509 authentication is based on public key cryptography.

For two parties, *A* and *B,* to authenticate themselves to one another, each needs a certified public key of the other. Typically these certificates would be obtained from a certification authority perhaps well in advance. Or *A* and *B* can exchange keys directly. Protocols of varying strength are defined for X.509; we describe here the strongest one—three-way authentication. (The protocol messages optionally contain application data; this is omitted from our description.)

From a CA, *A* obtains public key certificates for itself and *B*. *A* sends to *B* its own identity plus other items that are signed with *A*'s private key. (Recall that a signed message includes the message plus the signature, and that verification confirms both the identity of the sender and the integrity of the message.) Here the signed items include a nonce and *B*'s identity. *B* uses *A*'s public key to decrypt the message. *B* thus verifies that the message came from *A* and was intended for *B,* and that the message is not altered. *B* can also save the nonce to check for later replay. *B* responds with a message, signed with *B*'s private key, that *A* verifies similarly. This message includes a new nonce, *A*'s identity, and the nonce sent by *A*. *A* verifies that the returned nonce is the same one it sent. *A* then sends a signed message containing *B*'s nonce, which *B* verifies. The protocol also specifies optional time stamps, which are used by the two-way X.509 protocols.

Public key authentication, as in X.509, has the advantage that no on-line authentication server is needed. Given signed public key certificates (which can be distributed in many ways, using untrusted servers), the parties need only each other for authentication.

KryptoKnight

The KryptoKnight system, developed at IBM, provides authentication and key distribution services. It supports single sign-on, mutual authentication of parties, and data authentication. The KryptoKnight protocols were designed for devices with a wide range of computational capability, all of which must interoperate. The protocol implementations are intended to be freely exportable. These goals led to a family of protocols that use encryption sparingly. Instead, they use:

- *One-time padding,* which protects a small secret by exclusive-ORing it with a one-time random number.
- *The one-way hash function* of a message concatenated with a secret key. A message sealed this way can be unsealed only by someone who knows the key. This hash function also generates a pseudorandom number that can be used for one-time padding.

Like Kerberos, KryptoKnight assumes a KDC (or AS) that shares a secret key with each party. However, KryptoKnight protocols do not assume that one party is a client and the other a server; the parties play symmetrical roles. KryptoKnight supports both the *push model* used by Kerberos (party *A* obtains a key before communicating with *B*) and the *pull model* (*A* contacts *B*, and *B* gets the key).

For a basic two-way authentication protocol, the message exchanges are

1. $A \rightarrow B$: A, B, N_a
2. $B \rightarrow A$: B, A, N_b, $\text{MAC}_{ab}\ (N_a, N_b, B)$
3. $A \rightarrow B$: A, B, $\text{MAC}_{ab}\ (N_a, N_b)$

where N_a and N_b are nonces and the message authentication code MAC_{ab} can be either (1) a cryptographic function computed with secret key K_{ab}, or (2) a hash function such as MD5 applied to the message field concatenated with the secret key. *A* knows that message 2 could only come from someone who knows K_{ab} and N_a. *B* verifies message 3 similarly. This protocol assumes that the two parties share the secret key. A key is transferred between two parties, such as the AS and *A*, in a *ticket*; the key is encrypted by exclusive-ORing it with the $\text{MAC}_{as,a}$ of the essential ticket fields.

Tickets are used for single sign-on. For each user, the AS maintains a secret key that is a one-way transformation of the user's password. KryptoKnight on the user's workstation first sends a message to the AS that contains the user's name and a value that is a function of a nonce and the password. The AS authenticates the user and replies with a ticket that is sealed with the secret key. If the entered password is correct, the local KryptoKnight can unseal the ticket. The ticket can be used for authentication (by way of the AS) to any number of remote services until the user logs off. A product based on KryptoKnight, NetSP, provides single sign-on, using a workstation as an authentication server. The tickets issued by NetSP are honored by various application services and by the Resource Access Control Facility (RACF). NetSP functions are used through the generic security interface, GSS-API.

S/KEY one-time passwords

S/KEY is a simple and highly practical scheme for transforming a user-chosen passphrase into a sequence of one-time passwords. The idea behind S/KEY was described by Leslie Lamport in 1981. A one-way hash function is applied to a secret passphrase n times; each time the function is applied to the result of the previous application. This process generates n one-time passwords, which then are used in reverse order for n logins. Since the hash function is one-way, an eavesdropper who collects a password cannot compute from it any password that remains to be used.

In an initialization phase, the password sequence is generated. The user chooses a secret passphrase and the value n (500, for example). The next step is performed by the user's computing device, which could be a trusted PC or a palmtop password calculator. The device applies the hash function n times to generate the first password, $n-1$ times for the second, and so on. Before the hash function is applied, a *seed* is concatenated with the passphrase. The seed allows the same passphrase to be used for different systems, with different seeds resulting in different password sequences. The seed, the value n, and the nth one-time password are sent to the authentication server.

For each login the AS issues a challenge containing the sequence number and seed, for example 96 and Unix3. The user enters these values and the secret passphrase into the password calculator, which computes and displays the 96th password. The user enters this at the terminal for transmission to the AS. Alternatively, the computations can be done by a trusted workstation.

For each user, the AS stores the seed, the current sequence number, and the password from the last successful login. To verify an authentication request, the AS applies the hash function once to the transmitted password. If the result equals the stored password, authentication succeeds. The new password is stored for the next use, and the sequence number is decremented.

The hash function produces a 64-bit output. Since a 64-bit password is hard for people to use, the calculator converts this value to an equivalent sequence of short words. S/KEY initialization can produce a printed list of the one-time passwords. Then the scheme can be used without any computing support (but the list must be closely guarded).

S/KEY is simple and inexpensive to implement. It has the virtue that no secret values have to be stored at either the workstation or the server. However, a dictionary attack on the secret password is still possible by an eavesdropper who collects one-time passwords and applies the hash function to password guesses. A weakness is that the AS does not authenticate itself to the user, opening the way for a *small n attack.* Suppose an intruder impersonates the AS. When a user attempts to log in, the intruder sends a challenge with a small sequence number, such as 50. The user's response of the 50th password allows the intruder to compute and use all the passwords between 50 and the real sequence number. This attack fails if the user spots the discrepancy between the new challenge and the previous challenge.

Access Control, Confidentiality, and Integrity

The descriptions of services in this section are brief, because the concepts and mechanisms are covered in other chapters.

Access control

Access control services for networks must go beyond those for individual systems. There are new issues because the objects are distributed. There are new kinds of objects, such as hosts, links, and connections. Access control must enforce the policies of different administrative domains.

Issues include where access control is enforced and where access control information is maintained. For resources such as files, enforcement typically is the responsibility of the host where the file resides. Authorization is based on the authenticated identity of the accessing principal. It is possible, however, to have a centralized access control server that is closely protected and managed—as with a centralized authentication server. A client could contact the access control server for a capability or ticket, or the application server could present the access request to the access control server for a decision. The ISO framework for access control distinguishes between the *decision function* and the *enforcement function,* and these could be implemented at different locations.

One mechanism is a *privilege attribute certificate* (PAC), which is signed by a party that is trusted by the decision function. A PAC contains information such as an authenticated user name, role memberships, security labels, and capabilities. It establishes the holder's identity for access control and audit. The PAC mechanism supports delegation of rights from users to their applications. (Delegation is sometimes called *access control forwarding*; it extends the idea of the Kerberos proxy ticket.) PACs are supported in SESAME V2.

Difficult access control problems result from the interconnection of different organizations, with different security policies. These administrative domains may handle their internal access control differently—have different schemes for identifying subjects and objects, different access control policies, different roles. So one problem is to translate access requests between domains. More pressing, though, is the need to enforce security policies about interdomain traffic. The policies often concern which hosts connect to one another and what kinds of data can be transmitted between them. Some networks must ensure that connections and data flow do not violate multilevel policies.

Interdomain access control often is implemented with *packet filtering:* routers make access control decisions based on source and destination addresses from packet headers, along with stored tables of rules. With *policy routing,* packets could be routed according to policy requirements about security and other attributes (such as performance and cost). Methods proposed for policy routing rely on signed certificates that accompany data units, so that routing devices can make their decisions simply and efficiently. In one scheme, a cryptographically sealed *visa* results from negotiation between access control servers in the source and destination domains. The visa authorizes a cross-domain connection, and each packet transmitted on the connection carries a *visa stamp* documenting its exit and entry permissions. (The stamp is a function of the packet's data and a secret value from the visa.) A *border router* (at the border of the source domain) then only has to check that the packet has a valid visa.

Confidentiality

Confidentiality in a computing system or network means that information is disclosed only in accordance with policy. Nearly all host policies restrict who can see information. When the hosts under a policy are connected—to one another and to the internetwork—policy enforcement must encompass the network. A company researcher should be able to transmit a confidential report from one company site to another without fear of eavesdropping. Electronic mail should go only to the sender's choice of recipients. People who order merchandise should not risk exposure of their credit card numbers. The OSI security architecture specifies two confidentiality services: data confidentiality and traffic confidentiality. The Trusted Network Interpretation uses the term *compromise protection,* which includes data confidentiality, traffic confidentiality, and selective routing. In principle, confidentiality could be provided either by preventing access to the data that flows on the network, or by making that data incomprehensible, as with encryption. Although both kinds of measures are used, encryption is by far the most important mechanism supporting confidentiality.

Providing traffic secrecy involves hiding how much traffic passes between end points, and what its pattern is. The two main mechanisms are *traffic padding* and routing control. Traffic padding adds random data to data units. Routing control allows users to restrict what links their data will take—to avoid insecure links. For example, they could specify a required level of *quality of service* for confidentiality.

Integrity and nonrepudiation

It is important to both the sender and receiver of a message that the message received have exactly the contents that were sent. Using Electronic Data Interchange, for example, AceComp Company orders 1000 computer chips from BestChip Company, but BestChip receives an order for 10,000. If BestChip acts on that information, a dispute—or worse—will ensue. The message could have been altered through communication error or through a malicious attack. Cryptographic mechanisms for message integrity include message authentication codes, hash functions, and digital signatures. When integrity mechanisms are applied to protect a single PDU or packet, the service provided is (in OSI terms) *connectionless integrity*. A transaction between AceComp and BestChip, however, probably involves a sequence of data units, and a sequence can be attacked in more ways. Data units can be deleted or inserted, and they can be repeated. The OSI service of *connection integrity* allows detection of any of these threats to data passing on a connection. The receiver can verify whether the data units arrived without modification, deletion, insertion, or replay. (But an intruder could still replay the entire sequence.) One way to provide sequence integrity is to number the data units in order and include the sequence numbers when the hash function or other check value is computed. Since integrity measures have a cost, partial protection is often a good option. For example, integrity protection might apply only to certain fields of a data unit (*selective field* integrity in OSI terms). This makes sense only at the application layer, where field meanings are understood.

Suppose that AceComp and BestChip communicate using a connection-oriented integrity service, and that some communications entity on a BestChip host detects a missing data unit. Rather than simply passing up an error indication, the entity can try to recover (by requesting retransmission of a data unit, for example) so that the error is never seen by higher layers and the EDI application. (This is *connection integrity with recovery.*)

BestChip needs to know that its connection is with AceComp and not with some party masquerading as AceComp; it needs peer entity authentication. The corresponding service for the connectionless case is *data origin authentication.* A recipient is assured that a data unit really came from the purported sender.

Suppose that BestChip fills AceComp's order for 1000 chips. Meanwhile, AceComp has had an unexpected and drastic drop in sales; it doesn't need the chips, and it can't pay for them. It claims it never ordered them. With *nonrepudiation service,* BestChip could prove that AceComp did place the order. In this example, since the sender denies sending, the service is "nonrepudiation with proof of origin." Protection against a receiver's denial of receiving is called "nonrepudiation with proof of delivery." Digital signatures provide a technical basis for nonrepudiation; an administrative and legal basis is also needed.

Digital signatures can support all of the integrity services—integrity, data origin authentication, and nonrepudiation—with the same transformations.

Network Management

Network management includes: keeping track of network configurations; monitoring performance; detecting breakdowns or intrusions—or conditions that could lead to them; gathering data to support decisions on equipment acquisition; controlling access to the network and its resources; and maintaining accounting information.

In the context of this book, network management is part of network security; it is a set of services that support network availability, confidentiality, and integrity. For network managers and those who provide their tools, however, network security is part of network management. Network management and security intersect in two ways. First, the security of the network management activities must be protected. An attack on network management is even more dangerous than an attack on a host, because it jeopardizes the very foundation of the network. An intruder who can modify routing tables, disable packet filtering, or add rogue devices or nodes can cause wide damage. Second, network management viewed broadly includes access control and audit services that directly support security. Sometimes it is viewed as including key management.

Network management is supported by software and hardware tools. The tools support management information databases that keep track of network objects, such as hosts, routers, links, and communications software and devices. The tools also support communications among the distributed network management components. Since networks are heterogeneous, standards are needed to allow network management tools to work together. Both OSI and the Internet have network management standards.

OSI Systems Management

The OSI term is *Systems Management.* Five functional areas are defined: fault management, accounting management, configuration management, performance management, and security management. Security management includes both the security of network management and the security of the managed objects. The entities of the OSI model include *managing systems, agents* at *managed systems,* and *managed objects* within managed systems. A *Common Management Information Protocol* (CMIP) allows managing systems to operate on managed objects through their agents. Since object-oriented techniques are used for representing the objects, any kind of object can be defined. Performance management, for example, could use a time series object. Built-in objects include counters, gauges, and logs. In addition to data and operations, the managed objects can have *events.* For example, an object could have an integrity violation event or a security violation event. This framework allows criteria to be set for asynchronous reporting and logging. Events are used by the security functions of OSI Systems Management, which include security alarm reporting and audit trail. Other security aspects are access control for managed objects and security features for CMIP.

SNMP

SNMP (Simple Network Management Protocol) is a set of Internet standards for managing TCP/IP networks. A second version, SNMPv2, was adopted in 1993. The data types defined for the *Management Information Base* (MIB) in SNMPv2 include counters, gauges, and time ticks; new objects can be defined. As with OSI, there is a manager-to-agent protocol, with message types including **get** and **set** of variables in the MIB. Agents can also asynchronously notify managers of events.

SNMPv1 has weak security. Authentication is based on a "community string" that appears in a message; in practice the method was equivalent to using a password. Messages are vulnerable to all the basic network attacks. SNMPv2 has much better security. It provides data-origin authentication, data integrity, protection against replay, and privacy (confidentiality). It introduces the concept of *party,* which is an execution context for an SNMP protocol. A party is associated with a transport address; it has authentication and privacy parameters and a restricted view of the MIB. This feature makes it possible to give different management privileges to different people.

Electronic Mail Security

Electronic mail is an essential part of the infrastructure for day-to-day business operation. But email often is not secure enough for the role that it plays. Unless a user takes steps to encrypt it, email is vulnerable to eavesdropping. A recipient has no assurance that the mail really came from the purported sender, and a sender has no assurance that the mail went to the intended recipients and no one else. Email systems have powerful features like distribution lists, forwarding, and logging. It becomes very easy to make an error that discloses confidential data to hundreds of people. With *computational email,* a message contains a command script that is executed automatically when the message is read. This feature is a convenient building block for multimedia applications, but it also provides a Trojan horse opportunity.

Privacy Enhanced Mail

Privacy Enhanced Mail (PEM) defines a comprehensive set of end-to-end services—not just privacy (confidentiality) as in the name, but also message integrity, message origin authentication, and support for nonrepudiation. The confidentiality service is optional, and the other services apply to all messages. PEM was developed by the Internet community and is an Internet standard.

PEM is designed to fit into the architecture of other messaging systems, such as those based on SMTP. PEM uses concepts from *X.400* (a standard developed by the ITU). PEM is not tied to any specific cryptographic algorithms (these are specified separately from the other protocols) but it originally specifies public key cryptography, in particular digital signatures. It uses the approach to public key certificates defined in X.509.

Mail system model. Figure 10.6 shows how PEM fits into a message-handling system, which is described according to the X.400 model. The responsibility for mail service at each host is shared by two components: a *user agent* (UA) and a *message transfer agent* (MTA). The user communicates with the UA, and the MTA communicates with other MTAs to get the message either directly to the recipient's UA or to a mailbox MTA, where it resides until the UA retrieves it. Figure 10.6 shows an originator at a multiuser host and a recipient at a workstation. Since the workstation is not continuously available, the

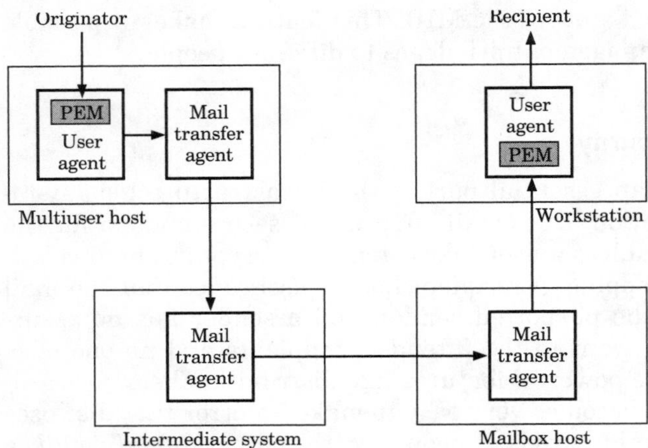

Figure 10.6 Mail system model for Privacy Enhanced Mail. [*Adapted from Kent (1993b). Copyright (©) 1993 Association for Computing Machinery, Inc. (ACM). Reprinted by permission.*]

message goes to an MTA at a mailbox host. PEM is designed to be transparent to MTAs. To make it easy to use, PEM is usually integrated into UAs.

Key management. An Internet certification authority is supposed to issue public key certificates. PEM specifies a hierarchy of authorities, each of which issues certificates to subordinate CAs or directly to users. At the highest level is the *Internet PCA Registration Authority* (IPRA). At the next level are *policy certification authorities* (PCAs), and at lower levels, CAs. The standards set up a framework for requiring PCAs to have documented certification policies. All PCAs must conform to the policy of the IPRA, but each can have its own policy as well. For example, a "high assurance" PCA for electronic commerce would require its CAs to use strong security technology for authentication and key management.

Integrity. Message integrity is based on a *message integrity code* (MIC), which is calculated by using a strong one-way hash function such as MD5. No specific algorithm is built into the standard. Of course the integrity of the MIC itself must be protected, and for message origin authentication it must be bound to the identity of the originator. Both purposes are accomplished with a digital signature. The MIC is encrypted with the originator's private key. To verify integrity, the recipient UA decrypts the MIC using the originator's public key, computes the MIC on the received message, and compares the computed MIC with the sent MIC. The UA informs the user that the message integrity has been verified, and it displays the authenticated identity of the originator.

For message origin and integrity verification, the recipient needs the public key certificate of the originator. One option that PEM allows is for the needed certificates to be passed in the message header; alternatively, certificates can be cached by UAs.

Confidentiality. The originator may ask for the message to be encrypted. Encryption is done after the message is signed, with a key that is generated by the originator and that is used for only one message. Even if the message has multiple recipients, it is encrypted only once, which means that the message key must be distributed safely to each recipient. This can be done by encrypting the message key with the public key of each recipient and including it in the message header. Other header fields specify the algorithm used for encryption and any parameters needed for decryption. For example, header fields might specify the DES in cipher block chaining mode and provide the initialization vector. Analogous fields describe how the message key was encrypted. When the message is received, it is decrypted before its integrity and origin are verified. Implementations of PEM use mainly RSA and DES.

PEM use. Privacy Enhanced Mail has been used less than expected. At an Internet workshop (Braden et al. 1994) some of the reasons were reviewed: slow arrival of high-quality implementations, use of patented cryptography, and export restrictions. There is no organizational infrastructure to provide the certification hierarchy and no directory service for obtaining certificates.

Pretty Good Privacy

While PEM seems to have languished, *Pretty Good Privacy* (PGP) has flourished. Both PEM and PGP use a combination of public key and symmetric methods. Their key management philosophies differ, however. PGP assumes no certification authority; instead public key certificates are distributed any way the users can work out. PGP was developed and made available as freeware by Philip Zimmermann. “PGP empowers people to take their privacy into their own hands. There’s a growing social need for it. That’s why I wrote it” (Zimmermann 1994). In a straightforward package, PGP provides email confidentiality and digital signatures, along with file encryption. It uses IDEA for data encryption, RSA for key encryption and digital signatures, and MD5 for the digital signature message digest. Our PGP descriptions use PGP terminology, which differs from the terminology for other systems. A *session* key is a secret key used to encrypt one message, and a *secret* key is the private key of a public-private pair.

Confidentiality. To send a confidential message, the user first builds a file containing the message. PGP compresses the file before encrypting it; this makes the encryption both faster and stronger. For each message sent, a 128-bit data-encrypting session key is generated randomly, based on keystroke timing. The session key is RSA-encrypted with the recipient's public key and sent along with the encrypted message. The recipient's secret key is used to decrypt the session key, which is then used to decrypt the message.

Digital signatures. A PGP user can also sign a message with her secret key. PGP uses MD5 to generate a 128-bit message digest, which is then RSA-encrypted using the sender's secret key. A *signature certificate* is attached to the cleartext message; the certificate includes the *key ID* of the key that was used to sign it, the signed message digest, and a time stamp. The recipient gets a cleartext message and a printable signature certificate. If the recipient asks PGP to verify signature integrity, PGP uses RSA with the sender's public key to decrypt the message digest, calculates a message digest of the received message, and checks if the two digests match. A signed message also can be encrypted for confidentiality.

Keys and key rings. PGP provides the user with two *key rings:*

- A secret key ring for the user's own key pairs
- A public key ring for other people's public keys

Each ring contains key certificates. At the user's request, PGP generates a public-secret key pair. The user chooses the key size, which can go up to more than a thousand bits. PGP prompts for a unique user ID (such as name and email address) and a passphrase that will be used to protect the secret key. A key certificate is built that includes the user's name, a time stamp, and the key ID, which is the low-order 64 bits of the public key. (The key ID is sent with an encrypted message; it is used by the recipient's PGP to find the right secret key for decrypting the session key.) Before a secret key is placed in the key ring, it is encrypted with a 128-bit digest of the passphrase; this means that the user must supply the passphrase whenever the secret key is used. The public key is stored in a public key certificate in the public key ring.

Public key management. PGP's trust model differs from the X.509 model, where the trust relationships are built into an infrastructure. PGP users decide whom they trust. They need not rely on trust being transitive; although Bob trusts Alice, who trusts Carol, Bob may not trust Carol. PGP users can obtain public keys by exchanging diskettes, by email combined with telephone, or from trusted key servers. Closest to the PGP spirit is to use *trusted introducers.* Bob trusts Alice to give him Carol's public key. Bob already has Alice's public key, so, if Alice signs Carol's key, Bob can verify Alice's signature. Bob might trust Alice as a key source more than he trusts Dave. PGP's public key ring supports these trust notions. Associated with any key in Bob's ring—say Alice's—is Bob's judgment of how much he trusts Alice to certify other keys. Associated with Alice's key in Bob's ring, there may be signatures of trusted introducers of that key. Using the number of signatures, along with Bob's trust in the introducers, PGP computes how much the key in Bob's ring is trusted to be Alice's valid public key. When Bob gives Alice's key to Dave, Dave gets all the signatures as well. Zimmermann's vision is that people will gradually accumulate keys from people they trust and there will emerge a "decentralized fault-tolerant web of confidence for all public keys."

If a user's secret key is compromised, the user has to revoke the corresponding public key by distributing, as widely as possible, a key revocation certificate. When this certificate is added to the recipient's key ring, the revoked key becomes unusable. Signed certificates can also be revoked; this means the revoker no longer certifies the public key.

Security of PGP. PGP seems to be a highly secure system. IDEA, which PGP uses for data encryption, is believed to be a strong algorithm. PGP allows very long RSA keys. It provides safeguards for stored secret keys. The source code is available for study.

Legal issues. Two legal issues whirled around the original freeware PGP. There were patent issues about its use of RSA technology, and Zimmermann was under government investigation because PGP had spread outside the United States in possible violation of cryptography export restrictions. The investigation was ended in 1996, and PGP can be used in the United States without the patent problem. For noncommercial use, the Massachusetts Institute of Technology (MIT) distributes a freeware PGP that uses a different RSA implementation under license. For commercial use, PGP is marketed by Viacrypt, which obtained the RSA licenses.

Internet Security

In the mid-1990s, the number of Internet break-ins was growing by 70 percent a year. Attacks compromised tens of thousands of passwords. As the potential of the Internet for electronic commerce became evident, the vulnerability of the Internet became lead news. It was no news to Internet old-timers. The original lower-layer protocols included minimal security services. The military networks based on the same protocols relied on carefully structured end-to-end measures; they assumed an insecure network between the ends. The Internet, in contrast, connects many hosts that are insecurely configured and administered and that use minimal end-to-end measures. A majority of Internet hosts run UNIX, whose vulnerabilities are well-known.

> Security vulnerabilities can exist in the underlying communications network and its nodes, in the internet protocols, in network administration, or in host systems. To use the highway analogy, a communications problem might be like a pothole, a bridge failure, or a closed road. A protocol problem might be like a mis-marked exit sign or a failure of slower traffic to stay in the slow lane. A network administration problem might be the lack of emergency vehicle access or notification and response procedures for accidents. Last, a host system problem might be likened to a store proprietor along the highway leaving the doors open and the store unoccupied. The problem is not the proximity of the highway, but the carelessness of the store proprietor (and the fact that not everyone on the highway is honest). (McNulty 1994)

Vulnerabilities

The TCP/IP protocols protect against some threats. Checksums protect against packet header modification. For TCP, sequence numbers protect against lost and duplicated packets, and other measures protect against reuse of packets. The protections are weak, however. IP packets carry no authenticators of their payload data (a weakness corrected in a new version of IP). There is no common place for identification and authentication information or services. For the most part, applications must do their own authentication. Telnet and FTP authentication relies on passwords transmitted in cleartext. The applications and accessories are probably easier to exploit than the lower-layer protocols. Intruders have exploited the Domain Name Service, X Windows, and others. Telnet and FTP are risky to a host that is not well-secured.

IP spoofing. Many Internet attacks have exploited *IP spoofing,* which allows one host to masquerade as another. A packet is sent from one host, but the source address in the packet is that of another host. This is dangerous because applications commonly use source addresses to identify requests from trusted hosts. So an attacker at Host *A,* whose target is Host *B,* impersonates Host *T,* which is trusted by *B.* A common attack exploits an IP feature called *source routing,* which allows the sender of a packet to specify its route and return route. If the route is (*A, B, C*), *C* must use the return route (*C, B, A*).

For the attack to succeed, the packet sent from *A* must appear to come from *T.* Further, if the attack is to accomplish anything, *B*'s reply must go to *A,* not *T.* First, the attacker takes control of Host *A* and changes its IP address to *T.* The attacker then sends a packet to *B,* specifying source routing with *A* as the last hop in the route. Host *B* accepts the request as coming from *T* and routes its reply packet through *A.*

A firewall can protect an internal network against IP spoofing attacks by rejecting incoming source-routed packets. The hosts inside the firewall should not specify any outside trusted hosts, and the firewall should reject any incoming packet whose source address is in the internal network. The firewall should also block outgoing packets whose source address is not in the internal network; this is to avoid being the origin of an attack.

Hijacked connections. An attacker who gains control of an ongoing session gains the rights of the legitimate user. Authentication and access control services are useless, since the session is taken over after authentication, and access control assumes the user who was authenticated. UNIX systems on the Internet have been hit with hijacking attacks. The attacker penetrates the system using any method, then modifies the kernel to allow the hijacking of any active session. By hijacking a connection with a remote system, the attacker also gets access to that system.

Sniffer attacks. The Internet has suffered attacks that collected passwords and other information that could be used for unauthorized logins. These are called *sniffer attacks* because they use network monitoring tools called *sniffers.* The monitoring relies on a network interface feature called *promiscuous mode,* which is useful for network management, but deadly for security. A computer whose network interface unit is in promiscuous mode can read *all* packets passing on the network. An attacker who takes over such a computer runs a program that captures the first data transmitted for each network session (such as Telnet and FTP). The data typically include a remote host name, account name, and password. Thus, a compromise of one computer on one LAN can lead to compromise of all the remote systems used by all the LAN users.

Firewalls

A firewall in a building provides a fireproof barrier between parts of the building, making it harder for a fire in one part of the building to spread to other parts. Similarly, a network firewall is built around a network or subnetwork to protect it from the outside. Just as the firewall of a building must have doors in it, the network firewall must have openings that selectively allow information to pass. Steven Bellovin and William Cheswick (1994) define a *firewall* as a collection of components placed between an inner network and an outer network to achieve the following goals:

- All traffic must pass through the firewall.
- Only traffic that is authorized by the inner network's security policy is allowed to pass.
- The firewall cannot be penetrated.

The firewall may protect a poorly secured network from external threats, or it may protect a highly secure network from a wider, less secure one. Most corporate networks that connect to the Internet limit their exposure with firewalls. The most important firewall mechanisms are *packet filtering* and *application gateways.* Many firewalls use both. Firewalls often provide authentication service.

Examples of policies that a firewall can enforce are

- Allow two-way traffic only with hosts at the same sensitivity level
- Limit outside traffic to electronic mail

Many useful services (such as Sendmail and Telnet) are vulnerable. Their use across the firewall can be prevented, while use inside the firewall is allowed. A firewall can guard against routing-based attacks. It can provide authentication for all outside access, using one-time passwords. The authentication software only has to be installed on the firewall components and not on every host. A firewall can help a site hide information that might be useful to intruders, such as the user information provided by the UNIX **finger** command or the site information provided by the Domain Name System. A firewall can keep an audit trail of network connections and can detect possible intrusions.

Firewalls for security build on mechanisms that were developed for other functions: routers and gateways. Each of these mechanisms connects networks and controls network traffic passing through it. A router uses a network layer destination address and possible routing instructions to determine a route to the destination. A gateway, which operates on higher-layer PDUs, can connect two networks that use different protocols; it can translate from one protocol to another, such as TCP/IP to SNA, or X.400 mail to SMTP. Since routers and gateways already control traffic, they are natural points for additional security controls.

By concentrating resources and effort on a security control point, an organization can try to compensate for weaker security within the firewall. The firewall components can be very carefully managed and audited. A firewall is no substitute for good internal security, but it adds a layer of protection; it may be the only practical way to gain the benefits of network connection.

Packet filtering. Packet filtering allows only certain packets to pass through the firewall. The criteria used for filtering can include anything in the network layer header; for TCP/IP, this is the IP header, which contains the source and destination host addresses. *Address filtering* uses the source and destination addresses as criteria. In practice, packet filtering often also uses TCP header information, especially the destination port identifier. Port numbers can be used to filter packets based on application, since TCP/IP networks use fixed port numbers (the well-known ports) for applications. Since ISO has no counterpart to well-known ports, packet filtering is less useful with ISO protocols. Packet filtering enforces access control; the host source identifies a subject and the destination (host, port) identifies an object. This access control is rough-grained, however. For example, the filter can disallow Telnet, but it cannot allow Telnet to some applications and not others. Some of the policies that filtering commonly enforces are

- Allow two-way email and directory services and outgoing Telnet; disallow everything else
- Allow communication only with a designated set of hosts
- Disallow incoming traffic to a designated set of ports (because they provide services that are risky)
- Allow only email and directory services

Routers are often used for building packet-filtering firewalls around LANs. Commercial boxes that cost about the same as a workstation allow LAN administrators to specify their own firewall policies. Routers perform well and are transparent to users. A router can also redirect a packet, so that a remote user's traffic goes through a gateway computer that implements more comprehensive authentication and audit before allowing a remote user to access the target host.

Packet filtering has several serious drawbacks. It relies on addresses whose integrity cannot be guaranteed; IP spoofing can defeat any access control based on source host. If the security policy is not very simple, the packet-filtering rules become complex and hard to write correctly. Packet filtering cannot readily filter for services that are invoked via Remote Procedure Call (see Chap. 11), since the port numbers are not fixed in advance.

Application gateways. Compared to packet filtering, an application gateway uses higher-layer protocol information and implements additional security services, as well as more complex and customized policies. It is typically implemented on one or most host computers and involves custom software developed for the organization. An application gateway provides *proxy services* that control access to the real services, such as Telnet, FTP, and X Windows. For Telnet, this would work as follows (Wack and Carnahan 1994):

1. A user Telnets to the gateway and enters the name of a target host.
2. The gateway checks the source IP address and accepts or rejects the attempt.
3. The user is authenticated.
4. The proxy service creates a Telnet connection between the gateway and the target host.
5. The proxy service passes data between the two connections.
6. The gateway logs the connection.

An outside user cannot use a service that has no proxy.

Many organizations use mail gateways. A gateway can perform user identification and authentication for remote users. It can allow carefully limited traffic between two subnetworks. Suppose, for example, that a military network has a classified segment and an unclassified segment. A trusted application gateway can attach to both segments and allow unclassified data to pass between the segments. A gateway can also control outgoing information flow; a gateway used by DEC limited outgoing data on Telnet connections to 1200 baud, in order to limit the amount of information that an intruder could transfer. A gateway has been used to reduce the very serious risks from X Window clients that are outside the firewall.

A disadvantage of application gateways is their incompatibility with end-to-end encryption that is done at the transport or network layer. The gateway needs to look at application-layer protocol information, so it would have to decrypt and reencrypt. Then the encryption would not be end-to-end.

The versatility of gateways makes them very attractive. A major drawback is that new code must be written for every policy, and the code may not correctly implement policy.

Firewall issues and problems. A firewall is far from a complete solution to network security problems. It provides no protection at all against insider misuse. Further, an insider can cooperate with an outsider to tunnel under the firewall. *Tunneling* means encapsulating a data unit from one protocol in a data unit of another (or the same) protocol. For example, IP packets can be hidden in TCP packets. Any modem can provide a back door through the firewall. The firewall does not prevent attacks in which the content of a message activates a vulnerability of a service, as in the 1988 Worm's exploitation of **finger.** It does not protect against a *data-driven* attack, in which a host executes something it receives (the Worm and **sendmail**).

Protocol enhancement

A significant step for Internet security is the adoption of an enhanced IP protocol standard, *IPv6.* This protocol supports authentication of data origin, data integrity, and encryption for confidentiality. All implementations of IPv6 must provide all the features, but the confidentiality components can be deleted to satisfy export restrictions. IPv6 provides two mechanisms, which can be used in various ways. An *Authentication Header* supports integrity and data origin authentication; an *Encapsulating Security Payload* (ESP) supports these services and encryption for confidentiality. The new protocol can interoperate with the previous version, IPv4.

IPv6 uses the concept of a *security association,* which is the security information for a network connection or set of connections. For example, a host might have one security association for all its users, for a specific destination address, or it might have one security association per user and destination. The security association includes such information as the authentication algorithm being used, the encryption algorithm, cryptographic keys and initialization vector, and sensitivity level, such as Secret or Unclassified. A receiving host can check if a packet's source address is compatible with its security association.

The ESP has two modes of use. *Tunnel mode* encrypts an entire IP packet, including headers, within another IP packet. With *transport mode* (used for frames of transport-layer protocols, such as TCP or UDP) the original header is not encrypted. The default algorithm for integrity is keyed MD5; for confidentiality it is DES in CBC mode. Alternative algorithms may be used.

Network-layer security mechanisms are essential for a strong Internet infrastructure, but they are only part of the complex picture of Internet security.

World Wide Web security

The *World Wide Web* (WWW) rapidly became the favorite way to navigate the Internet. The user sees a hypertext or hypermedia document, with links to resources that may reside anywhere on the Internet. Resources can be of many types, including FTP, Gopher, Telnet, and files. A *Universal Resource Locator* (URL) specifies each resource's type, host, and location on the host. Web clients and servers cooperate using *Hypertext Transfer Protocol* (HTTP). One type of client is a graphical *browser*.

Security threats. Both clients and servers are exposed to security threats. Client systems are exposed to the usual network threats that are countered by authentication, integrity, and confidentiality measures. They are vulnerable to Trojan horse attacks, since client software executes Web resources received from servers, such as the *applets* written in the *Java* programming language. (Java has security safeguards.) Since a client can write data to a server and even invoke server transactions, a server with weak security can be subverted.

Electronic commerce. Web protocols are emerging as the likely base for doing business over the Internet. The security requirements for electronic transactions (see Chap. 2) include: transaction integrity; confidentiality of all parts of the transactions; mutual authentication of parties (such as customer, merchant, and bank); nonrepudiation; timely service; record keeping; and protection of the participating systems against intrusion and insider abuse. As one step toward meeting those requirements, the basic Web protocols must be enhanced for security. Further, servers must be secured. For electronic banking, for example, a "Secure Web Platform" was developed that uses a trusted operating system (SecureWare 1996).

Protocol enhancements. Two security enhancements of Web protocols are being used: *Secure Socket Layer* (SSL) and *Secure Hypertext Transfer Protocol* (S-HTTP). SSL fits between TCP and HTTP (or other application protocols). Using RSA public key technology, SSL provides server authentication, message integrity, and encryption. S-HTTP is an enhanced version of HTTP. It provides more flexibility than SSL, allowing for negotiation between the client and server about the key management methods, security policies, and cryptographic algorithms and message formats. S-HTTP provides authentication of client and server, message integrity, and encryption. Each of these services may be selected (or not) independently.

Netscape security. Netscape, which dominates the market for browsers, has used SSL on its server. Every server that uses the security features must have a public key certificate. Clients are not authenticated to the server, so do not need certificates. (This is fine for credit card purchases, since the merchant cares about the buyer's credit, not identity.) The X.509 certificates are issued, for a fee, by RSA Inc.'s certification service and sent to the server administrator by email. Data encryption uses RC4, with a 128-bit key in the United States and a 40-bit key for export. Netscape users can distinguish documents that came from a secure server by the URL (*https* rather than *http*) and by a security icon displayed by the browser. Documents can also contain mixed secure and insecure information. Netscape agreed to also support S-HTTP, which is seen as a more open standard; this would allow S-HTTP browsers to use the Netscape SSL server. Other companies are working on toolkits for developing applications that will work with either SSL or S-HTTP.

By 1996, brute force attacks had succeeded on Netscape's 40-bit (exportable) encryption. This is not an immediate threat, since the attacks, which took 8 days, would have to be repeated for each transaction. However, the threat will become more serious as computers get faster.

Digital cash. Credit card transactions are quite costly. A less expensive form of network commerce is needed for selling inexpensive items such as small documents or small software items. There is also a need for anonymous, untraceable transactions. *Digital cash* schemes were developed to meet these needs. We describe here the *ecash* system developed by DigiCash.

Ecash is used very much like cash, but is implemented quite differently. A bank is involved in cash transfer between two parties. A purchase involves a buyer, a seller, and the bank; each party runs ecash software. Cash is represented as digital coins, each bearing a unique serial number and the digital signature of the bank. When Alice withdraws digital coins from her bank, the bank sends her messages that represent each coin, and Alice's ecash software stores the coins on her hard disk. To pay for a purchase from Bob, Alice sends him some of her coins. Bob's ecash software sends them on to the bank for validation and deposit. The bank's involvement is necessary to prevent abuses such as spending coins twice. The bank maintains a database of spent coins, which it can access by coin serial number. If the coins paid by Alice are valid, the bank stores them in the database and informs Bob that the payment is valid. Bob could also choose to "keep" the coins, in which case the bank sends him equivalent new ones.

The methods described so far would allow the bank, if it chose, to trace the coins that it issued to Alice. Chapter 5 described *blind signatures,* which allow a party to sign a message without knowing its content. Blind signatures allow the bank to sign digital coins that are untraceable. For anonymity, ecash at Alice's computer creates a coin with a random serial number, hides it in a digital "envelope," and sends it to the bank. The bank places its digital signature on the outside of the envelope and returns it to Alice. Alice's software removes the coin from its envelope. The bank has no way of recognizing the coin as issued to Alice.

Some Architectures

This section describes conceptual work and designs that consider network security as a whole.

Trusted Network Interpretation

The *Trusted Network Interpretation* (TNI) or Red Book of the TCSEC extends trusted system concepts to networks. It considers two kinds of networks:

1. Networks of separately accredited systems that are interconnected
2. Unified networks with an overall security policy, which are evaluated as a whole

A unified trusted network is seen as a special case of a trusted system. It is composed of trusted components interconnected by communications channels. The TCB for the network—the *NTCB*—is partitioned among the components. The first network view, called *interconnected accredited AIS,* recognizes that networks consist of systems that are independently managed and accredited, according to different standards. For example, systems belonging to the U.S. Department of Defense (DoD) and to the United Nations cannot be combined into a unified network, yet it is valuable to interconnect them.

A system is connected to the network with an *accreditation range* set by its accreditor. The system is trusted to communicate within that range of security levels, although it may contain information at lower levels. Consider, for example, a system that contains both Secret and Confidential information. If the system is not trusted to segregate them, its accreditation range includes only Secret. The TNI uses this range in an *interconnection rule* designed to ensure that systems get only information that they can properly mark and handle. For the TNI, a communication channel is between two I/O devices. The interconnection rule states that information exported at a given level can go only to an importing device whose accreditation range contains that level or a higher one. The importing device can relabel the information to satisfy the rule.

Even with the interconnection rule, network connection exposes information to greater risk. One problem is that accreditors may use different standards. The accreditor of one system may choose to accept a certain risk in accrediting it, and the network as a whole is exposed to that risk. The second problem exists when "...a penetrator can take advantage of network connections to compromise information across a range of security levels that is greater than the accreditation range of any of the component systems he must defeat to do so" (NCSC 1987: 249). This is the *cascading problem.* The example used in the TNI is of two systems, *A* containing Top Secret and Secret information and *B* containing Secret and Confidential. When they are connected so that Secret information can pass between them, the total system now has three levels of information. Suppose a penetrator at *A* manages to downgrade Top Secret to Secret, and sends it to *B,* where a penetrator downgrades it to Confidential. The information has been compromised across two levels, more than is possible at *A* or *B* alone. When cascade vulnerability exists (and this is complex to determine) the solution could be to eliminate certain connections, or to use end-to-end encryption.

DoD network security

The DoD supported the development of TCP/IP and the Internet. Its common network service is an internet based on TCP/IP. DoD network security approaches reflect an emphasis on confidentiality over the other security properties. Traditionally, communications security for the DoD (*COMSEC*) has relied primarily on hardware, while computer security (*COMPUSEC*) has relied on trusted software. Both are used for network security, with hardware dominating. Encryption devices are used at the link, MAC, and IP layers, and the MAC and IP layer devices also support integrity, access control, and data origin authentication.

Robert Shirey (1990) has described the 1990s security architecture as planned in the late 1980s. The goal was to carry multilevel traffic on a single *backbone.* (Intermediate systems on a backbone provide connectivity for an internet; all systems that can connect to the backbone have connectivity to each other.) An important mechanism was an end-to-end encryption system called *BLACKER,* which consists of several devices. One device, the *BLACKER front end* (BFE) separates each host from the network. BLACKER is trusted to restrict traffic so as to enforce the multilevel policy. Its cryptographic measures also permit the backbone to operate at a lower security level than some of the hosts. Each communication line is also protected cryptographically by link encryption devices developed by the NSA.

Clark Weissman (1992) describes BLACKER, also as of the late 1980s. The system includes four devices: the BFE, a small removable device used for installing keys and other parameters, a KDC, and an *access control center* (ACC). There is (logically) one KDC and one ACC for a network community. The ACC provides the human interface and manages the security specifications. It is also responsible for audit trails and alarms. The BFE enforces the Bell-LaPadula model. The host is the subject, and the object is a cryptographic connection between two hosts. Data permitted on a connection must be at levels within the intersection of the levels of the two hosts. The BLACKER devices rely on trusted software designed for A1 level certification.

The *DoD Goal Security Architecture* (DGSA) (DoD 1993) is part of a goal information system architecture. The DoD security requirements that the DGSA draft addresses include:

- Support of multiple security policies
- Secure distributed processing over multiple networks, using open systems architectures
- Secure use of common carrier communications systems

Working from the requirements, the draft specifies the network security services that are needed. In general, these follow ISO standards for security and security management.

Secure Data Network System

The BLACKER system was developed for TCP/IP networks. The NSA sponsored a project called *Secure Data Network System* (SDNS) for networks built on the OSI model. (It formerly was the strategy to move to OSI networks for U.S. government use.) SDNS considered both military and commercial needs, and commercial organizations such as AT&T participated.

SDNS includes four types of functions: key management, access control, system management, and secure communications.

Asymmetric cryptography is used. The *SDNS device* plays a role similar to that of the BLACKER front end. When a device first goes into operation, certificates for it are obtained from a key management center. The certificates contain the access policy that the device is to enforce. Certificates cannot be forged, and they are valid for a long time, so the key management center does not have to be on line. To set up a secure session, two SDNS devices exchange certificates, and each device verifies the credentials of the other. If the security rules allow them to communicate, access control privileges are negotiated, and the devices determine what security services are used for the session. Confidentiality and connectionless integrity services are provided. A "traffic key" for the session is generated. There are two kinds of access control. When a session is set up, the SDNS device determines what information may be communicated. During the session, the SDNS device and the hosts perform further access control checking, based on security labels, for example. For less trusted hosts, the device takes on more of the responsibility. SDNS resulted in two protocols, SP3 and SP4, that were published as NIST standards, and in some commercial products. SP3 fits in the network layer just below the transport layer, and SP4 extends the transport protocol. These protocols had a major influence on IPv6 and on the ISO security protocols NLSP and TLSP.

Summary

Networking technology and applications are advancing rapidly, and network security is struggling to catch up. Networking is the source of many computer security threats, and it magnifies others. Secure computing depends on secure networks, and secure networking depends on secure computing.

A computer network is a collection of hosts that communicate over links provided by transmission media. Local-area networks are connected to one another and to metropolitan-area and wide-area networks. Separate networks are connected to form an internet; the best-known internet is the Internet. Most networks use packet-switching: a message is broken into packets that make their ways independently to their destination. Information is transmitted over copper wire and optical fiber, or by wireless methods. Communications security is about protecting transmitted information. Network security includes both communications security and measures that support secure computing in a network environment. *Distributed systems* are networks whose components cooperate on tasks. Most distributed systems follow the client-server model: a client requests a service, and a server somewhere in the network provides it. The security services needed for operating systems are also needed for networks. They must cope with harder problems in a network environment, and additional services are needed.

A network architecture describes network functions and the protocols by which they are performed. Network architectures are layered. The lowest layers concern physical aspects, middle layers deal with messages and connections, and the highest layers define presentation and application protocols. The leading open systems architectures are ISO/OSI and the Internet protocols. A network architecture should be accompanied by a network security architecture. However, people who build and operate networks usually must develop their own security architectures.

Many standards address security. The OSI Reference Model provides a foundation for the OSI standards. According to the model, hardware and software entities at each layer carry out some part of the total network task. For each layer, protocols are carried out between peer entities at the same layer on different systems. The OSI Security Architecture identifies the security services and mechanisms, and positions them within the layers. The services identified are authentication, access control, confidentiality, integrity, and nonrepudiation.

The Internet is viewed as heterogeneous networks connected by routers. The Internet architecture also is layered. IP, TCP, UDP, and other protocols form the TCP/IP protocol suite. There is not yet an Internet security architecture.

Threats to networks can compromise confidentiality or integrity or can deny service. Attacks on confidentiality are called *passive,* and attacks on integrity and availability are called *active*. An attack can modify the transmitted data, replay a previously sent message, or alter the apparent origin of a message. A sender can repudiate a message, and a receiver can deny receiving. Cables are vulnerable to wiretapping, fiber less so than twisted pair and coaxial cable. Open transmission is open to eavesdropping and jamming. Certain points in a network are most vulnerable because of accessibility, difficulty of detecting an attack, or high payoff. In practice, network security is most threatened by penetrated hosts. Attack methods include systematically probing many hosts, exploiting trust relationships, impersonating another host, and eavesdropping on passwords.

Cryptography is the indispensable mechanism for network security, supporting all the security services. Link encryption is done at a low layer and is invisible to all higher layers. It occurs independently for each link. End-to-end encryption is done at the source, and decryption occurs only at the destination. Each approach has its advantages, and both can be used. End-to-end encryption is more secure, in that no intermediate nodes need be trusted.

Compared to authentication in operating systems, authentication in networks must solve a broader problem under circumstances of greater threat. The problem is broader because: not only users but also other entities need to be authenticated; mutual authentication is needed; users must authenticate themselves to many hosts and services; multiple domains of authority are involved; authentication service must be available despite network unreliability. The circumstances hold more threat in that: authentication information is subject to eavesdropping; attacks can modify messages, including protocol messages; parts of the network may not be trusted; intruders are harder to trace.

Simple authentication is one-way, with the proof of identity exposed to eavesdroppers. A commonly used proof of host identity is the network address in a packet. This address-based authentication is weak because network addresses can be impersonated. In an authentication protocol, the claimant and verifier carry out a sequence of steps involving message exchanges and computation. With strong authentication, the claimant does not risk disclosure of any secret. With strong mutual authentication, neither principal risks disclosure. Authentication often uses a trusted third party. This authentication server may act on line or may instead issue credentials that principals save for later use. Authentication with secret key methods involves on-line servers, whereas public key methods use off-line certification. Authentication protocols often rely on challenge-response; the response usually requires decrypting the challenge. An interleaving attack uses one message of a protocol as the basis for later messages. Interleaving and replay attacks are foiled if message freshness is ensured, with either a time stamp or a nonce.

Kerberos is the most widely used cryptographic method for authentication. It provides both user authentication and mutual authentication of client and server. The protocols rely on secret key encryption, assuming a trusted KDC. The secret key of a user is computed from the user's password. A client obtains from the KDC credentials for a server. Credentials can be used not only for authentication, but also for integrity and confidentiality of messages. Kerberos has some security weaknesses. Secret keys are briefly vulnerable to intruders at the client machine. Password-guessing attacks are possible.

X.509 authentication is based on public key cryptography. For mutual authentication, each party needs a certified public key of the other. The protocols make use of digital signatures and nonces. KryptoKnight supports single sign-on, mutual authentication, and data authentication. The protocols use encryption sparingly. S/KEY is a simple scheme for transforming a user-chosen passphrase into a sequence of one-time passwords. A one-way hash function is applied to a secret passphrase *n* times to generate n one-time passwords. No secret values have to be stored. However, a dictionary attack is possible.

Access control objects include hosts, links, and connections. The policies of different administrative domains must be enforced. In general, each host enforces access control for its resources; a centralized access control server is an alternative. The ISO framework for access control distinguishes between the decision function and the enforcement function, and these could be implemented at different locations. One mechanism is a privilege attribute certificate signed by a party that is trusted by the decision function. This mechanism supports delegation of rights from users to their applications. Interdomain access control often is implemented with packet filtering: routers make access control decisions based on source and destination addresses. Signed certificates accompanying packets could express policy requirements about security and other attributes.

Encryption supports confidentiality. To support traffic secrecy, traffic padding adds random data to data units, and routing control allows users to restrict what links their data will take.

Connectionless integrity service protects a single packet. Connection integrity allows detection of packet deletion, insertion, or repetition. Data origin authentication assures a recipient that a data unit came from the purported sender. Nonrepudiation with proof of origin protects against a sender's denial of sending; nonrepudiation with proof of delivery protects against a receiver's denial of receiving. Digital signatures can support all of the integrity services—integrity, data origin authentication, and nonrepudiation—with the same transformations.

An attack on network management jeopardizes the foundation of the network. Both OSI and the Internet specify standards for systems or network management, and both include security services.

Email often is not secure enough. Privacy Enhanced Mail defines a comprehensive set of end-to-end services for confidentiality and integrity. It is an Internet standard. It uses public key cryptography, following the X.509 approach for public key certificates. DES is used for data encryption. Pretty Good Privacy also uses a combination of public key and symmetric methods. However, PGP assumes no certification authority; instead public key certificates are distributed any way the users can work out. PGP provides email confidentiality and digital signatures. It uses IDEA for data encryption, RSA for key encryption and digital signatures, and MD5 for the digital signature message digest.

The Internet is vulnerable in many ways. The TCP/IP protocols have weak protection. Internet attacks have exploited IP spoofing, which allows one host to masquerade as another. Hijacking attacks have allowed attackers to gain control of sessions. By hijacking a connection with a remote system, the attacker also gets access to that system. Sniffer attacks exploit a network interface feature that allows a computer to read all packets passing on the network. These attacks capture session information such as host names, account names, and passwords.

A network firewall is built around a network or subnetwork to protect it from the outside. All traffic passes through the firewall. Only traffic that is authorized by the inner network's security policy is allowed to pass. Most corporate networks that connect to the Internet limit their exposure with firewalls. The most important firewall mechanisms are packet filtering and application gateways. Many firewalls use both. Address filtering uses the source and destination addresses as criteria. Packet filtering also uses TCP header information, especially the destination port, which identifies the service being requested. An application gateway uses higher-layer protocol information and implements additional security services, as well as more complex and customized policies. An application gateway provides proxy services that control access to the real services. Many organizations use mail gateways. A gateway can perform user identification and authentication for remote users. A firewall is far from a complete solution to network security problems. It does not protect against insider misuse, and an insider can cooperate with an outsider to tunnel under the firewall.

An enhanced IP protocol standard, IPv6, supports authentication of data origin, data integrity, and encryption for confidentiality. IPv6 uses the concept of a security association, which is the security information for a network connection or set of connections. Encryption has two modes. Tunnel mode encrypts an entire IP packet, including headers, within another IP packet. With transport mode the original header is not encrypted.

World Wide Web clients and servers are exposed to security threats. Client systems are vulnerable to Trojan horse attacks, and, since a client can write data to a server, a server with weak security could be subverted. Web protocols are the likely base for commerce over the Internet. To meet security requirements for commercial transactions, the Web protocols have been enhanced. Two security enhancements are being used: Secure Socket Layer (SSL) and Secure Hypertext Transfer Protocol (S-HTTP). Digital cash is a low-cost method for network commerce that can provide anonymous transactions.

The Trusted Network Interpretation considers two kinds of networks: (1) networks of separately accredited systems that are interconnected and (2) unified networks with an overall security policy. For the first kind, a system is connected to the network with an accreditation range. Using this range, an interconnection rule ensures that systems get only information that they can properly mark and handle. Even with the interconnection rule, network connection is risky because accreditors may use different standards and because information can be compromised across a range that is greater than the accreditation range of any of the systems.

Traditionally, DoD communications security relied primarily on hardware, while computer security relied on trusted software. Both are used for network security. As planned in the late 1980s, the goal for the 1990s was to carry multilevel traffic on a single backbone. An important mechanism is the BLACKER end-to-end encryption system, which is trusted to restrict traffic so as to enforce the multilevel policy.

Bibliographic Notes

Kaufman, Perlman, and Speciner (1995) are an excellent source on authentication and other network security topics. Stallings (1995) provides clear descriptions of the important systems and protocols. Janson and Molva (1991) survey network security problems and methods. Ford (1994) surveys network and communications security, with good coverage of standards, especially OSI. Davies and Price (1989) describe cryptographic measures and their use for network security. Textbooks on computer networks include Tanenbaum (1988) and Halsall (1992).

Architecture and standards

The OSI reference model is described by Ford (1994), Piscitello and Chapin (1993), and Stallings (1992). SNA and other architectures are covered by Cypser (1991). Chapter 2 discusses standards organizations. Lynch and Rose (1993) is a good resource on the Internet. Big-picture descriptions of the Internet architecture are lacking. Cerf and Cain (1983) describe an earlier state, and chapters of Lynch and Rose describe the various protocols. Cerf (1993) describes the TCP/IP protocols, and Clark (1988) discusses the original design goals for those protocols. Postel (1993) describes the main Internet applications. Kent (1993a) analyzes the OSI security architecture and considers what an Internet security architecture might be. Work on an Internet Security Architecture, by the Privacy and Security Research Group of the Internet Engineering Task Force is summarized by Oldehoeft (1994). Ford (1994), I'Anson and Pell (1993), and Stallings (1992) explain the OSI security architecture. Mirhakkak (1993) discusses TLSP. Security standards work is surveyed by Ford (1994). Chapin

(1994) gives the status of network standards. Maughan (1992) considers interoperability of ISO and SDNS secure protocols. The DSSA security architecture developed by DEC is described by Gasser et al. (1989), Linn (1990), and Gasser and McDermott (1990).

Asynchronous transmission mode (ATM) is a newer network paradigm that is expected to become dominant. It was developed to support applications that use many kinds of data and that need their data in real time. ATM networks have distinct security needs; for example, key distribution must be faster. ATM is described by Vetter (1995), ATM security by Stevenson, Hillery, and Byrd (1995).

Threats

Cooper (1989) provides a readable survey of communications vulnerabilities and countermeasures. Wells, Stone, and Miles (1993) discuss the eavesdropping vulnerability of fiber optics and propose a way to scramble light waves for secrecy. Threats to computing systems, including viruses and worms, are covered in Chap. 3.

Cryptography in network security

The issue of link-oriented versus end-to-end encryption is discussed by Popek and Kline (1979), Voydock and Kent (1985), and NCSC (1990). Saltzer, Reed, and Clark (1984) discuss the "end-to-end argument" for networks more generally. Walker (1985) discusses end-to-end encryption for networks of trusted systems. Chapters 2 and 5 discuss patent and export issues.

Authentication

An overview of authentication in distributed systems is provided by Woo and Lam (1992). Yahalom, Klein, and Beth (1993) consider trust relationships of entities involved in authentication. Gollmann, Beth, and Damm (1993) discuss services that depend on an authentication server. Boyd (1992) presents a formal framework for authentication, using LOTOS. Lampson et al. (1992) present a theory of authentication that is used by a prototype distributed system. Challenge-response methods are introduced in Chap. 8. Stubblebine (1995) analyzes the problem of revoking authentication. Our discussion of interleaving attacks is based on Bird et al. (1993). Burrows, Abadi, and Needham (1990) develop a logic for analyzing authentication protocols. Gong (1993) describes methods for replicating an authentication server.

The Kerberos authentication system is described by Steiner, Neuman, and Schiller (1988) and Schiller (1994). It is based on the work of Needham and Schroeder (1978). Two versions of Kerberos are used—Version 4 and Version 5. Our description is of Version 5 (Kohl and Neuman 1993; Kohl, Neuman, and Ts'o 1994; Neuman and Ts'o 1994). Kerberos is available from MIT. Bellovin and Merritt (1990) call attention to security problems in Kerberos and propose protocol changes. The SESAME extensions to Kerberos are described by McMahon (1995). Kotanchik (1994) describes protocols to add token-based authentication to Kerberos. Toussaint (1993) uses formal methods to analyze Kerberos protocols. Ganesan (1995) proposes modifications to Kerberos to allow use of public key methods. Protocols that protect against password guessing attacks are described by Bellovin and Merritt (1992, 1993), Gong et al. (1993), and Steiner, Tsudik, and Waidner (1994). X.509 directory authentication is described by Nechvatal (1992), Ford (1994), and Stallings (1995). An early version is analyzed in formal terms by Gaarder and Snekkenes (1991) and Toussaint (1993). Kaufman (1993) describes DASS, an authentication architecture and protocol developed by DEC, based on X.509 concepts. DASS is an updated version of SPX (Tardo and Alagappan 1991). References on KryptoKnight include Molva et al. (1992), Bird et al. (1993, 1995), and Tsudik and Van Herreweghen (1993). Linn (1990) discusses the advantages of using public key cryptography for authentication. S/KEY is described by Haller (1994, 1995). It is publicly available. McDonald, Atkinson, and Metz (1995) describe the U.S. Naval Research Laboratory's enhancement of S/KEY, also available. The small *n* attack is described by Kaufman, Perlman, and Speciner (1995). Rubin (1995) describes a scheme for generating one-time passwords that are independent of one another.

Access control, confidentiality, and integrity

Ford (1994) describes access control concepts from the OSI framework and the Directory standards. Policy routing is discussed by Nessett and Solo (1991) and by Tsudik (1992). Stubblebine and Gligor (1993) describe design methods to protect the integrity of cryptographic protocol messages. OSI nonrepudiation services are discussed by Ford (1994). The place of security services is considered by Walker (1989), Kent (1993a) and Ford (1994). Linn (1993a) describes GSS-API.

Network management

Stallings (1993) edits a collection of papers on network management. Znaty and Sclavos (1994) provide an annotated bibliography. OSI Systems Management is described by Yemini (1993) and Ford (1994). O'Mahoney (1994) describes work on access control for the management information base. Jansen (1992) shows how the framework is used for SDNS security management. SNMP is described by Stallings (1993) and Case (1993). SNMPv2 security is described by McCloghrie, Davin, and Galvin (1993) and Stallings (1995). Wood (1994) describes how security practitioners can take advantage of network management products.

Electronic mail security

Jaeger and Prakash (1994) discuss threats from computational email. Privacy Enhanced Mail is described by Kent (1993b) and Linn (1993b). Galvin and Balenson (1992) discuss an implementation of PEM. Bahreman (1995) describes a toolkit for building a certification hierarchy for PEM. X.400 is described by Ford. PGP is described by Zimmermann (1994) and Garfinkel (1995). Stallings (1995) gives the details of its operation.

Internet security

Wallich (1994) describes hazards related to the Internet. Haller and Atkinson (1994) discuss authentication techniques and their applicability to the Internet. Bellovin (1989) describes security weaknesses of TCP/IP and other network protocols; Kent (1989) replies and describes weaknesses in Bellovin's article. IP spoofing is described by Bellovin (1989) and by Cheswick and Bellovin (1994), Kaufman, Perlman, and Speciner (1995), and CERT (1995). Ioannidis and Blaze (1993) describe a software implementation of IP network-layer security under UNIX. This work influenced IPv6 (Atkinson 1995, Huitema 1996). Cheng et al. (1995) describe other IP-layer security protocols. Kumar and Crowcroft (1993) consider security threats to OSI and IP routing protocols and propose countermeasures. Bhimani (1996) considers security for electronic commerce on the Internet.

Firewalls are discussed by Kent (1993a), Bellovin and Cheswick (1994), Cheswick and Bellovin (1994), Wack and Carnahan (1994), and Chapman and Zwicky (1995). Kent (1993a) explains the idea of well-known ports and lists the ports. Chapman (1992) describes how IP packet filtering works and suggests improvements to the usual methods. Shirey (1990) describes ways to use gateways to connect classified and unclassified military networks. Kahn (1995) summarizes X Window risks and describes an X Gateway prototype. Rescorla and Schiffman (1995) describe S-HTTP.

The ideas behind ecash are described by Chaum (1992) and the system is described in DigiCash (1995). Dyson (1995), Morgan (1995), and Panurach (1996) provide overviews of electronic payment methods. Medvinsky and Neuman (1993) describe the NetCash system. Brands (1995) proposes a scheme that can operate without an on-line bank; the user needs a tamper-resistant device. Low, Maxemchuk, and Paul (1994) describe protocols for anonymous credit card transactions.

Some architectures

The Trusted Network Interpretation documents are NCSC (1987 and 1990). The TNI specifies network security services parallel to OSI's, but emphasizes mechanisms less and assurance more. DoD network security architecture is described by Shirey (1990) and Kent (1993a), who analyzes it in relation to Internet security. BLACKER is described by Weissman (1992). Oldehoeft (1994) summarizes the DGSA (DoD 1993) and compares it with other security architectures. SDNS is described by Karp, Barker, and Nelson (1988). SP3 is discussed by Birnbaum (1990). Burgoyne and Puga (1992) describe cryptographic products that were developed to SDNS standards. Fumy and Leclerc (1993) describe the SDNS key distribution scheme. The Trusted Systems Interoperability Group (TSIG), a group of vendors of multilevel secure systems, developed specifications for networking of their products; MaxSix is an implementation (Adams and Luther 1995).

Exercises

10.1. Why are cryptographic measures so important in network security?

10.2. Contrast Kerberos tickets with capabilities in an operating system.

10.3. List the systems or architectures described in the chapter that provide security services at the network layer of the OSI model. List those providing security services at the transport layer.

10.4. Compare the layering principles of the OSI architecture to the design principles of Chap. 6. What accounts for the similarities and differences?

10.5. Which transmission media are the most secure? Which are the least secure?

10.6. Does PEM provide end-to-end encryption?

10.7. In what ways is the firewall approach like the TCB approach? In what ways is it different?

10.8. Which security services (of those in the OSI architecture) are provided by a router used as a firewall?

10.9. How does the DoD guard against the vulnerabilities of TCP/IP networks that it uses?

10.10. Describe the role of a nonce in authentication protocols.

10.11. What are the advantages of public key cryptography for authentication? What are the advantages of secret key cryptography?

10.12. What problem described in this chapter parallels the protection problem that is solved by rights amplification in Hydra (Chap. 7)? Compare the solution with rights amplification.

10.13. Assume you are the administrator of a LAN that is connected to the Internet. Define a policy regarding what interactions are allowed between the LAN and the Internet. Could your policy be implemented by packet filtering?

10.14. If the single sign-on protections described in this chapter were available, would you recommend that your organization use single sign-on?

10.15. List some ways that communicating parties can exchange session keys.

10.16. Does the BLACKER front-end device enforce the Bell-LaPadula policy? If not, how does its policy differ?

References

Adams, John R., and David F. Luther. 1995. The evolution of MaxSix trusted networking. *Security Audit & Control Review* **13**(1): 7–11.

Atkinson, R. 1995. *Security Architecture for the Internet Protocol.* Internet Request for Comments 1825, August, 1995. Network Working Group.

Bahreman, Alireza. 1995. PEMToolKit: Building a top-down certification hierarchy for PEM from the bottom up. *Proceedings of the Symposium on Network and Distributed System Security,* 161–171. Los Alamitos, Calif.: IEEE Computer Society.

Bellovin, S. M. 1989. Security problems in the TCP/IP protocol suite. *Computer Communication Review* **19**(2): 32–48.

Bellovin, Steven M., and William R. Cheswick. 1994. Network firewalls. *IEEE Communications Magazine* **32**(9): 50–57.

Bellovin, S. M., and M. Merritt. 1990. Limitations of the Kerberos authentication system. *Computer Communication Review* **20**(5): 119–132.

______. 1992. Encrypted key exchange: Password-based protocols secure against dictionary attacks. *Proceedings of the 1992 IEEE Computer Society Symposium on Research in Security and Privacy,* 72–84. Los Alamitos, Calif.: IEEE Computer Society.

______. 1993. Augmented encrypted key exchange: A password-based protocol secure against dictionary attacks and password file compromise. *Proceedings of the 1st ACM Conference on Computer and Communications Security,* 244–250. New York: ACM Press.

Bhimani, Anish. 1996. Securing the commercial Internet. *Communications of the ACM* **39**(6): 29–35.

Bird, Ray, I. Gopal, Amir Herzberg, Philippe A. Janson, Shay Kutten, Refik Molva, and Moti Yung. 1993. Systematic design of a family of attack-resistant authentication protocols. *IEEE Journal on Selected Areas in Communications* **11**(5): 679–693.

______. 1995. The KryptoKnight family of light-weight protocols for authentication and key distribution. *IEEE/ACM Transactions on Networking* **3**(1): 31–41.

Birnbaum, William C. 1990. SP3 peer identification. *Proceedings of the 1990 IEEE Computer Society Symposium on Research in Security and Privacy,* 41–48. Los Alamitos, Calif.: IEEE Computer Society.

Boyd, Colin. 1992. A formal framework for authentication. *Computer Security—ESORICS 92. Proceedings of the Second European Symposium on Research in Computer Security,* 273–292. Berlin: Springer-Verlag.

Braden, R., D. Clark, S. Crocker, and C. Huitema. 1994. *Report of IAB Workshop on Security in the Internet Architecture.* Internet RFC 1636, June 1994. Network Working Group.

Brands, Stefan. 1995. Electronic cash on the Internet. *Proceedings of the Internet Society Symposium on Network and Distributed System Security,* 64–84. Los Alamitos, Calif.: IEEE Computer Society.

Burgoyne, Ernie, and Ralph G. Puga. 1992. An SDNS platform for trusted products. *Proceedings of the 15th National Computer Security Conference,* 564–573. NIST/NCSC.

Burrows, Michael, Martín Abadi, and Roger Needham. 1990. A logic of authentication. *ACM Transactions on Computer Systems* **8**(1): 18–36.

Case, Jeffrey D. 1993. Network management. In Lynch, Daniel C., and Marshall T. Rose, eds. *Internet System Handbook,* 493–519. Reading, Mass.: Addison-Wesley.

Cerf, Vinton G. 1993. Core protocols. In Lynch, Daniel C., and Marshall T. Rose, eds. *Internet System Handbook,* 79–155. Reading, Mass.: Addison-Wesley.

Cerf, Vinton G., and Edward Cain. 1983. The DOD Internet architecture model. *Computer Networks* **7**(5): 307–318.

CERT. 1995. *IP Spoofing Attacks and Hijacked Terminal Connections.* CERT Advisory, January 1995.

Chapin, A. Lyman. 1994. Status of standards. *Computer Communication Review* **24**(2): 109–136.

Chapman, Brent, and Elizabeth Zwicky. 1995. *Building Internet Firewalls.* Sebastopol, Calif.: O'Reilly & Associates, Inc.

Chapman, D. Brent. 1992. Network (in)security through IP packet filtering. *Proceedings of UNIX Security Symposium III,* 63–76. Berkeley, Calif.: USENIX Association.

Chaum, David. 1992. Achieving electronic privacy. *Scientific American,* August: 96–101.

Cheng, Pau-Chen, Juan A. Garay, Amir Herzberg, and Hugo Krawczyk. 1995. Design and implementation of modular key management protocol and IP secure tunnel on AIX. *Proceedings of the Fifth USENIX UNIX Security Symposium,* 41–54. Berkeley, Calif.: USENIX Association.

Cheswick, William R., and Steven M. Bellovin. 1994. *Firewalls and Internet Security: Repelling the Wily Hacker.* Reading, Mass.: Addison-Wesley.

Clark, David D. 1988. The design philosophy of the DARPA Internet protocols. *Computer Communication Review* **18**(4): 106–114.

Cooper, James Arlin. 1989. *Computer and Communications Security: Strategies for the 1990s.* New York: McGraw-Hill.

Cypser, R. J. 1991. *Communications for Cooperating Systems: OSI, SNA, and TCP/IP.* Reading, Mass.: Addison-Wesley.

Davies, D. W., and W. L. Price. 1989. *Security for Computer Networks: An Introduction to Data Security in Teleprocessing and Electronic Funds Transfer.* 2d ed. Chichester: John Wiley & Sons.

DigiCash. 1995. *An Introduction to ecash.* WWW document. DigiCash.

DoD. 1993. *DoD Goal Security Architecture Version 1.0.* Center for Information System Security, Defense Information Systems Security Program, August 1993. Fort Meade, Md.: Defense Information Systems Agency.

Dyson, Peter E. 1995. Toward electronic money: Some Internet experiments. *Seybold Report on Desktop Publishing* **9**(10): 3(9).

Ford, Warwick. 1994. *Computer Communications Security.* Englewood Cliffs, N.J.: PTR Prentice Hall.

Fumy, Walter, and Matthias Leclerc. 1993. Placement of cryptographic key distribution within OSI: design alternatives and assessment. *Computer Networks and ISDN Systems* **26**(2): 217–225.

Gaarder, Klaus, and Einar Snekkenes. 1991. Applying a formal analysis technique to the CCITT X.509 strong two-way authentication protocol. *Journal of Cryptology* **3**(2): 81–98.

Galvin, James M., and David M. Balenson. 1992. Security aspects of a UNIX PEM implementation. *Proceedings of UNIX Security Symposium III,* 119–131. Berkeley, Calif.: USENIX Association.

Ganesan, Ravi. 1995. Yaksha: Augmenting Kerberos with public key cryptography. *Proceedings of the Internet Society Symposium on Network and Distributed System Security,* 132–143. Los Alamitos, Calif.: IEEE Computer Society.

Garfinkel, Simson L. 1995. *PGP, Pretty Good Privacy.* Sebastopol, Calif.: O'Reilly & Associates.

Gasser, Morrie, Andy Goldstein, Charlie Kaufman, and Butler Lampson. 1989. The Digital Distributed System Security Architecture. *Proceedings of the 12th National Computer Security Conference,* 305–319. NIST/NCSC.

Gasser, Morrie, and Ellen McDermott. 1990. An architecture for practical delegation in a distributed system. *Proceedings of the 1990 IEEE Computer Society Symposium on Research in Security and Privacy,* 20–30. Los Alamitos, Calif.: IEEE Computer Society.

Gollmann, Dieter, Thomas Beth, and Frank Damm. 1993. Authentication services in distributed systems. *Computers & Security* **12**(8): 753–764.

Gong, Li. 1993. Increasing availability and security of an authentication service. *IEEE Journal on Selected Areas in Communications* **11**(5): 657–662.

Gong, Li, Mark A. Lomas, Roger M. Needham, and Jerome H. Saltzer. 1993. Protecting poorly chosen secrets from guessing attacks. *IEEE Journal on Selected Areas in Communications* **11**(5): 648–656.

Haller, N. M. 1994. The S/Key one-time password system. *Proceedings of the Internet Society Symposium on Network and Distributed Systems Security,* 151–157. Reston, Va.: Internet Society.

Haller, N. 1995. *The S/KEY One-Time Password System.* Internet Request for Comments 1760, February 1995. Network Working Group.

Haller, N., and R. Atkinson. 1994. *On Internet Authentication.* Internet RFC 1704, October 1994. Network Working Group.

Halsall, Fred. 1992. *Data Communications, Computer Networks, and Open Systems.* 3rd ed. Wokingham, England: Addison-Wesley.

Huitema, Christian. 1996. *IPv6: The New Internet Protocol.* Upper Saddle River, N.J.: Prentice-Hall PTR.

I'Anson, Colin, and Adrian Pell. 1993. *Understanding OSI Applications.* Englewood Cliffs, N.J.: Prentice Hall.

IEEE. 1993. *IEEE Standards for Local and Metropolitan Area Networks: Interoperable LAN/MAN Security (SILS).* IEEE standard 802.10-1992. New York: IEEE.

Ioannidis, John, and Matt Blaze. 1993. The architecture and implementation of network-layer security under Unix. *Proceedings of UNIX Security Symposium IV,* 29–39. Berkeley, Calif.: USENIX Association.

Jaeger, Trent, and Atul Prakash. 1994. Support for the file system security requirements of computational e-mail systems. *2d ACM Conference on Computer and Communications Security,* 1–9. New York: ACM.

Jansen, Wayne A. 1992. SDNS security management. *Proceedings of the 15th National Computer Security Conference,* 574–583. NIST/NCSC.

Janson, P., and R. Molva. 1991. Security in open networks and distributed systems. *Computer Networks and ISDN Systems* **22**(5): 323–346.

Kahn, Brian L. 1995. Safe use of X Window system protocol across a firewall. *Proceedings of the Fifth USENIX UNIX Security Symposium,* 105–116. Berkeley, Calif.: USENIX Association.

Karp, Bennett C., L. Kirk Barker, and Larry D. Nelson. 1988. The Secure Data Network System. *AT&T Technical Journal,* May/June: 19–27.

Kaufman, C. 1993. *DASS: Distributed Authentication Security Service.* Internet Request for Comments RFC 1507, September 1993.

Kaufman, Charlie, Radia Perlman, and Mike Speciner. 1995. *Network Security: Private Communication in a Public World.* Englewood Cliffs, N.J.: PTR Prentice Hall.

Kent, Stephen. 1989. Comments on "Security problems in the TCP/IP protocol suite." *Computer Communication Review* **19**(3): 10–19.

______. 1993a. Architectural security. In Lynch, Daniel C., and Marshall T. Rose, eds. *Internet System Handbook,* 369–419. Reading, Mass.: Addison-Wesley.

______. 1993b. Internet Privacy Enhanced Mail. *Communications of the ACM* **36**(8): 48–60.

Kohl, John T., B. Clifford Neuman, and Theodore Y. Ts'o. 1994. The evolution of the Kerberos authentication service. In Brazier, F. M. T. and D. Johansen, eds. *Distributed Open Systems,* 78–95. Los Alamitos, Calif.: IEEE Computer Society.

Kohl, J., and C. Neuman. 1993. *The Kerberos Network Authentication Service (V5).* Internet Request for Comments RFC 1510, September 1993.

Kotanchik, J. 1994. *Kerberos and Two-Factor Authentication.* RFC 59.0, March 1994. OSF DCE SIG.

Kumar, Brijesh, and Jon Crowcroft. 1993. Integrating security in inter-domain routing protocols. *Computer Communication Review* **23**(5): 36–51.

Lamport, Leslie. 1981. Password authentication with insecure communication. *Communications of the ACM* **24**(11): 770–772.

Lampson, Butler, Martin Abadi, Michael Burrows, and Edward Wobber. 1992. Authentication in distributed systems: Theory and practice. *ACM Transactions on Computer Systems* **10**(4): 265–310.

Linn, John. 1990. Practical authentication for distributed computing. *Proceedings of the 1990 IEEE Computer Society Symposium on Research in Security and Privacy,* 31–40. Los Alamitos, Calif.: IEEE Computer Society.

______. 1993a. *Generic Security Service Application Program Interface.* Internet Request for Comments RFC1508, September 1993. Network Working Group.

______. 1993b. *Privacy Enhancement for Internet Electronic Mail.* Internet Request for Comments RFC 1421, February 1993.

Low, Steven H., Nicholas F. Maxemchuk, and Sanjoy Paul. 1994. Anonymous credit cards. *2d ACM Conference on Computer and Communications Security,* 108–117. New York: ACM.

Lynch, Daniel C., and Marshall T. Rose. 1993. *Internet System Handbook.* Reading, Mass.: Addison-Wesley.

Maughan, W. Douglas. 1992. Standards for computer systems security: An interoperability analysis of SDNS SP3 and ISO NLSP. *Proceedings of the Eighth Annual Computer Security Applications Conference,* 193–201. Los Alamitos, Calif.: IEEE Computer Society.

McCloghrie, Keith, James R. Davin, and James M. Galvin. 1993. SNMP security. In Stallings, William, ed. *Network Management,* 247–251. Los Alamitos, Calif.: IEEE Computer Society.

McDonald, Daniel L., Randall J. Atkinson, and Craig Metz. 1995. One time passwords in everything (OPIE): Experiences with building and using stronger authentication. *Proceedings of the Fifth USENIX UNIX Security Symposium,* 177–186. Berkeley, Calif.: USENIX Association.

McMahon, P. V. 1995. SESAME V2 public key and authorisation extensions to Kerberos. *Proceedings of the Internet Society Symposium on Network and Distributed System Security,* 114–131. Los Alamitos, Calif.: IEEE Computer Society.

McNulty, F. Lynn. 1994. *Security on the Internet.* Statement before the U.S. House of Representatives, March 22, 1994.

Medvinsky, Gennady, and B. Clifford Neuman. 1993. NetCash: A design for practical electronic currency on the Internet. *Proceedings of the 1st ACM Conference on Computer and Communications Security,* 102–106. New York: ACM Press.

Mirhakkak, Mohammad. 1993. A distributed system security architecture: applying the Transport Layer Security Protocol. *Computer Communication Review* **23**(5): 6–16.

Molva, Refik, Gene Tsudik, Els Van Herreweghen, and Stefano Zatti. 1992.

KryptoKnight authentication and key distribution system. *Computer Security—ESORICS 92. Proceedings of the Second European Symposium on Research in Computer Security,* 155–174. Berlin: Springer-Verlag.

Morgan, Lisa. 1995. Cashing in: The rush is on to make net commerce happen. *Internet World,* February: 48–51.

NCSC. 1987. *Trusted Network Interpretation.* Report NCSC-TG-005. Fort Meade, Md.: National Computer Security Center.

______. 1990. *Trusted Network Interpretation Environments Guideline: Guidance for Applying the Trusted Network Interpretation.* Report NCSC-TG-011. Fort Meade, Md.: National Computer Security Center.

Nechvatal, James. 1992. Public key cryptography. In Simmons, Gustavus J., ed. *Contemporary Cryptology: The Science of Information Integrity,* 177–288. Piscataway, N.J.: IEEE Press.

Needham, R. M., and M. D. Schroeder. 1978. Using encryption for authentication in large networks of computers. *Communications of the ACM* **21**(12): 993–999.

Nessett, D., and D. Solo. 1991. Policy route certification: requirements and techniques. *Information Security: Proceedings of the IFIP TC11 Seventh International Conference on Information Security, IFIP/Sec '91,* 87–98. Amsterdam: North-Holland.

Neuman, B. Clifford, and Theodore Ts'o. 1994. Kerberos: An authentication service for computer networks. *IEEE Communications Magazine* 32(9): 33–38.

Oldehoeft, Arthur E. 1994. *An Assessment of the DOD Goal Security Architecture (DGSA) for Non-Military Use.* NISTIR 5570, November 1994. Gaithersburg, Md.: National Institute of Standards and Technology.

O'Mahoney, Donal. 1994. Security considerations in a network management environment. *IEEE Network Magazine* **8**(3): 12–17.

Panurach, Patiwat. 1996. Money in electronic commerce: Digital cash, electronic fund transfer, and Ecash. *Communications of the ACM* **39**(6): 45–50.

Piscitello, David M., and A. Lyman Chapin. 1993. *Open Systems Networking: TCP/IP and OSI.* Reading, Mass.: Addison-Wesley.

Popek, Gerald J., and Charles S. Kline. 1979. Encryption and secure computer networks. *ACM Computing Surveys* **11**(4): 331–356.

Postel, Jon. 1993. Main applications. In Lynch, Daniel C., and Marshall T. Rose, eds. *Internet System Handbook,* 183–274. Reading, Mass.: Addison-Wesley.

Rescorla, E., and A. Schiffman. 1995. *The Secure HyperText Transfer Protocol.* Internet-Draft, July 1995. Web Transaction Security Working Group.

Rubin, Aviel D. 1995. Independent one-time passwords. *Proceedings of the Fifth USENIX UNIX Security Symposium,* 167–176. Berkeley, Calif.: USENIX Association.

Saltzer, J. H., D. P. Reed, and D. D. Clark. 1984. End-to-end arguments in system design. *ACM Transactions on Computer Systems* **2**(4): 277–288.

Schiller, Jeffrey I. 1994. Secure distributed computing. *Scientific American* 271, November: 72–76.

SecureWare. 1996. *Secure Web Platform Whitepaper.* Web document, February 1996.

Shirey, Robert W. 1990. Defense Data Network security architecture. *Computer Communication Review* **20**(2): 66–71.

Stallings, William. 1992. A network security primer. In Stallings, William, ed. *Computer Communications: Architectures, Protocols, and Standards,* 34–39. Los Alamitos, Calif.: IEEE Computer Society.

______, ed. 1993. *Network Management.* Los Alamitos, Calif.: IEEE Computer Society.

______. 1995. *Network and Internetwork Security: Principles and Practice.* Englewood Cliffs, N.J.: Prentice-Hall.

Steiner, Jennifer G., Clifford Neuman, and Jeffrey I. Schiller. 1988. Kerberos: An authentication service for open network systems. *Proceedings of the 1988 USENIX Winter Conference,* 191–202. Berkeley, Calif.: USENIX Association.

Steiner, Michael, Gene Tsudik, and Michael Waidner. 1994. Refinement and extension of Encrypted Key Exchange. *Operating Systems Review* **29**(3): 22–30.

Stevenson, Daniel, Nathan Hillery, and Greg Byrd. 1995. Secure communications in ATM networks. *Communications of the ACM* **38**(2): 45–52.

Stubblebine, Stuart G. 1995. Recent-secure authentication: Enforcing revocation in distributed systems. *Proceedings of the 1995 IEEE Symposium on Security and Privacy,* 224–235. Los Alamitos, Calif.: IEEE Computer Society.

Stubblebine, Stuart G., and Virgil D. Gligor. 1993. Protocol design for integrity protection. *Proceedings of the 1993 IEEE Computer Society Symposium on Research in Security and Privacy,* 41–53. Los Alamitos, Calif.: IEEE Computer Society.

Tanenbaum, Andrew S. 1988. *Computer Networks.* 2d ed. Englewood Cliffs, N.J.: Prentice Hall.

Tardo, Joseph J., and Kannan Alagappan. 1991. SPX: Global authentication using public key certificates. *Proceedings of the 1991 IEEE Computer Society Symposium on Research in Security and Privacy,* 232–244. Los Alamitos, Calif.: IEEE Computer Society.

Toussaint, M. J. 1993. A new method for analyzing the security of cryptographic protocols. *IEEE Journal on Selected Areas in Communications* **11**(5): 702–714.

Tsudik, Gene. 1992. Policy enforcement in stub autonomous domains. *Computer Security—ESORICS 92. Proceedings of the Second European Symposium on Research in Computer Security,* 229–257. Berlin: Springer-Verlag.

Tsudik, Gene, and Els Van Herreweghen. 1993. On simple and secure key distribution. *Proceedings of the 1st ACM Conference on Computer and Communications Security,* 49–57. New York: ACM Press.

Vetter, Ronald J. 1995. ATM concepts, architectures, and protocols. *Communications of the ACM* **38**(2): 31–44, 109.

Voydock, Victor L., and Stephen T. Kent. 1985. Security in high-level network protocols. *IEEE Communications Magazine,* July: 12–24.

Wack, John P., and Lisa J. Carnahan. 1994. *Keeping Your Site Comfortably Secure: An Introduction to Internet Firewalls.* Special Publication 800-10, December 1994. Gaithersburg, Md.: National Institute of Standards and Technology.

Walker, Stephen T. 1985. Network security overview. *Proceedings of the 1985 Symposium on Security and Privacy,* 62–76. Silver Spring, Md.: IEEE Computer Society.

______. 1989. Network security: The parts of the sum. *Proceedings of the 1989 IEEE Computer Society Symposium on Security and Privacy,* 1–9. Washington, D.C.: IEEE Computer Society.

Wallich, Paul. 1994. Wire pirates. *Scientific American,* March: 90–101.

Weissman, Clark. 1992. BLACKER: Security for the DDN: Examples of A1 security engineering trades. *Proceedings of the 1992 IEEE Computer Society Symposium on Research in Security and Privacy,* 286–292. Los Alamitos, Calif.: IEEE Computer Society.

Wells, Willard, Russell Stone, and Edward Miles. 1993. Secure communications by optical homodyne. *IEEE Journal on Selected Areas in Communications* **11**(5): 770–777.

Woo, Thomas Y. C., and Simon S. Lam. 1992. Authentication for distributed systems. *Computer* **25**(1): 39–52.

Wood, Charles Cresson. 1994. Using network management systems to achieve information security. *Computer Security Journal* **X**(1): 11–21.

Yahalom, R., B. Klein, and Th. Beth. 1993. Trust relationships in secure systems—A distributed authentication perspective. *Proceedings of the 1993 IEEE Computer Society Symposium on Research in Security and Privacy,* 150–164. Los Alamitos, Calif.: IEEE Computer Society.

Yemini, Yechiam. 1993. The OSI network management model. *IEEE Communications Magazine* **31**(May): 20–29.

Zimmermann, Philip. 1994. *PGP User's Guide,* vol. I: *Essential Topics.* October 1994.

______. 1995. *The Official PGP User's Guide.* Cambridge, Mass.: MIT Press.

Znaty, Simon, and Jean Sclavos. 1994. Annotated bibliography on network management. *Computer Communication Review* **24**(1): 37–56.

Chapter

11

Distributed System Security

This chapter continues with network security, concentrating on modes of distributed processing. The topics include local area networks, distributed file systems, network operating systems, and distributed computing environments.

Concepts and Definitions

There are many ways to use the connections that a network provides. Users can send and receive mail, for example, or transfer files. With a *distributed file system,* they can use files located elsewhere on the network just as they use files at their own workstations. A *network operating system* (NOS), while not a complete operating system, provides far more than distributed files. Leaving local services to the local (or *client*) operating system, such as UNIX or Windows 95, the NOS provides services specifically for resource sharing and interaction. For example, it provides user accounts, security, and intermachine communications. It typically supports different client operating systems on the same network. A *distributed operating system* is a complete operating system designed specifically for a distributed environment. Mach, for example, is a distributed operating system. *Environments* for *distributed computing* or *distributed processing* provide the services that are needed to build and execute distributed applications.

An important building block for distributed systems, and for their security, is the *remote procedure call* (RPC). A remote procedure call is very much like a procedure call in programming for one machine. A process or thread issues a call, supplying parameters. It then blocks until the call is complete. One remote call, for example, would read a record from a remote file. The RPC mechanism takes care of constructing call messages and determining where to send them, collecting results, and all the other details.

Overview of the Chapter

The next section is about local-area networks (LANs): their hardware and topology; what security threats they face; and what LAN security services are needed. The section covers LAN integrity and availability, virus protection for LANs, and multilevel LANs. Then the security aspects of two important distributed file systems are described. Next we discuss security in the leading network operating system—Novell NetWare. The problem of providing single sign-on to multiple systems is discussed next. Then we describe ways to secure remote access to LANs. The special problems of mobile computing are discussed. The final section deals with distributed computing. It discusses security aspects of remote procedure call and of DCE, an industry standard for distributed computing, and describes the authentication theory of the Taos distributed operating system.

Security of Local-Area Networks

For most users who work in organizations, a workstation attached to a LAN is the entry point for all computing services. These users also get many services directly from LANs. As LANs replaced mainframes and minicomputers, security suffered; surveys show it is a top concern of network managers. Organizations that controlled security effectively when data and services were centralized lost control when they were distributed. Small organizations that moved from separate workstations to LANs failed to cope with the new threats of that environment. This section describes these threats and summarizes the safeguards. It begins with a brief overview of local-area networks.

Local-area networks: Uses and characteristics

Figure 11.1 shows a LAN for an enterprise site. Departmental LANs in four buildings are connected to one another and to a mainframe. Figure 11.2 shows a departmental LAN. LAN servers provide file storage and access, printing, electronic mail, and support for group work—such as scheduling meetings and cooperating on writing documents. Servers also provide administrative and security services, such as user registration, authentication, accounting, and access control. Specialized servers in some departments provide databases and

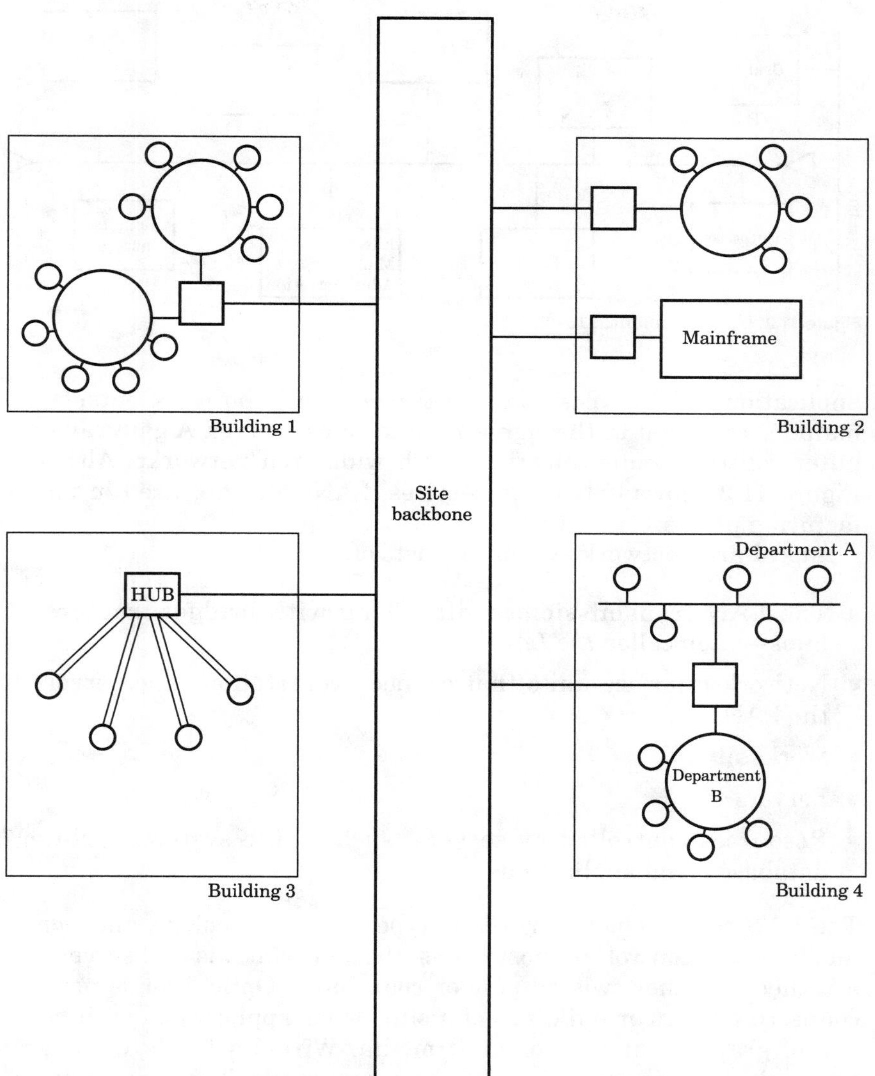

Figure 11.1 An enterprise LAN.

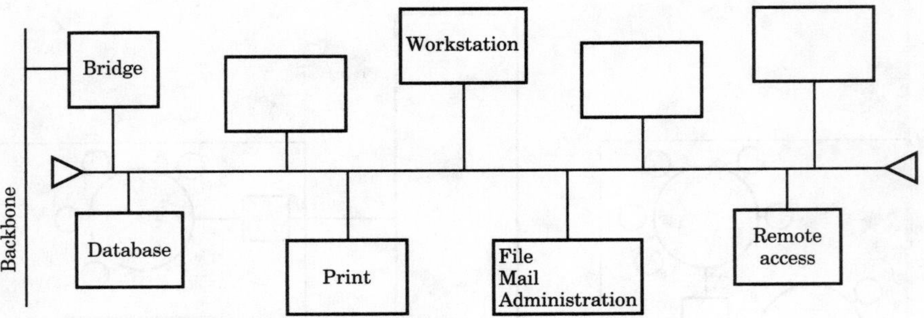

Figure 11.2 A departmental LAN.

applications. Employees who are traveling or who work outside the main location dial in through a remote-access server. A gateway computer controls communications with wide-area networks. Although Figure 11.2 shows only office services, LANs also are used in manufacturing plants.

A local-area network system consists of:

- The LAN transmission media, along with bridges, routers, or hubs—often called *the LAN*
- Network interface units that connect workstations and servers to the LAN
- Workstations
- Servers
- Resources controlled by servers, such as file systems, printers, databases, and applications

The LAN can be characterized by type of cable, topology, and type of media access control. In most LANs, the workstations and servers are attached to either twisted pair or coax cable. Optic fiber is used for connecting floors or buildings of a site, or for applications with heavy use of graphics, image, or multimedia. Wireless LANs with radio transmission are also used, but less commonly. The most common topologies are bus and ring. Department A of Fig. 11.1 has a bus topology LAN, and Department B uses a ring topology. Building 3 uses a hub topology, with the wires of the ring or bus going through a central unit. It is also possible to use a hierarchy of hubs, with a central hub for an entire site.

The purpose of a media access control discipline is to ensure that all devices on the network get their fair share of the transmission medium. The two disciplines covered by standards are *CSMA/CD*—carrier-sense multiple access with collision detection, also known as

Ethernet—and *control token*. Although the methods work differently, both allow one device to observe packets addressed for another. Because of the shorter distances, LAN data rates can be much higher than WAN rates. A standard for fiber LANs is the *Fiber Distributed Data Interface* (FDDI), a token ring at 100 million bits per second. Other standards are IEEE 802.3 (CSMA/CD), 802.4 (token bus) and 802.5 (token ring). *ATM* (asynchronous transfer mode) provides greater flexibility in function and implementation. It is expected to become dominant for both LANs and WANs.

Hub topologies are used increasingly. Earlier hub devices simply received and retransmitted signals at a central wiring closet. Hubs quickly evolved into centers for monitoring and managing the wiring of an entire enterprise, and hub devices added many functions: switching, routing, and collection of statistics. These products are part of a trend toward more central control of LANs.

Security threats and security advantages

LANs are vulnerable to the generic network security threats described in Chap. 10. Salient threats to LANs include:

- Connection of unauthorized devices to the LAN
- Workstations observing data intended for other stations on the LAN
- Workstations impersonating other workstations
- Unauthorized access to file server data or LAN services
- Hardware or software failures that cause loss of data or deny service
- Unauthorized remote access to LAN resources by way of other networks or by dialing in
- Propagation of viruses over the LAN.

On the other hand, joining a set of workstations into a LAN can improve security. File servers can provide far greater integrity and availability of data than separate workstations, and better access control. Servers can use more costly storage devices with better integrity and availability. The LAN can provide redundancy of data and of servers. Servers can be kept in physically protected locations and administered with extra care. LAN operating systems help administrators to keep track of users and LAN resources, and to control access. Using a LAN enhances integrity by ensuring that everyone uses the same information. A LAN makes it possible to limit the flow of information outside the organization by disabling removable-disk drives.

Despite these potential security advantages, organizations that moved work from mainframes to LANs often discovered that they had weakened security. Improved tools for managing LANs are beginning to close the gap.

LAN security services

Like any computing system, a LAN must control system entry and must authenticate users. It must control access to shared resources. It must protect its own integrity, protect data, and keep its services up and running. It must offer tools for managing the LAN and for collecting and analyzing audit data. Very often, a LAN is the user's portal to all services, local and remote. Users need a simple way to access these services without repeatedly identifying and authenticating themselves. Remote users will want to access the LAN over telephone lines, and so will intruders; the LAN must provide secure remote access. Some LANs must support multilevel security policies.

Integrity and availability

A great advantage of a LAN over separate workstations is that, because storage and administrative chores are shared, more resources and more attention can be devoted to data integrity and service availability. If these efforts succeed, critical applications can run on LANs. Integrity and availability depend on the design, implementation, and management of the entire network. Fault-tolerant designs are used for hubs, routers, and other network components. Unavailability of a server affects many users and may cause operational applications to go down. Protection of a server's data is even more crucial.

Server integrity and availability

The main way to protect data and provide high availability is through redundancy. An entire server and its data can be replicated, so that one server can quickly take over the work of the other. Alternatively, a single server computer can maintain redundant data and have other fault-tolerance properties.

Disk integrity, mirroring, and duplexing. An essential step in ensuring integrity is getting the data onto the disk correctly in the first place. A server reads back what it has just written—"read-after-write"—and verifies that the data on disk agree with the data in memory. Servers also maintain in duplicate the data that would be needed to reconstruct a disk—specifically the root directory and file allocation table.

A straightforward way to provide complete data redundancy is *disk mirroring*. Each update is written twice, to two different disks, so there are always two valid copies of all the data. If one disk fails, its mirror disk can replace it immediately, with no loss of availability or of data. Some disk controllers implement mirroring, or NOS software can do it. The cost is that half the storage is used only as insurance. Although there are two copies of the data, if the disk controller fails, both copies become unavailable. More reliability is provided by *disk duplexing,* where a separate controller is used for each drive. Disk duplexing is implemented by NOS software.

Disk arrays. Many storage devices are built out of large numbers of small disks. With these disk arrays, or *RAID* systems, each logical unit of data gets spread over many disks, a technique called *striping*. (The acronym RAID originally stood for *redundant arrays of inexpensive disks*; the scheme is now used with expensive disks too, providing very high performance.) RAID systems were developed for cost and performance reasons, not for integrity. Without any compensating features, they would degrade integrity very badly. The failure of a conventional disk affects only the files stored on that disk. With disk arrays, a failure affects every file that is striped across the disk. With n disks storing files conventionally, $1/n$ files would be lost; with striping, $1/n$ of each file would be lost. Similarly, the mean time to failure of the array is inversely proportional to the number of disks. Fortunately, RAID devices compensate for these properties by data redundancy. Either data is replicated or its integrity is protected with parity information.

With replicated data, each block of data is written multiple times. Replication hurts performance on writes but helps performance on reads, since each read can be directed to the disk where it will encounter the least delay. Various replication schemes are used. One is simple mirroring, where each disk is mirrored on another. More sophisticated replication schemes aim at keeping an array's performance balanced, no matter where failures occur. Parity-based methods compute parity information and store it on a separate disk. Then, any lost data can be reconstructed from the remaining data plus the parity information. Parity methods need less redundant data than replication does, but they use more extra disk accesses to update parity information.

When a failure occurs in an array, performance suffers and so does reliability, because there are now fewer disks. It is important to replace the disk and rebuild its data as quickly as possible. Arrays often include spare "hot disks" so that rebuild can start immediately. Depending on application needs, rebuild can proceed in parallel with normal use, or it can claim exclusive use of the array.

Physical security. Physical access to servers must be controlled. Hub configurations make it possible to centralize servers in a protected and access-controlled room, even if those servers belong to different departments and serve different sets of workstations. An operations staff with the necessary skills can then perform backups and other maintenance for all of the servers. Only an authenticated, authorized user should be able to boot up a server, and there should be a way to lock the display and keyboard until another authentication occurs.

Superservers. *Superservers* are computers that are configured specifically for the server role; they provide both high performance and high availability. Superservers often have redundant disk storage, multiple processors, error-checking memory, and redundant power supplies. They provide sophisticated diagnostic tools and allow a failed component to be replaced without taking down the server—a "hot fix." Superservers provide disk mirroring and disk duplexing, and they may include RAID devices that provide transparent redundancy of disk storage.

Backup

No matter how fault-tolerant the servers, their data still must be backed up to off-line storage, and so must the data of workstations on the LAN. A LAN architecture opens up many flexible options for backup. Redundant storage makes it easier for data to be backed up at the same time it is being used. Some products automatically take image backups at intervals, and others do continuous backup of all writes to a removable volume. Backup is usually to tape or optical disk. It can be done over the network to a "virtual tape" that is really a mainframe. There should be a way to back up a volume, saving its complete structure. Access control lists should be backed up along with the files and restored with them. Critical workstation data can be copied to a file server to ensure that it is backed up, or (in some systems) privileged users can back up workstation data directly.

LAN operating systems or add-on packages provide tools to keep track of backups and to enforce some access control. For example, Windows NT's backup program allows a user to back up only volumes or files that the user has access to. However a special backup right overrides this normal control. It could be used, for example, to allow operators to back up workstation data. Windows NT labels a backup tape with the user ID and machine of the person who created it. The tape can then be accessed only by that person, the system administrator, or someone with the backup right.

Transaction support

Transaction-processing applications and database systems need server support for transactions. They should be able to tell the server that a sequence of updates constitutes a transaction. Then, if a server goes down in the middle of a transaction, the recovery procedure backs out all the updates of the incomplete transaction.

Virus protection

A LAN provides a path for viruses to spread. On balance, however, a LAN environment is more secure against viruses than separate workstations. For one thing, users have less need to share diskettes or download from remote and uncertified sources. Executable files reside at servers, where administrators can ensure that antivirus measures are applied. Antivirus software for LANs scans server files and looks for suspicious activity on them. A LAN also makes it easier to ensure that workstations apply antivirus measures. When a workstation logs on, its files can be scanned, and its operating system can be checked for signs of a virus.

Multilevel security

Several systems have been developed to provide multilevel secure LANs. We describe here *VSLAN*.

VSLAN relies on trusted devices that connect nodes to the LAN. The VSLAN architecture is shown in Fig. 11.3. A host (which may be a workstation) is attached to an Ethernet LAN through a *network security device* (NSD), which takes the place of a standard Ethernet network interface unit. A *network security center* (NSC) maintains security information, provides the interface for a network security officer, and handles authentication and audit. The NSDs enforce the security policy by enforcing the interconnection rule defined in the Trusted Network Interpretation (Chap. 10). Each host is assigned a range of levels by the security officer—its *accreditation range*. This could be a single level. According to the interconnection rule, information exported at a given level can go only to a host whose range contains that level or a higher one. Discretionary access control is also enforced; it determines which hosts can communicate, independent of security level. The NSDs work at the link layer, providing datagram service plus security service.

Token devices identify VSLAN users and certify their rights to use specific hosts. A user inserts the token into a reader that is part of the NSD. Network connection is allowed only if the user is authenticated

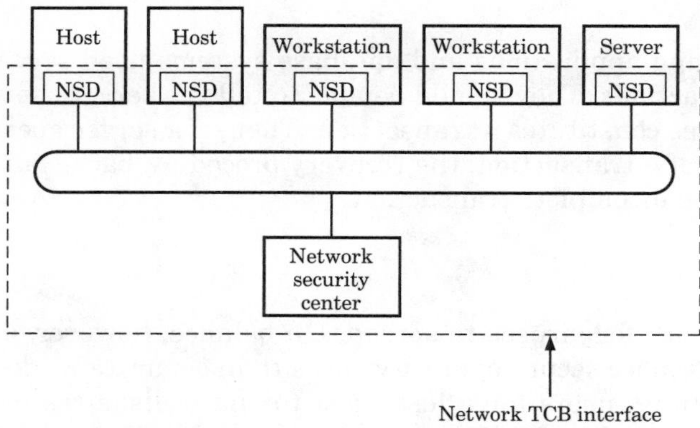

Figure 11.3 VSLAN architecture. [*From King* (*1990*).]

and also is authorized to use the host. The NSC then downloads to the NSD a list of hosts that it is allowed to communicate with. (This is for discretionary access control.) For a send operation, the NSD of the sending host gets a packet and its security label from a trusted component of host software. The NSD determines whether the interconnection rule and DAC permit the packet to go to the destination. If so, the NSD appends the identity of the host and the user, computes checksums for the label and the data, inserts these into the packet, and encrypts the packet for transmission. The NSD at the receiving end also enforces the interconnection rule. It passes to the host the security label and the IDs of the sending host and the user. The receiving host can use these for access control.

Distributed File Systems

Distributed file systems enlarge the file system view of users to include a global shared file system. Except for its scope, this global system appears almost exactly like a local one at a host or workstation. The file system is shared, as on a multiuser host, but the files reside at various hosts, or on specialized file servers. A distributed file system provides many advantages. Workstation users can share up-to-date versions of the same data and can cooperate to jointly maintain schedules, documents, or databases. Sharing the cost of the storage devices is a major advantage. Specialized file servers can also enhance performance, data protection, and availability. Security in a distributed file system differs from file security in a multiuser host. Mutual authentication is needed, the confidentiality of data in transit is at risk, and access control cannot rely on protection mechanisms of a single operating system.

Network File System

The predominant distributed file system is *Network File System* (NFS). NFS is a product sold by Sun Microsystems with its UNIX. NFS is also a specification that is supported in many environments. NFS is aimed at heterogeneous environments, and its protocols are specified as RPCs that can be implemented in different ways.

NFS allows file sharing between any pair of machines. All the mechanism is hidden from applications, which can use remote files just like local ones. A server machine offers one or more of its file systems for export, specifying which machines are allowed to use them. A client machine issues a **mount** request for the remote file system, specifying the name of the server. Only a superuser can invoke this remote mount. If the client host is on the approved list, the server returns a handle to the file. Using this handle, client processes issue the normal file system calls, which get translated into RPCs (by a *redirector* component at the client) and handled by the server.

NFS uses a *stateless* approach, which means that the server keeps no information about remotely opened files. Each request is handled independently. A stateful approach would keep track of open files and which records have been read or written, using some connection-oriented abstraction. The advantage of the stateless approach is that recovery is far simpler: a server can crash and restart quickly without any special measures, and a client crash causes no problem at the server. The downside is that request messages are longer, specifying not only the handle but also an explicit file offset, and processing of each request is more complex. A stateful system should perform better, but in practice NFS performance is very good. One reason is that it caches sizable chunks at the client, so that many file system calls can be handled locally.

The main security mechanism of NFS is a file on the server machine that lists the exported file systems along with the hosts and netgroups that can mount them. (Netgroups are defined groups of hosts.) In some systems this file can also specify the type of access—read only or read-write. Another file contains a list of the exported file systems that clients have mounted; a **showmount** command allows administrators to view this information. At a client, administrators can view what remote file systems are mounted. Another security feature is that the superuser cannot access remote files with superuser status. Some implementations relax this restriction because remote superuser access is very useful. *Secure NFS,* introduced in SunOS 4.0, is based on Sun Secure RPC, which uses encrypted time stamps to authenticate packets. Kerberos also can be used with NFS. A defect in NFS security is that a client could retain file system handles and continue to use them, although the server machine no longer trusts the client machine.

Andrew file system and AFS

AFS is based on the file system developed at Carnegie Mellon University for its Andrew distributed computing environment. Andrew was largely built on file sharing, and much attention was paid to scalability, availability, and security of the file system. File servers were dedicated trusted machines that resided in a physically secure environment and ran no user software. Workstations, in contrast, were considered insecure, as was the network. The design therefore included end-to-end encryption. The authentication scheme was based on Needham and Schroeder's (see Chap. 10). Originally, whole files were cached at the client workstations. Andrew included the concept of a *cell*—a separately administered Andrew system, with its own users, file servers, and authentication. Multiple cells shared the same global name space. Authentication tokens were valid only for the cell in which they were issued, but workstation software largely hid this location awareness from users and application programs.

The AFS product has been marketed by Transarc, and its technology is incorporated into the distributed file system of the Open Software Foundation's Distributed Computing Environment. AFS clients cache 64 kbytes of data (not whole files) on local disk or in memory. A call-back scheme notifies clients if their cached data becomes invalid because of file changes. AFS has stronger security than NFS. For availability and data integrity, AFS files can be replicated on different servers of a cell. The replicas are read-only. Replication improves performance as well as availability. AFS provides access control via access control lists at the directory level, with UNIX access control for individual files. Protection groups of users can be defined by users as well as administrators. AFS uses Kerberos authentication and encryption. An AFS utility monitors file servers and alerts administrators when a server's status is abnormal. A backup system allows backups to be taken without loss of availability: disk volumes are "cloned" and then backed up to tape.

Novell NetWare Security

A LAN operating system can be *peer-to-peer* or *dedicated server.* In a peer-to-peer system, any workstation can act as a server, offering to share its files or hardware devices. Peer-to-peer systems are used mainly for small networks where dedicated servers would be too costly. For larger networks, dedicated servers offer many advantages in performance, availability, and security. Novell NetWare is a good example of the dedicated-server approach. It is the dominant network operating system. Some others are Banyan VINES, Microsoft LAN Manager and Windows NT, and IBM LAN Server.

The architecture of a NetWare LAN system is shown in Fig. 11.4. The NetWare operating system runs on a dedicated server machine, providing file and print service, internetwork routing, administration, and backup. Other services can be added, using software provided by Novell or by other vendors. Examples are remote access and database systems. Client workstations are of different flavors: Windows, OS/2, Macintosh, and UNIX. This means that NetWare must support multiple file systems, with different naming structures. The NFS interface is supported. NetWare uses its own proprietary file format. Clients run network software and redirector software, which examines calls and decides whether to handle them locally or pass them to the server. Similarly, the redirector examines input from the server and decides what local software to direct it to. The server runs the NetWare software directly (not on top of another operating system). Our description is of NetWare v.4.

Objects, directory services, and administrators

The entities involved in NetWare security are files, directories, and *objects* known to the directory services. *NetWare Directory Services*

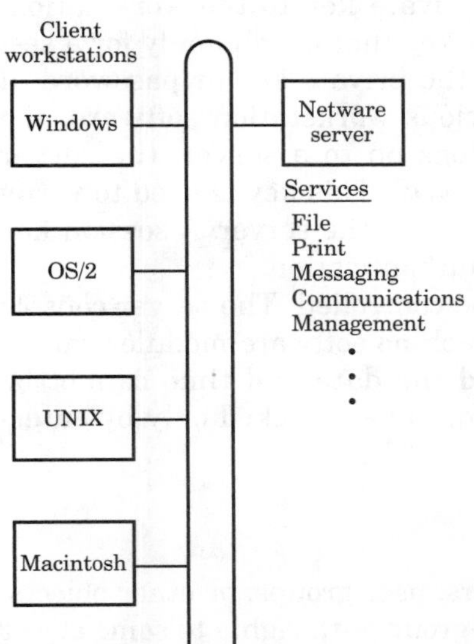

Figure 11.4 Novell NetWare architecture.

(NDS) are based on a global distributed database that is hierarchically organized and partitioned among the servers of an internetwork. Partitions can be replicated, and time-stamp-based protocols maintain consistency of replicas. The objects that the directory keeps track of include users, user groups, roles, organizational units, servers, workstations, and resources such as printers. Storage volumes are objects. Some objects are *containers* that contain other objects; for example, a company object can contain department objects. Access control applies to files, directories, objects, and *properties* of objects. Properties of a user object, for example, include login restrictions and group memberships. The network administrator can delegate control over portions of the internetwork to *supervisors*; they have unrestricted rights over their domains.

Control of system entry and authentication

To use the network, a user must have an account (a user object) and must log on, using a password. A user can be limited to specific workstations or designated times of day. A user account may also have an expiration date. Administrators can set password criteria such as length, complexity, and divergence from recent passwords. Password expiration times can be used. A single logon gives a user access to all the internetwork services that he is authorized for.

NetWare uses public key authentication protocols. The NDS keeps all the private keys, which are stored encrypted with the user's password. First, the workstation proves to the NDS that it knows the password. The NDS then sends the private key to the workstation, where it is converted into a temporary key that is valid only for a session. The workstation does not store the private key or password; if the temporary key is stolen by malicious workstation software, the damage is limited. When the user logs on to a server, the server obtains the user's public key from the NDS. This key is used to verify the workstation's signature of a message to the server. A session key is established that is used for packet authentication.

Access to the NetWare server can be controlled. The server console can be put into a secured mode, in which no software modules can be loaded, no patches can be made, and the date and time cannot be altered. The console can also be locked, to be unlocked only by entering the password again.

Access control

The subjects for access control are users, user groups, or other objects, such as organizational units. A user or group with rights to some object is a *trustee* of the object. Access control lists keep track of trustees and their rights. For files, access can be controlled at the file level or at the directory level. A user with rights to a directory has the same rights, by default, to its subdirectories and files. Similarly, rights to a container imply rights to the contained objects. This inheritance can be blocked, however, by an *inherited rights filter* on the contained object. The filter for a directory could specify, for example, that only read rights can be inherited from its parent directory. (Supervisor rights are not blocked by filters.) When a container becomes a trustee, all its contained objects also become trustees. For example, Department *A* becomes trustee for Directory *Y,* and all the members of Department *A* also become trustees of *Y.* User *templates* in containers can simplify the task of assigning rights to users; they allow default rights and restrictions to be specified before adding users to the container.

Rights can be inherited (as allowed by the filter), explicitly assigned, based on group membership, and based on *security equivalents.* (One object can be made completely equivalent to another in security rights and restrictions.) *Effective rights* actually govern access. Suppose the object is Directory *X.* Tim's effective rights to it are based on his assigned rights to *X,* his rights to *X*'s parent directory, the inherited rights filter on *X,* rights granted to groups Tim belongs to, and any security equivalences for Tim.

To grant rights for a file or directory, a user needs the *access control* right. To grant rights to an object, a user needs write access to its access control list.

The administrator interface allows rights to be assigned quite easily. The administrator selects the icon for Tim (the trustee-to-be) and drags it onto the icon for Directory *X.* A dialog box opens showing the current and possible rights, and the administrator selects those to assign. The administrator can view Tim's assigned rights and effective rights to any object, and can view all the trustees of *X.*

An organizational role object can be given the rights appropriate to some role. If a new person takes over the role, that person becomes trustee of the role object.

Integrity and availability

The NetWare file system has several data integrity features. If a bad spot on the disk is found during operation, that spot is marked as unusable and an alternative disk location is chosen to replace it (the hot fix redirection area.) The normal mode for write operations is to read back the data after writing and compare the data with the buffer in memory. A failure is interpreted as a new bad spot, and the information is written in the hot fix redirection area. Crucial information on the disk is duplicated—the root directory structure and the file allocation table.

A feature called *system fault tolerance* (SFT) allows two separate disks to be used, one disk mirroring the other. For still greater reliability each disk can have its own controller—disk duplexing. If one disk fails, or its data are lost, service can immediately switch to the other. An optional feature allows a complete second server to be used, connected to the primary server by a high-speed link. Given a high-speed connection, the second server can even be in a different building where it would be more likely to survive a disaster affecting the primary server. Disk mirroring is done by software, but special disk hardware can also be used for NetWare servers. Superservers can be used.

File locking and the *transaction tracking system* support file integrity. Transaction tracking is applied to files that have a "transactional" attribute. If a server failure occurs before a transaction is complete, all the transactions's updates are backed out. Several file attributes support integrity. Files can be designated as not deletable, not renamable, hidden, or read-only. "Execute only" files cannot be copied (for software license protection). Deleted files are not really deleted, but are kept and flagged as deleted. They can be kept for a specified minimum time or until there is no more room, when the oldest files are purged. Salvaged files are restored with their access control intact.

NetWare has defined a specification for backing up server and workstation data in a common system-independent format. The data can be restored to any type of disk or operating system—not just the type it was backed up from.

Packet integrity

In 1992, university students in the Netherlands discovered that any NetWare client could forge packets that gave its user supervisor status; the user could completely take over the network. *Packet signature* was added to protect against this threat; it requires the client and server to sign each packet. Since packet signature slows performance, different levels of use can be selected. The signature of each packet is based on the session key established during authentication, a hash function of the packet data, and the signature of the previous packet.

Audit and C2

A user designated as auditor controls event recording and produces reports. The usual events can be audited, including login and logout, granting rights, and changing passwords. Novell announced that it was working toward NCSC certification at the C2 level. Part of this work is to provide application program interfaces that allow client products to use NetWare security services.

Single Sign-on

The typical user of a distributed system must log on many times—to her department's NetWare LAN, another department's network that uses LAN Manager, an MVS system, the CICS subsystem on the MVS system, a database server on the LAN, a financial application running on a LAN server, CompuServe, an Internet gateway, and so on. Each system may have different format requirements for user IDs and passwords, and different criteria for password aging. A person may need a half-dozen IDs and a dozen passwords. Inevitably, people write them down or store them in logon profiles.

Requirements

What is needed is *single sign-on:* a user provides an ID and password just once per work session, and any further logons happen as if by magic. That is the functional requirement. A security requirement is that passwords should not be stored or transmitted in plaintext. Without standards, this is hard to achieve. Given the plaintext password, there is the problem of applying the right one-way transformation—the one used by the system that the password is being forwarded to. If an authentication server is doing the forwarding, and it has only a transformed password, it cannot recover the plaintext to transform it in a different way.

Some single sign-on products work entirely at the user's workstation, and others involve authentication servers. Most of the products work with the local operating system.

Implementations

One popular product is *SSO-DACS,* part of the *PC/DACS* security package. Using a combination of preprogramming and learning, SSO-DACS gathers the needed user IDs and passwords, stores them in encrypted form, and then supplies them as needed without bothering the user. SSO-DACS can work entirely at the local workstation, or can use a LAN server for storing the IDs and passwords. The LAN server approach is a better way to go if workstations are shared by different users. Other workstation-based packages prompt the user for the single password before proceeding with secondary logons.

Windows NT provides single sign-on to Windows NT workstations and servers. As described in Chap. 8, a Windows NT network is organized into domains. There can be a central (but replicated) security database for the entire domain. A user can log on to any workstation in the domain and automatically receive appropriate privileges. One domain can also handle a logon to another domain, and a single user account can have privileges that apply to many domains. The *trust relationships* of domains are explicit; for example, Domain *A* trusts Domain *B*, but *B* does not trust *A*. If a server in Domain *A* receives a logon request from a user in Domain *B*, it passes the request to *B* for authentication.

Kerberos supports single sign-on through its *authentication forwarding* capability. If a user's initial request to the authentication server includes a *forwardable* option, the AS will issue a ticket-granting ticket flagged as forwardable. This TGT can be forwarded to another system to authenticate the user without another password entry. When the ticket-granting server receives a forwarded TGT, it issues a ticket with a *forwarded* flag, so that servers can choose to treat forwarded tickets differently.

NetSP, an IBM product for single sign-on, is described in Chap. 10.

Remote Access

In addition to protecting against the errors and misuse of internal users, LANs must also protect against threats from remote users. The term *remote access* is used for access to LAN resources over telephone lines. Remote access has become more important because of increased mobile computing and telecommuting, which lets employees work at home or at satellite locations, connected to the department LAN by remote access. Remote access exposes the LAN to a serious security threat. Without special safeguards, anyone who can learn the telephone number of the LAN (by being told or by attack dialing) and can provide a user ID and password gets access to LAN resources.

How remote access works

When a computer sends data over a telephone line, a modem must convert the data to the form that the telephone system expects for voice communications. A LAN can use either individual modem devices or more complex equipment that provides a pool of modems—from two to hundreds. A common configuration is for a *remote access server* to support a modem pool, using specialized software products or hardware/software LAN modems. The same server may also support dialing out from LAN workstations.

The remote computer's software directs the remote modem to dial the number of the LAN, where the call is answered, completing the connection. There are two main types of remote access: *remote control* and *remote node*. With remote control, the remote user connects to a workstation on the LAN (her own, we hope). With remote node, everything runs on the remote computer, which behaves as if it were attached to the LAN. Remote access servers usually provide both types of access. Any workstation with a modem can (with inexpensive software) provide remote control, with security measures up to the workstation owner. This is a potential LAN intrusion path.

Authentication

The remote access server is a logical place for security measures. Authentication usually is based on *callback,* extra passwords, and cryptographic methods. Callback relies on a table listing the users who are authorized for remote access; the table also gives their telephone numbers. When a call is answered, the user enters an ID and password, and the system hangs up. The system looks up the user ID in the table, finds the telephone number, and dials it. The user typically has to enter a second password (which may be a common password for all users). Except for the minor inconvenience of the two-phase call, callback works well. It does nothing to prevent eavesdropping on the password, however. Some phone systems do not disconnect a call until the caller hangs up; this might allow an intruder to spoof the modem when callback is attempted. A good safeguard is to use different lines for the incoming and outgoing calls.

The main weakness of callback is that a user must be at a fixed number—not in a hotel room or at an airport. So callback is a good solution for employees working at home, but not for mobile users. Some schemes allow several alternative numbers for callback. This is useful, for example, for service personnel who regularly work with several customers. Flexible telephone services, such as call forwarding, may threaten the security of callback. Intruders have succeeded in forwarding other people's calls to their own numbers. A second password can be used with or without callback, to provide an additional level of protection for remote access.

Cryptographic challenge-response also is used. The Windows NT remote access server, for example, can use *Challenge Handshake Authentication Protocol* (CHAP), a challenge-response protocol that protects the password against eavesdropping and allows encryption of communications. Remote access servers often can negotiate either CHAP or weaker protocols—in order to support remote users who do not have token devices. A remote access server also can use a separate authentication server (AS). A central AS can maintain a larger database of users and authentication information, and it can use the best authentication technology. This approach allows large organizations to centralize remote-access authentication. A draft standard, *Remote Authentication Dial-In User Service* (RADIUS), covers protocols for remote access servers' use of a separate AS.

Other security services

A remote access server (or any component that handles remote access) should provide other services besides authentication. It should send alerts to network management systems or to the system operator when security-related events occur. (An example would be a callback that is not answered.) The server should maintain an audit trail of all calls. There should be a way to put the LAN in a mode that permits no remote access, and to selectively disable incoming lines. Whether or not callback is used, remote access should be limited to designated users. Multiuser systems need to protect against attacks that exploit the behavior of modems, ports, or sessions. When a user logs out, the modem should hang up. A remote user who hangs up should be logged out immediately, to prevent another caller from connecting to the same session.

With remote control, security at the LAN workstation is an issue. Some remote control products allow the remote user to clear the screen and lock the keyboard. The session can be disconnected after a specified period with no activity, and the workstation can automatically reboot after the user hangs up.

Telephone company and other services

Telephone companies provide service that allows a business to easily switch telephone numbers among its telephone lines; this helps restrict knowledge of dial-in numbers. Caller ID may be useful. With LAN dial-in services, all calls go through the management and security of a commercial service.

Mobile Computing and Wireless Communication

With digital wireless communications, computing and networking services are available from any place. People can communicate with other people and access their organizations' systems. New security and privacy problems arise from mobility itself and from the use of wireless communications.

One problem is that a portable computer or device—and its data—can be lost or stolen. Locks and passwords can help, but they are breakable. File encryption keeps data confidential even if it is stolen. One way to safeguard against data loss is to mirror updates to a home location very frequently. A distributed file system could handle this automatically, if the network connection was maintained. With wireless communications, however, there can be many brief disconnections and occasional longer ones, as the user moves into a new zone.

Large or intelligently managed caches at the mobile computer could allow these interruptions to be managed.

Wireless networks are much more vulnerable to eavesdropping than fixed networks, so encryption becomes an essential safeguard. A new privacy threat arises: eavesdroppers can learn not only message content and traffic patterns, but also where people are. Location information can also be learned by mail correspondents of a user, and by the services used. This is a matter of policy for employers and employees, but also a broader societal issue. Technical measures can be developed that will allow continuous network access while at the same time protecting location privacy. One measure is to broadcast to a large area containing the recipient; then the recipient's exact location is not revealed. Cryptographic protocols have been proposed for a trusted message service that preserves anonymity and location privacy of senders and receiver.

Authentication for mobile users is special in that, as a user moves about, the network access point changes, and so may the administrative domain that controls the access point. This *visited domain* needs to authenticate the user—to prevent fraudulent use of its services—but it probably does not have the authentication information. The safest assumption is that only the user's *home domain* has this information. Since the same authentication problem must be solved for digital wireless telephone, the methods used there are relevant. The different domains communicate over the wire network, and current authentication schemes assume—optimistically—that it is secure.

An important standard for wireless telephone is *Groupe Special Mobile* (GSM), used in Europe. A subscriber to GSM receives a smart card containing a secret key. When a mobile unit moves into a new local domain, it contacts the switching center for that domain. The visited domain sends a request to the home domain, passing it the ID and location of the mobile unit. The home domain obtains from its local authentication server and forwards to the visited domain the following items: a random number challenge, an expected signed response, and a session key. The visited network sends the challenge to the mobile unit, where the smart card computes the signed response using the secret key. The visited domain checks the signed response against the expected one. The secret key never leaves the AS of the home domain. All the encryption algorithms used by GSM are unpublished. GSM and other schemes have been criticized for their vulnerability to attacks on the wire network. Also, with heavy traffic, it may become impractical to always contact the home domain. Public key methods have not been used because of their computational demands on mobile phones, but this is not a problem for mobile computers.

Distributed Computing

This section looks at security in distributed computing and in the supporting services and structures.

Secure remote procedure call

Many distributed applications are written with remote procedure calls. RPC is a straightforward extension of a familiar programming construct—the procedure call. An RPC has call parameters, and it may return results. Each RPC is independent, with no state retained by either the caller or the callee. There is an Internet standard for RPC (based on Sun RPC) and an ISO standard called the *remote operations service element* (ROSE). RPC is a good anchor for security measures. Andrew Birrell argues this in an article about secure RPC for a Xerox research internetwork. RPC in that system takes place in the context of a *conversation* between two principals. A client creates a conversation by interacting with an authentication service, presenting the client name, private key, and name of the other principal. With that done, an RPC within the conversation guarantees some security properties. The caller is guaranteed that the call will be handled by the named callee. The callee is told the true name of the caller. There can be no eavesdropping on calls, except for their length, no modifications, and no replay. These are the basic guarantees that are needed for secure RPC.

Sun RPC has a secure version that can be used for communicating with other systems that also use the secure version. The name server acts as a key distribution center in this protocol. At login, the user's record is obtained from the name server's database; this record contains the user's name, a public key, and a secret key encrypted by the user's password. The login program decrypts the secret key and combines it with the public key to produce a session key. Encrypted authentication information goes into the header of each packet.

Distributed Computing Environment

Distributed Computing Environment (DCE) is a framework and a set of components for building and running distributed applications. Initially UNIX-oriented, DCE is reaching into other environments, such as MVS and NetWare. The RPC used in Windows NT conforms to the DCE specification.

DCE components fit between the local operating system and applications, and they use the local OS services and communication services. The core services of DCE are: thread service, remote procedure call, cell directory service, distributed time service, and security service. Threads are used to support RPC, which is the basic building block of DCE. A time service is needed for many distributed functions, including authentication and distributed files. The security service includes authentication, access control, and the *registry,* which is a trusted repository of security information. RPC uses aspects of the security service.

The registry contains information about accounts, groups, passwords, and security policy. Since the registry editor uses RPC, administrators can maintain it remotely. The registry can also have replicas, as described for AFS. To log on to DCE, a user needs an account entry in the registry. Authentication uses Kerberos extended with *privilege* service. The authentication server returns to the client a response that the client can pass to a *privilege server.* The privilege server certifies the client's user ID and group IDs and, interacting with the ticket-granting server (TGS), seals them in a *privilege TGT.* The client presents the privilege ticket-granting ticket to the TGS to get a ticket for a server, and that ticket also contains the privileges.

Each server controls access to its objects, using local access control lists. The access control manager at the server checks the privileges in a ticket against those in the ACL for the object. RPC has two phases: execution of an authentication protocol, and execution of the call itself. The call data can be encrypted. Once the call is received, the ticket privileges are checked. Thus authentication, confidentiality, and access control are all part of DCE's remote procedure call.

Authentication in a distributed operating system

This chapter has described security services and products that meet immediate, practical needs. Since the market is one where different operating systems interoperate, security is implemented "in front of," "beside," or above the operating system. That is, in communications protocols, in servers, or at the application layer. An instructive contrast is the Taos distributed operating system, a DEC research project. Taos security is based on an elegant theory, whose constructs are built right into the operating system.

Taos uses the notion of *compound principals* for all the different kinds of entities that can make access requests. According to the theory, principals make statements. If *s* is a statement, authentication answers the question "Who said *s?*", and the answer is a principal. Authorization answers another question. If *o* is an object, authorization answers "Who is trusted to access *o?*". Principals can be people or machines (these are *simple* principals); they can be *channels,* such as network addresses or encryption keys. Only a channel can make a direct statement to a computer. Principal *A* "speaks for" another principal B if, when A makes a statement, we can believe that B makes it too. The speaks-for relation represents indirection. For example, since a user cannot make a direct statement, the channel from her workstation must speak for her. A *handoff* axiom states that a principal has the right to allow any other principal to speak for it; from this axiom is derived a handoff rule: if A says B speaks for it, then B does speak for A. There is also a delegation axiom; delegation is somewhat weaker than handoff. A user hands off to a channel, but delegates to a workstation.

Other kinds of principals include groups, principals in roles, and conjunctions of principals. Roles serve to limit authority; people who hold a role speak for the role and not for themselves. The theory can describe encryption as a means of authenticating a channel, which means finding a principal that it speaks for.

A certification authority (CA) speaks for everyone, so it is trusted when it says that a channel (such as a key) speaks for a principal. The public key of the CA speaks for the CA. The CA issues a certificate for each principal A saying that A's public key speaks for A. Certificates are signed statements, and sets of them make up larger units called credentials that are maintained for each principal. Credentials are the proofs of authenticity. Special kinds of certificates are used for authenticating programs and machines. An *image certificate* authenticates an executable program (to ensure the program's integrity and proper use). The image certificate states that an image digest (a hash function of the code) speaks for a role, where the role is the name of a program or program category. A *boot certificate* states that a specific machine (or rather its key) speaks for a specific node key.

The purpose of authentication is for access control to know the source of an access request. An access control list for an object is a set of principals, each with some rights to the object. A request by A will be granted if A speaks for B and B is on the ACL, and B has all the rights needed for the request. The task of the reference monitor is to prove that A speaks for B or to determine that no such proof exists. Since each access control decision is based on a proof, the steps in the proof can be recorded in the audit trail to document why access was granted or denied.

Each Taos node has an authentication agent consisting of four components. A secure channel manager sets up channels between processes—which can be on different nodes—and links channels to the principals they speak for. An authority manager keeps track of principals and stores their credentials. A credentials manager builds, stores, and checks credentials. A certification library maps from keys to names and from group members to groups.

Summary

The ways to use networks include mail, file transfer, and distributed file systems. There are network operating systems, distributed operating systems, and environments for distributed computing. *Remote procedure call* (RPC) is an important building block.

For many users, a workstation attached to a LAN is the entry point for all computing services. A LAN system consists of: transmission media, along with bridges, routers, or hubs; network interface units; workstations; servers; and resources controlled by servers. In most LANs, workstations and servers are attached to twisted pair or coax cable; optic fiber is used for connecting floors or buildings. Hubs often serve as centers for monitoring and managing LANs.

Salient threats to LANs include: connection of unauthorized devices; observing data intended for other devices; impersonating other devices; unauthorized access to file server data or LAN services; failures that deny service or cause loss of data; unauthorized remote access; propagation of viruses over the LAN.

Joining a set of workstations into a LAN can improve security. Servers provide better integrity, availability, and access control. The LAN can provide redundancy of data and of servers. Servers can be well protected and administered, and LAN OSs help administrators to maintain control.

The most important technique for LAN integrity and availability is redundancy. An entire server and its data are replicated, or a single server maintains redundant data and has other fault-tolerance properties. Servers perform “read-after-write” to verify that data were written to disk properly; they maintain in duplicate the data that would be needed to reconstruct a disk. With disk mirroring, each update is written to two different disks. With disk duplexing, a separate controller is used for each drive. Redundant storage makes it easier for data to be backed up during use. Some products automatically take backups at intervals, and others do continuous backup. RAID devices, which are built out of large numbers of small disks, provide a great deal of data redundancy.

Physical access to servers must be controlled; they can be centralized in a protected room. Superservers (computers built to be servers) often have redundant disk storage, multiple processors, error-checking memory, and redundant power supplies.

Although a LAN provides a path for viruses, on balance it is more secure against viruses than separate workstations. Antivirus software for LANs scans server files and monitors for suspicious activity. A LAN makes it easier to ensure that workstations apply antivirus measures.

VSLAN is one of several multilevel secure LAN projects. VSLAN relies on trusted devices that connect hosts to the LAN. The devices enforce the interconnection rule of the Trusted Network Interpretation.

Security in a distributed file system differs from file security in a multiuser host. Access control cannot rely on the operating system, mutual authentication is needed, and eavesdropping is a risk. NFS is the dominant distributed file system. Its main security mechanism is a file on the server machine that lists exported file systems, along with the hosts that can mount them and (in some systems) the type of access. Secure NFS is based on Sun Secure RPC, which uses encrypted time stamps to authenticate packets. AFS has stronger security than NFS. Files can be replicated on different servers. AFS provides access control lists at the directory level, and UNIX access control for individual files. Backups can be taken without loss of availability.

Novell NetWare is the leading NOS. The entities for NetWare security are files, directories, and objects known to the directory services. These objects include users, user groups, roles, organizational units, servers, workstations, and resources such as printers. The administrator can delegate control over portions of the internetwork. A single logon gives a user access to all the internetwork services that he is authorized for. NetWare uses public key authentication protocols. The directory service keeps all the private keys, which are stored encrypted with the user's password. Access to the NetWare server can be controlled. File access can be controlled at the file or directory level. A user's effective rights to an object are based on his assigned rights and other factors, such as rights to a parent directory and group memberships. Data integrity features include read-after-write and replication of the root directory structure and the file allocation table. The system fault tolerance feature allows disk mirroring or duplexing. A complete second server can be connected to the primary server by a high speed link. If a server failure occurs before a transaction is complete, all the transactions's updates are backed out. Optional packet signature protects against packet forging.

With single sign-on, a user provides an ID and password just once per work session, although many systems and services may be used. One product, SSO-DACS, gathers the needed user IDs and passwords, stores them at the workstation in encrypted form, and then supplies them as needed without bothering the user. Kerberos supports single sign-on through its authentication forwarding capability.

Remote access exposes a LAN to a serious security threat. Without safeguards, anyone who can dial the LAN and provide a user ID and password gets access to LAN resources. Typically, a remote access server supports a modem pool. There are two main types of remote access. With remote control, the remote user connects to a workstation on the LAN; with remote node, a remote computer behaves as if it were attached to the LAN. Authentication is based on callback, extra passwords, and cryptographic methods. With callback, the user enters an ID and password, and the system hangs up. If the user is in a table of users authorized for remote access, the system calls the number given in the list. The limitation is that a user must be at a fixed number. Challenge-response methods are coming into greater use. An audit trail should be kept of all calls, and there should be a way to disable remote access.

New security and privacy problems arise from mobility and from the use of wireless networks, which are more vulnerable to eavesdropping than fixed networks. Eavesdroppers can learn not only message content and traffic patterns, but also where people are. Authentication is complicated because, as a user moves about, the network access point changes, and so may the administrative domain.

The focus of attention for network security is moving toward the services that support distributed applications. RPC is a good anchor for security measures. Some basic guarantees are needed for secure RPC. The caller is guaranteed that the call will be performed by the named callee. The callee is told the true name of the caller. There can be no eavesdropping, modification, or replay.

Distributed Computing Environment (DCE) is a framework and a set of components for building and running distributed applications. DCE security service includes authentication, access control, and a trusted repository of security information. Authentication, confidentiality, and access control are all part of DCE's remote procedure call. Authentication uses Kerberos extended with privilege service. Each server controls access to its objects.

According to the theory of authentication of the Taos distributed operating system, principals make statements. If *s* is a statement, authentication answers the question "Who said *s*?" Principal *A* "speaks for" another principal *B* if, when *A* makes a statement, we can believe that *B* makes it too. An access request by *A* is granted if *A* speaks for *B*, and *B* is on the ACL, and *B* has all the needed rights. The reference monitor either proves that *A* speaks for *B* or determines that no such proof exists.

Bibliographic Notes

LAN technology is described by Halsall (1992) and Berson (1992). A potpourri of LAN security information, including product names and vendor addresses, can be found in Stang and Moon (1993). Levy and Silberschatz (1990) survey distributed file systems, including NFS and Andrew. NFS security is described by Curry (1992) and Farrow (1991). Andrew security is described by Satyanarayanan (1989). AFS is described by Cohen (1993). Calas (1994) describes the design of a multilevel secure distributed file system.

Bates (1994) covers disaster recovery planning for LANs. Storage integrity measures are described in Chap. 8. Disk arrays are discussed by Ganger et al. (1994). Chen et al. (1994) provide a comprehensive RAID survey and annotated bibliography. A good source on Novell NetWare and its security features, and on LANs in general, is Sheldon (1993). NetWare authentication is described by Kaufman, Perlman, and Speciner (1995). It uses a variant of the Guillou and Quisquater method, described in Guillou, Ugon, and Quisquater (1992). Adamson, Rees, and Honeyman (1995) discuss issues in setting up a single login to Kerberos and NetWare realms. Windows NT security is described in Chap. 8. Windows NT network domains are described by Custer (1993) and Ruley et al. (1994). Williams (1990) and King (1990) describe the VSLAN system. Loscocco et al. (1992) describe the MLS LAN multilevel secure LAN.

Single sign-on is discussed in Janson and Molva (1991) and IBM (1993). Arnold (1993) and Curry (1992) discuss remote access security for UNIX. Rigney et al. (1995) describe RADIUS protocols. Baldwin and Kubon (1993) describe one company's use of a remote access server for UNIX LANs.

Forman and Zahorjan (1994) discuss security issues in mobile computing. Spreitzer and Theimer (1993) discuss privacy and security of location information. Brown (1993) describes and evaluates security services of digital radio telephone systems. So do Molva, Samfat, and Tsudik (1994), who also propose improved security algorithms. Beller, Chang, and Yacobi (1993) propose public-key methods to achieve location privacy. Carlsen (1994) proposes protocols for end-to-end authentication and privacy between two portable devices. Cooper and Birman (1995) describe protocols using a trusted message service for anonymity and location privacy; they assume vulnerability of the fixed network.

Birrell (1985) describes security features for RPC. The ISO remote operations service element is described by Halsall (1992). DCE is described by Johnson (1994), Bever et al. (1993), and Berson (1992). DCE security is described by Lin and Chandersekaran (1993) and Hu (1995), DCE protocols by Kaufman, Perlman, and Speciner (1995). The Taos theory of authentication is described by Lampson et al. (1992) and Wobber et al. (1994). A semantics for authorization in distributed systems is given by Woo and Lam (1993). Reiter, Birman, and Gong (1992) propose a security architecture for the Isis system, which is based on group multicast communication rather than RPC. Isis and its security are also described by van Renesse and Birman (1994).

Exercises

11.1. Does a hub topology for a LAN help or hurt security?

11.2. Explain why redundancy is more important for RAID disks than for conventional disks.

11.3. What are the two main RAID redundancy schemes?

11.4. Compare the security features of NFS and AFS.

11.5. In the context of NetWare Directory Services, what is a *container?* What is its significance for access control?

11.6. Explain the *inherited rights filter* of NetWare access control.

11.7. Explain how VSLAN enforces the interconnection rule of the Trusted Network Interpretation.

11.8. Describe how Kerberos supports single sign-on.

11.9. Explain how callback helps to secure remote access. What are its drawbacks?

11.10. Describe the authentication scheme used with GSM mobile telephones.

11.11. What is a remote procedure call, and why is it a popular mechanism for distributed applications?

11.12. Describe one security extension to remote procedure call.

11.13. What is the "speaks for" relationship in the authentication theory used for Taos?

References

Adamson, William A., Jim Rees, and Peter Honeyman. 1995. Joining security realms: A single login for NetWare and Kerberos. *Proceedings of the Fifth USENIX UNIX Security Symposium,* 157–166. Berkeley, Calif.: USENIX Association.

Arnold, N. Derek. 1993. *UNIX Security: A Practical Tutorial.* New York: McGraw-Hill.

Baldwin, Bob, and Jim Kubon. 1993. Dial-in security firewall software. *Proceedings of UNIX Security Symposium IV,* 59–62. Berkeley, Calif.: USENIX Association.

Bates, Regis J. Bud. 1994. *Disaster Recovery for LANs: A Planning and Action Guide.* New York: McGraw-Hill.

Beller, Michael J., Li-Fung Chang, and Yacov Yacobi. 1993. Privacy and authentication on a portable communications system. *IEEE Journal on Selected Areas in Communications* **11**(6): 821–829.

Berson, Alex. 1992. *Client / Server Architecture.* New York: McGraw-Hill.

Bever, M., K. Geihs, L. Heuser, M. Mühlhäuser, and A. Schill. 1993. Distributed systems, OSF DCE, and beyond. In Schill, Alexander, ed. *DCE—The OSF Distributed*

Computing Environment: Client/Server Model and Beyond, 1–20. Berlin: Springer-Verlag.

Birrell, Andrew D. 1985. Secure communication using remote procedure calls. *ACM Transactions on Computer Systems* **3**(1): 1–14.

Brown, Dan. 1993. Security planning for personal communications. *Proceedings of the 1st ACM Conference on Computer and Communications Security,* 107–111. New York: ACM Press.

Calas, Christel. 1994. Distributed file system over a multilevel secure architecture: Problems and solutions. *Computer Security—ESORICS 94. Proceedings of the Third European Symposium on Research in Computer Security,* 281–297. Berlin: Springer-Verlag.

Carlsen, Ulf. 1994. Optimal privacy and authentication on a portable communications system. *Operating Systems Review* **28**(3): 16–23.

Chen, Peter M., Edward K. Lee, Garth A. Gibson, Randy H. Katz, and David A. Patterson. 1994. RAID: High-performance, reliable, secondary storage. *ACM Computing Surveys* **26**(2): 145–185.

Cohen, David L. 1993. AFS: NFS on steroids. *LAN Technology* **9**(3): 51(9).

Cooper, David A., and Kenneth P. Birman. 1995. Preserving privacy in a network of mobile computers. *Proceedings of the 1995 IEEE Symposium on Security and Privacy,* 26–38. Los Alamitos, Calif.: IEEE Computer Society.

Curry, David A. 1992. *UNIX System Security: A Guide for Users and System Administrators.* Reading, Mass.: Addison-Wesley.

Custer, Helen. 1993. *Inside Windows NT.* Redmond, Wash.: Microsoft Press.

Farrow, Rik. 1991. *UNIX System Security: How to Protect Your Data and Prevent Intruders.* Reading, Mass.: Addison-Wesley.

Forman, George H., and John Zahorjan. 1994. The challenges of mobile computing. *Computer* **27**(4): 38–47.

Ganger, Gregory R., Bruce L. Worthington, Robert Y. Hou, and Yale N. Patt. 1994. Disk arrays: High-performance, high-reliability storage subsystems. *Computer* **27**(3): 30–36.

Guillou, Louis Claude, Michel Ugon, and Jean-Jacques Quisquater. 1992. The smart card: A standardized security device dedicated to public cryptology. In Simmons, Gustavus J., ed. *Contemporary Cryptology: The Science of Information Integrity,* 561–613. Piscataway, N.J.: IEEE Press.

Halsall, Fred. 1992. *Data Communications, Computer Networks, and Open Systems.* 3d ed. Wokingham, England: Addison-Wesley.

Hu, Wei. 1995. *DCE Security Programming.* Sebastopol, Calif.: O'Reilly & Associates.

IBM. 1993. *IBM Security Architecture: A Model for Securing Information Systems.* Publication No. SC28-8135-0. Kingston, N.Y.: IBM Corporation.

Janson, P., and R. Molva. 1991. Security in open networks and distributed systems. *Computer Networks and ISDN Systems* **22**(5): 323–346.

Johnson, Brad Curtis. 1994. A distributed computing environment framework: An OSF perspective. In Brazier, F. M. T., and D. Johansen, eds. *Distributed Open Systems,* 57–77. Los Alamitos, Calif.: IEEE Computer Society.

Kaufman, Charlie, Radia Perlman, and Mike Speciner. 1995. *Network Security: Private Communication in a Public World.* Englewood Cliffs, N.J.: PTR Prentice Hall.

King, Greg. 1990. Considerations for VSLAN integrators and DAAs. *Proceedings of the 13th National Computer Security Conference,* 201–210. NIST/NCSC.

Lampson, Butler, Martín Abadi, Michael Burrows, and Edward Wobber. 1992. Authentication in distributed systems: Theory and practice. *ACM Transactions on Computer Systems* **10**(4): 265–310.

Levy, Eliezer, and Abraham Silberschatz. 1990. Distributed file systems: Concepts and examples. *ACM Computing Surveys* **22**(4): 321–374.

Lin, Ping, and Sekar Chandersekaran. 1993. Integration of DCE and local registries: Design approaches. *Proceedings of the 1st ACM Conference on Computer and Communications Security,* 165–170. New York: ACM Press.

Loscocco, Peter A., William R. Kutz, Dale M. Johnson, and Ronald J. Watro. 1992. Dealing with the dynamics of security: Flexibility with utility in an MLS LAN.

Proceedings of the Eighth Annual Computer Security Applications Conference, 180–192. Los Alamitos, Calif.: IEEE Computer Society.

Molva, Refik, Didier Samfat, and Gene Tsudik. 1994. Authentication of mobile users. *IEEE Network Magazine* **8**(2): 26–34.

Reiter, Michael, Kenneth Birman, and Li Gong. 1992. Integrating security into a group oriented distributed system. *Proceedings of the 1992 IEEE Computer Society Symposium on Research in Security and Privacy,* 18–32. Los Alamitos, Calif.: IEEE Computer Society.

Rigney, Carl, Allan C. Rubens, William Allen Simpson, and Steve Willens. 1995. *Remote Authentication Dial In User Service (RADIUS).* Internet Draft, May 1995. Work in progress.

Ruley, John D., et al. 1994. *Networking Windows NT.* New York: John Wiley & Sons.

Satyanarayanan, M. 1989. Integrating security in a large distributed system. *ACM Transactions on Computer Systems* **7**(3): 247–280.

Sheldon, Tom. 1993. *Novell NetWare 4: The Complete Reference.* Berkeley, Calif.: Osborne McGraw-Hill.

Spreitzer, Mike, and Marvin Theimer. 1993. Scalable, secure mobile computing with location information. *Communications of the ACM* **36**(7): 27.

Stang, David J., and Sylvia Moon. 1993. *Network Security Secrets.* San Mateo, Calif.: IDG Books.

van Renesse, Robert and Ken Birman. 1994. Fault-tolerant programming using process groups. In Brazier, F. M. T., and D. Johansen, eds. *Distributed Open Systems,* 96–112. Los Alamitos, Calif.: IEEE Computer Society.

Williams, Timothy C. 1990. Usefulness of a network reference monitor. *Proceedings of the 13th National Computer Security Conference,* 788–796. NIST/NCSC.

Wobber, Edward, Martin Abadi, Michael Burrows, and Butler Lampson. 1994. Authentication in the Taos operating system. *ACM Transactions on Computer Systems* **12**(1): 3–32.

Woo, Thomas Y. C., and Simon S. Lam. 1993. A framework for distributed authorization. *Proceedings of the 1st ACM Conference on Computer and Communications Security,* 112–118. New York: ACM Press.

Part

4

Management and Analysis

Chapter 12

Managing Computer Security

Introduction

Is computer security a technical problem or is it a management problem? It is both, of course. This chapter is about managing security—what has to be done and how to get it done. The chapter revisits the problems and methods treated in earlier chapters, but from a more practical and more prescriptive viewpoint.

The job of security management

Computer security management is a terribly complex task. It relates to many areas of expertise and requires a wide variety of skills. It is also an area of rapid change, driven by changes in technology and in the way computing is organized.

Several names are used for security management programs, including *information security* and *information protection.* Whatever the activity is called, organizations are responsible—to society, to their customers, to their stockholders—for carrying out a computer security program. This means developing a security plan that defines the security objectives, policies, and procedures. It means setting up organizations to carry out the plan and assuring that the plan is being carried out.

Overview of the chapter

First we discuss possible organizational structures for security management, then consider how security policy is formed and implemented. Next comes a section on people and security. The issues include how to select employees, how to train them and alert them to security issues, what security roles people play, and how organizational and administrative controls contribute to security. Then we discuss how to operate computing systems securely. The following section deals with physical security: the threats that it protects against—such as intrusion, electrical problems, fire, flood—and the protective measures. Next comes contingency planning—planning for harmful events that might occur, such as natural disasters. The final section deals with response to computer security incidents.

Organizational Structure

Although every organization needs the right organizational structure for managing information security, there is no consensus on what that structure is. In the early days of computer security, an era of centralized computing, the security function usually resided in the computing department. But sweeping changes in how computing is done, along with deeper understanding of security needs, have led to other structures and to continuing debate.

Basic goals

In deciding which structure to adopt, an organization needs to consider some basic goals. People who manage security must be able to align security policy with business needs. They must understand technology and be able to explain technical risks and safeguards to the most senior management. Security managers need clout; they need to command resources and to project an image that draws the support of users. They need strong influence on application developers in order to get security into the development process. The highest-level security goals and policies should be consistent throughout the organization. (If they are not, users' view of policy is unclear, and resources are wasted on duplicate efforts.) The structure for security must provide this overall consistency while also supporting decentralized computing and end-user application development.

Possible management structures

The following paragraphs describe some possible management structures.

- Security is a function within an Information Systems or Information Technology organization. With this structure, a security program tends to lack independence and resources, and to get little management attention. Separating security from applications development and from operations gives it more autonomy. Or, it can be a staff function reporting to the Chief Information Officer.

- Security reports to a specialized business unit, such as corporate security, insurance, or legal. Although information security often is part of general security, that structure is not recommended. It gives users a low-prestige, low-technology image of information security and leads them to think that security is someone else's job.
- A structure that makes sense for many organizations is described by William Perry (1985). A *chief security officer* (CSO) is a senior manager reporting directly to the CEO. Depending on the size of the organization, computer security can be a full-time or part-time responsibility of the CSO. Each major operating unit [such as finance, marketing, information technology (IT)] also has a security officer who reports to the management of that unit. A computer security planning committee is composed of managers of the operating units (ideally all of them) and is chaired by the CSO. The committee identifies security tasks and assigns a sponsor to oversee each task; the sponsor is usually one of the security officers. The planning committee is the major force for security, and the CSO makes sure that the committee's plans are carried out. Perry also recommends a separate security quality assurance function, reporting to the CSO.
- Digital Equipment Corporation engineered a structure that also uses a security planning committee. A Corporate Security organization provides overall leadership; some members of the executive committee of the corporation act as a security board and oversee Corporate Security. Policy is developed by a council of senior managers, and strategies are developed by a committee of managers—both council and committee representing Digital organizations. Finally, sites or organizations have security coordinators. This structure deemphasizes formal security organizations and security jobs in favor of making security part of everyone's job.
- Mainly for U.S. government agencies, the National Institute of Standards and Technology (NIST) has described a multilevel structure with (as a minimum) a central agency level and a "system" level. Many agencies will need four or five levels; for example: agency level, unit level, computer facility level, and application level. The central security program does what it can do best: set policy, exercise authority, articulate and enforce standards, provide training, and get the best price on security hardware and software. The system levels can meet the specific needs of a unit or platform or application. Security programs at these levels evaluate vulnerabilities, implement safeguards, administer users and resources, and respond to security problems.

Organizations vary so greatly that no one structure can possibly suit all. Each organization needs to develop its own security management structure, based on the basic goals and its own structure and culture.

Computer Security Policy

Whatever the chosen structure, security policy is what governs security management. In Chap. 4, a "real-world" security policy was defined as "the set of laws, rules, and practices that regulate how an organization manages, protects, and distributes resources to achieve its security objectives." Security management needs a real-world security policy for computing, networking, and information. The policy defines the organization's view of security and how it plans to realize that view. It provides a framework and guide for security management and a basis for assessing how well the organization is achieving its security objectives. The organization's business goals, its culture, its environment, and the technology available—all of these determine what goes into the security policy.

Security policies vary greatly in scope. An owner-operated company with 300 employees can cover everything it needs in one fairly simple policy. A loosely managed entity, such a cooperative educational network, needs a broad policy framework to be fleshed out by its members' individual policies. A large corporation fits somewhere between these extremes. Whatever its scope, a security policy should be as simple and clear as possible.

Types of policies

Since computer security is a complex endeavor involving business needs, human behavior, and technology, it is not surprising that different kinds of security policies are needed. The Information Technology Security Evaluation Criteria (ITSEC), for example, define a *corporate security policy* as "the set of laws, rules and practices that regulate how assets including sensitive information are managed, protected, and distributed within a user organisation" (ITSEC 1991: 112). A *system security policy* pertains not to the organization as a whole, but to a specific system. Finally, a *technical security policy* is defined as "the set of laws, rules and practices regulating the processing of sensitive information and the use of resources by the hardware and software of an IT system or product."

The NIST makes still finer distinctions with respect to corporate (or government agency) policy and system policy. A *program-level policy* creates an organization's security program, defining its goals and scope, and assigning management responsibilities. A *program-frame-*

work policy defines an organization's overall approach to computer security, and assigns management responsibilities. A framework policy might state, for example, that every unit of the organization must have business continuity plans. It might spell out the philosophy of access control—for example, role-based or following the DoD policy. Guidelines for secure operation of the Internet (Fig. 12.1) could be considered a program-framework policy. *System-specific policies* pertain to applications, computing platforms, or facilities. Finally, *issue-specific policies* (Fig. 12.2) might deal with the security vulnerabilities of new technologies, how to handle specific threats or problems, or how to use specific safeguards. For example, an organization that collects personal data from its customers needs a policy about collection, handling, and use of that data.

No fixed set of policy types will apply to all environments. Realms of activity need their own policies, and they also must conform to—or make demands on—the policies of other realms. Take, for exam-

1. Users are responsible for understanding and respecting the security policies of the systems they use and are accountable for their own behavior.
2. Users are responsible for protecting their own data and for helping to protect the systems they use.
3. Service providers are responsible for the security of the systems they operate and for keeping users informed about their security policies.
4. Vendors and system developers are responsible for providing sound and secure systems.
5. Users, service providers, and vendors are responsible for cooperating to provide security.
6. Technical improvements in Internet security should be sought. Designers and developers of new protocols, hardware or software are expected to consider security.

Figure 12.1 Guidelines for secure operation of the Internet. [*Summarized from Pethia, Crocker, and Fraser (1991).*]

- The issue
- The organization's position on the issue
- Applicability
- Roles and responsibilities
- Compliance
- Contacts and supplementary information

Figure 12.2 Suggested format for issue-specific policies. [*From NIST-CSL (1994).*]

ple, a local-area network (LAN) that implements a local part of a large bank's loan processing system. This LAN is governed by the overall security policy of the bank, and also by the policy of the loan processing application. But security managers for the LAN interpret and augment those policies for their environment. Security managers for the loan application make sure that the LAN's security policy suffices.

An organization's overall policy (corporate, or program-level and program-framework) lays out the security philosophy and goals. It may refer to the laws and regulations that motivate and constrain it. It may rank the security attributes, stating for example that data integrity and availability are more important to the organization than confidentiality. The overall policy defines the scope of the security program—which resources and people it covers. It sets up the management structure and delineates roles and responsibilities (more about these later). It may set minimum requirements for units of the organization. It may define an organizationwide data classification scheme. It may authorize the use of penalties for noncompliance. The overall policy, especially for a large organization, is not very detailed and does not deal with specific technologies.

Setting policy

Who sets security policy for an organization? Since the policy must make sense technically and must be enforceable, its framers need both know-how and power. Overall policy is the responsibility of top management. Responsibility for other levels of policy corresponds to the organization's general structure and to its structure for managing security. If each operating unit has a security officer, that person sets policy for the unit, or creates a committee that sets policy. Policy should be developed in consultation with the people who run the computing systems, people technically knowledgeable about security, and the users (who can best judge its effect on their work). Policy developers should consult other people concerned with asset protection, such as auditors and physical security people—both to help set the right policy and to get their cooperation in implementing it. A policy reflects the decisions made—based on risk assessment—about priorities for security.

The aim of policy is to guide or influence the behavior of many people, including users, security administrators, and those responsible for setting priorities or undertaking new security initiatives. Before a policy goes into effect, it needs publicizing, full discussion in meetings, and a period for comments and revisions.

Policy issues

We have mentioned some issues that an overall policy typically covers. Other issues are so pervasive that most organizations need to address them at some level of policy.

Authorized use. An explicit policy is needed about who may use each system, and for what purposes. The overall policy might specify, for example, that systems may be used only by employees unless system-level policies authorize use by contractors or customers. Most commercial organizations authorize use for business purposes only. A university, though, may allow experimenting and even game playing. Most organizations require users to be individually authorized. For some organizations, such as libraries with on-line catalogs, policies of open access are appropriate. The authorized use policy defines what forms of network connection are allowed, such as remote access or Internet connection. If telecommuting is used, the policy must cover it.

Roles and responsibilities. The policy defines generic security roles and spells out the responsibilities of each role. For example, as described in Chap. 4, a company's policy might define the role of information resource *owners*—managers who are responsible for the security of the resources they own. Other roles are *user* and *supplier of services.* Each role carries a distinct set of responsibilities. For example, the owner of an application is responsible for providing access control based on user ID. The user is responsible for using systems only in authorized ways. The supplier of services is responsible for a disaster recovery plan. Although different organizations will view roles differently, most will define the responsibilities of:

- Users
- Managers of sites, applications, and systems
- Service providers
- System administrators
- Security organizations

The responsibilities for these roles will reflect policy decisions on many issues, as can be seen in Table 12.1, from a proposed security policy for a research network.

Ethics. The policy should explicitly require ethical behavior of all users. The policy statement may include a code of ethics or may refer to codes developed by professional organizations or universities.

TABLE 12.1 Security Responsibilities

Role	Responsibilities
Users	Know and respect laws, codes of ethics, and security policies. Use available security mechanisms to protect their own information, and advise others who fail to do so. Notify a system administrator or management about any detected security violation or failure. Do not exploit security weaknesses. Supply correct and complete information for authentication. Use network and computing resources ethically.
System administrators	Rigorously apply available security mechanisms to enforce local policies; implement available improvements promptly. Advise management on the workability of existing policies and on technical considerations for possible improvements. Secure systems and networks within the site and interfaces to global networks. Respond to emergency events in a timely and effective way. Use standard and generally approved auditing tools to help detect security violations and actively participate in educating users who, through carelessness or ignorance, violate security. Keep informed on network policies and recommended practices and keep local users and management informed. Communicate and cooperate with other sites and emergency response centers about threats or violations. Judiciously exercise their "extraordinary" privileges. Give user privacy major consideration.

SOURCE: Excerpted and summarized from Oldehoeft (1992).

Policies that cover users of open networks should refer to the codes of ethics for those networks.

Classification of information. Overall policies often define classes of information that are more or less sensitive—or that differ in what access is allowed. Classification allows an organization to apply security measures where they are most needed. Although most organizations have simpler needs than the DoD, many also classify information according to its sensitivity. An organization might have three levels of sensitivity, such as: Unclassified, Internal Use Only, and Confidential. It might also categorize information as Business Confidential (for sensitive business results), Personal and Confidential (for personnel information), and Proprietary (for trade secrets). Classification is especially important for trade secrets. An organization may need to show in court that it treated specific information as proprietary. In 1994, for example, American Airlines charged that Northwest Airlines stole portions of a proprietary fare-setting system. The data were transferred to Northwest by American employees who left for jobs at Northwest. The employees claimed they believed the information was not confidential.

Highest level allowed. Information classification policies are fleshed out with guidelines and procedures for handling each level or category of data. If a system does not meet the requirements for "Company Confidential," it cannot accept that level of data. The system-level policy then would be "no Company Confidential data."

Licensed software. A typical policy states that licensed software can be used only if properly licensed and only in the way specified in the license agreement.

System administration. The policy assigns responsibility for system administration and security administration. For example, system administration for departmental systems is the responsibility of the departments' administrative managers.

Response to policy violation. What does the organization do when policy is violated? The policy must address both investigation and what follows. Will a violator be counseled or dismissed or prosecuted? Sometimes it is another organization's policy that is violated. For example, a BioWidget employee who uses a supplier's system repeatedly picks weak passwords.

Implementing policy

In the broadest sense, all of computer security is about implementing security policy. Here we mean translating policy into concrete terms, interpreting it, and making sure that everyone knows and understands it.

Policy is a high-level statement that needs to be amplified. The policy may state, for example, that all users must be authenticated, but not say how. The NIST has distinguished three types of policy-implementing tool:

- *Standards,* which specify the uniform use of some measures throughout the organization. For example: the same kind of smart card for all user authentication.

- *Guidelines,* which allow for more flexibility. For example: a strong authentication technique such as smart cards. "Guidelines...help ensure that specific security measures are not overlooked, although they can be implemented, and correctly so, in more than one way" (NIST-CSL 1994).
- *Procedures,* which spell out in detail the steps in some security-related task. For example: security procedures to follow when an employee leaves the company.

Policy, standards, guidelines, and procedures can go into a single handbook.

Employees or users often perceive the security policy differently from the managers who promulgate it. A survey can reveal these discrepancies and allow security managers to resolve them. Also, the policy is bound to be ambiguous on some points, so someone must have the last word on policy issues. That authority might be, for example, the committee that sets policy.

A difficult management task is to make people aware of security policy and to convince them it is important. Employees get many policies and directives—and understandably ignore some of them. Some suggestions:

- Use meetings or videos, as well as printed and on-line memos, to show that management puts high priority on security.
- Convey the content of the policy through a security handbook (or chapter in a more general handbook) and in meetings.
- Produce or purchase security videos.
- Bring in outside security experts as guest speakers.
- Discuss one security item at each staff meeting.

Security policy keeps changing as the organization changes and as threats and technology change, and people need to know the current policy.

People and Security

Nothing is more important in the computer security picture than people's behavior. Management must find the right people, give them the skills that they need, and motivate them to follow secure practices. Management must make people keenly aware of security needs and must set up controls that guide behavior toward security. This must be done without violating dignity or rights to privacy. Security measures should not make work harder or unpleasant. After all, security is one goal among many.

Selecting employees

One consideration in staffing an organization is how well people will support computer security. Employment applications can request information that is needed to evaluate security risk. The law restricts what can be asked, and privacy guidelines have to be observed. Outside bureaus are often used for background checks, which require the applicant's permission. Some bureaus have better records on privacy and responsible operation than others. The most common background checks are for credit history and criminal record. It is important to verify references, employment history, and academic transcripts. Danger signals in the application include unexplained gaps in employment, frequent job moves, or a salary or educational level that is unusual for the job that was held.

Since most computer security losses result from error, hiring qualified people furthers security. The job description can include security, stating, for example, that the job requires care in handling confidential material. It is valuable for security managers to maintain close relationships with people in the human resources department, encouraging them to consider security needs when they gather and use information about applicants.

Training and awareness

Ideally, all employees and all computer users are highly skilled in their jobs and in security practices. Ideally, everyone is aware of computer security issues and motivated to take security seriously. Ideally, everyone considers security to be part of his job and not the exclusive concern of specialists. It is the job of security managers to approach that ideal through training and through measures that highlight security and convince people of its importance. To motivate people, organizations use a combination of carrot and stick, with the stick predominating too often. Good security tends to go unnoticed and unrewarded, and the cost savings and other gains are not measured as they might be.

Orientation for new employees is the place to start imparting security awareness, attitudes, and skills. At that time, employees get their first exposure to the organization's security policy. They get a copy of the security handbook and perhaps some tutorial instruction. But security is not a one-time thing. There needs to be continuing reinforcement of the idea that security is important and has management behind it. To show the breadth of concern about security, newspaper or magazine stories can be used—stories about critical systems going down or assets being lost. A security-awareness poster might be distributed in March, a brochure in June, and so on through the year. Senior managers can attend seminars on computer security and can take a visible interest in cases of misuse—investigate them, make the causes known. Often it pays to hire an external consultant for a security review. Special expertise is obtained, and, if the consultant is brought in by senior management, the recommendations may actually get implemented.

Computer security audits are essential, as is the consideration of security in EDP audits and financial audits—both internal and external. Email or login messages can tell about new security features, warn of new threats, or give tips on using security software. Some security experts suggest putting computer security in all performance plans. Although this goes too far, managers certainly can consider security in performance reviews. At any time managers can notice and praise time and effort spent on security.

Useful for both training and awareness are hands-on demonstrations and tutorials of security features. Since these features are often hard to use, the person who gets no easy introduction may use them ineffectively or not at all.

Security roles and responsibilities

An organization's security policy spells out roles with respect to security and what responsibilities go with each role. Here we discuss three kinds of roles: users, their managers, and security officers (the people in charge of security for some level of an organization).

Security responsibilities of users. Users are the first line in security. They are responsible for knowing what the policy is and following it. They are also responsible for observing ethical standards that may not be explicit in the policy. Users are responsible for learning the tools and skills that they need in order to abide by the policy. They are responsible for encouraging good security behavior on the part of other users—sharing their expertise, giving help when asked. They can suggest improvements in procedures or tools. For example, a user needs to grant other people certain kinds of access to her files, but finds this laborious with the current security software. With an additional feature, this granting could be easy and quick. If she alerts her management or security management, they can push the vendor to add that feature, or can buy an add-on package.

Security responsibilities of managers. The manager of a department or unit has to provide the people in that unit with the resources to carry out their security responsibilities. That includes training; it often includes security software and hardware. Managers can convey attitudes about security. They can give rewards in the form of comments on performance reviews, acknowledgments at meetings, and special recognitions. In addition to these general responsibilities, managers will have specific responsibilities spelled out by security guidelines and procedures. For example, it is typically an employee's manager who requests a new account and specifies its privileges.

Security officer role and qualifications. Every organization defines some role as responsible for computer security in a unit of the organization; this is the *security officer* (SO); the Department of Defense (DoD) uses the term *Information Systems Security Officer* (ISSO). There are security officers at various levels of an organization, and the organization as a whole may have a chief security officer (CSO). The scope of the job varies greatly. For a small department that operates a LAN, for example, the security officer may be one and the same as the systems administrator, and even that may be a part-time job. For a large site with many systems, a professional security officer may supervise several specialized groups.

The job of security officer is relatively new and not yet highly codified. One thing is clear: a security officer needs a broad array of skills. An SO needs a good technical background in hardware and software, especially the particular systems being used. In addition to understanding the principles and practices of computer security, an SO must know management procedures. An SO must be good at interacting with people, because he or she has to stay in touch with and influence many people and organizations. Figure 12.3 shows the minimum qualifications for an ISSO.

Two years of experience in a computer-related field
One year of experience in computer security, or a computer security training course
Familiarity with the operating system being used
Technical degree desirable in computer science, mathematics, electrical engineering, or a related field

Figure 12.3 Qualifications for an Information Systems Security Officer. [*From NCSC* (*1992*).]

Responsibilities of the security officer. The security officer of a unit participates in setting policy for the unit and is responsible for writing its detailed security procedures. She sets up training programs or coordinates them with others, such as the personnel department for orientation. She is responsible for developing security awareness. The security officer should be well-known to all the users and available to them. They should know whom to ask for help, whom to contact right away about security problems.

A security officer also has planning responsibilities. One is contingency planning: how do the computing systems go on operating if there is an emergency? The SO also participates in planning what to do in case of a security incident. The security officer makes sure that safeguards are installed in the computing systems: that there is proper access control, identification and authentication, and backup. Another responsibility is configuration management: keeping track of the installed software, hardware, and documentation, and making sure that they are authentic and that they conform to the policy. If the policy prohibits access via telephone lines, for example, the system configuration should make it impossible. Working with other groups, the SO ensures physical security for the whole computing environment.

The SO reviews audit trails regularly—probably daily—and promptly investigates anything suspicious. For example, if the audit trail shows repeated login failures, the SO contacts the owner of the user ID and, if that person was not responsible, tries to find out who was. The security officer is responsible for maintaining the audit trail archives.

In government or defense environments, the ISSO must also make sure that all users, and all who maintain equipment or software, have the necessary security clearances. Records have to be kept of all these clearances. The ISSO is involved in getting systems certified and accredited. The ISSO supervises the declassification or downgrading of data and equipment.

Distributing security responsibilities. It is simpler to write about the security officer as a single person; in reality, an entire department may be involved. Some responsibilities are best distributed to user organizations. For example, one large company improved its security by setting up "guardians." An application guardian owns an application, and a user guardian owns a set of user IDs. The application guardians control access to databases and transactions.

Certifying information security professionals

The practice of information security is quite a new discipline, and the practitioners have no common academic or work experience background, common set of understandings, or common body of knowledge. This is in contrast to professions such as accounting, for example, with well-established prerequisites and understandings and professional certification. There are advantages to certification for computer security professionals. For the field of computer security as a whole, there is the advantage of high standards and continuing competence. For the individual professional, there is the advantage of a recognized profession and a more rewarding career. Several organizations are now involved in certifying information security professionals. Setting up a certification program involves agreeing on criteria, defining a course of study covering a "common body of knowledge," and specifying the amount of work experience needed to qualify for certification (particularly important for security because there have been no academic programs.) A testing program has to be set up and examinations developed. A code of ethics is needed. Certification has to be a continuing process, with periodic recertification based on additional education and possibly reexamination.

Organizational and administrative controls

Just as important as the technical safeguards for security are administrative controls that guide behavior.

Information security agreements. One important control is an *information security agreement,* typically required when an employee joins the organization or when a new user account is set up. The person agrees that he or she has read and understood the computer security policy and knows the sanctions for violations—such as termination or, for lawbreakers, prosecution. The agreement must be renewed periodically, such as once a year. This practice forces people to pay attention to the policy—because they are signing something—and it reinforces the impression that computer security policy is important. Without a clear policy and a clear indication that a person understood it and agreed to abide by it, disciplinary action or prosecution may be impossible. An employee could claim she never knew that keeping the accounts for her outside business on the company computer was not allowed. Of course, the person gets a copy of the agreement. Some organizations also give a copy to anyone who leaves the organization, reminding the departing person that certain information is confidential or proprietary.

User administration. User administration includes maintaining user accounts, providing for identification and authentication, making sure that privileges and access rights are appropriate and up-to-date, and auditing for improper use of accounts. User administration is an area where security policy must be supplemented with a detailed set of procedures to follow. One procedure is for giving out new accounts. Typically, the user's manager makes a request to the system manager or perhaps to the security administrator. The security policy defines what approvals are needed. For example, every employee may automatically get an account on the departmental system, but application managers may need to approve accounts on other systems. Users are sometimes asked to sign receipts for accounts.

User administration is time-consuming, and administrators tend to get behind in handling requests. For good security, people who need access must get it quickly, and those who no longer need it must not have it. Similarly, privileges and authorizations must be kept up-to-date. One way to reduce the bottleneck is to decentralize administration of accounts. Also, there need to be ways to make temporary changes in accounts, as when a person fills in for someone else. (This is easier if access rights are based on role.) When someone gets a temporary authorization, that authorization must end when the need is gone. Every authorization—temporary or not—has to be reaffirmed periodically by the authorizer.

Reviews of controls. Just setting up controls is not enough; they also must be reviewed or audited to make sure that they are really effective. Periodically, an outside or parallel organization should conduct a review of the administrative controls, as part of an external or internal audit.

Personnel practices. Personnel practices can be effective in controlling security risk. One example is requiring employees to take their vacations; misuse is most likely to be noticed during the person's absence. There can be periodic rescreening of the type done at hiring. Government organizations formalize this as renewal of security clearance, at which time background checks are repeated. If, for example, a person's lifestyle has become lavish, although his salary has remained modest, that raises a suspicion.

The procedures to follow when any employee leaves include:

- If the employee was responsible for any data or programs, make sure that his departure will not affect their availability. For example, he has to reveal the keys for any encrypted data. Have him document how he handles his computer applications, or make sure that he has taught someone else.
- Remind a departing employee about what is proprietary information; remind him of the nondisclosure agreements and information security agreements that he has signed, and give him copies.

- Tell other employees that he is leaving.
- Pay special attention to unfriendly departures, particularly of systems personnel, who have the knowledge and the access to destroy data or plant time bombs. Have a fired employee leave immediately rather than staying at work during the notice period.

The altered workplace

Much of the common wisdom about security management is based on a vision of well-managed companies with a stable work force, treated well, and with good morale. Fewer and fewer computer users fit this image of the happy employee of the happy company. Many users are not employees at all but vendors, contractors, or the employees of other companies. They may be temporary employees, who make up more and more of the work force. Another deviation from the image is that many employees work at home; that is, employee and employer agree that the employee will work at home several days a week, using a computer at home. Telecommuting poses all the problems of remote access, including communications security and authentication. Another problem is the physical insecurity of the home workplace. There is no way that an employer can control access to home computers and data. It is essentially up to the employee, who has to be trusted. Many companies gamble that their employees will take good care of data and equipment if there are clear security guidelines for the home workplace, and the employees and managers know what the guidelines are. Many telecommuters are happy with the arrangement, which may save them unpleasant commutes through heavy traffic and polluted air; they may enjoy working at home. But some are pressured into home work as an expense-cutting measure; they no longer have a full-time office and they must provide part of their home for an office. These employees may be less motivated to be careful about security.

Typical security guidelines for telecommuting require a physically secure environment for the company-owned computer and for the work that is produced; they may require measures such as surge protectors. The guidelines specify that the computer is to be used only for business purposes and only by the employee. The guidelines usually say what kind of dial-out access is allowed, specify what software can be installed and prohibit the copying of software.

Perhaps the greatest risk is the loss of data; fortunately, this risk is controlled if telecommuters back up their work regularly. They could back up to diskettes and bring them to the office periodically, but it is better to upload to the central work location—perhaps once or twice a day. Less easily solved is the problem of confidentiality. At the very least, an organization needs to be clear about which data classifications can be used at home. For example, if a company has three levels of sensitivity for information, it may allow only the least sensitive of the three to be used at home.

Service personnel

It is easy to overlook a large population that has access to secure areas and to computing equipment: people who service equipment or do custodial work or catering. Many of them work outside the usual hours, largely unobserved. Aside from physical security, the main controls are education and clear guidelines:

- Brief custodial and service people on what the organization's security procedures are, particularly with respect to computing equipment. (In a 1994 incident, several computers and part of a network went down when a vacuum cleaner was plugged into the power strip attached to a server's power supply.)
- Tell regular employees and security guards what behavior is appropriate for service, vendor, and catering personnel.
- Maintain an up-to-date list of authorized service personnel and make it available to operations and security people.

Operations Security

The task of keeping a system secure in its day-to-day functioning is *operations security.* This means keeping the system available, protecting the hardware, ensuring the right software is installed, and protecting the data. Operations security typically spans several departments of an organization and several roles. The people responsible include system administrators, security administrators, systems programmers, operators, and auditors. In the context of trusted systems, the term *trusted facility management* refers to secure system configuration, administration, and operation.

Well-planned and well-implemented operations are among the most effective security controls. On the other hand, the operations area is a source of risk, because operations people hold powerful privileges. An authorized person could deliberately or accidentally misuse her authority. For example, she could change the hardware or software configuration in unauthorized ways. Or, an impersonator could take over a role—security administrator, for example—and misuse its privileges. These threats come from positive acts. Perhaps a greater threat is failure to act: not taking backups, for example, or not caring properly for storage media.

Organization and roles

A common weakness in organization has been that security administration is in the operations department, where it lacks independence and authority and does not get the right resources or management attention. Even without security administration, however, the operations department has crucial security responsibilities. A centralized computing facility is an extremely complex environment, serving perhaps tens of thousands of users and operating around the clock. The operations department often includes several units. In addition to the actual operations, there may be technical support groups and groups responsible for storage media. The type of organization will continue to change along with changes in the role of central facilities.

The organization for operations should follow two basic security principles: least privilege and separation of duty. According to least privilege, people should be authorized only for the resources they need to do their jobs. For example, an operator does not need access to documentation about operating system internals. According to separation of duty, functions should be divided between people, so that no one person can commit fraud undetected. It is especially important to separate system design and programming from operations. Many organizations have completely separate machines for development and testing. It is sometimes advised that operators not know programming, but this removes a traditional job advancement path. The media library can be a separate unit. The Trusted Computer System Evaluation Criteria (TCSEC) specify separation of the roles of operator, system administrator and security administrator, and separation of security-relevant functions from others. The criteria for B3, for example, separate the operator role from the "secure operator" role. Table 12.2 shows the functions associated with each of the roles in trusted facility management. Control of the media library ideally is separate as well. Least privilege then can be enforced by, for example, releasing a sensitive data tape only to operators and only at the job's scheduled time.

Good separation of duty is hard to implement. It can make jobs terribly dull unless steps are taken to enliven them, such as giving an operator other part-time assignments. An ideal separation is costly in time and money, and it is possible only for a large operations staff. For a smaller installation, one or a few people may have to fill all the operations roles.

Many central operations departments support distributed operations and also try to introduce some control and uniformity into workstation software and hardware use. These departments include "information centers," staffed with people who know the applications and the relevant software packages, and in-house "computer stores" that

TABLE 12.2 Roles in Trusted Facility Management and Some of Their Functions

Role	Functions

Security administrator	Identification and authentication
	  Setting login and password parameters
	  Defining user and group profiles
	Mandatory access control
	  Maintaining the security label map
	  Setting limit and default levels for systems, users, groups, devices, and file systems
	  Labeling imported data and media
	  Reclassifying objects
	Discretionary access control
	  Setting group administrators' privileges
	  Defining group membership
	  Setting privileges on file systems
	  Changing object ownership
	  Controlling object privileges (if owners cannot)
	Consistency checks on security profiles
	Consistency checks on TCB
	Verifying system configuration
	Testing system integrity
	Supervising system maintenance
	Responding to real-time alarms
	Setting up and maintaining security databases

Secure operator	System start-up and shutdown Locating damaged data for repair Routine TCB database maintenance, including backup Testing devices Responding to mount and import/export requests
Auditor	Defining and selecting events for audit log recording Managing audit files Setting parameters for covert channel handling Generating and analyzing audit reports
Operator	Backing up user data Measuring system performance Responding to user requests Adjusting resource quotas
System programmer	Trusted system distribution Setting of system configuration parameters Nonroutine TCB maintenance

SOURCE: Summarized from NCSC (1989).
TCB: Trusted Computing Base.

centralize purchasing and maintain lists of approved hardware and software. The information center and the computer store can contribute to security by reducing complexity, selecting secure products, and helping users control equipment and software.

Controls at interfaces

One operations responsibility is to control the interfaces to the computing system. All data that cross an interface with operator help must cross in complete and accurate form and must be recorded. None of the data may be lost and no data may be added.

Operations people play only a small role in controlling input, since most of it comes from on-line transactions, whose interface controls are software controls. As for output controls, each print job should be set off by time-stamped header and trailer pages that identify the originator and specify the data classification. Some installations use locked cabinets for distributing output, with individual compartments assigned to users. Each compartment has two openings: one in the computer room for the operator and the other a locked door that opens onto a hallway, where the recipient unlocks the door to pick up the output.

One crucial interface is the operator's console, which should be in a physically secure location. Some consoles can be used to modify the computing system itself, changing the contents of memory locations, for example. It is best if the operator has no access to such capabilities. The operator should use a software-controlled console except under special circumstances and with the cooperation of someone in a different role. Even with these controls, an operator could load the wrong operating system, shut down the system inappropriately, or change the address of a device, so that the wrong input is read or output goes to the wrong place.

Media control

Every organization, small or large, has a media control responsibility. Every volume in the media library has to be labeled in both human-readable and machine-readable forms. Color coding can be used to distinguish volumes with different purposes; for example, black for backup and red for production programs. It is important to keep a media control log that records each entry of a volume into the library, each removal of a volume, and each return. Other media-control tasks are

- Cleaning and checking tapes and other media on a scheduled basis
- Taking inventories and reconciling them with the log

- Storing on-site backups in a protected area
- Erasing each volume at the end of its retention period. This is important for volumes that will be reused and also for those to be thrown away, given away, or sold. This caution also applies to the hard disks of PCs that are disposed of. Commercial media destruction services are available.

Backup

Backup protects against almost any threat—accidental or deliberate—that causes loss or destruction of data. Many organizations do full backup of all files every night; others do an incremental backup every night. Software is available that automatically schedules and carries out backups. At any time there should be at least three copies of every file: the copy that is used, an on-site backup, and an off-site backup. Backups—on-site and off-site—should be stored in fire-retardant and access-controlled enclosures or rooms. The operations staff should verify that a backup can be read. Backup software can optionally verify by reading back, and this option should be chosen. The staff should rehearse procedures for restoring from backups after a failure.

Configuration management

Operations, along with development and maintenance groups, has configuration management responsibilities. Software obtained from vendors or retailers should be checked to make sure that it is authentic and intact. When new versions are received that have fixes for security exposures, it is important to verify that the fixes really work, that the exposures are indeed gone. No one person should have complete authority over configurations.

Physical Security

Many computer security measures ultimately depend on physical security. Physical security has been defined as "the application of physical barriers and control procedures as preventive measures or countermeasures against threats to resources and sensitive information" (NCSC 1988: 35).

What physical security protects

What are the resources and sensitive information that must be protected by physical security? People come first; they may be at risk specifically because of their association with computing. The availability of systems must be protected against physical threats. Also to be protected are

- Data, wherever it resides or travels, including computer memories, fixed disks, tapes in a storage cabinet, LAN cables, paper documents, even waste materials
- Equipment, such as computers, storage devices, printers, network hardware, file cabinets
- Facilities, including sites, buildings, computer rooms, offices, server areas, wiring closets
- Support systems, including electricity, air conditioning, and telephone systems
- Supplies, such as tapes, disks, and printed forms

Resources are widely distributed—in offices, on plant floors, in homes, airplanes, and hotel rooms. Every organization has, however, some relatively centralized resources, including servers, shared printers, network hardware, and mainframes.

Threats

What are the threats that physical security counters?

Intruders. Intruders can steal equipment (in the office, on the road, or at home) learn confidential information or steal computing services. They can tamper with hardware or software so as to make it insecure. They can sabotage buildings and systems.

Utility problems. Every computer needs a power supply, which it gets from a utility company, a local generator, or batteries. Unfortunately, power is not consistently there to be relied on; it is not always consistent and not always there. Inconsistencies include spikes, which are brief and intense increases in voltage; surges, which are longer and less intense increases; and dips. Spikes, surges, and dips can be caused by other equipment that shares the same power supply. They can be caused by faulty switches, power company actions, or electrical storms. They can have disastrous effects on computing devices and computing results. During periods of extreme demand (such as hot weather) power companies may intentionally reduce the voltage. Computing equipment can be vulnerable to these brownouts. Most disruptive are extended power interruptions. In 1987, for example, the Nasdaq stock market was closed for 40 minutes because of a power failure (attributed to a squirrel carrying aluminum foil). The New York Stock Exchange was closed for almost half an hour in 1991 by a dip in power.

Computing equipment is also subject to interference from electromagnetic sources, such as motors. Defective electrical equipment can cause fires or explosions. Nearly all organizations depend on telephone facilities that are largely outside their control. Telephone outages are especially damaging because they can disable security controls, such as automatic dialing of alarms.

Natural disasters and other emergencies. Some of the most serious disruptions have been caused by floods, earthquakes, snow storms or lightning storms, and hurricanes. Brush fires have threatened facilities.

Fire and smoke. Fire threatens not only people, but also computing equipment, tapes, and disks. The burning of plastics in office furniture, for example, releases toxic fumes that damage equipment.

Water. The worst effect of a fire may be from the water used to put it out. Other sources of water damage are flooded rooms, leaking pipes above or below, rain coming in through windows, doors, roofs or other openings, and the morning coffee spilled on the keyboard.

Operating environment hazards. Many mainframes cannot operate without air conditioning. Personal computers tolerate a wider range of temperature and humidity, but they too can suffer from extremes, and from dirt, contaminants, and static electricity.

Emanations. Electrical equipment, including computing equipment, emits electromagnetic radiation through the air in a way that can jeopardize security. For example, the emanations from a display terminal can be read with relatively simple equipment some distance away. In some circumstances, a strong electromagnetic field can erase media, such as tapes or disks; this is unlikely, but possible.

Management considerations

Like many computer security management tasks, physical security depends on cooperation with other security groups and with the people whose decisions affect physical security; security managers cannot do it themselves. Especially needed is cooperation with those responsible for site security, which includes security guards, visitor control, and monitoring systems. A crucial decision is about where to locate new or relocated data centers. This decision is usually based on factors unrelated to computer security; security managers need to make sure that physical security is weighed along with other factors.

Safeguards

Physical security measures can be pervasive and apply to a wide variety of threats—backup is a good example—or they can be specific to a set of threats. Pervasive measures include selecting a good site. They include backup of data, offsite storage of copies of documents and data, and backup sites for processing if something happens to the main site. They include having spare personal computers and spare parts for putting ailing machines back into operation quickly. They include clear policies about physical security, knowledge of responsibilities, and rehearsing the responses to emergencies.

A tricky problem is that the safeguards themselves can be disabled by the very threats they are intended to counter, or by concomitant threats. Suppose that an alarm system is supposed to dial a phone number to report a water problem at an unattended site; this won't work if the hurricane has taken out the telephone system. The documentation and records about physical security controls could also become unavailable.

Protecting against intrusion

Site selection. For a major new data center or for a small office, the site is an important security consideration. This is true whether facilities are built, bought, or leased. Some of the questions to ask are: Is this a high-crime area? Is the site in an earthquake or hurricane area? Does its location make it vulnerable to accidents? For example, is it in the approach path to an airport or adjacent to a freeway? Is the area prone to flooding? Could brush fires in nearby areas reach the facility? Do the utilities that supply electricity and telephone service have good records of reliability? Is the site close to a nuclear power plant? Is there good access to the site for emergency service personnel? Might terrorists attack? Could a truck build up momentum to crash into a building, or are there barriers that would stop such an attack?

Is good fire service and police service readily available? Are medical facilities available quickly? Are the buildings that will house computing equipment strong—able to support the weight of the equipment and to sustain forces such as winds, earthquakes and snow? If the building houses a centralized data center, does it have as few openings as possible—that is, few windows, doors, or other types of entries?

Security perimeters. As with logical security in software and hardware, physical security involves establishing security perimeters and guarding the few gates through those perimeters. The outermost perimeter may be a fence or wall around a site or a building. Outside lights are needed; television cameras and other monitoring devices, preferably with alarms, can be installed to detect potential threats at the perimeter. A guard station protects the "gate" on the road that enters the site. Doors to buildings have to be guarded—in a way that depends on the level of security needed. It may suffice to give a key to everyone who needs access, or badges can be coded to open specific doors. Or a guard may observe badges and also put them into a reader to verify a person's access to the building. Concrete barriers outside the building can prevent attacks by fast-moving, large vehicles. Some high-security buildings have holding areas or "mantraps," which a person enters through a first door which then locks behind him. While in the holding area, he has to present authenticating information to enter the building via a second door. An unauthorized person is trapped in the holding area until a security officer investigates.

Inside buildings, perimeter security protects computer rooms, rooms where servers are kept, or other secure areas. Some software-based entrance control systems can control both building and room entrances. Often they operate from a different site than the one being controlled. These systems maintain databases of users and their physical access rights; they create audit trails and activate alarms. As for locks on doors, the most secure are digital combination locks. The combination must be changed regularly, so that only those who currently need access will know it. If keys are used, lock and key should be changed frequently.

Protecting equipment. Just as the site must be protected, and within the site the building, and within the building individual rooms, so also pieces of equipment need to be protected against theft, tampering, or other misuse. Equipment that is not within other security perimeters needs even more protection. In one case, criminals modified an automatic teller machine (ATM) to do what they wanted—recording the user's personal identification number. (More precisely, the criminals attached a fraudulent front to the ATM.) Enclosures around equipment can protect against theft and tampering, and also against accidental damage from disasters or from everyday wear and tear. Some tables, for example, come equipped with protective covers that can be locked over a workstation when it is not in use. This protects to a degree against hazards and also prevents unauthorized use. Another method uses a locked device that fits between a PC's cord and its power source. Bolting a small computer to a heavy table helps prevent theft.

Physical security for equipment must be maintained during shipment and delivery. [The National Computer Security Center (NCSC) criteria address this need as *Trusted Distribution.*] Equipment often is delivered in a tamper-resistant container; it may be equipped with an alarm that goes off when the container is opened. The same protective enclosure can also be used during the life of the equipment. A problem is that, since there must be a way to reset the alarm when the enclosure is opened for normal maintenance, an intruder might also be able to reset it. Another method is to display a new random number each time the enclosure is opened, so that a change in number indicates tampering. Equipment can also be shrink-wrapped in a material that cannot be removed or broken or penetrated without detection. Or a paper seal can be used that cannot be removed without being destroyed. A paper seal needs to carry an authenticating stamp, or it could be replaced by an intruder. Cryptographic methods could be used with physical enclosures to get a high level of confidence that the equipment has not been tampered with.

Policies about visitors. Since documents and computing equipment are scattered throughout offices, laboratories, and open hallways, visitors pose a risk. An unescorted visitor can look at confidential information on paper that is exposed on desks, peruse an unattended display, or poke at a keyboard. The best policy is to escort visitors at all times and to challenge any unescorted visitor—recognized by the visitor badge.

Protecting against emergencies

We are only too familiar with natural disasters and other emergencies that can devastate critical operations. These include floods, earthquakes, and hurricanes. They also include terrorist attacks. Each type of disaster brings its own threats, but all have a great deal in common. The first thing is to plan for these contingencies (more about this later). Close attention should be paid to warnings for those emergencies—hurricanes, for example—that are somewhat predictable. Emergency phone numbers—for medical care, fire fighting and police—should be posted. There must be a system for communicating with people in the building during emergencies. Access to secured areas must not depend on a single power source that might fail in an emergency; there has to be a backup way of gaining access. Drills for emergencies should be held on a predetermined schedule. In earthquake areas, computing equipment should be placed or fastened so that it cannot fall or be hit by a falling object.

Protecting against electrical problems

One insurance company found that it had more computer loss claims for power problems than for theft, fire, or natural disaster. Mainframe computers are the most sensitive to transient electrical events, but, since they come with equipment that stabilizes their voltage supply, these events usually are not threatening. The main concern for mainframes is extended power outages. If at all possible, power should be obtained from a utility with a good record on continuity of service. A backup power supply also is essential. The backup source might be a diesel generator, for example, or a different power station. Although electrical problems are often blamed on the power company, problems within the building may also cause failures. Improper grounding is one source; difficulty with the building wiring is another; air conditioners, elevators, and refrigerators can cause power transients when they go on and off. Electronic equipment is subject to noise that comes from the power source and also from the grounding circuit; ironically, devices that are used to smooth the power supply can contribute to this problem.

Several types of devices are used to improve power supply quality. Power conditioners provide a smooth source of voltage, eliminating spikes, surges, and dips. Power monitors detect abnormal power conditions and either log them for future analysis or, if they exceed certain limits, set off alarms or automatically shut down systems. The most common device is the surge suppressor, which protects primarily against spikes. Many surge suppressors work by diverting excess energy to ground, and this can cause problems in any equipment that is connected to the same electrical system. Also, since networks may use the same ground as a signal reference ground, surge suppressors can propagate surges through a network. It is better to use surge suppressors that absorb the excess energy instead of diverting it to ground. Finally, an *uninterruptible power supply* (UPS) is a source of power that allows computing equipment to run during a power outage. UPS systems use various technologies: batteries, flywheels whose inertia keeps them going through a brief power failure, and motors, diesel for example, that run ac generators. There are comprehensive systems that provide all these power supply services and also monitor, maintain audit trails, and generate alarms.

There must be procedures for regularly checking batteries and for checking auxiliary motors to make sure they are operable and that they have fuel. Firms that consult on power will review the electrical system for an organization or a building or a computer installation. In addition to ensuring a power supply, an organization needs to ensure that: emergency power-off switches are at all the exits from a computing center, electrical cabling goes through metal conduits, all connections are properly grounded, and the components of the physical security system itself (including fire alarm systems and doors with power locks) have backup power supply.

Protecting against fire

To prevent and control fire, buildings should be constructed of fire-resistant materials and contain fire-resistant furnishings and fixtures. A no-smoking policy helps greatly. (No smoking is good physical security in another way, because smoke particles damage magnetic media.) The term "firewall" is a metaphor in the context of network security, but not here; a firewall may be able to keep a fire from spreading to other parts of a building. Areas that contain critical computing resources need full floor-to-ceiling walls of fire-retardant material, and all the openings in the walls should be well-sealed. Pieces of equipment that are susceptible to fires, such as printers and copiers, need their own enclosures, with good firewalls. Flammable supplies, like cleaning supplies and solvents, should be kept in closed, fire-resistant storage. Magnetic media are flammable and also give off toxic fumes when they burn. They should be kept in strong fire-resistant containers, in a media library separated from the computer room by a good fire barrier.

If a fire does occur, quick detection is important. Smoke detectors should be installed on ceilings, underneath raised floors, and in air ducts. If an alarm is raised, it should sound at the place of detection, in a local monitoring area such as a guard station, and at the fire station. Smoke detectors need to be tested and serviced regularly. Since a likely place for fire to be detected is under the floor, floor pullers should be stored in well-marked and well-known locations, preferably the same place as fire extinguishers.

If a fire is detected, the steps to take are: first start getting the people out, then call the fire department, and then try to put the fire out. A common fire suppression mechanism is fixed automatic sprinklers, typically in the ceiling. Water is excellent for putting out fires, but it has definite drawbacks for use on computing equipment. For one thing, water conducts electricity, and electricity often is involved in computer fires. Water can also damage the computing equipment badly, especially if the water is impure. As a result, many computing facilities use other methods.

One method uses carbon dioxide. Either an entire room is flooded with carbon dioxide, to put out the fire by depriving it of oxygen, or carbon dioxide is directed at specific fires with hoses. Unfortunately the people are also deprived of oxygen. Probably the most widely used systems for protecting computer rooms use Halon gas. Halon is less dangerous to people and it does smother fires. It is used both in fixed systems and in portable fire extinguishers. However, Halon is restricted for environmental reasons because it contains chlorofluorocarbon compounds (CFCs). Other gases are available that behave much like Halon but do not contain CFCs.

Large plastic sheets should be available to cover equipment where water may be used. This will probably happen if the fire department is called and it will happen if an automatic sprinkler system is used.

Personal computers and other computing equipment often survive water baths, if they get plenty of time to dry out before being used. They have the best chance if the water is relatively clean and pure. The water used in sprinkler systems often comes from holding tanks, where it can sit for a long time and get quite dirty. The water level and quality in these tanks should be monitored.

Every organization needs a plan for fire prevention and fire response (see the checklist in Fig. 12.4).

Protecting against water damage

An organization cannot prevent a flood caused by a river, but many water problems can be prevented by good building maintenance—keeping the roof sound and the plumbing working. There should be watertight electrical outlets in floors; waterproof doors and windows, and no steam or water pipes under the floor of a computer room or overhead. Other preparations will help if water does threaten a facility: pumps in basement areas and large plastic sheets available to cover equipment quickly (also to be used if fires are extinguished with water). PCs should be kept away from windows that might leak. Mainframes and servers should be above the ground floor. Monitoring systems can detect leaks under raised floors and above suspended ceilings. Some of these systems use cables or tapes that are strung along a large area and that detect moisture anywhere in their course. They then trigger an alarm that can pinpoint where the leak is detected. Another type of detector is placed at low spots where water might collect.

Contingency Planning

People in every organization need to ask themselves: "If a disaster occurs, can we stay in business?" Too often the answer has to be "No."

Test fire alarms and hold fire drills regularly.
Assign clear responsibilities in case of fire.
Post emergency phone numbers.
Service and test smoke detectors regularly.
Place fire extinguishers carefully and visibly; instruct employees on their use.
Verify that employees know how to override fire suppression systems.
Verify that security personnel know what to do if fire occurs after hours.

Figure 12.4 Fire preparation checklist. [*Adapted from ACM SIGSAC. Copyright (©) 1993 Association for Computing Machinery, Inc. (ACM). Reprinted by permission.*]

Contingency planning has to do with the steps that will allow the organization to continue functioning even though its normal operations are disrupted. Contingency planning covers the steps to take both before and after any contingency occurs. The source of the disruption can be a natural disaster or something else. For example, the organization may totally rely on a software application, and the software vendor may fail. The computers may be infected by viruses. A contingency is some event that might occur and—if it did—would require special measures to handle it. A risk analysis can be used to rank contingencies according to how disruptive they are.

The value of contingency planning

It is obvious that a mail-order company will suffer a dramatic loss of revenue if its computing systems are down for a day. Other types of operations are equally though less obviously dependent on computing. A survey of companies in the United Kingdom revealed that 70 percent would have to stop their normal business operation if they lost their computer systems for more than 2 days. Many of these would eventually go out of business. Without contingency planning, then, an emergency can cost dearly in the form of:

- Lost business
- The effects on customers of interrupted service or poor service
- The very real chance of going out of business

In addition, there are legal reasons for contingency planning. In the United States, many state laws require businesses and other organizations to do emergency planning. On the national level, the Foreign Corrupt Practices Act requires businesses to exercise care over their stockholders' assets. Other legislation authorizes standards for employee safety. Having a contingency plan indicates that an organization did take due care, that it was not negligent. Further, customers are concerned about the availability of function. If your organization is a bank, your customers need to get their account balances and to withdraw cash; they will not be tolerant of failures.

A contingency plan is defined as "a plan for emergency response, backup operations, and post-disaster recovery maintained by an activity as a part of its security program that will ensure the availability of critical resources and facilitate the continuity of operations in an emergency situation...(NCSC 1988: 11). The terms *contingency plan* and *disaster recovery plan* are used quite interchangeably. "Contingency" reminds us that it does not take a magnitude-8 earthquake to seriously threaten an organization's viability. Recovering from a contingency is not just a matter of restoring computing service; rather, it is a matter of restoring business processes. The term *business continuity planning* emphasizes this business-oriented point of view.

Contingency planning steps

The steps to take in contingency planning include:

- *Develop a plan.* Assign one person to coordinate developing, and perhaps also carrying out, the plan. The contingency planning process is valuable in itself even if no emergency arises. Consider getting help from a consulting service that has experience in contingency planning.
- *Set up a contingency team* that will carry out the plan if necessary. Communicate the plan to the team and train the team.
- *Test the plan periodically.* Have it reviewed and analyzed. Rehearse it with simulated disasters.
- *Build partnerships.* It is nearly always necessary to work with other organizations. These include: other units of the same large organization; neighboring organizations; city or county emergency planning units. Others to work with are consultants and vendors who provide commercial disaster recovery services.

Developing a contingency plan

The crucial part of contingency planning is the planning process itself. There is value, however, in a formal written plan. It helps in getting cooperation from people, and it is evidence that due care was taken. There are many software tools—some highly sophisticated—that can assist in developing a contingency plan. Some of these are specialized for specific business (such as banks) or for specific computing environments (such as LANs). These tools can help educate staff about disaster recovery, and the planning process itself is an educational experience.

Planning should use data about which emergencies are most frequent—government weather records and earthquake histories, for example. But even the statistically rare event can occur. Some experts recommend ranking disasters from minor to catastrophic and estimating the potential loss for each level. The plan can then prescribe different responses for the different levels of emergency.

Developing a contingency plan is a substantial effort. For example, a plan for a large university computing center took 6 months, with the coordinator working half-time on the plan, and many other people contributing part-time.

What the contingency plan covers

Many problems and measures must be considered in a contingency plan. This section discusses those items that apply broadly to many organizations. Organizations differ enormously in their needs, and some have unique needs.

Off-site storage. After a disaster, the main processing site may be totally unavailable, along with everything that is stored there. It is essential to store in a different place everything that would be needed to recover operations after a disaster. Data and important documents should be backed up offsite at a secure location. The organization could maintain its own site or contract to a commercial vendor. A specialized vendor can more efficiently maintain the environment needed for safe backup storage.

The items to be stored off site include backup volumes, paper forms, and copies of records that exist only on paper. Also copies of all documents that will be needed for disaster recovery, such as key telephone numbers. Employees should have a convenient place to drop off diskettes and documents for transfer to off-site storage by a regular courier.

Security controls for the storage site need to match the level of the organization's own controls, providing good physical security, access control, and personnel security. Also, physical and personnel security must be good for the transfer to the backup site. If a commercial service is used, it should be financially able to cover any losses due to lost data. Commercial services will accept backup data over communication lines and then store it. This probably is more secure than a physical transport of volumes. Backup can be performed automatically according to a schedule. Incremental backups can be taken every day, for example.

Backup processing. The organization that has lost a processing site has several alternatives for backup processing. One alternative is reciprocal agreements with other organizations to take over one another's processing in case of an emergency. This is a low-cost contingency arrangement and is worth considering for that reason. However, it makes sense mainly for small or batch-oriented operations. If both the organizations are heavily on-line, the partner is unlikely to have enough capacity to handle both its own load and that of the distressed partner.

If the same organization has spare computing power at another location, that is a good solution. This might well be the case for a large state university system, or a federal agency. If the emergency processing capability is limited, some processing can be deferred—if on-line requirements permit it. Another solution is to get the hardware replaced quickly. Most vendors will try to cooperate. The hardware could go into a cold site or, if only the equipment was damaged, into the main site. (There are two kinds of backup sites. A *cold site* is some space that is computer-ready but contains no computing equipment. A *hot site* is a complete computing facility ready to be used. It has power supply, air conditioning, and communications. It may have office space for staff.)

A good alternative, but a costly one, is a commercial service for disaster recovery or business recovery. Some computer vendors provide this service for users of their equipment, and other organizations are in the disaster-recovery service business. There is a membership fee plus an additional fee during use, and the usage time is limited—to 6 weeks, for example. The commercial sites have to limit their membership and ensure a variety in member geographic area, so as to decrease the chance that several members will need the service at once. Some services provide transportation to the site for people and also provide extra staff to help with data recovery and other postemergency needs. The service may also replace lost media. Some services offer mobile recovery sites—vans that can be moved to the customer's location or a convenient location. In choosing a commercial site, the same types of security considerations apply as in selecting the organization's own sites.

Work space for employees. If buildings are destroyed or their services do not work, replacement space and services (such as telephone and email) must be found for the people who are essential to the critical business processes and the critical computing services.

Security during the emergency. In selecting an approach to restoring data and processing, consider who will have access to the data. If an outside service is used, are its employees screened? Will the service take responsibility for data losses or data confidentiality exposures? Could an attacker deliberately cause an emergency, in order to use the disarray as a chance to breach security?

The critical processes. Everything will not come back up at once. There will be shortages of processing power and of people's time for restoring data. So the contingency plan must rank the business processes or (for a service bureau type of operation) the users. One way to figure out the critical processes for a computing facility is for each staff member to review his or her job and list its critical needs. For business processes, a high level of management must make the decisions.

Testing the plan. A contingency plan must include measures for testing whether the plan itself is adequate and also how people will behave in carrying out the plan. The best test is a realistic simulation, repeated on a regular schedule such as every 6 months.

Software vendor failure. A software vendor may go out of business. As a protection, an organization can insist on a software escrow, which keeps the source code in trust. This may not help, however, if the software is badly dysfunctional. Also, a promised software system may not materialize. The software for the Denver airport baggage-handling system, for example, was in such bad shape 9 months after its projected completion date that the airport chose to invest in a whole new alternative system. The delay in opening the airport was costing over $1 million a day.

Insurance. Insurance must be adequate. Being insured is not enough, though, because it may take a long time to collect. A year after the 1994 Northridge earthquake, many businesses were still awaiting approval of their repairs, and many others no longer existed because they could not wait. It may be necessary to arrange in advance a line of credit that can be used for the emergency expenses. Some of the disaster recovery services are combined with insurance packages into a total disaster protection plan.

The contingency team

An important result of contingency planning is a team, with a leader and well-defined roles for the team members. Some members are permanent, and others—with specialized skills or information—participate in the planning process and the simulations as needed. These participants might be, for example, from the legal department or the purchasing department or facilities management. There may be different teams for different stages of the emergency. The plan specifies who to notify of the emergency, who does the notifying, and where the team will meet. The plan says who will communicate with users and the press, who will assess the damage, and who will decide on the level of the emergency and the course to be taken. Each member of the team needs to have a responsibility for action and to know who to coordinate with. Listing specific people rather then roles reduces confusion, but since a person might be ill or on vacation, each team member must have a backup.

Stages

Philip Fites and Martin Kratz (1993) distinguish five stages that are typical for a disaster:

- *The event* itself.
- *The initial response,* such as evacuating buildings, calling ambulances, assessing damage and notifying people.
- *Impact assessment.* At this stage the team determines the damage and losses and identifies the most critical processing needs. Decisions are made about which plan alternatives to follow.
- *Start-up.* The start-up team is larger, because much work has to be done and special skills are needed. Depending on the plan and the nature of the emergency, start-up activities vary enormously.
- *Full recovery.* At this time, the normal operating team has taken over from the contingency team and operations are fully restored. This is a good time to analyze the entire event, document what was learned, and change the contingency plan accordingly.

Incident Response

Traditional contingency planning, which emphasizes response to physical or environmental events, has been less effective for computer security incidents, which often exploit software weaknesses. Networking makes these incidents particularly dangerous, since they can spread extremely rapidly from one system to another, and a compromise in one organization can affect other organizations, making for legal and financial complications. An organization may be quite unaware that its system was penetrated and used to launch attacks on systems of other organizations. The computer security field has paid more attention to prevention and protection, and less to the handling of incidents when they do occur.

The traditional responses have been ineffective for security incidents and can even make things worse. What is needed is a special incident response capability that includes skilled people, policies and procedures, and sophisticated techniques. Incident response involves much cooperation among organizations, with centralized reporting and tracking. It aims at fast and efficient response. A series of Internet security incidents led to the creation of incident response centers in government agencies, academia, and industry. These centers help their constituencies and the whole Internet community.

What are the advantages of having a coherent incident response capability? First, if safety-critical systems are involved, fast response can save lives. System downtime can be reduced by containing incidents more quickly. Both the planning and the actual response are more efficient if trained people do them. Greater user awareness of security is a side effect, because incident response planning transfers information between groups—alerts to new viruses, for example.

Legal liability can be prevented that might result if one site is used to attack another.

Incident response and computer abuse teams

An incident response team needs people with technical knowledge, excellent communication skills, and, since security incidents are emotionally charged, the ability to calm the situation. The team needs a technically expert person to act as a single point of contact and to coordinate the response. The coordinator also maintains contact with external security groups and with local law enforcement agencies and investigative agencies such as the FBI. A single coordinator can make a better presentation of evidence if legal action is brought. The coordinator is not necessarily the decision maker.

The functions of an incident response team overlap with those of a "computer abuse team," which focuses less on quick response and more on dealing with abusers. The computer abuse team determines policy about abuse (which will influence the response to an incident), investigates incidents, preserves evidence, and preserves options about legal action. It also protects the organization against legal action. It takes the lead in identifying abusers and advises management on the options for dealing with them.

About investigation

An abuser may escape sanctions because of a legal technicality or bad handling of the evidence. For these reasons, a computer abuse team needs access to an attorney. The incident response or computer abuse team needs to know how to maintain a trail of evidence that could be used in court. It also needs to know how to avoid liability; for example, it has to know limits on questioning of a possible abuser. As few people as possible should handle a piece of evidence (another reason why having a single coordinator is important). People on the team need to learn, before incidents occur, to act as witnesses in legal proceedings.

It is good to make contacts with investigative agencies in advance and to notify them as soon as an incident occurs. The same applies to local law enforcement, corporate security, or campus police. The organization's legal counsel should be notified as soon as an incident is detected. Since cooperating with law enforcement can result in negative publicity and other risks, the policy of many organizations is to not report cases of abuse. The issue may arise whether to leave the system up and running in order to collect more evidence, but at the risk of damage to other sites on a network (with possible legal liability), or take the system down and learn less about who was responsible or how the intrusion was done. (There also may be liability if users are monitored without being informed.) It is important to address this issue in policies and procedures, and to have legal counsel evaluate them.

Before incidents occur

The items in an incident response plan include:

- The goals and priorities. For example, the decision could be that saving data is more important than maintaining availability.
- The actions to be taken and their priorities.
- How to quickly notify every member of the team. For example, each member carries a card containing home and work telephone numbers for every other member.

Everyone should know how to contact the coordinator 24 hours a day. The coordinator needs to keep up-to-date lists of all the people to notify in case of an incident. The incident response team needs the latest information about threats and solutions; it can get much of this through the Internet. Other preparations include:

- Set up backup procedures and methods for identifying damaged files, such as by recording checksums for system files.
- Keep good records of the initial configuration and setup of system software and of each subsequent change.
- Set up monitoring procedures to detect intrusions or viruses.
- Create an operations handbook (see Fig. 12.5).
- Maintain a library of books, reports, guides, and references. Make sure that the latest information is there when needed. Also keep on-line information readily available.
- Test the procedures with dry runs.
- Update the policies, procedures, and tools at a fixed interval and after any security incident.

During an incident

The following activities are needed during an incident.

1. *Detection and evaluation.* Monitoring tools may provide the first indication that something is wrong—virus detection software, for example. Other possible symptoms of an incident are shown in

Staffing information

Hotline use

Procedures for communicating with constituents

Incident reports

Procedures for logging and handling sensitive information and incident summaries

Policies and procedures and configurations for the center's computing equipment

Administrative procedures

Contacts: investigative agencies, vendors, others

Dealing with the press

Figure 12.5 Contents of an incident response center's operations handbook. [*Summarized from Wack (1991)*].

Fig. 12.6. A snapshot of the system should be taken at the first inkling of any problem—to help in identifying the problem and preserving evidence. A log book should be started, with a record of every system event, every action taken, and every telephone conversation. It is important to determine at this stage just how big the problem is. That is, how many computers are affected, whether other sites are involved, what the potential damage is, and how many people are needed to deal with the incident.

System crashes

Unexplained new accounts

High activity on a formerly inactive account

New files with strange names

Accounting anomalies

Changes in file lengths or dates

Attempts to write to system files

Disappearing files

Denial of service

Unexplained poor performance

Anomalous displays or sounds

Many unsuccessful login attempts from other sites

Suspicious browsing

Figure 12.6 Possible symptoms of a security incident. [*Adapted from Holbrook and Reynolds (1991)*.]

2. *Notification.* The coordinator must notify management, all members of the incident response team, software or hardware vendors if their products are involved, law enforcement, service providers, investigative agencies, and the public relations office if there is one. Communications should be open, explicit and factual. Team members need to learn what other people are doing and how to communicate with them. Others to notify are users (if that is appropriate), other sites (if they are threatened or may be sources of the problem) and incident response centers. A nontechnical description of the problem is needed for communicating with higher levels of management, who will have to make decisions, and for the press. Public communications should not divulge evidence, speculate, or describe system weaknesses that hackers may exploit.

3. *Containment.* The incident must be contained as quickly as possible. Forest fire containment is a good analogy, since security incidents also spread rapidly. Although some containment is possible without knowing the incident's cause (disconnecting from networks, for example) most steps require an understanding of the problem. The whole system is a potential problem source, but the system software is the most likely source. If a vulnerability is found, it should be removed if fixes are available. If not, fixes may have to be developed. The vendor should be notified as soon as possible and told of the flaw in detail. One way to contain a problem is to take the system down completely. This, however, may deny services unnecessarily and may prevent finding the source of the problem.

4. *Eradication.* Any viruses must be eradicated, any bogus system files deleted, and disks cleaned. It is important to clean all backups to avoid reinfection.

After an incident

The following steps should be taken after an incident:

1. Inventory the effects. Examine system files for irregularities and look for abnormal patterns in logs.
2. Develop a written plan for recovery, based on the damage assessment, and document what recovery steps are taken. Decide with care which backups to recover from, since the incident may have gone on a long time and affected many backups, or the abuser may be an insider who could subvert backups. In the worst case, reinstall the system from the original distribution media and redo all subsequent changes.
3. Keep any command procedures that the team developed for containing, cleaning up, and recovering. Periodically run those that check for abnormality.

4. If system vulnerabilities were discovered, install fixes or (if they are not available) set up compensating administrative controls.
5. Since more problems can be lurking, continue close monitoring.
6. If the policy calls for it, investigate and possibly prosecute.
7. Fully analyze the incident and write a report. The report covers what happened, how the problem was found, what losses occurred, who was responsible, what was done to remove vulnerability, how operation was restored, how security was maintained or restored, and what monitoring is continuing. Also, what lessons were learned, such as: the response team needs someone with experience in a particular software package, or systems people must keep better records of software changes.
8. Revise (if necessary) the incident response plan and the security policy.

Summary

Computer security is both a technical problem and a management problem. Organizations are responsible for carrying out an information security program. This means developing a security plan, setting up organizations to carry out the plan, and assuring that the plan is being carried out.

The people who manage security must be able to align security policy with business needs; they must understand technical risks and safeguards and be able to explain them to senior management. The highest-level security policies should be consistent throughout the organization. Some organizations use a structure in which a chief security officer, who is a senior manager, reports directly to the CEO. Each major operating unit has a security officer who reports to the unit's management. A computer security planning committee is composed of managers of the operating units and is chaired by the CSO; the CSO makes sure that the committee's plans are carried out.

Security management is governed by security policy. An organization's overall (or corporate) policy is the responsibility of top management; it lays out the security philosophy and goals. It sets up the management structure, delineates roles and responsibilities, sets minimum requirements for units, defines a data classification scheme, and authorizes penalties for noncompliance.

A policy issue addressed by most organizations is authorized use: who may use each system, and for what purposes. Generic security roles and responsibilities must be defined. Policy should: explicitly require ethical behavior of all users, assign responsibility for system administration and security administration, and define the response to policy violation. Implementing policy involves translating it into concrete terms (through standards, guidelines, and procedures), interpreting it, and making sure that everyone knows and understands it.

Hiring qualified people furthers security. Orientation for new employees is the place to start imparting security awareness, attitudes, and skills. There needs to be continuing reinforcement of the idea that security is important and has management behind it. Computer security audits are essential. Users are responsible for: knowing and following security policy; observing ethical standards, learning the tools and skills, encouraging good security on the part of others, and suggesting improvements. Managers are responsible for providing people with the resources to carry out their security responsibilities.

A security officer (SO) is responsible for computer security in a unit. The SO participates in setting policy for the unit and is responsible for its security procedures, training and awareness efforts, contingency planning, making sure that safeguards are installed, working with other groups to ensure physical security, and reviewing audit trails. Some SO responsibilities are best distributed to user organizations. There are certification programs for information security professionals.

One important administrative control is an information security agreement, in which a person agrees that he or she has read and understood the computer security policy and knows the sanctions for violations.

User administration includes maintaining user accounts, providing for identification and authentication, making sure that privileges and access rights are appropriate and up-to-date, and auditing for improper use of accounts. User administration is time-consuming, and administrators tend to get behind; one way to reduce the bottleneck is to decentralize user administration.

Personnel practices can be effective security controls. One example is requiring employees to take their vacations. Security guidelines for telecommuting usually require a physically secure environment for the computer and the work that is produced; the computer is to be used only for business purposes and only by the employee. The procedures to follow when any employee leaves include: ensuring continued availability of programs and data and reminding the employee about proprietary information and nondisclosure and information security agreements. A large nonemployee population has access to secure areas and to computing equipment: people who service equipment or do custodial work or catering. The main controls are physical security, education, and clear guidelines.

Operations security typically spans several departments of an organization and several roles, including system administrators, security administrators, systems programmers, operators, and auditors. The operations area has the potential for effective security control and also for risk, which derives from powerful privileges. The organization should follow the principles of least privilege and separation of duty; especially important is separating system design and programming from operations. Every volume in the media library has to be labeled in both human-readable and machine-readable forms. A media control log must be kept. Other media-control tasks are: cleaning and checking media, taking inventories and reconciling them with the log, storing on-site backups in a protected area, and erasing volumes. There should be three copies of every file: the copy that is used, an on-site backup, and an off-site backup. Software obtained from vendors should be checked to make sure that it is authentic and intact. When fixes for security exposures are received, it is important to verify that the fixes really work.

Many computer security measures ultimately depend on physical security. Physical security must protect people, system availability, data, equipment, supplies, facilities, and support systems. Physical security counters threats from intruders, inconsistent power or extended power interruptions, telephone outages, natural disasters and other emergencies, fire and smoke, water, operating environment hazards, and emanations. Physical security measures include selecting a good site, backing up data, off-site storage of documents and data, providing backup processing sites, providing spare personal computers and spare parts, stating clear policies about physical security, ensuring knowledge of responsibilities, and rehearsing the responses to emergencies.

For protecting against intrusion, the choice of site is important. Physical security involves establishing security perimeters, both outside and inside buildings, and guarding the few gates through those perimeters. Equipment needs to be protected against theft, tampering or other misuse; its security must be maintained during shipment and delivery. Visitors should be escorted to reduce the risk of their seeing confidential information or getting access to computers.

It is necessary to plan for natural disasters and other emergencies. If possible, electrical power should be obtained from a utility with a good record on continuity of service. Problems within the building may also cause failures. Safeguards include power conditioners and power monitors. An uninterruptable power supply (UPS) allows computing equipment to run during a power outage. To prevent and control fire, buildings should be constructed of fire-resistant materials and contain fire-resistant furnishings and fixtures. There should be a no-smoking policy. Areas that enclose critical computing resources need walls of fire-retardant material. Printers and copiers need their own enclosures. Magnetic media should be kept in fire-resistant containers, separated from the computer room by a fire barrier. Smoke detectors should be installed on ceilings, underneath raised floors, and in air ducts. Water is excellent for putting out fires, but it can damage computing equipment. Many computer rooms have systems that use Halon or other gases. Many water problems can be prevented by good building maintenance. Other preparations include pumps in basements and plastic sheets for covering equipment quickly. PCs should be kept away from windows. Mainframes and servers should be above the ground floor. Monitoring systems can detect leaks under raised floors and above suspended ceilings.

Contingency planning prepares for the steps that will allow the organization to continue functioning even though its normal operations are disrupted. A contingency is some event that might occur and—if it did—would require special measures to handle it. An emergency can be costly in lost business, effects on customers, and possibly going out of business. There are also legal reasons for contingency planning. Recovering from a contingency is a matter of restoring business processes.

The contingency plan covers off-site storage, backup processing, work space for employees, security during the emergency, software vendor failure, insurance, and priorities for restoring business processes. The plan must include measures for its own testing. An important result of contingency planning is a team, or different teams for different stages of the emergency, such as: the event itself, the initial response, impact assessment, start-up, and full recovery.

Traditional contingency planning has been less effective for computer security incidents. These need a special incident response capability that includes skilled people, policies and procedures, and sophisticated techniques. Incident response involves much cooperation among organizations. An incident response team needs people with technical knowledge and excellent communication skills. The team must know how to maintain a trail of evidence that could be used in court. Investigative and law enforcement agencies should be contacted in advance. Since cooperating with law enforcement can result in negative publicity and other risks, many organizations do not report cases of abuse; others report incidents immediately. The main activities during an incident are: detection and evaluation; notification of management, team members, and others; containment; and eradication. After an incident: inventory the effects; develop a written plan for recovery; document what recovery steps are taken; if vulnerabilities were discovered, install fixes or set up administrative controls; continue close monitoring; possibly investigate and prosecute; fully analyze the incident and write a report; if necessary, revise the incident response plan and the security policy.

Bibliographic Notes

Fites and Kratz (1993) provide wide-ranging coverage of security professional responsibilities. A good overview of security controls is given by Fites, Kratz, and Brebner (1989). Smith (1993) provides a readable, nontechnical guide for security managers.

Perry (1985) gives a prescription for security management and recommends management structures. Peltier (1994) considers alternative management structures. Schweitzer (1991) describes the security organization planned by DEC. NIST-CSL (1993b) describes how federal agencies can set up multilevel structures for managing security. White and Farrell (1994) advocate transforming security administration from a technically oriented function to a business process that adds value for the organization. Wright (1993) reports on a survey of CEO involvement in computer security.

Chapter 4 treats security policy in general and also specific policies. Different types of security policy are defined in the glossary of the ITSEC (1991). NIST-CSL (1994) differentiates types of policies. Fites and Kratz (1993) reprint several model security policies. Oldehoeft (1992) sketches a security policy for the National Research and Educational Network. Pethia, Crocker, and Fraser (1991) give security guidelines for the Internet. Ethical considerations are discussed in Chap. 2. The American/Northwest Airlines case is described by Carley (1994). Information classification policies are described in Chap. 4.

The use of guardians is described by Allen (1993). The role of the ISSO is described in NCSC (1992). The National Research Council study (1991) calls for certification of security professionals; certification is discussed by Schou et al. (1993). One organization involved in certification is the International Information Systems Security Certification Consortium, or $(ISC)^2$, whose work is described by Fites and Kratz (1993) and by the Committee on the Common Body of Knowledge (1993).

NIST-CSL (1993a) discusses people and security. Wood (1994) describes information security agreements. Security problems of telecommuting are discussed by Power (1994). Threats in remote access are discussed in Chap. 11.

Operations security is covered by Fites and Kratz (1993). NCSC (1989) describes separation of duty in operations. Recovery methods are described in Chap. 8. The vacuum cleaner incident is reported in Neumann (1994). Chapter 6 discusses configuration management.

A comprehensive checklist for physical security is found in ACM SIGSAC (1993). Stang and Moon (1993) also provide good material on physical security. A catalog of security products, including many for physical security, is published by the Computer Security Institute

(1995). Tamper-resistant enclosures are discussed by Bianco (1992) and by Yeh and Smith (1991). Wood (1993) discusses policies about visitors. Power supply issues are discussed by Sheldon (1993). Emanations and TEMPEST measures are described by Cooper (1989) and by Russell and Gangemi (1991).

Contingency planning is discussed by Snoyer and Fischer (1993), Rohde and Haskett (1990), ACM SIGSAC (1993), Bodnar (1993), Cerullo et al. (1994), and NIST-CSL (1995). Bates (1992) is oriented to telecommunications. Commercial disaster recovery services are offered by Comdisco, Hewlett-Packard, IBM, Wang Laboratories, an AT&T subsidiary, and others. Riggs (1994) mentions companies that provide LAN disaster recovery services. Gibbs (1994) gives examples of software systems that did not get done or failed to work right.

Our discussion of incident response draws on the detailed Internet RFC by Holbrook and Reynolds (1991). The ISSO's responsibilities for incident reporting are described in NCSC (1992). Fithen and Fraser (1994) describe the CERT incident response center located at the Software Engineering Institute at Carnegie Mellon University. Incident response groups have joined together in a coalition called the *Forum of Incident Response and Security Teams* (FIRST). Wack (1991) explains how to build an incident response capability, addressing legal issues, staffing, and operation. Legal background on evidence is provided by Fites and Kratz (1993: Chap. 11) and Wack (1991) tells how to keep an incident response log book as evidence. Wood (1995) discusses the issue of whether to report incidents to law enforcement.

Exercises

12.1 Should computer security management be a responsibility of the computer operations department? Explain your answer.

12.2 Consider your organization, or an organization that you are familiar with (for example, a university department). Write an overall security policy for that organization.

12.3 What is meant by an *authorized use* policy? Write one for your organization.

12.4 In what way does hiring qualified people contribute to computer security?

12.5 What is the value of information security agreements?

12.6 Discuss the impact on computer security of telecommuting.

12.7 If you were the computer security officer for your organization, what would you do to make people more aware of computer security?

12.8 How should computer operations be organized to follow the principle of separation of duty? Answer for (1) a centralized university computing center and (2) a LAN that serves the Psychology Department.

12.9 Describe threats from power irregularities and failures. Describe the main protections against these threats.

12.10 What is a *software escrow?*

12.11 What is meant by *business continuity planning?* How does it relate to contingency planning and disaster recovery?

12.12 Outline a contingency plan for your organization. Cover each of the items the chapter lists for contingency plans to consider.

12.13 Why do computer security incidents need a different kind of response from other contingencies, such as fire or flood?

12.14 What steps should be taken in the aftermath of a computer security incident?

References

ACM SIGSAC. 1993. Checklist for security and contingency planning. *Security Audit & Control Review* **11**(1): 3–16.

Allen, Peter. 1993. On guardian: CSX's information security relies on decentralization of duties. *Computer Security ALERT* (129), December: 1.

Bates Jr., Regis J. 1992. *Disaster Recovery Planning: Networks, Telecommunications, and Data Communications.* New York: McGraw-Hill.

Bianco, Mark. 1992. A tamper-resistant seal for trusted distribution and life-cycle integrity assurance. *Proceedings of the 15th National Computer Security Conference,* 670–679. NIST/NCSC.

Bodnar, George H. 1993. Data security and contingency planning. *Internal Auditing* 8, Winter: 74–80.

Carley, William M. 1994. Did Northwest steal American's systems? The court will decide. *The Wall Street Journal,* July 7.

Cerullo, Michael J., R. Steve McDuffie, and L. Murphy Smith. 1994. Planning for disaster. *CPA Journal* **64**(6): 34–38.

Committee on the Common Body of Knowledge. 1993. CISSP Common Body of Knowledge. *Computer Security Journal* **IX**(1): 79–89.

Computer Security Institute. 1995. *Computer Security Products Buyers Guide.* San Francisco: Computer Security Institute.

Cooper, James Arlin. 1989. *Computer and Communications Security: Strategies for the 1990s.* New York: McGraw-Hill.

Fites, Philip E., and Martin P. J. Kratz. 1993. *Information Systems Security: A Practitioner's Reference.* New York: Van Nostrand Reinhold.

Fites, Philip E., Martin P. J. Kratz, and Alan F. Brebner. 1989. *Control and Security of Computer Information Systems.* Rockville, Md.: Computer Science Press.

Fithen, Katherine, and Barbara Fraser. 1994. CERT incident response and the Internet. *Communications of the ACM* **37**(8): 108–113.

Gibbs, W. Wayt. 1994. Software's chronic crisis. *Scientific American,* September: 86–95.

Holbrook, J. Paul, and Joyce K. Reynolds. 1991. *Site Security Handbook.* Internet Request for Comments RFC 1244, July 1991.

ITSEC. 1991. *ITSEC: Information Technology Security Evaluation Criteria.* Luxembourg: European Communities—Commission.

National Research Council. 1991. *Computers at Risk: Safe Computing in the Information Age.* Washington, D.C.: National Academy Press.

NCSC. 1988. *Glossary of Computer Security Terms.* NCSC-TG-004, October 1988. Fort Meade, Md.: National Computer Security Center.

______. 1989. *A Guide to Understanding Trusted Facility Management.* Report NCSC-TG-015. Fort Meade, Md.: National Computer Security Center.

______. 1992. *A Guide to Understanding Information System Security Officer Responsibilities for Automated Information Systems.* NCSC-TG-027. Fort Meade, Md.: National Computer Security Center.

Neumann, Peter G. 1994. Risks to the public in computers and related systems. *Software Engineering Notes* **19**(3): 4–12.

NIST-CSL. 1993a. *People: An Important Asset in Computer Security.* Bulletin, October 1993. NIST Computer Systems Laboratory.

______. 1993b. *Security Program Management.* Bulletin, August 1993. NIST Computer Systems Laboratory.

______. 1994. *Computer Security Policy: Setting the Stage for Success.* Bulletin, January 1994. NIST Computer Systems Laboratory.

______. 1995. *Preparing for Contingencies and Disasters.* Bulletin, September 1995. NIST Computer Systems Laboratory.

Oldehoeft, Arthur E. 1992. *Foundations of a Security Policy for Use of the National Research and Educational Network.* NISTIR 4734, PB92-172030. Gaithersburg, Md.: National Institute of Standards and Technology.

Peltier, Tom. 1994. Who should the information protection staff report to? *Computer Security ALERT* (131): 2.

Perry, William E. 1985. *Management Strategies for Computer Security.* Boston: Butterworth.

Pethia, R., S. Crocker, and B. Fraser. 1991. *Guidelines for the Secure Operation of the Internet.* Internet Request for Comments RFC 1281, November 1991.

Power, Richard. 1994. Telecommuting may be the wave of the future, but what about the undertow? *Computer Security ALERT* (136), July: 1.

Riggs, Brian. 1994. Companies scramble to provide LAN disaster recovery. *Computer* **27**(9): 8–9.

Rohde, Renate, and Jim Haskett. 1990. Disaster recovery planning for academic computing centers. *Communications of the ACM* **33**(6): 652–657.

Russell, Deborah, and G. T. Gangemi Sr. 1991. *Computer Security Basics.* Sebastopol, Calif.: O'Reilly & Associates.

Schou, Corey D., W. Vic Machonachy, F. Lynn McNulty, and Arthur Chantker. 1993. Information security professionalism for the 1990s. *Computer Security Journal* **IX**(1): 27–37.

Schweitzer, James A. 1991. Laying the groundwork for a model information security program. *Information Security: Proceedings of the IFIP TC11 Seventh International Conference on Information Security, IFIP/Sec '91,* 77–85. Oxford, U.K.: Elsevier Science.

Sheldon, Tom. 1993. *Novell NetWare 4: The Complete Reference.* Berkeley, Calif.: Osborne McGraw-Hill.

Smith, Martin. 1993. *Commonsense Computer Security: Your Practical Guide to Information Protection.* 2d ed. London: McGraw-Hill.

Snoyer, Robert S., and Glenn A. Fischer, eds. 1993. *Managing Microcomputer Security.* Homewood, Ill.: Chantico Publishing Co., Inc.

Stang, David J., and Sylvia Moon. 1993. *Network Security Secrets.* San Mateo, Calif.: IDG Books.

Wack, John P. 1991. *Establishing a Computer Security Incident Response Capability (CSIRC)*. NIST Special Publication 800-3, PB92-123140. Gaithersburg, Md.: National Institute of Standards and Technology.

White, Daniel E., and Mark H. Farrell. 1994. Reengineering information security administration. *Computer Security Journal* **X**(1): 23–37.

Wood, Charles Cresson. 1993. Reduce the risk posed by visitors; require escorts. *Computer Security ALERT* (128), November.

______. 1994. Annual compliance agreement signatures. *Computer Security ALERT* (136), July.

______. 1995. When to report computer crimes to law enforcement. *Computer Security ALERT* (151), October.

Wright, Phillip C. 1993. Computer security in large corporations: Attitudes and practices of CEOs. *Management Decision* **31**(7): 56–60.

Yeh, Phil C., and Ronald M. Smith. 1991. ESA/390 Integrated Cryptographic Facility. *IBM Systems Journal* **30**(2): 192.

Chapter

13

Analyzing Security

Introduction

This chapter describes four different ways to analyze and evaluate security. The goal of *risk analysis* is to help with selecting cost-effective safeguards. Risk analysis involves estimating potential losses and how much safeguards could reduce them, to determine if the safeguards are worth their cost. *Information systems auditing* is an extension of traditional financial auditing. It collects and evaluates evidence to determine whether a computer system is secure, effective, and efficient. *Vulnerability testing* examines systems for known kinds of security weakness. *Intrusion detection* systems automatically collect and analyze traces of user activity, trying to identify instances of misuse.

Overview of the chapter

The section on risk analysis describes how assets are identified and valued, how threats and vulnerabilities are evaluated, how risks are calculated, and how safeguards are analyzed. Methodologies and tools are described. Problems with the risk analysis approach are discussed.

The section on information systems auditing begins with some background on financial auditing, then describes the work of auditors, the concepts of controls and auditability, and auditing tasks and techniques. The auditor's role in system development is discussed.

The next section briefly describes how systems are tested for vulnerability.

The final section describes intrusion detection, first delineating alternative detection approaches and design approaches. An intrusion detection model is presented, and several prototype systems are described. The section concludes with the challenges facing intrusion detection.

Risk Analysis

One way to look at computer security practice is as risk management—identifying threats and vulnerabilities, and selecting safeguards or countermeasures to control them. Since it is not practical to implement every possible safeguard, security managers must decide which threats to control, and with which safeguards. This decision is clearly difficult to make. Is it better to invest in smart cards for better authentication or in a firewall system to protect the internal network? To aid their decision making, security practitioners use *risk analysis,* which is the "process of analyzing threats to and vulnerabilities of an information system to determine the risks (potential for losses), and using the analysis as a basis for identifying appropriate and cost-effective measures" (NCSC 1994: 41). The main goal of risk analysis is to help with selecting cost-effective safeguards. Risk analysis involves estimating the potential losses and how much the safeguards could reduce them and using these results to determine if the safeguards are worth their cost. Cost-effectiveness is not the only possible basis for security decisions, and a focus on cost-effectiveness can sometimes damage longer-range security. (We return to this issue later.)

For hundreds of years, risk analysis has been used in insurance. It is applied to finance, health, and the environment. Since the 1970s, risk analysis has been applied to computer security. Ideally, risk analysis is an integral part of the development methodology and of the system development life cycle. In practice, it often is applied to existing systems on a one-time or periodic basis. One reason for the wide use of risk analysis is government mandate. In the United States, federal agencies and their contractors must perform risk analyses at various stages of system procurement, development, and operation. The mandate applies to systems that handle unclassified, but sensitive, information and applications.

Risk analysis has its own costs. Software tools alone can cost tens of thousands of dollars, and a complete formal risk analysis can be very costly in time. The results are imprecise and lack empirical validation. Other criticisms abound. Still, risk analysis is worth doing, even when not mandated. It provides insight into security and improves security awareness, and sometimes it is the only way to justify expenditures on security. Risk analysis gives managers a familiar kind of information—measures of costs and potential gains and losses. "Management rarely attempts to control what it cannot observe through the accounting system...what is not measured is not controlled. Conversely, what is measured is controlled" (Perry 1985: 56). Risk analysis "...facilitates the expression of the interpretive knowledge of the security designer, and the communication of this knowledge to the investment decision-makers in management" (Baskerville 1991: 763).

A simple example

Risk analysis often measures potential losses in terms of an *annual loss expectancy* (ALE), which is the loss, in money units, that can be expected in a year. ALE can be computed for individual assets as exposed to specific threats. ALE is computed as

$$e = pv$$

where e is the expectancy, p is the annual probability of loss, and v is the value of the asset. Suppose the asset is a LAN server with peripherals, valued at $150,000, and the probability that it will be destroyed by fire within a year is .01. The ALE would be $1500. This ALE is a measure of the *risk* associated with the server's vulnerability to fire.

Extending the example, we consider three assets of the BioWidget company—the LAN server, workstations located in offices, and workstations located on the shop floor—and two threats: fire and flood (Table 13.1) and compute the risk to each asset from each threat. This simplified example assumes that loss is total. It also ignores an extremely important factor in realistic risk calculation—safeguards.

The analysis of Table 13.2 introduces safeguards and uses, not the total value of the asset, but the *impact* of the threat event. For this

TABLE 13.1 Annual Loss Expectancies (ALEs) for Three Assets and Two Threats

	Assets and their values		
Threats and their probabilities	Server 150,000	Office workstations 100,000	Shop workstations 200,000
Fire .01	1500	1000	2000
Flood .02	3000	2000	4000

TABLE 13.2 Annual Loss Expectancies (ALEs) with Safeguards

	Assets and their values		
Threats and their probabilities	Server 150,000	Office workstations 100,000	Shop workstations 200,000
Fire .01	Impact 150,000 ALE ~~1500~~ With safeguard (cost = 5000) *ALE 750*	Impact 100,000 ALE 1000	Impact 200,000 ALE 2000
Flood .02 With safeguard (cost = 12,000) *.01*	Impact 100,000 ALE ~~2000~~ *ALE 1000*	Impact 50,000 ALE ~~1000~~ *ALE 1000*	Impact 100,000 ALE ~~2000~~ *ALE 1000*

example, fire's impact is the total value of each asset, and flood's impact varies for the different assets. Table 13.2 shows the new ALE values (in italics) that would result from the contemplated safeguards. Safeguards can affect the probability of the threat, or its impact, or both. In the example, a fire-extinguishing system for the server room would cut the fire impact on the server by half, and thus cut the ALE by half (by $750). (This safeguard would not affect the workstations.) Since the fire work costs $5000, and has a life of 5 years, it does not appear to be a cost-effective safeguard. Installing drainage around the building affects the likelihood of flooding, affecting the ALE for all the assets. The total ALE reduction is $2000. Since the drainage work costs $12,000 and has a lifetime of 10 years, it is cost-effective.

This example begins to reveal the complexities and quandaries of risk analysis. First, although the server hardware could be replaced for $150,000, a fire would in reality have far greater impact. So it is necessary to analyze intangibles, such as unavailability of services and the work needed to replace, reconfigure, and restore the server. If these were considered, the fire safeguards might well seem cost-effective. Identifying and valuing assets is by no means straightforward. Fire and flood may have well-known probabilities, but other threats do not. How likely is unauthorized transaction use by insiders, or system penetration by a hacker? The impact of a threat event may also be hard to quantify. How much is lost through the unauthorized transaction? Another difficult estimate is how much a safeguard reduces a risk. How much does access-control software reduce the risk from the insider threat? Countermeasures that reduce one risk may increase another; for example, a sprinkler system reduces the fire risk but increases the water risk. Risk analysis must contend with uncertainty in every variable it considers.

Steps in a risk analysis

A risk analysis involves the following steps:

1. Identify the assets and assign monetary values to them.
2. Identify the threats and the vulnerabilities—(which assets are vulnerable to which threats). Estimate the likelihood of occurrence of each threat. For each vulnerable asset, estimate the impact of the threat.
3. Calculate the exposure (ALE) of each asset to each threat.
4. Identify potential safeguards and estimate how much they reduce the exposures. Estimate the costs of the safeguards and determine which ones are cost-effective.

(Later sections expand on each step.) Step 4 can be repeated with varying selections of safeguards, and other steps may be repeated as well. The risk analysis results, along with other factors (such as the funds available) determine what safeguards are actually implemented.

The risk analysis draws on the expertise of the asset owners, computer security managers, application users, and people who understand threats (such as system software experts and physical security experts).

Identifying and valuing assets

An *asset* is any component or aspect of an information system. Assets include hardware, software, data, people, processes, and customer goodwill. There are *tangible* assets and *intangible* assets. A LAN server is an example of a tangible asset, whose value is easily measurable in dollars—as the replacement cost, for example. An example of an intangible asset is an accounts database, whose valuation is more difficult. Its value might include the interest lost due to delayed billing, plus the labor and computer time required to rebuild the database, plus the value of the information permanently lost. Even less tangible is customers' image of the company as efficient and responsive. Using checklists or interviews, risk analysts identify the assets and the *impact* on them of threat events. Risk analysis methodologies often aggregate assets of the same type for the purpose of analysis.

Often, an organization's most significant assets are its information system's services. It is worth something to someone (clients or the organization itself) to have a service performed. Consider an on-line database that charges $25 per hour of connect time. When the database is down for an hour, the database provider could lose $25 of revenue for each likely user. Knowing the value of a service helps the analyst value the assets that go into providing it.

Units of value. Usually, value is assigned to assets in monetary units, such as dollars. There are arguments against using money units. Since asset values often are rough estimates, a better scale might be *valuable, highly valuable, extremely valuable.* But the case for monetary units is strong. People are comfortable with money units, which they use all the time when considering costs and losses. Money is used as the common measure for all kinds of things—even human lives and suffering. In some risk analysis methodologies, people estimate value in orders of magnitude. An estimate would be given as 4 or 5, for example, rather than $10,000 or $100,000. This method has the advantage of removing any illusions about the precision of the estimate. Direct dollar estimates, though, are usually easier and more valid.

Ways to assign value. Two ways to assign value to tangible assets are

- *Standard accounting.* This method uses the book value of the asset—the value in the accounting records of the company. The estimated value is the sum of the book value and the accumulated depreciation.
- *Replacement cost.* If the LAN server is destroyed by flood, it can be replaced. Its value is the cost (at the time of the analysis) of a replacement.

The value of intangible assets includes the value of each of their security attributes: confidentiality, integrity, and availability. Many factors can go into each of these values. Loss of confidentiality could harm individuals (who might sue), give away trade secrets, or reveal closely guarded market information. For defense-related information, confidentiality may be the main determinant of value. Loss of availability can mean lost business—postponed or lost forever—as well as loss of goodwill. (A company may have historical data to support value estimates for availability.) Factors to consider in relation to loss of each attribute include: liability, lost business, loss of goodwill, lost competitive advantage, and failure to meet contractual or regulatory obligations.

Value estimates can be useful without being precise. It is a mistake to spend too much time on refining estimates, at least until the risk analysis reveals where finer estimates are needed.

The results of this step. Just identifying the assets and assigning values to them is already a significant achievement. The data are now there for the next steps of the risk analysis. Just as important, a clearer picture emerges of just how valuable the assets are. This picture may well motivate stronger management backing for the risk analysis and for other computer security efforts.

Analyzing threats and vulnerabilities

A *threat* is a circumstance or event that could cause damage by impairing security. A *vulnerability* is a security weakness that could be exploited by a threat. For risk analysis, vulnerability is the openness of a specific asset to damage from a specific threat. The BioWidget LAN server has a low level of vulnerability to fire (because its room is fire-resistant), and the shop-floor workstations have a high level. Vulnerabilities have rough or yes-no values, and threats have probabilities or likelihoods. Risk analysis usually starts with assets and goes on to threats and vulnerabilities.

Identifying threats. The analyst must select which threats to consider, using threat information gathered from a variety of sources. Checklists or questionnaires are filled out by the appropriate people—physical security people about fire and electrical problems, software experts about hackers. Analysts interview users about the environment and the organization's history of threat events. The organizational structure and personnel can be analyzed to determine which people or roles are likely sources of threats. Users of applications can be observed. Like a penetration testing team, the risk analysis team can hold brainstorming sessions. Threat scenarios can be developed, either on paper or with the aid of software. (Some experts feel that threat scenarios are too risky because they may fall into the wrong hands.)

Weather and geological bureaus publish statistics about natural disasters, as do insurers. Investigative agencies publish data on crime and insurance companies on losses. Other sources of threat information are books about computer security and the newsletters of computer security organizations and auditors' organizations. Government agencies [such as the *National Institute of Standards and Technology* (NIST) in the United States] publish reports about threats. The online RISKS forum has logged many years of computer security incidents. Incident response centers warn of new threats. One reason to make risk analysis an ongoing activity is that the relative importance of different classes of threats changes all the time.

Estimating likelihood of threats. Although there is some historical data, risk analysis relies heavily on people's estimates of threat probabilities. The time period of 1 year is customary, since people are used to yearly budgets and yearly reports. According to many risk analysis experts, people are better at estimating how often an event might occur than at estimating a probability. That is, people are better able to say that an electrical failure is expected every 2 years than to say its probability for a year is .5. Some methodologies allow people to select from alternatives such as "once in 10 days" or "once in 3 years." The choice is transformed into a value that is used to calculate the ALE or look it up in a table. The term *likelihood* is used in risk analysis. It has the advantage of carrying less connotation of precision (which would be misleading) than the term *probability.* As with value estimates, risk analysis often uses very rough likelihood estimates.

Various sources and methods can be used for estimating threat likelihood. Weather and geological bureaus and insurers are sources for natural threats. Police departments and insurance companies have crime data. Manufacturers of equipment may provide data on failure rates. Some risk analysis tools include threat databases based on such sources. For the more common intrusions, an excellent source is local history, which should be available in audit reports and archives. For estimates that are primarily judgment calls, integrating the calls of different judges can increase validity. With the *Delphi* technique, participants make individual estimates, then can revise them after learning what the other participants did.

An estimation of the likelihood of a deliberate intrusion can consider factors that motivate the intruder, such as, according to Deborah Bodeau (1992):

- The relative gain from this intrusion compared to all possible ones
- The amount of effort required
- The strength of safeguards that might lead to the attacker's apprehension

Although single-point estimates of likelihood are common, some methods work with *ranges* of likelihood.

Analyzing vulnerabilities and impacts. Having considered assets and threats, a risk analysis then proceeds to how specific threats affect specific assets. The goal is to arrive at a risk or ALE value for each (asset, threat) pair—a measure of the expected loss in the absence of any additional safeguards. The risk is a function of the threat's likelihood and its *impact*—its damaging effect on the asset. A technique called *exposure analysis* has been suggested for finding the assets most exposed to threats from nature, accident, or insider roles. Some risk analysis software supports use of the Delphi method to rank threat impacts.

Some vulnerabilities may be so obvious, and the safeguards for them so standard, that the course of action is clear. These vulnerabilities can be omitted from the risk analysis.

Calculating risks

Assume that the likelihood of electrical failure having an impact on BioWidget's LAN server is .2, and that the impact is

Availability	60,000
Integrity	10,000
Confidentiality	0
Total impact	70,000

Then the impact is multiplied by the likelihood, .2×70,000, to obtain an ALE of 14,000. If likelihood ranges are used instead of single-point estimates, the result is a risk curve. If the software tool does not provide this feature, the analysis can be repeated, varying the likelihood estimate, to see how sensitive the results are to the variation. The same type of sensitivity analysis can be applied to impact estimates.

We have described one simple form of risk calculation. Risk analysis tools may use more sophisticated algorithms.

Analyzing safeguards

A safeguard can reduce risk by changing any of the variables that go into it. For example, disabling remote access reduces the likelihood of a penetration attempt. The impact can be reduced by encrypting sensitive files or by removing sensitive data from the computing system. By analyzing the relationship between safeguard cost and risk reduction, risk analysis provides a basis for selecting a cost-effective set of safeguards.

Safeguard costs are usually easier to estimate than threat impacts. There are two kinds of costs: the cost to acquire the safeguard, and the cost to maintain it. Suppose the safeguard is installing RACF. In addition to the license fee, the cost includes training of security administrators and users, the ongoing demands on their time, and additional computer resources. As with assets, some safeguard costs are intangible. Disabling remote access adversely affects the work of some users. Removing data from the system makes someone's job harder. A safeguard might conceivably have negative cost. For example, installing RACF might provide the security needed for a profitable new application.

In the final steps of the risk analysis, safeguards are identified to control as many risks as possible. Some risk analysis tools include databases of safeguards to select from. For a system being designed, the security measures specified in the design are used. The costs of the safeguards are estimated, as are their effects on threat likelihood and impact. (There is no point in estimating safeguard costs more precisely than risks.) Then the amount of ALE reduction for each safeguard can be calculated and compared with the cost to see if the safeguard is cost-effective.

Usually, there is a fairly fixed budget for safeguards, so that, even considering only cost-effective safeguards, their total cost may well exceed the available funds. Not all the risks can be controlled. Most organizations will decide to accept some level of risk. Then they must decide how to allocate the limited resources among the potential safeguards. James Cooper (1989) identifies three resource allocation strategies to consider:

1. Allocate resources in proportion to the risk.
2. Disregard very small risks, and allocate proportionally among the rest.
3. Address the largest risk, then the next in order, until the budget is used up.

Risk analysis tools support "what if" analysis of safeguard choices.

Risk analysis methodologies and tools

Most risk analysis is done with the help of software tools. Their functions include gathering and storing data, computing risk measures, evaluating cost-effectiveness of countermeasures, and presenting the results in effective form.

Desirable features for software tools. Some organizations have developed their own methodologies and tools, some use commercially available tools, and others use methodologies and tools developed for governments. Selecting a tool generally implies also selecting a methodology. Methodologies are sometimes characterized as *quantitative* or *qualitative,* depending on how finely risk variables are assessed. A qualitative assessment might be *low, medium,* or *high,* as opposed to a probability value or a dollar value. Some organizations choose qualitative methods because they are easier to use. With qualitative methods, users are less likely to overestimate how precise the results are. Properties of a good software tool are shown in Fig. 13.1.

Example methodology: CRAMM. One of the most fully-developed and important methodologies is *CRAMM*—CCTA Risk Analysis and Management Methodology. CRAMM has been adopted as a standard by the CCTA, the Central Computer and Telecommunications Agency of the U.K. government. Although originally a stand-alone method, CRAMM has been linked to another U.K. standard methodology, Structured Systems Analysis and Design Method (SSADM), so that risk analysis can accompany all stages of design.

A CRAMM analysis begins with identifying the assets, assigning values to them, and determining potential impacts. Four kinds of impact are considered: disclosure, modification, unavailability, and destruction. CRAMM provides questionnaires for obtaining this information from the asset owners. It provides guidance on how to value tangible assets by replacement or reconstruction cost, and data assets

- Can model a wide variety of systems
- Applies to systems being developed as well as operational ones
- Can represent assets at a fine enough granularity
- Can start with imprecise or informal analyses and go on to more precise and formal ones as necessary
- Includes training facilities
- Makes clear to users how the results are obtained, and what their precision is
- Serves as an educational tool
- Serves as a repository of risk data and documentation
- Documents the risk analysis process, including who performed it and where the data came from
- Has its own security features to prevent misuse
- Includes an iterative safeguard evaluation
- Produces outputs that clearly and graphically convey the issues and results of the analysis and that are meaningful to security decision-makers

Figure 13.1 Desirable properties for risk analysis tools.

in relation to "political embarrassment, commercial confidentiality, personal privacy, personal safety, and financial and legal implications" (Charette 1990: 407). Assets can be organized into groups, all the assets in a group being analyzed together. Using a built-in list of generic threats, the software generates customized questionnaires that elicit from the owners each group's vulnerability to each threat, expressed as low, medium, or high. The software then calculates a risk number (from 1 to 5) for each impact (disclosure, modification, unavailability, and destruction).

Finally, countermeasures are considered. CRAMM provides a database of hundreds of countermeasures, and the system's existing countermeasures are also considered. The countermeasures are grouped according to what they are (for example, hardware, communications, personnel) and how they affect risk. CRAMM considers four ways that countermeasures can reduce risk: by making a threat less likely, by reducing its impact, by detecting an occurrence, or by facilitating recovery. The software compiles a list of recommended countermeasures to be added. The analysts can try out various countermeasure selections and determine their cost-effectiveness.

CRAMM has features that support periodic updates and reviews of the risk analysis. When CRAMM is used in conjunction with the SSADM design methodology, the results of a design stage are fed into

CRAMM, which suggests countermeasures that can be introduced into the design. Although risk analysis is not really integrated into the design methodology, it is linked to it.

Example methodology: ARiES. The Aerospace Risk Evaluation System (*ARiES*) is an example of a quantitative risk analysis methodology. ARiES implements and enhances the Livermore Risk Assessment Methodology (LRAM), which is a detailed description of the steps risk analyzers should take. ARiES estimates of risk are based on assets, threats, controls, and consequences. (*Consequences* are what we have called *impacts.*) A threat has an initiator, such as a human attacker or a natural disaster, and a path to the asset. Controls are of two kinds: preventive controls are placed on the path from the threat to the asset, and mitigative controls are placed between the asset and the consequences. For example, access control to files is a preventive control, and file backup is a mitigative control. A *risk element* (RE) is the combination of a threat initiator, its path, an asset, the consequence, and the effectiveness of the controls, as shown in Fig. 13.2. Risk is computed as

$$R = EF \times PCF \times MPL$$

where *EF* is the expected annual frequency of the threat, *PCF* is the probability of controls failure, and *MPL* is the expected loss if the controls fail and the consequence is realized.

The methodology has six stages: (1) project planning, (2) information gathering and management input, (3) risk element definition and screening, (4) risk acceptability assessment, (5) cost-benefit assess-

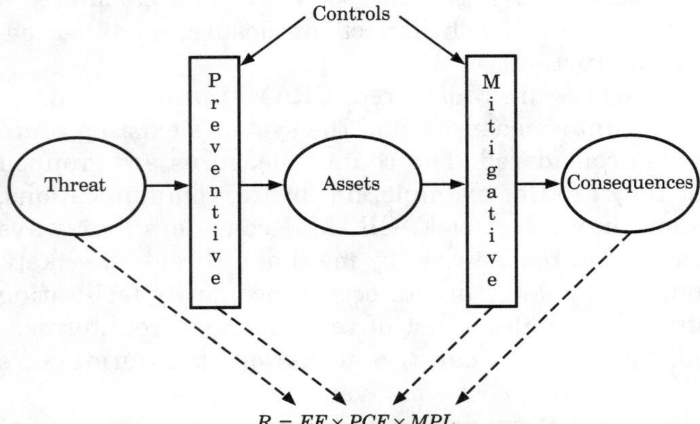

Figure 13.2 Risk analysis model for the ARiES system. [*From Lavine, Lindell, and Guarro (1994).*]

ment, and (6) prioritization of control sets. In Stage 2, the assets are identified and assigned monetary values and also values based on criticality, sensitivity, and classification. The analyst can define thresholds for loss, which can be used to screen out assets, retaining only important ones for later stages. In Stage 3 the analyst defines threats, consequences, and risk elements. Risk elements can also be screened to eliminate insignificant ones. In Stage 4, controls are defined, each having an installation cost, annual operating cost, and useful lifetime. Sets of controls are associated with risk elements and their failure probability is estimated. Then a *loss potential indicator* (*LPI*) is calculated for the risk element:

$$LPI = PCF \times MPL$$

The *LPI* is the loss expected if the threat against the asset materializes, given the strength of the controls. For those risk elements with unacceptable *LPI*, additional controls are proposed and new *LPI*s are calculated. This step is repeated until the *LPI*s are acceptable for all the risk elements, or until nothing more can be done for the unacceptable ones. In Stage 5, ARiES evaluates the cost-benefit of proposed control sets. For each risk element with proposed control enhancements, a cost-benefit ratio is computed by dividing the reduction in risk by the cost of the additional controls. In Stage 6, control sets are selected. ARiES supports this decision process by calculating control priorities according to several different criteria.

Methodology issues. Risk analysis ideally is an integral part of system development. Development methods increasingly emphasize modeling—of the system, the enterprise, and the environment. Similarly, recent risk analysis research focuses on modeling of systems and threats. Systems are composed of other systems, and systems are networked. The modeling has to represent how risks in one system affect another system, or how one system's assets become another system's threats (as when customer access that is profitable to one unit of a company threatens other systems on the company network). Although no standard risk model yet exists, some prototypes have carefully modeled restricted threat environments and restricted forms of assets and impacts.

Many criticisms have been aimed at risk analysis methodologies. Most lack any integration with system development methodologies. The modeling of assets, threats, and impacts does not allow enough specificity and richness. Networks or complex systems of systems cannot be represented. Better support is needed for valuing intangible assets and for determining type and level of impact. The checklists or databases of assets, threats, and safeguards keep growing larger, as technology changes, and they need to be updated frequently. Safeguards do not fit into a security architecture, but are unrelated entities pulled from a safeguard basket.

Evaluation of risk analysis

In addition to weaknesses in risk analysis methodologies, there are problems with the basic notions behind risk analysis.

The statistical basis of risk analysis may apply badly to computer security, where some threats are deliberate. "In particular, traditional risk analysis relies on statistical models that assume that unlikely events remain unlikely after they have occurred once" (National Research Council 1991: 19). Of course, once a computer security vulnerability has been discovered, its exploitation becomes far more likely. Another problem is that the danger of rare, but catastrophic, threats tends to be obscured. A cost-effective security solution may leave a company at risk of going out of business. Measured in ALE, a $1,000,000 loss expected once every 100 years is equivalent to a $10,000 loss expected once a year. But only the $1,000,000 loss threatens the company's existence. Another widely recognized problem is the lack of validation for the estimates (such as likelihoods and impacts) that go into a risk analysis; they may or may not be close to reality.

Even more fundamental is that the cost-benefit framework is narrowly applied. Monetary units do not properly represent all risk, and reduction in ALE does not fully describe the value of security measures. For one thing, the risk analysis may ignore certain impacts, because they are borne by persons outside the scope of the risk analysis. Suppose a health maintenance organization (HMO) conducts a risk analysis of its medical-record system. A patient's loss of privacy, although it might cause great upheaval in his personal life, enters into the risk analysis only as a potential legal liability that is within the HMO's acceptable risk level. For another example, consider the benefits system of a county welfare department. The department suffers no monetary impact if the benefit checks are late because of a system outage; it is the clients who suffer. These examples show that a cost-effectiveness approach to security can yield quite different results from a baseline or due-care approach.

The cost-benefit approach can also be short-sighted. Donald Davies cites the example of credit card fraud, which "has built up a formidable industry to exploit the system's weaknesses. New countermeasures are met by a determined response from the criminals, who see their income threatened. We see here an example of a system which initially was not secure enough, though it has probably met the 'profit and loss' criterion at each stage of its history" (Davies 1991: 462).

The lesson for security practitioners and managers is that risk analysis is a tool to be used with care. Its results must feed into thoughtful, prudent, and ethical design and decision. If used wisely, though, risk analysis enhances understanding and contributes to secure designs and effective security management.

Information Systems Auditing

Information systems auditing (also called *EDP auditing*) grew out of traditional financial auditing. An auditor collects and evaluates evidence about an organization, determining if its financial statements are accurate, and communicating the results of the examination. "EDP auditing is the process of collecting and evaluating evidence to determine whether a computer system safeguards assets, maintains data integrity, achieves organization goals effectively, and consumes resources efficiently" (Weber 1988: xiii). Safeguarding information or other assets and maintaining data integrity are clearly computer security concerns, and organizational goals usually imply system availability.

There are two categories of auditors: external and internal. External auditors are independent of the organizations they audit. In the United States, private companies are audited by Certified Public Accountants, and government agencies (and their contractors) are audited by the General Accounting Office, which is an independent government agency. Internal auditors, in contrast, work for the organization that they audit. Still, they too are independent; internal audit is a separate function within an organization, typically reporting to an audit committee of the board of directors. The auditor—external or internal—must evaluate the organization's system of *internal control,* which is intended to ensure that the organization's objectives are met: that it operates effectively, complies with laws and regulations, and prepares reliable financial data. Audits have varying objectives. There are financial audits, performance audits, and security audits, as well as hybrid and special-purpose audits. Financial audits cover the controls for computer-based systems, and security audits focus specifically on those controls. Auditing standards are promulgated (in the United States) by the American Institute of Certified Public Accountants (AICPA), and by the Institute for Internal Auditors, which is an international organization. The General Accounting Office has it own standards, which build on those of the AICPA. Changes in technology and business practices are so rapid that auditing standards tend to lag behind.

In the 1960s it became apparent that auditors lacked the knowledge to audit computer-based systems, and that computer people did not understand controls and auditing. The EDP audit function was created to bridge the gap, with EDP auditors coming from both sides. EDP auditors were (and are) specialists employed by CPA firms or as internal auditors. The standards for external auditors were revised to make clear that auditors needed their own computer expertise; they could not rely on computer specialists.

The financial auditing process

The financial auditing process has three main phases:

- Understanding the internal control structure
- Assessing control risk
- Substantive testing

Understanding the internal control structure. The auditor must understand the internal control structure in order to perform other phases of the audit. If internal controls are strong, the auditor can reduce the amount of substantive testing.

One element of the control structure is the overall *control environment,* including management's attitudes, the functioning of the board of directors and its audit committee, the quality of internal auditing, and personnel policies. One auditor, commenting on the BCCI bank fraud case, said that a "control culture" is needed—"when a problem comes up, you do something about it...." Sometimes the control problem goes all the way to the top, and prominent accounting firms have failed to detect fraud because they did not probe the control environment. Other elements of the control structure are risk assessment, control activities (which include operating controls, financial information controls, and compliance controls), information and communication (how information flows through an organization), and monitoring of the internal control system. *Safeguarding controls* are those designed to prevent or detect unauthorized transactions or unauthorized access to assets. The auditor must understand the safeguarding controls to spot security risks.

Assessing control risk. The auditor, after gaining an understanding of the control structure, assesses the *control risk* for specific assertions of the financial statement. If control risk is low, less substantive testing of that assertion is needed. An auditor who assesses control risk as "below the maximum" must identify the controls that are relevant to the assertion, test if they are effective, and document the tests.

Substantive testing. With *substantive testing,* the auditor collects evidence to form and support an opinion on the financial statements. Here the issue is the amounts themselves: whether the balances are accurate and properly documented, and whether they properly reflect all transactions. The tests involve examining records and documentation and real assets, as well as analyzing relationships among pieces of financial information. For example, this year's actual results are compared with forecasts, or sales expenses are compared with industry averages.

Information systems auditing

IS auditors. Both internal and external auditors do information systems (IS) auditing. For internal auditing, smaller organizations often use audit consultants (who may work for public accounting firms) or security consultants. Different organizations set different qualifications for internal IS auditors. Many look for a CPA, IS auditing certification, and a computing background. (Since much of auditing deals with computer-based systems, an IS audit specialty may become inappropriate. Rather, most auditors would be IS auditors, and some auditors would specialize in specific information technologies or products.)

Many organizations obtain crucial information services from other organizations—everything from payroll to stockholder services. The service organization becomes a significant factor in the user organization's internal control structure. Although auditors of service organizations must report on their controls, the standards say that a user auditor cannot rely on these reports alone and must assess how the service organization's controls affect those of the user organization.

The IS auditor's scope includes effectiveness and efficiency, not just security; our focus here is on security.

Controls and auditability. The concept of *controls* is used in both financial auditing and computer security. Computer security safeguards—technical, physical, and organizational—are controls. Auditors bridge the two contexts when they evaluate internal controls for computer-based systems. *General controls* are in the realm of entire organizations and their computing environments; *application controls* are provided by specific applications. Both general and application controls include safeguarding controls. General controls include technical security services and mechanisms, as well as personnel, physical, and organizational controls. An auditor's review of general controls might cover the following areas: management and organization, physical security, contingency planning, computer operations, data integrity, computer and network security, and programming change controls. With advancing technology, controls tend to migrate from applications to systems or subsystems, so that general controls become relatively more important. For example, data integrity controls that used to be in applications are now supported by database management systems (DBMSs).

Auditing is a process of collecting and evaluating evidence. To be *auditable,* automated systems must provide counterparts to traditional paper evidence, such as order forms, signed authorizations, and procedures manuals. An auditable system produces and maintains evidence that can be used to reconstruct transactions and processing. The system of internal controls protects the evidence.

Tasks in an information systems audit. An information systems auditor gathers evidence about general and application controls, using interviews, observations, and reviews of documentation. That is, the auditor gains an understanding of how the controls are supposed to work. For example, documentation indicates that the LAN administrator backs up the server once a day. Then the auditor does compliance testing—determining if the internal control system works the way it is supposed to. Does the daily backup actually occur? What happens when the administrator is on vacation? Finally, the auditor does substantive testing. The external auditor's goal in substantive testing is to determine if the financial statements are correct. The internal auditor's goal is to learn if losses have occurred or could occur. Substantive testing includes identifying erroneous processing, assessing data integrity, and comparing data with outside sources and with real assets. The same auditing tests may contribute to both review of controls and substantive testing. Auditing standards require auditors to report any significant deficiencies in the internal control system.

Computer security figures in any audit's review of internal controls, and some audits are specifically computer security audits.

Techniques and tools. Software tools help auditors to plan their work, to understand the system, and to gather and analyze evidence. Public accounting firms and others have developed generalized audit software, which can be used for many clients. Other audit software is specialized for specific industries or specific forms of data—such as relational databases or spreadsheets. For analytical testing, auditors use both spreadsheets and specialized tools. To verify the accuracy of processing, auditors feed test transactions or test data through the system and observe if they are handled correctly. The problem of developing good test data is the same problem faced during system development, and many of the same methods apply. Data integrity is verified through analytical testing and through tools provided by DBMSs and other generalized software.

Instead of gathering evidence only during periodic audits, *concurrent auditing* tests processing as it occurs and data as they are used. This more timely testing can detect errors and problems before they propagate through the system. One form of concurrent auditing, called an *integrated test facility,* involves creating dummy entities, such as employee, customer, or department. During normal operation, test data for the dummy entities (known only to the auditor) is processed along with real data for real entities. Another concurrent auditing technique (which can be used with the integrated test facility) embeds audit modules in system or application software to collect data about transactions as they are processed. *Continuous process auditing* takes concurrent auditing further by continuously gathering and analyzing financial data, detecting anomalies, and alerting the auditor to key results.

Auditor participation in systems development

Auditors have two kinds of involvement with systems development. They participate in the development of application systems, and they evaluate the system development process in general.

It has been argued that participation in systems development compromises the auditor's independence. This is a valid argument, but other arguments are overriding. Without auditor participation during development, the resulting system may lack proper safeguarding controls and may be difficult to audit. Once the system has been built, incorporating controls and auditability is far more costly, and it may not ever happen. For that reason, some companies give priority to system development audits over operational audits. Independence can be enhanced if different auditors participate in system development and in later audits.

A U.S. government task force studied the problem of developing controlled and auditable systems—especially large systems that handle sensitive information. The study resulted in an auditing guide (Ruthberg et al. 1988) organized around the phases of the system development life cycle (SDLC), as shown in Table 13.3. The guide includes some activities that could be handled by security designers, but auditors have a different constituency and a different view of financial controls and system auditability. We present some points from the guide, along with other comments.

One role of the auditor is to ensure that a new system is both needed and cost-justified. This means including security controls in the needs statement and doing a risk analysis. To be valid, a cost justification must take into account security risks and controls. The auditor

TABLE 13.3 Primary Audit Objective of Each SDLC Phase

Phase	Primary audit objective
Initiation	Ensure that the system need is established and that the cost to satisfy that need is justified
Definition	Ensure that users' needs have been clearly defined and translated into requirements statements which incorporate adequate controls and conform to established standards
System design	Ensure that system requirements are adequately incorporated into design specifications, including controls that ensure auditability
Programming and training	1. Ensure that the program/system fully implements the design specifications 2. Ensure that documentation and training provide for a usable and maintainable system
Evaluation and acceptance	Ensure that the total system and data are validated as fully meeting all user and internal-control-related requirements
Installation and operation	[Not specified]

SOURCE: From Ruthberg et al. (1988)

makes sure that risks are not underestimated in order to justify the project. The auditor also evaluates whether management has set up a project control structure that can lead to a secure system.

Functional requirements for security and internal control benefit from an auditing viewpoint on separation of duty and minimizing error. The auditor ensures consideration of the new system's effect on people's jobs, and thus their attitudes. The auditor ensures that the system incorporates the traditional financial controls; that sensitive and critical data, assets, and processes are identified; and that the effect of system failure is considered.

The main auditing goal in the design phase is for the controls of the system definition to be represented in the design. The auditor ensures that the system will be auditable: that it maintains an audit trail and that it includes components that capture and analyze data specifically for audit purposes. The auditor may help design these components or may advise purchasing them. The auditor verifies that the user interfaces contribute to data integrity—that they help elicit correct input and do not produce misleading output. The auditor's scope includes both components developed in-house and purchased ones. For purchased software, the auditor ensures that the security, controls, and auditability features of competing products are compared.

The auditor ensures that the project development teams are rationally organized, with separation of duties, and that the developers are qualified. The auditor reviews development logs to verify that the project follows its development methodology and standards, including its change control procedures. With regard to testing, the auditor: reviews the plan and standards, interviews the people involved, and reviews the results; designs tests to validate the most important system functions; and verifies that tests have been done for backup and recovery, system failure, and the contingency plan. The auditor verifies that the system implementation is complete.

People need training to use a new system. The auditor reviews the training plan and the user documentation. Other aspects of conversion, especially security measures, also need to be audited. Once the system is operational, a postinstallation review verifies that the controls are working as they should, and the auditor designs a strategy for ongoing system auditing.

This description of life-cycle auditing applies to large development organizations developing large systems. For applications developed by end users, auditors play a different role, since they cannot be involved in all projects. What they can do is to make user-developers aware of security needs and of the controls that are possible.

Vulnerability Testing

A system's security is not just a function of its hardware and software security features. The security of a specific system at a specific moment depends on how those features are deployed and how people use them. History is full of examples of bad deployment and use: insecure default security options that were never changed, bug fixes never installed, inappropriate file access rights, and weak passwords. Over the years, security professionals have developed procedures and tools for detecting these holes in systems. As systems grow in number and complexity, automated tools for *vulnerability testing* become essential. Both security administrators and auditors test systems for vulnerability.

Testing approaches

Vulnerability tests can be passive or active. A passive test examines the system statically, looking for dangerous conditions. An active test probes the system, trying to exploit a vulnerability. For example, a passive test would analyze the password file off line, looking for weak passwords. An active test would try to change an account password to a weak one, or try to break in by exploiting weak passwords. Although active tests can be extremely effective, they are also risky. An active test that exploits a vulnerability is a weapon if an attacker gets hold of it.

Often, a single administrator must test for vulnerabilities at many network hosts. Each host can be probed from the administrator's site, or tests can be run at each host and the results sent to the administrator's site. Either way, security of communications is crucial, since traces of tests or reports of vulnerabilities could be highly valuable to an intruder.

Testing techniques

Some of the main items to test are

1. *System configurations.* For example, what are the default rights for access to new files? Is remote access inadvertently allowed where not intended?
2. *Login scripts.* Since a login script is always executed, it is a good place for an attacker to plant a Trojan horse. The main goal of the testing is to ensure that only the owner can modify the file—and all the other files that the script invokes. The actions of the script can also be audited. Does it, for example, set weak default file protection for files to be created?
3. *Security fixes.* As vulnerabilities are discovered in operating systems and network operating systems, the vendors develop and distribute security fixes. System administrators may not realize that the fixes apply to their systems, or they just may not get around to installing them. A passive test checks the system files' sizes and checksums to verify that the fixes are in. An active test tries to exploit the vulnerability.
4. *Changes to files.* Certain files, including executable ones, are not supposed to change. If baseline checksums have been computed (when the files were considered to be intact) the vulnerability test compares the current checksums with the baseline checksums.
5. *Passwords.* Password files can be examined to find passwords that are vulnerable to attack.

These are only the most general items; every system has many specific items to test.

Vulnerability testing should be done regularly (monthly, weekly, or even daily), with critical systems tested the most frequently and thoroughly. Testing is also needed at certain special times. When new system software is installed, a new change-detection baseline must be computed, and the security settings must be rechecked. Testing is needed after any intrusion, or suspected intrusion, because a Trojan horse may have been planted. Testing can use both general and customized software. A general vulnerability-testing tool is a collection of tests plus an analyzer that combines the results of the tests to assess overall vulnerability. *COPS* (Computer Oracle and Password System), which tests UNIX systems, is in the public domain and is distributed with some UNIX products. Tripwire (described in Chap. 8) detects file changes. *Security Profile Inspector* (SPI), which comes in UNIX and VMS versions, was developed by the U.S. Department of Energy and has limited availability. SPI includes the following tests:

- *Access control:* determines if there is any path by which a specific insecure state can be reached, given the existing file permissions and ownerships and group memberships.
- *Binary authentication:* checks authenticity of system object files and currency of patches, using checksum tables.
- *Change detection:* detects changes to file attributes such as permissions, ownerships, modification time, and checksums. Also detects new and missing files.
- *Password security inspection:* tries to crack user passwords using dictionaries and variants of words from the user's account.
- *Quick system profile:* tests for operating system vulnerabilities.

SATAN (Security Administrator Tool for Analyzing Networks) attracted much anxious attention when it became available on the Internet, because it can help crackers as well as administrators. SATAN probes other systems, over the network. It tests for more vulnerabilities than earlier tools (but they are all previously known vulnerabilities), and it allows new tests to be added by users. SATAN can proceed from probing one system to probing other systems that it trusts. SATAN has an easy-to-use World Wide Web interface.

Intrusion Detection

Misuse must be detected quickly to contain damage, act against perpetrators, and prevent more exploitation of the same vulnerabilities. Vulnerability testing reveals only known types of vulnerabilities, and only potential—not actual—misuse. The audit trail is a rich source of information, but auditors do not have the time to study it promptly or thoroughly, and some of what it has to reveal is not apparent. *Intrusion detection systems* (IDSs) automatically collect traces of user activity and analyze them, trying to identify instances of misuse. (The name *intrusion detection* is a bit misleading, since IDSs look for insider misuse as well as intrusion by outsiders.) Although it is still a research area, intrusion detection promises to become an important security measure.

Approaches

The main problem to be solved in intrusion detection is this: given the actions recorded in the audit trail, how does the IDS recognize an instance of misuse? There are distinct ways to approach this problem:

1. Detect statistical anomalies. The thesis here is that misuse activity is unusual for the purported user. This is reasonable; human auditors do look for the unusual in reviewing audit trails. If an intrusion detection system develops profiles of normal behavior from historical data, it can recognize departures from the norm.
2. Use expert systems whose knowledge is derived from expert human auditors. The expert system tries to do what the auditor would do, more promptly, and with greater speed, scope, and accuracy (see Fig. 13.3).
3. Develop models of intrusions, based on past intrusions, and build systems that can recognize occurrences that fit the models. The term *signature* is used for the pattern of events of an attack.
4. Build systems that learn to recognize intrusion patterns, using methods such as neural networks.
5. Use a composite approach. Several approaches can be used together. For example, whatever their main focus, most intrusion detection systems include an expert system component. The composite system must integrate the results from the different approaches.

System design issues

Issues arise about how to construct an intrusion detection system.

Sources of data. Intrusion detection works on data about user actions, such as logins or file reads. Ideally, an IDS would obtain whatever data would be most useful. But an IDS has to take what it can get: what the operating system provides, or what can be observed passing over a network. The information may not be at the level the IDS needs. For example, an IDS monitoring a LAN sees packets and needs to interpret packet sequences as significant entities such as network service requests. The validity of the data cannot be assumed; if a sys-

> Expert systems use techniques from artificial intelligence, including automatic logical processing, or inference. A part of the expert system, called the *inference engine,* processes the knowledge available to it using the rules of inference and generalized methods of searching for problem solutions. An expert system is developed by building a knowledge base, which typically consists of **if-then** rules that express the expert knowledge. When the conditions of its **if** part hold, a rule *fires,* and its **then** part is executed.

Figure 13.3 Expert system

tem is penetrated, its audit trail could be turned off or subverted. An IDS may be unable to interpret network traffic that is encrypted.

Target systems and auditing systems. Intrusion detection involves much data and much computation. To do it on the *target* system—the one being audited—would be to risk an unacceptable performance hit. (Even generating accounting records is more than some system managers are willing to do.) Also, the IDS would be vulnerable to subversion by the very intruders it is trying to detect, and a version of the IDS would have to be developed for each different type of audited system. To avoid these problems, and to allow one IDS to audit multiple target systems at once, most IDSs analyze the audit data on a dedicated system. An IDS component on each target system gathers the data, does some preliminary analysis, possibly reduces the data, and converts the data to a common format for use by the auditing system. Even with this architecture, if the target-system component is not trusted, or the data path is not trusted, the results are vulnerable.

Intrusion detection systems

Several prototype intrusion detection systems have been built and used, and at least one is a commercial product. The following sections describe some of the IDSs, and others appear in the bibliographic notes.

The IDES model and IDES/NIDES systems. The anomaly-detection approach was articulated in a model developed by Dorothy Denning. The model provided a framework for SRI's *IDES* (Intrusion Detection Expert System) project and its successor *NIDES,* and for other intrusion detection work.

The IDES model. The model has six components: *subjects* (normally users), *objects* (such as files), *audit records* that are generated by the target system, *profiles* of subject behavior, *anomaly records* that are generated when abnormal behavior is detected, and *activity rules* that drive the actions of the intrusion detection system.

An audit record represents an action by a subject on an object. For example, an audit record might represent login, or the execution of a specific program. The audit record specifies the resources used (such as records written or CPU time) and any exception conditions raised by the action.

An activity profile characterizes the "normal" activity of a subject on an object, in terms of a metric and a statistical model of a random variable. Types of metrics are: event counter (such as the number of password failures in a minute), interval timer (how long between two related events), and resource measure (such as CPU time consumed by the execution of a program). The statistical model specifies how abnormal values of a metric are recognized. For example, using a "mean and standard deviation" model, an observation would be considered abnormal if it deviated from the mean by more than some threshold number of standard deviations. The profile also specifies which audit events are measured by the random variable. Finally, a "value" component of the profile represents the distribution of previous values, as learned from previous audit records that match this profile.

Although its behavior is specified by activity rules, the IDES *model* is not an expert system in the sense of expressing expertise in rules.

The IDES system. IDES consists of a "realm interface" component, a statistical anomaly detector, an expert system anomaly detector, and a user interface. Audit data are collected by the realm interface component, which is split between the target machine and the IDES processor. Data are collected about: file access, system access (login, logout, change to/from superuser status), resource consumption, and process creation. When auditing a Sun UNIX system, IDES uses data logged by the SunOS auditing system, the UNIX accounting system, and an auditing facility that Sun developed to meet TCSEC Class C2 requirements.

The statistical component. The NIDES statistical component identifies anomalous behavior by comparison with historical norms. This component has no knowledge of intrusive behavior (since that is in an expert system component) but relies totally on the audit records. It develops profiles of subjects' long-term behavior and compares them, in real time, with subjects' short-term behavior, interpreting a large discrepancy as cause for an alert. NIDES works with single events, such as file reads or logins, not grouping the events into higher-level events. An event is described by a fairly long vector of measures (some listed in Table 13.4), and subject profiles contain

TABLE 13.4 Examples of Measures Used by the IDES Statistical Component

Counting measures
CPU usage
I/O usage
Categorical measures
Physical location of use
Window command usage
General system call usage
File usage, by file name
Remote network activity by type
Intensity measure
Volume of audit records per unit of time

summary statistics for the measures. Profiles are updated daily, and they go through an aging process that gives greater weight to more recent history.

Using all or some of the measures, NIDES develops a statistic T^2 that summarizes the abnormality of a subject's "near past" behavior. T^2 is the average of statistics that describe the abnormality on each of the measures for recent behavior, such as the last 20 remote logins or the last 500 file accesses. When T^2 exceeds some threshold, an alert is generated.

Although these methods have been reasonably successful, the purely statistical approach has drawbacks. Some users have such erratic work patterns that it is almost impossible to detect deviations from them. An insider with knowledge of the monitoring could deliberately behave so as to alter his long-term profile in the direction of the intended misuse. The IDES project has broadened its approach by including an expert system and by investigating model-based reasoning and neural-network approaches.

Wisdom and Sense. *Wisdom and Sense* (W&S) was developed at Los Alamos National Laboratory. Like IDES, W&S uses statistical methods to decide which events are anomalous. It automatically generates a rule base, from historical data about a system. Very many overlapping and redundant rules are generated for a target system. Some of these appear meaningless, but are still useful in detecting misuse. W&S generates its rules by examining how field values are associated in the historical data. The left-hand side of each rule specifies the conditions (in terms of audit record field values) for the rule to fire, and the right-hand side the conclusions (also field values). The intent is for human auditors to review the rule base and also to add their own rules.

Some rules are more valuable than others as evidence of anomaly. When a rule fires, W&S determines if the conclusion is satisfied—if the audit record passes or fails the rule. Each rule is assigned a passing strength and a failing strength, based on its historical rates of passing and failing. W&S prunes its rule base on the basis of strength and other criteria.

When processing audit records (transactions), W&S computes a figure of merit (FOM) for each field of a transaction. The FOM is based on the strengths of the rules failed by the field. The transaction FOM is the sum of the individual field FOMs. A large field or transaction FOM causes W&S to flag an anomaly. Unlike IDES, which works only with individual audit records, W&S aggregates individual transactions into *threads* based on field-value criteria. An example is a user session thread. A thread's FOM is computed from its constituent transaction FOMs, and a large thread FOM also indicates an anomaly.

HAYSTACK. Another system based on anomaly detection is *HAYSTACK,* developed for auditing of U.S. Air Force computers. HAYSTACK analyzes entire user sessions, measuring about two dozen features, such as time of work, number of files created, and pages printed. Unlike IDES and W&S, HAYSTACK maintains profiles of specific types of intrusions and compares each session against these. Each feature is assigned (not automatically) a weight for relevance in detecting each intrusion type; these weights constitute the profile. Users who have similar system privileges and work characteristics—such as "day shift accounting data entry"—are grouped together. From historical data, HAYSTACK computes the expected range of each security feature for each security group.

For each session, HAYSTACK computes a "suspicion quotient" describing how closely the session resembles one of the profiled intrusions. The quotient is based on (1) which features were outside the expected range for the security group and (2) how closely these feature results resemble the profile of the intrusion. HAYSTACK also looks for trends in a user's behavior, comparing recent sessions to earlier ones.

Network Security Monitor. The systems described so far obtain their raw data from audit trails of individual systems. Another source of data is network traffic. In a LAN environment, for example, any local intrusion or misuse would be reflected in LAN activity. Using network traffic as a source has several advantages. Since network traffic follows standard protocols, there is no need to convert data in auditing heterogeneous systems. The data are available immediately and cannot be turned off or changed. There is no performance degradation.

Single-system IDSs can fail to detect common attacks that are launched over networks, such as the "doorknob" attack, which may fall below the threshold for each host's intrusion detection. Only when the network is considered as a whole is the intrusion revealed.

Network Security Monitor (NSM), developed at the University of California, Davis, observes packets on a LAN and derives from them higher-level objects, such as connections, and representations of network activity at individual hosts and on the network as a whole. These objects are one type of input to an expert system. The expert system uses profiles describing what services (such as **Telnet** or **mail**) look like, what network activity is expected, how much capability each service provides, and what level of authentication it requires. The expert system knows a security level for each computer, and it knows signatures of past attacks. It uses all of its knowledge to identify likely intrusive behavior.

NSM has performed well on a LAN at UC Davis. Two limitations are that it cannot detect attacks via remote access (which might generate no LAN traffic) and it cannot analyze encrypted traffic.

Distributed Intrusion Detection System. *Distributed Intrusion Detection System* (DIDS) widens the scope of monitoring to include both the LAN and the networked hosts. With DIDS, each host does its own monitoring, data reduction, and some analysis, and a centralized component does higher-level analysis. DIDS models the target environment more explicitly than the other IDSs we have described.

Figure 13.4 shows the components of DIDS: a *host monitor* for each host, a *LAN monitor* for each LAN segment, and a centralized *director* that does high-level analysis. The DIDS design puts as much of the work as possible on the host and LAN monitors. A host monitor selects events on its machine to communicate to the director, and it reports on anomalous session behavior, which it detects using the HAYSTACK algorithm. The LAN monitor audits connections, network services used, and traffic volume. The director includes an expert system that draws conclusions about the security of each host and about the system as a whole.

Host monitors transform their raw audit data into higher-level *events*; events are actions (such as session-start or read) on categories of objects. This transformation lets the expert system work at a higher level of abstraction, and with less operating-system dependence.

The LAN monitor, which is based on NSM, reports to the director on significant events, including the use of **Telnet** or **rlogin,** use of security-related services, and changes in network traffic patterns.

The director expert system tries to arrive at high-level hypotheses about intrusions and about the overall security of the network. The expert system rules undergo training, using feedback from the security officer about false alarms.

A system like DIDS, however successful in its own LAN, cannot track down intruders from outside the LAN. That requires network-wide cooperation.

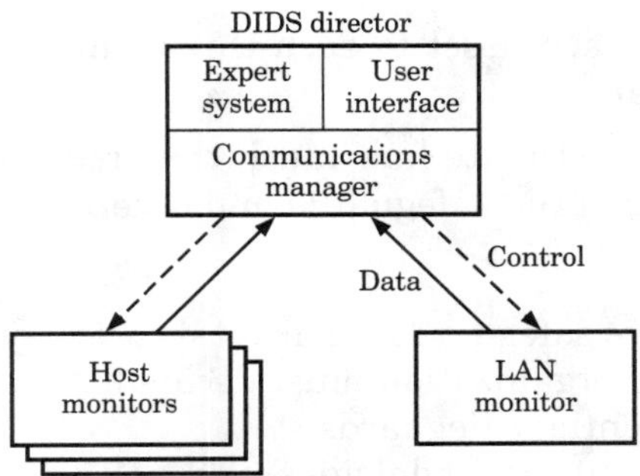

Figure 13.4 Components of the DIDS system. [*From Snapp et al. (1991).*]

Challenges. Intrusion detection research has broadened from statistical anomaly detection to include many techniques. Intrusion detection is practical and effective, although better measures of effectiveness are needed. The challenges are to build frameworks that can integrate the various techniques, to apply intrusion detection to heterogeneous wide-area networks, and to use it along with other network security activities. As more and finer analysis of users' activities becomes practical, a harder challenge is to protect users' privacy.

Summary

Four different ways to analyze and evaluate security are risk analysis, information systems auditing, vulnerability testing and intrusion detection.

The main goal of risk analysis is to help with selecting cost-effective safeguards. Risk analysis involves estimating the potential losses from threats, and how much the safeguards could reduce them. Risk analysis provides insight into security and improves security awareness; sometimes it is the only way to justify expenditures on security.

Risk analysis often measures risk in terms of an *annual loss expectancy* (ALE), which is the loss, in money units, that can be expected in a year. Safeguards can affect the ALE by affecting the likelihood of the threat, or its impact, or both. A risk analysis involves the following steps:

1. Identify the assets and assign monetary values to them.
2. Identify the threats and the vulnerabilities. Estimate the likelihood of each threat. For each asset vulnerable to the threat, estimate the impact of the threat.
3. Calculate the exposure (ALE) of each asset to each threat, in the absence of any additional safeguards.
4. Identify potential safeguards and estimate how much they reduce the exposures. Estimate the costs of the safeguards and determine which ones are cost-effective.

Even considering only cost-effective safeguards, their total cost may well exceed the available funds. The organization must decide how to allocate its resources among the potential safeguards.

Most risk analysis uses structured methodologies and software tools that gather and store data, compute risk measures, evaluate cost-effectiveness, and present the results in effective form.

An important risk analysis methodology is CRAMM, a U.K. government standard. A CRAMM analysis begins with identifying the assets, assigning values to them, and determining potential impacts. Using a built-in list of threats, CRAMM software generates questionnaires that elicit the vulnerability of each asset group to each threat. The software then calculates a risk number for each impact. Finally, existing countermeasures and others from CRAMM's database are considered. A countermeasure can reduce risk by making a threat less likely, reducing its impact, detecting an occurrence, or facilitating recovery.

Risk analysis methodologies have been criticized for lack of integration with system development methodologies, inadequate modeling, and inadequate support for valuing assets and determining impact. The checklists or databases of threats and safeguards must be updated frequently. Safeguards do not fit into a security architecture. More fundamentally, the statistical basis of risk analysis does not apply to deliberate threats. The danger of rare, but catastrophic, threats tends to be obscured. The estimates that go into a risk analysis are not validated. The cost-benefit approach can be short-sighted, and it is narrowly applied. If used wisely, though, risk analysis contributes to secure designs and effective security management.

Information systems auditing grew out of traditional financial auditing. External auditors are independent of the organizations they audit. Internal auditors work for the organization that they audit, but are somewhat independent. The auditor must evaluate the organization's system of internal control, which is intended to ensure that the organization operates effectively, complies with laws and regulations, and prepares reliable financial data. The financial auditing process has three main phases: understanding the internal control structure, assessing control risk, and substantive testing. If internal controls are strong, the auditor can reduce the amount of substantive testing. With substantive testing, the auditor collects evidence to form and support an opinion on the financial statements.

After gaining an understanding of how the controls are supposed to work, an IS auditor does compliance testing—determining if the controls work the way they are supposed to. Auditing standards require auditors to report any significant deficiencies in the internal control system. Finally, the auditor does substantive testing. This includes identifying erroneous processing, assessing data integrity, and comparing data with outside sources and with real assets. To be auditable, automated systems must provide counterparts to traditional paper evidence.

Auditors participate in the system development process. One role is to ensure that a new system is both needed and cost-justified. To be valid, a cost-justification must take into account security risks and controls. Auditors should participate in each stage of the systems development life cycle, addressing the controls of both the system being developed and the development process.

The security of a system at a specific moment depends on how its security features are deployed and how people use them. Vulnerability testing analyzes these aspects. A passive test examines the system statically, and an active test probes, trying to exploit a vulnerability. Vulnerability testing should be done regularly and also at special times, such as when new system software is installed, and after any intrusion. A general vulnerability-testing tool is a collection of tests plus an analyzer. Examples are COPS, Security Profile Inspector, and SATAN.

Intrusion detection systems (IDSs) automatically collect traces of user activity and analyze them, trying to identify instances of misuse. The main approaches to identifying misuse are: detect statistical anomalies; use expert systems whose knowledge is derived from human auditors; develop models of intrusions, based on past intrusions, and build systems that can recognize occurrences that fit the models; build systems that learn to recognize intrusions. The approaches can be used together.

Several prototype IDSs have been built and used. IDES (Intrusion Detection Expert System) includes both a statistical anomaly detector and an expert system anomaly detector. The statistical approach alone cannot cope with erratic work patterns and could be subverted by an insider with knowledge of the monitoring. IDES collects data about file access, system access, resource consumption, and process creation. The statistical component identifies anomalous behavior by comparison with historical norms. It develops profiles of users' long-term behavior and compares them with short-term behavior. Wisdom and Sense also uses statistical methods to decide which events are anomalous. It automatically generates a rule base from historical data about a system, tracks performance of each rule, and eliminates weaker rules. HAYSTACK maintains profiles of specific types of intrusions and compares each user session against these.

Network traffic is a good source of activity traces, and network monitors can detect attacks that single-system monitors cannot detect. Network Security Monitor observes packets on a LAN. It includes an expert system that knows about services, expected network activity, and signatures of past attacks. Another prototype, DIDS, combines LAN and host monitoring. Each host does its own monitoring, data reduction, and some analysis, and a centralized component does higher-level analysis.

The research results indicate that intrusion detection is practical and effective. The challenges are more integration and broader application, without endangering privacy.

Bibliographic Notes

Risk analysis

Baskerville (1993) analyzes the history of security design methods, including risk analysis, relating security methods to generations of system design methods. This survey article also describes risk analysis methodologies and tools. Anderson (1991) analyzes existing risk analysis methodologies and their strengths and (mostly) weaknesses. He suggests attributes for ideal methodologies and tools. Fites and Kratz (1993) cover risk analysis. Our risk analysis example is adapted from Cooper (1989). Some risk analysis methodologies are based on a U.S. government publication, FIPS 65 (National Bureau of Standards 1979), which in turn was based on work by Robert Courtney of IBM (Courtney 1977). The FIPS 65 publication contains a thorough (but dated) outline of risks.

Bodeau (1992) and Bodeau and Chase (1993) describe the modeling constructs used in a prototype risk analysis tool. The tool is intended for analysis of complex "systems of systems." Dennison and Toth (1991) propose risk and threat models and a risk analysis methodology. A selection from the RISKS forum appears in Neumann (1995a).

Gilbert (1989) reviews what is desirable in a risk analysis tool, and Gardner (1989) describes five software packages. CRAMM is described by Charette (1990) and Baskerville (1993). ARiES is described by Lavine et al. (1994). Charette (1991) describes the risks involved in using risk analysis. Baskerville (1991) argues that, although risk analysis flunks when evaluated by the rules of natural science, it is a valuable social artifact for communication between security designers and managers.

Information systems auditing

Textbooks on EDP auditing are Weber (1988) and Watne and Turney (1990). Perry (1988) provides a manual for application auditing. Bodnar (1992) reviews the Institute of Internal Auditors' 1991 study of control and audit practices, which found managers' top control concerns to be data security and contingency planning. Studying 114 fraud cases, Calderon and Green (1994) found that 45 percent involved managerial and professional employees, and that the greatest exposures were inadequate internal controls and poor separation of duties. Davis and Dykman (1993) describe what an IS auditor does. Morris (1992) summarizes the phases of an IS audit. Cerullo and Cerullo (1992) asked audit experts to rank in importance the factors to consider in an EDP operational audit. The highest-ranked factors were data security, physical security, and data control. Roufaiel and Dorweiler (1994) describe laws and standards that pertain to the external auditor's responsibilities regarding internal control. Rezaee (1994) describes a revised definition of internal control that integrates different viewpoints. Warner (1992) discusses auditing standards relating to service organizations that process transactions for others.

The system development life cycle and methods for developing secure systems are described in Chap. 6. Ruthberg et al. (1988) present a general prescription for system development audits that can be customized to specific environments.

Vulnerability testing

Much of our discussion of vulnerability testing is based on Polk (1992). CERT (1995) tells how to assess site vulnerability, summarizes common vulnerabilities, and lists useful tools. SATAN is described by its authors, Farmer and Venema, and by Fisher (1995), who also discusses safeguards against SATAN. Neumann (1995b) summarizes the debate about openness of vulnerability information and testing tools. Automated change detection is described in Chap. 8, along with other services that support vulnerability testing.

Intrusion detection

Mukherjee, Heberlein, and Levitt (1994) provide a comprehensive survey of intrusion detection systems. Lunt (1993) reviews approaches to intrusion detection, and Lunt (1988) reviews early work.

Denning (1987) describes the IDES model. The IDES system is described by Lunt and Jagannathan (1988) and Lunt et al. (1992). The NIDES statistical component is described by Javitz and Valdes (1991, 1994). Anderson et al. (1993) describe a test of the statistical component where its task was to consider applications (not users) as subjects and to detect the unauthorized use of applications. Garvey and Lunt (1991) propose using model-based reasoning for intrusion detection.

Vaccaro and Liepins (1989) describe Wisdom and Sense, and Liepins and Vaccaro (1992) give results of tests of the W&S approach. Helman et al. (1992) present a formalism for intrusion detection. They model computer transactions as a stochastic process that is a mixture of two auxiliary stochastic processes: normal transactions and misuse transactions. Misuse detector functions estimate the likelihood of a transaction being a misuse transaction.

Smaha (1988, 1990) describes HAYSTACK. Smaha and Winslow (1994) describe a commercially available misuse detection tool.

Network attacks are discussed in Chaps. 3 and 10. Snapp et al. (1991) and Mukherjee et al. (1994) describe the DIDS architecture and summarize its detection methods. Ko et al. (1993) describe the algorithm used by DIDS to recognize a single user across various network manifestations, and to correctly attribute network activity. The network security monitor (NSM) on which the LAN monitor is based is described by Heberlein et al. (1990), Heberlein et al. (1991), and Mukherjee et al. (1994). Heberlein et al. (1992) describe the Internet Security Monitor model, which extends DIDS and NSM concepts to large-scale networks. White et al. (1996) describe a distributed IDS that does not rely on a central director. Ko et al. (1994) describe an approach for detecting vulnerabilities in privileged UNIX programs; the audit trail for a program is compared with what is expected from a model of the program's behavior.

Hochberg et al. (1993) describe the NADIR expert system, developed to help auditors of a network at Los Alamos National Laboratory. Winkler (1990) and Winkler and Landry (1992) describe the Information Security Officer's Assistant (ISOA). Tsudik and Summers (1990) describe an expert system developed at IBM for auditing RACF reports. Teng et al. (1990) describe a system that builds its rule base by rule induction on historical audit data and that deals with sequences of events. The system can relate a specific event to a generalized description. For example, JOHN ISSUES THE COMMAND EMACS AT 2 PM becomes A MEMBER OF THE XYZ PROJECT INVOKES AN EDITOR DURING BUSINESS HOURS. This description allows the event to be checked against a security policy. Dowell and Ramstedt (1990) describe the ComputerWatch expert system developed and marketed by AT&T for its System V/MLS system. Neural network methods for intrusion detection are described by Debar, Becker, and Siboni (1992), and a pattern-oriented model by Shieh and Gligor (1991). Porras and Kemmerer (1992) describe an approach that models intrusions as series of state transitions. Kumar and Spafford (1994) describe a pattern-matching model. Frank (1994) surveys the use of AI in IDSs for data reduction and behavior classification. Schaefer (1992) discusses intrusion detection and other monitoring in relation to employee privacy.

Exercises

13.1 Give a rationale for defining risk as the annual loss expectancy (ALE). Try to come up with a different definition that fits our intuitive notions about risk.

13.2 Describe the factors that go into assigning values to intangible assets for a risk analysis.

13.3 What techniques can be used in a risk analysis to compensate for the roughness of likelihood estimates?

13.4 In relation to assumptions about their probability, how do computer security threats differ from threats such as fire or flood?

13.5 Using the risk analysis model and methodology of ARiES, do a risk analysis for the information system of a college library. The system, which uses a mainframe and terminals, handles cataloging and circulation. It is connected to the Internet. Consider five threats and some existing safeguards. Propose new safeguards and determine if they are cost-effective.

13.6 What is meant by the term *control environment?* Why is it important for computer security?

13.7 Compare "continuous process auditing" with intrusion detection. What are their similarities and differences?

13.8 Why should auditors participate in system development?

13.9 Which of the operating system services described in Chap. 8 are most important in making a system auditable? Are operating system services enough?

13.10 Assume you are assigned to test the vulnerability of a system to unauthorized file access. Describe a passive test and an active test to learn if sensitive files are world-writable.

13.11 Compare the IDES and DIDS systems in their allocation of responsibility between target system and auditing system.

13.12 What are some criticisms of a purely statistical approach to intrusion detection?

13.13 What is meant by "training" of rules in an IDS? Explain how training works in Wisdom & Sense.

13.14 Summarize the advantages and disadvantages of using LAN traffic as a data source for intrusion detection.

References

Anderson, A. M. 1991. Comparing risk analysis methodologies. *Information Security: Proceedings of the IFIP TC11 Seventh International Conference on Information Security, IFIP/Sec '91,* 301–311. Amsterdam: North-Holland.

Anderson, Debra, Teresa F. Lunt, Harold Javitz, Ann Tamaru, and Alfonso Valdes. 1993. *Safeguard Final Report: Detecting Unusual Program Behavior Using the NIDES Statistical Component.* Report, December 1993. Menlo Park, Calif.: SRI International.

Baskerville, Richard. 1991. Risk analysis as a source of professional knowledge. *Computers & Security* **10**(8): 749–764.

______. 1993. Information systems security design methods: Implications for information systems development. *ACM Computing Surveys* **25**(4): 375–414.

Bodeau, Deborah J. 1992. A conceptual model for computer security risk analysis. *Proceedings of the Eighth Annual Computer Security Applications Conference,* 56–63. Los Alamitos, Calif.: IEEE Computer Society.

Bodeau, Deborah J., and Frederick N. Chase. 1993. Modeling constructs for describing a complex system-of-systems. *Proceedings of the Ninth Annual Computer Security Applications Conference,* 140–148. Los Alamitos, Calif.: IEEE Computer Society.

Bodnar, George H. 1992. SAC II: Systems auditability and control report. *Internal Auditing,* Summer: 75–80.

Calderon, Thomas G., and Brian P. Green. 1994. Internal fraud leaves its mark: Here's how to spot, trace and prevent it. *National Public Accountant* **39**(8): 17–19.

CERT. 1995. *CERT Coordination Center Generic Security Information.* January 1995. Carnegie Mellon University Software Engineering Institute.

Cerullo, Virginia, and Michael J. Cerullo. 1992. Factors considered in EDP operational reviews. *EDP Auditor Journal* **III:** 53–65.

Charette, Robert N. 1990. *Applications Strategies for Risk Analysis.* New York: McGraw-Hill.

Charette, Robert. 1991. The risks with risk analysis. *Communications of the ACM* **34**(6): 106.

Cooper, James Arlin. 1989. *Computer and Communications Security: Strategies for the 1990s.* New York: McGraw-Hill.

Courtney Jr., R. H. 1977. Security risk assessment in electronic data processing systems. In *AFIPS Conference Proceedings,* **46,** 97–104. Montvale, N.J.: AFIPS Press.

Davies, Donald W. 1991. Information security—theory and practice. In Lindsay, David T. and Wyn L. Price, eds. *Information security: Proceedings of the IFIP TC11 Seventh International Conference on Information Security, IFIP/Sec '91,* 461–467. Amsterdam: North-Holland.

Davis, Charles K., and Charlene A. Dykman. 1993. Information systems auditors: Friend or foe. *Journal of Systems Management* **44**(6): 25–27.

Debar, Hervé, Monique Becker, and Didier Siboni. 1992. A neural network component for an intrusion detection system. *Proceedings of the 1992 IEEE Computer Society Symposium on Research in Security and Privacy,* 240–250. Los Alamitos, Calif.: IEEE Computer Society.

Denning, Dorothy E. 1987. An intrusion-detection model. *IEEE Transactions on Software Engineering* **SE-13**(2): 222–232.

Dennison, Mark W. L., and Kalman C. Toth. 1991. Practical models for threat/risk analysis. *Proceedings 14th National Computer Security Conference,* 427–435. NIST/NCSC.

Dowell, Cheri, and Paul Ramstedt. 1990. The ComputerWatch data reduction tool. *Proceedings of the 13th National Computer Security Conference,* 99–108. NIST/NCSC.

Farmer, Dan, and Wietse Venema. *Improving the security of your site by breaking into it.* Electronic document posted at FIRST WWW site.

Fisher, John. 1995. *A Look at SATAN.* CIAC Notes Number 95-07, March 29, 1995. U.S. DOE's Computer Incident Advisory Capability.

Fites, Philip E., and Martin P. J. Kratz. 1993. *Information Systems Security: A Practitioner's Reference.* New York: Van Nostrand Reinhold.

Frank, Jeremy. 1994. Artificial intelligence and intrusion detection: Current and future directions. *Proceedings of the 17th National Computer Security Conference,* 22–33. NIST/NCSC.

Gardner, Phillip E. 1989. Evaluation of five risk assessment programs. *Computers & Security* **8:** 479–485.

Garvey, Thomas D., and Teresa F. Lunt. 1991. Model-based intrusion detection. *Proceedings of the 14th National Computer Security Conference,* 372–385. NIST/NCSC.

Gilbert, Irene E. 1989. *Guide for Selecting Automated Risk Analysis Tools.* NIST Special Publication 500-174. Gaithersburg, Md.: National Institute of Standards and Technology.

Heberlein, L. Todd, Gihan V. Dias, Karl N. Levitt, Biswanath Mukherjee, Jeff Wood, and David Wolber. 1990. A network security monitor. *Proceedings of the 1990 IEEE Computer Society Symposium on Research in Security and Privacy,* 296–304. Los Alamitos, Calif.: IEEE Computer Society.

Heberlein, L. T., K. N. Levitt, and B. Mukherjee. 1991. A method to detect intrusive activity in a networked environment. *Proceedings of the 14th National Computer Security Conference,* 362–371. NIST/NCSC.

Heberlein, L. T., B. Mukherjee, and K. N. Levitt. 1992. Internet security monitor: An intrusion-detection system for large-scale networks. *Proceedings of the 15th National Computer Security Conference,* 262–271. NIST/NCSC.

Helman, Paul, Gunar Liepins, and Wynette Richards. 1992. Foundations of intrusion detection. *The Computer Security Foundations Workshop V,* 114–120. Los Alamitos, Calif.: IEEE Computer Society.

Hochberg, Judith, Kathleen Jackson, Cathy Stallings, J. F. McClary, David DuBois, and Josephine Ford. 1993. NADIR: an automated system for detecting network intrusion and misuse. *Computers & Security* **12:** 235–248.

Javitz, Harold S., and Alfonso Valdes. 1991. The SRI IDES statistical anomaly detector. *Proceedings of the 1991 IEEE Computer Society Symposium on Research in Security and Privacy,* 316–326. Los Alamitos, Calif.: IEEE Computer Society.

______. 1994. *The NIDES Statistical Component: Description and Justification.* Annual Report, A010, March 1994. Menlo Park, Calif.: SRI International.

Ko, Calvin, George Fink, and Karl Levitt. 1994. Automated detection of vulnerabilities in privileged programs by execution monitoring. *Proceedings of the Tenth Annual Computer Security Applications Conference,* 134–144. Los Alamitos, Calif.: IEEE Computer Society.

Ko, Calvin, Deborah A. Frincke, Terrence Goan Jr., L. Todd Heberlein, Karl Levitt, Biswanath Mukherjee, and Christopher Wee. 1993. Analysis of an algorithm for distributed recognition and accountability. *Proceedings of the 1st ACM Conference on Computer and Communications Security,* 154–165. New York: ACM Press.

Kumar, Sandeep, and Eugene H. Spafford. 1994. A pattern matching model for misuse intrusion detection. *Proceedings of the 17th National Computer Security Conference,* 11–21. NIST/NCSC.

Lavine, Charles H., Anne M. Lindell, and Sergio B. Guarro. 1994. The Aerospace Risk Evaluation System (ARiES): Implementation of a quantitative risk analysis methodology for critical systems. *Proceedings of the 17th National Computer Security Conference,* 431–440. NIST/NCSC.

Liepins, G. E., and H. S. Vaccaro. 1992. Intrusion detection: its role and validation. *Computers & Security* **11:** 347–355.

Lunt, Teresa F. 1988. Automated audit trail analysis and intrusion detection: A survey. *Proceedings of the 11th National Computer Security Conference.* NIST/NCSC.

______. 1993. A survey of intrusion detection techniques. *Computers & Security* **12:** 405–418.

Lunt, Teresa F., and R. Jagannathan. 1988. A prototype real-time intrusion-detection expert system. *Proceedings of the 1988 IEEE Symposium on Security and Privacy,* 59–66. Los Alamitos, Calif.: IEEE Computer Society.

Lunt, Teresa F., Ann Tamaru, Fred Gilham, R. Jagannathan, Caveh Jalali, Peter G. Neumann, Harold S. Javitz, Alfonso Valdes, and Thomas D. Garvey. 1992. *A Real-Time Intrusion-Detection Expert System (IDES).* Final Technical Report, February 1992. Menlo Park, Calif.: SRI International.

Morris, Gordon F. 1992. Securing your computer system with an EDP audit. *Corporate Controller* **4**(3): 36.

Mukherjee, Biswanath, L. Todd Heberlein, and Karl N. Levitt. 1994. Network intrusion detection. *IEEE Network Magazine* **8**(3): 26–41.

National Bureau of Standards. 1979. *Guideline for Automatic Data Processing Risk Analysis.* FIPS PUB 65, August 1979. National Bureau of Standards.

National Research Council. 1991. *Computers at Risk: Safe Computing in the Information Age.* Washington, D.C.: National Academy Press.

NCSC. 1994. *Introduction to Certification and Accreditation.* NCSC-TG-029. Fort Meade, Md.: National Computer Security Center.

Neumann, Peter G. 1995a. *Computer-Related Risks.* Reading, Mass.: Addison-Wesley.

______. 1995b. Computer vulnerabilities: Exploitation or avoidance. *Communications of the ACM* **38**(6): 138.

Perry, William E. 1985. *Management Strategies for Computer Security.* Boston: Butterworth.

______. 1988. *A Standard for Auditing Computer Applications.* Boston: Auerbach.

Polk, W. Timothy. 1992. *Automated Tools for Testing Computer System Vulnerability.* NIST Special Publication 800-6. Gaithersburg, Md.: National Institute of Standards and Technology.

Porras, Phillip A., and Richard A. Kemmerer. 1992. Penetration state transition analysis: A rule-based intrusion detection approach. *Proceedings of the Eighth Annual Computer Security Applications Conference,* 220–229. Los Alamitos, Calif.: IEEE Computer Society.

Rezaee, Zabihollah. 1994. Implementing the COSO report. *Management Accounting* **76**(1): 35–37.

Roufaiel, Nazik S., and Vernon Dorweiler. 1994. White-collar computer crimes: A threat to auditors and organization. *Managerial Auditing Journal* **9**(3): 3–12.

Ruthberg, Zella G., Bonnie T. Fisher, William E. Perry, John W. Lainhart IV, James G. Cox, Mark Gillen, and Douglas B. Hunt. 1988. *Guide to Auditing for Controls and Security: A System Development Life Cycle Approach.* NBS Special Publication 500-153. Gaithersburg, Md.: National Bureau of Standards.

Schaefer, Lorrayne. 1992. Employee privacy and intrusion detection systems: Monitoring activities on the job. *EDPACS* **XX**(6): 1–7.

Shieh, Shiuhpyng Winston, and Virgil D. Gligor. 1991. Pattern-oriented intrusion-detection model and its applications. *Proceedings of the 1991 IEEE Computer Society Symposium on Research in Security and Privacy,* 327–342. Los Alamitos, Calif.: IEEE Computer Society.

Smaha, Stephen E. 1988. Haystack: An intrusion detection system. *Proceedings of the Fourth Aerospace Computer Security Applications Conference,* 37–44. Los Alamitos, Calif.: IEEE Computer Society.

______. 1990. *HAYSTACK Audit Trail Analysis System.* Status report, April 1990. Austin, Tex.: Haystack Laboratories.

Smaha, Stephen E., and Jessica Winslow. 1994. Misuse detection tools. *Computer Security Journal* **X**(1): 39–49.

Snapp, Steven R., James Brentano, Gihan V. Dias, Terrance L. Goan, L. Todd Heberlein, Che-Lin Ho, Karl N. Levitt, Biswanath Mukherjee, Stephen E. Smaha, Tim Grance, Daniel M. Teal, and Doug Mansur. 1991. DIDS (Distributed Intrusion Detection System)—motivation, architecture, and an early prototype. *Proceedings of the 14th National Computer Security Conference,* 167–176. NIST/NCSC.

Teng, Henry S., Kaihu Chen, and Stephen C.-Y. Lu. 1990. Adaptive real-time anomaly detection using inductively generated sequential patterns. *Proceedings of the 1990 IEEE Computer Society Symposium on Research in Security and Privacy,* 278–284. Los Alamitos, Calif.: IEEE Computer Society.

Tsudik, Gene, and Rita Summers. 1990. AudES—an expert system for security auditing. *Proceedings of the Second Annual Conference on Innovative Applications of Artificial Intelligence,* 71–75. Menlo Park, Calif.: American Association for Artificial Intelligence.

Vaccaro, H. S., and G. E. Liepins. 1989. Detection of anomalous computer session activity. *Proceedings of the 1989 IEEE Computer Society Symposium on Security and Privacy,* 280–289. Washington, D.C.: IEEE Computer Society.

Warner, Paul D. 1992. SAS 70: Reports on the Processing of Transactions by Service Organizations. *CPA Journal* **62**(11): 30–36.

Watne, Donald A., and Peter B. B. Turney. 1990. *Auditing EDP Systems.* 2d ed. Englewood Cliffs, N.J.: Prentice Hall.

Weber, Ron. 1988. *EDP Auditing: Conceptual Foundations and Practice.* 2d ed. New York: McGraw-Hill.

White, Gregory B., Eric A. Fisch, and Udo W. Pooch. 1996. Cooperating security managers: A peer-based intrusion detection system. *IEEE Network Magazine* **10**(1): 20–23.

Winkler, J. R. 1990. A UNIX prototype for intrusion and anomaly detection in secure networks. *Proceedings of the 13th National Computer Security Conference,* 115–124. NIST/NCSC.

Winkler, J. R., and J. C. Landry. 1992. Intrusion and anomaly detection: ISOA update. *Proceedings of the 15th National Computer Security Conference,* 272–281. NIST/NCSC.

List of Acronyms

ACC	access control center
ACL	access control list
AICPA	American Institute of Certified Public Accountants
AIS	automated information system
ALE	annual loss expectancy
ANSI	American National Standards Institute
AOS	authorization object schema
APF	Authorized Program Facility
ARiES	Aerospace Risk Evaluation System
AS	authentication server
ASD	Advanced Secure DBMS
ATM	asynchronous transfer mode
ATM	automatic teller machine
BLP	Bell-LaPadula model
C-list	capability list
CA	certification authority
CAS	Controlled Application Set
CBC	cipher block chaining
CDI	constrained data item
CFB	cipher feedback
CHAP	Challenge Handshake Authentication Protocol
CLEF	Certified Licensed Evaluation Facility
CMIP	Common Management Information Protocol
CMW	Compartmented Mode Workstation
COMPUSEC	computer security (DoD)
COMSEC	communications security (DoD)
COPS	Computer Oracle and Password System
CPL	current privilege level

CRAMM	CCTA Risk Analysis and Management Methodology
CRC	Cyclic Redundancy Check
CSMA/CD	carrier-sense multiple access with collision detection
CSO	chief security officer
CTCPEC	Canadian Trusted Computer Product Evaluation Criteria
DAC	discretionary access control
DACL	discretionary access control list
DBA	database administrator
DBMS	database management system
DCE	Distributed Computing Environment
DCL	data control language
DDL	data description language
DES	Data Encryption Standard
DGSA	DoD Goal Security Architecture
DIDS	Distributed Intrusion Detection System
DMA	direct memory access
DML	data manipulation language
DoD	Department of Defense
DPB	Denial-of-Service Protection Base
DS	descriptor segment
DSA	Digital Signature Algorithm
DSS	Digital Signature Standard
ECB	electronic codebook
ECMA	European Computer Manufacturers Association
ECPA	Electronic Communications Privacy Act
EDI	electronic data interchange
EDIFACT	EDI for Administration, Commerce, and Transport
EDP	electronic data processing
EES	Escrowed Encryption Standard
EPL	effective privilege level
ESP	Encapsulating Security Payload
EU	European Union
FCRA	Fair Credit Reporting Act
FDDI	Fiber Distributed Data Interface
FDM	Formal Development Method
FEAL	Fast Data Encryption Algorithm
FHM	flaw hypothesis methodology
FTLS	formal top-level specification

FTP	File Transfer Protocol
gcd	greatest common divisor
GSM	Groupe Special Mobile
GSS-API	Generic Security Service Application Program Interface
GSSP	Generally Accepted System Security Principles
HRU	Harrison, Ruzzo, and Ullman model
HTTP	Hypertext Transfer Protocol
IDEA	International Data Encryption Algorithm
IDES	Intrusion Detection Expert System
IDS	Intrusion detection system
IEEE	Institute of Electrical and Electronics Engineers
IETF	Internet Engineering Task Force
IP	Internet Protocol
IPRA	Internet PCA Registration Authority
IS	Information systems
$(ISC)^2$	International Information Systems Security Certification Consortium
ISO	International Organization for Standardization
ISSO	Information Systems Security Officer
ITSEC	Information Technology Security Evaluation Criteria
ITU	International Telecommunication Union
IV	initialization vector
IVP	integrity verification procedure
KD	data key
KDC	key distribution center
KK	key encrypting key
KKM	highest-level key encrypting key
KU	Device Unique Key
LAN	local-area network
LDV	LOCK Data Views
LEAF	Law Enforcement Access Field
LFSR	linear-feedback shift-register
LNS	local name space
LOCK	Logical Coprocessing Kernel
LRAM	Livermore Risk Assessment Methodology
MAC	message authentication code
MAC	media access control layer
MAC	mandatory access control

MAN	metropolitan-area networks
MDC	manipulation detection code
MIB	Management Information Base
MIC	message integrity code
MIPS	millions of operations per second
MTA	message transfer agent
MVTO	time-stamp ordering algorithm
NCIC	National Crime Information Center
NCSC	National Computer Security Center
NDS	NetWare Directory Services
NFS	Network File System
NII	national information infrastructure
NIST	National Institute of Standards and Technology
NLSP	network-layer security protocol
NOS	network operating system
NPD	named protection domain
NSA	National Security Agency
NSD	network security device
NSM	Network Security Monitor
OECD	Organization for Economic Cooperation and Development
OFB	output feedback
OODBMS	object-oriented DBMS
ORCON	originator controlled
OSI	Open Systems Interconnection
PAC	privilege attribute certificate
PCA	policy certification authority
PDU	protocol data unit
PEM	Privacy Enhanced Mail
PGP	Pretty Good Privacy
PIN	personal identification number
PLB	protection lookaside buffer
PRL	process resource list
RACF	Resource Access Control Facility
RADIUS	Remote Authentication Dial In User Service
RAID	redundant arrays of inexpensive disks
RAMP	Ratings Maintenance Phase
RE	risk element
RISC	Reduced Instruction Set Computer

ROSE	remote operations service element
RPC	remote procedure call
RPL	requester privilege level
RSA	Rivest-Shamir-Adleman system
S-HTTP	Secure Hypertext Transfer Protocol
SACL	system access control list
SAM	Security Account Manager
SATAN	Security Administrator Tool for Analyzing Networks
SCCS	Source Code Control System
SCOMP	Honeywell Secure Communications Processor
SDB	statistical database
SDE	Secure Data Exchange
SDLC	systems development life cycle
SDNS	Secure Data Network System
SDW	segment descriptor word
SFT	system fault tolerance
SGID	set group id
SHA	Secure Hash Algorithm
SID	security identifier
SMF	systems management facility
SMTP	Simple Mail Transfer Protocol
SNA	System Network Architecture
SNMP	Simple Network Management Protocol
SO	security officer
SPI	Security Profile Inspector
SPM	Security Protection Module
SRT	Secure Release Terminal
SSADM	Structured Systems Analysis and Design Method
SSL	Secure Socket Layer
SSN	Social Security number
SUID	set user ID
SVC	supervisor call
TCB	Trusted Computing Base
TCP	Transmission Control Protocol
TCSEC	Trusted Computer System Evaluation Criteria
TDI	Trusted Database Management System Interpretation
TFE	trusted front end
TFM	Trusted Facility Manual

TGS	ticket-granting server
TGT	ticket-granting ticket
TLB	translation lookaside buffer
TLSP	transport-layer security protocol
TMach	Trusted Mach
TNI	Trusted Network Interpretation
TOCTTOU	time-of-check-to-time-of-use
TOE	target of evaluation
TP	transformation procedure
TRM	Transformation Model
UA	user agent
UBD	untrusted back-end DBMS
UDI	unconstrained data item
UDP	User Datagram Protocol
UIC	user identification code
UID	Device Unique ID
UPS	uninterruptable power supply
URL	Universal Resource Locator
VLSI	very large scale integration
VM	virtual machine
VMM	virtual machine monitor
W&S	Wisdom and Sense
WAN	wide-area network
WWW	World Wide Web

Index

ABOUT THE AUTHOR

Rita C. Summers has over 30 years of experience in software design and development, research, and management. Before retiring, she was a member of IBM's Senior Technical Staff and a manager at their Scientific Center. She has taught industry and university courses on computer security, and is the coauthor of *Database Security and Integrity*.